TOEFL® iBT

新托福

真词汇

胡敏◎主编

CTPC 中国出版传媒股份有限公司
中国对外翻译出版有限公司

图书在版编目（CIP）数据

新托福真词汇 / 胡敏主编．—北京：中国对外翻译出版有限公司，2013.6
ISBN 978-7-5001-3746-7

Ⅰ．①新… Ⅱ．①胡… Ⅲ．① TOEFL—词汇—自学参考资料 Ⅳ．① H313

中国版本图书馆 CIP 数据核字（2013）第 121100 号

出版发行 / 中国对外翻译出版有限公司
地　　址 / 北京市西城区车公庄大街甲 4 号物华大厦六层
电　　话 /（010）68338545　68353673　68359101
邮　　编 / 100044
传　　真 /（010）68357870
电子邮箱 / book@ctpc.com.cn
网　　址 / http：// www.ctpc.com.cn

策划编辑 / 吴良柱　吴　蓉
责任编辑 / 顾　恬　邹丽娜

印　　刷 / 三河市东方印刷有限公司
经　　销 / 新华书店

规　　格 / 787 × 1092 毫米　1/16
印　　张 / 27.25
字　　数 / 600 千字
版　　次 / 2013 年 6 月第 1 版
印　　次 / 2013 年 9 月第 2 次

ISBN 978-7-5001-3746-7　　定价：49.00 元

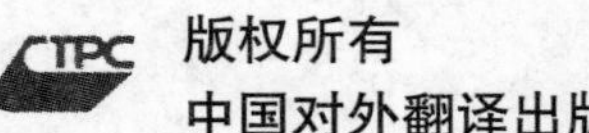

新航道图书编委会

知真，方能有灼见

《庄子》里，有一则小故事：

厨师给梁惠王宰牛。手接触的地方，肩膀倚靠的地方，脚踩的地方，膝盖顶的地方，哗哗作响，进刀时豁豁地，没有不合音律的：合乎汤时《桑林》舞乐的节拍，又合乎尧时《经首》乐曲的节奏。于是梁惠王就问："你解牛的技术怎么竟会高超到这种程度啊？"厨师放下刀回答说："我追求的，是道，已经超过一般的技术了。"

现实中，考出一个理想的分数，相信是每一个考生的愿望。但如何才能实现这一目标？"庖丁解牛"的故事告诉我们：做事情要想成功，不能一味地重视"技"，只有按照"道"去思考、去实践，最终才能做到"游刃有余"。而这里的"道"，就是规律，也就是真知灼见。

因此，知真，方能有灼见。试想，如果庖丁每天是在羊身上练习刀法，有一天当他需要解牛的时候，他是否还可以做到如此游刃有余呢？答案是否定的。同样，对于托福学习而言，要想获得托福的"真知灼见"，首先要选对备考素材。什么素材才能最好地揭示托福考试规律呢？答案自然是真题。

这就是《新托福真词汇》的由来。

众所周知，将英语学习到出神入化的人，其掌握的单词都不是以点状呈现的，而是以典型的网状结构存储在大脑中的。例如以一个词为中心，联想出其近义词、反义词、派生词等。编者根据自身多年的教学经验，通过对托福考试命题规律、备考方法的全面把握，从托福TPO中精心挑选出重点、难点、考点词汇，并从同义、反义、派生、逆构等角度对其进行深度拓展。这样，编者就将托福TPO庞大的真题库所涵盖的词汇精华浓缩在了一起，由厚到薄；而考生在学习的时候又能通过核心词汇拓展、联想、举一反三，由薄到厚。而真知灼见的获得不也正是源自考生由厚到薄，再由薄到厚的领悟过程吗？另外，本书的每一个词条都配有真题例句，旨在让考生学习词汇的同时，预先熟悉托福真题句，从而在真实考场中做到笃定泰山、从容不迫。

苏格拉底被称为“人类中最智慧的人”，他的学生柏拉图说过一句话“真理可能在少数人一边”。准备托福的学生很多，最终可以真正洞悉托福考试规律、洞悉英语学习奥秘的人，可能是少数，而真正成功实现自己梦想的人，也往往是少数。孔子曰“朝闻道，夕死可矣”，本书试图探索出托福考试的词汇之“道”，为考生提供一条科学、有效的词汇备考思路。希望广大考生及英语学习者，能够按照本书提供的思路灵活学习，躬亲实践，以“道”为所好，必可在英语学习上“游刃有余”，成为少数中的精英。

新航道国际教育集团总裁兼校长——

2013 年 6 月

前言

托福考试迈进中国已有三十余年，市面上各种托福词汇书早已是层出不穷。面对形形色色的“奇葩”词汇书，你是否也在其前流连忘返却难以抉择过？因为这些书本身的内容大同小异，你很难有将它们买走的冲动。我们也一直在思考，究竟什么样的词汇书才能使考生的单词学习更有效率呢？显然，这种书也是目前市场最缺乏、考生最迫切需要的。《新托福真词汇》正是在广大考生的这种急切呼唤下应运而生的。本书的与众不同之处在于：在使用的过程中，考生不仅能将托福真题词汇收入囊中，还能近距离接触托福考试最真实的模样。本书的编写耗时两年之久。俗话说：“慢工出细活，慢笔写好书”。本书从选词、选意到斟酌、成书，每一个细节都经过编者们反复思考、仔细推敲、精心提炼，才最终“成就”了如今的这本《新托福真词汇》。

何谓“真词汇”？《新托福真词汇》的“真”意味着“真实、精准”。本书所有的核心词汇均是从 TPO 1—TPO 23 收录的托福官方真题中精挑细选而来，可谓是与托福考试结合最为紧密的词汇。这些词汇真实、准确地反映了托福考试的难度，并且最有可能在考试中重复出现。因此，掌握了这些“真词汇”，便是为托福学习和备考打下了坚实的基础。

本书有以下优势：

一、词汇量大　本书词汇量高达 6500 多，其中包含近 3200 个核心词汇。这些核心词汇均源自真题，是托福词汇的重中之重，所以本书对这部分词汇进行了详细注释。我们为每个核心词条提供了其在真题句中的原意以及拓展意。同时，我们对核心词条从派生词、近义词、反义词、搭配以及逆构词五个角度进行同步拓展，帮助考生成倍地扩大词汇量。

二、词频分类　本书所有核心词汇都有词频标注，托福词条，孰轻孰重，考生可以一目了然，进而迅速拿下重中之重的核心词条。对于想要拿高分的考生来说，掌握全部核心词汇是必须的；如果对分数要求不高、复习时间又比较紧张，那么只专注于高频词是比较明智的选择，这样可以最大化地利用有限的时间，从而达到最满意的效果。

三、科学记忆 将相关联的词放在一起记忆是非常科学、有效的途径之一。尤其可以使所记单词在考生的记忆存储中有序、整齐地分布，记忆牢靠的同时也方便考生随时提取合适词条。我们尽可能地为核心词条提供相关的同义词、反义词、派生词，还有词组搭配及词条的逆构形式。让单词的“亲朋好友”在考生的记忆中紧密的排列组合在一起，形成覆盖全面的单词网络。

四、真题例句 本书所有例句均选自托福 TPO，为考生学习单词提供了最真实、最准确的语言环境。同时，考生在记忆单词的过程中可以熟悉托福真题。尤其对于托福考试阅读词汇部分的真题例句，考生可在潜移默化中提高托福阅读水平。另外，所有的真题例句都配有精准的中文译文，供考生参考。对于例句的出处也有非常明确的标注。

五、返记菜单 鉴于很多考生都有着“茫茫词海，背过就忘”的苦恼，本书在每页下方都设有“返记菜单”板块，便于考生及时复习背过的单词，为考生都学过哪些单词提供一条清晰的思路。

六、独立切分的单词音频 不同于以往将所有同类词汇整合成一个音频文件的传统做法，本书附赠的音频文件将每个单词都做成了一个独立的小音频，并按照书中的单元分类归为 50 个文件夹，方便考生查找、播放某个特定的单词。例如，如果考生对“aesthetic”这类比较复杂的单词无法做到听一遍就掌握，而是想反复多听几次，那么就可以到“Word List 19”的文件夹轻松地找到“aesthetic”这个单词独立的音频，在电脑上反复播放、学习。另外，所有的独立切分的音频也可以在电脑或随身音乐播放器里连续播放，不会造成任何麻烦。本书附赠的音频内容可以到托福读者服务群里面下载。

本书在编排的过程中，严格按照托福考试最新趋势选取词条，以 TPO 真题题库为依托，每个词条都是严加斟酌，每个真题句都是原汁原味，每个例句翻译都经过多次润色，旨在为大家提供优质的图书，提供最为便捷的帮助。希望它能让在托福备考路上迷茫的考生找到方向，直达胜利的彼岸。祝愿每一位拿到此书的“你”都有一个美好的、享受的阅读体验。

编者

2013 年 6 月

目录

Word List 1

time[576] [taɪm] 

【释义】*v.* 计时,测定…的时间 *n.* 1. 时间,时代,时期 2. 倍;次数

【例句】Consequently, the timing and rhythms of biological functions must closely match periodic events like the solar day, the tides, the lunar cycle, and the seasons. (TPO13, R, S2, T1) 生物的计时与交替循环的机能也就理所应当地必须与像昼夜交替、潮涨潮落、月圆月缺和四季更迭这样的周期性事件保持大体的一致。

【派生】timer *n.*(电子)定时器,计时器

【搭配】time zone 时区

will[528] [wɪl]

【释义】*n.* 愿望(intention, wish);决心,意志 *aux.* 将;愿意;必须 *v.* 主观促成;遗赠

【例句】He criticizes that people of his time for abandoning their own minds and their own wills for the sake of conformity and consistency. (TPO4, L, S1, L2) 他批评他同时代的人为了随大流而放弃自己的思想和愿望。

【派生】willing *a.* 愿意的
willingness *n.* 乐意,愿意

【搭配】at will 随意;任意
with a will 有决心地;努力地

way[385] [weɪ]

【释义】*ad.* 远远地,大大地 *n.* 1. 方法,方式,手段(method) 2. 路,道,街,径

【例句】However, the reading is way too optimistic in its assessment of hydrogen-based fuel-cell engines. (TPO9, W, Q1) 然而,文章却过于乐观地估计了燃料电池发动机。

【搭配】by the way 顺便说说,顺便提起

well[369] [wel] 

【释义】*n.* 井;源泉 *ad.* 很好地,相当地 *int.*【口】好吧,啊 *a.* 健康的;良好的,适宜的

【例句】Gas pressure gradually dies out, and oil is pumped from the well. (TPO4, R, S2, T2) 气压逐渐消失,油从井中被抽出来。

【搭配】as well 也;同样地;还不如
as well as 也;和…一样;不但…而且
do well in 在…方面干得好
well versed in 精通
well off 富裕的;处境好的
go well with 协调,和…很相配

into[334] [ˈɪntʊ]

【释义】*prep.*〈口语〉很喜欢

【例句】Everyone's into sports and I'm more artsy, you know, into music. (TPO5, L, S1, C1) 每个人都喜欢运动,而我,你知道的,更有艺术天分,我喜欢音乐。

live[220] 

【释义】[laɪv] *a.* 直播的;活的 [lɪv] *v.* 居住;生活

【例句】But the movies differed significantly from these other forms of entertainment, which depended on either live performance or the active involvement of a master of ceremonies who assembled the final program. (TPO2, R, S2, T2) 但是电影与其他形式的娱乐活动有着很大的不同,电影无需依赖现场表演,也不需要串联全场节目的主持人的积极参与。

【派生】lively *a.* 活泼的,生动的

【搭配】live through 度过,经受过
live up to 不辜负,做到
live with 忍受,承受

find[203] [faɪnd] 

【释义】*n.* 发现;(有价值的)发现物(discovery, finding)*v.* 找到,发现(discover)

【例句】An even more exciting find was reported in 1994, also from Pakistan. (TPO2, R, S2, T1) 1994年报道了一项更让人兴奋的发现,这次重大发现仍然是在巴基斯坦。

【搭配】find out 查明(真相)

found[193] [faʊnd] 

【释义】*v.* 创立,创办,创建 (establish)

【例句】Egyptians were known to have founded

other great civilization. (TPO5, R, S2, T1) 人们认为是埃及人开创了另一个伟大的文明。

【派生】foundation *n.* 基础；基金会
founded *a.* 有基础的

place[188] [pleɪs]

【释义】*v.* 使（某人）处于某处境；将（某物）放置 (put, situate) *n.* 地方；地位

【例句】Life places us in a complex web of relationships with other people. (TPO13, R, S1, T1) 生活使我们置身于与其他人复杂的社会关系网之中。

【派生】placement *n.* 布置；定位球；人员配置

【搭配】place sb. in a dilemma 使某人进退两难

might[185] [maɪt]

【释义】*n.* 力量，威力，权力 (power) *v.* 可能，也许（may 的过去式）

【例句】As always, there are the power worshippers, especially among historians, who are predisposed to admire whatever is strong, who feel more attracted to the might of Rome than to the subtlety of Greece. (TPO7, R, S2, T1) 通常总会有对权威的崇拜者，尤其是在历史学家中，他们倾向于钦佩强大的事物，相对于希腊的微妙，罗马的强大威力对他们更有吸引力。

【搭配】Might is right. 强权就是公理。

cause[182] [kɔːz]

【释义】*n.* 1. 原因，缘故 (reason) 2. 事业，原则，目标 3. 诉讼案 *v.* 引起，促使，使发生

【例句】The first reason why pollution seemed the more likely cause was that there were known sources of it along the Alaskan coast. (TPO10, W, Q1) 之所以污染似乎是更可能的原因，首先在于阿拉斯加海岸沿线有已知的污染源。

【搭配】in the cause of 为了…

course[181] [kɔːs]

【释义】*n.* 课程 (lesson, lecture)；路线；一道菜

【例句】I'm supposed to do a literature review for my psychology course. (TPO1, L, S1, C1) 我需要针对我的心理学课程写一篇文献综述。

【派生】coursebook *n.* 教科书

present[177]

【释义】[prɪ'zent] *v.* 1. 出现，出席；显示 (show, display) 2. 赠与，交给 ['prezənt] *a.* 1. 现在的，目前的 2. 出席的，到场的 *n.* 1. 礼物，赠品 (gift) 2. 现在，目前

【例句】A recent study of some of the formations presents some new theories about the area's past. (TPO9, L, S2, L1) 近期的地质构造研究就该地区过去的情况提出了新的理论。

【派生】presently *ad.* 不久，一会儿
presentation *n.* 介绍，陈述；节目，演出；赠送物

century[175] ['sentʃʊrɪ] 

【释义】*n.* 百年，世纪

【例句】The introduction of new screen formats was put off for a quarter century, and color, though utilized over the next two decades for special productions, also did not become a norm until the 1950s. (TPO12, R, S2, T1) 新的屏幕形式的使用被推迟了25年，而色彩，尽管在接下来的20年中被用于特殊生产，也是直到20世纪50年代才变成了一种规范。

summary[175] ['sʌmərɪ]

【释义】*n.* 摘要，总结

【例句】Wildman and Niles make a summary comment: "Perhaps the most important thing we learned is the idea of the teacher-as-reflective-practitioner will not happen simply because it is a good or even compelling idea." (TPO9, R, S2, T1) Wildman 和 Niles 作出了一个总结性的评论："或许我们学到的最重要的观点就是教师不会因为这是一个好的或者不得不接收的观点而自发地开展教学反思。"

【派生】summarily *ad.* 概括地，扼要地

【搭配】in summary 简要地说

being[170] ['biːɪŋ]

【释义】*n.* 1. 人，生物 2. 存在 (existence) 3. 生命，本质

【例句】They were designed to be put in places where these beings could manifest themselves in order to be the recipients of ritual actions. (TPO11, R, S1, T1) 它们被放置在特定的位置上，使那些神灵和人物得以显现，通过仪式活动来接受人们的膜拜。

【搭配】come into being 形成，产生
for the time being 暂时

land[170] [lænd]

【释义】*n.* 1. 土地，陆地 2. 国土 *v.* 着陆，使着陆

【例句】Today I want to talk about a way in which we are able to determine how old a piece of land, or some other geologic feature is—dating techniques. (TPO1, L, S1, L2) 今天我想讲一种方法，通过这种方法我们能够判断一块土地的年龄或是其他的一些地质特征，这就是年代鉴定技术。

【派生】landlady *n.* 女房东，女地主
landmark *n.* 地标，路标
landscape *n.* 风景

element[166] ['elɪmənt]

【释义】*n.* 要素，元素 (factor, component)；基本原则

【例句】What are the elements of Realism we should be looking for in Frantzen's work? (TPO1, L, S1, L1) 我们应该从Frantzen的作品里找寻哪些现实主义的元素呢？

【派生】elemental *a.* 基本的；自然力的
elementary *a.* 基本的，初级的

through[163] [θruː]

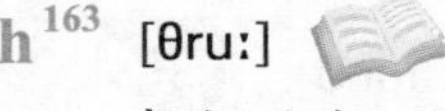

【释义】*prep.* 1. 穿过，通过 2. 从头到尾，自始至终 3. 经由，以 4. 因为，由于 *ad.* 1. 从头到尾，自始至终 2. 彻底，完全 *a.* 1. 直达的，直通的 2. 完成的，结束的

【例句】This same arrangement found in an old-fashioned stream radiator, in which the coiled pipes pass heat back and forth as water courses through them. (TPO15, R, S2, T1) 老式的蒸汽式暖气片上有着相同的构造，当水通过这些盘绕着的管子时热量就进行了交换。

【派生】throughout *ad.* 自始至终；到处；全部 *prep.* 贯穿，遍及

population[153] [ˌpɒpjʊ'leɪʃən]

【释义】*n.* 人口，(全体)居民，群体

【例句】The vast majority of the population used their own regional vernacular in all aspects to their lives. (TPO12, L, S2, C1) 多数人在生活的方方面面都使用他们自己的方言。

【逆构】populate *v.* 居住于；构成人口

【搭配】population census 人口普查

book[151] [bʊk]

【释义】*v.* 预订，预约 (register, make reservation) *n.* 书

【例句】Anyway, now the music building's fully booked. (TPO16, L, S1, C1) 不管怎样，音乐楼现在已经全被预订了。

film[151] [fɪlm]

【释义】*n.* 1. 影片，电影 (movie) 2. 胶片，胶卷 3. 薄层，薄膜

【例句】In the peepshow format, a film was viewed through a small opening in a machine that was created for that purpose. (TPO2, R, S2, T2) 在通过西洋镜播放电影的年代里，人们只能通过仪器上的一个专门设置的小窗孔来看电影。

【派生】filmy *a.* 非常薄的

species[148] ['spiːʃɪz]

【释义】*n.* 物种，种 (kind, class)

【例句】These changes— in plant numbers and the mix of species— are cumulative. (TPO3, R, S1, T2) 植物数量和种类混合的变化是慢慢积累的。

【派生】specimen *n.* 范例，标本

sound[146] [saʊnd]

【释义】*a.* 1. 明智的，可靠的，合理的 (reasonable, right) 2. 健全的，完好的 *n.* 声音，响声 *v.* 1. 发(音) 2. 测…的深度

【例句】Wildman and Niles observed that systematic reflection on teaching required a sound ability to understand classroom events in an objective manner. (TPO9, R, S2, T1) Wildman和Niles观察到，系统的教学反思

返记菜单

land[170] element[166] through[163] population[153] book[151]
film[151] species[148] sound[146]

需要一种可靠的能力,从而以一种客观的方式来理解教室中所发生的事。

【派生】sounder *n.* 音响器

soundly *ad.* 坚实地,牢固地

【搭配】sound off 高声谈论

system[145] ['sɪstəm]

【释义】*n.* 1. 制度,体制 2. 理论体系

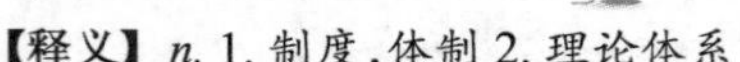

【例句】Some socities make use of a barter system. (TPO2, S, Q6) 一些社会很好地利用了物物交换体制。

light[142] [laɪt]

【释义】*v.* 1.(使)发光,照亮 2. 点火,点燃 *a.* 1. 光线充足的,明亮的 (bright) 2. 浅色的 *n.* 1. 光,光线 2. 光源,电灯,发光体

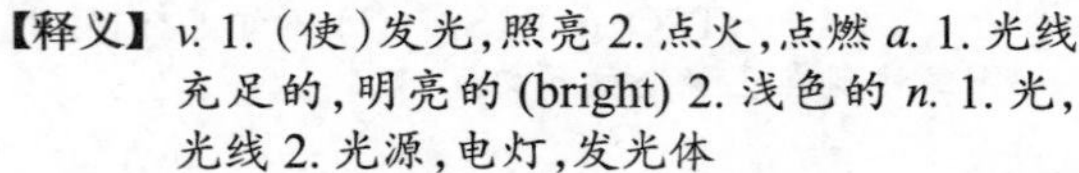

【例句】When an animal is signaling in an area with green-to-yellow lighting conditions, its signal will not be visible if the backgroud is brightly lit. (TPO17, R, S2, T1) 当动物在黄绿光波的光线条件下发出视觉信号时,如果光照背景特别强的话信号是不能被发现的。

【派生】lightless *a.* 不发光的,暗的

【搭配】in the light of 根据,考虑到

suggest[138] [sə'dʒest]

【释义】*v.* 1.(间接地)表明,意思是,意味着 (indicate, signify) 2. 建议,提议 (advise) 3. 暗示 (imply)

【例句】There's some indications to suggest that the population of the Nightcap Oak has not declined over the last many hundreds of years. (TPO6, L, S1, L2) 有一些迹象表明夜冠橡树的数量在过去的几百年里并没有下降。

【派生】suggestion *n.* 建议,意见

surface[137] ['sɜːfɪs]

【释义】*v.*(使)浮出水面;使成平面 *n.* 1. 外表 2. 平面 *a.* 表面的,外表上的

【例句】And what happens is, they inhibit each other, they cancel each other out in a way, and a third seemingly irrelevant behavior surfaces through a process that we call 'Disinhibition'. (TPO4, L, S1, L1) 而出现的情况是,他们互相抑制,在某种程度上相互抵消,于是一种似乎不相干的第三种行为通过一个我们称之为"抑制解除"的过程浮出水面。

【搭配】on the surface 在表面上,外表上

body[135] ['bɒdɪ]

【释义】*n.* 身体;团体;主体,主要部分

【例句】The numerous small bodies include asteroids, comets, and meteoroids. (TPO16, R, S2, T2) 无数的小天体包括小行星、彗星和流星。

【搭配】main body 主体

in a body 全体,整体

a body of 大量的

own[133] [əʊn]

【释义】*v.* 有,拥有 (have, hold, possess) *a.* 自己的

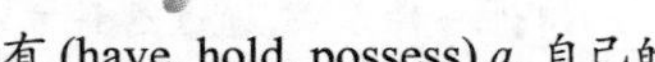

【例句】Will that pay checking include all the money I am owned? (TPO12, L, S2, C1) 那张工资支票上包含我所拥有的所有的钱吗?

【派生】owner *n.* 所有者

process[133]

【释义】['prəʊses] *n.* 1. 工序 2. 过程 3. 程序,手续 (procedure) [prə'ses] *v.* 1. 加工,处理 (dispose)

【例句】Animals, even insects, carry out what look like very complex decision making processes. (TPO16, L, S2, L1) 动物们,甚至是昆虫,执行着看似复杂的决策过程。

【派生】procession *n.* 行列,队伍

processive *a.* 前进的,进行的

around[132] [ə'raʊnd]

【释义】*a.* 存在的,活的;可看到的 *ad.* 到处,在周围 *prep.* 到处,在…附近,围绕

【例句】I should say that Uranium-Lead Dating has been around for quite a while. (TPO1, L, S1, L2) 应该说铀铅测年法已经存在了很长时间了。

material[132] [mə'tɪərɪəl]

【释义】*n.* 1. 材料,原料(stuff) 2. 素材,资料 *a.* 1. 物质的,物欲的 2. 重要的,重大的 3. 实质性的,客观存在的

【例句】She needs his help to find resource materials.

(TPO6, L, S2, C1) 她需要他的帮助来寻找资源材料。

【搭配】raw material 原料

region[131] [ˈriːdʒən] 

【释义】*n.* 1. 地区，区域（area, district）2. 范围（scope, span）3.（身体的）部位

【例句】This region has a semiarid climate, and for 50 years after its settlement, it supported a low-intensity agricultural economy of cattle ranching and wheat farming. (TPO3, R, S1, T1) 这一地区属半干旱气候，在人们定居于此的 50 年间，都保持着以畜牧业和小麦种植为主的低密度农业经济。

【派生】regional *a.* 地方的，地域性的
regionalization *n.* 分成地区，按地区安排
regionalism *n.* 地域性，地方分权主义

【搭配】in the region of 大约，接近

effect[129] [ɪˈfekt] 

【释义】*n.* 作用，影响，效果（consequence, result）*v.* 使发生，引起（cause, generate, produce）

【例句】For example, one principle of social interaction, audience effects, suggests that individuals' work is affected by their knowledge that they are visible to others. (TPO2, S, Q4) 例如，关于社会互动的理论之一——观众效应表明，如果个体知道自己能被别人看见，那么他的工作将会受到影响。

【派生】effective *a.* 有效的
effectual *a.* 奏效的

【搭配】bring/carry/put into effect 实行，实施
have an effect on/upon 对…有影响
of no effect 无用，无效
take effect（药等）见效，（法规等）生效
side effect 副作用

mark[128] [mɑːk] 

【释义】*v.* 1. 标明（sign, indicate）2. 纪念 3. 打分 *n.* 1. 痕迹；记号 2. 分数

【例句】The last event marks the beginning of the Cambrian period. (TPO5, R, S2, T2) 最后的这一事件标志着寒武纪时代的开始。

【派生】marked *a.* 有记号的；显著的
marker *n.* 书签

behavior[127] [bɪˈheɪvjə] 

【释义】*n.* 行为，举止，态度（conduct, manner, action）

【例句】For today's discussion, we'll review the case study on how some animals have behaviorally adapted to their environments. (TPO1, L, S2, L2) 在今天的讨论中，我们将对这一个案进行讨论，看看一些动物是如何在行为上适应它们所处的环境的。

【派生】behavioral *a.* 行为的
behaviorally *ad.* 行为举止上

【逆构】behave *v.* 表现，举止

fact[125] [fækt] 

【释义】*n.* 事实，真相（truth）

【例句】As a matter of fact, science is still working on it, trying to find ways of enhancing energy storage techniques so that coming of night or cloudy days really wouldn't matter. (TPO12, L, S2, L2) 事实上，科学仍在努力寻求增强能量储备技术的方法，这样夜间或阴天的时候也都无关紧要了。

【派生】factor *n.* 因素；代理人

【搭配】in fact/as a matter of fact 事实上

amount[119] [əˈmaʊnt] 

【释义】*v.* 1. 合计，总计（totalize）*n.* 数量，总额（sum, quantity）

【例句】Estimates indicate that the aquifer contains enough water to fill Lake Huron, but unfortunately, under the semiarid climatic conditions that presently exist in the region, rates of addition to the aquifer are minimal, amounting to about half a centimeter a year. (TPO3, R, S1, T1) 据估计，（奥加拉拉）蓄水层的含水量足以填满休伦湖，但不幸的是，在目前该地区半干旱的气候条件下，（奥加拉拉）蓄水层的蓄水能力极低，每年仅半厘米左右。

【搭配】amount to 总计…

bet[116] [bet]

【释义】*v.* 1. 确信，保证 2. 打赌 *n.* 1. 打赌 2. 赌注

【例句】I bet if they did that, they'd get plenty of students riding those buses. (TPO2, S, Q3)

返记菜单

region[131] effect[129] mark[128] behavior[127] fact[125]
amount[119] bet[116]

我敢保证，如果他们那样做的话，肯定会有很多学生乘坐校车。

【搭配】accept/take up a bet 同意与别人打赌
an even bet 成败参半的机会
bet on the wrong horse 估计（或判断）错误
You bet! 当然！没问题！

event[114] [ɪ'vent]

【释义】*n.* 1. 事件，大事 2. 运动项目

【例句】In fact, damage to the environment by humans is often much more severe than damage by natural events and processes. (TPO3, R, S1, T2) 事实上，人类对环境造成的破坏通常要比自然事件和自然演变对环境的损害严重得多。

【派生】eventless *a.* 平静无事的，平凡的

【搭配】in the event of 如果发生…，万一

last[112] [lɑːst]

【释义】*v.* 持续（continue）*a.* 最后的

【例句】Frankly, I can't believe you've lasted this long. (TPO5, L, S2, C1) 坦率地说，我真不敢相信你已经坚持了这么久。

【搭配】last for ever 直到永远

design[109] [dɪ'zaɪn]

【释义】*v.* 设计，计划（plan）*n.* 1. 图样，设计图 2. 设计，布局 3. 目的，打算

【例句】But still, the program's been designed to progress through certain stages. (TPO5, L, S2, C1) 但是，这个项目计划通过某些阶段取得进展。

【派生】designer *n.* 设计者

【搭配】by design 有计划地；有意地

major[109] ['meɪdʒə]

【释义】*a.* 较大的；主要的（main, principal）；主修的 *n.* 少校；主修科目 *v.*〈美〉主修，专攻

【例句】Of all the visual arts, architecture affects our lives most directly for it determines the character of the human environment in major ways. (TPO3, R, S1, T1) 在所有的视觉艺术当中，建筑最直接地影响着我们的生活，因为它在很多方面决定了我们的生存环境的特征。

【反义】minor

【派生】majority *n.* 大多数，大半；多数票

【搭配】major course 主修课

essential[108] [ɪ'senʃəl]

【释义】*a.* 1. 本质的，必要的，重要的（basic, fundamental, substantial）*n.* 要素；必需品

【例句】When plants do not absorb sufficient amounts of essential minerals, characteristic abnormalities result. (TPO5, R, S1, T1) 当植物没有吸收到足够多必要的矿物质时，异常特征就会出现。

【派生】essentiality *n.* 重要性；本质
essentially *ad.* 本质上，根本上

soil[107] [sɔɪl]

【释义】*n.* 1. 泥土，土壤，土地 2. 国土，领土 *v.* 弄脏；污辱

【例句】The soil is the source of these minerals which are absorbed by the plant with the water from the soil. (TPO5, R, S1, T1) 土壤是这些矿物质的来源，植物通过土壤中的水分来吸收矿物质。

community[103] [kə'mjuːnɪtɪ]

【释义】*n.* 1.（动植物的）群落 2. 社区，社会（district, society）3. 社团，团体

【例句】Plant communities assemble themselves flexibly, and their particular structure depends on the specific history of the area. (TPO3, R, S1, T2) 植物群体可以自由地聚集，其特殊结构取决于聚集区域的具体历史。

story[101] ['stɔːrɪ]

【释义】*n.* 1. 楼层 (=storey)（floor）2. 故事

【例句】The settlements of Chaco Canyon in the New Mexico in the American Southwest were notable for their "great houses", massive stone buildings that contain hundreds of rooms and often stand three or four stories high. (TPO5, W, Q1) 居住在美国西南部新墨西哥州的查克峡谷中的人们以其"大房子"而出名，那些房子都是大型的石头建筑，包含几百间屋子，而且常常有三、四层楼高。

experience[100] [ɪks'pɪərɪəns] 

【释义】*v.* 经历，体验（undergo）*n.* 经验；体验，经历

【例句】Even when the region experiences unfortunate climatic conditions, the rates of addition of water continue to increase. (TPO3, R, S1, T1) 即使该地区经历不好的气候状况时，水的增加率也是继续上升的。

house[100] [haʊs]

【释义】*v.* 1.覆盖 2.给…房子住 *n.* 1.房屋（dwelling） 2.家庭（home）3.机构，议院

【例句】These canals house nerves and blood vessels that allow the living animal to grow quickly, and rapid body growth is in fact a characteristic of endothermy. (TPO4, W, Q1) 这些管道覆盖了神经和血管，使得动物可以快速生长，而身体生长快速实际上是恒温动物的特点之一。

【搭配】on the house 免费，由店家出钱
in house 内部的，固有的
greenhouse 温室，花房

affect[99] [ə'fekt] 

【释义】*v.* 1.影响（influence）2.（在感情上）打动（move, touch）3.（疾病、疼痛等）侵袭，感染（afflict）4.假装，佯装（fake）

【例句】People take each other into account in their daily behavior and in fact, the very presence of others can affect behavior. (TPO2, S, Q4) 人们在日常行为中会将他人的因素考虑在内，所以，事实上，其他人在场会影响人们的行为表现。

【派生】affection *n.* 影响；喜爱
affectionate *a.* 深情的
affective *a.* 情感(上)的

ancient[99] ['eɪnʃənt]

【释义】*a.* 1.古代的，古老的（primitive）2.老年的（aged, old）

【例句】Another ancient Greek philosopher we need to discuss is Aristotle—Aristotle's ethical theory. (TPO2, L, S2, L1) 我们需要讨论的另一位古希腊哲学家是亚里士多德——亚里士多德的伦理学。

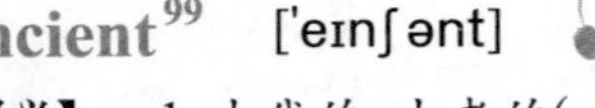

imply[98] [ɪm'plaɪ] 

【释义】*v.* 1.暗示，暗指（suggest）2.说明，表明 3.（思想、行为等）必然包含，使有必要

【例句】So basic ecological principles imply a strong tendency within pastoralist lifeways toward nomadism. (TPO14, R, S2, T2) 所以，基本的生态原则暗示了牧民的生活方式强烈倾向于游牧方式。

state[98] [steɪt] 

【释义】*n.* 1.情况，状况，状态（condition）2.国家（nation）3.州 *v.* 说明，陈述（express）*a.* 官方的；国家的，政府的

【例句】Even nitrogen, which is a gas in its elemental state, is normally absorbed from the soil as nitrate ions. (TPO5, R, S1, T1) 即使是常态下以气体形式存在的氮，通常也是以硝酸盐的形式从土壤中吸收的。

source[97] [sɔːs] 

【释义】*n.* 信息来源；来源，出处（origin）

【例句】The article I just copied is from that journal, so I've got to look at other sources. (TPO1, L, S1, C1) 我刚刚拷贝过来的文章出自那个期刊，所以我得再看看其他的资料来源。

【搭配】energy source 能源
at source 从源头，从一开始

order[96] ['ɔːdə] 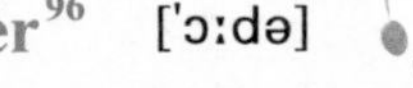

【释义】*v.* 1.订购，定制（request）2.命令，嘱咐（command）3.整理，布置 *n.* 1.次序，顺序（arrangement）2.秩序 3.命令，嘱咐（instruction）

【例句】To find out how to order a book for a course. (TPO10, L, S2, C1) 弄明白如何订购一本教科书。

【搭配】in order 整齐，秩序井然；按顺序；状况良好

factor[95] ['fæktə] 

【释义】*n.* 1.因素，要素（element, ingredient）2.因子，系数

【例句】Further observation revealed the tendency of teachers to evaluate events rather

返记菜单

experience[100]	house[100]	affect[99]	ancient[99]	imply[98]
state[98]	source[97]	order[96]	factor[95]	

than review the contributory factors in a considered manner by standing outside the situation. (TPO9, R, S2, T1) 进一步的观察发现,教师们更倾向于评价事件,而不是站在事件之外以一种深思熟虑的方式洞察一个事件的促成因素。

【搭配】factor in 包括,把…计算在内

minute[95]

【释义】[maɪ'nju:t] *a.* 1. 细微的,极小的(tiny)2. 仔细的,详细的 ['mɪnɪt] *n.* 分钟,片刻

【例句】Consolidated sediments, too, contain millions of minute water-holding pores. (TPO1, R, S2, T2) 那些坚固的沉淀物也有以数百万计的小孔来容纳水。

【反义】broad, immense

【搭配】minute memory 短暂记忆

location[94] [ləʊ'keɪʃən]

【释义】*n.* 1. 位置,地点(site, position)2. 外景拍摄地

【例句】The researchers Peter Ucko and Andree Rosenfeld identified three principal locations of paintings in the caves of western Europe. (TPO4, R, S2, T1) 研究人员 Peter Ucko 和 Andree Rosenfeld 确定了西欧的洞穴画的三个主要地点。

【逆构】locate *v.* 找到…位置,使坐落于

【搭配】on location 出外景;现场拍摄

target location 目标位置

particular[94] [pə'tɪkjʊlə]

【释义】*a.* 1. 特别的,独特的(unique, special)2. 特定的 3. 详细的,具体的 4. 挑剔的 *n.* 详情

【例句】I'm going to talk about a particular dating technique. (TPO1, L, S1, L2) 我将要讲到的是一种特别的年代鉴定技术。

【派生】particularity *n.* 特质,个性;讲究

particularize *v.* 例举,使特殊;详细说明

【搭配】particular about 过分讲究的,难以取悦的

technique[94] [tek'ni:k]

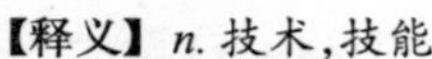

【释义】*n.* 技术,技能

【例句】Today I want to talk about a way in which we are able to determine how old a piece of land, or some other geologic feature is — dating techniques. (TPO1, L, S1, L2) 今天我想讲一种方法,通过这种方法我们能够判断一块土地的年龄或是其他的一些地质特征,这就是年代鉴定技术。

determine[93] [dɪ'tɜ:mɪn]

【释义】*v.* 1. 决定,下决心(decide)2. 确定 3. 支配,影响

【例句】Of all the visual arts, architecture affects our lives most directly for it determines the character of the human environment in major ways. (TPO3, R, S1, T1) 在所有的视觉艺术当中,建筑最直接地影响着我们的生活,因为它在很多方面决定了我们的生存环境的特征。

【派生】determination *n.* 决心,果断

determinant *n.* 决定因素

【搭配】determine on sth. / to do sth. 决定做某事

term[93] [tɜ:m]

【释义】*v.* 把…称为,把…叫做 *n.* 1. 学期;任期,期限 2. 措词;术语,专门用语

【例句】But the Maya homeland lies more than sixteen hundred kilometers from the equator, at latitudes 17 to 22 degrees north, in a habitat termed a "seasonal tropical forest." (TPO14, R, S2, T1) 但玛雅人的家园距离赤道 16000 多公里,位于北纬 17° 到 22° 之间一个被称为"季节性热带森林"的地方。

Word List 2

view[93] [vjuː]

【释义】*v.* 1. 认为，考虑(think, perceive) 2. 观看(电视、电影等)(watch) *n.* 1. 看法，意见(opinion) 2. 景色，风景

【例句】The researchers estimate that the initial training of the teachers to view events objectively took between 20 and 30 hours, with the same number of hours again being required to practice the skills of reflection. (TPO9, R, S2, T1) 研究者认为，最初训练教师客观地看待事件需要20到30个小时，之后还需要花同样多的时间练习反思技能。

【派生】viewable *a.* 看得见的

【搭配】in full view 尽收眼底

specific[92] [spɪ'sɪfɪk]

【释义】*a.* 1. 特定的，特有的(particular, special) 2. 具体的，明确的(explicit)

【例句】When we're being observed specifically, we tend to increase the speed at which we perform that activity. (TPO2, S, Q4) 当我们作为特定对象被人观察时，我们趋于加快正在从事的某项活动的速度。

【派生】specifically *ad.* 特定地
specification *n.* 规格；说明书

【逆构】specify *v.* 明确说明

habitat[91] ['hæbətæt]

【释义】*n.* 栖息地，产地

【例句】Birds will take the most direct migratory route to their new habitat. (TPO11, R, S2, T1) 鸟类会采取最直接的迁徙路线去往它们的新栖息地。

【派生】habitation *n.* 居住

【搭配】habitat condition 居住条件

crop[90] [krɒp]

【释义】*n.* 1. 农作物，庄稼 2. 平头 *v.* 收割，收获(harvest)

【例句】Now they did hunt and they also raised cereal crops and kept sheep, but we don't know why so many of the paintings are of hunting scenes. (TPO1, L, S2, L1) 他们现在确实还在狩猎，而且还种植谷物、饲养羊群，但是我们并不知道为什么这么多画都是有关狩猎场景的。

【派生】cropped *a.* 剪裁不正的

【搭配】crop yield 粮食产量
crop rotation 轮作
in crop (土地)种着庄稼

remain[89] [rɪ'meɪn]

【释义】*n.* 残骸；遗体 *v.* 1. 保持；继续；仍然处于；依然(continue) 2. 留下，逗留

【例句】The coastal hypothesis has gained increasing support in recent years because the remains of large land animals, such as caribou and brown bears, have been found in southeastern Alaska dating between 10,000 and 12,500 years ago. (TPO9, R, S1, T1) 海岸走廊假设近些年得到了越来越多的支持，因为人们在阿拉斯加东南部地区发现了一些大型陆地动物(比如北美驯鹿和棕熊)的残骸，可追溯至10000年到12500年前。

【派生】remaining *a.* 剩余的，剩下的

likely[87] ['laɪklɪ]

【释义】*a.* 1. 可能的，可信的 2. 合适的 *ad.* 可能

【例句】The likely explanation is that an area of underground freshwater underlies the Yucatan Peninsula, but surface elevation increases from north to south, so that as one moves south the land surface lies increasingly higher above the water table. (TPO14, R, S2, T1) 可能的解释是在尤卡坦半岛有一处地下淡水，但地表海拔是从北到南逐渐升高的，所以越往南走，地表就会越高于地下水位。

name[86] [neɪm]

【释义】*v.* 命名，取名；明确说出 *n.* 名字

【例句】The fossil was officially named Pakicetus in honor of the country where the discovery was made. (TPO2, R, S2, T1) 这块化石被官

返记菜单

view[93] specific[92] habitat[91] crop[90] remain[89]
likely[87] name[86]

方命名为 Pakicetus，以纪念这一发现的所在国家。

【同义】 call

【搭配】 name after 以…命名

reach[85] [riːtʃ]

【释义】 *v.* 1. 到达，达成（approach）2. 取得联系 *n.* 1. 范围（stretch）2. 影响力 3. 河段

【例句】 The path a person takes can only be seen clearly after the destination has been reached. (TPO4, L, S1, L2) 一个人所选择的路只有在其到达终点后才会清晰地呈现出来。

【搭配】 reach out 伸出
reach for 伸手去拿
reach an agreement 达成协议；取得一致意见，达成共识
out of reach 够不着

space[85] [speɪs]

【释义】 *n.* 1. 空地 2. 太空 3. 期间，空间 *v.* 间隔开

【例句】 It's gotten really tough to find a space. (TPO2, S, Q3) 现在找个停车位真是太困难了。

【派生】 spacious *a.* 宽敞的
spatial *a.* 空间的
spaceship/spacecraft *n.* 宇宙飞船

【搭配】 look into space 茫然直视
make space for 为…腾出地方

though[85] [ðəʊ]

【释义】 *conj.* 虽然，尽管；即使 *ad.* 然而，可是，不过

【例句】 To understand this though, we first need to look at the early form of drama known as the well-made play. (TPO7, L, S1, L1) 然而，为了理解这一思想，我们首先需要了解一下被称作"佳构剧"的早期戏剧形式。

require[84] [rɪˈkwaɪə]

【释义】 *v.* 1. 需要（need）2. 要求，命令（demand）

【例句】 Research has shown that certain minerals are required by plants for normal growth and development. (TPO5, R, S1, T1) 研究表明，植物正常的生长发育需要一定的矿物质。

【派生】 requirement *n.* 需求，要求，必要条件

【搭配】 be required to do sth. 要求做某事

organism[83] [ˈɔːgənɪzəm]

【释义】 *n.* 有机体，生物体，有机组织

【例句】 Why did it take so long for multicellular organisms to develop? (TPO5, R, S2, T2) 为什么多细胞生物的生长需要这么长时间？

【派生】 organismal *a.* 生物的，有机体的

【逆构】 organ *n.* 器官

turn[83] [tɜːn]

【释义】 *n.* 转向，轮流 *v.* 翻转，旋转，转动，转向，轮流

【例句】 Up close, it seems a little all over the place, but from farther away, the true path shows and in the end it justifies all the turns along the way. (TPO4, L, S1, L2) 从眼前看，好像走了很多弯路，但从长远看，这是一条正确的道路并且最终证明了一路上所有的兜兜转转都是合理的。

【搭配】 in turn 轮流，依次
turn off 关掉；拐弯
turn into 变成
turn on 打开，发动
turn out 生产；结果是
turn over 移交给；翻阅；把…翻过来
turn in 上交
turn down 拒绝
turn from 对…感到厌恶
turn away 避开；解雇

character[80] [ˈkærɪktə]

【释义】 *n.* 人物，角色（role）；特征，性格（feature, personality）

【例句】 But all the other elements, like the location or characters, might be modified for each audience. (TPO5, L, S2, L2) 但是其他所有的因素，比如地点和人物，可能会根据不同的观众作出修改。

【派生】 characteristic *a.* 独特的，典型的 *n.* 特性，特征

project[80]

【释义】 [prəˈdʒekt] *v.* 1. 放映（show, screen）2. 计划，规划（plan, design）3. 预测，推想 4. 投掷，发射（fire, shoot）[ˈprɒdʒekt] *n.* 1. 方案

(scheme) 2. 课题,项目,工程

【例句】The cinema did not emerge as a form of mass consumption until its technology evolved from the initial "peepshow" format to the point where images were projected on a screen in a darkened theater. (TPO2, R, S2, T2) 电影放映技术从最初的西洋镜形式演变为将影像投射到幽暗的影院屏幕上,这一转变使得电影开始成为大众消费。

【派生】projection *n.* 发射
projectionist *n.* 放映员
projector *n.* 放映机
projectile *n.* 发射物,投掷物

rate[80] [reɪt] 

【释义】*n.* 1. 比率,率 2. 价格 3. 速度 4. 等级 *v.* 1. 评级 2. 估价 3. 把…列为

【例句】Estimates indicate that the aquifer contains enough water to fill Lake Huron, but unfortunately, under the semiarid climatic conditions that presently exist in the region, rates of addition to the aquifer are minimal, amounting to about half a centimeter a year. (TPO3, R, S1, T1) 据估计,(奥加拉拉)蓄水层的含水量足以填满休伦湖,但不幸的是,在目前该地区半干旱的气候条件下,(奥加拉拉)蓄水层的蓄水能力极低,每年仅半厘米左右。

【搭配】at this/that rate 按照这种情形;既然如此

image[79] ['ɪmɪdʒ] 

【释义】*n.* 1. 形象,印象 2. 镜像,影像,图像,雕像 3. 意象,比喻

【例句】The cinema did not emerge as a form of mass consumption until its technology evolved from the initial "peepshow" format to the point where images were projected on a screen in a darkened theater. (TPO2, R, S2, T2) 电影放映技术从最初的西洋镜形式演变为将影像投射到幽暗的影院屏幕上,这一转变使得电影开始成为大众消费。

【逆构】brand image 品牌形象
public image 公众形象

site[79] [saɪt] 

【释义】*n.* 位置,场所,地点(location, place, position) *v.* 使坐落在;设置

【例句】In addition to other artworks, figurines representing the human female in exaggerated form have also been found at Upper Paleolithic sites. (TPO4, R, S2, T1) 除了其他艺术品外,形式夸张的女性形象的雕像也在旧石器时代的遗址中被发掘出来。

【搭配】off site 不在现场

cave[78] [keɪv] 

【释义】*n.* 洞穴,山洞 *v.* (使)塌陷,倒塌

【例句】Some of the world's oldest preserved art is the cave art of Europe, most of it in Spain and France. (TPO3, L, S2, L1) 一些世界上保存最古老的艺术是欧洲的洞窟艺术,其中大部分在西班牙和法国。

cover[78] ['kʌvə]

【释义】*v.* 1. 覆盖 2. 包含 3. 掩护 4. 报导 *n.* 1. 封面 2. 盖子,套子 3. 表面

【例句】We've been covering rocks and different types of rocks for the last several weeks. (TPO4, L, S2, L1) 在过去几周里我们谈到了岩石和岩石的不同种类。

【搭配】from cover to cover 从头至尾
under cover 隐藏着;秘密地
cover up 掩盖
cover for 代替
cover in 用泥土填,遮盖住
take cover 躲藏,隐蔽

movement[78] ['muːvmənt]

【释义】*n.* 1. 移动;运动;活动 2. 动作,姿势 3. 量的变化,增减

【例句】So you've probably studied both of these movements separately, Realism and Impressionism. (TPO1, L, S1, L1) 你们可能已经分别学习了这两种运动:现实主义(运动)和印象主义(运动)。

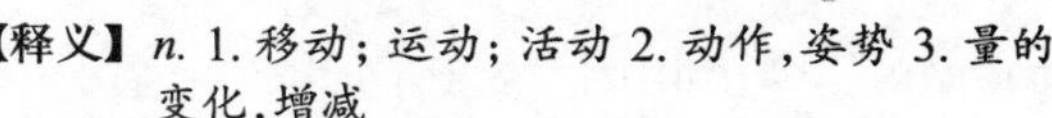

返记菜单

rate[80] image[79] site[79] cave[78] cover[78]
movement[78]

once[78] [wʌns]

【释义】*conj.* 一旦 *ad.* 1. 一次 2. 曾经

【例句】But still, once all the construction is over, more people will probably want to live in the dorms, right? (TPO11, S, Q3) 但是，一旦所有的建设完成，可能会有更多的学生愿意住在宿舍里，对吧？

【搭配】once again 再一次
at once 立刻，马上
once and for all 彻底地，永远地
once in a while 偶尔，间或
once upon a time 从前

advertise[77] ['ædvətaɪz]

【释义】*v.* 1. 为…做广告，宣传（promote）2. 公布，公告

【例句】Another strategy they use is to get a celebrity to advertise a product. (TPO3, S, Q6) 他们所使用的另一个策略就是请一位名人来为产品做宣传。

【派生】advertisement *n.* 广告
advertising *n.* 广告业，广告的总称

main[77] [meɪn]

【释义】*a.* 主要的，重要的（major, important, dominant）*n.* 1. 总管道，干线 2. 体力

【例句】This used to be an agricultural area and we already know that where the main lecture hall now stands, there once were farm house and barn that were erected in the late 1700s. (TPO3, L, S2, C1) 这里过去是一片农场，我们已经知道，现在主讲厅所在的地方曾经是18世纪后期时建立起来的农舍和仓库。

【搭配】by main force 尽全力

means[77] [miːnz]

【释义】*n.* 1. 方法，办法（way, approach）2. 金钱，财产

【例句】If I value something as a means to something else, then it has what we will call "extrinsic value." (TPO2, L, S2, L1) 如果我认为某一事物是获取另一事物的手段，那么这个事物就具有了我们所说的"外在价值"。

【搭配】by means of 依靠，通过，借助于
leave no means untried 千方百计，想尽一切办法

style[77] [staɪl]

【释义】*n.* 1. 风格；式样，类型（manner）2. 时尚（fashion）*v.* 设计

【例句】In other words, the arguments both for and against government funding of the arts are as many and as varied as the individual styles of the artists who hold them. (TPO4, L, S2, L2) 换言之，赞成和反对政府为艺术提供资金的争论就如同拥有这些艺术品的艺术家的个人风格一样纷繁复杂，且具有多样性。

【派生】stylish *a.* 时髦的
stylistic *a.* 风格上的

【搭配】in style 流行，时髦地
out of style 过时的

pattern[76] ['pætən]

【释义】*n.* 1. 模式，方式 2. 花样，图案 3. 模型，样本 *v.* 1. 仿制，复制 2. 用图案装饰

【例句】Well, this pattern is known as Bode's Law. (TPO2, L, S2, L2) 这种模式被称为波德定律。

【派生】patterned *a.* 有图案的

【搭配】after the pattern 仿照…
pattern oneself after 模仿（某人的）样子
pattern something upon/on 仿照…式样制造某物

involve[75] [ɪn'vɒlv]

【释义】*v.* 包含，牵涉，使卷入

【例句】It no longer involves radioactive elements. (TPO1, L, S1, L2) 它不再包含放射性元素。

【派生】involvement *n.* 牵连，包含
involved *a.* 卷入的，有关的，复杂的

【搭配】involve in 涉及，包含，牵涉到

lead[75] [liːd]

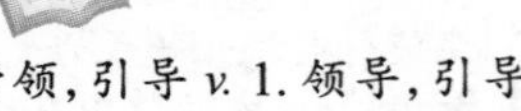

【释义】*n.* 1. 铅 2. 带领，引导 *v.* 1. 领导，引导 2. 通向，导致，引起

【例句】Research has focused on the toxic effects of heavy metals such as lead, cadmium, mercury, and aluminum. (TPO5, R, S1, T1) 研究集中在诸如铅、镉、汞和铝等重金属的

毒性上。
【派生】leaden *a.* 浅灰色的；铅制的
leaded *a.* 加铅的

desert[74]

【释义】['dezət] *n.* 沙漠，不毛之地 *a.* 荒凉的，荒芜的 [dɪ'zɜːt] *v.* 1. 舍弃，遗弃 2. 擅离职守（尤指从军队中开小差）
【例句】Death valley is this desert plane, a dry lake bed in California surrounded by mountains and on the desert floor these huge rocks, some of them hundreds of pounds. (TPO4, L, S2, L1) 死亡谷是这样一片沙地，位于加利福利亚的一处干涸的湖床，周围群山环绕，而这些沙地上的巨石，有的重达几百磅。
【派生】deserted *a.* 荒芜的，荒废的

infant[74] ['ɪnfənt]

【释义】*n.* 婴儿，幼儿 *a.* 1. 婴儿的 2. 初期的
【例句】Within them, infants and children are introduced to the ways of their society. (TPO13, R, S1, T1) 在这个群体里，幼儿和儿童被引入社会。
【派生】infancy *n.* 婴儿期，幼年时代
【搭配】premature infant 早产儿
infant industry 新生工业

relate[74] [rɪ'leɪt]

【释义】*v.* 1. 联系，使有关联（connect）2. 讲述，叙述（narrate, state）
【例句】The first is support from administrators in an education system, enabling teachers to understand the requirements of reflective practice and how it relates to teaching students. (TPO9, R, S2, T1) 首先是来自教育系统管理层的支持，这使得教师们明白了反思实践的必要条件以及它与教学之间的联系。
【派生】related *a.* 有关系的
relation *n.* 关系，联系

shape[73] [ʃeɪp]

【释义】*n.* 形状，形式；身材 *v.* 塑造，定形，使…成形
【例句】It's really the visual components of the work, things like color, texture, shape, lines and how these elements work together, that tell us something about the work. (TPO4, S, Q6) 其实是作品中的视觉要素，比如颜色、质地、形状、线条以及这些元素如何组合在一起，才让我们对作品有了一些了解。
【搭配】in shape 处于良好状态
take shape 形成；体现
out of shape 走样；身体状况不佳

social[73] ['səʊʃəl]

【释义】*a.* 社会的，社交的；群居的 *n.* 社交聚会
【例句】A country as vast as China with so long-lasting a civilization has a complex social history. (TPO10, R, S1, T1) 像中国这样一个地域广阔、有着悠久文明的国家一般都有着复杂的社会历史。
【派生】socialize *v.* 使社会化

solar[73] ['səʊlə]

【释义】*a.* 太阳的，太阳能的
【例句】So since Jupiter, the planet, is the largest planet in our solar system, it's like the king of the planets, like Jupiter was the king of all the gods. (TPO1, L, S2, C1) 由于木星是我们太阳系中最大的行星，所以它就像所有行星中的王者，正如朱庇特是众神之王一样。
【派生】solarium *n.* 日光浴室
solarization *n.* 日晒
【搭配】solar calendar 阳历
solar radiation 太阳辐射，日光照
solar cell 太阳能电池

available[72] [ə'veɪləbl]

【释义】*a.* 可用的，可得到的（obtainable, accessible）；有空的（free）
【例句】Groundwater is the word used to describe water that saturates the ground, filling all the available spaces. (TPO1, R, S2, T2) 地下水是指渗入到地下并填满所有可能的缝隙的水。
【派生】availablity *n.* 可用性，实效性

square[72] [skweə]

【释义】*a.* 正方形的；平方的 *n.* 正方形；平方；广场

返记菜单

desert[74] infant[74] relate[74] shape[73] social[73]
solar[73] available[72] square[72]

v. 使成正方形；求平方；使打成平局

【例句】The Ogallala aquifer is a sandstone formation that underlies some 583,000 square kilometers of land extending from northwestern Texas to southern South Dakota. (TPO3, R, S1, T1) 奥加拉拉蓄水层属于砂岩结构，从德克萨斯州西北部到南达科塔州南部一直绵延了583000平方公里。

effective[71] [ɪ'fektɪv] 

【释义】a. 1. 有效的，生效的(efficient, powerful) 2. 事实上的，实际的 3. 显著的(striking)

【例句】This process took time and patience and effective trainers. (TPO9, R, S2, T1) 这个过程需要时间、耐心以及有效的受训者。

【派生】effectuate v. 实行，完成
effectively ad. 有效地；实际上
effectiveness n. 效力

【逆构】effect n. 结果，效力

【搭配】effective measures 有效措施

glass[71] [glɑːs] 

【释义】n. 1. 玻璃 2. 玻璃杯 3.[pl.] 眼镜

【例句】For example, solar energy is gathered through large glass panels facing the sun. (TPO12, L, S2, L2) 例如，太阳能是通过朝向太阳的大玻璃板收集起来的。

【派生】glasshouse n. 温室，暖房
glassware n. 玻璃器皿

whale[71] [weɪl] 

【释义】n. 鲸，鲸目动物

【例句】It should be obvious that cetaceans—whales, porpoises, and dolphins—are mammals. (TPO2, R, S2, T1) 显然，鲸类动物——鲸、鼠海豚和海豚——都是哺乳动物。

campus[70] ['kæmpəs] 

【释义】n. 校园；场地

【例句】The administration has plans to acquire a new sculpture for campus. (TPO1, S, Q3) 管理部门打算在校园中设立一座新的雕塑。

【搭配】on campus 在校内

cell[70] [sel] 

【释义】n. 1. 细胞 2. 小房间 3. 小组 4. 电池

【例句】I was so impressed with the way you handle the microscope and the samples of onion cells. (TPO15, L, S2, C1) 你操作显微镜的方式以及洋葱细胞的样本都令我如此印象深刻。

【搭配】cell phone 手机

compute[70] [kəm'pjuːt] 

【释义】v. 计算，估算(calculate, count)

【例句】All the checks are computed automatically in the system. (TPO12, L, S2, C1) 所有的工资都是在系统里自动计算的。

【派生】computer n. 计算机

feature[70] ['fiːtʃə] 

【释义】v. 以…为特色(characterize)；(电影)由…主演 n. 特点，特征(characteristic)；容貌(countenance)

【例句】Many incomplete skeletons were found but they included, for the first time in an archaeocyte, a complete hind leg that features a foot with three tiny toes. (TPO2, R, S2, T1) 尽管发现的这些骨骼并不完整，但这是专家们第一次在原始动物身上发现完整的后肢，其主要特征是有三个小脚趾的足部。

【派生】featureless a. 没有特点的

recent[70] ['riːsnt]

【释义】a. 最近的，近来的(late, modern)

【例句】The deserts, which already occupy approximately a fourth of the Earth's land surface, have in recent decades been increasing at an alarming pace. (TPO2, R, Sl, T1) 沙漠已经占据地球表面约四分之一的面积，近几十年来仍在以惊人的速度扩张。

【反义】ancient, old

【派生】recently ad. 最近，近来

sediment[70] ['sedɪmənt] 

【释义】n. 沉淀物，沉积物

返记菜单

effective[71]	glass[71]	whale[71]	campus[70]	cell[70]
compute[70]	feature[70]	recent[70]	sediment[70]	

【例句】Several skeleton of another early whale, Basilosaurus, were found in sediments left by the Tethys Sea and now exposed in the Sahara desert. (TPO2, R, S2, T1) 人们在古地中海残留的沉积物中发现了另一类早期鲸鱼——龙王鲸的一些骨骸，这些骨骸如今暴露在撒哈拉大沙漠上。

【派生】sedimentary *a.* 沉积的，沉淀性的

observe[69] [əb'zɜːv]

【释义】*v.* 1. 注意到，察觉 2. 观察 3. 评论 4. 遵守，遵循

【例句】All the words you know, all the scientific theories you've learned, the rules your parents taught you to observe, all are memes that have been passed on from person to person. (TPO5, L, S1, L1) 你知道的所有单词、学过的所有科学理论，以及父母教导你去遵守的规则，所有这一切都是一个人传递给另一个人的文化基因。

【派生】observer *n.* 观察者；遵守者

【搭配】observe on 评论
observe professional ethics 恪守职业道德
observe the discipline 遵守纪律

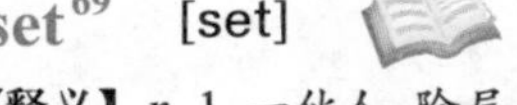

set[69] [set]

【释义】*n.* 1. 一伙人，阶层 2. 一套 *v.* 1. 放置 2. 设定，规定 3. 调整，分配 *a.* 做好准备的

【例句】Indeed, if you take baby tree swallows out of a nest for an hour feeding half the set and starving the other half, when the birds are replaced in the nest, the starved youngsters beg more loudly than the fed birds, and the parent birds feed the active beggars more than those who beg less vigorously. (TPO11, R, S2, T2) 确实，如果你把树燕幼鸟从巢中拿出来一小时，其中一半的鸟喂食，而另一半饿着，那么当把它们放回巢中时，挨饿的幼鸟的乞食声就比喂过的鸟大，而相比求食不够活跃的幼鸟，父母会更多地喂食给积极求食的幼鸟们。

【搭配】set up 建立；装配；开业
a set of 一套(组，副)
set out 出发；开始；陈述
set in 到来；流行
set forth 陈述，提出
set off 出发；分开
set by 把…搁在一旁

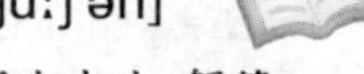

solution[69] [sə'ljuːʃən]

【释义】*n.* 1. 溶液 2. 解决办法，解答

【例句】Much of the research on nutrient deficiencies is based on growing plants hydroponically, that is, in soilless liquid nutrient solutions. (TPO5, R, S1, T1) 很多有关营养缺乏的研究都是基于水栽培植物，也就是生长在无土壤的营养液中的植物。

【派生】solutionist *n.* 解密专家，解答者

【逆构】solute *v.* 解决

yawn[69] [jɔːn]

【释义】*v.* 1. 打呵欠 2. 张开裂开 *n.* 1. 呵欠 2.〈口〉乏味的人(或事)

【例句】Unfortunately, the few scientific investigations of yawning have failed to find any connection between how often someone yawns and how much sleep they have had or how tired they are. (TPO18, R, S2, L1) 但遗憾的是，少数对于打呵欠的科学研究并没有找到任何关于打呵欠频率与个人睡眠时长或者疲劳程度之间的联系。

lay[68] [leɪ]

【释义】*v.* 1. 产(蛋，卵) 2. 放置，放下，铺设，使处于 3. 筹划，设置 4. 提出，提交

【例句】For example, the common housefly reproduces by laying several thousand eggs. (TPO5, L, S1, L1) 比如，普通的苍蝇通过产下几千颗卵来繁衍后代。

characteristic[67] [ˌkærɪktə'rɪstɪk]

【释义】*n.* 特征，特性(feature, property) *a.* 独特的，特有的(distinctive, peculiar)；典型的(typical)

【例句】They have one more characteristic that's very important, and that is that they are exceptionally resistant to salt water. (TPO2, L, S1, L2) 它们还有另外一个重要的特点，那就是它们对盐水的抵抗力异常地强。

【派生】characteristically *ad.* 典型地

【逆构】character *n.* 特点，特征

返记菜单

observe[69] set[69] solution[69] yawn[69] lay[68] characteristic[67]

impact[67]

【释义】['ɪmpækt] *n.* 1. 影响，作用（influence, effect）2. 冲击，撞击（collision）[ɪm'pækt] *v.* 1. 对某事物有影响（affect）2. 冲撞，冲击

【例句】One of the most far-reaching examples is the impact of the fine ninth-century AD. (TPO10, R, S1, T1) 意义最为深远的例子之一是公元第九世纪的影响。

【搭配】impact of…的影响
impact on 影响；对…冲击，碰撞

run[67] [rʌn]

【释义】*v.* 1. 行驶，运转 2. 跑，奔跑 3. 竞赛，竞选 4. 流动，延伸 5. 经营

【例句】I ran that by the group. (TPO16, L, S1, C1) 我跟组内的成员讨论过了。

【搭配】run across 偶然碰到
run after 追赶，追求
run away 抛开，逃走
run down 停掉；耗尽；撞倒
run into 偶然遇到；陷入；合计
run out 用完，耗尽
run on 继续做
in the long/short run 从长远 / 短期来看

surprise[67] [sə'praɪz]

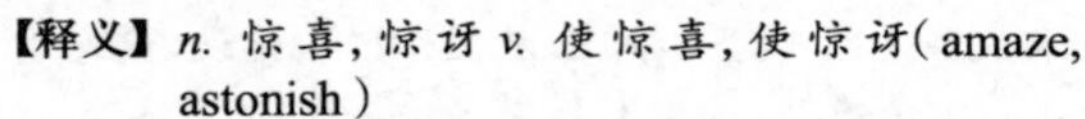

【释义】*n.* 惊喜，惊讶 *v.* 使惊喜，使惊讶（amaze, astonish）

【例句】Anyway, Uranium-Lead Dating has produced some surprises. (TPO1, L, S1, L2) 不管怎样，铀铅测年法已经带来了很多惊喜。

【派生】surprised *a.* 感到惊讶的，出人意料的
surprising *a.* 令人感到惊讶的

illustrate[65] ['ɪləstret]

【释义】*v.* 1. 举例说明 2.（为书）作插图，图解

【例句】It is a monumental scientific achievement, and its development illustrates the essential interplay between observation, prediction, and testing required for scientific progress. (TPO16, R, S2, T1) 周期表是一项科学的创举，它的发展表明了面向科学进步的观察、预测和验证之间的相互作用。

【派生】illustration *n.* 插图，例证
illuatrated *a.* 有插图的

【搭配】illustrate with 用…来说明；给…加插图

chemical[64] ['kemɪkəl]

【释义】*n.* 化学物 *a.* 化学的

【例句】But when we analyze the cells chemically we find something very interesting, a chemical in them, and an enzyme called telomerase. (TPO12, L, S1, L1) 但是当我们从化学角度分析这些细胞的时候，我们会发现一些很有趣的物质，它们中有一种化学物质，是一种叫做端粒酶的酶素。

【派生】chemically *ad.* 从化学角度，以化学方法

【逆构】chemistry *n.* 化学

mass[64] [mæs]

【释义】*n.* 1. 块，团，堆 2. 大量 3. 群众 *a.* 大规模的，大量的 *v.* 集中

【例句】Glaciers are slowly moving masses of ice that have accumulated on land in areas where more snowfalls during a year than melts. (TPO15, R, S1, T1) 冰川是一种缓慢移动的巨大冰块，这些冰块在每年降雪多于融雪的地方积聚形成。

【搭配】mass of 成堆的，大量的
mass media 大众传媒

Word List 3

individual[63] [ˌɪndɪˈvɪdjʊəl] 

【释义】*a.* 1. 个别的,单独的 2. 独特的(special) *n.* 个人

【例句】Individual fish may be replaced, but the number of fish will tend to be the same from one year to the next. (TPO3, R, S1, T2) 个别鱼类可能会被替代,但每年鱼的总数都趋于一致。

【派生】individually *ad.* 各自地,分别地
individualism *n.* 个人主义

subject[63] 

【释义】[ˈsʌbdʒɪkt] *n.* 1. 主题(theme, topic) 2. 科目 3. 对象 *a.* 1. 易患…的 2. 受…支配的,服从的 [səbˈdʒekt] *v.* 使服从,使隶属

【例句】Researchers have proposed several different explanations for the fact that animals were the most common subjects in the cave paintings. (TPO4, R, S2, T1) 对于石窟壁画最常以动物为主题这一情况,研究者已经提出了几种不同的解释。

【派生】subjection *n.* 征服,隶属
subjective *a.* 主观的,个人的

【搭配】on the subject 就某话题
subject line 标题; 主题行

survive[63] [səˈvaɪv] 

【释义】*v.* 1. 幸存,幸免于难 2. 艰难度过,挺过 3. 比…活得长

【例句】According to Fladmark, Native American languages have survived the longest along the west coast of the Americas. (TPO9, R, S1, T1) 根据Fladmark的说法,在沿美洲西海岸这一带,美国本土语言的存在时间是最长的。

【反义】perish

【派生】survival *n.* 生存,幸存
survivor *n.* 幸存者,生还者

semester[62] [sɪˈmestə] 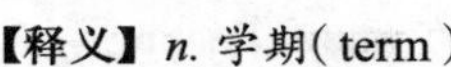

【释义】*n.* 学期(term)

【例句】Remember I said that at some point during this semester I wanted you to attend an exhibit at the Fairy Street Gallery and then write about it? (TPO1, L, S1, L1) 我说过让你们这个学期找个时间去童话街画廊参观展览,然后写一些东西,还记得吗?

tend[62] [tend] 

【释义】*v.* 趋向,朝向(incline); 照料,管理

【例句】Trees trend to attain greater heights on ridges. (TPO1, R, S1, T1) 生长在山脊上的树趋向于长得更高。

【派生】tendency *n.* 倾向,趋势; 癖好

【搭配】tend to 有…的倾向; 易于

within[62] [wɪðˈɪn] 

【释义】*prep.* 1.(表示位置)在…里面,在…内部 2.(表示时间、举例)不超过

【例句】The structure of biological communities depends on the types of relationships that exist among the species within. (TPO17, R, S2, T2) 生物群落的结构取决于物种内部存在的关系类型。

【反义】beyond

power[61] [ˈpaʊə] 

【释义】*n.* 1. 能,动力 2. 力量(strength) 3. 能力,本领(ability) 4. 权力,权威 *v.* 1. 给…提供动力(stimulate) 2. 促进,推动

【例句】In Britain one of the most dramatic changes of the Industrial Revolution was the harnessing of power.(TPO6, R, S1, T1)在英国,工业革命带来的最大的变化之一就是动力的运用。

【派生】powerful *a.* 有力的
powerless *a.* 无力的

【搭配】beyond/out of one's power 力所不及
fall into the power of 落入…手中
in power 掌权的,在位的
out of power(政党)在野的

返记菜单

individual[63] subject[63] survive[63] semester[62] tend[62]
within[62] power[61]

brief[60] [briːf]

【释义】*a.* 1. 短暂的，简短的(short, fleeting) 2. 简洁的(concise) *v.* 作概述，作总结(summarize) *n.* 摘要，概要

【例句】Some of the proposed mechanisms required a very brief period during which all extinctions suddenly took place, other mechanisms would be more likely to have taken place more gradually, over an extended period. (TPO15, R, S2, T2) 一些假设的生物机制在很短的时间内就会灭绝，而另外一些生物机制的灭绝则是逐渐发生的，需要较长一段时间。

【派生】briefing *n.* 简报，简介
briefly *ad.* 简要地，剪短地

carry[60] [ˈkærɪ]

【释义】*v.* 1. 运送，传送 2. 负载，容纳 3. 传递，传播 4. 拿，挑，提，搬 5. 支撑，支持

【例句】The sounds made as each wing is opened carry extremely well over distance. (TPO17, R, S2, T1) 翅膀张开时发出的声响能够传送到极远的距离之外。

【搭配】carry out 实行，运作

identify[60] [aɪˈdentɪfaɪ]

【释义】*v.* 1. 认出，识别(distinguish, recognize) 2. 找到，发现 3. 确认，鉴定

【例句】Four specific activities have been identified as major contributions to the desertification process. (TPO2, R, Sl, T1) 四种特定活动被确定为促进沙漠化进程的罪魁祸首。

【派生】identification *n.* 鉴别
identifiable *a.* 可鉴别的

minor[60] [ˈmaɪnə]

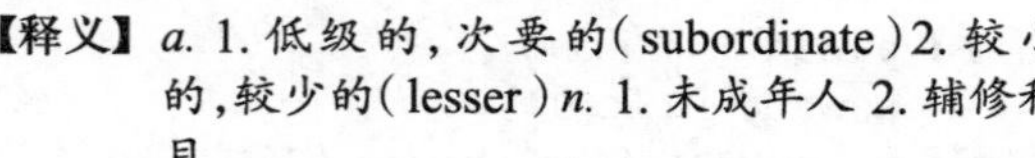

【释义】*a.* 1. 低级的，次要的(subordinate) 2. 较小的，较少的(lesser) *n.* 1. 未成年人 2. 辅修科目

【例句】Minor characters are sometimes called, well, just the opposite, “flat”. (TPO6, L, S2, L1) 次要角色恰恰相反，有时被叫做“扁平人物”。

【反义】major

【派生】minority *n.* 少数；少数民族

【搭配】in a minor key 轻描淡写的

practice[60] [ˈpræktɪs]

【释义】*n.* 练习，实习；习惯；业务；执行，实践(exercise)

【例句】Some early societies stopped using myths in their religious practices when rites ceased to be seen as useful for social well-being. (TPO1, R, S2, T1) 当人们不再认为宗教仪式有益于社会福祉的时候，一些早期的社会团体就停止在其宗教实践中运用神话了。

【派生】practiced *a.* 熟练的，有经验的，老练的

【搭配】in practice

room[60] [ruːm]

【释义】*n.* 1. 机会，余地 2. 室，房间 3. 空间，空位(space)

【例句】You’re next on the waiting list, so now there’s room for you to come along. (TPO2, S, Q5) 你在候补名单上，所以现在你有机会同去。

【派生】roomer *n.* 房客
roomful *n.* 满房间；全屋的人
roomy *a.* 宽敞的
roommate *n.* 室友

【搭配】make room for 让地方(或位置)给…
single/double room 单人/双人房间

nest[59] [nɛst]

【释义】*n.* 巢，穴，窝 *v.* 筑巢；置于巢中

【例句】A classic example is noisy begging by nestling songbirds when a parent returns to the nest with food. (TPO11, R, S2, T2) 一个典型的例子是尚未离巢的幼小鸣鸟看见父母带着食物归巢后发出的喧闹的鸣叫。

【搭配】nest egg 储蓄金，储备金

original[59] [əˈrɪdʒənəl]

【释义】*a.* 1. 原始的，最初的(first, primary) 2. 独创性的，原版的(novel) *n.* 原件，原作

【例句】When such statues are viewed in isolation, out of their original context and without knowledge of their function, it is easy to criticize them for their rigid attitudes that

remained unchanged for three thousand years. (TPO11, R, S1, T1) 当脱离了其原来的环境而孤立地看这些雕像，且不了解其作用时，很容易会对其三千年来都保持不变的僵硬姿态提出批判。

【派生】originally *ad.* 最初，起初，本来
originality *n.* 创意，新奇

【逆构】origin *n.* 起源，由来；出身，血统

working[59] ['wɜːkɪŋ]

【释义】*a.* 1.（涉及）工作的 2.（想法等）可作为基础的，有效用的 *n.* 运作方式

【例句】To be architecture, a building must achieve a working harmony with a variety of elements. (TPO3, R, S1, T1) 从建筑学上来说，一幢建筑物必须实现各种要素的和谐搭配。

【逆构】work *v.*（使）工作，（使）运作

【搭配】working time 工作时间

charge[58] [tʃɑːdʒ]

【释义】*v.* 1. 索（价）；收（费）2. 记账，赊账 3. 控诉，控告；指责（accuse）*n.* 1. 费用（bill）2. 指责，指控，控告（accusation）3. 感染力，震撼力

【例句】Exhibitors, however, wanted to maximize their profits, which they could do more readily by projecting a handful of films to hundreds of customers at a time (rather than one at a time) and by charging 25 to 50 cents admission. (TPO2, R, S2, T2) 然而，影院老板希望将收益最大化。要想更容易地做到这一点，他们可以一次性向数百名观众放映几部电影（而不是一次一位观众），每位观众的入场费是25到50美分。

【派生】chargeable *a.* 可以控诉的；可充电的

【搭配】in charge 负责，主管

claim[58] [kleɪm]

【释义】*v./n.* 1. 声称，断言，主张（assert）2. 要求（demand, require, request）3. 索赔

【例句】To make a comparison that supports the claim that, in general, stability increases with diversity. (TPO3, R, S1, T2) 为了做个对比来支持"一般而言，稳定性随着多样性而增强"这一论断。

【反义】disclaim

【派生】claimable *a.* 可要求的

compare[58] [kəm'peə]

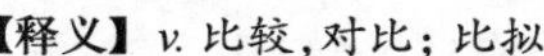

【释义】*v.* 比较，对比；比拟

【例句】But she's got a very unusual style, compared to some of the artists we've looked at this term. (TPO1, L, S1, L1) 但是，同我们这学期见过的艺术家相比，她的风格不同寻常。

【派生】comparable *a.* 可比的，比得上的
comparison *n.* 比较，对比

【搭配】compare to 把…比作
compare with 与…相比

function[58] ['fʌŋkʃən]

【释义】*v.* 运行；起作用（operate, perform）*n.* 功能，机能，作用（role, task）

【例句】The Kinetoscope functioned in a similar way. (TPO2, R, S2, T2) 电影放映机的运行方式与之类似。

【派生】functional *a.* 功能的，起作用的
functionalism *n.* 功能主义
functionally *ad.* 功能地
functionalist *n.* 功能主义者
multifunctional *a.* 多功能的
malfunction *n.* 故障

【搭配】fulfil a function 完成职责

sense[58] [sens]

【释义】*v.* 意识到，感觉到 *n.* 1. 感官，官能 2. 感觉 3. 判断力 4. 意义，意思

【例句】A long long time ago, a dog sensing danger would get ready to bite whatever animal was threatening him. (TPO17, S, Q4) 很久很久以前，一旦狗发现危险，就会准备好去咬任何威胁到它们的动物。

【反义】senseless

【逆构】make sense 言之有理；理解，明白
in a sense 从某种意义上说

article[57] ['ɑːtɪkl]

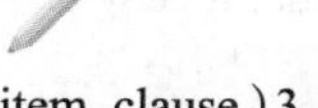

【释义】*n.* 1. 文章 2. 条款（item, clause）3. 冠词 4. 物件（object, thing）

【例句】Then to help draw up the preservation plan to do the research in a professional scientific

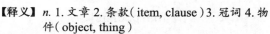

返记菜单

working[59] charge[58] claim[58] compare[58] function[58]
sense[58] article[57]

manner and finally to process the data and write reports and articles. (TPO16, W, Q1) 然后帮助起草保护方案，秉着专业科学的态度进行研究，最后处理数据，写出报告文章。

establish[57] [ɪsˈtæblɪʃ]

【释义】*v.* 1. 建立，成立，设立（build, found, enact, set）2. 安置，使定居（settle）3. 确定，证实

【例句】And then individual states throughout the country started to establish their own state arts councils to help support the arts. (TPO4, L, S2, L2) 之后全国各州相继开始建立起本州的艺术委员会来支持艺术。

【反义】demolish, destroy, ruin

【派生】establishment *n.* 建立，确立，建立的机构
established *a.* 已建立的，已确立的

formation[57] [fɔːˈmeɪʃən]

【释义】*n.* 1. 形成，组成 2. 形成物 3. 队形，排列

【例句】In other words, if you want to know how a land formation was formed, the first thing you probably want to know is how old it is. It's fundamental. (TPO1, L, S1, L2) 换言之，如果你想要知道一个地质构造是怎样形成的，那么可能你首先要知道的就是它形成有多长时间了。这是最根本的。

【搭配】form *n.* 形状，形态 *v.* 构成，组成

review[57] [rɪˈvjuː]

【释义】*v./n.* 1. 检查，复查 2. 复习 3. 回顾，反省 4. 评论

【例句】Further observation revealed the tendency of teachers to evaluate events rather than review the contributory factors in a considered manner by, in effect, standing outside the situation. (TPO9, R, S2, T1) 进一步的观察发现，教师们更倾向于评价事件，而不是站在事件之外以一种深思熟虑的方式洞察一个事件的促成因素。

【派生】reviewer *n.* 评论员，评论家

【搭配】under review 在审查中

hypothesis[56] [haɪˈpɒθɪsɪs]

【释义】*n.* 假说，假设

【例句】There are several hypotheses, including warming or cooling of Earth, changes in seasonal fluctuations or ocean currents, and changing positions of the continents. (TPO15, R, S2, T2) 有几种假说，包括：地球变暖或变冷、季节的变动或洋流的变化，以及大陆位置移动。

【逆构】hypothesize *v.* 假设，假定

hold[55] [həʊld]

【释义】*v.* 1. 持有，拿着，控制 2. 认为 3. 容纳 4. 保持 5. 举行 *n.* 1. 控制，把握 2. 影响

【例句】In other words, the arguments both for and against government funding of the arts are as many and, and as varied as the individual styles of the artists who hold them. (TPO4, L, S2, L2) 换言之，赞成和反对政府为艺术提供资金的争论就如同拥有这些艺术品的艺术家的个人风格一样纷繁复杂，且具有多样性。

【搭配】hold on 不挂断电话，等一下；继续
on hold 暂停；尚未办理的事情；等候接听
get hold of 把握；抓住
take hold 抓住；扛着；固定下来
hold in 抑制，约束
hold up 举起；阻挡，拦截
hold on to sth. 抓住…不放
hold back 隐瞒；退缩；抑制；阻止
hold out 坚持；伸出；提供；维持

price[55] [praɪs]

【释义】*v.* 标价；定价 *n.* 1. 价格，价钱 2. 代价

【例句】Some of the most priced tulips were white with purple stricks, or red with yellow stricks on the paddles, even a dark purple tulip that was very much priced. (TPO6, L, S1, L1) 一些很贵重的郁金香是有着紫条的白色花，或是有着黄条的红色花，甚至暗紫色的郁金香也是很值钱的。

【派生】priceless *a.* 无价的，贵重的，无法估价的

【搭配】at any price 不惜任何代价；无论如何

data[54] [ˈdeɪtə]

【释义】*n.* 数据，资料（information）

【例句】I've got all my data. (TPO2, L, S1, C1) 我已经收集好了所有需要的数据。

【搭配】data storage/transfer/retrieval 数据存储/传输/获取

figure[53] ['fɪgə]

【释义】*n.* 1. 外形，轮廓(outline) 2. 图形，图表(diagram) 3. 数字 4. 人物 5. 身材，体型(shape) *v.* 1. 认为，领会到 2. 演算，估算

【例句】The stone between the arms and the body and between the legs in standing figures or the legs and the seat in seated ones was not normally cut away. (TPO11, R, S1, T1) 石像人物的手臂与身体之间、站立姿态下的两腿之间或者坐姿下的双腿与座位之间的石头通常都不会被削去。

【搭配】figure out 解决；算出；弄明白
figure in 算进
figure on [美口] 指望；[英口] 打算；料想
figure for 谋取
go figure 猜猜看

portrait[53] ['pɔːtrɪt]

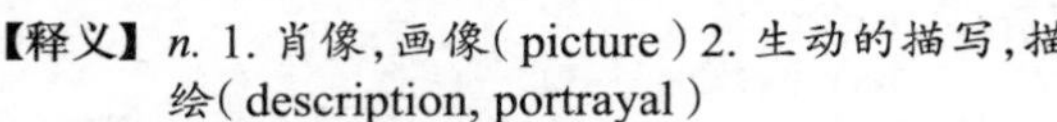

【释义】*n.* 1. 肖像，画像(picture) 2. 生动的描写，描绘(description, portrayal)

【例句】One such painting is known as attributed to Rembrandt because of its style, and indeed the representation of the woman's face is very much like that of portraits known to be by Rembrandt. (TPO3, W, Q1) 有一幅画因其风格特点而被认为是伦勃朗的作品，而画面中女人的脸部肖像的画法也的确与伦勃朗的作画方式颇为一致。

【派生】portraitist *n.* 肖像画家
portraiture *n.* 画像，肖像；画像技法

short[53] [ʃɔːt]

【释义】*a.* 1. 短的，矮的，近的 2. 短期的，短暂的 3. 短缺的，不足的(insufficient, deficient) 4. 粗暴无礼的 *ad.* 突然地；不足，达不到

【例句】Hey, don't sell yourself short. (TPO18, L, S2, C1) 嘿，别看轻自己。

【反义】long, tall

【派生】shortage *n.* 不足

【搭配】short of 缺乏，不足；除…以外
in short 总之，简言之
short in 在…方面短(缺)的
for short 作为…的缩写

statuary[53] ['stætʃuəri]

【释义】*n.* 组雕，雕塑艺术

【例句】Why did the Egyptians not develop sculpture in which the body turned and twisted through space like classical Greek statuary? (TPO11, R, S1, T1) 为什么埃及人不把雕像制作成像古希腊雕像那样的翻转或弯曲的样子？

benefit[52] ['benɪfɪt]

【释义】*n.* 1. 利益，好处，恩惠 2. 津贴，保险金 *v.* 得益于，使受益(profit)

【例句】Ah, it's just a term that describes this situation, when people in the group seek to get the benefits of being in a group without contributing to the work. (TPO4, L, S2, C1) 嗯，就是这个词语，它描述了团队成员并未对团队工作作出贡献却试图从中获益的情形。

【派生】beneficial *a.* 有益的
beneficiary *n.* 受益人，受惠者

【搭配】for the benefit of 为…的利益
benefit by/from 得益于
in benefit 有资格得到救济金

dinosaur[52] ['daɪnəsɔː]

【释义】*n.* 恐龙

【例句】Paleontologists have argued for a long time that the demise of the dinosaurs was caused by climatic alterations. (TPO8, R, S2, T1) 在很长一段时期，古生物学家都争辩说，恐龙的灭绝是由气候变化引起的。

【派生】dinosaurian *a.* 恐龙的，似恐龙的

display[52] [dɪ'spleɪ]

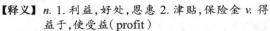

【释义】*v./n.* 1. 显示，显露(illustrate, show) 2. 陈列，展览(exhibit) 3. 展示(demonstrate)

【例句】Because this region has been settled the longest, it also displays the greatest diversity in Native American languages. (TPO9, R, S1, T1) 由于这一地区是人们定居时间最长的，因此它最大程度地展示了美国本土语言上的多样性。

返记菜单

figure[53] portrait[53] short[53] statuary[53] benefit[52]
dinosaur[52] display[52]

【反义】conceal, hide
【派生】displayer *n.* 显示仪,显示器
【搭配】on display 正在展览中

position[52] [pəˈzɪʃən]

【释义】*v.* 安置(install);定位 *n.* 1. 位置(location, place)2. 职位 3. 立场 4. 姿势,状态
【例句】But running is efficient only if an animal's legs are positioned underneath its body, not at the body's side, as they are for crocodiles and many lizards. (TPO4, W, Q1) 但是,只有当动物的腿长在身体下方时才可以跑得快,而不是像鳄鱼和很多蜥蜴那样长在身体两侧。
【派生】positional *a.* 位置的,地位的
【搭配】in position 就位;在适当的位置;在原位
in a position to 能够…,可以…
in the position of 处在…位置上

public[52] [ˈpʌblɪk]

【释义】*a.* 1.公众的,公共的 2.公开的 *n.* 公众,民众,大众(people)
【例句】If you wanted to save yourself the trouble of hunting down the second driver, well, what about public transportation? (TPO1, S, Q5) 如果你想省去找第二个司机的麻烦,那么,使用公共交通怎么样啊?
【反义】private
【派生】publicise *v.* 宣传,宣扬;公布
publicity *n.* 宣传;公开
【搭配】in public 公开地,当众
go public 公开发售股票

cool[51] [kuːl]

【释义】*a.* 1.〈俚〉酷的,了不起的 2. 凉爽的,凉的(chilly)3. 冷静的,冷漠的(calm)*v.* 1.(使)变凉,(使)冷却 2.(使)冷静
【例句】Market research was showing that new customers said they would be more interested in buying our computers if they looked cooler. (TPO1, S, Q4) 市场调查表明,顾客认为要是我们的电脑看起来更酷的话,他们将更有兴趣购买。
【派生】cooler *n.* 冷却剂

exchange[51] [ɪksˈtʃeɪndʒ]

【释义】*v.* 1. 交换,兑换(change)2. 交易(trade)*n.* 1. 交换,兑换 2. 交流 3. 交易(所)
【例句】People exchange goods and services for coins or paper bills. (TPO2, S, Q6) 人们将商品和服务兑换成硬币或纸币。
【搭配】in exchange (for) 作为(对…的)交换
New York Stock Exchange 纽约证券交易所

lack[51] [læk]

【释义】*v./n.* 缺乏,不足(shortage, deficiency)
【例句】First, contributors to a communal online encyclopedia often lack academic credentials, thereby making their contributions partially informed at best and downright inaccurate in many cases. (TPO6, W, Q1) 在线百科全书的编撰者经常缺乏学术可信度,因此使他们的成果只有一部分比较好,而大部分都是完全不准确的。
【派生】lacking *a.* 缺少的,没有的
【搭配】lack of 没有,缺乏
lack in 缺少…;在…缺乏

decline[50] [dɪˈklaɪn]

【释义】*n./v.* 1. 下降,减少(descend)2. 变弱,衰退(decay, fade)3. 拒绝(refuse)4. 倾斜
【例句】Deer populations naturally fluctuate, but early settlers in the Puget Sound environment caused an overall decline in the deer populations of the area at that time. (TPO4, R, S1, T1) 鹿群的数量会自然波动,但早期移民在皮吉特海湾定居造成了当时该地区鹿群数量的整体下降。
【派生】declination *n.* 倾斜;偏差
declined *a.* 下降的;被拒绝的
【搭配】decline to 下降至

focus[50] [ˈfəʊkəs]

【释义】*v.*(使)集中,聚集(concentrate)*n.* 焦点,焦距;中心
【例句】Some theorists of theater development focus on how theater was used by group leaders to govern other members of society. (TPO1, R, S2, T1) 一些戏剧发展的研究者关注的是集

团统治者们是如何运用戏剧来统治其集团成员的。

【反义】distract
【派生】focused *a.* 聚焦的，关注的
【搭配】focus on/upon 集中（注意力等）于…

phrase[50] [freɪz]

【释义】*v.* 措辞，表达，叙述；将文章断句 *n.* 短语，词组，用语
【例句】In nearly every language, however the words are phrased, the most basic division in cinema history lies between films that are mute and films that speak. (TPO12, R, S2, T1) 几乎在每一种语言里，不管言语是怎样表达的，电影史上最基本的划分在于无声电影和有声电影。
【派生】phrasal *a.* 短语的；习惯用语的

complex[49] ['kɒmpleks]

【释义】*a.* 复杂的，费解的（complicated, intricate）*n.* 综合体，集合体
【例句】They take a long time to build as a result of their complex construction methods. (TPO3, R, S1, T1, Q8) 由于建筑方法复杂，他们需要很长的时间来建筑。
【派生】complexity *n.* 复杂性

lower[49] ['ləʊə]

【释义】*v.* 降低，减弱，跌落（reduce, decrease）*a.* 较低的；下级的
【例句】It might be that yawning helps to clear out the lungs by periodically lowering the pressure in them. (TPO18, R, S2, T1) 可能打呵欠会通过定期降低肺部压力来帮助清理肺部。
【反义】raise, heighten
【搭配】lower oneself 有失身份；自甘堕落

meet[49] [mi:t]

【释义】*v.* 遇见，碰见，会见；满足（要求），应付 *n.* 运动会，比赛
【例句】In order for the structure to achieve the size and strength necessary to meet its purpose, architecture employs methods of support that, because they are based on physical laws, have changed little since people first discovered them—even while building materials have changed dramatically. (TPO3, R, S1, T1) 建筑结构必须在大小和强度上达到必要的要求，以实现其建筑目的，因此建筑学上采用了一些支撑的方法，因为这些方法都是以物理定律为基础的，所以尽管建筑材料已经发生了翻天覆地的变化，这些支撑的方法却自人们发现他们以来就鲜有变化。
【搭配】meet the case 适用，符合要求

remove[49] [rɪ'mu:v]

【释义】*v.* 1. 移走；排除；移开；拿开（get rid of, eliminate）2. 脱去（衣服等），摘下（take off）3. 开除；免除，解除（职务等）
【例句】In other cases, the finer particles may be removed. (TPO2, R, Sl, T1) 在另一些地区，细沙可能会被风吹走。
【派生】removal *n.* 移动
removable *a.* 可移动的
【搭配】be removed from... 与…疏远的（远离的）；与…不一样

resource[49] [rɪ'sɔ:s]

【释义】*n.* 1. 资源 2. 资料 3. 才智，谋略
【例句】The impact of rainfall upon the surface water and groundwater resources of the desert is greatly influenced by landscape. (TPO12, R, S2, T2) 降水量对沙漠中的地表水和地下水资源的影响在很大程度上受地貌的限制。
【派生】resourceful *a.* 资源丰富的；足智多谋的
【搭配】resource utilization 资源利用

advantage[48] [əd'vɑ:ntɪdʒ]

【释义】*n.* 优势，有利条件；优点 *v.* 有利于
【例句】The low growth form can also permit the plants to take the advantage of the insulation provided by a winter snow cover. (TPO1, R, S1, T1) 低矮生长形态也使得植物可以利用冬天雪的覆盖带来的隔离优势。
【反义】disadvantage
【派生】advantaged *a.* 占有利地位的，有优势的
advantageous *a.* 有利的，有帮助的
【搭配】take advantage of 利用；占便宜

返记菜单

phrase[50] complex[49] lower[49] meet[49] remove[49]
resource[49] advantage[48]

evolve[48] [ɪ'vɒlv] 

【释义】*v.* 发展，进化（develop, grow）

【例句】A closely related theory sees theater as evolving out of dances that are primarily pantomimic, rhythmical or gymnastic, or from imitation of animal noises and sounds. (TPO1, R, S2, T1) 另外一种比较相关的理论认为，戏剧主要是从哑剧舞蹈、韵律舞蹈、体操或者对动物声音的模仿中逐渐发展进化而来的。

【派生】evolution *n.* 发展，演变
evolutionary *a.* 发展的，进化的

grain[48] [greɪn] 

【释义】*n.* 1. 谷粒，谷物 2. 微量，一点儿 3.（木、织物等的）纹理 *v.*（使）成粒状

【例句】In addition, 40 percent of American grain-fed beef cattle are fattened here. (TPO3, R, S1, T1) 此外，美国40%以谷物饲养的肉牛是在这里被养肥的。

【搭配】against the grain 格格不入，违反意愿
a grain of 一粒

highlight[48] ['haɪlaɪt] 

【释义】*v.* 1. 突出，使显著（emphasize, stress）2. 标注记号 *n.* 最显著或重要的部分

【例句】The complex interplay of species in symbiotic relationships highlights an important point about communities: Their structure depends on a web of diverse connections among organisms. (TPO17, R, S2, T2) 处于共生关系的物种间的相互作用揭示了有关群落的重要一点：他们的结构取决于生物体之间多样化的联系。

【搭配】to be a highlight of 为…中最突出的事物

insect[48] ['ɪnsekt] 

【释义】*n.* 昆虫

【例句】Animals, even insects, carry out what look like very complex decision making processes. (TPO16, L, S2, L1) 动物，甚至昆虫，都会执行看似很复杂的决策过程。

internal[48] [ɪn'tɜːnl] 

【释义】*a.* 1. 内在的，内部的（inner, interior）3. 国内的，内政的

【例句】Leatherbacks apparently do not generate internal heat the way we do, or the way birds do, as a by-product of cellular metabolism. (TPO15, R, S2, T1) 表面上来看，棱皮龟产生内部热量的方式不同于我们或是鸟类，我们或者鸟类产生的热量是细胞新陈代谢的副产品。

【反义】external

【派生】internalize *v.* 使内在化；使藏在心底

【搭配】internal affairs 内部事务
internal organs 内脏

stream[48] [striːm] 

【释义】*n.* 小河，溪流（brook, creek）；（人、车、气、水）流 *v.* 流出，流动（flow,）

【例句】Streams flowed where nature intended them to, and water-driven factories had to be located on their banks, whether or not the location was desirable for other reasons. (TPO6, R, S1, T1) 水的流向是由自然因素决定的，因此，不论适不适合工厂选址，利用水力生产的工厂都必须建造在河流的岸边。

【搭配】go with/against the stream 顺（逆）潮流行事，（不）随波逐流

Word List 4

locate[47] [ləʊ'keɪt]

【释义】*v.* 1. 找出，定位 2. 设置（settle）

【例句】The paintings were located where many people could easily see them, allowing groups of people to participate in the magical-religious activities. (TPO4, R, S2, T1) 这些画位于很多人都能看到的地方，从而使得人们可以参与到这些神秘的宗教活动中来。

【派生】location *n.* 位置，地点

nutrient[47] ['nju:trɪənt]

【释义】*n.* 营养物，滋养物 *a.* 营养的，滋养的

【例句】So we've been talking about nutrients, the elements in the environment that are essential for living organisms to develop, live a healthy life and reproduce. (TPO10, L, S2, L1) 所以，我们一直在谈论营养物质，也就是环境中适合有机体生存、发展以及繁殖的必要元素。

deposit[46] [dɪ'pɒzɪt]

【释义】*n.* 1. 沉淀物，堆积物（sediment）2. 定金，存款 *vt* 1. 使沉淀，堆积（lay down, accumulate）; 2. 寄存; 放置（place）3. 储蓄

【例句】This has been so since ancient times, partly due to the geology of the area, which is mostly limestone and sandstone, with few deposits of metallic ore and other useful materials. (TPO16, R, S1, T1) 自古以来就是这样，部分原因在于该地的地质，这里的地质以石灰石、砂岩为主，只有少量金属矿藏和其他有用的原料。

【派生】deposition *n.* 沉积作用; 沉积物
depositor *n.* 存款人

【搭配】term deposit 定期存款

infer[46] [ɪn'fɜː]

【释义】*v.* 推论，推断

【例句】They inferred that the Egyptians even crossed the Pacific to found the great civilizations of the New World (North and South America). (TPO5, R, S2, T1) 他们推测埃及人甚至穿过了太平洋才发现伟大的新世界文明（北美洲和南美洲）。

【派生】inferable *a.* 可推论的
inference *n.* 推论，推断

significant[46] [sɪg'nɪfɪkənt]

【释义】*a.* 有意义的，重要的，重大的（meaningful, noteworthy, important, remarkable）

【例句】It had a significant effect on European society of that time. (TPO16, L, S1, L2) 这对当时的欧洲社会影响深远。

【反义】insignificant *a.* 无意义的，无关紧要的

【派生】significance *n.* 意义，重要性

air[45] [eə]

【释义】*n.* 1. 样子，神态，姿态（appearance）2. 天空，大气，空气 3. 气氛 *v.* 播送，广播

【例句】So these spices took on an air of mystery. (TPO18, L, S2, L1) 所以这些香料有一点神秘的味道。

【搭配】air separation 空气分离
in the air 广泛的，流行的
up in the air 尚未确定的

biological[45] [baɪə'lɒdʒɪkəl]

【释义】*a.* 生物的，生物学的（biologic）

【例句】In the absence of solid linguistic, archaeological, and biological data, many fanciful and mutually exclusive theories were devised. (TPO5, R, S2, T1) 由于缺乏确凿的语言学、考古学和生物学数据，人们想出了很多不切实际的、互相矛盾的理论。

【派生】biologically *ad.* 生物学上，生物学地

【搭配】biological clock 生物钟

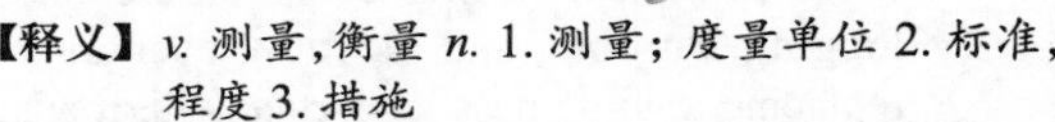

measure[45] ['meʒə]

【释义】*v.* 测量，衡量 *n.* 1. 测量; 度量单位 2. 标准，程度 3. 措施

【例句】The basin measures an amazing 2500km in diameter. (TPO5, L, S1, L2) 这一盆地的直径竟然有 2500 千米。

返记菜单

locate[47]	nutrient[47]	deposit[46]	infer[46]	significant[46]
air[45]	biological[45]	measure[45]		

【派生】measureless *a.* 无限的，不可量的
measurement *n.* 衡量，尺寸
【搭配】measure up to 符合，达到
measure out 按量配给

parenting[45] ['peərəntiŋ]

【释义】*n.* 父母对子女的养育
【例句】OK, today we are going to continue our discussion of the parenting behaviors of birds. (TPO11, L, S1, L1) 好的，今天我们将继续讨论鸟类父母抚养子女的行为。
【逆构】parent *n.* 父亲，母亲
【搭配】parenting style 教养方式

raise[45] [reɪz]

【释义】*v.* 1. 提起，举起，竖起(lift) 2. 增加，提升 3. 饲养，养育(rear) 4. 引起 5. 提出
【例句】They are typically crops raised for food. (TPO5, R, S1, T1) 它们是典型的种来作粮食的庄稼。
【反义】lay, lower
【派生】raised *a.* 凸起的；浮雕的
【搭配】raise a question 提出问题
raise sb.'s spirits 使振奋

supply[45] [sə'plaɪ]

【释义】*n.* 供应(量)，贮备，补给 *v.* 供应，供给(provide)；弥补(不足)
【例句】The paintings were inspired by the need to increase the supply of animals for hunting. (TPO4, R, S2, T1) 绘画的灵感来自于为动物们增加猎物供给的需要。
【搭配】supply sth. to sb./supply sb. with sth. 向某人提供某物

clear[44] [klɪə]

【释义】*v.* 清空，清除(eliminate) *a.* 清楚的，明显的，清澈的 *ad.* 清楚地，彻底地
【例句】A worsening of the plight of deer was to be expected as settlers encroached on the land, logging, burning, and clearing, eventually replacing a wilderness landscape with roads, cities, towns, and factories. (TPO4, R, S1, T1) 随着移民侵占土地、伐木、烧林和清理等活动的进行，最终空旷的原野会被公路、城镇和工厂所取代，可以预见鹿群的处境会越来越恶劣。
【派生】clearing *n.* (森林中的)空地；清除；结算
【搭配】make clear 显示；解释清楚
in the clear 不受阻碍
clear up 清理；放晴

current[44] ['kʌrənt]

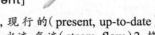

【释义】*a.* 1. 当今的，现行的(present, up-to-date) 2. 流通的 *n.* 1. 水流，气流(steam, flow) 2. 趋势，潮流(tendency)
【例句】Some experts explained these observations by suggesting that ocean currents or other environmental factors may have created uneven concentrations of pollutants along the coast. (TPO10, W, Q1) 一些专家指出这些发现标明可能是洋流或其它环境因素造成了沿海岸线污染物的不均衡聚集。
【派生】currently *ad.* 现在，当今

decrease[44] [diː'kriːs]

【释义】*v.* (使)减少，缩减，缩小(diminish, reduce) *n.* 减少；减少量
【例句】However, what is astonishing about this is not that Dutch agriculture was affected by critical phenomena such as a decrease in sales and production, but the fact that the crisis appeared only relatively late in Dutch agriculture. (TPO23, R, S2, T1) 不过令人惊讶的不是荷兰农业受到这些危机现象的影响而导致产量和销售量的降低，而是这些危机在荷兰农业中发生的相当晚。
【反义】increase
【搭配】decrease to 减少到
decrease from 从原来的…减少

picture[44] ['pɪktʃə]

【释义】*n.* 1. 影片；照片 2. 画，图画 3. 画面 *v.* 1. 描绘(describe) 2. 构想，想象
【例句】The shift from silent to sound film at the end of the 1920s marks, so far, the most important transformation in motion picture history. (TPO12, R, S2, T1) 20世纪20年代末期无声电影向有声电影的转变是迄今为止电影史上最重要的转变。

【派生】picturesque *a.* 生动的；独特的
【搭配】picture sb./sth. as sth. 把某人或某物描述成

primary[44] ['praɪmərɪ]

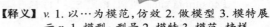

【释义】*a.* 1. 首要的，主要的(chief, dominant) 2. 基本的(basic, fundamental) 3. 最初的，初步的(first)
【例句】It may also explain why beavers forage primarily during the evenings. (TPO16, L, S2, L1) 这或许也解释了为什么海狸主要在晚上捕食。
【反义】secondary
【搭配】primary school 小学

range[44] [reɪndʒ]

【释义】*n.* 1. 范围(scope, extent) 2. 一系列 3. 山脉 *v.* 1. (在某范围内)变动 2. 闲逛；散布
【例句】Remember that the ranges of many animal species were different back then so all these animals actually lived in the region at that time. (TPO3, L, S2, L1) 别忘了，许多动物种类的范围在那时是不同的，所以这些动物过去的确在那个地区存在过。
【搭配】in/within range of 在可及的范围内
range from 延伸；(在一定范围内)变化

shrub[44] [ʃrʌb]

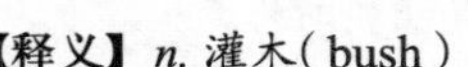

【释义】*n.* 灌木(bush)
【例句】Where the forest inhibits the growth of grass and other meadow plants, the black-tailed deer browses on huckleberry, salal, dogwood, and almost any other shrub or herb. (TPO4, R, S1, T1) 在草和其它草地植物的生长受到森林抑制的地方，黑尾鹿便以越橘、沙巴叶、山茱萸和几乎任何其它灌木或草本植物为食。

stage[44] [steɪdʒ]

【释义】*n.* 1. 阶段，步骤(period, phase) 2. 舞台(platform) *v.* 1. 上演 2. 举办
【例句】But still, the programme's been designed to progress through certain stages. (TPO5, L, S2, C1) 但是，这个项目是为度过某些阶段而设计的。
【派生】stagecraft *n.* 编剧才能
stagewise *a.* 有喜剧效果的；阶梯的

check[43] [tʃek]

【释义】*v.* 1. 检查，核对 2. 加以控制，制止(control, suppress, restrict) *n.* 1. 检查 2. 支票
【例句】To find out the procedure for checking out journal articles. (TPO1, L, S1, C1) 找出核对期刊文章的步骤。
【派生】checkbook *n.* 支票簿
paycheck *n.* 付薪水的支票
checkout *n.* 检验，校验
【搭配】check in 登记，报到
check out 付账后离开
check up on 核实，查证

model[43] ['mɒdl]

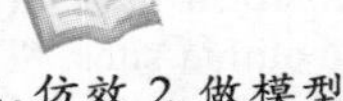

【释义】*v.* 1. 以…为模范，仿效 2. 做模型 3. 模特展示 *n.* 1. 模型；型号 2. 模特 3. 模范，榜样
【例句】The Kinetoscope arcades were modeled on phonograph parlors. (TPO2, R, S2, T2) 这些电影播放厅是仿照留声机播放厅设计的。
【搭配】new model 新模型，新型号

store[43] [stɔː]

【释义】*v.* 储存，贮藏，保存(keep) *n.* 商店；仓库
【例句】It has the capacity to store large amounts of water. (TPO1, R, S2, T2) 它能容纳大量的水。
【派生】storeroom *n.* 储藏室
【搭配】store away 把…放起来；储藏
in store 即将来临的

vary[43] ['veərɪ]

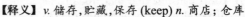

【释义】*v.* 改变，变化，使多样化(alter, change, differ)
【例句】Most things that are enjoyed in and of themselves vary from person to person. (TPO2, L, S2, L1) 很多本身非常享受的事物会因人而异。
【派生】varying *a.* 变化的，不同的
【搭配】vary from 不同于

reduce[42] [rɪ'djuːs]

【释义】*v.* 减少，缩减，降低(decrease, diminish, lessen)
【例句】Water absorption is greatly reduced,

返记菜单

primary[44] range[44] shrub[44] stage[44] check[43]
model[43] store[43] vary[43] reduce[42]

consequently runoff is increased, resulting in accelerated erosion rate. (TPO2, R, Sl, T1) 水分的吸收大量减少，结果径流量增加，从而导致侵蚀率也随之增加。

【反义】increase

【派生】reduction *n.* 减少
reducer *n.* 减少者，还原剂
reducible *a.* 可减少的
reducibility *n.* 可减少性

represent[42] [ˌriːprɪˈzent]

【释义】*v.* 1. 代表，象征，表示（stand for, symbolize）2. 表现，描绘（depict, illustrate）

【例句】In addition to other artworks, figurines representing the human female in exaggerated form have also been found at Upper Paleolithic sites. (TPO4, R, S2, T1) 除了其他艺术品外，以夸张的形式代表女性形象的雕像也在旧石器时代的遗址中被发掘出来。

【派生】representation *n.* 表示，表现（法）
representative *a.* 有代表性的 *n.* 代表

seed[42] [siːd]

【释义】*n.* 种子 *v.* 播种

【例句】But I can imagine that, for instance, seed disposal might be a factor. (TPO6, L, S1, L2) 但是我可以想象，例如，种子传播可能是一个因素。

assume[41] [əˈsjuːm]

【释义】*v.* 1. 假定，设想（suppose, presume）2. 承担，就职 3. 假装，佯作

【例句】It had been assumed that the ice extended westward from the Alaskan/Canadian mountains to the very edge of the continental shelf, the flat, submerged part of the continent that extends into the ocean. (TPO9, R, S1, T1) 人们猜测，冰从阿拉斯加/加拿大山脉向西延伸到大陆架的边缘，也就是大陆延伸到海洋中而被淹没的平坦的部分。

【派生】assumption *n.* 假设，假想

【搭配】assume full responsibility 负完全责任

contribute[41] [kənˈtrɪbjuːt]

【释义】*v.* 1. 贡献，捐款（donate）2. 有助于 3. 投稿

【例句】I've tried to get in touch with the club members, but only four have gotten back to me and said they'd contribute some money to the cost. (TPO13, S, Q5) 我尽力联系了俱乐部成员，但是只有4个人回电话说能拿点儿钱出来。

【派生】contribution *n.* 贡献；捐献物；稿件

free[41] [friː]

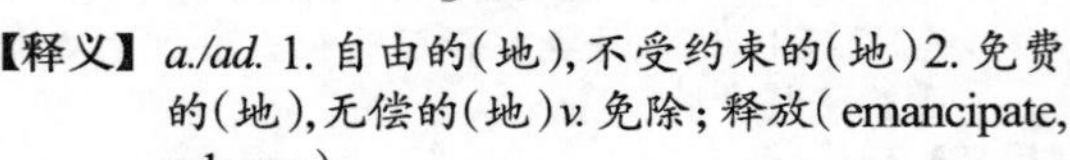

【释义】*a./ad.* 1. 自由的（地），不受约束的（地）2. 免费的（地），无偿的（地）*v.* 免除；释放（emancipate, release）

【例句】I know your office hours are tomorrow, but I was wondering if you had a few minutes free now to discuss something. (TPO2, L, S1, C1) 我知道你的办公时间是明天，但是我想知道你现在是否能抽出几分钟空闲时间讨论点儿事情。

【反义】busy, bound, restrict

【搭配】pain-free 无痛的
fat-free 无脂肪的

mammal[41] [ˈmæməl]

【释义】*n.* 哺乳动物

【例句】It should be obvious that cetaceans—whales, porpoises, and dolphins—are mammals. (TPO2, R, S2, T1) 显然，鲸类动物——鲸、鼠海豚、海豚——都是哺乳动物。

【派生】mammalian *a.* 哺乳动物的

note[41] [nəʊt]

【释义】*v.* 1. 注意（notice）2. 记录（write, record）*n.* 1. 笔记 2. 便条（memorandum）3. 音符 4. 钞票

【例句】Here he notes, with some frustration, people disagree. (TPO2, L, S2, L1) 他注意到，人们对此看法不一，这让他有点沮丧。

【派生】noted *a.* 著名的，出名的
notable *a.* 值得注意的，显著的；著名的 *n.* 名人

【搭配】note down 记录某事
note payable 应付票据

presence[41] [ˈprezns]

【释义】*n.* 1. 出席，到场（attendance）2. 存在（existence）3. 仪表，仪态（appearance）

【例句】People take each other into account in their daily behavior and in fact, the very presence of others can affect behavior. (TPO2, S, Q4) 人们的日常行为会考虑到他人的因素，所以，事实上，其他人在场会影响人们的行为表现。

【逆构】present *a.* 出席的 *v.* 呈现

【搭配】in the presence of 在…的面前

visual[41] [ˈvɪzjʊəl]

【释义】*a.* 视觉的，看得见的 *n.* 画面，图像

【例句】A country as vast as China with so long-lasting a civilization has a complex social and visual history. (TPO10, R, S1, T1) 像中国这样一个地大物博、有着悠久文明的国家是有着复杂的社会和影像历史的。

【派生】visualize *v.* 形象化

【搭配】visual arts 视觉艺术

assignment[40] [əˈsaɪnmənt]

【释义】*n.* 1. 分配，指派（distribution, appointment）2. 工作，任务（task, job）

【例句】There's a room assignment sheet on the bulletin board outside this office. (TPO3, L, S1, C1) 办公室外面的公告牌上有一张教室分布情况表。

【逆构】assign *v.* 分配，指派

【搭配】do one's assignment 做作业

contrast[40] [ˈkɒntræst]

【释义】*n.* 对比，差别 *v.* 对比，对照（compare）

【例句】Any contrast, the Olympic marmots? What about them? (TPO1, L, S2, L2) 那么奥林匹亚旱獭和他们又有什么区别呢？

【搭配】contrast with 与…形成对比

draw[40] [drɔː]

【释义】*v.* 1. 吸引，招引（attract, entice）2. 绘画，描绘（picture, sketch）3. 引起，激起 4. 提取，支取；抽出 *n.* 平局，不分胜负

【例句】They were concerned that many would be "drawn to these new, refreshing" conceptions of teaching only to find that the void between the abstractions and the realities of teacher reflection is too great to bridge. (TPO9, R, S2, T1) 他们担心很多人会被这种全新的教育理念所吸引，结果却发现教师反思的抽象概念和现实之间的鸿沟实在太大而无法逾越。

【搭配】draw back 退后

drive[40] [draɪv]

【释义】*n.* 1.（心理）驱动力；欲望 2. 驾车 3. 车道 *v.* 1. 驾驶 2. 驱赶；猛击

【例句】Displacement activities are activities that animal's engaging in when they have conflicting drives. (TPO4, L, S1, L1) 替换活动是当动物产生相矛盾的动机时所从事的活动。

【派生】driving *n.* 驾驶；操纵
driver *n.* 驾驶员，司机

【搭配】drive in 钉入；运球突破
drive away 赶走；离去
drive out 乘车出去；驱赶出去
drive up 抬高，迫使…上升

fuel[40] [fjʊəl]

【释义】*n.* 燃料 *v.* 为…提供燃料

【例句】Oxygen could be used to breathe, and hydrogen could be turned into fuel, rocket fuel. (TPO5, L, S1, L2) 氧气可以用来呼吸，氢气可以转化成燃料，火箭燃料。

【搭配】fossil fuel 矿物燃料
nuclear fuel 核燃料

sample[40] [ˈsæmpl]

【释义】*n.* 样品，样本，范例（specimen, example）

【例句】Much of the water in a sample of water-saturated sediment or rock will drain from it if the sample is put in a suitable dry place. (TPO1, R, S2, T2) 如果把充满水分的沉淀物或岩石样本放在适合的干燥环境中，其中的大部分水分都会流干。

【派生】sampler *n.* 取样器，取样员

【搭配】sample data 样本数据

sculpture[40] [ˈskʌlptʃə]

【释义】*n.* 雕塑；雕像，雕刻品（statue）

【例句】In addition, there was an important group of sculptures, the majority of which were

produced in earthenware. (TPO10, R, S1, T1) 此外,还有一类重要的雕塑,其中大多数都是陶器。
【派生】sculptural *a.* 雕刻的,雕刻般的
sculptor *n.* 雕刻家
【搭配】ice sculpture 冰雕

side[40] [saɪd]

【释义】*n.* 面;侧面;边 *a.* 1. 侧面的,边的 2. 次要的,附带的 *v.* 支撑,支持;站在…的一边
【例句】But running is efficient only if an animal's legs are positioned underneath its body, not at the body's side, as they are for crocodiles and many lizards. (TPO4, W, Q1) 但是只有当动物的腿长在身体下面时才可以跑得快,而不是像鳄鱼和很多蜥蜴那样长在身体两侧。
【搭配】from side to side 从左到右

signal[40] ['sɪgnl]

【释义】*n.* 信号;标志(mark, sign, indication) *v.* 发信号;示意 *a.* 显著的,重大的
【例句】When we speak with other people face-to-face, the nonverbal signals we give—our facial expressions, hand gestures, body movements, and tone of voice—often communicate as much as, or more than, the words we utter. (TPO4, S, Q4) 当我们面对面交流时,我们所使用的非语言信号——面部表情、手势、肢体动作和声调——所传达的信息通常跟我们说的话一样多,甚或更多。
【派生】signalize *v.* 向…发信号

sort of[40] [sɔːt ɒv]

【释义】有几分,有那么点儿(kind of)
【例句】Maybe a particular sunspot was sort of square, then later it would become more lopsided, then later something else. (TPO18, L, S1, L1) 也许有个别独特的太阳黑子有点像正方形的,然后变得更加不对称,再变成别的什么样子。

spot[40] [spɒt]

【释义】*n.* 1. 地点,场所(location, place, site) 2. 污点,斑点(stain) *v.* 认出,发觉(recognize)
【例句】The artists had removed rough spots on the cave walls. (TPO4, R, S2, T1) 艺术家把洞壁上不平整的地方给去掉了。
【派生】spotlight *n.* 聚光灯
potty *a.* 多斑点的,多污点的
【搭配】on the spot 立刻,当场
scenic spot 风景区,景点

aspect[39] ['æspekt]

【释义】*n.* 1. 方面,层面(facet) 2. 外观,外表(look) 3. 方位,朝向
【例句】From a practical aspect this protected the figures against breakage and psychologically gives the images a sense of strength and power, usually enhanced by a supporting back pillar. (TPO11, R, S1, T1) 从实用的方面来看,这样可以保护人像不受破坏,而且从心理上给人一种力量感,这种力量感通常会通过其后部的柱子得以强化。
【派生】aspectual *a.* (动词)体的
【搭配】a nonessential aspect 非本质方面

concern[39] [kən'sɜːn]

【释义】*n.* 1. 关心,忧虑 2. 有关的事;(利害)关系 *v.* 1. 涉及,关系到(involve) 2. 使关心,使忧虑
【例句】In modern agriculture, mineral depletion of soils is a major concern, since harvesting crops interrupts the recycling of nutrients back to the soil. (TPO5, R, S1, T1) 在现代农业中,土壤中矿物质的消耗是一个值得担忧的问题,因为收割庄稼会扰乱土壤养分回归土壤的循环。

familiar[39] [fə'mɪliə]

【释义】*a.* 1. 熟悉的 2. 常见的,普通的
【例句】Ok, the next kind of animal behavior I want to talk about might be familiar to you. (TPO4, L, S1, L1) 好了,接下来我将讨论的一种你们可能很熟悉的动物行为。
【反义】strange
【派生】familiarity *n.* 亲密的行为;精通
【搭配】be familiar to sb. 为…所熟知,了解
be familiar with sth. 对…通晓,熟悉

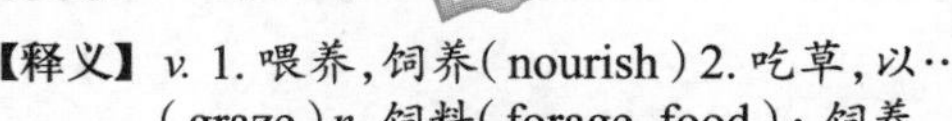

feed[39] [fiːd]

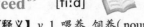

【释义】*v.* 1. 喂养，饲养(nourish) 2. 吃草，以…为生(graze) *n.* 饲料(forage, food)；饲养

【例句】Finally, the growing population was probably fed by increasing the number and size of irrigated fields. (TPO8, R, S1, T1) 最后，不断增长的人口可能要通过增加灌溉土地的数量和面积来养活。

【搭配】off one's feed 没胃口

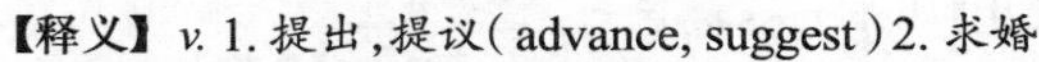

propose[39] [prəˈpəuz]

【释义】*v.* 1. 提出，提议(advance, suggest) 2. 求婚

【例句】Storytelling has been proposed as another alternative. (TPO1, R, S2, T1) 讲故事被认为是另外一种选择。

【派生】proposal *n.* 建议；求婚

【搭配】propose to do 提议做某事

microclimate[38] [ˈmaɪkrəuˌklaɪmɪt]

【释义】*n.* 小气候，微气候

【例句】And that's body is colder or warmer than the surrounding environment, because it's a microclimate. (TPO14, L, S1, L2) 那是由于身体比周围的环境冷或者热，因为它是一种微气候。

reveal[38] [rɪˈviːl]

【释义】*v.* 1. 泄露，透露(disclose, uncover) 2. 显示，露出(expose)

【例句】Finally, examination of the back of the painting reveals that it was painted on a panel made of several pieces of wood glued together. (TPO3, W, Q1) 最后，查看一下画作的背面，你会发现，这幅画是画在一块由胶水将几块木头粘合在一起而组成的木板上的。

【反义】conceal, cover, hide

【派生】revelation *n.* 显示，揭露；新发明

serve[38] [sɜːv]

【释义】*v.* 1. 向…供应(supply) 2. 接待，服务 3. 对…有用，能满足…的需要

【例句】Beginning next month, Dining Services will no longer serve hot breakfast foods at university dining halls. (TPO3, S, Q3) 从下个月开始，学校餐厅将不再供应热的早餐。

【派生】server *n.* 侍者

【搭配】serve someone right 给某人应得的惩罚；得到某人应得的

sign[38] [saɪn]

【释义】*v.* 1. 做手势，示意 2. 署名 *n.* 1. 记号(mark) 2. 标志，符号(signal, symbol) 3. 手势(gesture)

【例句】Did he happen to look at people who sign? (TPO2, L, S1, L1) 他是不是偶然看到过使用手语的人？

【派生】signature *n.* 签名

【搭配】sign a contract 签订合同
sign language 手语；符号语言
traffic sign 交通标志

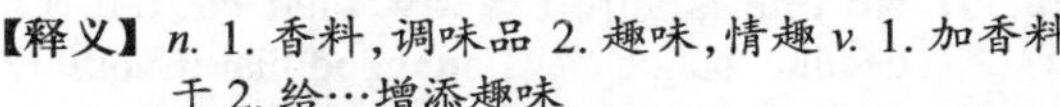

spice[38] [spaɪs]

【释义】*n.* 1. 香料，调味品 2. 趣味，情趣 *v.* 1. 加香料于 2. 给…增添趣味

【例句】Spices were the most sought-after commodities. (TPO17, R, S1, T1) 香料开始变成最为普遍的日用品。

【同义】flavor

【派生】spicy *a.* 辛辣的

surround[38] [səˈraund]

【释义】*v.* 1. 包围，圈住(embrace) 2. 与…紧密相关，围绕(circle)

【例句】Quartz is quartz—a silicon ion surrounded by four oxygen ions—there's no difference at all between two-million-year-old Pleistocene quartz and Cambrian quartz created over 500 million years ago. (TPO6, R, S2, T1) 石英是一种由四个氧离子包围一个硅离子的化合物。两百万年前的更新世石英和五亿年前形成的寒武纪石英并无差别。

【派生】surrounding *n.* 周围的事物，环境

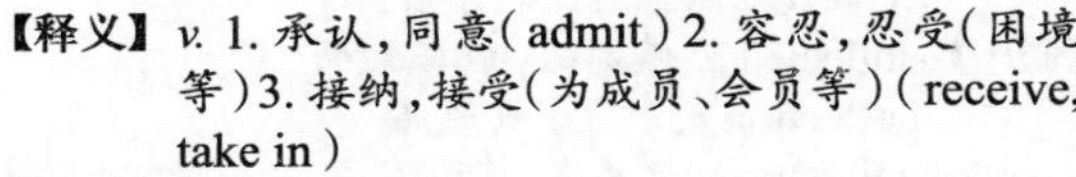

accept[37] [əkˈsept]

【释义】*v.* 1. 承认，同意(admit) 2. 容忍，忍受(困境等) 3. 接纳，接受(为成员、会员等)(receive, take in)

【例句】It has long been accepted that the Americas

were colonized by a migration of peoples from Asia, slowly traveling across a land bridge called Beringia (now the Bering Strait between northeastern Asia and Alaska) during the last Ice Age. (TPO9, R, S1, T1) 人们长久以来都认为：美洲被一群来自亚洲的移民殖民统治着，他们在上一个冰河时代慢慢地跨越了一个叫做白令的大陆桥（位于东北亚和阿拉斯加之间的现在的白令海峡）来到美洲。

【反义】refuse

【派生】acceptable *a.* 可接收的，合意的
acceptance *n.* 接受，接纳
acceptability *n.* 可接受性

chance[37] [tʃɑːns]

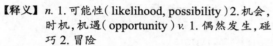

【释义】*n.* 1. 可能性（likelihood, possibility）2. 机会，时机，机遇（opportunity）*v.* 1. 偶然发生，碰巧 2. 冒险

【例句】No one is sure exactly what caused the decline, but chances are good that if nothing is done, Torreya will soon become extinct. (TPO17, W, Q1) 没有人确切地知道是什么导致了数量的减少，但如果不采取任何措施，榧属极可能很快就会灭绝。

【搭配】chance one's arm 冒险一试，碰碰运气

channel[37] ['tʃænl]

【释义】*n.* 1. 水道，航道；通道（path, way）2. 渠道，途径 3. 频道（TV station）

【例句】Two types of flow features are seen: runoff channels and outflow channels. (TPO8, R, S2, T2) 我们可以看到两种类型的流动特征：径流河道和外流河道。

collect[37] [kə'lekt]

【释义】*v.* 1. 收集（gather, accumulate）2. 聚集，集合（assemble, convene, congregate）3. 征收 4. 鼓起（勇气），打起（精神）

【例句】Most of the evidence he has collected contradicts it. (TPO2, L, S1, L1) 他收集的大多数证据都与此相矛盾。

【派生】collected *a.* 镇定的；收集成的
collection *n.* 收集；收藏品
collector *n.* 收集者，收藏家
collective *a.* 集体的，共同的

【搭配】collect oneself 镇定下来，使自己平心静气

huge[37] [hjuːdʒ]

【释义】*a.* 巨大的，庞大的（tremendous, immense）

【例句】Instead, they are probably the paths taken by huge volumes of water draining from the southern highlands into the northern plains. (TPO8, R, S1, T1) 相反，它们很可能是由南部高地流向北部平原的大量水流所经过的通道。

【反义】small, tiny

【派生】hugeness *n.* 巨大，广大，庞大

additional[36] [ə'dɪʃənl]

【释义】*a.* 另外的，附加的，额外的（extra）

【例句】The library only recently got approval to hire additional staff. (TPO14, L, S1, C1) 图书馆只是在最近才得到另外招人的批准。

【逆构】addition *n.* 附加物

【搭配】additional security 追加保证金；额外的安全性

Word List 5

challenge[36] ['tʃælɪndʒ] 

【释义】*n.* 1. 挑战 2. 质问，质疑 *v.* 1. 向…挑战 2. 对…质疑

【例句】They found exploration challenging and exciting. (TPO5, R, S2, T1) 他们发现探险既富有挑战性又刺激。

【派生】challenging *a.* 有挑战性的

【搭配】challenge to 对…的挑战

date[36] [det] 

【释义】*n.* 1. 日期，日子 2. 时期，年代 3. 约会；约会对象 *v.* 1. 注明日期，确定…的年代 2. 与…约会

【例句】But I think the problem is the route's out of date. (TPO2, S, Q3) 但我认为问题在于原来的公交路线已经过时了。

【搭配】to date 迄今为止，直到现在
date back to 追溯到，始于
blind date 相亲

eventually[36] [ɪ'ventjʊəlɪ] 

【释义】*ad.* 最终地（finally, ultimately）

【例句】Eventually through, each role has been assumed by a different person. (TPO1, R, S2, T1) 最终，故事的每一个角色都由不同的人来担当。

【反义】initially

fall[36] [fɔːl]

【释义】*v.* 1. 降落，落下 2. 跌倒；垮塌 3. 来临，发生 *n.* 1. 跌落，下落 2.〈美〉秋天（autumn）

【例句】Remember that the reader needs to know how your character is different from other people who might fall in the same category. (TPO6, L, S2, L1) 切记读者需要知道你的故事中的主角在遇到同样的情形时和其他人有什么不同。

【搭配】fall back 退回；撤退
fall apart 破坏，倒塌
fall behind 落后；拖欠
fall down 失败

glacial[36] ['gleɪsjəl] 

【释义】*a.* 1. 冰川（期）的 2. 极冷的 3. 冷漠的

【例句】With additional time, pressure, and refrozen meltwater from above, the small firn granules become larger, interlocked crystals of blue glacial ice. (TPO15, R, S1, T1) 有了额外的时间、压力以及那些位于上方的融雪重新结冰，那些较小的积雪颗粒就会变成更大的、互相连结的蓝色冰川晶体。

【逆构】glacier *n.* 冰川，冰河

key[36] [kiː]

【释义】*n.* 关键；钥匙；键；答案（answer）*v.* 用键盘输入（信息等）*a.* 重要的；基本的（pivotal）

【例句】Um, the key to the pacific islanders' success was probably their location near the equator. (TPO14, L, S2, L1) 太平洋岛上的居民成功的关键可能在于他们的地理位置靠近赤道。

【派生】keyboard *n.* 键盘

【搭配】key point 关键点，要点
key factor 关键因素，主要因素
key in [计] 键入

particle[36] ['pɑːtɪkl]

【释义】*n.* 1. 微粒，质点 2. 极小量

【例句】We usually look at the grain type within sandstone, meaning the actual particles in the sandstone, to determine where it came from. (TPO1, L, S1, L2) 我们经常会观察砂岩里的颗粒类型，也就是那些存在于砂岩里的实际颗粒，来判断它来自哪里。

【派生】particleboard *n.* 木屑板，碎料板

perform[36] [pə'fɔːm] 

【释义】*v.* 1. 做，进行，运行 2. 履行，执行（handle, execute）3. 表演，演出（play）

【例句】When we're being observed specifically, we tend to increase the speed at which we perform that activity. (TPO2, S, Q4) 当我们作为特定对象受到观察时，我们趋于加快正在从事的某项活动的速度。

【派生】performance *n.* 表现；演出

返记菜单

challenge[36] date[36] eventually[36] fall[36] glacial[36]
key[36] particle[36] perform[36]

performer *n.* 执行者；表演者

【搭配】perform in the role of 扮演…的角色
perform one's place 履行职责，尽义务

reflection[36] [rɪ'flekʃən]

【释义】*n.* 1. 反映，沉思 2. 反射，倒影

【例句】Teachers, it is thought, benefit from the practice of reflection, the conscious act of thinking deeply about and carefully examining the interactions and events within their own classrooms. (TPO9, R, S2, T1) 人们认为，教师是受益于反思实践的，这是一种有意识地深入思考并仔细观察教室中发生的事件以及相互影响的行为。

【逆构】reflect *v.* 反射，反映

reservoir[36] ['rezəvwɑː]

【释义】*n.* 1. 水库，蓄水池 2. 储藏，汇集

【例句】The explanation is that the Maya excavated depressions, or modified natural depressions, and then plugged up leaks in the karst by plastering the bottoms of the depressions in order to create reservoirs, which collected rain from large plastered catchment basins and stored it for use in the dry season. (TPO14, R, S2, T1) 可以这样解释：玛雅人挖掘出洼地或者改造了天然的洼地，并将洼地的底部涂上水泥来堵住喀斯特地形漏水处，这样便建造出了水库，从而可以利用涂抹了水泥的大集水盆地来收集雨水以备旱季使用。

【搭配】oil reservoir 油箱，储油器
reservoir engineering 油藏工程

revise[36] [rɪ'vaɪz]

【释义】*v.* 1.修改，改变（alter, change）2.修订（amend, rewrite）3. 复习，温习

【例句】I was actually thinking about revising some of my poems and sending them into places for publication. (TPO2, L, S2, C1) 事实上，我想修改一些诗歌并把它们寄给出版社。

【派生】revision *n.* 修订；修订版

turtle[36] ['tɜːtl]

【释义】*n.* 海龟，鳖，甲鱼

【例句】If true, though, why did cold-blooded animals such as snakes, lizards, turtles, and crocodiles survive the freezing winters and torrid summers? (TPO8, R, S2, T1) 如果情况属实的话，那为什么像蛇、蜥蜴、龟、鳄鱼这样的冷血动物能在寒冷的冬天和炎热的夏天幸存下来？

bark[35] [bɑːk]

【释义】*n.* 1. 树皮（outer covering, skin）2. 狗叫，咆哮 *v.*（狗等）吠，叫

【例句】The birch tree has white bark, and this tough protective outer layer of the tree, this white bark, is waterproof. (TPO7, L, S2, T1) 桦树有着白色的树皮，这种坚硬的保护外皮，也就是这种白色树皮，是防水的。

【搭配】sb's bark is worse than his bite 虽然某人嘴很厉害，但心并不坏

concept[35] ['kɒnsept]

【释义】*n.* 观念，概念，想法（idea, notion）

【例句】Without this knowledge we can appreciate only the formal content of Egyptian art, and we will fail to understand why it was produced or the concepts that shaped it and caused it to adopt its distinctive forms. (TPO11, R, S1, T1) 没有这些知识，我们就只能欣赏埃及艺术形式上的内容，而无法了解其产生的原因或者塑造以及造成其独特形式的理念。

【派生】conceptual *a.* 概念的
conception *n.* 思想，观念

marketing[35] ['mɑːkɪtɪŋ]

【释义】*n.* 市场营销

【例句】I'm actually in marketing, but there seems to be a connection. (TPO5, L, S2, C1) 我的专业实际上是市场营销，但是看起来是有联系的。

【逆构】market *n.* 市场

property[35] ['prɒpətɪ]

【释义】*n.* 1. 性质，特性，性能（characteristics）2. 财产，所有物（asset, estate, possession）

【例句】Genes are replicators that pass on

information about properties and characteristics of organisms. (TPO5, L, S1, L1) 基因是传递有关生物体特征信息的复制因子。

【搭配】 state property 国家财产

suppose[35] [sə'pəuz]

【释义】 *v.* 推想，假设(presume, assume, conjecture)

【例句】 Second, the supposed error with light and shadow. (TPO3, W, Q1) 其次，假定的关于光和影子的错误。

【派生】 supposition *n.* 假定，推测，推断
supposedly *ad.* 按说，应该

【搭配】 a supposed case 假设情况

vegetation[35] [ˌvedʒɪ'teɪʃən]

【释义】 *n.* 植物(总称)；植被，植物群落

【例句】 The protein content of shade-grown vegetation, for example, was much lower than that for plants grown in clearings. (TPO4, R, S1, T1) 比如，在荫蔽处成熟的植物的蛋白质含量要远低于在空地上长熟的植物。

【派生】 vegetable *n.* 蔬菜，植物
vegetarian *n.* 素食者

apply[34] [ə'plaɪ]

【释义】 *v.* 1. 敷，涂 2. 应用，适用 3. 申请，请求

【例句】 So first of all, you'll need to know the techniques Rembrandt used when he applied paint to canvas. (TPO5, L, S2, L1) 所以，首先，你需要知道当伦勃朗把颜料涂在画布上的时候所使用的技巧。

【派生】 application *n.* 应用；申请；应用程序
applicable *a.* 可应用的；合适的
applicant *n.* 申请人

【搭配】 apply sth. to sth. 把…运用到…上
apply for 申请…

expand[34] [ɪks'pænd]

【释义】 *v.* 1. 扩张，扩展，膨胀(dilate, enlarge, extend)

【例句】 Literature encourages us to exercise our imaginations, empathize with others, and expand our understanding of language. (TPO11, W, Q1) 文学有助于我们锻炼自己的想象力、与他人产生共鸣，还可以拓展我们对语言的理解。

【反义】 condense, shrink

【派生】 expansion *n.* 扩充，扩张
expanding *a.* 扩大的，增加的

melt[34] [melt]

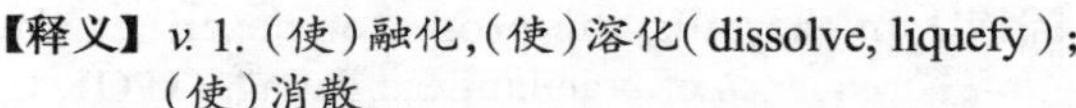

【释义】 *v.* 1. (使)融化，(使)溶化(dissolve, liquefy)；(使)消散

【例句】 Water ice could be melted and purified for drinking. (TPO5, L, S1, L2) 固态水可以被消融和净化以供饮用。

【搭配】 melt into 溶解成；消散在…中
melt away 融化；消散

periodic[34] [pɪərɪ'ɒdɪk]

【释义】 *a.* 周期的；定期的

【例句】 In places, the water table is declining at a rate of a meter a year, necessitating the periodic deepening of wells and the use of ever-more-powerful pumps. (TPO3, R, S1, T1) 有的地方地下水位的下降速度甚至达到了每年1米，因而迫使人们周期性地加深水井并使用更有力的水泵。

【逆构】 period *n.* 阶段，周期

【搭配】 periodic law 周期律

potential[34] [pə'tenʃ(ə)l]

【释义】 *n.* 潜力，潜能；可能性 *a.* 潜在的；可能的(possible, latent)

【例句】 The semiarid lands bordering the deserts exist in a delicate ecological balance and are limited in their potential to adjust to increased environmental pressures. (TPO2, R, Sl, T1) 紧邻沙漠的半干旱地区处在一个十分脆弱的生态平衡中，其适应不断增加的环境压力的潜能也很有限。

【派生】 potentially *ad.* 潜在地
potentiality *n.* 潜力，潜能

route[34] [ru:t]

【释义】 *n.* 1. 路线，线路(course, path) 2. 途径，渠道 *v.* 按指定路线发送

【例句】 But I think the problem is the route's out of date. (TPO2, S, Q3) 但我认为问题在于原来的(公交)路线已经过时了。

【搭配】 en route 在途中

返记菜单

suppose[35] vegetation[35] apply[34] expand[34] melt[34]
periodic[34] potential[34] route[34]

route map 路线图
escape route 脱险通道

sequence[34] ['si:kwəns]

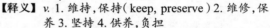

【释义】*n.* 顺序,次序 *v.* 按顺序排好

【例句】In the talk, the professor describes the sequence of uranium-lead dating. (TPO1, L, S1, L2) 在这个讲座中,教授描述了铀铅测年法的步骤。

stand[34] [stænd]

【释义】*v.* 1. 坐落,位于 2. 站立 3. 忍受,容忍(tolerate, endure) *n.* 1. 站立 2. 主张,立场,态度 3. 货摊

【例句】This used to be an agricultural area and we already know that where the main lecture hall now stands, there once were farm house and barn that were erected in the late 1700s. (TPO3, L, S2, C1) 这里过去是一片农场,而且我们已经知道主讲厅现在坐落的位置曾经是 18 世纪末建立的农舍和仓库。

【搭配】stand for 代表,象征
stand by 站在…的旁边;支持;做好准备;袖手旁观
stand out 站出来;突出;顶住
stand up 起立,站得住脚

absorb[33] [əb'sɔ:b]

【释义】*v.* 1. 吸收,吸取(take in, receive) 2. 使全神贯注 3. 理解,掌握

【例句】The soil is the source of these minerals which are absorbed by the plant with the water from the soil. (TPO5, R, S1, T1) 土壤是这些矿物质的来源,植物通过水分从土壤中吸收矿物质。

【派生】absorption *n.* 吸收

【搭配】absorb in 全神贯注于,集中精力做某事

demonstrate[33] ['demənstreɪt]

【释义】*v.* 1. 说明,阐释,论证(confirm, prove) 2. 演示(show) 3. 示威游行

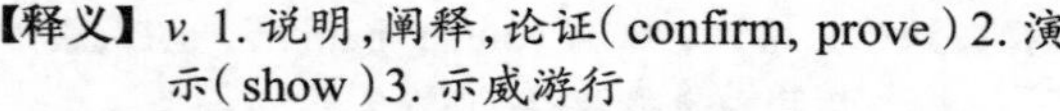

【例句】Once the idea of planting diffused, Africans began to develop their own crops, such as certain varieties of rice, and they demonstrated a continued receptiveness to new imports. (TPO7, R, S2, T2) 栽培的想法一经传播,非洲就开始培养自己的农作物了,比如某些水稻品种,并且他们一直愿意接收新的进口物种。

【派生】demonstration *n.* 论证;演示;示威游行

【搭配】demonstrate against (游行)抗议或示威反对

goods[33] [gʊdz]

【释义】*n.* 1. 商品,货物 2. 动产

【例句】People exchange goods and services for coins or paper bills, and they use this money to obtain other goods and services. (TPO2, S, Q6) 人们将商品和服务兑换成硬币或纸币,再用这些钱去购买其他商品和服务。

【搭配】deliver the goods 交货;遵守诺言
catch someone with the goods 〈美〉人赃俱获地抓获某人

maintain[33] [men'teɪn]

【释义】*v.* 1. 维持,保持(keep, preserve) 2. 维修,保养 3. 坚持 4. 供养,负担

【例句】For instance, humans are endotherms and maintain an internal temperature of 37℃, no matter whether the environment is warm or cold. (TPO4, W, Q1) 例如,人类是恒温动物,能够把体内温度稳定地维持在 37 摄氏度,不论处在温暖还是寒冷的环境中。

【派生】maintenance *n.* 维修,保养

【搭配】maintain in 维持…;保持…
maintain contact with 与…保持联系

metal[33] ['metl]

【释义】*n.* 金属 *v.* (以金属)覆盖,装配

【例句】Statues were normally made of stone, wood, or metal. (TPO11, R, S1, T1) 雕像通常由石头、木头或者金属制成。

【派生】metallic *a.* 金属的,含金属的

native[33] ['neɪtɪv]

【释义】*a.* 1. 出生地的,原产的,土著的(indigenous) 2. 天生的,天然的(natural) *n.* 土生土长者,本地(国)人

【例句】Programs to replant flowers native to humming bird habitats are not succeeding. (TPO3, L, S1, L1, Q10) 重新种植蜂鸟栖息

地的本土花类的项目没有继续进行。
【派生】natively *ad.* 生来地；天然地
【搭配】native plants 土生植物

replace[33] [rɪ(:)'pleɪs]

【释义】*v.* 1. 替代(substitute) 2. 归还，把…放回原处
【例句】Trees are replaced by low shrubs, herbs, and grasses. (TPO1, R, S1, T1) 树木被低矮的灌木、药草和牧草所代替。
【派生】replacement *n.* 更换；代替者
replaceable *a.* 可置换的，可替换的

analyze[32] ['ænəlaɪz]

【释义】*v.* 分析，研究
【例句】And then, they analyze the echoes, how the waves bound back. (TPO7, L, S1, L2) 接下来他们分析回声，声波是如何反射回来的。
【派生】analysis *n.* 分析，分解

approach[32] [ə'prəʊtʃ]

【释义】*n.* 方法，手段(measure, way) *v.* 靠近，接近
【例句】You've been observing Mr. Grable's third-grade class for your approaches to education paper, right? (TPO1, L, S2, C1) 你为了找到完成教育论文的方法一直在观察格莱伯先生所教的三年级课程，对吗？
【派生】approachability *n.* 可接近性；易接近
【搭配】approach to 接近；约等于；通往…的方法

concentrate[32] ['kɒntsəntreɪt]

【释义】*v.* 1. 集中(注意力)(focus) 2. 集合 3.(使浓缩)
【例句】These people settled at first in scattered hunting-and-gathering bands, although in some places near lakes and rivers, people who fished, with a more secure food supply, lived in larger population concentrations. (TPO7, R, S2, T2) 这些人最初以零散的狩猎采集的形式定居下来，不过在一些靠近河湖的地区，人们以捕鱼为生，食物供给更为稳定，在那里人口聚集密度更大。
【反义】distract
【派生】concentration *n.* 集中；专心；浓度，密度
【搭配】concentrate the/one's mind 使某人急切地、认真地考虑某事

differ[32] ['dɪfə]

【释义】*v.* 不同，相异(disagree, vary)
【例句】But the movies differed significantly from these other forms of entertainment. (TPO2, R, S2, T2) 但是电影与其他形式的娱乐活动有着很大的不同。
【派生】difference *n.* 差别，差异
different *a.* 不同的
differently *ad.* 不同地
【搭配】agree to differ 各自保留不同意见；求同存异

extend[32] [ɪks'tend]

【释义】*v.* 延长，延伸；扩大(stretch, expand, prolong, increase)
【例句】The proposed areas of the domestication of African crops lie in a band that extends from Ethiopia across southern Sudan to West Africa. (TPO7, R, S2, T2) 建议对非洲作物进行本土化的地区是从埃塞俄比亚穿过苏丹南部一直到西非的这一地带。
【反义】contract, shrink
【派生】extendable *a.* 可延长的，可扩张的

further[32] ['fɜːðə]

【释义】*v.* 促进 *ad.* 另外(地)；更远(地)
【例句】The growth of independent guilds was furthered by the fact. (TPO16, R, S1, T1) 这一事实促进了独立行会的增长。

recognize[32] ['rekəgnaɪz]

【释义】*v.* 1. 识别，辨认(distinguish, identify) 2. 认可，赏识(acknowledge)
【例句】I hope you can recognize by my saying that how much you do know about the subject. (TPO2, L, S1, C1) 我希望通过我的话，你能意识到你对这个项目了解多少。
【派生】recognized *a.* 公认的
recognition *n.* 认出；承认
recognizable *a.* 可辨认的

scene[32] [siːn]

【释义】*n.* 1. 景色(setting, view) 2. 地点，现场(spot,

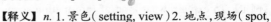

返记菜单

replace[33] analyze[32] approach[32] concentrate[32] differ[32]
extend[32] further[32] recognize[32] scene[32]

location）3.（戏剧的）一场，（电影或电视的）一个镜头 4. 场面

【例句】It didn't depict scenes or models exactly as they looked. (TPO1, L, S1, L1) 这并没有描绘出景色或者模型本身的样子。

【派生】scenery *n.* 风景，景色

attend[31] [ə'tend] 

【释义】*v.* 1. 入学 2. 出席，参加（present）3. 照顾，看管（take care of）4. 专心，注意

【例句】She attended art school, but was told by one of her instructors that she was not good at illustration. (TPO1, L, S1, L1) 她上了一所艺术学校，但是她的一位老师却说她并不擅长画画。

【派生】attendance *n.* 出席，参加；照料
attendant *n.* 侍者，护理人员 *a.* 伴随的

enjoy[31] [ɪn'dʒɔɪ] 

【释义】*v.* 享受，喜欢（like）

【例句】Some scientists speculate that Mars may have enjoyed an extended early period during which rivers, lakes, and perhaps even oceans adorned its surface. (TPO8, R, S2, T2) 一些科学家推测，火星可能经历了一个很长的早期发展阶段，在这期间，河流、湖泊甚或海洋点缀着火星的表面。

【派生】enjoyable *a.* 有趣的，愉快的
enjoyment *n.* 享受，愉快，乐趣

enter[31] ['entə] 

【释义】*v.* 1. 开始处理某事物 2. 进入 3. 参加

【例句】There is not much glory, but we are looking for someone with some knowledge of anthropology who can enter the articles. (TPO7, L, S1, C1) 这没什么吸引人的，但是，我们正在寻找一位懂一点人类学、可以处理这些文章的人。

【搭配】enter into sth. 开始处理某事物

obtain[31] [əb'teɪn] 

【释义】*v.* 1. 获得，得到（gain, acquire, procure）2. 通用，流行

【例句】To explain what kind of information scientists hope to obtain from the mantle. (TPO5, L, S1, L2) 解释一下科学家们希望从地幔上获得什么样的信息。

【派生】obtainable *a.* 能得到的

perceive[31] [pə'siːv] 

【释义】*v.* 1. 感知 2. 察觉，发觉（detect）

【例句】Humans are constantly perceiving visual and auditory stimuli. (TPO12, S, Q5) 人类正不断地感受到视觉和听觉上的刺激。

【派生】perceivable *a.* 可察觉的；可感知的

shift[31] [ʃɪft] 

【释义】*n.* 1. 转移，改变（change）2. 轮班（turn）*v.* 移动，改变位置或方向（change, turn）

【例句】This technological shift caused profound changes in the complexity of African societies. (TPO7, R, S2, T2) 这一技术变革使非洲社会的复杂性发生了深刻转变。

【派生】shifter *n.* 移动装置

valley[31] ['vælɪ] 

【释义】*n.* 山谷；流域

【例句】It's got peaks and valleys, vegetation, rocky areas, and some sea animals have developed permanent colors or shapes to resemble these environmental features. (TPO13, S, Q6) 这里有顶峰，有低谷，有植物，有岩石地区，而且一些海洋动物已经形成了永恒的颜色或形状来保持与这些环境特征的一致。

【搭配】the Nile valley 尼罗河流域

valuable[31] ['væljuəbl] 

【释义】*a.* 贵重的，宝贵的

【例句】No, there's plenty of culturally valuable material that isn't written—music and movies for example. (TPO11, W, Q1) 不，还有很多文化方面的宝贵资料不是用笔写的——比如音乐和电影。

【反义】valueless

advance[30] [əd'vɑːns] 

【释义】*v.* 1. 提出（propose）2. 前进（proceed）3. 提高，发展，进步（progress）*n.* 进展，前进

【例句】Another (answer), advanced in the twentieth

返记菜单

attend[31] enjoy[31] enter[31] obtain[31] perceive[31]
shift[31] valley[31] valuable[31] advance[30]

century, suggests that humans have a gift for fantasy. (TPO1, R, S2, T1) 另一个在20世纪提出的答案表明人类拥有幻想的天赋。

【派生】advanced *a.* 高级的，先进的
advancement *n.* 进步，进展

【搭配】in advance 提前，预先

credit[30] ['kredɪt]

【释义】*n.* 1. 学分 2. 信用，信誉 3. 信贷 *v.* 1. 相信，信任 2. 把…归功于（attribute, ascribe）

【例句】Otherwise I'll be short six credits. (TPO2, L, S2, C1) 否则我就会差六个学分。

【派生】creditable *a.* 值得赞扬的；信誉好的
creditor *n.* 债权人，贷方

【搭配】on credit 赊账，赊（购）
have/lose credit with 得到 / 失去…的信任
add to sb.'s credit 增添某人的光彩

evolution[30] [ˌiːvə'luːʃən]

【释义】*n.* 演变，进化，发展（progression, development）

【例句】These were eventually published as fairy tales, but not before undergoing a process of evolution. (TPO5, L, S2, L2) 这些最后都是以童话故事的形式出版的，但那也是经历了一番演变了的。

【派生】evolutional *a.* 进化的
evolutionary *a.* 进化的，发展的

fee[30] [fiː]

【释义】*n.* 费用；酬金（charge, fare）

【例句】The university has announced that it will charge a small additional fee for these dinners in order to pay for the special gourmet food ingredients that will be required. (TPO5, S, Q1) 学校已经宣布这些晚餐会收取一点儿额外的费用用以支付这些特别的美味所需要的原材料。

【搭配】tuition fee 学费

gather[30] ['gæðə]

【释义】*v.* 1. 收集，采集 2. 聚集 3. 逐渐增加

【例句】Because it is hard to gather it? (TPO12, L, S2, L2) 因为把它收集起来很难吗？

【反义】distribute

【派生】gatherer *n.* 采集者，收集器

【搭配】gather in 收集；尽量收集起来
gather up 收集起；概括
gather round 聚集

phenomenon[30] [fɪ'nɒmɪnən]

【释义】*n.* 1. 现象 2. 非凡的人（或事物）

【例句】It is a very common phenomenon. (TPO6, L, S2, C1) 这是一种很正常的现象。

【派生】phenomenal *a.* 现象的；非凡的，格外的

【搭配】social phenomenon 社会现象

policy[30] ['pɒləsɪ]

【释义】*n.* 1. 政策，方针 2. 保险单

【例句】A mandatory policy requiring companies to offer their employees the option of working a four-day workweek for four-fifths (80 percent) of their normal pay would benefit the economy as a whole as well as the individual companies and the employees who decided to take the option. (TPO1, W, Q1) 一项强制政策要求公司给其员工一周工作四天并领取正常工资的五分之四的选择权，这将在总体上有利于经济发展，同时也有利于那些想要行使这项权力的公司和个人。

【派生】policymaker *n.* 政策制定者；决策人
policyholder *n.* 投保人；保险客户

summarize[30] ['sʌməraɪz]

【释义】*v.* 概述，简要概括（outline, brief）

【例句】The process perceived by these anthropologists may be summarized briefly. (TPO1, R, S2, T1) 这些人类学家观察到的这一过程可以被简要地总结概括。

wide[30] [waɪd]

【释义】*a.* 1. 宽阔的；广泛的（broad, extensive）2. 偏离目标的 *ad.* 广泛地；完全地

【例句】First of all, a group of people has a wider range of knowledge, expertise, and skills than any single individual is likely to possess. (TPO2, W, Q1) 首先，一个团队较单独个体有更广泛的知识和专业技能。

【反义】narrow

【派生】widen *v.* 使变宽

返记菜单

credit[30] evolution[30] fee[30] gather[30] phenomenon[30]
policy[30] summarize[30] wide[30]

clay[29] [kleɪ]

【释义】*n.* 黏土，泥土（earth, mud）

【例句】The impact of raindrops on the loose soil tends to transfer fine clay particles into the tiniest soil space, sealing them and producing a surface that allows very little water penetration. (TPO2, R, Sl, T1) 雨滴落在松软的泥土表面，会把黏土微粒转移至土壤最小的缝隙之内，并把黏土微粒固定住，这样形成的地表是水分几乎无法渗透的。

【派生】clayey *a.* 黏土的

combine[29] [kəm'baɪn]

【释义】*v.*（使）结合，（使）联合（merge, unite）*n.* 1. 联合企业 2. 联合收割机

【例句】They decided how to combine various components of the film program. (TPO2, R, S2, T2) 他们决定如何把电影节目的不同元素结合在一起。

【反义】divide, part

【派生】combination *n.* 结合，联合

【搭配】combined effects 联合作用，综合影响

connect[29] [kə'nekt]

【释义】*v.* 连接；联系；联合（link, joint, relate）

【例句】Sure, the painting has long been somewhat loosely connected to Austen's family and their descendents, but this hardly proves it's a portrait of Jane Austen as a teenager. (TPO12, W, Q1) 当然，这幅肖像与简·奥斯汀家族及其后代间或许有些松散的联系，但是这很难证明这就是一幅简·奥斯汀少女时期的画像。

【派生】connection *n.* 联系，关联
disconnect *v.* 分离，断开

【搭配】connect up 连接，连上
connect with 连接；与…联系

continent[29] ['kɒntɪnənt]

【释义】*n.* 大陆，洲

【例句】Offshore drilling platforms extend the search for oil to the ocean's continental shelves—those gently sloping submarine regions at the edges of the continents. (TPO4, R, S2, T2) 寻找石油的近海钻井平台已经拓展到了大陆架——那些大陆边缘逐渐向海底倾斜的区域。

【派生】continental *a.* 大陆的，大陆性的
supercontinent *n.* [地]超大陆
transcontinental *a.* 横贯大陆的，大陆那边的

define[29] [dɪ'faɪn]

【释义】*v.* 下定义，解释，限定（explain, outline）

【例句】Polynesia is the central Pacifc area in the great triangle defined by Hawaii, Easter Island and New Zealand. (TPO5, R, S2, T1) 波利尼西亚是太平洋地区的中心，位于夏威夷、复活岛和新西兰围成的三角形区域里。

【派生】definition *n.* 定义

【搭配】define as 解释为

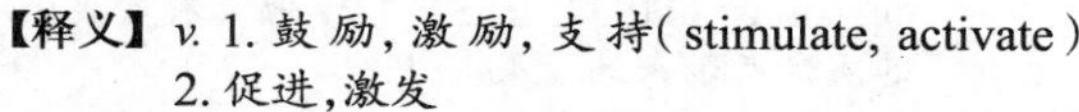

Word List 6

encourage[29] [ɪn'kʌrɪdʒ]

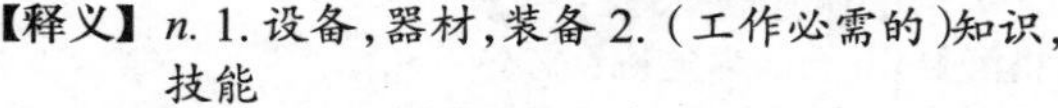

【释义】*v.* 1. 鼓励，激励，支持（stimulate, activate）2. 促进，激发

【例句】Literature encourages us to exercise our imaginations, empathize with others, and expand our understanding of language. (TPO11, W, Q1) 文学鼓励我们运用自己的想象力，与他人产生共鸣，并拓展对语言的理解力。

【反义】discourage

【派生】encouragement *n.* 鼓励，激励

equipment[29] [ɪ'kwɪpmənt]

【释义】*n.* 1. 设备，器材，装备 2.（工作必需的）知识，技能

【例句】Of course in early architecture—such as igloos and adobe structures—there was no such equipment, and the skeleton and skin were often one. (TPO3, R, S1, T1) 当然，在早期的建筑中，比如圆顶建筑和土坯建筑，并没有这样的设施，支撑架和外壳也往往是合在一起的。

【逆构】equip *v.* 装备，配备

external[29] [eks'tɜːnl]

【释义】*a.* 1. 外面的，外部的（exterior, outer）2. 外来的，对外的

【例句】There appear to be many unexplored matters about the motivation to reflect – for example, the value of externally motivated reflection as opposed to that of teachers who might reflect by habit. (TPO9, R, S2, T1) 关于反思的动力存在许多未知的问题，例如，外部驱动的反思的价值与习惯性反思的价值是不同的。

【反义】internal

【派生】externally *ad.* 在（或从）外部；外表上

heavy[29] ['hevi]

【释义】*a.* 1. 严重的，过度的 2. 重的（weighty）3. 大量的

【例句】In the early twentieth century, the American ecologist Frederic Clements pointed out that a succession of plant communities would develop after a disturbance such as a volcanic eruption, heavy flood, or forest fire. (TPO19, R, S2, T1) 在二十世纪初，Fredeic Clements 指出，在经过比如火山爆发、大洪水或者森林火灾的混乱后，会有一系列植物群落形成。

【反义】light, trivial

【派生】heavily *ad.* 严重地；大量地

【搭配】heavy going 难对付的；乏味的

landscape[29] ['lændskeɪp]

【释义】*n.* 风景；风景画（scenery）*v.* 美化…的景观

【例句】A worsening of the plight of deer was to be expected as settlers encroached on the land, logging, burning, and clearing, eventually replacing a wilderness landscape with roads, cities, towns, and factories. (TPO4, R, S1, T1) 随着移民侵占土地、伐木烧林和清理等活动的进行，最终空旷的原野会被公路、城镇和工厂所取代，可以预见鹿群的处境会越来越恶劣。

nature[29] ['neɪtʃə]

【释义】*n.* 1. 性质 2. 自然，自然界，自然状态 3. 本性

【例句】Whether teachers can overcome the difficulties involved in reflection may depend on the nature and intensity of their motivation to reflect. (TPO9, R, S2, T1) 教师们能否克服反思中遇到的困难取决于他们的反思动机的性质和强烈程度。

【搭配】in nature 本质上，事实上
by nature 天生地；生性
nature reserve 自然保护区

relative[29] ['relətɪv]

【释义】*n.* 1. 亲戚（kin）2. 相关物 *a.* 1. 相关的 2. 比较而言的，相对的（comparative）

【例句】If you wish to impress your friends and

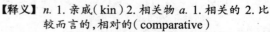

返记菜单

encourage[29] equipment[29] external[29] heavy[29] landscape[29]
nature[29] relative[29]

relatives, you can change this simple process into a magic trick. (TPO2, L, S1, L1) 如果你想让你的朋友或亲戚大开眼界，你可以把这个简单的过程变成魔术。

【派生】 relatively *ad.* 比较而言，相对地
relativity *n.* 相对性；[物理] 相对论

【搭配】 a close/distance relative 近 / 远亲

share[29] [ʃeə]

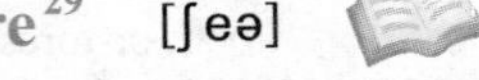

【释义】 *n.* 一份；份额(apportion) *v.* 1. 共享，共用 2. 分配，均分(distribute, divide) 3. 参与

【例句】 Joint-stock companies provided permanent funding of capital by drawing on the investments of merchants and other investors who purchased shares in the company. (TPO10, R, S2, T2) 股份制公司通过让商人和其他投资者购买公司的股份所募集的投资来提供长期的资金储备。

【搭配】 share with 分配；和…分享
share in 分享，分担

tie[29] [taɪ]

【释义】 *v.* 1. (用绳、带、线等) 系，拴(bind, fasten) 2. 打成平局 *n.* 1. 领带 2. 平局

【例句】 If you wanna tie your anchor to it and drop it right into the ocean, that's no problem, because plant fibers can stand up for months, even years, in direct contact with salt water. (TPO2, L, S1, L2) 如果你想用它系住锚、然后直接扔到海里，那也没有问题，因为植物纤维可以直接与盐水接触，好几个月甚至好几年都不会被腐蚀。

【反义】 release, untie

【搭配】 tie the knot [非正式] 结婚

access[28] ['ækses]

【释义】 *n./v.* 接近(的机会) *n.* 入口，通道(entrance, entry)

【例句】 In other parts of the world problems with rights or access to equipment delayed the shift to sound production for a few more years. (TPO12, R, S2, T1) 在世界上的其他地方，设备使用权方面的问题使得向声音生产上的转化又推迟了好几年。

【派生】 accessible *a.* 可进入的，可接近的
accessory *n.* 零件，附件

consequence[28] ['kɒnsɪkwəns]

【释义】 *n.* 1. 结果，后果(result, outcome) 2. 重要(性)，重大

【例句】 He did not consider the consequences of his decisions. (TPO4, L, S1, L2) 他没有考虑到其决定所带来的后果。

【派生】 consequent *a.* 结果的
consequently *ad.* 从而，因此

【搭配】 take/bear the consequences 承担后果

fair[28] [feə]

【释义】 *a.* 1. 公平的，合理的 2. 晴朗的；纯洁的 3. 相当的 *ad.* 公平地；直接地 *n.* 展览会，市集

【例句】 But that's not fair. (TPO11, L, S1, C1) 但是这不公平。

【派生】 fairly *ad.* 公正地，相当地
fairness *n.* 公正；晴朗

【搭配】 for fair 肯定地；完全
to be fair 公平地说

farming[28] ['fɑːmɪŋ]

【释义】 *n.* 农业，耕作

【例句】 This region has a semiarid climate, and for 50 years after its settlement, it supported a low-intensity agricultural economy of cattle ranching and wheat farming. (TPO3, R, S1, T1) 这一区域属半干旱气候，在人们定居于此后的 50 年间，这里都是以畜牧业和小麦种植为主的低密度农业经济。

【逆构】 farm *n.* 农田，农场

game[28] [geɪm]

【释义】 *n.* 1. 猎物 2. 游戏；运动 3. (比赛等的)一局 4. 计策

【例句】 Cave art seems to have reached a peak toward the end of the Upper Paleolithic period, when the herds of game were decreasing. (TPO4, R, S2, T1) 石窟艺术似乎在旧石器时代末达到了顶峰，当时猎物的数量正在下降。

【搭配】 play the game 玩游戏；行动光明正大；遵守比赛规则
on the game 偷窃；卖淫，为娼

game theory 博弈论，对策论

migrate[29] [maɪ'greɪt] 

【释义】v. 迁居，移居，迁徙

【例句】In addition, there were other immigrants who migrated west in search of new homes, material success, and better lives. (TPO20, R, S1, T1) 此外，还有一些移民迁到西部是为了找寻新的家园，获得物质上的成功，过上更好的生活。

【派生】migration n. 定期迁徙，迁居

generate[28] ['dʒenəˌreɪt] 

【释义】v. 1. 产生，发生，引起(cause, produce, originate) 2. 产卵

【例句】It generated a very large number of ancient fossil beds containing soft-bodied animals. (TPO5, R, S2, T2) 这产生了大量含有软体动物标本的古化石层。

【派生】generation n. 产生；一代

【搭配】generate electricity 发电

marine[28] [mə'riːn] 

【释义】a. 1. 海的，海产的(oceanic) 2. 海事的，海运的(maritime) n.(尤指美国或英国皇家)海军陆战队士兵

【例句】Extinct but already fully marine cetaceans are known from the fossil record. (TPO2, R, S2, T1) 从化石记录可以了解一些灭绝的、但已经完全进化为海洋生物的鲸类。

motion[28] ['məʊʃən] 

【释义】n. 1. 运动，动作(action, movement) 2. 提议 v. 打手势，示意

【例句】The molecular motion of a gas depends on temperature. (TPO16, R, S2, T2) 气体分子的运动取决于温度。

【派生】motionless a. 不动的，静止的

【搭配】relative motion 相对运动
in motion 在开动中，在运转中

organic[28] [ɔː'gænɪk] 

【释义】a. 1. 器官的 2. 有机(体)的，有机物的 3. 自然的

【例句】Petroleum, consisting of crude oil and natural gas, seems to originate from organic matter in marine sediment. (TPO4, R, S2, T2) 由原油和天然气组成的石油似乎来自于海洋沉积物中的有机物。

【派生】organism n. 生物体，有机体

【逆构】organ n. 器官

【搭配】organic matter 有机物
organic synthesis [化] 有机合成
organic chemistry 有机化学

preserve[28] [prɪ'zɜːv] 

【释义】v. 保护；保存；维持(conserve, keep)

【例句】So help them survive, we need to preserve their habitats. (TPO3, L, S1, L1) 所以为了帮助它们生存下来，我们需要保护它们的栖息地。

【派生】preservation n. 保存

principle[28] ['prɪnsəpl] 

【释义】n. 1.(表示自然规律的)基本原理 2. 行为准则，原则(law, rule) 3. 主义，信条(belief)

【例句】Explain how the examples of tying shoes and learning to type demonstrate the principle of audience effects. (TPO2, S, Q4) 解释一下系鞋带和学打字的例子是如何证明观众效应原理的。

【搭配】on the principle of 根据…的原则
stick up for one's principles 坚持原则

recommend[28] [rekə'mend] 

【释义】v. 1. 推荐(nominate) 2. 劝告，建议(advise, suggest)

【例句】Then maybe you could recommend some extra reading I can do to catch up? (TPO5, L, S2, C1) 那么或许你能向我推荐一些使我能跟上进度的额外的阅读材料吗？

【派生】recommendation n. 推荐；介绍信
recommendable a. 可推荐的，值得推荐的

【搭配】recommend to 交付；向…推荐

spring[28] [sprɪŋ] 

【释义】n. 1. 泉，源泉 2. 春天 v. 蹦，跳，跃起(jump, leap)；突然活动

【例句】The aquifer's water comes from

underground springs. (TPO3, R, S1, T1) 蓄水层的水来自地下泉水。

sum[28] [sʌm]

【释义】*n.* 1. 金额（amount）2. 总数 *v.* 总结，合计

【例句】An Amsterdam merchant purchasing soap from a merchant in Marseille could go to an exchanger and pay the exchanger the equivalent sum in guilders, the Dutch currency. (TPO10, R, S2, T2) 一位从马赛商人那里购买肥皂的阿姆斯特丹商人可以找到一位兑换人，然后付给那位兑换人等值的荷兰货币——荷兰盾。

【搭配】sum up 总结，概述
in sum 总而言之；大体上
a large sum of 一大笔；大量的

traditional[28] [trəˈdɪʃən(ə)l]

【释义】*a.* 传统的，惯例的（conventional）

【例句】Possibilities for trade seemed promising, but no hope existed for maintaining the traditional routes over land. (TPO17, R, S1, T1) 交易的可能性似乎指日可待，但是要保持传统的陆上路线却是毫无希望的。

【派生】traditionist *n.* 传统主义者

【逆构】tradition *n.* 传统，惯例

【搭配】traditional culture 传统文化

underground[28] [ˈʌndəgraʊnd]

【释义】*a.* 1. 地下的 2. 秘密的 *ad.* 1. 在地下 2. 秘密地

【例句】The aquifer's water comes from underground springs. (TPO3, R, S1, T1) 蓄水层的水来自地下泉水。

visible[28] [ˈvɪzəbl]

【释义】*a.* 1. 可见的，有形的（noticeable）2. 明显的（apparent）

【例句】The light that we see with our human eyes as a band of rainbow color falls in a range of what's called visible light. (TPO3, L, S2, L2) 我们肉眼看到的彩虹带的光被称作可见光。

【反义】invisible, obscure

【派生】visision *n.* 视力，视觉
visual *a.* 视觉的，直观的

consist[27] [kənˈsɪst]

【释义】*v.* 由…组成，构成（comprise, make up）2. 在于 3. 符合

【例句】The total volume of the water in the saturated sample must therefore be thought of as consisting of water that can, and water that cannot, drain away. (TPO1, R, S2, T2) 试验样本的总含水量因此被认为既包括可以流干的水，也包括不可以流干的水。

【派生】consistency *n.* 一致性，相容性
consistent *a.* 始终如一的，一致的

【搭配】consist of 由…构成
consist in 在于

contact[27] [ˈkɒntækt]

【释义】*n.* 1. 接触，联系 2. 熟人 *v.* 使接触，与…联系

【例句】Moreover, the city had economic and perhaps religious contacts with most parts of Mesoamerica (modern Central America and Mexico). (TPO8, R, S1, T1) 此外，这座城市还在经济或许还有宗教方面与大部分中美洲国家（现代中美洲和墨西哥）保持联系。

【搭配】contact with/between 两者之间的联系
be/get/stay/keep in contact (with sb.)（和某人）保持联系

efficient[27] [ɪˈfɪʃənt]

【释义】*a.* 效率高的；有能力的

【例句】Now, for this group of people, business people, the company will have to show how efficient their phone is, how it can handle all business easily and maybe even save money. (TPO5, S, Q2) 现在，针对这些商人来说，手机公司将不得不向其展示他们的手机是多么有效，以及这手机是怎样轻松处理所有商业事务或许甚至还能省钱。

【派生】efficiency *n.* 效率，功效

encyclopedia[27] [enˌsaɪkləʊˈpiːdɪə]

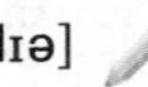

【释义】*n.* 百科全书

【例句】Communal online encyclopedias represent one of the latest resources to be found on the Internet. (TPO6, W, Q1) 公共在线百科全书

代表了一种在互联网上发现的最新资源。

fiber[27] ['faɪbə]

【释义】*n.* 1. 纤维 2. 性格，品质（character）

【例句】In the last class, we started talking about useful plant fibers. (TPO2, L, S1, L2) 上节课，我们开始讨论了有用途的植物纤维。

【搭配】natural/synthetic/man-made fibre 天然 / 合成 / 人造纤维

issue[27] ['ɪsjuː]

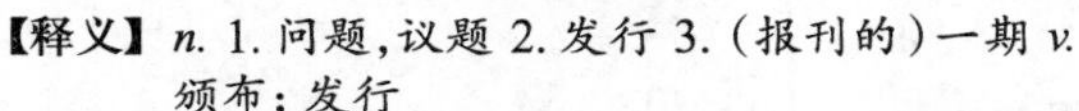

【释义】*n.* 1. 问题，议题 2. 发行 3.（报刊的）一期 *v.* 颁布；发行

【例句】These are generally fed by groundwater springs, and many issue from limestone massifs. (TPO12, R, S2, T2) 这些通常都是源自地下泉水，还有很多是从石灰岩断层中流出的。

【搭配】at issue 待解决的，争议中的

previous[27] ['priːvjəs]

【释义】*a.* 先前的，以前的（preceding, prior）

【例句】The expansion of desertlike conditions into areas where they did not previously exist is called desertification. (TPO2, R, Sl, T1) 沙漠区向非沙漠区的不断扩张被称作沙漠化。

【派生】previously *ad.* 以前地

【搭配】previous to 在…以前

reliable[27] [rɪ'laɪəbl]

【释义】*a.* 可靠的，值得信赖的（dependable, trustworthy）

【例句】Furthermore, even the most reliable waterpower varied with the seasons and disappeared in a drought. (TPO6, R, S1, T1) 再者，即便是最可靠的水资源也会随季节而变化或因干旱而枯竭。

【派生】reliability *n.* 可靠性

【逆构】rely *v.* 依靠

setting[27] ['setɪŋ]

【释义】*n.* 1. 环境（surroundings）2. 背景（background, context）3. 布景

【例句】So more energy can be put into other elements of the story like character and setting. (TPO5, L, S2, L2) 所以人们将更多的精力放在故事的其他因素上，比如人物和场景上。

sunspot[27] ['sʌnspɔt]

【释义】*n.* 太阳黑子

【例句】We are going to start a study of sunspots today, and I think you'll find it rather interesting. (TPO18, L, S1, L1) 今天我们将开始关于太阳黑子的研究，我想你们会觉得这个研究是相当有趣的。

toad[27] [təʊd]

【释义】*n.* 蟾蜍，癞蛤蟆

【例句】Many species of amphibians (frogs and toads) and reptiles (lizards and snakes) are able to change their color patterns to camouflage themselves. (TPO17, R, S2, T1) 很多两栖动物（青蛙和蟾蜍）和爬行动物（蜥蜴和蛇）都可以通过改变体色来伪装自己。

attempt[26] [ə'tempt]

【释义】*n./v.* 尝试，努力（effort, try, endeavor）

【例句】But the first attempt the United States government made to support the arts was the Federal Art Project. (TPO4, L, S2, L2) 但美国政府支持艺术的首次尝试就是联邦艺术计划。

【搭配】attempt at 企图，努力；尝试
attempt to do 尝试去做
make an attempt 试图

aware[26] [ə'weə]

【释义】*a.* 知道的，意识到的

【例句】A society becomes aware of forces that appear to influence or control its food supply and well-being. (TPO1, R, S2, T1) 社会意识到了那些可能会影响或者控制其食物供应和社会安康的力量。

【派生】awareness *n.* 意识，明白，知道
unaware *a.* 未意识到的

【搭配】be aware of 意识到

climatic[26] [klaɪ'mætɪk] 

【释义】*a.* 气候上的

【例句】The glacial system is governed by two basic climatic variables: precipitation and temperature. (TPO15, R, S1, T1) 冰川系统主要受两个基本的气候变量所控制：降雨和温度。

【派生】climatically *ad.* 气候上的，由气候引起的

【逆构】climate *n.* 气候

【搭配】climatic change 气候变化

convince[26] [kən'vɪns] 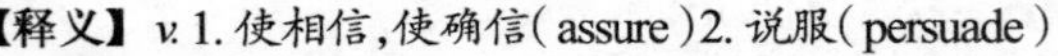

【释义】*v.* 1. 使相信，使确信（assure）2. 说服（persuade）

【例句】And then there was another occasion when a couple influencers convinced the group that a plan of theirs was "highly creative." (TPO2, W, Q1) 还有一种情形：一些具有影响力的人使团队里面的人确信他们的计划具有"高度创造性"。

【派生】convinced *a.* 确信的，深信的
convincible *a.* 可说服的，可使信服的
convincing *a.* 令人信服的

【搭配】convince sb. of sth. 使某人相信某事

decade[26] ['dekeɪd] 

【释义】*n.* 十年，十年间

【例句】The deserts, which already occupy approximately a fourth of the Earth's land surface, have in recent decades been increasing at an alarming pace. (TPO2, R, Sl, T1) 沙漠已经占据地球表面约四分之一的面积，近几十年来仍在以惊人的速度扩张。

【搭配】over the past decade 在过去的十年里

directly[26] [dɪ'rektlɪ] 

【释义】*ad.* 1. 直接地 2. 立即（instantly）3. 正好地

【例句】But now I decided that succeeding in school meant only doing well in the classes that related directly to my future career, I eliminated the conflict, at least in my mind. (TPO3, S, Q4) 但是现在，我认为学业上的成功只意味着在和未来职业相关联的学科上成绩优秀，至少在我的思想中矛盾消除了。

distinguish[26] [dɪs'tɪŋgwɪʃ] 

【释义】*v.* 1. 辨别，区分（differentiate, recognize）2. 使出众，使著名

【例句】Another difference, very important today for distinguishing between older lake beds and newer ones, is the location of the limestone formations. (TPO9, L, S2, L1) 对于今天区分旧湖床和新湖床的另一个很重要的不同是石灰岩形成的位置。

【反义】confuse

【派生】distinguished *a.* 卓著的，高贵的

recall[26] [rɪ'kɔːl] 

【释义】*v.* 回忆起，回想起（remember）*n.* 回忆

【例句】Recall the fate of the Columbian white-tailed deer, now in a protected status. (TPO4, R, S1, T1) 回想一下哥伦比亚白尾鹿的命运，它们现在处于被保护的状态。

【反义】forget

stuff[26] [stʌf] 

【释义】*n.* 原料，材料（material）*v.* 1. 填满 2. 吃饱

【例句】You know, we have two introductory courses that are supposed to be taken before you get to my course, one in film art, techniques, technical stuff and another in film history. (TPO5, L, S2, C1) 你知道的，我们有两门课程是在你上我的课前应该上的，一个是关于电影艺术、技术和一些工艺上的东西，另一个是关于电影历史的。

【派生】stuffed *a.* 已经喂饱了的；塞满了的

【搭配】stuff with 用…装 / 填
stuff and nonsense 胡说八道

version[26] ['vɜːʃən] 

【释义】*n.* 1. 版本 2. 译文，译本

【例句】Different people remembered different versions of a story. (TPO5, L, S1, L1) 不同的人记住了同一个故事的不同版本。

gene[26] [dʒiːn]

【释义】*n.* 基因，遗传因子

【例句】Because close relatives have many of the

same genes, animals that harm their close relatives may in effect be destroying some of their own genes.（TPO1, R, S2, T2）因为近亲中有很多相同的基因，所以伤害其近亲的动物其实也是在破坏一些它们自己的基因。

【派生】genetic *a.* 基因的，遗传学的

appeal[25] [ə'piːl]

【释义】*n.* 1. 感染力，吸引力（attraction, charm）2. 呼吁，恳求 *v.* 1. 恳求，呼吁（plead）2. 吸引（attract, fasinate）3. 上诉，申诉（challenge）

【例句】You think your product will appeal most to teachers aged twenty to thirty, so you decide to put your advertisement in their favor magazine, the one about classroom activities.（TPO11, L, S2, L2）你认为你的产品将会吸引20岁到30岁的老师们，因此你决定将广告放在他们喜欢的杂志上，例如放在有关课堂活动的杂志上。

【派生】appealing *a.* 吸引人的；令人同情的

【搭配】public appeal 号召力

beaver[25] ['biːvə]

【释义】*n.* 海狸，海狸皮毛 *v.* 卖力工作

【例句】Well, um…, how about beavers—ecosystems with beavers in waterways. (TPO13, L, S1, L2) 呃，讨论一下海狸怎么样——生活在水中的海狸的生态系统。

canoe[25] [kə'nuː]

【释义】*n.* 独木舟 *v.* 乘独木舟，用独木舟运

【例句】Detailed studies of the winds and currents using computer simulations suggest that drifting canoes would have been a most unlikely means of colonizing the Pacific. (TPO5, R, S2, T1) 通过电脑模拟的对风和水流的详细研究显示，漂流的独木舟是一种最不可能用来完成太平洋殖民的工具。

【派生】canoeist *n.* 乘独木舟的人

climax[25] ['klaɪmæks]

【释义】*n.* 1. 顶点，极点；高潮（culmination, peak）*v.* 达到高潮

【例句】The first community in a succession is called a pioneer community, while the long-lived community at the end of succession is called a climax community. (TPO3, R, S1, T2) 演替过程中的第一个群落被称作先锋群落，而处于演替过程最后的那个长期存在的群落被称为顶级群落。

【搭配】come to a climax 达到高潮

conflict[25]

【释义】['kɒnflɪkt] *n.* 冲突；战斗；矛盾 [kən'flɪkt] *v.* 冲突，抵触，争执

【例句】Displacement activities are activities that animal's engaging in when they have conflicting drives. (TPO4, L, S1, L1) 替换活动是当动物产生相矛盾的动机时所从事的活动。

【派生】confliction *n.* 冲突，抵触

【搭配】conflict of interest 利益冲突

detect[25] [dɪ'tekt]

【释义】*v.* 发觉，察觉；探测，侦查（discover, discern, sense, identify）

【例句】Mineral deficiencies can often be detected by specific symptoms such as chlorosis (loss of chlorophyll resulting in yellow or white leaf tissue), necrosis (isolated dead patches), anthocyanin formation (development of deep red pigmentation of leaves or stem), stunted growth, and development of woody tissue in an herbaceous plant. (TPO5, R, S1, T1) 矿物质的缺乏通常可以通过一些特别的症状表现出来，比如萎黄病（水溶性叶绿素的缺乏导致的黄色或白色的叶片组织）、坏死（分离的枯死的叶片）、花色素甙生成（叶子或枝干上深红色色素的扩散），生长萎缩以及草本植物中木质组织的发展。

【反义】conceal, hide

【派生】detectible *a.* 可看穿的，可发觉的
detective *a./n.* 侦探（的）

extra[25] ['ekstrə]

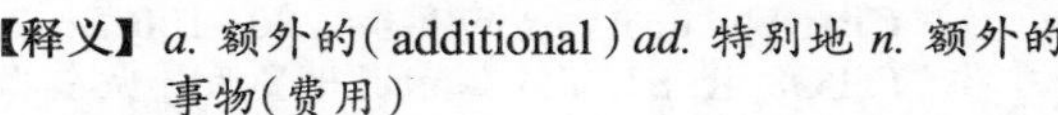

【释义】*a.* 额外的（additional）*ad.* 特别地 *n.* 额外的事物（费用）

【例句】Then maybe you could recommend some extra reading I can do to catch up? (TPO5, L, S2, C1) 那么或许你能向我推荐一些使我能

跟上进度的额外的阅读材料吗?

flood[25] [flʌd]

【释义】v. 淹没;充满 n. 1. 洪水 2. 大量,大批

【例句】One team of scientists flooded an area of the desert with water, then try to establish how much wind force would be necessary to move the rocks. (TPO4, L, S2, L1) 有一组科学家曾经往沙漠的一块地区灌水,然后试图测试需要多大的风力才能将岩石移动。

【搭配】in flood 泛滥
flood in 涌入
a flood of 一大批
at the flood 正当高潮

instrument[25] ['ɪnstrʊmənt]

【释义】n. 乐器;工具,仪器

【例句】We've seen the technical advances in the development of some of the instruments, uh, you remember the transverse flute, the clarinet and so on. (TPO16, L, S1, L2) 我们已经从一些乐器的发展中看到了技术的进步,呃,你还记得横笛、竖笛等乐器吧。

【派生】instrumental a. 仪器的;有帮助的
instrumentalist n. 器乐家

【搭配】musical instruments 乐器

lab[25] [læb]

【释义】n. 实验室

【例句】Listen to a conversation between a student and the language lab manager (TPO13, L, S2, C1) 听一段学生与语言实验室管理员之间的对话。

lie[25] [laɪ]

【释义】v. 1. 躺,卧 2. 位于,坐落在 3. (比赛时)名列,排名 4. 说谎 n. 谎言

【例句】The city of Teotihuacán, which lay about 50 kilometers northeast of modern-day Mexico City, began its growth by 200 -100 B. C. (TPO8, R, S1, T1) 位于现代墨西哥城东北50千米处的特奥蒂瓦坎城发源于公元前200年到公元前100年。

【搭配】lie heavy on sb. 使某人痛苦
lie in 在于

military[25] ['mɪlɪtərɪ]

【释义】a. 军人的,军事的(martial) n. [the ~] 军队,武装力量

【例句】The physical bonds included the network of military garrisons, which were stationed in every province, and the network of stone-built roads that linked the provinces with Rome. (TPO7, R, S2, T1) 物质上的联结包括安置在各省的军事驻防网络以及连接各省与罗马的石筑公路网。

【搭配】military spending 军费开支

normal[25] ['nɔːməl]

【释义】a. 1. 正常的,平常的(ordinary);正规的(standard) n. 常态,标准

【例句】A mandatory policy requiring companies to offer their employees the option of working a four-day workweek for four-fifths (80 percent) of their normal pay would benefit the economy as a whole as well as the individual companies and the employees who decided to take the option. (TPO1, W, Q1) 一项强制政策要求公司给其员工一周工作四天并领取正常工资的五分之四的选择权,这将在总体上有利于经济发展,也有利于那些想要行使这项权力的公司和个人。

【反义】abnormal

【派生】normally ad. 正常地;通常地
nomality n. 常态;规定浓度

【搭配】normal school 师范学校

notice[25] ['nəʊtɪs]

【释义】v. 注意到(heed, detect, discern) n. 1. 通知,布告 2. 注意,留心

【例句】Ideomotor action is an activity that occurs without our noticing it. (TPO2, L, S1, L1) 观念运动是一种我们自身不会注意到的活动。

【反义】ignore, overlook

【派生】noticeable a. 容易察觉的

【搭配】escape sb.'s notice 逃过某人的注意
take no notice of 不理会
without notice 未事先通知的

Word List 7

psychology[25] [saɪ'kɒlədʒɪ]

【释义】 *n.* 心理,心理学

【例句】 I'm supposed to do a literature review for my psychology course. (TPO1, L, S1, C1) 我要为我的心理学课程写一篇文献综述。

【派生】 psychologist *n.* 心理学家
psychological *a.* 心理学的

rainfall[25] ['reɪnfɔːl]

【释义】 *n.* 雨量

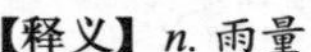

【例句】 Rainfall is not completely absent in desert areas, but it is highly variable. (TPO12, R, S2, T2) 在沙漠地区,降雨量不是完全没有的,但变化却相当大。

【搭配】 rainfall amount 雨量

stable[25] ['steɪbl]

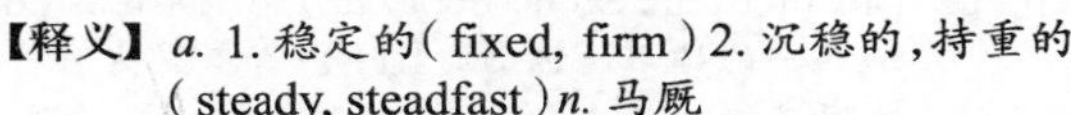

【释义】 *a.* 1. 稳定的(fixed, firm) 2. 沉稳的,持重的(steady, steadfast) *n.* 马厩

【例句】 The plot is the only stable element. (TPO5, L, S2, L2) 情节是唯一稳定的元素。

【派生】 stableness *n.* 稳定性
stability *n.* 稳定性,可靠性

strategy[25] ['strætɪdʒɪ]

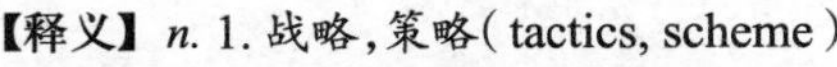

【释义】 *n.* 1. 战略,策略(tactics, scheme)

【例句】 They designed an experimental strategy for a group of teachers in Virginia and worked with 40 practicing teachers over several years. (TPO9, R, S2, T1) 他们给弗吉尼亚的一组教师设计了一个实验策略,并在几年内对40位教师进行了实验。

【派生】 strategic *a.* 战略的,战略上的
strategist *n.* 战略家

tiny[25] ['taɪnɪ]

【释义】 *a.* 极小的,微小的(small, miniature, little)

【例句】 These plants propagate by producing spores – tiny fertilized cells that contain all the instructions for making a new plant – but the spore are unprotected by any outer coating and carry no supply of nutrient. (TPO9, R, S2, T2) 这些植物通过产生孢子来繁殖,孢子是一些有营养的细胞,它们携带了一株新的植物生长所需要的所有遗传物质,但它没有任何外部表皮的保护,也没携带任何供应营养的组织。

【反义】 large, gigantic

【派生】 tininess *n.* 极小,微小

adapt[24] [ə'dæpt]

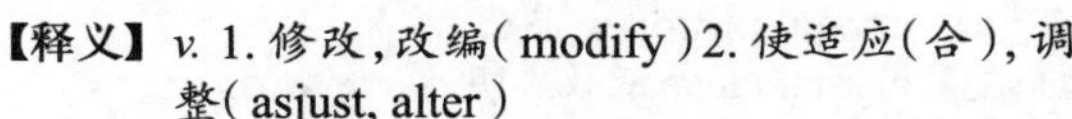

【释义】 *v.* 1. 修改,改编(modify) 2. 使适应(合),调整(asjust, alter)

【例句】 So essentially the same tale could be told in different communities, with certain aspects of the tale adapted to fit the specific community. (TPO5, L, S2, L2) 所以在本质上,不同的社群可以讲述同一个故事,只是这故事的某些方面被改编,以适应特定的社群。

【派生】 adaption *n.* 适应,改编
adaptable *a.* 能适应的,适应性强的
adaptive *a.* 适应的;适合的

capacity[24] [kə'pæsɪtɪ]

【释义】 *n.* 1. 能力,才能(ability, capability) 2. 容量(volume, content)

【例句】 The first is the heat capacity of the materials that constitute the city, which is typically dominated by concrete and asphalt. (TPO23, R, S1, T1) 第一个原因是组成城市的主要典型物质沥青和混凝土的热容量。

【搭配】 capacity crowd 观众满座,爆满
capacity for…的能力

civilization[24] [ˌsɪvəl-aɪ'zeɪʃən]

【释义】 *n.* 文明,文化,教养

【例句】 They inferred that the Egyptians even crossed the Pacific to found the great civilizations of the New World (North and South America). (TPO5, R, S2, T1) 他们推测埃及人甚至曾经穿过太平洋去寻找新世界的伟大文明(北美洲和南美洲)。

crystal[24] ['krɪstl] 

【释义】*n.* 水晶；结晶(体) *a.* 透明的，清澈的
【例句】You all know when you take a crystal prism and pass a beam of sunlight through it, you get a spectrum, which looks like a continuous band of rainbow colors. (TPO3, L, S2, L2) 大家都知道，当一束光通过一个水晶棱镜时，你会看到一个光谱，这个光谱如同一个连续的彩虹色带。
【派生】crystalline *a.* 水晶制的，透明的
crytallize *v.* (使)结晶；(使)明确
crystallization *n.* 晶化，结晶
【搭配】crystal clear 清澈透明的；晴朗的

cue[24] [kjuː] 

【释义】*n.* 线索，暗示，提示(hint) *v.* 给…以提示
【例句】There is accumulating evidence indicating that birds navigate by using a wide variety of environmental cues. (TPO11, R, S2, T1) 有成堆的证据可以表明鸟类用各种环境线索来导航。
【搭配】on cue 恰好在这个时候
cue in 插入；提供消息

density[24] ['densɪtɪ] 

【释义】*n.* 密度，浓度，比重(compactness, thickness)
【例句】The cultivation of crops has expanded into progressively drier regions as population densities have grown. (TPO2, R, Sl, T1) 由于人口密度增加，作物耕种区域已经延伸到越来越干旱的地区。
【逆构】dense *a.* 密集的
【搭配】population density 人口密度

depth[24] [depθ]

【释义】*n.* 深度，厚度
【例句】Timberline trees are strongly influenced by the duration and depth of the snow cover. (TPO1, R, S1, T1) 积雪层存留的时间和厚度会强烈地影响到林木线上的树木。
【搭配】in the depth of 在…里面

expansion[24] [ɪks'pænʃən] 

【释义】*n.* 扩张，扩大，膨胀
【例句】Among the key factors behind this growth were increased agricultural productivity and an expansion of trade. (TPO10, R, S2, T2) 拉动经济增长最关键的因素是农业生产力的提高和贸易规模的扩大。
【反义】contraction
【搭配】business expansion 业务扩张

expose[24] [ɪks'pəʊz] 

【释义】*v.* 1. 暴露，显露 2. 曝光，揭穿
【例句】But I thought being exposed to radiation is dangerous. (TPO3, L, S2, L2) 但是我觉得接触辐射是一件很危险的事。
【反义】conceal, cover, hide
【派生】exposure *n.* 暴露，揭露，曝光
【搭配】expose a conspiracy 揭露阴谋

freeze[24] [friːz] 

【释义】*v.* (使)结冰，(使)凝固 *n.* 冰冻，冰冻期
【例句】But there are some areas in Florida that do freeze. (TPO11, L, S2, L1) 但佛罗里达有些地方也会结冰。
【反义】melt
【逆构】freezing *a.* 冷冻的
【搭配】freeze in 冰封
freeze up 冻结；怯场
freeze over 冻结；使…凝固；全面结冰
freeze out 冻死；逼走，排挤
credit freeze 信用冻结

hemp[24] [hemp] 

【释义】*n.* 大麻，大麻类植物
【例句】Now, for some strange reason, many people believe that Manila hemp is a hemp plant. (TPO2, L, S1, L2) 现在，由于某种未知的原因，很多人认为马尼拉麻(蕉麻)属于大麻类植物。

limestone[24] ['laɪmstəʊn] 

【释义】*n.* 石灰岩
【例句】This has been so since ancient times, partly

due to the geology of the area, which is mostly limestone and sandstone, with few deposits of metallic ore and other useful materials. (TPO16, R, S1, T1) 自古以来就是这样，部分原因在于该地的地质，这里的地质以石灰石、砂岩为主，只有少量金属矿藏和其他有用的原料。

【搭配】limestone cave 灰岩洞
limestone soil 石灰土

merchant[24] [ˈmɜːtʃənt]

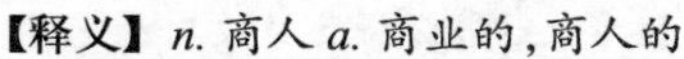

【释义】*n.* 商人 *a.* 商业的，商人的

【例句】They had access to urban merchants, markets, and trade routes. (TPO10, R, S2, T2) 这些乡镇邻近城市的商人、市场以及贸易路线。

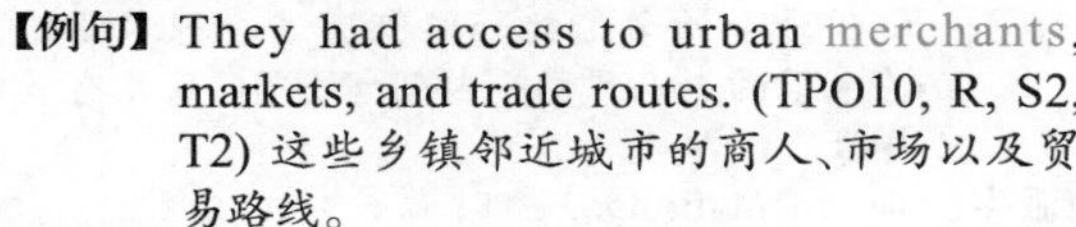

【搭配】merchant bank 商业银行

perception[24] [pəˈsepʃən]

【释义】*n.* 1. 感知(能力)，觉察(力) 2. 观念，看法

【例句】A study of children in Hong Kong, however, found that the presence of celebrities in advertisements could negatively affect the children's perceptions of a product if the children did not like the celebrity in question. (TPO14, R, S1, T1) 然而，一项针对香港儿童所做的研究表明，名人在广告中出现也会对孩子们对产品的认知带来负面影响，如果孩子们不喜欢广告中的这个名人的话。

【派生】perceptive *a.* 敏感的，有洞察力的
perceptivity *n.* 知觉，理解力

poetry[24] [ˈpəuɪtri]

【释义】*n.* 1. 诗歌，诗集(poem, verse) 2. 诗情，诗意 3. 诗歌艺术

【例句】So you are not writing any poetry I imagine. (TPO2, L, S2, C1) 我想你该不会是写诗吧？

【逆构】poet *n.* 诗人 poetic *a.* 诗歌的；诗意的

respond[24] [rɪsˈpɒnd]

【释义】*v.* 1. 回答，答复(reply) 2. 响应，反应(react)

【例句】It was also found that older children responded more positively to products in host selling advertisements. (TPO14, R, S1, T1) 我们还发现，年龄稍大些的孩子对主持销售广告中的产品反响更积极。

【派生】respondency *n.* 响应，一致
respondent *n.* 回答者；被告 *a.* 回答的，有反应的

【搭配】respond to 对…做出反应，响应
respond with 回复
respond by 以…方式反应

responsible[24] [rɪsˈpɒnsəbl]

【释义】*a.* 1. 有责任的(accountable) 2. 负责的，可靠的(trustworthy)

【例句】The domesticated horse is primarily responsible for Inner Eurasian pastoralism's success in mobility and warfare. (TPO14, R, S2, T2) 驯化的马匹是印欧内陆的游牧主义能成功迁徙和在战争中取胜的主要原因。

【派生】responsibility *n.* 责任，职责

【搭配】responsible for 是…的原由；为…负责
be responsible to sb. 对某人负责

section[24] [ˈsekʃən]

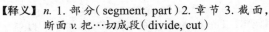

【释义】*n.* 1. 部分(segment, part) 2. 章节 3. 截面，断面 *v.* 把…切成段(divide, cut)

【例句】And also be sure you include a good reference section where all your published and unpublished data came from. (TPO2, L, S1, C1) 同时也要确保你论文中的参考书目要包括你所参考的所有已经出版和未出版的资料、数据。

【派生】sectional *a.* 部分的；可拆卸组合的

【搭配】cross section 剖面(图)

series[24] [ˈsɪəriːz]

【释义】*n.* 1. (单复同)系列，连续 2. 丛书，连续剧

【例句】Why does the fossil record not document the series of evolutionary changes during the evolution of animals? (TPO5, R, S2, T2) 为什么化石标本没有记录下动物进化过程中的一系列演变呢？

【搭配】series of 一系列，一连串

settle[24] [ˈsetl]

【释义】*v.* 1. 安排；安放 2. 安家，定居 3. 解决 4. 决定 5. 调停 6. (鸟等)栖息

【例句】The vast grasslands of the High Plains in the

返记菜单

merchant[24] perception[24] poetry[24] respond[24] responsible[24]
section[24] series[24] settle[24]

central United States were settled by farmers and ranchers in the 1880s. (TPO3, R, S1, T1) 19世纪80年代，在美国中部北美大草原上定居着农民和农场主们。

【搭配】settle down 定居；静下心来
settle in/into 习惯于，适应

urban[24] [ˈɜːbən]

【释义】*a.* 城市的

【例句】They had access to urban merchants, markets, and trade routes. (TPO10, R, S2, T2) 这些乡镇邻近城市的商人、市场以及贸易路线。

【反义】rural

【派生】urbanism *n.* 都市生活，都市化
urbanize *v.* 使城市化，使都市化
urbanite *n.* 都市人
urbanization *n.* 城市化

vessel[24] [ˈvesl]

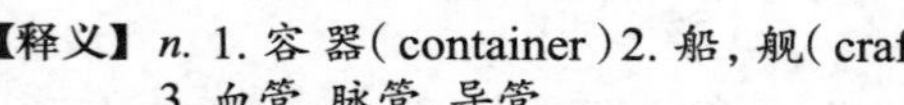

【释义】*n.* 1. 容器(container) 2. 船，舰(craft, ship) 3. 血管，脉管，导管

【例句】The ceramics fall into three broad types—earthenware, stoneware, and porcelain—for vessels, architectural items such as roof tiles, and modeled objects and figures. (TPO10, R, S1, T1) 陶制瓷器从广义上可以被分为3大类：陶器、石器以及瓷器，比如容器、瓦片等建筑材料以及物体和人物模型。

【搭配】vessel wall 血管壁；器壁

volcanic[24] [vɒlˈkænɪk]

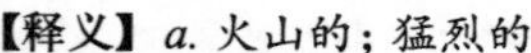

【释义】*a.* 火山的；猛烈的

【例句】The last factor is the impact of natural disasters, such as the volcanic eruptions of the late first millennium B. C. (TPO8, R, S1, T1) 最后一个因素是自然灾害的影响，比如公元前一千年后期的火山喷发。

【逆构】volcano *n.* 火山

【搭配】volcanic rock 火山岩
volcanic ash 火山灰

anyway[23] [ˈenɪweɪ]

【释义】*ad.* 不管怎样，无论如何

【例句】But anyway, Frantzen's style is what she herself calls Realistic Impressionism. (TPO1, L, S1, L1) 但是不管怎样，用弗兰岑自己的话来说，她的风格是现实印象主义。

argument[23] [ˈɑːgjʊmənt]

【释义】*n.* 1. 理由，论据 2. 争论，争吵(debate, disputation)

【例句】In other words, the arguments both for and against government funding of the arts are as many and, and as varied as the individual styles of the artists who hold them. (TPO4, L, S2, L2) 换言之，赞成和反对政府为艺术提供资金的争论就如同拥有这些艺术品的艺术家的个人风格一样纷繁复杂，且具有多样性。

【派生】argumentation *n.* 论证；辩论
argumental *a.* 好争辩的，辩论的

【逆构】argue *v.* 争论

【搭配】argument with sb. about sth. 同某人争论某事

associate[23] [əˈsəʊʃɪeɪt]

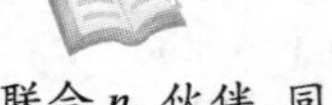

【释义】*v.* (使)发生联系，(使)联合 *n.* 伙伴，同事 *a.* 非正式的；副的

【例句】Even the kind of stability defined as simple lack of change is not always associated with maximum diversity. (TPO3, R, S1, T2) 即使是这种被定义为缺乏变化的稳定性也并非总是与最大多样性联系起来。

【派生】associated *a.* 联合的，关联的
association *n.* 联想；协会

【搭配】associate professor 副教授

bacteria[23] [bækˈtɪərɪə]

【释义】*n.* 细菌

【例句】I realize we're supposed to research food-born bacteria, but food packaging must play a role in all of that, right? (TPO 9, L, S1, C1) 我意识到我们应该研究食品细菌，但食品包装肯定是其中很重要的一个环节，对吧？

【派生】bacterial *a.* 细菌的
bacterin *n.* 疫苗，菌苗

cafe[23] [ˈkæfeɪ]

【释义】*n.* 餐厅；咖啡馆；酒吧

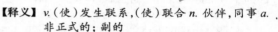

【例句】Well, a lot of impressionist artists painted everyday scenes, like people on the streets and in cafes, lots of nature scenes, especially landscapes. (TPO1, L, S1, L1) 很多印象主义画家画过日常景物，比如路上的行人或咖啡店里的闲客；还画过许多自然景色，尤其是风景。

central[23] ['sentrəl] 

【释义】*a.* 1. 主要的，核心的，起支配作用的（chief, main, pricipal）2. 中心的，中央的 *n.* 中心枢纽；中央办公室
【例句】Helping this group of teachers to revise their thinking about classroom events became central. (TPO9, R, S2, T1) 帮助这组教师修正他们对于课堂事件的认识变成了主要的问题。
【反义】marginal, local
【派生】centrality *n.* 中心，中央
【搭配】Central Park 中央公园

ceramic[23] [sɪ'ræmɪk] 

【释义】*n.* 1.（用作单）制陶术 2.（用作复）陶器
【例句】The function and status of ceramics in China varied from dynasty to dynasty. (TPO10, R, S1, T1) 中国陶瓷在不同朝代的功能和地位是不同的。

compete[23] [kəm'pi:t] 

【释义】*v.* 竞争；竞赛（contend, contest）
【例句】Lichens and ferns competed to grow in the same rocky environments. (TPO9, R, S2, T2) 地衣和蕨类植物在同样的岩石环境下竞相生长。
【派生】competition *n.* 竞争，竞赛
competitive *a.* 竞争的，竞赛的

drill[23] [drɪl] 

【释义】*v./n.* 1. 钻孔，打眼 2. 训练
【例句】Proxy temperature records have been reconstructed from ice core drilled out of the central Greenland ice cap. (TPO10, R, S2, T1) 通过钻取自格陵兰冰冠中部的冰核，替代温度记录已被重建。
【搭配】fire drill 消防演习

exercise[23] ['eksəsaɪz] 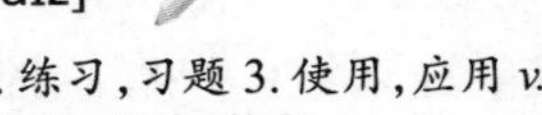

【释义】*n.* 1. 运动，锻炼 2. 练习，习题 3. 使用，应用 *v.* 1. 锻炼，训练 2. 运用；行使，执行
【例句】Literature encourages us to exercise our imaginations, empathize with others, and expand our understanding of language. (TPO11, W, Q1) 文学有助于锻炼我们的想象力，与他人产生共鸣，还可以拓展我们对语言的理解力。
【搭配】take/do exercise 做运动；做练习
physical exercise 体育运动
aerobic exercise 有氧运动

host[23] [həʊst] 

【释义】*n.* 1. 东道主，主人 2.（电视等的）主持人 3.（寄生动植物的）寄主，宿主 *v.* 作东；请客
【例句】In the recent past, the role of celebrities in advertising to children has often been conflated with the concept of host selling. (TPO14, R, S1, T1) 前不久，在针对儿童的广告中，人们常常将名人的角色和主持人销售的概念合并在一起。
【派生】hostess *n.* 女主人；旅馆女老板
【搭配】a host of 众多，大量
host country 东道国，主办国
play host to 招待

marsh[23] [mɑ:ʃ] 

【释义】*n.* 沼泽，湿地
【例句】It is native to lowlands and marshes. (TPO4, R, S1, T1) 它原产于低地和沼泽。
【派生】marshy *a.* 沼泽的
【搭配】marsh gas 甲烷，沼气
salt marsh 盐沼，盐碱滩

quantity[23] ['kwɒntɪtɪ] 

【释义】*n.* 量，数量，大量
【例句】Greek civilization had quality; Rome, mere quantity. (TPO7, R, S2, T1) 希腊文明拥有的是质量，而罗马拥有的仅仅是数量。
【搭配】a large quantity of sth. 大量

返记菜单

central[23] ceramic[23] compete[23] drill[23] exercise[23]
host[23] marsh[23] quantity[23]

release[23] [rɪ'liːs]

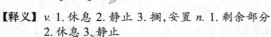

【释义】*v./n.* 1. 释放(discharge, liberate)2. 发布，发行(issue)

【例句】More promising have been recent experiments for releasing capillary water (water in the soil) above the water table by injecting compressed air into the ground. (TPO3, R, S1, T1) 最近一些有希望获得成功的实验试图通过向土壤中注入压缩空气来释放水层上方的土壤毛管水。

【派生】releasable *a.* 能释放的；可免除的

rest[23] [rest]

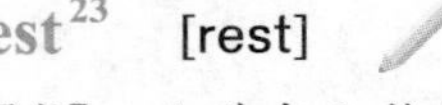

【释义】*v.* 1. 休息 2. 静止 3. 搁，安置 *n.* 1. 剩余部分 2. 休息 3. 静止

【例句】The shortened workweek would increase company profits because employees would feel more rested and alert. (TPO1, W, Q1) 缩短工作周将提高公司的利润，因为职员们将会感到更放松、更机敏。

【派生】rested *a.* 精力充沛的，休息得好的

【搭配】at rest 睡眠的；静止的；死的
put/lay to rest 埋葬；解决

rural[23] ['ruər(ə)l]

【释义】*a.* 1. 乡村的，农村的(country, rustic)2. 田园的

【例句】In turn, a deep attachment to the land, and to the stability which rural life engenders, fostered the Roman virtues: gravitas, a sense of responsibility, pietas, a sense of devotion to family and country, and justitia, a sense of the natural order. (TPO7, R, S2, T1) 反之，对土地和平稳的乡村生活的深深依恋孕育了罗马人的美德：庄重，一种责任感；敬重，对祖国和家庭奉献的使命感；正义，对自然秩序的遵循。

【反义】urban

solid[23] ['sɒlɪd]

【释义】*a.* 1. 实心的 2. 固体的 3. 结实的；稳定的(firm)*n.* 固体

【例句】They were used to outline figures to show boundaries just like you might use solid lines in a pencil drawing. (TPO16, L, S2, L2) 他们被用来勾画边界的轮廓，就好像你在画铅笔画时会用实心线一样。

【派生】solidify *v.*(使)凝固，巩固
solidarity *n.* 团结，一致

transport[23]

【释义】[træn'spɔːt] *v.* 运输；传播 ['trænspɔːt] *n.* 运输；运输系统，运输工具

【例句】In the face of the upcoming water supply crisis, a number of grandiose schemes have been developed to transport vast quantities of water by canal or pipeline from the Mississippi, the Missouri, or the Arkansas rivers. (TPO3, R, S1, T1) 在即将到来的水资源供应危机面前，人们提出了一些宏伟的计划，将密西西比河、密苏里河或者阿肯色河的水通过运河或管道输送到需要用水的地方。

【派生】transportation *n.* 运输，运送

archaeologist[22] [ˌɑːkɪ'ɒlədʒɪst]

【释义】*n.* 考古学家

【例句】The most influential proponent of the coastal migration route has been Canadian archaeologist Knut Fladmark. (TPO9, R, S1, T1) 海岸移民路线的最有影响力的支持者是加拿大考古学家 Knut Fladmark。

bat[22] [bæt]

【释义】*n.* 蝙蝠

【例句】Well, bats, since there are all blind, have to use sound for, you know, keeping them from flying into things. (TPO7, L, S1, L2) 啊，蝙蝠，由于它们看不见，所以不得不使用声音来防止飞行时撞到东西。

【搭配】like a bat out of hell 迅速地，以最高的速度

due[22] [djuː]

【释义】*a.* 1. 到期的；预期的(scheduled)2. 应支付的(unpaid, payable)3. 正当的，适当的

【例句】It typically runs between 50 and 60 percent on the day the research paper is due. (TPO2, L, S1, L2) 在研究论文上交截止当天，它(出勤率)通常会在 50% 至 60% 之间。

【派生】overdue *a.* 迟到的；过期的

subdue *v.* 征服
【搭配】due to 应归于…，因为
give credit where credit is due 谁值得表扬就表扬谁
pay one's dues 尽责任，尽义务

extensive[22] [ɪks'tensɪv]

【释义】*a.* 1. 广阔的，广大的 2. 广泛的，大量的
【例句】This drift has been studied extensively in many animals and in biological activities ranging from the hatching of fruit fly eggs to wheel running by squirrels. (TPO13, R, S2, T1) 在许多动物和生物活动中对这种漂移进行了广泛的研究，从果蝇卵的孵化到松鼠的滚轮跑。
【搭配】agriculture of the extensive type 粗放型农业

extreme[22] [ɪks'triːm]

【释义】*a.* 极度的，极端的 *n.* 极端，极限
【例句】Over a period of about 100, 000 years, while the seas pulled back, climates around the world became dramatically more extreme: warmer days, cooler nights; hotter summers, colder winters. (TPO8, R, S2, T1) 在大约10万年的时期里，随着海洋的回落，世界各地的气候变得急剧极端：白天更暖，夜里更凉；夏天更热，冬天更冷。
【反义】moderate, proper, temperate
【派生】extremity *n.* 末端，极度 [*pl*]（人的）手足
【搭配】in the extreme 极其

imagination[22] [ɪˌmædʒɪ'neɪʃən]

【释义】*n.* 1. 想象，想象力 2. 空想，幻想
【例句】But when people think fiction, they may assume the characters come from the author's imagination. (TPO6, L, S2, L1) 但当人们想到小说的时候，他们可能会认为其中的角色都源自作者的想象。
【派生】imaginable *a.* 可想象的
imaginary *a.* 想象中的
imaginative *a.* 想象的，虚构的
【逆构】imagine *v.* 想象

innovation[22] [ˌɪnəʊ'veɪʃən]

【释义】*n.* 改革，创新（novelty）
【例句】Over the course of the history of building, innovations in materials and methods of construction have given architects ever greater freedom to express themselves. (TPO3, R, S1, T1) 在建筑史上，材料和建筑方法的创新使得建筑师们可以更加自由地表达自己的想法。
【派生】innovative *a.* 革新的，富有创新精神的
【逆构】innovate *v.* 创新，革新

invent[22] [ɪn'vent]

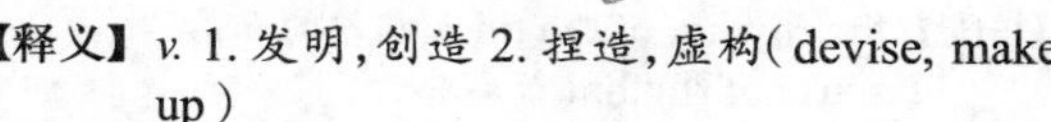

【释义】*v.* 1. 发明，创造 2. 捏造，虚构（devise, make up）
【例句】What did they do before glasses were invented? (TPO8, L, S2, L1) 在眼镜发明之前，他们做什么呢？
【派生】inventor *n.* 发明家，发明者

leatherback[22] ['leðəˌbæk]

【释义】*n.* 棱皮龟
【例句】When it comes to physiology the leatherback turtle is, in some ways, more like a reptilian whale than a turtle. (TPO15, R, S2, T1) 从生理学角度来说，棱皮龟在某些方面更像是一种爬行类的鲸鱼，而不是海龟。

modify[22] ['mɒdɪfaɪ]

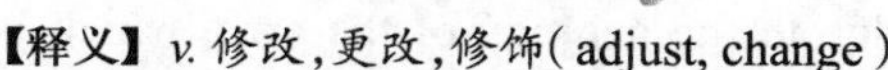

【释义】*v.* 修改，更改，修饰（adjust, change）
【例句】But all the other elements, like the location or characters, might be modified for each audience. (TPO5, L, S2, L2) 但是其他所有的因素，比如地点或人物，可能会根据不同的观众而进行更改。

navigate[22] ['nævɪgeɪt]

【释义】*v.* 航行，航海，航空
【例句】Kramer initiated important new kinds of research regarding how animals orient and navigate. (TPO11, R, S2, T1) Kramer 开创了关于动物如何确定方向和前行的重要的新研究。
【搭配】navigation *n.* 航行，航海（术）

rhythm[22] ['rɪðəm]

【释义】*n.* 节奏,韵律

【例句】Consequently, the timing and rhythms of biological functions must closely match periodic events like the solar day, the tides, the lunar cycle, and the seasons. (TPO13, R, S2, T1) 因此,生物的计时与交替循环的机能也必须与像昼夜交替、潮涨潮落、月圆月缺和四季更迭这样的周期性事件保持一致。

【派生】rhythmic *a.* 有节奏的,有韵律的

【搭配】the rhythm of the tides 潮汐的涨落
sense of rhythm 节奏感

ritual[22] ['rɪtjʊəl]

【释义】*n.* 1.(宗教等的)仪式 2. 惯例 *a.* 1. 仪式的 2. 习惯的,例行公事的

【例句】They were designed to be put in places where these beings could manifest themselves in order to be the recipients of ritual actions. (TPO11, R, S1, T1) 他们被放置在特定的位置上,使那些神灵和人物得以显现,通过仪式活动来接受人们的膜拜。

sandstone[22] ['sændstəʊn]

【释义】*n.* 砂岩

【例句】This has been so since ancient times, partly due to the geology of the area, which is mostly limestone and sandstone, with few deposits of metallic ore and other useful materials. (TPO16, R, S1, T1) 自古以来就是这样,部分原因在于该地的地质,这里的地质以石灰石、砂岩为主,只有少量金属矿藏和其他有用的原料。

【搭配】quartz sandstone 石英砂岩

separate[22] ['sepəreɪt]

【释义】*a.* 分开的;单独的,个别的 *v.* 1. 分离 2. 区别,划分 3. 分居

【例句】The arms could be held away from the body and carry separate items in their hands; there is no back pillar. (TPO11, R, S1, T1) 手臂可以从躯干上面卸除,手上的部件也可以被分开;没有后背支柱。

【派生】separation *n.* 分离,分开
separable *a.* 可分离的

【搭配】separate from 把…和…分开
separate out 析出;分出
separate into 把…分离成

vision[22] ['vɪʒən]

【释义】*n.* 1. 视力;视觉(sight) 2. 眼光,洞察力 3. 幻想,幻影(fantasy, illusion)

【例句】Actually, there are some species of bats, the ones that don't use echolocation that do rely on their vision for navigation, but it's true for many bats, that their vision is too weak to count on. (TPO7, L, S1, L2) 事实上,有些种类的蝙蝠是不用回声定位法而是依靠自己的视力来导航的,但是确实对于大多数蝙蝠来说,它们的视力太差了,无法指望。

【派生】visible *a.* 明显的,看得见的;现有的

accumulate[21] [ə'kjuːmjʊleɪt]

【释义】*v.* 1. 堆积,积累,积聚(assemble, collect, gather)

【例句】In other cases, the finer particles may be removed, while the sand-sized particles are accumulated to form mobile hills or ridges of sand. (TPO2, R, Sl, T1) 在另一些地区,细沙可能会被风吹走,而粗沙则逐渐堆积成小山状或山脊状的流沙。

【反义】dissipate

【派生】accumulation *n.* 积累
accumulative *a.* 积累的

Word List 8

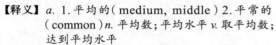

average[21] ['ævərɪdʒ]

【释义】*a.* 1. 平均的(medium, middle) 2. 平常的(common) *n.* 平均数;平均水平 *v.* 取平均数;达到平均水平

【例句】It's within 10 percent of the average distance to Mars from the Sun. (TPO2, L, S2, L2) 误差在火星与太阳的平均距离的10%以内。

【派生】averagely *ad.* 平均地

【搭配】on (the) average 平均而言,一般说来
above the average 在一般水平(或平均数)以上
average price 平均价格
average value 平均值

capable[21] ['keɪpəbl]

【释义】*a.* 有能力的,有技能的(able, competent)

【例句】Modern irrigation devices, each capable of spraying 4.5 million liters of water a day, have produced a landscape dominated by geometric patterns of circular green islands of crops. (TPO3, R, S1, T1) 日喷水量达450万升的现代灌溉设备,形成了一个以圆形绿岛作物为主的景观。

【反义】incapable, unable

【派生】capability *n.* 能力,技能

【搭配】capable of sth./of doing sth. 有能力做某事

contemporary[21] [kən'tempərərɪ]

【释义】*a.* 当代的,现代的,同时代的(modern, present, current) *n.* 同时代的人

【例句】Contemporary literature, English style, um...a teaching seminar, and I still have to do my student teaching. (TPO2, L, S2, C1) 现代文学、英语文体,还有教学研讨会,另外我还得继续做我的教学实习。

divide[21] [dɪ'vaɪd]

【释义】*v.* 1. [数学]除 2. 分开,划分 3. 分裂 *n.* 1. 分歧,不合 2. 分水岭

【例句】I divided all those numbers by 10 by putting in a decimal point. (TPO2, L, S2, L2) 我给所有的数字都添加一个小数点,这样就相当于所有数字都除以10。

【反义】unite

【派生】divisible *a.* 可分的;可除尽的
division *n.* 除法;部门;分割

【搭配】divide into 把…分成
digital divide 数字鸿沟
divide by 除以;用…除
divide and conquer 分而治之,各个击破

echo[21] ['ekəʊ]

【释义】*n.* 1. 回声,回音 2. 反响,反应 3. 共鸣 4. 重复 *v.* 1. 回响,回荡 2. 重复,仿效

【例句】And then, they analyze the echoes, how the waves bound back. (TPO7, L, S1, L2) 接下来他们分析回声,声波是如何反射回来的。

【搭配】echo effect 回声效应;回音效果

extinct[21] [ɪks'tɪŋkt]

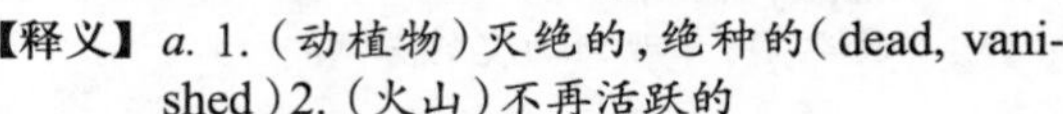

【释义】*a.* 1.(动植物)灭绝的,绝种的(dead, vanished) 2.(火山)不再活跃的

【例句】A local population that goes extinct is quickly replaced by immigrants from an adjacent community. (TPO3, R, S1, T2) 当地物种灭绝后,马上就会被相邻群落的移民所取代。

【派生】extinction *n.* 熄灭,消失,灭绝

fine[21] [faɪn]

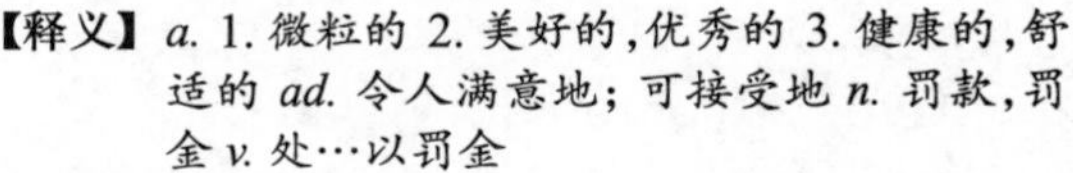

【释义】*a.* 1. 微粒的 2. 美好的,优秀的 3. 健康的,舒适的 *ad.* 令人满意地;可接受地 *n.* 罚款,罚金 *v.* 处…以罚金

【例句】In other cases, the finer particles may be removed. (TPO2, R, Sl, T1) 在另一些地区,更为精细的沙粒可能会被风吹走。

【反义】coarse

introduction[21] [ˌɪntrə'dʌkʃən]

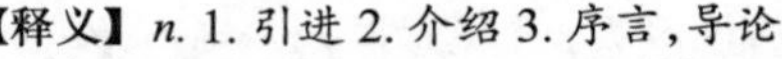

【释义】*n.* 1. 引进 2. 介绍 3. 序言,导论

【例句】And this was the thinking of European astronomers until the introduction of the telescope, which brings us to our old friend, Galileo. (TPO18, L, S1, L1) 欧洲天文学家

一直抱有这种想法，直到望远镜的引进，这又要提到我们的老朋友伽利略了。

【逆构】introduce *v.* 介绍；引进；提出，提倡

match[21] [mætʃ]

【释义】*v.* 匹配(suit) *n.* 1. 比赛(contest) 2. 对手(opponent)

【例句】Consequently, the timing and rhythms of biological functions must closely match periodic events like the solar day, the tides, the lunar cycle, and the seasons. (TPO13, R, S2, T1) 生物的计时与交替循环的机能也就理所应当地必须与像昼夜交替、潮涨潮落、月圆月缺和四季更迭这样的周期性事件保持大体的一致。

【派生】matchable *a.* 对等的，匹配的

medieval[21] [ˌmedɪ'iːvəl]

【释义】*a.* 中世纪的

【例句】I needed to talk to you about the medieval history test. (TPO16, L, S2, C1) 我需要跟你谈谈有关中世纪历史的考试。

memoir[21] ['memwɑː]

【释义】*n.* 回忆录；自传

【例句】Toward the end of his life, the Chevalier de Seingalt (1725-1798) wrote a long memoir recounting his life and adventures. (TPO7, W, Q1) 在走向人生尽头的时候，Chevalier de Seingalt (1725-1798) 写下了长长的回忆录，记载了他的人生和经历。

positive[21] ['pɒzətɪv]

【释义】*a.* 1. 积极的，肯定的(definite) 3. 正的，阳性的

【例句】The picture of Teotihuacán that emerges is a classic picture of positive feedback among obsidian mining and working, trade, population growth, irrigation, and religious tourism. (TPO8, R, S1, T1) 浮现出的特奥蒂瓦坎的画面是一个正面反映黑曜石开采和加工、贸易、人口增长、灌溉、宗教旅游的经典画面。

【反义】negative

【派生】positivity *n.* 积极性

proposal[21] [prə'pəʊzəl]

【释义】*n.* 1. 提议，建议(suggestion) 2. 求婚

【例句】The proposal to add the classes is a response to student complaints that daytime computer classes have become increasingly overcrowded and there are no longer enough computers available. (TPO4, S, Q3) 增班的建议是对学生抱怨白天的电脑班越来越挤而且电脑不够用所做的回应。

【搭配】proposal for sth./doing sth. 建议做某事

pump[21] [pʌmp]

【释义】*v.* 1. 用泵抽 2. 打气 3. 盘问 *n.* 泵，抽水机，打气筒

【例句】Gas pressure gradually dies out, and oil is pumped from the well. (TPO4, R, S2, T2) 气压逐渐消失，油被从井中抽出来。

【搭配】pump up 打气；使振奋
heat pump 热泵，蒸汽泵
water pump 抽水机，水泵

rare[21] [reə]

【释义】*a.* 1. 稀有的，罕见的(peculiar, scarce) 2. (肉类等)半熟的

【例句】The rare and valuable metals and stones were found in Middle Eastern deserts. (TPO16, R, S1, T1) 这些稀有而珍贵的金属和宝石是在中东沙漠里发现的。

【反义】ordinary

【派生】rareness *n.* 珍奇，罕见

【搭配】rare metal 稀有金属

reserve[21] [rɪ'zɜːv]

【释义】*v.* 储备；预订，保留(keep, retain)

【例句】Help her reserve a rehearsal space on campus. (TPO16, L, S1, C1) 帮她在学校预定一个排练场地。

【派生】reserved *a.* 保留的；含蓄的
reservation *n.* 预订，储备

【搭配】in reserve 备用的，留下的

skeleton[21] ['skelɪtən]

【释义】*n.* 1. 骨骼(bones) 2. (建筑物等的)骨架，框

架(frame)3. 梗概,提要(sketch)

【例句】However, some modern architectural designs, such as those using folded plates of concrete or air-inflated structures, are again unifying skeleton and skin. (TPO2, R, Sl, T1) 但是,一些现代建筑设计,例如使用折板的实体结构或充气结构,再一次使骨架和表面成为一体。

substance[21] [ˈsʌbstəns] 

【释义】*n.* 1. 本质,实质(essence, nature) 2. 物质,东西(material) 3. 主旨,要义

【例句】The substance of the movies themselves is mass-produced, prerecorded material that can easily be reproduced by theaters with little or no active participation by the exhibitor. (TPO2, R, S2, T2) 电影的本质是大量生产的、提前录制好的胶片,它们能够很容易被剧院复制播放而无需放映者的积极参与。

texture[21] [ˈtekstʃə] 

【释义】*n.* 1. 质地 2.(材料等的)结构

【例句】It's really the visual components of the work, things like color, texture, shape, lines and how these elements work together, that tell us something about the work. (TPO4, S, Q6) 其实是作品的视觉要素,如颜色、质地、形状、线条及这些元素如何组合在一起,让我们了解了作品。

【派生】textured *a.* 有织纹的,有特定结构的

transfer[21] [trænsˈfɜː] 

【释义】*v.* 1. 转移 2.(使)调动,转学 3. 转移(感情);传染(疾病);让与 *n.* 1.(运动员)转会 2. 中转,换乘

【例句】The impact of raindrops on the loose soil tends to transfer fine clay particles into the tiniest soil space, sealing them and producing a surface that allows very little water penetration. (TPO2, R, Sl, T1) 雨滴落在松软的泥土表面,会把黏土微粒转移至土壤最小的缝隙之内,并把黏土微粒固定住,这样形成的地表是水分几乎无法渗透的。

【派生】transferable *a.* 能转移的
transference *n.* 转移,传输

【搭配】transfer…into… 将…改变成…

unique[21] [juːˈniːk] 

【释义】*a.* 1. 独一无二的,唯一的(singular, peerless) 2. 独特的,特有的(particular)

【例句】It takes geniuses, people like, say, Shakespeare, who're unique because when they have a glimpse at this truth, this universal truth, they pay attention to it and express it and don't just dismiss it like most people do. (TPO4, L, S1, L2) 这需要天赋,比如像莎士比亚这样的人,他们是独一无二的,因为他们只需瞥一眼这些真理,这些普遍的真理,他们就会予以关注并将其表达出来,而不像多数人那样忽略掉。

【派生】uniqueness *n.* 独特,独一无二
uniquely *ad.* 唯一地,独特地

appropriate[20] 

【释义】[əˈprəupri-ɪt] *a.* 适当的,相称的(suitable, proper)[əˈprəuprieɪt] *v.* 1. 占用,挪用 2. 拨款

【例句】It's appropriate under the circumstances. (TPO4, L, S1, L1) 在这种情况下这是恰当的。

【反义】inappropriate, unsuitable, improper

【派生】inappropriate *a.* 不恰当的
appropriately *ad.* 适当地

【搭配】as appropriate 酌情
if appropriate 任选地;如果有的话
be appropriate for 适合于

band[20] [bænd] 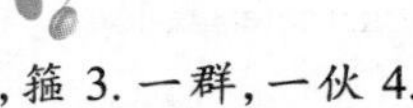

【释义】*n.* 1. 条纹 2. 带,箍 3. 一群,一伙 4. 乐队 *v.* 用带绑扎;联合,结合(unite)

【例句】And then we place an extremely lightweight band on one of its legs, well, what looks like a leg, although technically it's considered part of the bird's foot. (TPO3, L, S1, L1) 接下来我们在蜂鸟的一条腿上放一条非常轻的看起来像腿的带子,技术上我们将它当做蜂鸟的一只足的一部分。

【搭配】waist band 腰带

返记菜单

substance[21] texture[21] transfer[21] unique[21] appropriate[20] band[20]

calendar[20] ['kælɪndə]

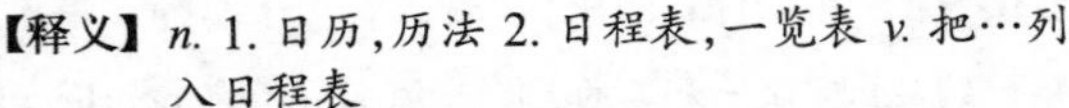

【释义】*n.* 1. 日历，历法 2. 日程表，一览表 *v.* 把…列入日程表

【例句】Okay, so one of the challenges that faced ancient civilizations like Egypt was timekeeping, calendars. (TPO17, L, S2, L1) 那么像埃及这样的古代文明面临的一大挑战是如何记录时间，即历法。

【派生】calendarian *a.* 日历的

【搭配】lunar/chinese calendar 阴历
solar calendar 阳历
desk calendar 台历

cereal[20] ['sɪərɪəl]

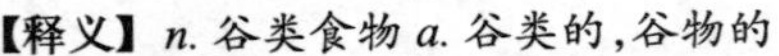

【释义】*n.* 谷类食物 *a.* 谷类的，谷物的

【例句】Now they did hunt and they also raised cereal crops and kept sheep, but we don't know why so many of the paintings are of hunting scenes. (TPO1, L, S2, L1) 他们现在确实还在狩猎，而且还种植谷物、饲养羊群，但是我们并不知道为什么这么多画都是有关狩猎场景的。

characterize[20] ['kærɪktəraɪz]

【释义】*v.* 1. 以…为特征 2. 描述（人或物）的特性，描绘

【例句】The arch is among the many important structural breakthroughs that have characterized architecture throughout the centuries. (TPO3, R, S1, T1) 而拱只是表现了近百年来建筑发展的众多重要建筑结构突破之一。

【派生】characterization *n.* 刻画，描绘

communicate[20] [kə'mjuːnɪkeɪt]

【释义】*v.* 1. 交流（converse, talk）2. 传递（convey, transmit）3. 传染

【例句】He argued that for very young children, thinking is really talking out loud to oneself because they talk out loud even if they're not trying to communicate with someone in particular. (TPO2, L, S1, L1) 他认为，对于非常小的孩子来说，思考就是大声地同自己讲话，因为小孩子即使不与特定的人交流也会大声讲话。

【派生】communication *n.* 交流；通讯
communicative *a.* 交际的；通信的
communicator *n.* 交流者
communicable *a.* 传染性的

confuse[20] [kən'fjuːz]

【释义】*v.* 混淆，搞乱；使困惑（bewilder, confound, disorient）

【例句】He had a special way of fusing, or some people might say confusing, science and fiction. (TPO3, L, S1, L2) 他有一种特别的方式来把科学和小说融合在一起，或者一些人可能会说是混淆在一起。

【反义】clarify

【派生】confused *a.* 困惑的；混乱的
confusion *n.* 混乱，混淆

content[20]

【释义】['kɒntent] *n.* 1. 内容 2. 容量，含量 3. 满足
[kən'tent] *a.* 满足的，满意的 *v.* 使满足，使满意

【例句】Without this knowledge we can appreciate only the formal content of Egyptian art, and we will fail to understand why it was produced or the concepts that shaped it and caused it to adopt its distinctive forms. (TPO11, R, S1, T1) 没有这些知识，我们就只能欣赏埃及艺术形式上的内容，而无法了解其产生的原因或者塑造及造成其独特形式的理念。

【反义】discontent

【派生】contentment *n.* 满足
contented *a.* 满足的，心安的

【搭配】content with 满足于…，对…感到满意

context[20] ['kɒntekst]

【释义】*n.* 上下文，语境（circumstance, setting）

【例句】Up until now, we've been talking about the development of musical styles and genres within the relatively narrow social context of its patronage by the upper classes. (TPO16, L, S1, L2) 直到目前，我们一直在谈论音乐风格和流派在相对狭隘的上层阶级的社会背景下的发展情况。

【搭配】in the context of 在…情况下
in this context 关于这点

device[20] [dɪ'vaɪs]

【释义】*n.* 1. 装置，设备（apprtus, equipment, instrument）2. 手段，策略（strategy）

【例句】Thomas Edison's peepshow device, the Kinetoscope, was introduced to the public in 1894.(TPO2, R, S2, T2) 1894年，托马斯·爱迪生发明的西洋镜设备——活动电影放映机公布于众。

【搭配】leave sb. to his own devices 任凭，听任

emerge[20] [ɪ'mɜːdʒ]

【释义】*v.* 出现，浮现，显露（appear, spring up）

【例句】Archaeological evidence suggests that by 3000 B. C. , and perhaps even earlier, there had emerged on the steppes of Inner Eurasia the distinctive types of pastoralism that were to dominate the region's history for several millennia. (TPO14, R, S2, T2) 考古学的证据表明在公元前3000年甚至更早的时候，在亚欧大陆内陆的大草原上出现了独特的畜牧主义，并一直主宰着该地区的历史达数千年。

【派生】emergency *n.* 紧急情况，突发事件
emergence *n.* 形成，出现

engineer[20] [ˌendʒɪ'nɪə]

【释义】*v.* 设计，策划；建造 *n.* 工程师，机械师

【例句】Farmers will be forced to switch to genetically engineered crops. (TPO3, R, S1, T1) 农民们将被迫改种转基因作物。

【搭配】chief engineer 总工程师

fund[20] [fʌnd]

【释义】*v.* 为…提供资金，给…拨款（finance）*n.* 基金；资金（money, capital）

【例句】For most of the twentieth century, archaeology was funded mostly through government funds and grants. (TPO16, W, Q1) 二十世纪的大部分时间里，考古学的资金主要来源于政府基金和拨款。

【派生】funding *n.* 专款，基金

【搭配】in funds 手头有钱

interaction[20] [ˌɪntər'ækʃən]

【释义】*n.* 相互作用，相互影响

【例句】Teachers, it is thought, benefit from the practice of reflection, the conscious act of thinking deeply about and carefully examining the interactions and events within their own classrooms. (TPO9, R, S2, T1) 人们认为，教师是受益于反思实践的，这是一种有意识地深入思考并仔细观察教室中发生的事件以及相互影响的行为。

【逆构】interact *v.* 互相作用，互相影响

【搭配】exchange interaction 交换作用

law[20] [lɔː]

【释义】*n.* 1. 定律 2. 法律，法令 3. 法律学

【例句】It isn't really a scientific law. (TPO2, L, S2, L2) 实际上，它并不是一条科学定律。

【派生】lawful *a.* 合法的，法定的
lawyer *n.* 律师

【搭配】by law 根据法律，在法律上
break the law 违法
obey the law 遵守法律
criminal law 刑法
civil law 民法

moth[20] [mɒθ]

【释义】*n.* 蛾

【例句】For example, one echo they quickly identified is one way associated with moth, which is common prey for a bat, particularly a moth meeting its wings. (TPO7, L, S1, L2) 例如，它们能够快速识别的一种回声与飞蛾相关，尤其是与正在煽动翅膀的飞蛾有关，飞蛾是蝙蝠的主要猎物。

pastoralism[20] ['pæstərəˌlɪzəm]

【释义】*n.* 畜牧主义，田园风格

【例句】Pastoralism is a lifestyle in which economic activity is based primarily on livestock. (TPO14, R, S2, T2) 畜牧主义是一种将经济活动主要建立在牲畜上的生活方式。

【逆构】pastoral *a.* 田园的 *n.* 田园诗，牧歌

返记菜单

device[20] emerge[20] engineer[20] fund[20] interaction[20]
law[20] moth[20] pastoralism[20]

practical[20] [ˈpræktɪkəl]

【释义】*a.* 实用的；实际的；实践的（effective, useful）

【例句】There would be a very practical value for a future moon base for astronauts. (TPO5, L, S1, L2) 对宇航员来说，这对未来的月球基地将非常具有实用价值。

【派生】practically *ad.* 实际上；几乎，简直
practicality *n.* 实用性

【搭配】practical value 实际价值
practical work 社会实践，实习作业

reproduce[20] [ˌriːprəˈdjuːs]

【释义】*v.* 再生；复制；繁殖

【例句】Someday we may be able to take any cell and keep it alive functioning and reproducing itself essentially forever through the use of telomerase. (TPO12, L, S1, L1) 有一天我们或许能够取出任意一种细胞，使其存活并保持机能，而且还能通过利用端粒酶使其永远自我繁殖下去。

【派生】reproduceable *a.* 能再生长的；能复制的
reproductive *a.* 复制的；生殖的

secondary[20] [ˈsekəndərɪ]

【释义】*a.* 1. 第二的，次要的（subordinate）2. 中级的，中等的 3. 伴随的

【例句】Also, large blocks thrown aside by the impact would form secondary craters surrounding the main crater. (TPO15, R, S2, T2) 撞击也会把一些大石块抛出去，在主要陨石坑周围形成次级陨石坑。

【搭配】secondary school 中学

unlikely[20] [ʌnˈlaɪklɪ]

【释义】*a.* 1. 不大可能的 2. 难以相信的，不能信服的

【例句】General knowledge of categories of events such as a birthday party or a visit to the doctor's office helps older individuals encode their experiences, but again, infants and toddlers are unlikely to encode many experiences within such knowledge structures. (TPO6, R, S2, T2) 对生日聚会或者看医生这类事件的基本认识可以帮助成年人记忆他们的经历，但是，婴幼儿在这样的知识结构下却不太可能记住很多经历。

【反义】likely

【派生】unlikelihood *n.* 未必有，不可信

volunteer[20] [vɒlənˈtɪə (ɒ)]

【释义】*n.* 志愿者；志愿兵 *v.* 自愿做

【例句】Well, I'm sure you can probably find a volunteer. (TPO1, S, Q5) 那么我肯定你可能会找到一个志愿者。

【派生】volunteerism *n.* 志愿精神；志愿服务
voluntary *a.* 自愿的，志愿的

【搭配】volunteer service/work 志愿服务，志愿活动

accurate[19] [ˈækjʊrɪt]

【释义】*a.* 准确无误的，精确的（correct, precise）

【例句】And it took a long time before you got results. It just wasn't very efficient. And it wasn't very accurate. (TPO1, L, S1, L2) 你要很长时间之后才能得到结果。那不是很高效，结果也未必很准确。

【反义】inaccurate

【派生】accuracy *n.* 精确度，准确性

adopt[19] [əˈdɒpt]

【释义】*v.* 1. 采用，采纳（accept, take on）2. 收养（raise, foster）

【例句】Without this knowledge we can appreciate only the formal content of Egyptian art, and we will fail to understand why it was produced or the concepts that shaped it and caused it to adopt its distinctive forms. (TPO11, R, S1, T1) 没有这些知识，我们就只能欣赏埃及艺术形式上的内容，而无法了解其产生的原因或者塑造以及造成其独特形式的理念。

【反义】reject

【派生】adoptive *a.* 采取的；收养的
adoption *n.* 采取；正式通过；收养

cattle[19] [ˈkætl]

【释义】[*pl.*] *n.* 牛

【例句】And the Sales Barn, it was basically this place where the local farmers bought and sold their cattle, their farm animals. (TPO1, L, S1, L1) Sales Barn 主要是一个当地农民

买卖牛和其他农场动物的地方。
【派生】 cattleman *n.* 畜牧者，牧场主人

elite[19] [eɪ'liːt] 

【释义】 *a.* 优秀的，卓越的 *n.* 精英，主力
【例句】 In order to understand ancient Egyptian art, it is vital to know as much as possible of the elite Egyptians' view of the world and the functions and contexts of the art produced for them. (TPO11, R, S1, T1) 想要了解古埃及艺术，尽可能多地了解埃及上层人士的世界观和为他们所创造的艺术品的功能及背景是非常重要的。
【派生】 elitist *a.* 上等的，高级的
【搭配】 elite education 精英教育

estimate[19] 

【释义】 ['estɪmeɪt] *v.* 估计，估量(judge, evaluate)；估价(value) ['estɪmət] *n.* 1. 估计 2. 估价 3. 评价，看法
【例句】 It is estimated that at current withdrawal rates, much of the aquifer will run dry within 40 years. (TPO3, R, S1, T1) 据估计，如果按照现在的下降速度，大部分地下蓄水将在40年内耗尽。
【派生】 estimated *a.* 估算的，估计的
underestimate *v./n.* 低估

length[19] [leŋθ] 

【释义】 *n.* 长，长度
【例句】 They can easily be several feet in length and they're also very strong, very flexible. (TPO2, L, S1, L2) 它们很容易就能长到若干英尺高，茎杆很强壮，也很柔韧。
【逆构】 long *a.* 长的
【搭配】 at full length 详尽地
at length 最后，最终
go to great lengths 不遗余力地
keep at arm's length 与…保持一定距离，疏远

linguistic[19] [lɪŋ'gwɪstɪk] 

【释义】 *a.* 语言的，语言学的
【例句】 In the absence of solid linguistic, archaeological, and biological data, many fanciful and mutually exclusive theories were devised. (TPO5, R, S2, T1) 由于没有确凿的语言学、考古学和生物学数据，人们想出了很多充满幻想、互相矛盾的理论。
【派生】 linguistical *a.* 语言学的，语言上的
linguisitician *n.* 语言学家
【搭配】 linguistic context 语言环境，语境

meme[19] [miːm] 

【释义】 *n.* 弥母(文化基因)
【例句】 Well, both the song and the story are examples of memes. (TPO5, L, S1, L1) 歌曲和故事都是文化基因的范例。

orientation[19] [ˌɒ(ː)rɪen'teɪʃən] 

【释义】 *n.* 1. 方向，方位 2. 定位 3. (任职等前的)培训
【例句】 Orientation is simply facing in the right direction; navigation involves finding one's way from point A to point B. (TPO11, R, S2, T1) 定位只是指要朝着正确的方向，而导航则是要找出从A地到B地的路线。
【逆构】 orient *v.* 使适应，以…为方向
【搭配】 market orientation 市场导向

portray[19] [pɔː'treɪ] 

【释义】 *v.* 描绘；描述；饰演(depict)
【例句】 He confused his audience in the way he portrayed the animals he filmed, mixing up on notions of the categories of humans and animals. (TPO3, L, S1, L2) 他在电影中饰演动物的方式混淆了人类和动物范畴的概念，这让观众感到迷惑。
【派生】 portrayal *n.* 描画；饰演
portrayer *n.* 肖像画家

scale[19] [skeɪl] 

【释义】 *n.* 1. 规模 2. 刻度 3. 比例 4. 等级，级别 5. 鳞，鳞状物 *v.* 1. 攀登，爬 2. 剥落
【例句】 The sheer scale of the investment it took to begin commercial expansion at sea reflects the immensity of the profits that such East-West trade could create. (TPO17, R, S1, T1) 用于海上商业扩张的单纯的投资规模反映出了这种东西方贸易所能带来的巨大利润。
【派生】 scaled *a.* 有鳞的；成比例的

返记菜单

elite[19] estimate[19] length[19] linguistic[19] meme[19]
orientation[19] portray[19] scale[19]

【搭配】 scale up 按比例增加
scale down/back 缩减,按比例减少
on a large scale 大规模地
in scale 成比例,相称

seminar[19] ['semɪnɑː]

【释义】 n. 研讨会,(大学的)研究班
【例句】 Currently, all of the seminar classes in the history department are three hours long. (TPO7, S, Q3) 当前,历史系的所有研讨课时长为三小时。
【派生】 seminary n. 神学院;发源地
【搭配】 seminar room 研究室

shallow[19] ['ʃæləʊ]

【释义】 a. 1. 浅的,薄的 2. 肤浅的(supreficial, skin-deep) v.(使)变浅
【例句】 It has been suggested that Pakicetus fed on fish in shallow waters and was not yet adapted for life in the open ocean. (TPO2, R, S2, T1) 据推测,巴基鲸以浅水鱼类为食,还未能适应在辽阔的大海里生活。
【派生】 shallowly ad. 浅地,肤浅地
shallowness n. 浅,肤浅
【搭配】 the shallows 浅滩

standard[19] ['stændəd]

【释义】 n. 标准,准则(createrion, model, role) a. 标准的,规范的(normative)
【例句】 That said, even by the standards of the 20s and 30s, Painlevé's films were unique, a hybrid of styles. (TPO3, L, S1, L2) 也就是说,即便是用20、30年代的标准来衡量,培乐威的电影也是独特的,是多种风格的混合体。
【派生】 standardize v. 使符合标准,使标准化
standardization n. 标准化

strength[19] [streŋθ]

【释义】 n. 1. 力,力量;体力,活力 2. 长处,优点,优势 3. 强度;效能
【例句】 The fact that the greatest diversity of Native American languages occurs along the west coast of the Americas lends strength to Fladmark's hypothesis. (TPO9, R, S1, T1, Q6) 美国本土语言多样化在美洲西海岸的出现有力地证明了弗莱德马克假说的正确性。
【反义】 weakness
【派生】 strengthen v. 加强,巩固
【搭配】 on the strength of 在…的基础上

tail[19] [teɪl]

【释义】 n. 1. 尾巴,尾部(end, rear, back) v. 跟踪,尾随(follow, track)
【例句】 The whale retained a tail and lacked a fluke, the major means of locomotion in modern cetaceans. (TPO2, R, S2, T1) 这只鲸仍有尾巴,但是缺少现代水生鲸类动物用于行动的主要身体部位——尾片。
【派生】 tailed a. 有…(状)尾的
【搭配】 turn tail 逃跑
tail away 减少
with one's tail between one's legs 夹着尾巴,垂头丧气

terrestrial[19] [tɪ'restrɪəl]

【释义】 a. 陆地的,陆生的,地球的
【例句】 But that makes it easier to identify something as a meteoroid, as it opposed to…to just a terrestrial rock. (TPO13, L, S2, L2) 但是,这样就会更容易鉴别出某物是流星体,因为它与地球上的岩石是不同的。

Word List 9

track[19] [træk]

【释义】*n.* 1. 踪迹，轨迹 2. 跑道 3. 小路 *v.* 追踪，跟踪

【例句】They leave long trails behind them, tracks you might say as they move from one point to another. (TPO4, L, S2, L1) 它们在身后留下了长长的轨迹，你会认为那是它们从一个地点移动到另一个地点留下的踪迹。

【搭配】track and field 田径，田径赛
on track 走上正轨
keep track of 记录；与…保持联系
track down 追捕
back on track 重回正轨；改过自新

warbler[19] [ˈwɔːblə]

【释义】*n.* 鸣鸟；用颤音歌唱的人

【例句】Let's look at the blue warbler. (TPO8, L, S1, L1) 下面我们来看蓝林莺。

academic[18] [ˌækəˈdemɪk]

【释义】*a.* 1. 学术的 2. 学院的 3. 理论的 *n.* 大学教师，学者，大学生

【例句】Well, let's start with the academics. (TPO5, L, S1, C1) 那我们就先从学习开始说起吧。

【派生】academy *n.* 研究院；学会

【搭配】academic qualification 学历；学术资格
academic background 学术背景

acquire[18] [əˈkwaɪə]

【释义】*v.* 获得，取得（gain, obtain）

【例句】And she wants to acquire it for her museum. (TPO5, L, S2, L1) 她想要为她所在的博物馆购买这幅画。

【派生】acquired *a.* 后天的；已获得的
acquirement *n.* 取得；才学成就

apparent[18] [əˈpærənt]

【释义】*a.* 1. 显然的，明白的（distinct, obvious）2. 表面上的，貌似（真实）的

【例句】Then, if he tries to talk with her, maybe her father get furious, for no apparent reason. (TPO7, L, S1, L1) 那么，如果他试图跟她说话，她父亲可能会莫名其秒的愤怒。

【反义】obscure; concealed

【派生】apparently *ad.* 显然地

bear[18] [beə]

【释义】*v.* 1. 开花，结果 2. 支持，支撑（hold, support）3. 承担，忍受（stand）4. 生产，生育（produce, yield）5. 怀有（某种感情），具有 *n.* 熊

【例句】It's actually a member of the banana family—it even bears little banana-shaped fruits. (TPO2, L, S1, L2) 事实上它是芭蕉科的一种——它甚至可以结出香蕉形的小果实。

【派生】unbearable *a.* 无法忍受的

【搭配】bear in mind 记着某事
bear the responsibility 承担责任

birch[18] [bɜːtʃ]

【释义】*n.* 桦树，桦木

【例句】Birch is one of the few species of tree that can survive in the extreme environments of the upper timberline. (TPO1, R, S1, T1) 桦树是少数能在上层林木线的极端环境中生存的树种之一。

cast[18] [kɑːst]

【释义】*v.* 1. 铸造（mould）2. 投掷，投射（throw, project）*n.* 演员阵容

【例句】By contrast, wooden statues were carved from several pieces of wood that were pegged together to form the finished work, and metal statues were either made by wrapping sheet metal around a wooden core or cast by the lost wax process. (TPO11, R, S1, T1) 相比之下，木雕是由钉在一起的几块木头雕刻而成的，而金属雕塑要么是金属片包裹着一块木质核心，要么是用脱蜡铸造法铸成的。

【搭配】cast off 丢弃，摆脱
cast out 驱逐，逐出
cast away 丢掉，浪费；使失事
cast aside 抛弃；废除
cast about 搜寻；想方设法

返记菜单

track[19] warbler[19] academic[18] acquire[18] apparent[18]
bear[18] birch[18] cast[18]

ceremony[18] ['serɪmənɪ] 

【释义】*n.* 典礼,仪式;礼节(ritual, rite)

【例句】To allow them to fulfill their important role in ceremonies of Egyptian life. (TPO11, R, S1, T1) 让他们完成在埃及生活的仪式中的重要作用。

【派生】ceremonious *a.* 讲究礼节的
ceremonial *a.* 仪式上的

【搭配】opening ceremony 开幕式

crater[18] ['kreɪtə] 

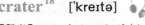

【释义】*n.* 1. 火山口 2. 坑(如陨石坑,弹坑等)

【例句】We could do this in theory by studying an enormous impact crater, known as the South-Pole-Aitken Basin. (TPO5, L, S1, L2) 我们可以通过研究一个巨大的陨石坑——著名的月球南极艾特肯盆地来从理论上做到这一点。

【派生】cratered *a.* 有坑洞的,多坑的
crateriform *a.* 漏斗状的;似火山的

creature[18] ['kriːtʃə] 

【释义】*n.* 生物,动物,人

【例句】Because we all know that very few fairy tales actually have those tiny magical creatures in them. (TPO5, L, S2, L2) 因为我们都知道童话故事中其实很少有那些小巧而神奇的生物。

custom[18] ['kʌstəm] 

【释义】*n.* 1. 习惯,风俗,惯例(tradition, habit) *a.* 定做的,定制的

【例句】And it maybe this burial custom that explain why the houses were packed in so tightly without streets. (TPO 1, L, S2, L1) 或许这种丧葬习惯可以解释为什么房屋建得满满当当的,连街道都没留。

【派生】customarily *ad.* 通常,习惯上
customer *n.* 消费者
customs *n.* 关税

deposit[18] [dɪ'pɒzɪt] 

【释义】*v.* 1. 沉积,沉淀 2. 储蓄,存款 3. 放置,寄存
n. 1. 定金,存款 2. 沉积物

【例句】The water was always laden with pebbles, gravel, and sand, known as glacial outwash, that deposited as the flow slowed down. (TPO1, R, S2, T2) 水里总会携带些石子、砾石和沙子,也就是所谓的冰水沉积,这些颗粒会随水流的减缓而沉淀下来。

【派生】deposited *a.* 堆积的,存放的
deposition *n.* 矿床,沉积

description[18] [dɪs'krɪpʃən] 

【释义】*n.* 1. 描述,形容 2. 种类,类型

【例句】See, I've never had a linguistics class before, so I was sort of, I mean, I was looking over the course description and a lot of the stuff you described there, I just don't know what it is talking about, you know, or what it means. (TPO6, L, S2, C1) 您知道,我过去从来没有上过语言学这门课,所以我看了课程描述和您介绍的关于这门课的东西,但我还不明白它主要讲的是什么,或者是什么意思。

【逆构】describe *v.* 描写,叙述

【搭配】beyond description 无法形容

doll[18] [dɒl] 

【释义】*n.* 1. 玩具娃娃 2. 美貌女子,有吸引力的人
v. 打扮

【例句】In this experiment, a baby is shown a doll on the table. (TPO1, S, Q5) 在这个实验里,人们把一个玩具娃娃摆在桌子上让婴儿看。

dolphin[18] ['dɒlfɪn] 

【释义】*n.* 海豚

【例句】It should be obvious that cetaceans—whales, porpoises, and dolphins—are mammals. (TPO2, R, S2, T1) 显然,鲸类动物——鲸、鼠海豚、海豚——都是哺乳动物。

fantasy[18] ['fæntəsɪ]

【释义】*n.* 想象,幻想(fancy, illusion, imagination)

【例句】Another (answer), advanced in the twentieth century, suggests that humans have a gift for fantasy. (TPO1, R, S2, T1) 另一个在20世纪提出的答案表明人类拥有幻想的天赋。

【派生】 fantasyland *n.* 梦境

favor[18] ['feɪvə] 

【释义】 *n.* 1. 赞同，支持 2. 偏爱，好意 *v.* 1. 偏爱 2. 给予 3. 支持

【例句】 It searches for means to win the favor of these forces. (TPO1, R, S2, T1) 寻找可以赢得这些力量支持的方法。

【派生】 favourite *a.* 最喜欢的

【搭配】 in favor of 支持，赞同
do sb. a favor 帮某人忙
owe sb. a favor 欠某人的情

imitate[18] ['ɪmɪteɪt] 

【释义】 *v.* 模仿，仿效(mimic, simulate)

【例句】 For many, Rome is at best the imitator and the continuator of Greece on a larger scale. (TPO7, R, S2, T1) 对许多人来说，罗马在很大程度上最多也不过是希腊的模仿者和继承者。

【派生】 imitation *n.* 模仿，效法

inspire[18] [ɪn'spaɪə] 

【释义】 *v.* 1. 鼓舞，激励(encourage) 2. 赋予灵感，启迪 3. 触动

【例句】 It often inspired French novelists to write great pieces of literature. (TPO12, L, S2, L1) 它常常给法国小说家们带来创作伟大文学作品的灵感。

【派生】 inspiration *n.* 灵感；鼓舞

【搭配】 inspire sb. to do sth. 鼓舞某人做某事

muscle[18] ['mʌsl] 

【释义】 *n.* 1. 体力 2. 肌肉

【例句】 There were three sources of power: animal or human muscles; the wind, operating on sail or windmill; and running water. (TPO6, R, S1, T1) 当时的驱动力有三种：动物或人力；风力，用于航行或风车；流水产生的动力。

【派生】 muscular *a.* 肌肉发达的
musculature *n.* 肌肉组织

【搭配】 muscle in [informal] 侵入，强夺

narrow[18] ['nærəʊ] 

【释义】 *a.* 1. 狭义的 2. 狭窄的 3.（心胸、目光）狭隘的 4. 勉强的，很险的 *v.*（使）狭窄

【例句】 Typically people think of coins and paper "bills" as money, but that's using a somewhat narrow definition of the term. (TPO2, S, Q6) 一般来说，人们认为硬币和纸币就是钱，但是这只是"钱"这一术语的狭义概念。

【反义】 broad, wide

【派生】 narrowly *ad.* 狭窄地
narrowness *n.* 狭小，狭窄

【搭配】 narrow escape 九死一生，幸免于难
narrow victory 险胜

originate[18] [ə'rɪdʒɪneɪt] 

【释义】 *v.* 1. 起源于，产生 2. 发起，创办

【例句】 It is now generally believed that these prerequisites originated with people speaking Austronesian languages. (TPO5, R, S2, T1) 普遍认为这些先决条件起源于那些说南岛语的人。

【搭配】 originate from 发源于

outline[18] ['aʊtlaɪn] 

【释义】 *v.* 1. 画出…的轮廓，勾勒 2. 概述 *n.* 1. 提纲，概要 2. 外形，轮廓(profile)

【例句】 You have to meet with your department chair to outline a plan for the rest of your time here. (TPO8, L, S1, C1) 你必须见见你们系主任，然后勾勒出一个你待在这里的剩余时间的计划。

path[18] [pɑːθ] 

【释义】 *n.* 1. 小路，小径 2. 路线，轨道 3. 途径

【例句】 And for better or for worse, we chose to go down that path. (TPO12, L, S2, L2) 不管怎样，我们选择沿着那条路走下去。

polar[18] ['pəʊlə] 

【释义】 *a.* 1. 极地的，两极的 2. 对立的

【例句】 The upper timberline is lowest in the polar regions. (TPO1, R, S1, T1) 上层树带界限在极地地区是最低的。

返记菜单

favor[18]	imitate[18]	inspire[18]	muscle[18]	narrow[18]
originate[18]	outline[18]	path[18]	polar[18]	

【派生】 polarize *v.* 使极化，截然对立

regular[18] ['regjʊlə]

【释义】 *a.* 1. 常规的，普通的(common, normal) 2. 惯例的，有规律的(orderly) 3. 匀称的 4. 规则的
【例句】 The pots in the pile could be regular trash too. (TPO5, W, Q1) 土堆里的罐子可能也就是些普通的垃圾。
【派生】 regularity *n.* 规则性；匀称
regularise *v.* 使合法化
regularly *ad.* 有规律地；经常

similarity[18] [ˌsɪmɪ'lærɪtɪ]

【释义】 *n.* 相似性，类似，相似(uniformity, likeness)
【例句】 But that's pretty much where the similarities end. (TPO3, L, S1, L2) 那正是缺乏相似性的地方。
【反义】 diffirence
【逆构】 similar *a.* (~ to) 相似的，类似的

total[18] ['təʊtl]

【释义】 *a.* 1. 完全的(complete) 2. 总的，全体的(whole) *n.* 总数，合计 *v.* 共计，总计
【例句】 Yeah, but it was totally unconvincing. (TPO1, S, Q3) 是啊，但是那完全是不可信的。
【反义】 partial
【派生】 totally *ad.* 完全地
【搭配】 in total 总计

toxic[18] ['tɒksɪk]

【释义】 *a.* 有毒的，中毒的(noxious, poisonous) *n.* 有毒物质
【例句】 And in fact, the leaves of the potato plant are quite toxic. (TPO10, L, S1, L2) 事实上，马铃薯的叶子毒性很大。
【搭配】 toxic effect 毒性作用，毒效

trend[18] [trend]

【释义】 *n.* 趋势，倾向
【例句】 In an effort to counteract the trend, the college has announced a plan to renovate its on-campus housing. (TPO11, S, Q3) 为了抵制这一倾向，校方宣布了一项整修校园内房屋的计划。
【派生】 trendy *a.* 时髦的，流行的

vast[18] [vɑ:st]

【释义】 *a.* 巨大的，广阔的，大量的(huge, immense, large)
【例句】 Vast areas along the coast may have been deglaciated beginning around 16,000 years ago, possibly providing a coastal corridor for the movement of plants, animals, and humans sometime between 13,000 and 14,000 years ago. (TPO9, R, S1, T1) 沿海的辽阔地区的冰川大约在16000年前开始融化，这就为13000年到14000年前的某一段时间内植物、动物和人类的迁移提供了一个海岸走廊。
【反义】 narrow
【派生】 vastitude *n.* 广度

beneath[17] [bɪ'ni:θ]

【释义】 *prep./ad.* 在…之下(below, under)
【例句】 Vast numbers of them fall on the ground beneath the mother plants. (TPO9, R, S2, T2) 大量的孢子降落在母体植物下面的土地上。

drain[17] [dreɪn]

【释义】 *v.* (使)排出，(使)流光(draw off, flow out) *n.* 1. 下水道，排水管 2. 消耗
【例句】 Instead, they are probably the paths taken by huge volumes of water draining from the southern highlands into the northern plains. (TPO8, R, S2, T2) 相反，它们很可能是由南部高地流向北部平原的大量水流所经过的通道。
【派生】 drainage *n.* 排水，排水装置
【搭配】 down the drain 浪费掉，化为乌有

eliminate[17] [ɪ'lɪmɪneɪt]

【释义】 *v.* 排除，消除(eradicate, abolish)
【例句】 But sadly all these ideas have been eliminated as possibilities. (TPO4, L, S2, L1) 不过悲哀的是，这些想法实现的可能性都被排除了。

返记菜单

regular[18] similarity[18] total[18] toxic[18] trend[18]
vast[18] beneath[17] drain[17] eliminate[17]

【派生】elimination *n.* 排除，除去

fail[17] [feɪl] 

【释义】*v.* 1. 不及格，未达成 2. 失败 3. 停止，用尽 *n.*（考试）不及格

【例句】I was failing chemistry. (TPO3, S, Q4) 我的化学不及格。

【派生】failure *n.* 失败，不成功

【搭配】without fail 一定，必定

geology[17] [dʒɪ'ɒlədʒɪ] 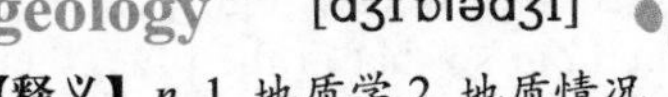

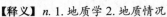

【释义】*n.* 1. 地质学 2. 地质情况

【例句】Listen to part of a lecture in a geology class. (TPO1, L, S1, L2) 听一段地理课讲座。

【派生】geological *a.* 地质的，地质学的
geologic *a.* 地质的，地质学的

geometric[17] [dʒɪə'metrɪk] 

【释义】*a.* 几何学的，几何学图形的

【例句】And why did they not discover the geometric perspective as European artists did in the Renaissance? (TPO11, R, S1, T1) 为什么他们没有像文艺复兴时期的欧洲艺术家那样发现几何视角呢？

【逆构】geometry *n.* 几何（学）

hire[17] ['haɪə] 

【释义】*v.* 雇佣，租用 *n.* 租用

【例句】I think you know that the department is looking to hire a new professor, are you familiar with our hiring process? (TPO11, L, S2, C1) 我想你知道系里正要招聘一位新教授，你熟悉我们的招聘流程吗？

kilometer[17] ['kɪləmiːtə] 

【释义】*n.* 千米，公里

【例句】The city of Teotihuacán, which lay about 50 kilometers northeast of modern-day Mexico City, began its growth by 200 -101 B. C. (TPO8, R, S1, T1) 位于现代墨西哥城东北50公里处的特奥蒂瓦坎城发源于公元前200年到公元前101年。

liquid[17] ['lɪkwɪd] 

【释义】*a.* 1. 液体的，液态的 2. 清澈的；流畅的 *n.* 液体

【例句】Photographic evidence suggests that liquid water once existed in great quantity on the surface of Mars. (TPO8, R, S2, T2) 影像证据表明，火星表面上曾经存在着大量的液态水。

【派生】liquidity *n.* 流动性，流畅

log[17] [lɒg] 

【释义】*v.* 1. 伐木 2. 正式记录 *n.* 1. 圆木（wood）2.（航海、飞行）日志

【例句】A worsening of the plight of deer was to be expected as settlers encroached on the land, logging, burning, and clearing, eventually replacing a wilderness landscape with roads, cities, towns, and factories. (TPO4, R, S1, T1) 随着移民侵占土地、伐木烧林和清理等活动的进行，最终空旷的原野会被公路、城镇和工厂所取代，可以预见鹿群的处境会越来越恶劣。

【搭配】log cabin 小木屋

mate[17] [meɪt] 

【释义】*v.*（使）配对；结伴 *n.* 1. 配偶（spouse）2. 伙伴（fellow）

【例句】You may have seen, for example, a bird that's in the middle of a mating ritual, and suddenly it stops and preens, you know, takes a few moments to straighten its feathers, and then returns to the mating ritual. (TPO4, L, S1, L1) 比如，你们会看到鸟在配对过程中会突然停下来梳理羽毛，你们知道，它们会花一阵功夫理顺羽毛后，再回到配对过程中。

【搭配】mate with 使紧密配合
soul mate 情人，性情相投的人

negative[17] ['negətɪv] 

【释义】*a.* 1. 消极的 2. 否定的 3. 负面的，负的

【例句】I hate to sound so negative here, but honestly, they are taking credit for things they shouldn't take credit for. (TPO4, L, S2,

返记菜单

fail[17]	geology[17]	geometric[17]	hire[17]	kilometer[17]
liquid[17]	log[17]	mate[17]	negative[17]	

C1) 我讨厌这样消极，但事实上，他们就是在不劳而获。
【反义】affirmative, positive
【派生】negativity *n.* 否定性，消极性
【搭配】in the negative 否定的（地）；反对的（地）

obvious[17] ['ɒbvɪəs]

【释义】*a.* 明显的，显然的（apparent, clear, distinct）
【例句】Of course, the obvious question is how did that sand end up so far west? (TPO1, L, S1, L2) 当然，一个明显的问题就是那些沙子是怎么跑到那么远的西部地区的呢？
【反义】obscure
【派生】obviousness *n.* 显而易见；显著性
obviously *ad.* 明显地

operate[17] ['ɒpəreɪt]

【释义】*v.* 1. 运营 2. 运转，运行 3. 操作 4. 做手术
【例句】Few students ride the buses and the buses are expensive to operate. (TPO2, S, Q3) 很少有学生乘坐校车，而且运营校车的费用很高。
【派生】operation *n.* 运转；手术
operative *a.* 有效的
operational *a.* 运转的，操作上的
【搭配】operate on 对…动手术；对…起作用

overall[17] ['əʊvərɔːl]

【释义】*a.* 全部的，总体的，全面的（general, comprehensive）*ad.* 总的来说 *n.* 罩衫，工作服
【例句】Deer populations naturally fluctuate, but early settlers in the Puget Sound environment caused an overall decline in the deer populations of the area at that time. (TPO4, R, S1, T1) 鹿群的数量会自然地波动，但早期移民在皮吉特海湾定居造成了当时该地区鹿群数量的整体下降。
【搭配】overall situation 大局；总体形势
overall development 综合开发

pigment[17] ['pɪgmənt]

【释义】*n.* 1. 天然色素，颜料
【例句】From the Middle East the Chinese acquired a blue pigment—a purified form of cobalt oxide unobtainable at that time in China—that contained only a low level of manganese. (TPO10, R, S1, T1) 中国人从中东地区得到了一种蓝色的颜料，这种颜料在当时的中国还没有，是氧化钴经过提纯后的一种成分，只含有少量的锰。
【搭配】red pigment 红色颜料，红颜料
pigment printing 染印

pot[17] [pɒt]

【释义】*n.* 罐，壶，锅 *v.* 把…装罐
【例句】Whereas in fact they were carefully and precisely worked out so that at the time, their meaning was clear, so it is with Chinese pots. (TPO10, R, S1, T1) 然而，它们实际上是被精心制作出来的，所以在当时，其意义是显而易见的，中国的陶器也是如此。

proportion[17] [prə'pɔːʃən]

【释义】*n.* 比例，部分 *v.* 使成比例
【例句】The price of pianos dropped to the point that a larger proportion of the population could afford to own them. (TPO16, L, S1, L2) 钢琴的价格降到了大部分人都能买得起的程度。
【派生】proportional *a.* 成比例的，均衡的
proportionate *a.* 成比例的 *v.* 使成比例
【搭配】out of proportion 不成比例
in proportion 成比例

rely[17] [rɪ'laɪ]

【释义】*v.* 依靠，信任
【例句】Since the climate's not too bad, the Eastern marmots don't have to rely on each other too much and they really don't need to stay together as a family to survive either. (TPO1, L, S2, L2) 因为天气并不太糟糕，所以东部土拨鼠并不需要过多地互相依赖，也并不需要待在一起作为一个家族才能够生存。
【搭配】rely on 依靠，指望

retain[17] [rɪ'teɪn]

【释义】*v.* 保留，保持（conserve, keep, preserve）
【例句】Stone statues were worked from single rectangular blocks of material and retained the compactness of the original shape.

返记菜单

obvious[17] operate[17] overall[17] pigment[17] pot[17]
proportion[17] rely[17] retain[17]

(TPO11, R, S1, T1) 石像是由一整块矩形石料加工而成的，保留了其原型的简洁性。
【派生】 retainable *a.* 可保留的，能保持住的

somewhat[17] ['sʌmwɒt] 

【释义】 *ad.* 稍微，有点
【例句】 One necessary condition seems to be a somewhat detached view of human problems. (TPO1, R, S2, T1)（戏剧发展的）一个必要条件似乎是有点超脱地看待人类的问题。

sophisticated[17] [sə'fɪstɪkeɪtɪd] 

【释义】 *a.* 1. 复杂的，精密的（complicated, advanced）2. 老练的，富有经验的（worldly）
【例句】 The Mutoscope was a less sophisticated earlier prototype of the Kinetoscope. (TPO2, R, S2, T2) 早期电影放映机是活动电影放映机的早期原型，它相对而言没有那么复杂。
【反义】 unsophisticated
【派生】 sophistication *n.* 老练；精密，高端
【逆构】 sophisticate *v.* 使变得世故；使复杂精密 *n.* 老于世故的人

sufficient[17] [sə'fɪʃənt] 

【释义】 *a.* 足够的，充足的（adequate, enough）
【例句】 The second is the availability of sufficient time and space. (TPO9, R, S2, T1) 第二就是要有足够的时间和空间。
【反义】 insufficient
【派生】 sufficiency *n.* 充足，自满
【逆构】 suffice *v.* 足够，有能力

tissue[17] ['tɪsjuː] 

【释义】 *n.* 1. 组织 2. 薄纱，棉纸
【例句】 Mineral deficiencies can often be detected by specific symptoms such as chlorosis (loss of chlorophyll resulting in yellow or white leaf tissue), necrosis (isolated dead patches), anthocyanin formation (development of deep red pigmentation of leaves or stem), stunted growth, and development of woody tissue in an herbaceous plant. (TPO5, R, S1, T1) 矿物质的缺乏通常可以通过一些特别的症状表现出来，比如萎黄病（水溶性叶绿素的缺乏导致的黄色或白色的叶片组织）、坏死（分离的枯死的叶片）、花色素甙生成（叶子或枝干上深红色色素的扩散），生长萎缩以及草本植物中木质组织的发展。

abundant[16] [ə'bʌndənt] 

【释义】 *a.* 丰富的，充裕的（affluent, rich）
【例句】 The salt and gypsum, the faunal changes, and the unusual gravel provided abundant evidence that the Mediterranean was once a desert. (TPO7, R, S1, T1) 盐和石膏、动物群体的变化以及非同寻常的砾石都为证明"地中海曾经是一个沙漠"这一观点提供了充足的证据。
【反义】 lacking, scarce
【派生】 abundance *n.* 丰富，充裕
【搭配】 abundant in sth. 富有，富于

acknowledge[16] [ək'nɒlɪdʒ] 

【释义】 *v.* 1. 答谢，致谢 2. 承认，确认（recognize, admit）
【例句】 Many of your cultural establishments in the United States will have a plaque somewhere acknowledging the support—the money they received from whatever corporation. (TPO4, L, S2, L2) 在美国，许多文化机构都会挂有一个牌匾，用以标明它们所得到的支持——从某些公司获得的资助。
【派生】 acknowledgment *n.* 承认

balance[16] ['bæləns] 

【释义】 *n.* 1. 平衡，均衡 2. 差额，余款 3. 天平，秤 *v.* 使平衡，使均衡（equilibrate）
【例句】 The balance of deer species in the Puget Sound region has changed over time, with the Columbian white-tailed deer now outnumbering other types of deer. (TPO4, R, S1, T1) 皮吉特海湾地区鹿群种类的平衡已经随着时间而改变了，目前是哥伦比亚白尾鹿的数量多于其他种类的鹿群。
【反义】 unbalance

celebrity[16] [sɪ'lebrɪtɪ] 

【释义】 *n.* 1. 名人，名流 2. 名声，名誉
【例句】 Um, another strategy they use is to get a celebrity to advertise a product. (TPO3, S,

返记菜单

somewhat[17] sophisticated[17] sufficient[17] tissue[17] abundant[16]
acknowledge[16] balance[16] celebrity[16]

Q6) 他们所采用的另一个策略就是找名人来为产品做广告。

choir[16] [kwaɪə]

【释义】*n.* 唱诗班，合唱队

【例句】I came from the choir. (TPO16, L, S1, C1) 我来自一个合唱队。

conduct[16]

【释义】[kən'dʌkt] *v.* 1. 实施，进行（实验或研究等）2. 引导，带领（guide）3. 传导 4. 管理，指挥 ['kɒndʌkt] *n.* 1. 举止，行为（behavior）2. 管理（方式），实施（方式）

【例句】She thinks that the amount of research conducted on the topic is excessive. (TPO10, L, S2, L1) 她认为对于这个话题的研究太多了。

【派生】conductor *n.* 导（电、热等）体
conductivity *n.* 导电率，传导率

consume[16] [kən'sjuːm]

【释义】*v.* 1. 吃，喝（eat up）2. 消费，消耗（use up, spend）3. 毁灭

【例句】To keep 40 people alive that winter, they consumed approximately 150 elk and 20 deer. (TPO4, R, S1, T1) 为了保证让 40 个人活过那个冬天，他们吃掉了大约 150 只麋鹿和 20 只鹿。

【反义】produce

crisis[16] ['kraɪsɪs]

【释义】*n.* 危机，危急关头，关键时刻

【例句】In the face of the upcoming water supply crisis, a number of grandiose schemes have been developed to transport vast quantities of water by canal or pipeline from the Mississippi, the Missouri, or the Arkansas rivers. (TPO3, R, S1, T1) 在即将到来的水资源供应危机面前，人们提出了一些宏伟的供水计划，比如将密西西比河、密苏里河或者阿肯色河的水通过运河或管道输送到需要用水的地方。

【搭配】economic crisis 经济危机

critical[16] ['krɪtɪkəl]

【释义】*a.* 1. 非常重要的；危急的（crucial, acute, essential）2. 评论的，批评的

【例句】The situation is most critical in Texas, where the climate is driest, the greatest amount of water is being pumped, and the aquifer contains the least water. (TPO3, R, S1, T1) 这种情况在德克萨斯州尤为严重，那里气候最为干旱，大量的水被抽走，蓄水层含水量最少。

【派生】criticize *v.* 批评，责备

【逆构】critic *n.* 批评家，评论家

【搭配】critical moment 紧急关头
critical point 临界点

Word List 10

depict[16] [dɪˈpɪkt]

【释义】*v.* 1. 描画，描绘（portray, picture）2. 描述，描写（describe, illustrate）

【例句】Apart from statues representing deities, kings, and named members of the elite that can be called formal, there is another group of three-dimensional representations that depicts generic figures, frequently servants, from the nonelite population. (TPO11, R, S1, T1) 除了代表神明、国王和上层精英人士的这种正式的雕像以外，还有另外一种立体的表现手法，用以描绘一般民众，通常是来自非上层人群中的仆人。

【派生】depiction *n.* 描写，叙述
depictive *a.* 描写的，描述的

dramatic[16] [drəˈmætɪk]

【释义】*a.* 戏剧的，戏剧性的；引人注目的（spectacular, striking）

【例句】A search of sedimentary deposits that span the boundary between the Cretaceous and Tertiary periods shows that there is a dramatic increase in the abundance of iridium briefly and precisely at this boundary. (TPO15, R, S2, T2) 对从白垩纪时期到第三纪时期的沉积物的调查显示：在这两个时期交替的时候，铱元素的含量有显著增加。

【派生】dramatical *a.* 戏剧的
dramatically *ad.* 戏剧性地；显著地

【逆构】drama *n.* 戏剧，戏剧艺术，戏剧性事件

enhance[16] [ɪnˈhɑːns]

【释义】*v.* 提高，增加，加强（improve, raise）

【例句】From a practical aspect this protected the figures against breakage and psychologically gives the images a sense of strength and power, usually enhanced by a supporting back pillar. (TPO11, R, S1, T1) 从实用的方面来看，这样可以保护人像不受破坏，而且从心理上给人一种力量感，这种力量感通常会通过其后部的柱子得以强化。

【反义】diminish, decrease

【派生】enhancement *n.* 增进，增加

except[16] [ɪkˈsept]

【释义】*conj.* 只是；除…外；除非 *prep.* 除…外 *v.* 不包括，不计（exclude）

【例句】I'm fine; except I have a question about my paycheck. (TPO12, L, S2, C1) 除了对我的薪水有点疑问之外，我挺好的。

【派生】exception *n.* 例外，异议

【搭配】except for 除了…之外
except as 除…之外

exhibit[16] [ɪɡˈzɪbɪt]

【释义】*v.* 展览，陈列 *n.* 展览，展品

【例句】Nitrogen-deficient plants exhibit many of the symptoms just described. (TPO5, R, S1, T1) 缺氮的植物就表现出很多刚才提到过的症状。

【派生】exhibition *n.* 展览，展览会

【搭配】on exhibit 展览

explore[16] [ɪksˈplɔː]

【释义】*v.* 1. 勘探，探险 2. 考察，探究（probe, search, investigate）

【例句】These expeditions were likely driven by population growth and political dynamics on the home islands, as well as the challenge and excitement of exploring unknown waters. (TPO5, R, S2, T1) 很有可能是母岛上人口的增长和政治变动以及开发未知水域的挑战和兴奋推动了这些远征探险活动。

【派生】exploration *n.* 探测，探究

fault[16] [fɔːlt]

【释义】*n.* 1.（地壳运动造成的）断层（处）2. 不足，缺陷（defect, flaw）3. 过错，误差（error）

【例句】As a result of crustal adjustments and faulting, the Strait of Gibraltar, where the Mediterranean now connects to the Atlantic, opened, and water cascaded spectacularly back into the Mediterranean. (TPO7, R, S1, T1) 由于地壳运动发生断层现象，致使现在连接地中海和大西洋的直布罗陀海峡裂开，

返记菜单

depict[16] dramatic[16] enhance[16] except[16] exhibit[16]
explore[16] fault[16]

海水如瀑布般地流回地中海，十分壮观。
【搭配】 at fault 有责任，有错
find fault 挑错，找错
to a fault 过度地

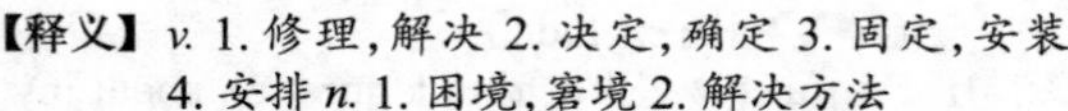

fix[16] [fɪks]

【释义】 *v.* 1. 修理，解决 2. 决定，确定 3. 固定，安装 4. 安排 *n.* 1. 困境，窘境 2. 解决方法
【例句】 And apparently, it's gonna take about two weeks to fix the problem. (TPO9, S, Q5) 很显然，这个问题需要两周才能解决。
【派生】 fixed *a.* 固定的，不变的
fixture *n.* 固定物；设备
【搭配】 fix up 修理好，修补

import[16]

【释义】 [ɪm'pɔːt] *v.* 进口，输入 ['ɪmpɔːt] *n.* 1. 进口商品，输入额 2. 意义，要旨，重要性
【例句】 Chinese porcelain wares imported into the Arab world. (TPO10, R, S1, T1) 中国的瓷器已进入阿拉伯国家。
【反义】 export
【搭配】 import from 从…输入；从…进口
import and export 进出口；输入和输出

massive[16] ['mæsɪv]

【释义】 *a.* 1. 大而重的，庞大的（enormous, colossal, immense）2. 可观的（considerable）
【例句】 It was this midcontinental corridor between two massive ice sheets—the Laurentide to the east and the Cordilleran to the west—that enabled the southward migration. (TPO9, R, S1, T1) 正是这一连接在两大冰盖（东部的劳伦太德冰盖和西部的科迪勒拉冰盖）之间的大陆中部走廊使得向南的迁移成为可能。

musical[16] ['mjuːzɪkəl]

【释义】 *n.* 音乐剧 *a.* 1. 音乐的 2. 喜爱音乐的，有音乐天赋的 3. 悦耳的
【例句】 Previously, large audiences had viewed spectacles at the theater, where vaudeville, popular dramas, musical and minstrel shows, classical plays, lectures, and slide-and-lantern shows had been presented to several hundred spectators at a time. (TPO2, R, S2, T2) 先前，大批观众在剧院观看表演，在那里，数百名观众可以同时观看轻歌舞剧、流行戏剧、音乐剧或歌唱表演、古典音乐、演讲和幻灯片放映。

orbit[16] ['ɔːbɪt]

【释义】 *n.* 1. 轨道（path, circle）2. 活动范围 *v.* 绕轨道运行
【例句】 Unlike earlier lunar missions, Clementine didn't orbit only around the moon's equator. (TPO5, L, S1, L2) 与早期登月任务不同，克莱芒蒂娜（1994 年发射的环月轨道探测器）并不只是环绕月球赤道运行。
【派生】 orbital *a.* 轨道的
【搭配】 orbit the earth 绕地球飞行

pellet[16] ['pelɪt]

【释义】 *n.* 颗粒状物，小子弹 *v.* 使成弹丸状；用子弹打
【例句】 What happens is that small (millimeter-to centimeter-size) pellets of ice form in the cold upper regions of the cloud. (TPO18, R, S2, T2) 所发生的情况就是微小的冰粒子（从几毫米到几厘米大小）会在云层的较冷的上层形成。

perfect[16] ['pɜːfɪkt]

【释义】 *v.* 使完美（improve, refine）*a.* 完美的；最好的（flawless, ideal）
【例句】 About a year after the opening of the first Kinetoscope parlor in 1894, showmen such as Orville and Woodville Latham (with the assistance of Edison's former assistant, William Dickson) perfected projection devices. (TPO2, R, S2, T2) 1894 年，第一个电影放映室向大众开放。一年之后，在爱迪生的前任助理威廉·迪克森的帮助下，放映商如奥维利和伍德维尔·莱瑟姆改进了放映设备。
【反义】 imperfect
【派生】 perfection *n.* 尽善尽美，完成
【搭配】 practice makes perfect 熟能生巧

plain[16] [pleɪn]

【释义】 *n.* 平原 *a.* 1. 简单的，朴素的 2. 清楚的，明白

的

【例句】The other species, the Columbian white-tailed deer, in earlier times was common in the open prairie country; it is now restricted to the low, marshy islands and flood plains along the lower Columbia River. (TPO4, R, S1, T1) 另一物种——哥伦比亚白尾鹿，以前常见于开阔的大草原上；现在却只限于地势低而湿软的岛上以及哥伦比亚河沿岸的冲积平原。

possess[16] [pəˈzes]

【释义】*v.* 1. 占有，拥有(have, own) 2.(感觉、情绪等)支配，控制

【例句】First of all, a group of people has a wider range of knowledge, expertise, and skills than any single individual is likely to possess. (TPO2, W, Q1) 首先，一个团队较单独个体有更广泛的知识和专业技能。

【派生】possession *n.* 拥有，占有；财产
possessive *a.* 物主的，占有的
possessor *n.* 持有人

profit[16] [ˈprɒfɪt]

【释义】*v.* 获益，得利(益)于 *n.* 1. 利润，收益，赢利 2. 益处(benefit, gain)

【例句】That same year, our competitor came out with a new design that attracted some of our customers and prevented us from profiting on potential new customers. (TPO1, S, Q4) 就在同一年，我们的竞争对手推出了一款新的设计，吸引了我们的一些顾客，并且影响了我们从潜在顾客身上获利。

【派生】profitable *a.* 有利可图的；有益的

【搭配】profit by 得益于
profit from 得益于；利用

resemble[16] [rɪˈzembl]

【释义】*v.* 像，类似(take after, be similar to)

【例句】Complex equipment inside buildings is the one element in modern architecture that resembles a component of the human body. (TPO3, R, S1, T1) 建筑内部的复杂装备是现代建筑的一个元素，如同人体的一个构成部分。

【反义】differ

【派生】resemblant *a.* 相似的，摹仿的
resemblance *n.* 相似，形似物

rule[16] [ruːl]

【释义】*n.* 1. 统治，支配 2. 规则，条例，规律 *v.* 1. 支配，统治 2. 裁决，裁定

【例句】China has one of the world's oldest continuous civilizations, despite invasions and occasional foreign rule. (TPO10, R, S1, T1) 尽管曾遭到侵略和偶尔受外国势力统治，但中国仍然是世界上最古老的源远流长的文明之一。

【搭配】as a rule 通常，照例
rule out 把…排除在外

sail[16] [seɪl]

【释义】*n.* 1. 帆，帆状物 2. 航行 *v.* 启航，航行(navigate)

【例句】The principal seagoing ship used throughout the Middle Ages was the galley, a long, low ship fitted with sails but driven primarily by oars. (TPO17, R, S1, T1) 中世纪使用的主要海船是单层甲板帆船，这种船的船体低矮狭长，配有船帆，但是主要靠船桨驱动。

selection[16] [sɪˈlekʃən]

【释义】*n.* 1. 选择，挑选 2. 挑选出来的人或事物

【例句】Well, last time we talked about passive habitat selection, like plants for example, they don't make active choices about where to grow. (TPO8, L, S1, L1) 那么，上次我们讲到了被动的生存环境选择，比如植物，它们并不主动地选择在哪里生长。

【逆构】select *v.* 选择

stress[16] [stres]

【释义】*v.* 1. 强调(emphasize) 2. 重读 *n.* 1. 压力(pressure) 2. 重要性(importance) 3. 强调(emphasis) 4. 重音，重读

【例句】The reason I think this painting is so important is that it stresses the impressionist aspect of Frantzen' style. (TPO1, L, S1, L1) 我认为这幅画非常重要，因为它强调了弗兰岑风格中印象主义的一面。

【派生】stressed *a.* 感到有压力的；紧张的

返记菜单

possess[16] profit[16] resemble[16] rule[16] sail[16]
selection[16] stress[16]

stressful *a.* 充满压力的，紧张的

succession[16] [səkˈseʃən]

【释义】*n.* 1. 连续 2. 一连串，一系列 3. 继承，继承权，继承人

【例句】Ecologists use the term "succession" to refer to the changes that happen in plant communities and ecosystems over time. (TPO3, R, S1, T2) 生态学家用"演替"来诠释植物群落和生态系统随着时间推移所发生的变化。

【派生】successive *a.* 连续的；继承的
successional *a.* 接连着的，连续性的

tension[16] [ˈtenʃən]

【释义】*n.* 紧张(stress)；张力，拉力

【例句】They are designed to withstand the forces of compression (pushing together), tension (pulling apart), bending, or a combination of these in different parts of the structure. (TPO3, R, S1, T1) 通过结构设计使建筑的不同部分能对抗压力、拉力、弯曲力或者以上各种压力的综合作用。

【逆构】tense *v.* 紧张的，拉紧的

thaw[16] [θɔː]

【释义】*v./n.* 1. 解冻，融化(melt, defrost) 2.(关系等)缓和

【例句】And because of the cold temperatures, the tundra has two layers: top layer, which is called the active layer, is frozen in the winter and spring, but thaws in the summer. (TPO9, L, S1, L2) 由于气温较低，冻土带分为两层，上层称为活跃层，会在冬天和春天冻结，而夏天就会融化。

transform[16] [trænsˈfɔːm]

【释义】*v.* 改变，转换，使改观(alter, change, convert)

【例句】The remains of microscopic organisms transform into petroleum once they are buried under mud. (TPO4, R, S2, T2) 微生物的遗体一旦被埋在泥土下后就会转化成石油。

【派生】transformable *a.* 可变化的
transformation *n.* 转换，改变
transformer *n.* 变压器

tundra[16] [ˈtʌndrə]

【释义】*n.* 苔原，冻土地带

【例句】The transition from forest to treeless tundra on a mountain slope is often a dramatic one. (TPO1, R, S1, T1) 从山坡上的树林转变为光秃秃的苔原的这一过程通常是显著而迅速的。

unit[16] [ˈjuːnɪt]

【释义】*n.* 1.(计量或计数等使用的)单位 2.(机械等的)元件，部件

【例句】In astronomical units—not perfect, but tantalizingly close. (TPO2, L, S2, L2) 这是天文单位——并不能保证丝毫不差，但是尽量接近正确数值。

【派生】unity *n.* 单一，个体

【搭配】absolute units (一般指国际通用的)绝对单位

varied[16] [ˈveərɪd]

【释义】*a.* 各种各样的，各不相同的(different, diverse)

【例句】Even though the northern part of the continent allowed for a more varied economy, several early human groups quickly moved south. (TPO9, R, S1, T1) 尽管大陆北部允许经济的多样性，但一些早期的人们却迅速南移。

【派生】variety *n.* 变化，多样性

【搭配】a varied topography 复杂的地形

virtually[16] [ˈvɜːtjʊəlɪ]

【释义】*ad.* 实际上；几乎(nearly, almost, practically)

【例句】On virtually every team, some members got almost a "free ride" ...they didn't contribute much at all, but if their team did a good job, they nevertheless benefited from the recognition the team got. (TPO2, W, Q1) 事实上，每个团队里面都有一些人坐享其成，他们不为团队做任何贡献，但如果他们的团队取得了不错的成绩，他们同样会从团队获得的认可中受益。

【逆构】virtual *a.* 实际上的，事实上的

arch[15] [ɑːtʃ]

【释义】*n.* 拱，拱门 *v.*(使)成拱形

【例句】The arch was used by the early cultures of the Mediterranean area chiefly for underground drains, but it was the Romans who first developed and used the arch extensively in aboveground structures. (TPO3, R, S1, T1) 在地中海地区的早期文化中拱主要是用来建设地下水渠，是罗马人最先开发并把拱广泛应用在地面建筑中。

【搭配】a triumphal arch 凯旋门

association[15] [əˌsəusɪˈeɪʃən]

【释义】*n.* 1. 关联，联合，联系(connection) 2. 协会(union, club)

【例句】When an association continues long enough for two people to become linked together by a relatively stable set of expectations, it is called a relationship. (TPO13, R, S1, T1) 当两个人的联系持续的时间足够长，使其能够通过相对稳定的期望联系在一起时，这种联系称为关系。

circle[15] [ˈsɜːkl]

【释义】*n.* 1. 圈子，界，阶层 2. 圆，圆圈 3. 循环 *v.* 包围，环绕

【例句】And Painlevé is still highly respected in many circles. (TPO3, L, S1, L2) 培乐威在很多圈子里仍然备受尊重。

compose[15] [kəmˈpəuz]

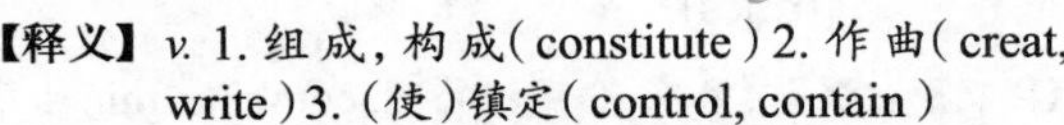

【释义】*v.* 1. 组成，构成(constitute) 2. 作曲(creat, write) 3. (使)镇定(control, contain)

【例句】By grouping the fibers you greatly increase their breaking strength—that bundle of fibers is much stronger than any of the individual fibers that compose it. (TPO2, L, S1, L2) 把单个纤维捆成一束可以大大提高它们的抗断强度——一束纤维合在一起比其中任何一根都要更强韧。

【派生】composer *n.* 作曲家
composition *n.* 构造；作文，曲子
composed *a.* 镇定的
composure *n.* 泰然自若

【搭配】be composed of 由…组成
compose oneself 镇静下来，安下心来

conclude[15] [kənˈkluːd]

【释义】*v.* 1. 得出结论，推断出(deduce, infer) 2. 结束，终止(end, finalize)

【例句】Ecologists concluded that the apparent stability of climax ecosystems depended on their complexity. (TPO3, R, S1, T2) 生态学家们得出的结论是：顶级生态系统表面上的稳定性取决于其复杂化程度。

【派生】conclusion *n.* 结论，推论
conclusive *a.* 决定性的；最后的

【搭配】conclude a speech 结束演说

encode[15] [ɪnˈkəud]

【释义】*v.* 编码，译码

【例句】A third likely explanation for infantile amnesia involves incompatibilities between the ways in which infants encode information and the ways in which older children and adults retrieve it. (TPO6, R, S2, T2) 对于婴幼儿期记忆缺失的第三种可能的解释是婴幼儿记忆信息的方式与年龄大些的儿童及成人不一致。

【派生】encoder *n.* 译码器，编码器

engage[15] [ɪnˈgeɪdʒ]

【释义】*v.* 1. 吸引 2. 订婚 3. (使)从事于，(使)忙于(involve)

【例句】Storytellers continually make their stories more engaging and memorable. (TPO1, R, S2, T1) 讲故事的人继续使他们的故事更吸引人，更难以忘怀。

【派生】engagement *n.* 约会；交战；婚约
engaged *a.* 忙碌的

【搭配】engage in (doing) sth. 从事于某事

existence[15] [ɪgˈzɪstəns]

【释义】*n.* 1. 存在 2. 生存，生活(方式)

【例句】Rayleigh and Ramsay postulated the existence of a new group of elements. (TPO16, R, S2, T1)) 瑞利和拉姆齐假设存在一组新的元素。

【逆构】exist *v.* 存在，生活
existent *a.* 存在的，生存的

返记菜单

association[15] circle[15] compose[15] conclude[15] encode[15]
engage[15] existence[15]

flipper[15] [ˈflɪpə] 

【释义】*n.* 鳍状肢，脚蹼

【例句】Insulation protects the leatherback everywhere but on its head and flippers. (TPO15, R, S2, T1) 这个防水层可以保护棱皮龟身上除头部和鳍之外的所有地方。

folk[15] [fəʊk]

【释义】*n.* 1.（口）大伙儿 2. 民间 3. [常作 folks] 人们，（某类或来自某个地方的）人 4. 双亲，亲属 *a.* 民间的

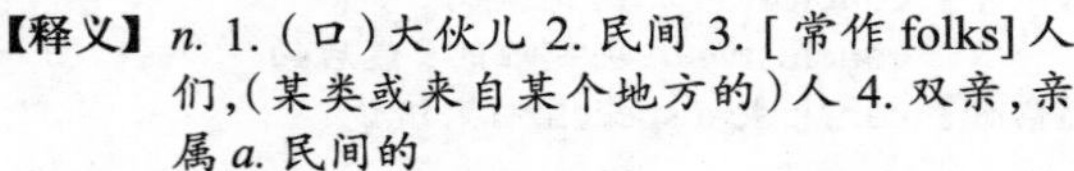

【例句】All right folks, let's continue our discussion of alternative energy sources and move on to what's probably the most well-known energy source—solar energy. (TPO12, L, S2, L2) 好的，伙计们，我们来继续讨论替代性能源，话题将推进到可能最众所周知的能源——太阳能。

【派生】folksy *a.* 有民间风味的；和气的；无拘束的
folkloric *a.* 民间传说的；民俗的

【搭配】folk music 民俗音乐

freeze[15] [friːz]

【释义】*v.*（使）结冰，（使）凝固 *n.* 冰冻，冻结

【例句】We bring in the day's catch to a floating-processor boat where the fish got cleaned, packaged and frozen right at sea. (TPO9, L, S1, C1) 我们把当天捕到的鱼带到一艘流动的加工船上，在这里对鱼进行清洗、包装，冷冻，这一切都在海上完成。

【搭配】frozen food 冷冻食品

gym[15] [dʒɪm] 

【释义】*n.* 1. 体育馆，健身房 2. 体育课

【例句】For example, I go to the gym several times a week. (TPO5, S, Q2) 比如说，我一周去几次体育馆。

【派生】gymnast *n.* 体操运动员

【搭配】gym class 体育课

lung[15] [lʌŋ]

【释义】*n.* 肺

【例句】They (the walls) ended up with a layer of black soot on them, and so did people's lungs. (TPO 1, L, S2, L1) 最终这些墙被一层黑灰覆盖，人们的肺也是如此。

【搭配】lung capacity 肺活量

map[15] [mæp]

【释义】*v.* 1. 绘制地图 2. 在地图上标示出 3. 计划 *n.* 地图

【例句】And he started keeping tracks of sunspots, mapping them, so he wouldn't confuse them with any potential new planet. (TPO18, L, S1, L1) 他开始跟踪记录太阳黑子的活动，把它们绘制成图，这样就不会将它们与可能出现的任何新行星弄混了。

【派生】mappable *a.* 可在图上标示的，可用图表示的

【搭配】on the map 存在的，重要的，出名的
off the map 不重要的；不存在的；不易到达的
map out 在地图上标出；筹划

mine[15] [maɪn]

【释义】*v.* 1. 开矿，采矿 2. 在…布雷 *n.* 1. 矿，矿井 2. 地雷；水雷 *pron.*（I 的所有格）我的（东西）

【例句】So that's the reason people mine rocks that contain a lot of Phosphorus to help the agriculture? (TPO10, L, S2, L1) 所以，那就是人们开采含有磷元素的矿石来帮助农业发展的原因？

【搭配】coal mine 煤矿

mix[15] [mɪks]

【释义】*v.* 混合，掺入，合成（blend, combine, mingle）*n.* 1. 混合（物）2. 融合

【例句】The theory is that huge rivers and wind carried the sand west where it mixed in the sand that was already there. (TPO1, L, S1, L2) 原理就是大河和狂风把沙子一路带到西部地区，这些沙子和那儿的沙子混合在一起。

【派生】mixed *a.* 混合的；弄糊涂的；形形色色的
mixture *n.* 混合；混合物

【搭配】mix up 使混乱，混淆；牵连

pebble[15] [ˈpebl] 

【释义】*n.* 卵石；[地] 水晶石 *v.* 用卵石铺

【例句】The sample consisted of pebbles of hardened

sediment that had once been soft, deep-sea mud, as well as granules of gypsum and fragments of volcanic rock. (TPO7, R, S1, T1) 样本中包含由曾经柔软的深海泥浆硬化沉积而成的卵石以及石膏微粒和火山岩碎片。

【搭配】not the only pebble on the beach 并非唯一要紧的人

pick[15] [pɪk]

【释义】*v.* 1. 挑选，选择（choose, select）2. 拾，捡，采摘 *n.* 1. 拾，捡，选择 2. 精华

【例句】Usually we can pick the hours we want to work. (TPO14, L, S1, C1) 通常我们能自己选择我们想要工作的时间。

【派生】picker *n.* 采摘者

【搭配】pick up 捡起；获得；收拾
pick out 挑选出
pick on 挑选；找茬
pick off 摘掉；拔去；截取
pick at 弹，拉；吃一点点
pick (someone) to piece 严厉批评
pick holes in 挑剔
pick (one's) way 寻找出路

progression[15] [prəˈgreʃən]

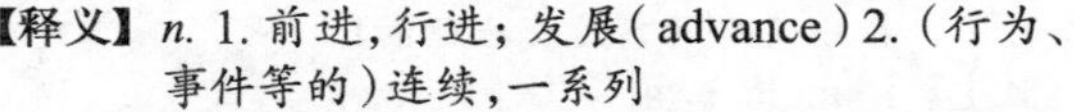

【释义】*n.* 1. 前进，行进；发展（advance）2.（行为、事件等的）连续，一系列

【例句】Fossil formation like the Burgess Shale show that evolution cannot always be thought of as a slow progression. (TPO5, R, S2, T2) 像伯吉斯岩层那样的化石构造显示，进化不总像是我们想的那样，是一个缓慢的过程。

【派生】progressional *a.* 级数的；前进的；进步的

【逆构】progress *n.* 过程

publish[15] [ˈpʌblɪʃ]

【释义】*v.* 1. 出版，刊印 2. 公布，发表

【例句】He wrote an essay that was published in a magazine. (TPO16, L, S2, C1) 他写的一篇文章在一本杂志上发表了。

purchase[15] [ˈpɜːtʃəs]

【释义】*v.* 购买 *n.* 购买，购买物

【例句】He refused to develp projection technology, reasoning that if he made and sold projectors, then exhibitors would purchase only one machine—a projector—from him instead of several. (TPO2, R, S2, T2) 他不愿研究投影技术，因为他认为如果研发并且销售投影机，影院老板就只会买一台投影机而不是几台。

【派生】purchaser *n.* 购买者

recover[15] [rɪˈkʌvə]

【释义】*v.* 1. 恢复，复原（renew）2. 重获（regain）3. 收回

【例句】The clearing of wilderness land for construction caused biotic changes from which the black-tailed deer population has never recovered. (TPO4, R, S1, T1) 清理荒野作为建筑用地带来的生态变化使黑尾鹿的数量一直无法恢复。

【派生】recovery *n.* 恢复，防御
recoverable *a.* 可重获的

【搭配】recover from 恢复；恢复知觉

respect[15] [rɪsˈpekt]

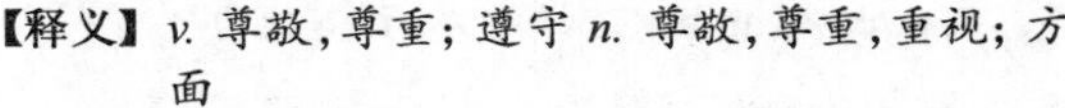

【释义】*v.* 尊敬，尊重；遵守 *n.* 尊敬，尊重，重视；方面

【例句】And Painlevé is still highly respected in many circles. (TPO3, L, S1, L2) 培乐威在很多圈子里仍然备受尊重。

【派生】respectable *a.* 可敬的，高尚的
respective *a.* 分别的，各自的
respectively *ad.* 分别地，各自地

【搭配】in respect of/with respect to 关于，至于；就…而言

sketch[15] [sketʃ]

【释义】*n.* 1. 草图，素描（draft）2. 梗概（outline）*v.* 1. 素描 2. 概述

【例句】For a long time, the only accepted image of Austen was an amateur sketch of an adult Austen made by her sister Casandra. (TPO12, W, Q1) 很长时间以来，唯一被接受的奥斯汀的形象来自一幅由其妹妹卡珊德拉所画的成年奥斯汀的非专业素描。

【搭配】sketch out 概略地描述；草拟

返记菜单

pick[15] progression[15] publish[15] purchase[15] recover[15]
respect[15] sketch[15]

spore[15] [spɔː]

【释义】*n.* 孢子 *v.* 产生孢子

【例句】Spores light enough to float on the breezes were carried thousands of miles from more ancient lands and deposited at random across the bare mountain flanks. (TPO9, R, S2, T2) 孢子很轻,可以随着微风,从更古老的陆地飘过几千英里,然后被随意地撒播在荒芜的山腰上。

【搭配】an asexual spore 无性孢子

verbal[15] ['vɜːbəl]

【释义】*a.* 1. 用言语的,用文字的 2. 口头的 3. 动词的 *n.* 动名词

【例句】When our nonverbal signals, which we often produce unconsciously, agree with our verbal message, the verbal message is enhanced and supported, made more convincing. (TPO4, S, Q4) 非语言信号通常在我们不经意间产生,当其与我们的语言信息一致时,语言信息得以强化和证实,从而变得更有说服力。

【搭配】verbal communication 语言通信
verbal ability 言语能力;语言能力

yield[15] [jild]

【释义】*v.* 1. 生产,带来(produce, provide) 2. 放弃,让步 3. 变形,弯曲 *n.* 产量,收益(output)

【例句】It's been shaped by constraints over vast stretches of time, all of which comes down to the fact that the best foraging strategy for beavers isn't the one that yields the most food or wood. (TPO16, L, S2, L1) 它是在长时间的限制之下形成的,所有这一切都归结于这样一个事实,就是对海狸来说,最好的觅食策略并不是得到最多的食物或木头。

【搭配】high yield 高产,高收益

zone[15] [zəʊn]

【释义】*n.* (划分出来的)地区,区域,地带(region, district) *v.* 将…划分

【例句】At least in temperate zones, maximum diversity is often found in mid-successional stages, not in the climax community. (TPO3, R, S1, T2) 至少在温带地区,最大多样性通常会出现在中期演替阶段,而不是在顶级群落中。

【派生】zonally *ad.* 地带地,区域地

【搭配】zone out 走神;失去意识

achieve[14] [ə'tʃiːv]

【释义】*v.* 完成,实现;取得,获得(win, accomplish, fulfill)

【例句】The effect is altogether lighter and freer than that achieved in stone, but because both perform the same function, formal wooden and metal statues still display frontality. (TPO11, R, S1, T1) 其效果比用石头做的更轻更不受限制,但因其所起的功用都是一样的,所以正式的木雕或金属雕塑仍然采用正面描绘手法。

【派生】achievement *n.* 成绩,成就

angle[14] ['æŋgl]

【释义】*n.* 1. 角,角度 2. 立场,观点 *v.* 1. 把…放置成一角度 2. 使(新闻、报道等)带有倾向性

【例句】Moreover, just look at the sculpture: several 60-foot long steel plates, jutting out of the earth at odd angles! (TPO1, S, Q3) 而且,就看看雕塑本身吧:有好几块60英尺的凌钢板以奇怪的角度突出地面!

【派生】triangle 三角
rectangle 矩形

appearance[14] [ə'pɪərəns]

【释义】*n.* 1. 出现,显露,露面 2. 外貌,外表

【例句】Both animals and plants have different appearances in these various lighting conditions. (TPO17, R, S2, T1) 在不同的光照条件下,动植物都会有相应的不同表现。

【反义】disappearance

【搭配】respectable appearance 体面的外表

返记菜单

spore[15] verbal[15] yield[15] zone[15] achieve[14] angle[14] appearance[14]

Word List 11

block[14] [blɒk] 

【释义】 *n.* 1. 石块，木块 2. 街区 *v.* 阻塞；阻碍，妨碍

【例句】 Stone statues were worked from single rectangular blocks of material and retained the compactness of the original shape. (TPO11, R, S1, T1) 石像是由单块的方形石块加工出来的，保留了其原型的简洁。

【派生】 blockade *v.* 封锁 *n.* 阻塞

【搭配】 in block 块装；整批
block in 草拟，画草图
block up 阻碍；垫高；停用；阻塞
a block of 一块，一大块
on the block 出售中；在拍卖中

boundary[14] [ˈbaʊndərɪ] 

【释义】 *n.* 边界，分界线（barrier, border, division）

【例句】 Hawaii, Easter Island, and New Zealand mark the boundaries of Polynesia. (TPO5, R, S2, T1) 夏威夷、复活节岛和新西兰构成了波利尼西亚的边界。

【派生】 boundaryless *a.* 无边界的

carve[14] [kɑːv] 

【释义】 *v.* 1. 雕刻 2. 切，分割

【例句】 By contrast, wooden statues were carved from several pieces of wood that were pegged together to form the finished work, and metal statues were either made by wrapping sheet metal around a wooden core or cast by the lost wax process. (TPO11, R, S1, T1) 相比之下，木雕是由钉在一起的几块木头雕刻而成的，而金属雕塑要么是金属片包裹着一块木质核心，要么是用脱蜡铸造法铸成的。

【派生】 carving *n.* 雕刻物，雕刻品

【搭配】 carve out 雕刻；创业，开拓
carve up 瓜分，划分
carve out of 从…切出（引申为修建）

chamber[14] [ˈtʃeɪmbə] 

【释义】 *n.* 1. 室，房间，会议厅 2. 腔

【例句】 As you move around chamber, the volume of the sound goes way up and way down, depending on where you are and these standing waves. (TPO14, L, S2, L2) 当你在房间周围走动的时候，根据你所处的位置以及位置的变化，声音的音量也会或高或低。

clarify[14] [ˈklærɪfaɪ] 

【释义】 *v.* 阐明，澄清，净化（illustrate, elucidate）

【例句】 To ask the man to clarify his request. (TPO4, L, S1, C1) 让那个男人说明白他的要求。

【反义】 confuse, obscure

【派生】 clarification *n.* 澄清，净化
clarity *n.* 清晰，明晰

comet[14] [ˈkɒmɪt] 

【释义】 *n.* 彗星

【例句】 We think meteors that crashed into the moon or tails of passing comets may have introduced water molecules. (TPO5, L, S1, L2) 我们认为撞进月球的流星或途经的彗星的尾巴有可能带去了水分子。

【搭配】 Halley's Comet 哈雷彗星

considerable[14] [kənˈsɪdərəbl] 

【释义】 *a.* 相当多的，相当大的；相当可观的（large, great, significant）

【例句】 In areas where considerable soil still remains, though, a rigorously enforced program of land protection and cover-crop planting may make it possible to reverse the present deterioration of the surface. (TPO2, R, Sl, T1) 在那些仍有大量土壤存在的地区，严格执行土地保护政策并种植护田作物可能会扭转目前不断下降的土地质量。

【派生】 considerably *ad.* 相当地

countercurrent[14] [ˈkauntəˌkʌrənt] 

【释义】 *n.* 逆流，反向电流

【例句】 The leatherback accomplishes this by arranging the blood vessels in the base of its flipper into a countercurrent exchange system. (TPO15, R, S2, T1) 棱皮龟通过将血管分布在鳍的底部从而形成一个反向的交换系统来达到(保持体温)这一目的。

distribute[14] [dɪ'strɪbjuːt]

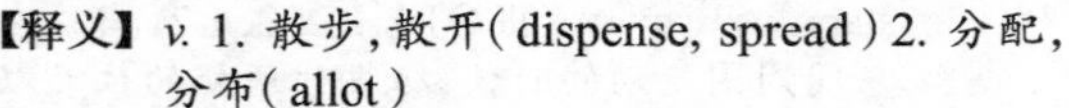

【释义】*v.* 1. 散步,散开(dispense, spread) 2. 分配,分布(allot)

【例句】In the second case, pollinators (insects, birds) obtain food from the flowering plant, and the plant has its pollen distributed and seeds dispersed much more efficiently than they would be if they were carried by the wind only. (TPO17, R, S2, T2) 第二种情形是,传粉者(昆虫、鸟类)从开花的植物中获取食物,植物通过这种渠道使其花粉得到分散,种子也得到扩散,这远比通过风来扩散高效的多。

【反义】assemble, collect, gather

【派生】distribution *n.* 分布,分配

domesticate[14] [də'mestɪkeɪt]

【释义】*v.* 驯养,驯化(cultivate, tame)

【例句】The proposed areas of the domestication of African crops lie in a band that extends from Ethiopia across southern Sudan to West Africa. (TPO7, R, S2, T2) 建议对非洲作物进行本土化的地区是从埃塞俄比亚穿过苏丹南部一直到西非的这一地带。

【搭配】domesticate animals 驯养动物

entire[14] [ɪn'taɪə]

【释义】*a.* 全部的,整体的(whole, total)

【例句】Until the early 1970s, most archaeologists did not consider the coast a possible migration route into the Americas because geologists originally believed that during the last Ice Age the entire Northwest Coast was covered by glacial ice. (TPO9, R, S1, T1) 直到20世纪70年代早期,大部分考古学家都不认为海岸可能是进入美洲的移民路线,因为地理学家一开始就坚信整个西北海岸在上个冰河期都是被冰川冰覆盖的。

favorable[14] ['feɪərəbl]

【释义】*a.* 1. 有利的,顺利的(beneficial, propitious) 2. 赞同的,值得赞扬的(pleasing)

【例句】Other species take into account the changing conditions of light by performing their visual displays only when the light is favorable. (TPO17, R, S2, T1) 一些其他的物种则只有在光照对它们有利的时候才会利用光照的变化来进行视觉表现。

【逆构】favor *n.* 好感,喜爱,偏爱;益处 *v.* 偏爱;关照;赞成

【搭配】favorable conditions 有利条件

fort[14] [fɔːt]

【释义】*n.* 堡垒,要塞(garrison, fortress)

【例句】David Douglas, Scottish botanical explorer of the 1830s, found a disturbing change in the animal life around the fort during the period between his first visit in 1825 and his final contact with the fort in 1832. (TPO4, R, S1, T1) 19世纪30年代的苏格兰植物学探险家大卫·道格拉斯,在其1825年首次探访这一要塞到其1832年最后一次访问要塞期间,发现了要塞周围动物生活的一个令人不安的变化。

hippopotamus[14] [ˌhɪpə'pɒtəməs]

【释义】*n.* 河马

【例句】At older lake sites, there are fossil remains from hippopotamuses, water buffalo, animals that spend much of their lives standing in water, and also, fossils of cattle. (TPO9, L, S2, L1) 在一些比较老的湖里,河马、水牛的化石仍有保存,还有其他大部分时间生活在水里的动物以及牛的化石也有保存。

ingredient[14] [ɪn'griːdɪənt]

【释义】*n.* 成分,原料,配料,因素(component, constituent, element)

【例句】Their key ingredients were not even known in Europe until quite recently. (TPO10, L, S1, L2) 其主要原料直到最近才在欧洲得以知晓。

【搭配】active ingredient 有效成分

intensity [14] [ɪn'tensɪtɪ]

【释义】 *n.* 强度；强烈

【例句】 Whether teachers can overcome the difficulties involved in reflection may depend on the nature and intensity of their motivation to reflect. (TPO9, R, S2, T1) 教师是否可以克服反思时遇到的困难可能取决于他们反思动机的性质和强度。

【派生】 intensify *v.* 加强，加剧

【搭配】 grow in intensity 愈演愈烈

interfere [14] [ˌɪntə'fɪə]

【释义】 *v.* 介入，干涉；妨碍(disrupt, intervene, obstruct)

【例句】 And their roots don't grow very deep, so the permafrost doesn't interfere with their growth. (TPO9, L, Sl, L2) 它们的根长得并不是很深，所以永久冻土层并不会妨碍其生长。

【派生】 interference *n.* 干涉

interpret [14] [ɪn'tɜːprɪt]

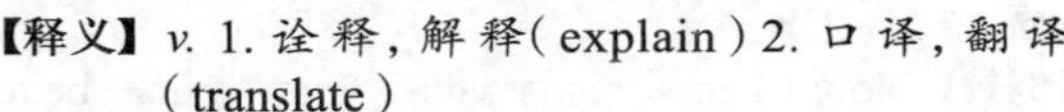

【释义】 *v.* 1. 诠释，解释(explain) 2. 口译，翻译(translate)

【例句】 This finding has been interpreted as evidence that people gathered at Pueblo Alto for special ceremonies. (TPO5, W, Q1) 这个发现证明人们聚集到巨屋是为了某种特殊的仪式。

【派生】 interpretation *n.* 解释；口译
interpreter *n.* 译员，口译者

interpretation [14] [ɪnˌtɜːprɪ'teɪʃən]

【释义】 *n.* 1. 解释，说明，诠释(explanation) 2.（表演的）艺术处理

【例句】 One interpretation regarding the absence of fossils during this important 100-million-year period is that early animals were soft bodied and simply did not fossilized. (TPO5, R, S2, T2) 对于在这重要的一亿年中却无化石这一现象的一种解释是，早期动物都是软体的，所以未能变成化石。

【逆构】 interpret *v.* 翻译，阐释

investigate [14] [ɪn'vestɪgeɪt]

【释义】 *v.* 调查，研究(examine, inspect, study)

【例句】 The main difference was that Cousteau simply investigated and presented the facts—he didn't mix in fiction. (TPO3, L, S1, L2) 最主要的区别就是库斯托仅仅是调查和呈现了事实，在他的小说中并没有混淆。

【派生】 investigation *n.* 调查，研究
investigative *a.* 调查的，调查研究的

mental [14] ['mentl]

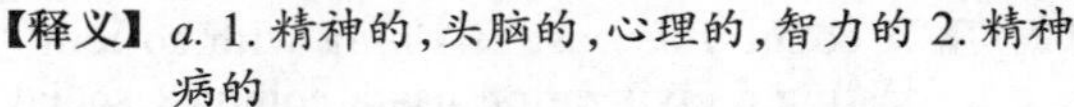

【释义】 *a.* 1. 精神的，头脑的，心理的，智力的 2. 精神病的

【例句】 They're not interested in mental processes. (TPO2, L, S1, L1) 他们对于心理活动过程不感兴趣。

【派生】 mentally *ad.* 精神上地
mentality *n.* 心智，智力

【搭配】 mental illness 精神病
make a mental note 牢记，铭记

opposite [14] ['ɒpəzɪt]

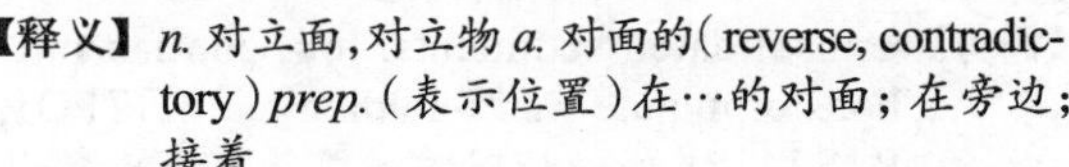

【释义】 *n.* 对立面，对立物 *a.* 对面的(reverse, contradictory) *prep.*（表示位置）在…的对面；在旁边；接着

【例句】 So it won't surprise you to learn that when the real contributors were asked how they felt about the group process, their attitude was just the opposite of what the reading predicts. (TPO2, W, Q1) 所以当团队中真正的贡献者被问及他对团队过程的感觉，他们的回答与阅读中预测到的完全相反时，你不必感到惊讶。

【派生】 oppositely *ad.* 相对地，对立地

【搭配】 the opposite sex 异性

parchment [14] ['pɑːtʃmənt]

【释义】 *n.* 羊皮纸，羊皮纸手稿

【例句】 And the material typically used for the pages was parchment, which is animal skin that stretched and dried under tension, so it becomes really fat and can be written on. (TPO15, L, S2, L1) 用于书页的典型材料是

intensity [14] interfere [14] interpret [14] interpretation [14] investigate [14]
mental [14] opposite [14] parchment [14]

羊皮纸，这种纸是在拉力下被拉展晾干的动物皮，所以这种纸就变得十分油腻，可用来书写了。

parlor[14] ['pɑːlə]

【释义】*n.* 客厅，接待室

【例句】It was designed for use in Kinetoscope parlors or arcades. (TPO2, R, S2, T2) 这种放映机仅适用于活动电影放映室或电影娱乐城。

porcelain[14] ['pɔːslɪn]

【释义】*n.* 瓷，瓷器

【例句】A country as vast as China with so long-lasting a civilization has a complex social and visual history, with which pottery and porcelain play a major role. (TPO10, R, S1, T1) 像中国这样一个地大物博、有着悠久文明的国家是有着复杂的社会和影像历史的，而陶器和瓷器在其中起着重要的作用。

【搭配】antique pottery and porcelain 陶瓷古玩

pore[14] [pɔː]

【释义】*n.* 小孔 *v.* 熟读，钻研，沉思

【例句】Consolidated sediments, too, contian millions of minute water-holding pores. (TPO1, R, S2, T2) 那些坚固的沉淀物也有以数以百万计的蓄水毛孔。

【派生】pored *a.* 有孔的

【搭配】pore over 注视

prairie[14] ['preərɪ]

【释义】*n.*（尤指北美的）大草原

【例句】The other species, the Columbian white-tailed deer, in earlier times was common in the open prairie country; it is now restricted to the low, marshy islands and flood plains along the lower Columbia River. (TPO4, R, S1, T1) 另一物种——哥伦比亚白尾鹿，以前常见于开阔的大草原上；现在却只限于地势低而湿软的岛上以及哥伦比亚河沿岸的冲积平原。

reject[14] [rɪ'dʒekt]

【释义】*v.* 拒绝，抵制，排斥；抛弃，摈弃（decline, refuse）

【例句】Discuss why the theory was rapidly accepted but then rejected. (TPO9, R, S1, T1) 讨论一下为什么这一理论在得到广泛的认同之后又遭拒绝。

【反义】accept, receive

【派生】rejection *n.* 拒绝
rejective *a.* 拒绝的，排斥的

remind[14] [rɪ'maɪnd]

【释义】*v.* 使想起，使记起（recall）

【例句】But then he suddenly changed the image or narration to remind us how different the animals are, how unlike humans. (TPO3, L, S1, L2) 但是他会突然改变图像或者叙事的方式，以提醒我们动物是多么不同，与人类多么不一样。

【搭配】remind sb. of/about sth. 使某人想起…

reporter[14] [rɪ'pɔːtə]

【释义】*n.* 记者

【例句】Now I know this is what I want to do—be a reporter. (TPO14, L, S2, C1) 现在我知道这就是我想做的——当一名记者。

【逆构】report *v./n.* 报导

【搭配】news reporter 新闻记者
TV reporter 电视台记者

scholar[14] ['skɒlə]

【释义】*n.* 1. 学者 2. 奖学金获得者

【例句】In addition to exploring the possible antecedents of theater, scholars have also theorized about the motives that led people to develop theater. (TPO1, R, S2, T1) 除了探索戏剧的起源外，一些学者还提出了关于人类发展戏剧的动机的理论。

【派生】scholarly *a.* 学者气质的，学者的
scholarship *n.* 奖学金

shadow[14] ['ʃædəʊ]

【释义】*n.* 1. 阴影，影子 2. 有点，些微 3. 鬼，幽灵 *v.*

1. 跟踪 2. 使有阴影，遮蔽 *a.* 阴影的；非正式的

【例句】Second, Rembrandt was a master of painting light and shadow, but in this painting these elements do not fit together. (TPO3, W, Q1) 其次，伦勃朗非常擅于处理光与阴影，但在这幅画中，这些元素并没有恰当地结合在一起。

【派生】shadowy *a.* 有阴影的，阴凉的

【搭配】shadow play 皮影戏

skull[14] [skʌl] 

【释义】*n.* 颅骨，头骨

【例句】The fossil consists of a complete skull of archaeocyte. (TPO2, R, S2, T1) 这块化石包含一个完整的原始动物的头盖骨。

somehow[14] ['sʌmhaʊ] 

【释义】*ad.* 以某种方式

【例句】Yet it would be wrong to suggest that Rome was somehow a junior partner in Greco-Roman civilization. (TPO7, R, S2, T1) 然而，认为罗马在某种程度上只是希腊罗马文明中的一个小角色也是错误的。

status[14] ['steɪtəs] 

【释义】*n.* 1. 地位，身份(standing, identity, position) 2. 情形，状况(condition)

【例句】The function and status of ceramics in China varied from dynasty to dynasty. (TPO10, R, S1, T1) 中国陶瓷在不同朝代的功能和地位不同。

suit[14] [sju:t]

【释义】*n.* 套装，一套衣服 *v.* 适合，适应(adapt, fit)

【例句】You mean, like get my resume together and wear a suit? (TPO6, L, S1, C1) 你的意思是备上一份简历，穿一身职业装？

【派生】suitable *a.* 合适的，相配的
suited *a.* 适合的，匹配的
suitcase *n.* 手提箱
lawsuit *n.* 诉讼(尤指非刑事案件)

【搭配】suit the action to the word 说到做到

telescope[14] ['telɪskəʊp]

【释义】*n.* 望远镜 *v.* 1.（使）套入，（使）叠进 2. 缩短，简略(compress, shorten)

【例句】But there wasn't anything obvious there, in the early telescopes. (TPO2, L, S2, L2) 通过早期望远镜观测，（天文学家）并未发现任何明显的物体。

【派生】telescopic *a.* 望远镜的

【搭配】astronomical telescope 天文望远镜

tube[14] ['tju:b] 

【释义】*n.* 管，电子管(pipe, hose)

【例句】In the phonograph parlors, customers listened to recordings through individual ear tubes. (TPO2, R, S2, T2) 在留声机播放厅中，顾客们通过独立的耳管收听已经录制好的声音。

【派生】tubular *a.* 管状的

wear[14] [wɪə]

【释义】*v.* 1. 穿，戴，蓄，留 2. 磨损 3. 耐用，持久 *n.* 穿戴的衣物；磨损；耐久性

【例句】European paintings often portrayed doctors or judges wearing glasses. (TPO8, L, S2, L1) 欧洲的绘画中描绘的医生或法官总是带着眼镜。

【搭配】wear down 磨损，用坏
wear off 逐渐消失
wear out 用坏，使耗尽，使疲乏

address[13] [ə'dres] 

【释义】*v.* 1. 处理 2. 演说 3. 写地址 *n.* 1. 地址 2. 演讲，致辞(speech)

【例句】The department has decided that despite some added expense, the most cost-effective way of addressing this problem is by adding computer classes in the evening. (TPO4, S, Q3) 系里已经决定，尽管要增加开支，但是解决这一问题最有效的方式是增开夜间电脑课。

【派生】addressee *n.* 收件人；被访地址
addresser *n.* 发信人；发言人

admire[13] [əd'maɪə]

【释义】*v.* 欣赏,钦佩;赞美,羡慕(esteem, appreciate, think highly)
【例句】The painters admired the beauty of these large animals. (TPO4, R, S2, T1) 绘画者们欣赏这些大型动物的美。
【反义】despise
【派生】admirer *n.* 赞美者
admiring *a.* 赞赏的
admirable *a.* 值得赞美的

alter[13] ['ɔːltə]

【释义】*v.* 改变,变化(change)
【例句】The presence of others tends to alter the way people behave or perform an activity. (TPO2, S, Q4) 有他人在场很可能会改变人们的行为举止或做某事的方式。
【反义】conserve, preserve
【派生】alteration *n.* 改变

appreciate[13] [ə'priːʃɪeɪt]

【释义】*v.* 1. 欣赏,赏识(admire) 2. 感激(be greatful of) 3. 领会,意识到(acknowledge) 4. 增值
【例句】Without this knowledge we can appreciate only the formal content of Egyptian art, and we will fail to understand why it was produced or the concepts that shaped it and caused it to adopt its distinctive forms. (TPO11, R, S1, T1) 没有这些知识,我们就只能欣赏埃及艺术形式上的内容,而无法了解其产生的原因或者塑造以及造成其独特形式的理念。
【派生】appreciation *n.* 重视,赏识;评价
appreciative *a.* 有欣赏力的;感激的

blend[13] [blend]

【释义】*v.* 1. (使)混合,(使)掺杂(combine, mix) *n.* 1. 混合物(mixture) 2. 混合,融合
【例句】Host selling involves blending advertisements with regular programming in a way that makes it difficult to distinguish one from the other. (TPO14, R, S1, T1) 主持销售涉及到把广告和常规节目进行融合,这样,两者就很难区分开来。
【搭配】blend in 混合,加入;调和
blend with 与…混和

catch[13] [kætʃ]

【释义】*n.* 1. 捕获量,捕获物 2. 抓,接 *v.* 1. 接住 2. 抓住,捕获 3. 赶得上 4. 感染,传染
【例句】We bring in the day's catch to a floating processor boat where the fish got cleaned, packaged and frozen right at sea. (TPO9, L, S1, C1) 我们把当天捕到的鱼带到一艘流动的加工船上,在这里对鱼进行清洗、包装,冷冻,这一切都在海上完成。
【派生】catching *a.* 传染性的;有魅力的,迷人的
【搭配】catch up 赶上,追上
catch on 理解,明白;变得流行
catch (one's) breath 喘口气,休息一下

comment[13] ['kɒment]

【释义】*n.* 注释,评论,意见 *v.* 作评论;谈论
【例句】Wildman and Niles make a summary comment: "Perhaps the most important thing we learned is the idea of the teacher-as-reflective-practitioner will not happen simply because it is a good or even compelling idea." (TPO9, R, S2, T1) Wildman 和 Niles 作出了一个总结性的评论:"或许我们学到的最重要的观点就是教师不会因为这是一个好的甚至强制性的观点而自发地开展教学反思。"
【派生】commentary *n.* 评论
commentator *n.* 评论员
【搭配】an inane comment 空洞的评论

convert[13] [kən'vɜːt]

【释义】*v.* 1. (使)转换(change, transform) 2. (使)改变信仰
【例句】Continued sedimentation—the process of deposits' settling on the sea bottom—buries the organic matter and subjects it to higher temperatures and pressures, which convert the organic matter to oil and gas. (TPO4, R, S2, T2) 持续的沉淀——沉积物沉淀到海底的过程——会将有机物埋在下面并使其经受高温和高压,这样有机物就转化成了原油和天然气。

【派生】converter *n.* 转换器
conversion *n.* 转变
【搭配】make a convert of sb. 使某人改变信仰

core[13] [kɔː]

【释义】*n.* 1. 果核 2. 核心，要点 *v.* 挖去果核
【例句】By contrast, wooden statues were carved from several pieces of wood that were pegged together to form the finished work, and metal statues were either made by wrapping sheet metal around a wooden core or cast by the lost wax process. (TPO11, R, S1, T1) 相比之下，木雕是由钉在一起的几块木头雕刻而成的，而金属雕塑要么是金属片包裹着一块木质核心，要么是用脱蜡铸造法铸成的。
【搭配】to the core 透顶的，十足的
at the core of 在…的中心

corridor[13] ['kɒrɪdɔː]

【释义】*n.* 走廊，通道
【例句】The first water craft theory about this migration was that around 11,000-12,000 years ago there was an ice-free corridor stretching from eastern Beringia to the areas of North America (south of the great northern glaciers). (TPO9, R, S1, T1) 关于此次迁徙的第一个水路理论是说大约在11000到12000年前，有一个不冻的走廊一直从白令海峡东部延伸到北美(大北部冰河的南部)，
【搭配】the corridors of power 权力走廊

destruction[13] [dɪs'trʌkʃən]

【释义】*n.* 破坏，毁灭(demolition, ruin)
【例句】And we were sound how important habitat selection is when we look at the habitat where some of the factors are removed, perhaps through habitats' destruction. (TPO8, L, S1, L1) 当我们看到一些要素或许是由于栖息地遭到破坏而消失的时候，我们就会知道栖息地的选择有多重要。
【派生】destructive *a.* 破坏性的，毁灭性的

dissolve[13] [dɪ'zɒlv]

【释义】*v.* 1.（使）溶解(melt) 2. 解散，（使）消失(disappear, end)
【例句】The organic matter may partially decompose, using up the dissolved oxygen in the sediment. (TPO4, R, S2, T2) 有机物会部分分解，耗尽沉淀物中溶解的氧。
【搭配】dissolve away 溶解掉
dissolve in 溶解入

distinct[13] [dɪs'tɪŋkt]

【释义】*a.* 1. 截然不同的，完全分开的(separate, different) 2. 清晰的，明显的(clear-cut, obvious) 3. 确实的
【例句】Throughout history buildings have been constructed like human bodies, needing distinct "organ" systems in order to function. (TPO3, R, S1, T1) 纵观历史，建筑物的构造都如同人的身体，需要有不同的"器官"来维持其功能。
【派生】distinction *n.* 差别，特性；显赫，声望
distinctive *a.* 特殊的，与众不同的

distract[13] [dɪs'trækt]

【释义】*v.* 使…分心，分散，转移(注意力等)(divert, disturb)
【例句】And the behaviors that the birds engaging in to distract predators are called distraction displays. (TPO11, L, S1, L1) 鸟类的这种分散捕食者注意力的行为被称为迷惑表演。
【派生】distraction *n.* 分心，分散注意力的事物
【搭配】distract from 转移；使从…分心

document[13] ['dɒkjʊmənt]

【释义】*v.* 用文件等证明，记载(record) *n.* 公文，文件，证件
【例句】Why does the fossil record not document the series of evolutionary changes during the evolution of animals? (TPO5, R, S2, T2) 为什么化石记录没有记载下动物进化过程中的一系列演变呢？

dust[13] [dʌst]

【释义】*n.* 尘土；粉尘 *v.* 1. 除去灰尘 2. 撒粉末于
【例句】The dust at the bottom of the SPA Basin really does have a fascinating story to tell. (TPO5, L, S1, L2) 关于SPA盆地(月球南极

返记菜单

core[13] corridor[13] destruction[13] dissolve[13] distinct[13]
distract[13] document[13] dust[13]

艾特肯盆地)底部的粉尘,确实有一个很引人入胜的故事要讲。

【派生】dusty *a.* 落满灰尘的
dustman *n.* 清洁工人

【搭配】dust coat 风衣

endure[13] [ɪn'djʊə]

【释义】*v.* 持久,耐久(last);忍受,容忍(bear, tolerate)

【例句】What happened is that the major divide in opera that endures today took place. (TPO12, L, S2, L1) 戏剧方面直到现在还存在着的主要分歧出现了。

【派生】endurance *n.* 忍耐;持久
endurable *a.* 能忍耐的;可忍受的

epic[13] ['epɪk]

【释义】*n.* 史诗,叙事诗 *a.* 1. 史诗般的 2. 宏大的

【例句】The french said you really cannot talk about real people who lived in opera and they relied on mythology to give them their characters and their plots, mythology, the past old traditions, the novels of chivalry or the epics of chivalry out of the middle ages. (TPO12, L, S2, L1) 法国人说你无法讨论那些真实存在于歌剧中的人,因此他们通过神话学来给予他们性格和特征。神话,就是那些过去的老传统,那些有关于中世纪骑士精神的小说或是史诗。

【派生】epical *a.* 英勇的;叙事诗的

【搭配】epic movie 史诗电影

epoch[13] ['iːpɒk]

【释义】*n.* 时期,时代,新纪元(age, era)

【例句】Researchers study sediment in order to learn about the characteristics of past geologic epochs. (TPO15, L, S1, L2) 研究人员对沉淀物进行研究,以期能够了解以往地质时期的特点。

【派生】epochal *a.* 划时代的,新纪元的

erosion[13] [ɪ'rəʊʒən]

【释义】*n.* 腐蚀,侵蚀;磨损(corrosion, eating away)

【例句】Desertification is accomplised primarily through the loss of stabilizing natural vegetation and the subsequent accelerated erosion of the soil by wind and water. (TPO2, R, Sl, T1) 由于加固土壤的自然植被消失,随后使得风力、流水对土壤的侵蚀速度加快,从而形成了沙漠化。

【派生】erosional *a.* 侵蚀的

【逆构】erose *v.* 侵蚀

exploit[13] [ɪk'splɔɪt]

【释义】*v.* 1. 开拓;开采,开发(explore, untilize)2. 剥削

【例句】All else being equal, this means they must exploit larger areas of land than do agriculturalists to secure the same amount of food, clothing, and other necesstities. (TPO14, R, S2, T2) 在其他条件相同的情况下,这意味着他们必须要比务农者开拓出更广阔的土地才能确保等量的食物、衣物和其他必需品。

【派生】exploitation *n.* 开发,开采

formal[13] ['fɔːməl]

【释义】*a.* 1. 形式上的,表面的 2. 正式的,正规的 *n.* 礼服

【例句】Without this knowledge we can appreciate only the formal content of Egyptian art, and we will fail to understand why it was produced or the concepts that shaped it and caused it to adopt its distinctive forms. (TPO11, R, S1, T1) 没有这些知识,我们就只能欣赏埃及艺术形式上的内容,而无法了解其产生的原因或者塑造和造成其独特形式的理念。

【派生】informal *a.* 非正式的
formality *n.* 形式

【逆构】form *n.* 形式

【搭配】formal education 正规教育;形式教育

Word List 12

genetic[13] [dʒɪ'netɪk]

【释义】 *a.* 遗传(学)的,基因的

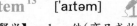

【例句】 For a population of trees to survive a disease, it needs to be relatively large and it needs to be genetically diverse. (TPO17, W, Q1) 一个树种要想在面临一种疾病时存活下来,就需要具有相对较多的数量,且基因也要具有多样性。

【派生】 genetics *n.* 遗传学

【搭配】 genetic information 遗传信息

item[13] ['aɪtəm]

【释义】 *n.* 1. 一件(商品或物品) 2. 条款,项目 3. (新闻等的)一则,一条

【例句】 Instead, students will be offered a wide assortment of cold breakfast items in the morning. (TPO3, S, Q3) 相反,(食堂)会在每天早上为学生供应各种各样的冷的早餐。

【搭配】 be an item 建立稳定的爱恋关系
item by item 逐项,逐条

journal[13] ['dʒɜːnl]

【释义】 *n.* 1. 杂志,期刊 2. 日志,日记

【例句】 I just copied an artical, but I still need three more on my topic from three different journals. (TPO1, L, S1, C1) 我只拷贝了一篇文章,但是我仍然需要就我的题目从三本不同的期刊里摘取三篇文章。

【派生】 journalist *n.* 新闻工作者

latitude[13] ['lætɪtjuːd]

【释义】 *n.* 纬度

【例句】 This is particularly true for trees in the middle and upper latitudes. (TPO1, R, S1, T1) 这对于那些生长在中高纬度上的树木来说尤其正确。

【反义】 longtitude

manager[13] ['mænɪdʒə]

【释义】 *n.* 经理,管理者,经纪人

【例句】 At first, more than half the group supported us. There were a few senior managers there though who didn't support the design change. (TPO1, S, Q4) 起初组里有半数以上的人支持我们。尽管还有几个不支持改变设计的高级管理人员。

【派生】 managerial *a.* 管理的;经理的
manageress *n.* 女经理

【逆构】 manage *v.* 管理,经营

mature[13] [mə'tjʊə]

【释义】 *v.* 使成熟;变成熟 *a.* 1. 成熟的,成年人的 2. 考虑周到的 3. 到期的

【例句】 Once a redwood forest matures, for example, the kinds of species and the number of individuals growing on the forest floor are reduced. (TPO3, R, S1, T2) 例如,红树林一旦成熟,在其森林地面上生长的的物种的种类以及单个物种的数量都会减少。

【反义】 immature

【派生】 maturely *ad.* 成熟地;充分地

motivate[13] ['məʊtɪveɪt]

【释义】 *v.* 作为…的动机;激发,诱发(prompt, propel)

【例句】 In other words, what motivates us to do what we do? (TPO5, S, Q2) 换言之,是什么激励我们做我们正在做的事呢?

【派生】 motivation *n.* 动机;推动

motor[13] ['məʊtə]

【释义】 *a.* 肌肉运动的;发动机的 *n.* 发动机,电动机

【例句】 The occurrence of these eye movements provides evidence that the moving pattern is perceived at some level by the newborn. Similarly, changes in the infant's general level of motor activity — turning the head, blinking the eyes, crying, and so forth — have been used by researchers as visual indicators of the infant's perceptual abilities. (TPO13, R, S2, T2) 眼球运动的发生证明移动的物体在一定程度上会引起的新生儿的注意。同

返记菜单

genetic[13] item[13] journal[13] latitude[13] manager[13]
mature[13] motivate[13] motor[13]

样，新生儿运动行为整体水平的变化，比如摆头、眨眼、哭泣等，已经被研究人员用做婴儿认知能力的视觉表现。

mud[13] [mʌd] 

【释义】*n.* 1. 泥，泥浆 2. 诽谤

【例句】Microscopic organisms settle to the seafloor and accumulate in marine mud. (TPO4, R, S2, T2) 微生物沉到海底并积聚成海泥。

【派生】muddy *a.* 泥泞的，浑浊的

【搭配】rock and mud slides 泥石流

occupy[13] [ˈɒkjʊpaɪ] 

【释义】*v.* 1. 使用，占用，占据 2. 忙于，从事

【例句】They occupy much less space than buildings constructed one hundred years ago. (TPO3, R, S1, T1, Q8) 现代建筑相比一百年前的建筑而言，占据的空间较少。

【派生】occcupant *n.* 占有者，居住者

【搭配】occupy a dominant position 占统治地位
occupy in 从事

otherwise[13] [ˈʌðəwaɪz] 

【释义】*ad.* 1. 否则，不然 2. 在其他方面 *a.* 别的，不同的

【例句】Otherwise I'll be short six credits. (TPO2, L, S2, C1) 否则我就会差六个学分。

【搭配】otherwise than 不像；除…外；与…不同

outer[13] [ˈaʊtə] 

【释义】*a.* 外面的，外部的，远离中心的(outside, external)

【例句】Also, because of their relative locations, the four Jovian planets are known as the outer planets. (TPO16, R, S2, T2) 同时，由于它们的相对位置，这四个木星行星被称为外行星。

【搭配】outer space 太空

phase[13] [feɪz] 

【释义】*n.* 1. 相位，方面 2. 阶段，时期(stage) *v.* 使分阶段进行

【例句】He believes that as far back as 30,000 B. C., hunters may have used a system of notation, engraved on bone and stone, to mark phases of the Moon. (TPO4, R, S2, T1) 他认为，早在公元前 30000 年，猎人们可能就使用了一种符号标记系统，把月相标记在骨头和石头上面了。

【搭配】in/out of phase 同相 / 异相；同步 / 不同步
phase sth. in/out 逐步或分阶段引进 / 中止某事物

physiological[13] [ˌfɪziəˈlɒdʒɪkəl] 

【释义】*a.* 生理的，生理学的

【例句】Another flaw of the tiredness theory is that yawning does not raise alertness or physiological activity, as the theory would predict. (TPO18, R, S2, T1) 疲倦论的另一大缺陷是，打呵欠并不能像该理论预测的那样提高警惕性或生理活跃度。

plate[13] [pleɪt] 

【释义】*n.* 1. 金属板，薄板 2. 盘子，碟(dish) 3. 版图，大片平面 *v.* 1. 覆盖 2. 电镀

【例句】However, some modern architectural designs, such as those using folded plates of concrete or air-inflated structures, are again unifying skeleton and skin. (TPO3, R, S1, T1) 然而，一些现代建筑设计，比如运用混凝土的折叠板材或充气材料，都是再次将骨架和外壳结合起来。

【派生】plateful *n.* (一)盘
plater *n.* 镀金匠，铁甲工

【搭配】on a plate 毫不费力

plot[13] [plɒt] 

【释义】*n.* 1. 故事情节 2. 密谋 3. 小块土地 *v.* 1. 制图，图示 2. 构想，密谋

【例句】Not the plot, the details of what happens in the story would remain constant. (TPO5, L, S2, L2) 不是在情节上(改动)，故事中发生的细节将会保持延续。

【搭配】plot against 暗算，阴谋策划

prey[13] [preɪ] 

【释义】*n.* 捕获物；牺牲品 *v.* 捕食；折磨

【例句】This unexpected display of color startles or confuses the predator and provides the would-be prey with an opportunity to

escape. (TPO8, S, Q4) 这种出人意料的颜色展示会吓到或迷惑捕食者,从而给可能的猎物提供了一个逃脱的机会。

【搭配】prey on 捕食,掠夺

realistic[13] [rɪə'lɪstɪk]

【释义】*a.* 1. 现实的; 现实主义的 2. 明智的 3. 逼真的

【例句】So in the original painting, light and shadow are very realistic and just what we would expect from Rembrandt. (TPO3, W, Q1) 因此在最初的作品中,光与影的搭配是切实可行的,正如我们期待伦勃朗所做的那样。

【派生】unrealistic *a.* 不切实际的,不实在的

recycle[13] ['riː'saɪkl]

【释义】*v.* 回收利用; 再利用(reuse, reprocess)

【例句】In modern agriculture, mineral depletion of soils is a major concern, since harvesting crops interrupts the recycling of nutrients back to the soil. (TPO5, R, S1, T1) 在现代农业中,土壤中矿物质的消耗是一个值得担忧的问题,因为收割庄稼会扰乱土壤养分回归土壤的循环。

【派生】recyclable *a.* 可回收利用的,可循环再造的

【搭配】recycle back 反向循环
recycle bin 回收站

reference[13] ['refrəns]

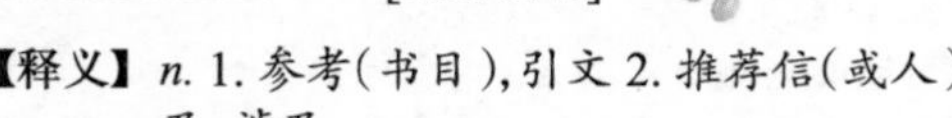

【释义】*n.* 1. 参考(书目),引文 2. 推荐信(或人)3. 提及,涉及

【例句】Well, we have copies of all the newspapers in the basement, and all the major papers publish reference guides to their articles reviews, etc. (TPO4, L, S1, C1) 我们地下室有全部的报纸,而且各大报纸都会刊登其评论文章的参考指南。

【逆构】refer *v.* 参考,提及

【搭配】for reference 以供参考; 备案
with/in reference to 关于

round[13] [raʊnd]

【释义】*n.* 1. 一回合,一连串,一套,一组 2. 圆,圆形物 *prep.* 1. (表示位置)在…四周,围绕于… 2. 从头至尾 *a.* 1. 圆形的,圆弧的 2. 大概的 3. 整数的 *ad.* 1. 围绕地; 在周围 2. 到处,各处,挨个地 *v.* 1. 环绕,围绕 2. 使变圆 3. 使发胖

【例句】For the price of 25 cents (or 5 cents per machine), customers moved from machine to machine to watch five different films (or, in the case of famous prizefight, successive rounds of a single fight). (TPO2, R, S2, T2) 观众花 25 美分(或者每台播放器的观看价格是 5 美分),便可以从一个播放器换到下一个播放器依次观看 5 场不同的影片(例如观看著名的职业拳击赛时,观众可以连续观看同一场比赛的几轮战况)。

【搭配】round and round 处处; 旋转不息地
make a round 兜个圈子,闲逛,漫步
round out 完成
round up 围捕; 使聚拢
in a round 围成一圈

spectrum[13] ['spektrəm]

【释义】*n.* 谱,光谱,频谱

【例句】It is an element whose presence in the Sun had been noted earlier in the spectrum of sunlight but that had not previously been known on Earth. (TPO16, R, S2, T1) 这种元素的存在早已在太阳光谱中发现了,但是之前还不曾在地球上发现。

【派生】spectrometer *n.* 光谱仪
spectra [*pl.*] 光谱,频谱

stem[13] [stem]

【释义】*n.* (植物的)茎,干 *v.* (~ from) 起源于,基于

【例句】Mineral deficiencies can often be detected by specific symptoms such as chlorosis (loss of chlorophyll resulting in yellow or white leaf tissue), necrosis (isolated dead patches), anthocyanin formation (development of deep red pigmentation of leaves or stem), stunted growth, and development of woody tissue in an herbaceous plant. (TPO5, R, S1, T1) 矿物质的缺乏通常可以通过一些特别的症状表现出来,比如萎黄病(水溶性叶绿素的缺乏导致的黄色或白色的叶片组织)、坏死(分离的枯死的叶片)、花色素甙生成(叶子或枝干上深红色色素的扩散),生长萎缩以及草本植物中木质组织的发展。

【派生】stemmy *a.* 多梗的

【搭配】from stem to stern 从头到尾

stencil[13] ['stensl]

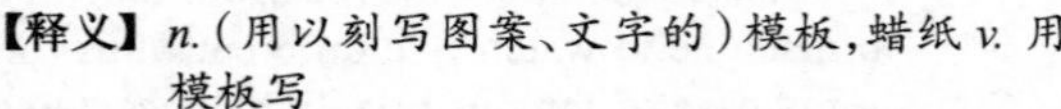

【释义】*n.*（用以刻写图案、文字的）模板，蜡纸 *v.* 用模板写

【例句】Much of the evidence about right-hand versus left-hand dominance comes from stencils and prints found in rock shelters in Australia and elsewhere, and in many Ice Age caves in France, Spain, and Tasmania. (TPO12, R, S1, T1) 在澳大利亚和其它一些地方的石窟以及法国、西班牙和塔斯马尼亚的许多冰河纪洞穴中发现的模板和印刷品都证明了右手较之左手的优势地位。

【派生】stenciler *n.* 模板工，模板印刷工具

threaten[13] ['θretn]

【释义】*v.* 威胁，恐吓（menace, intimidate）

【例句】It has been estimated that an additional one-fourth of the Earth's land surface is threatened by this process. (TPO2, R, Sl, T1) 据估计，地球表面另有四分之一的土地面临着沙漠化的危险。

【派生】threatening *a.* 威胁的，危险的

【逆构】threat *n.* 威胁

touch[13] [tʌtʃ]

【释义】*n.* 1. 格调 2. 接触，触觉 3. 少量 *v.* 1. 接触，触摸 2. 触及；联系

【例句】Another realistic touch was using three-dimensional objects on the set, like rocks and bushes as opposed to two-dimensional painted scenery. (TPO 9, L, S1, L1) 另一种现实的手法是在舞台上使用三维物体，例如岩石、灌木，而不是二维的风景画面。

【派生】touchable *a.* 可触的；可食用的

【搭配】a near touch 侥幸脱险，九死一生
get/keep in touch with 和…取得 / 保持联系
touch off 使爆炸；引发

trap[13] [træp]

【释义】*n.* 圈套，陷阱，困境（snare）*v.* 1. 诱捕，困住，使陷入绝境（catch, snare）

【例句】Cane toads can easily be caught in simple traps and can even be captured by hand. (TPO15, W, Q1) 通过简易的陷阱就能轻易捕捉到甘蔗蟾蜍，甚至用手也可以捕捉到。

typical[13] ['tɪpɪkəl]

【释义】*a.* 典型的，有代表性的（distinctive, symbolic）

【例句】Typically, older leaves are affected first as the phosphorus is mobilized to young growing tissue. (TPO5, R, S1, T1) 通常，较老的叶子会最先受到影响，因为磷会转移到生长中的幼嫩的组织。

virus[13] ['vaɪərəs]

【释义】*n.* 病毒；病毒性疾病

【例句】In 1950, myxoma virus, a parasite that affects rabbits, was deliberately introduced into Australia to control the rabbit population. (TPO17, R, S2, T2) 1950 年，澳大利亚特意引进了一种可以影响兔子的寄生虫——粘液瘤病毒，以便控制兔灾。

volume[13] ['vɒljuːm]

【释义】*n.* 1. 体积，容积（capacity, bulk）2. 书卷，册，卷 3. 量（amount）

【例句】Thus a proportion of the total volume of any sediment, loose or cemented, consists of empty space. (TPO1, R, S2, T2) 因此，不管沉淀物是疏松还是坚固，其整体中必有一部分为真空区。

【派生】volumetric *a.* 体积的，容积的

【搭配】volume production 批量生产

zinc[13] [zɪŋk]

【释义】*n.* 锌 *v.* 镀锌于

【例句】And it's red because of the zinc paint that goes on those stainless steel cables. (TPO2, L, S1, L2) 它之所以呈红色是因为那些不锈钢钢丝绳上面涂有锌漆。

accomplish[12] [ə'kɒmplɪʃ]

【释义】*v.* 完成，实现（achieve, complete）

【例句】So everything they accomplished, like building this town, they did with just stones, plus wood, bricks, that sort of thing. (TPO1,

L, S2, L1) 所以他们完成的一切，比如建造这个城镇，都是只用了石头，外加木头和砖块这样的东西。

【派生】 accomplishable *a.* 可完成的，可达成的
accomplishment *n.* 成就，完成；技艺
accomplished *a.* 熟练的，有技巧的；完成的

alternative[12] [ɔːl'tɜːnətɪv]

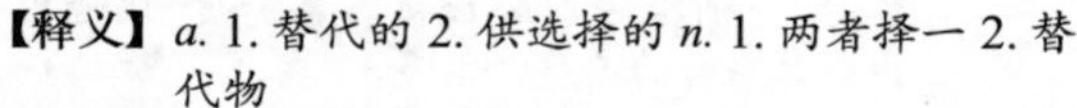

【释义】 *a.* 1. 替代的 2. 供选择的 *n.* 1. 两者择一 2. 替代物

【例句】 By far the most promising alternative source of energy for cars is the hydrogen-based fuel-cell engine, which uses hydrogen to create electricity that, in turn, powers the car. (TPO9, W, Q1) 到目前为止，最有前途的汽车动力替代能源是氢燃料电池发动机，它是利用氢燃料产生电能，进而为汽车提供动力。

【派生】 alternatively *ad.* 或者

【搭配】 alternative energy 替代能源，新能源
alternative medicine 非传统医学
have no alternative but 别无选择，只得

altitude[12] ['æltɪtjuːd]

【释义】 *n.* 1. 高度，海拔 2.[常 *pl.*] 高处，高地

【例句】 Potatoes grew better at higher altitudes than native Irish crops. (TPO10, L, S1, L2) 种植在较高海拔地区的土豆比当地的爱尔兰作物长得更好。

【搭配】 in one's altitude 飘飘然；自高自大

announce[12] [ə'naʊns]

【释义】 *v.* 1. 宣布，宣告 2. 声称，叙说 3. 预示

【例句】 In an effort to counteract the trend, the college has announced a plan to renovate its on-campus housing. (TPO11, S, Q3) 为了抵制这一倾向，校方宣布了一项整修校园内房屋的计划。

【派生】 announcement *n.* 通告；公告
announcer *n.* 播音员，广播员

annual[12] ['ænjʊəl]

【释义】 *a.* 每年的，年度的(yearly) *n.* 1. 年刊 2. 一年生植物

【例句】 An annual rainfall of four inches is often used to define the limits of a desert. (TPO12, R, S2, T2) 人们常用 4 英寸的年降水量来描述沙漠地区的局限性。

【派生】 annualize *v.* 按年计算
annially *ad.* 每年，一年一次

【搭配】 annual budget 年度预算

application[12] [ˌæplɪ'keɪʃən]

【释义】 *n.* 1. 应用 2. 申请 3. 敷用

【例句】 Someone give me an application of this principle. (TPO11, L, S1, L2) 有人给出了这一原理的一个应用。

【逆构】 apply *v.* 应用；申请

【搭配】 application for 申请…

artifact[12] ['ɑːtɪfækt]

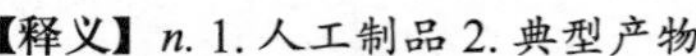

【释义】 *n.* 1. 人工制品 2. 典型产物

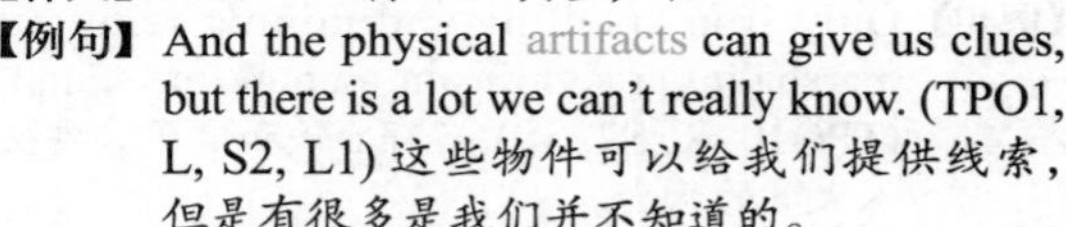

【例句】 And the physical artifacts can give us clues, but there is a lot we can't really know. (TPO1, L, S2, L1) 这些物件可以给我们提供线索，但是有很多是我们并不知道的。

【派生】 artifactual *a.* 人造的

artificial[12] [ˌɑːtɪ'fɪʃəl]

【释义】 *a.* 1. 人工的，人造的 2. 虚伪的，假的 3. 模拟的

【例句】 In experimenting with artificial suns, Kramer made another interesting discovery. (TPO11, R, S2, T1) 在用人造太阳进行实验的过程中，克莱默获得了另一个有趣的发现。

【反义】 natural, real

【派生】 artificiality *n.* 人工，人造物

【搭配】 artificial intelligence 人工智能
artificial leather 人造革

bulb[12] [bʌlb]

【释义】 *n.* 1. (植物的)鳞茎 2. 电灯泡

【例句】 And the Turks often gave the Europeans tulip bulbs as gifts which they would carry home with them. (TPO6, L, S1, L1) 土耳其人经常会给欧洲人一些郁金香的根作为礼物，让他们带回家。

【搭配】 electric light bulb 电灯泡

cage[12] [keɪdʒ] 

【释义】*v.* 关入笼中 *n.* 笼子；监狱

【例句】Early in his research, Kramer found that caged migratory birds became very restless at about the time they would normally have begun migration in the wild. (TPO11, R, S2, T1) 在其研究初期，克莱默发现，每到它们在野外时该开始迁徙的时候，关在笼子中的候鸟就会变得非常焦躁不安。

【派生】caged *a.* 困在笼中的

capital[12] ['kæpɪtəl] 

【释义】*n.* 1. 资本，资金 2. 首都，首府 3. 大写字母 *a.* 1. 重要的，一流的 2. 可判处死刑的 3. 大写的

【例句】Only iron smelting and mining required marshaling a significant amount of capital. (TPO10, R, S2, T2) 只有冶铁和采矿需要投入大量的资金。

【搭配】capital market 资本市场

colonize[12] ['kɒlənaɪz] 

【释义】*v.* 开拓殖民地，殖民，移民

【例句】The most recent geologic evidence indicates that it may have been possible for people to colonize ice-free regions along the continental shelf that were still exposed by the lower sea level between13,000 and 14,000 years ago. (TPO9, R, S1, T1) 最近的地质资料表明，在13000到14000年前，人们对因海平面低而裸露出来的大陆架沿岸的无冰区进行殖民是很可能的。

【派生】colonization *n.* 殖民地的开拓，殖民

confirm[12] [kən'fɜːm] 

【释义】*v.* 1. 确认，证实(affirm, substantiate, prove) 2. 批准(ratify) 3. 使坚定

【例句】Other studies confirm the same is true even when we're learning new activities. (TPO2, S, Q4) 其他研究证明，当我们学习做新鲜事情的时候也是如此。

【反义】deny

【派生】confirmation *n.* 确认，证实

conscious[12] ['kɒnʃəs] 

【释义】*a.* 1. 意识到的(aware) 2. 神志清醒的 3. 有意的(intended)

【例句】When they're conscious of being observed, they'll likely begin typing at a much faster rate than they would if they were alone. (TPO2, S, Q4) 当他们意识到自己在被人观察时，他们很可能会加快打字速度，比他们独自打字时的速度快很多。

【派生】consciously *ad.* 有意识地
consciousness *n.* 意识；知觉

【搭配】be conscious of 意识到

constant[12] ['kɒnstənt] 

【释义】*a.* 不变的，持续的(invariable, consistent, perpetual, continual) *n.* 常数，恒量

【例句】The shallow seas on the continents probably buffered the temperature of the nearby air, keeping it relatively constant. (TPO8, R, S2, T1) 大陆的浅海可能缓冲了附近空气的温度，使之保持相对恒定。

【派生】constancy *n.* 坚定不移，始终如一

dense[12] [dens] 

【释义】*a.* 密集的；浓厚的，浓稠的(thick, compact)

【例句】As evaporation continued, the remaining brine (salt water) became so dense that the calcium sulfate of the hard layer was precipitated. (TPO7, R, S1, T1) 随着蒸发继续，剩下的盐水变得非常稠，从而使硬层中的硫酸钙沉淀下来。

【派生】density *n.* 稠密；密度

division[12] [dɪ'vɪʒən] 

【释义】*n.* 1. 分开，分裂 2. 分配 3. 部门，部分 4. 分歧，不合 5. 除(法)

【例句】I was so impressed with the way you handle the microscope and the samples of onion cells, and with how carefully you observed and diagramed and interpreted each stage of cell division. (TPO15, L, S2, C1) 你操作显微镜和处理洋葱细胞样品的方式，以及你观察、绘制、阐释细胞分裂的每一步的认真程度，都给我留下了极为深刻的印象。

【派生】divisional *a.* 分割的；分区的
【逆构】devide *v.* 分开，划分

electronic[12] [ɪˌlek'trɒnɪk]

【释义】*v.* 电子的，电子设备的
【例句】You can access psychology databases or electronic journals and articles through the library computers. (TPO1, L, S1, C1) 你可以从图书馆的电脑里获取心理学的数据或电子期刊和文章。
【派生】electronics *n.* 电子学；电子设备
【搭配】electronic commerce 电子商务
electronic dictionary 电子词典

ensure[12] [ɪn'ʃuə]

【释义】*v.* 确保，担保(assure, guarantee)
【例句】In general, diversity, by itself, does not ensure stability. (TPO3, R, S1, T2) 一般来说，多样性本身并不能保证稳定性。
【派生】ensurance *n.* 保障

equator[12] [ɪ'kweɪtə]

【释义】*n.* 赤道
【例句】Unlike earlier lunar missions, Clementine didn't orbit only around the moon's equator. (TPO5, L, S1, L2) 与早期登月任务不同，克莱芒蒂娜不只是环绕月球的赤道而行。
【派生】equatorial *a.* 赤道的，近赤道的
equatorward *ad.* 朝赤道反向地

era[12] ['ɪərə]

【释义】*n.* 时代，纪元(age, epoch)
【例句】So they may be utilitarian, burial, trade-collector's, or even ritual objects, according to their quality and the era in which they were made. (TPO10, R, S1, T1) 所以，根据其质量和制造年代，它们可能是实用物品、陪葬品、艺术收藏品，或者甚至是宗教仪式上的法器。

evaporate[12] [ɪ'væpəreɪt]

【释义】*v.*(使)蒸发；消失(disappear, vanish)
【例句】Crustal movements closed the straits, and the landlocked Mediterranean began to evaporate. (TPO7, R, S1, T1) 地壳运动隔断了海峡，被陆地包围的地中海开始蒸发。
【派生】evaporation *n.* 蒸发；消失

format[12] ['fɔːmæt]

【释义】*n.* 版式，格式，模式(pattern, design)
【例句】Most of them are accessible in an electronic format. (TPO1, L, S1, C1) 它们中的大部分都可以在电子格式下使用。
【派生】formation *n.* 形成；编队；构造
formative *a.* 形成的；造型的；格式化的
【搭配】format error 尺度误差

fulfill[12] [fʊl'fɪl]

【释义】*v.* 1. 履行，实现(perform, execute) 2. 完成，达到；使满意
【例句】To allow them to fulfill their important role in ceremonies of Egyptian life. (TPO11, R, S1, T1) 让他们完成在埃及的仪式中的重要作用。
【派生】fulfillment *n.* 实行，履行
fulfilled *a.* 满足的
【搭配】fulfill oneself 完全实现自己的抱负

fur[12] [fɜː]

【释义】*n.* 毛皮，软毛；毛皮制品 *v.* 用毛皮覆盖
【例句】I mean if a bird's feathers get ruffled or an animal's fur, maybe it's not so strange for them to stop and tidy themselves up at that point. (TPO4, L, S1, L1) 我是说假如鸟或者动物竖起毛发，也许它们停下来整理一下自己，这并不奇怪。
【搭配】artificial fur 人造毛皮
fake fur 人造革；仿造皮毛

height[12] [haɪt]

【释义】*n.* 高度，高处，顶点
【例句】Trees tend to attain greater heights on ridges. (TPO1, R, S1, T1) 山脊上的树木会长得更高。

initial[12] [ɪ'nɪʃəl]

【释义】*a.* 开始的，最初的(beginning, first, primary)
n.(姓名的)首字母

【例句】The cinema did not emerge as a form of mass consumption until its technology evolved from the initial "peepshow" format to the point where images were projected on a screen in a darkened theater. (TPO2, R, S2, T2) 电影放映技术从最初的西洋镜形式演变为将影像投射到幽暗的影院屏幕上，这一转变使得电影开始成为大众消费。

【派生】initially *ad.* 最初地

【逆构】initiate *v.* 开始，创办

【搭配】initial stage/phase/period 开始阶段 / 时期

isolate[12] ['aɪsəleɪt]

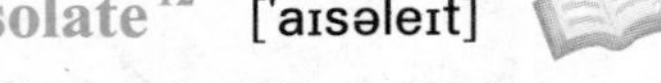

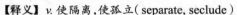

【释义】*v.* 使隔离，使孤立（separate, seclude）

【例句】Mineral deficiencies can often be detected by specific symptoms such as chlorosis (loss of chlorophyll resulting in yellow or white leaf tissue), necrosis (isolated dead patches), anthocyanin formation (development of deep red pigmentation of leaves or stem), stunted growth, and development of woody tissue in an herbaceous plant. (TPO5, R, S1, T1) 矿物质的缺乏通常可以通过一些特别的症状表现出来，比如萎黄病（水溶性叶绿素的缺乏导致的黄色或白色的叶片组织）、坏死（分离的枯死的叶片）、花色素甙生成（叶子或枝干上深红色色素的扩散），生长萎缩以及草本植物中木质组织的发展。

【派生】isolated *a.* 孤立的，分离的；与世隔绝的
isolation *n.* 隔离；孤立

【搭配】isolate sb./sth. from 把某人或某物从…中分离出来

limitation[12] [ˌlɪmɪ'teɪʃən]

【释义】*n.* 局限性；限制（limit, restriction）

【例句】The world's architectural structures have also been devised in relation to the objective limitations of materials. (TPO3, R, S1, T1) 世界上建筑物的建筑结构在设计时也要涉及到材料的客观局限性。

【逆构】limit *v.* 限制 *n.* 界限

【搭配】put/place/impose limitations on sth. 限制某事或某物

loan[12] [ləʊn]

【释义】*v.* 借出，贷与 *n.* 1. 贷款 2. 借，借出物

【例句】Bills of exchange contributed to the development of banks, as exchangers began to provide loans. (TPO10, R, S2, T2) 随着兑换人开始提供贷款服务，汇票对银行的发展起到了促进作用。

【派生】loanword *n.* 外来词，借用词

【搭配】on loan 借用；借贷；借调
mortgage loan 按揭贷款，抵押贷款

meteor[12] ['miːtiə]

【释义】*n.* 1. 流星（shooting star）2. 大气现象

【例句】If we had rock samples to study, we'd know whether the small craters were formed by impacts during the final stages of planetary formation, or if they resulted from later meteor showers. (TPO5, L, S1, L2) 如果有岩石样本可供研究，我们就能知道那些小火山是否是由行星形成后期的冲击力形成的，或者是否是由后来的流星雨造成的。

【搭配】meteor shower 流星雨

multiple[12] ['mʌltɪpl]

【释义】*a.* 多重的，多种多样的 *n.*〈数〉倍数

【例句】Ceramics produced during the Tang and Ming dynasties sometimes incorporated multiple colors. (TPO10, R, S1, T1) 唐代和明代制造的陶器有时会融合多种色彩。

【搭配】multiple choice 多项选择

Word List 13

novel[12] ['nɒvəl]

【释义】*a.* 新奇的，新颖的（new, innovative）*n.* 小说

【例句】Remember this is 1838, "Self-Reliance" was a novel idea at the time and the United State's citizens were less secure about themselves as individuals and as Americans. (TPO4, L, S1, L2) 记住，这是在1838年，"自立"在当时是个新颖的观点，而美国公民对他们作为个体和美国人的身份也没有太多的安全感。

numerous[12] ['njuːmərəs]

【释义】*a.* 为数众多的，许多的（abundant, many）

【例句】Critics also point out that the shallow seaways had retreated from and advanced on the continents numerous times during the Mesozoic. (TPO8, R, S2, T1) 批评者还指出，在中生代期间，浅海已经有过无数次进入大陆又退回（盆地）的过程。

【派生】numerously *ad.* 大量地

offspring[12] ['ɒfsprɪŋ]

【释义】*n.* 1. 子女，后代 2. 结果，产物

【例句】Then about six to eight weeks after birth, the offspring leave their mothers. (TPO1, L, S2, L2) 大约在出生六到八周后，孩子们就会离开它们的母亲。

oppose[12] [ə'pəuz]

【释义】*v.* 反对，对抗，使对立（object, resist）

【例句】There appear to be many unexplored matters about the motivation to reflect – for example, the value of externally motivated reflection as opposed to that of teachers who might reflect by habit. (TPO9, R, S2, T1) 关于反思的动力存在许多未知的问题，例如，外部驱动的反思的价值与习惯性反思的价值是不同的。

【反义】agree, correspond

【派生】opposite *a.* 相反的，对立的 *n.* 相反的事物 *prep.* 与…相对

opposition *n.* 反对，反对意见

payroll[12] ['peɪrəul]

【释义】*n.* 1. 工资单 2. 工薪总额

【例句】Hiring more staff would not result in additional payroll costs because four-day employees would only be paid 80 percent of the normal rate. (TPO1, W, Q1) 雇佣更多的员工不会造成额外的工资支出，因为工作四天的员工只能拿到正常工资的80%。

permit[12] [pə (:)'mɪt]

【释义】*v.* 许可，允许（admit, allow）

【例句】This permits them to make use of the higher temperature immediately. (TPO1, R, S1, T1) 这允许他们立刻利用这一较高的温度。

【反义】prohibit

【派生】permission *n.* 许可

【搭配】permit sb. to do sth. 允许某人做某事

perspective[12] [pə'spektɪv]

【释义】*n.* 1. 观点，看法，视角（viewpoint）2. 远景，展望（outlook）3. 透视

【例句】And why did they not discover the geometric perspective as European artists did in the Renaissance? (TPO11, R, S1, T1) 为什么他们没有像文艺复兴时期的欧洲艺术家那样发现几何视角呢？

【派生】perspectivity *n.* 透视性，明晰度

【搭配】in perspective 正确地；符合透视法地

pose[12] [pəuz]

【释义】*n.* 1. 姿态，姿势（posture. stance）2. 装腔作势 *v.* 1. 摆姿势 2. 形成，引起（cause）

【例句】Unlike formal statues that are limited to static poses of standing, sitting, and kneeling, these figures depict a wide range of actions, such as grinding grain, baking bread, producing pots, and making music, and they are shown in appropriate poses, bending and squatting as they carry out their tasks. (TPO11, R, S1, T1) 这些雕像不像正规雕像那样只有静止的站立、坐和跪的姿态，而是表现了各种不同的动

返记菜单

novel[12] numerous[12] offspring[12] oppose[12] payroll[12]
permit[12] perspective[12] pose[12]

作，比如磨谷物、烤面包、造壶罐，还有奏乐，而且进行这些活动时的姿态都很恰当，或弯腰，或蹲坐着。

【搭配】pose a threat 构成威胁

predictable[12] [prɪ'dɪktəb (ə) l]

【释义】*a.* 可预知的

【例句】Survival and successful reproduction usually require the activities of animals to be coordinated with predictable events around them. (TPO13, R, S2, T1) 生存并成功繁衍通常需要动物们的活动与周围可预知的事件保持协调。

reasonable[12] ['riːznəbl]

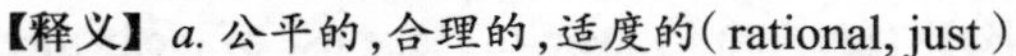

【释义】*a.* 公平的，合理的，适度的（rational, just）

【例句】So having us moved to a bigger space like the Lincoln Auditorium seemed like a reasonable idea. (TPO16, L, S1, C1) 所以我们搬到像林肯大教堂这样一个更大的空间似乎是一个合理的主意。

【搭配】reasonable price 合理的价格

regulate[12] ['regjʊleɪt]

【释义】*v.* 1. 调整，调节（adjust）2. 管理，控制

【例句】Without the external cue, the difference accumulates and so the internally regulated activities of the biological day drift continuously, like the tides, in relation to the solar day. (TPO13, R, S2, T1) 如果没有外部因素，这种差别会积聚，因而生物日内的内部规律性活动就会像潮水一样随着太阳日改变。

【搭配】regulate a clock 校准时钟

repeat[12] [ri'piːt]

【释义】*v./n.* 重复，反复

【例句】Perceiving an apparent connection between certain actions performed by the group and the result it desires, the group repeats, refines, and formalizes those actions into fixed ceremonies, or rituals. (TPO1, R, S2, T1) 当他们意识到自己的某些行为和期许的结果之间存在明显的联系以后，人们便开始重复并且完善这些行为，最终形成固定的典礼或宗教仪式。

【派生】repeated *a.* 反复的，重复的
repeatedly *ad.* 一再；多次

reverse[12] [rɪ'vɜːs]

【释义】*v.*（使）反转，（使）颠倒（overturn, invert）*a.* 相反的，颠倒的，反向的（opposite, contrary）*n.* 1. 相反 2. 背面（back, rear）

【例句】Or the situation may be reversed then a children's television show is written to characters that are based on already popular toys. (TPO10, S, Q4) 或者，情况可能会相反，那样的话，儿童电视节目的角色将会基于已经流行的玩具。

【搭配】in reverse *ad.* 相反，向相反方向

rough[12] [rʌf]

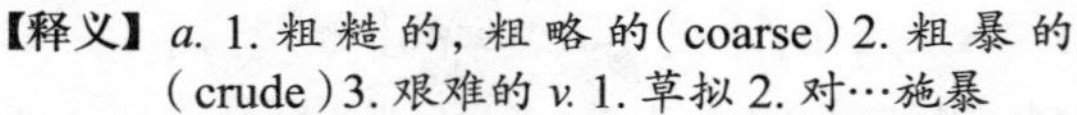

【释义】*a.* 1. 粗糙的，粗略的（coarse）2. 粗暴的（crude）3. 艰难的 *v.* 1. 草拟 2. 对…施暴

【例句】Now if you look at this rough drawing of one of them, one Chromosome is about to divide into two. (TPO12, L, S1, L1) 现在，如果你看看其中的这个草图的话，你就会发现一个染色体会分裂成两个。

【派生】roughly *ad.* 粗糙地；概略地
roughness *n.* 粗糙；粗暴

saturate[12] ['sætʃəreɪt]

【释义】*v.* 使浸透，使充满，使饱和

【例句】Both oil and gas are less dense than water, so they generally tend to rise upward through water-saturated rock and sediment. (TPO4, R, S2, T2) 油和气的密度比水的密度小，因此它们通常会通过饱含水的岩石及沉淀物而向上升。

【派生】saturated *a.* 饱和的，渗透的
saturation *n.* 饱和

silt[12] [sɪlt]

【释义】*n.* 淤泥 *v.*（使）淤塞

【例句】For centuries, the annual floods of the Nile, Tigris, and Euphrates, for example, have brought fertile silts and water to the inhabitants of their lower valleys. (TPO12, R, S2, T2) 例如，几百年来，每年源自尼罗河、底格里斯河以及幼发拉底河的洪水都会为下游

的居民们带去肥沃的淤泥和水。

【派生】silty *a.* 淤泥的；塞满了淤泥的

stain[12] [steɪn]

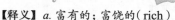

【释义】*n.* 污点，瑕疵(spot) *v.* 弄脏，染色；玷污

【例句】Yeah…there is a huge red stain on it. (TPO15, S, Q5) 是啊，上面有一大块红色的污渍。

【派生】stainable *a.* 染色的
stainless *a.* 纯洁的，无瑕疵的

【搭配】stain remover 去污剂

striking[12] ['straɪkɪŋ]

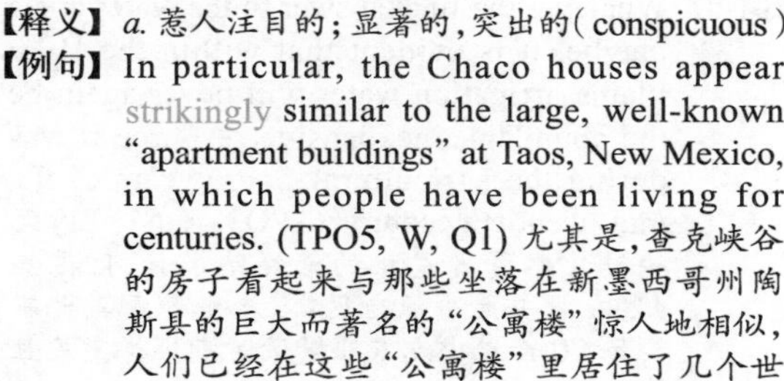

【释义】*a.* 惹人注目的；显著的，突出的(conspicuous)

【例句】In particular, the Chaco houses appear strikingly similar to the large, well-known "apartment buildings" at Taos, New Mexico, in which people have been living for centuries. (TPO5, W, Q1) 尤其是，查克峡谷的房子看起来与那些坐落在新墨西哥州陶斯县的巨大而著名的"公寓楼"惊人地相似，人们已经在这些"公寓楼"里居住了几个世纪。

temperate[12] ['tempərɪt]

【释义】*a.* 1. 温和的(gentle, mild) 2. 适度的，有节制的(moderate)

【例句】They reside throughout the eastern region of North America where is a temperate climate, where the growing season lasts for at least five months of the year, which is when they do all their mating, playing and eating. (TPO1, L, S2, L2) 它们在北美洲东部的各处栖息，那里气候温和，生长期至少有五个月，在那期间，它们完成全部交配、嬉戏和觅食活动。

【派生】temperately *ad.* 适度地，有节制地
temperature *n.* 温度

【搭配】temperate climate 温带气候

velocity[12] [vɪ'lɒsɪtɪ]

【释义】*n.* 速度，速率

【例句】They are more exposed to high-velocity winds. (TPO1, R, S1, T1) 它们更多地曝露于大风之中。

wealthy[12] ['welθɪ]

【释义】*a.* 富有的；富饶的(rich)

【例句】Moreover, an increased credit supply was generated by investments and loans by bankers and wealthy merchants to states and by joint-stock partnerships—an English innovation. (TPO10, R, S2, T2) 此外，信贷供应的增加是由银行家和富商们给国家投资和贷款以及股份合作带来的，这是一项英国的革新。

【反义】poor

web[12] [web]

【释义】*n.* 1. 网；网状物 2. 网络 3. 蹼 *v.* 结网；用网覆盖

【例句】Support for this idea came from the observation that long-lasting climax communities usually have more complex food webs and more species diversity than pioneer communities. (TPO3, R, S1, T2) 对这一观点的支持源于这样的观察结果，即：历时久远的顶级群落通常要比先锋群落具备更为复杂的食物网和更多的物种。

【派生】weblike *a.* 似网的

whereas[12] [weər'æz]

【释义】*conj.* 然而，但是；鉴于

【例句】Just as painted designs on Greek pots may seem today to be purely decorative, whereas in fact they were carefully and precisely worked out so that at the time, their meaning was clear, so it is with Chinese pots. (TPO10, R, S1, T1) 很多希腊陶罐上的绘画设计在今天看来可能纯粹是装饰性的，然而，实际上它们都是经过精心制作出来的，所以在当时有着明显的意义，中国的陶罐也是如此。

absence[11] ['æbsəns]

【释义】*n.* 1. 缺席，不在场 2. 缺乏，不存在(lack)

【例句】Their streamlined bodies, the absence of hind legs, and the presence of a fluke and blowhole cannot disguise their affinities with land dwelling mammals. (TPO2, R, S2, T1) 它们的身体呈流线型，没有后腿，长有尾

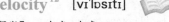

返记菜单

stain[12] striking[12] temperate[12] velocity[12] wealthy[12]
web[12] whereas[12] absence[11]

片和喷水孔，但这些都不能掩盖它们与陆生哺乳动物的相似性。

【派生】absent *a.* 缺席的
absentee *n.* 缺席的人
absenteeism *n.* 旷课，旷工

【搭配】absence of mind 心不在焉

---

agency[11] [ˈeɪdʒənsɪ]

【释义】*n.* 1. 代理，代理处 2. 政府机构

【例句】And by the mid 1970s, by 1974 I think, all fifty states had their own arts agencies, their own state arts councils that work with the federal government, with corporations, artists, performers, you name it. (TPO4, L, S2, L2) 到20世纪70年代中期，我想是到1974年，全部50个州都有了自己的艺术协会，与他们合作的有联邦政府、企业、艺术家、表演家，凡是你能说出来的。

【派生】agent *n.* 代理人，代理商

【搭配】news agency 新闻通讯社
travel agency 旅行社
agency business 代理业务

---

ancestor[11] [ˈænsəstə]

【释义】*n.* 祖先，祖宗；原型，先驱(forefather, forebear)

【例句】The fossil consists of a complete skull of archaeocyte, an extinct group of ancestors of modern cetaceans. (TPO2, R, S2, T1) 这块化石包含一个完整的原始动物的头盖骨，这种原始动物是现代鲸类的祖先，已经灭绝。

【反义】descendant, offspring

【派生】ancestral *a.* 祖先的，祖先传下的
ancestry *n.* 世系，出身

---

arise[11] [əˈraɪz] 

【释义】*v.* 1. 产生，形成，起源于 2. 起立 3. 上升

【例句】Many theorists believe that theater arises when societies act out myths to preserve social well-being. (TPO1, R, S2, T1) 许多理论学家认为当诸多社会群体为保持社会繁荣而演绎神话的时候，戏剧就产生了。

【派生】arisen *a.* 兴起的，产生的

【搭配】arise from 由…引起，起因于

---

attribute[11] [əˈtrɪbju(ː)t] 

【释义】*v.* 把…归于 *n.* 1. 品质，属性 2. 象征，标志

【例句】It attributes both desirable and undesirable occurrences to supernatural or magical forces. (TPO1, R, S2, T1) 他们把尽如人意和不尽如人意的偶发事件都归因于超自然的或魔法的力量。

【搭配】attribute to 把…归因于

---

boom[11] [buːm] 

【释义】*n.*（一段时间的）繁荣；行情暴涨 *v.* 1. 迅速发展(flourish, thrive) 2. 发出隆隆声

【例句】Whatever the final answer to the water crisis maybe, it is evident that within the High Plains, irrigation water will never again be the abundant, inexpensive resource it was during the agricultural boom years of the mid-twentieth century. (TPO3, R, S1, T1) 无论这次水资源危机的最终结果如何，很显然，在北美大平原地区，灌溉水资源再也不会像20世纪中期农业繁荣时期那样充足且廉价了。

【派生】booming *a.* 迅速发展的，兴旺的

【搭配】a boom town 一个新兴的城市

---

bust[11] [bʌst]

【释义】*n.* 1. 半身像 2. 胸部 *v.*（使）破产，（使）爆裂

【例句】We've already looked at portrait sculpture which are busts created to commemorate people who had died, and we've looked at relief sculpture, or sculpting on walls. (TPO18, L, S1, L2) 我们已经看过用来纪念死者的半身肖像雕塑了，而且我们还看了浮雕和壁雕。

【搭配】boom and bust 繁荣与萧条

---

capture[11] [ˈkæptʃə]

【释义】*v.* 1. 俘虏；捕获 2. 夺取，占领 3. 引起（注意、想像、兴趣等）*n.* 捕获，俘获

【例句】In fact, most of what we've known about humming birds comes from banding studies, where we capture a humming bird and make sure all the information about it, like its weight and age and length, are all recorded

and put into an international information database. (TPO3, L, S1, L1) 事实上，我们所知道的有关蜂鸟的大部分信息都来自标记研究，我们在捕获一只蜂鸟后，要确保关于这只蜂鸟的所有信息，比如体重、年龄、长度，都要记录下来并录入国际信息数据库。

【反义】release

cognitive[11] ['kɒgnɪtɪv] 

【释义】*a.* 认知的，认识的

【例句】Another possibility is that children younger than 3 lack some cognitive capacity for memory. (TPO10, L, S2, L2) 另一种可能性是3岁以下的儿童缺乏一些对记忆的认知能力。

【搭配】cognitive psychology 认知心理学

comparative[11] [kəm'pærətɪv] 

【释义】*a.* 比较的，相对的

【例句】In pastoral societies, gender inequality is comparatively mild because wealth is relatively evenly distributed and women have to learn most of the same skills that men do. (TPO14, R, S2, T2) 在农牧社会中，性别的不平等现象比较轻微，因为财富分配相对平均，且女人们需要掌握男人们所具有的大多数技能。

component[11] [kəm'pəunənt] 

【释义】*n.* 组成部分，要素（element, constituent, ingredient, part）*a.* 组成的，成分的

【例句】They decided how to combine various components of the film program. (TPO2, R, S2, T2) 他们决定如何把电影节目的不同元素结合在一起。

【搭配】key/major/essential component 主要组成部分

construct[11]

【释义】[kən'strʌkt] *v.* 1.建造（build）2.创立（found）['kɒnstrʌkt] *n.* 构想，概念

【例句】And they also use trees and tree branches to construct their homes in streams and lakes. (TPO16, L, S2, L1) 它们也会利用树和树枝在溪流和湖泊中建立家园。

【派生】construction *n.* 建造，建筑物
constructor *n.* 建设者

contradict[11] [kɒntrə'dɪkt] 

【释义】*v.* 与…相矛盾；反驳（clash, conflict, confront）

【例句】Most of the evidence he has collected contradicts it. (TPO2, L, S1, L1) 他收集的大多数证据都与此相矛盾。

【派生】contradiction *n.* 矛盾（性）；反驳
contradictory *a.* 矛盾的，反驳的 *n.* 对立面

【搭配】contradict oneself 自相矛盾

cooperation[11] [kəuˌɒpə'reɪʃən] 

【释义】*n.* 合作，协作

【例句】Biological hypotheses include ecological changes brought about by the evolution of cooperation between insects and flowering plants or of bottom-feeding predators in the oceans. (TPO15, R, S2, T2) 生物假说包括：由昆虫与开花植物之间合作式进化或海洋底层肉食动物进化引起的生态变化。

【派生】cooperationist *n.* 合作者论

【逆构】cooperate *v.* 合作

【搭配】in cooperation with 与…合作

deadline[11] ['dedlaɪn] 

【释义】*n.* 最后期限

【例句】It's kind of stressing me out, because we are getting close to the deadline and I feel like I'm doing everything for this project. (TPO4, L, S2, C1) 这让我有点力不从心，因为眼看就要到截止日期了，而我感觉好像我一个人在做这个项目的所有工作。

【搭配】meet the deadline 赶上最后期限，按期完成

decay[11] [dɪ'keɪ] 

【释义】*n./v.* 1. 腐烂，枯萎（decompose, disintegration, rot）2. 衰退，衰落（decline, worsen）

【例句】What keeps the black-tailed deer alive in the harsher seasons of plant decay and dormancy? (TPO4, R, S1, T1) 是什么使得黑尾鹿在植物枯萎和休眠的最严酷的季节里生存了下来呢？

【反义】flourish, prosper

【派生】decayable *a.* 易腐的；易衰败的

返记菜单

cognitive[11]	comparative[11]	component[11]	construct[11]	contradict[11]
cooperation[11]	deadline[11]	decay[11]		

decayless *a.* 不腐朽的；不衰败的
【搭配】fall into decay 损坏，腐烂；衰败

despite[11] [dɪs'paɪt]

【释义】*prep.* 尽管，不管 *n.* 憎恨，轻视
【例句】China has one of the world's oldest continuous civilizations, despite invasions and occasional foreign rule. (TPO10, R, S1, T1) 尽管曾遭到侵略和偶尔受外国势力统治，但中国仍然是世界上最古老的源远流长的文明之一。
【逆构】in despite of 尽管

dynasty[11] ['dɪnəsti]

【释义】*n.* 朝代，王朝
【例句】The function and status of ceramics in China varied from dynasty to dynasty. (TPO10, R, S1, T1) 在中国，陶瓷在各个朝代的功能和地位是不同的。

edge[11] [edʒ]

【释义】*n.* 1. 边(缘)(brink, perimeter) 2. 刃 3. 优势 *v.* 1. 使锋利；给…加上边 2. 侧着移动，徐徐移动
【例句】Offshore drilling platforms extend the search for oil to the ocean's continental shelves—those gently sloping submarine regions at the edges of the continents. (TPO4, R, S2, T2) 寻找石油的近海钻井平台已经拓展到了大陆架——那些大陆边缘逐渐向海底倾斜的区域。
【派生】edging *n.* 边饰
【搭配】on the edge of 几乎；濒于
on the edge 在边缘上；坐立不安
on edge 紧张，急切；竖着
edge in 挤进
edge on 怂恿，鼓励
on the cutting edge 处在最前沿的位置

episode[11] ['epɪsəʊd]

【释义】*n.* 一段情节，片段，轶事；(音乐的)插曲
【例句】Their calculations show that the impact kicked up a dust cloud that cut off sunlight for several months, inhibiting photosynthesis in plants; decreased surface temperatures on continents to below freezing; caused extreme episodes of acid rain: and significantly raised long-term global temperatures through the greenhouse effect. (TPO8, R, S2, T1) 他们的估算表明，这次撞击引起的尘埃云阻断阳光达数月之久，因而妨碍了植物的光合作用，使得地表温度降到了零度以下，并引起了酸雨的不断发生，从而由于温室效应导致了全球长期气温的显著提高。

flash[11] [flæʃ]

【释义】*a.* 火速的，突然的 *v.* 闪光；反射(flare, glare, sparkle) *n.* 闪光，闪烁
【例句】The onrushing water arising from these flash floods likely also formed the odd teardrop-shaped "islands" that have been found on the plains close to the ends of the outflow channels. (TPO8, R, S2, T2) 这突如其来的洪水产生的急流可能也形成了这种奇特的泪滴形状的"岛屿"，这些"岛屿"已经在靠近泄水渠末端的平原上被发现了。
【搭配】flash sb. a smile 冲某人迅速一笑

forage[11] ['fɒrɪdʒ]

【释义】*v.* 1. 搜寻粮草 2. 搜寻 *n.* 1. 粮草，饲料 2. 搜寻粮草
【例句】Such theories imply that the Indo-European languages evolved not in Neolithic (10,000 to 3,000 B. C.) Anatolia, but among the foraging communities of the cultures in the region of the Don and Dnieper rivers, which took up stock breeding and began to exploit the neighboring steppes. (TPO14, R, S2, T2) 这些理论意味着印欧语系不是在新石器时代(公元前一万年到三千年)的安纳托利亚演变发展的，而是在顿河和第聂伯河流域的牧民社区，他们当时已经发展了畜牧业并开始开拓邻近的大草原。
【逆构】forager *n.* 觅食者，强征(粮食)的人
【搭配】forage for 搜查

gallery[11] ['gælərɪ]

【释义】*n.* 1. 画廊，美术馆 2. 楼座，旁听席 3. 走廊，地道
【例句】Remember I said that at some point during

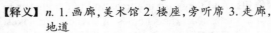

this semester I wanted you to attend an exhibit at the Fair Street Gallery and then write about it? (TPO1, L, S1, L1) 我说过让你们这个学期找个时间去菲尔大街的画廊参加一次展览然后写一些东西给我，还记得吗？

【搭配】public gallery 旁听席，公众旁听席

gravel[11] ['grævəl] 

【释义】n. 砾石；沙砾 v. 1. 用沙砾铺 2. 使迷惑，使困惑

【例句】The salt and gypsum, the faunal changes, and the unusual gravel provided abundant evidence that the Mediterranean was once a desert. (TPO7, R, S1, T1) 盐和石膏、动物群体的变化以及非同寻常的砾石都为证明"地中海曾经是一个沙漠"这一观点提供了充足的证据。

【搭配】a gravel path 石子路

groom[11] [grʊm] 

【释义】v. 1. 打扮，梳理毛发（preen）2. 准备 n. 1. 新郎（bridegroom）2. 马夫（stableman）

【例句】So, instead, it starts grooming itself. (TPO4, L, S1, L1) 于是，取而代之的是它开始梳理自己的羽毛。

hide[11] [haɪd] 

【释义】v. 1. 隐藏，躲避 2. 隐瞒 3. 遮蔽，覆盖

【例句】But the painters actually tried to hide them. (TPO16, L, S2, L2) 但事实上画家们试图把它们藏起来。

【搭配】hide from 隐瞒

highland[11] ['haɪlənd] 

【释义】n. 高地 a. 高地的

【例句】The valley, like many other places in Mexican and Guatemalan highlands, was rich in obsidian. (TPO8, R, S1, T1) 同墨西哥和瓜地马拉高地的许多地方一样，这个山谷蕴藏着丰富的黑曜石。

【反义】lowland

ideal[11] [aɪ'dɪəl] 

【释义】a. 1. 理想的，完美的（model, perfect）2. 空想的，假设的 n. 理想，典范，目标

【例句】Great tracts of lowland country deforested by logging, fire, or both have become ideal feeding grounds for deer. (TPO4, R, S1, T1) 低地的森林被大面积砍伐、焚烧，这样都成了鹿群理想的进食场所。

【派生】idealism n. 理想主义，唯心论

impressive[11] [ɪm'presɪv] 

【释义】a. 给人印象深刻的

【例句】This impressive display is clearly visible in the light spectrum illuminating the forest floor. (TPO17, R, S2, T1) 在照亮雨林底层的光谱环境下，这种表现尤其引人注目、令人印象深刻。

【派生】impressively ad. 令人难忘地

inhabit[11] [ɪn'hæbɪt] 

【释义】v. 居住于，栖息于（dwell, live）

【例句】This aquifer was named the Ogallala aquifer after the Ogallala Sioux Indians, who once inhabited the region. (TPO3, R, S1, T1) 因奥加拉拉苏族印第安人曾居住于这一地区，所以这一蓄水层被命名为奥加拉拉蓄水层。

【派生】inhabitant n. 居民，栖息的动物

intermediate[11] [ˌɪntə'miːdjət] 

【释义】a. 中间的，中级的，中等的（medium, middle）n. 调解人；中间事物 v. 调解；干涉

【例句】Most of Africa presents a curious case in which societies moved directly from a technology of stone to iron without passing through the intermediate stage of copper or bronze metallurgy, although some early copper-working sites have been found in West Africa. (TPO7, R, S2, T2) 非洲大部地区都呈现出一种奇特的情况：其社会是直接从石器时代过渡到铁器时代的，而没有经历青铜冶炼的中间阶段，虽然人们曾在西非地区发现炼铜厂的旧址。

返记菜单

gravel[11] groom[11] hide[11] highland[11] ideal[11]
impressive[11] inhabit[11] intermediate[11]

interview[11] [ˈɪntəvjuː]

【释义】*n.* 1. 面试 2. 访谈，谈话 *v.* 1. 面试 2. 采访，会见

【例句】Well, as you know, the career fair is generally an opportunity for local businesses to recruit new employees, and for soon-to-be graduates to have interviews with several companies they might be interested in working for. (TPO6, L, S1, C1) 你知道，人才招聘会通常是为当地企业招聘新员工和为应届毕业生与感兴趣的一些公司进行面试提供机会。

【派生】interviewee *n.* 接受面谈者；被接见者
interviewer *n.* 面试官

intrinsic[11] [ɪnˈtrɪnsɪk]

【释义】*a.* 内在的，固有的，本质的（essential, inherent, fundamental）

【例句】Increased agricultural production in turn facilitated rural industry, an intrinsic part of the expansion of industry. (TPO10, R, S2, T2) 农业生产的增加反过来促进了乡村工业的发展，乡村工业是整个工业发展中固有的一部分。

【搭配】intrinsic motivation 内在动机；内在激励
intrinsic property 固有特性

knight[11] [naɪt]

【释义】*n.* 骑士 *v.* 授予骑士地位

【例句】Now they were called songs of deeds because strangely enough, they were written to describe the heroic deeds or actions of warriors, the knights during conflicts. (TPO13, L, S2, L1) 现在，之所以称其为英雄颂歌，很大程度上是因为它们往往描写勇士的英雄事迹和行为，比如战争中的骑士。

【派生】knighthood *n.* 骑士的地位或资格

logical[11] [ˈlɒdʒɪkəl]

【释义】*a.* 逻辑（上）的，符合逻辑的；合理的（resonable, rational）

【例句】You think that the viewer would reach the logical conclusion that the slogan…er… misrepresents the product. (TPO3, S, Q6) 你觉得观众会得出广告语并没有真实地反映产品这样的逻辑结论。

【派生】logicality *n.* 逻辑性

magical[11] [ˈmædʒɪkəl]

【释义】*a.* 魔术的，有魔力的，神奇的

【例句】It attributes both desirable and undesirable occurrences to supernatural or magical forces. (TPO1, R, S2, T1) 他们把尽如人意和不尽如人意的偶发事件都归因于超自然或魔法的力量。

【派生】magically *ad.* 如魔法般地

mild[11] [maɪld]

【释义】*a.* 温和的，柔和的，轻微的（temperate, gentle, moderate）

【例句】Florida's winter is very mild; the temperature doesn't often get below freezing. (TPO11, L, S2, L1) 佛罗里达的冬天非常温暖，气温很少会降到冰点以下。

【反义】harsh, severe, strict, wild

【搭配】mild climate 温和的气候

muscular[11] [ˈmʌskjʊlə]

【释义】*a.* 肌肉的，肌肉发达的；强壮的

【例句】Right-handers tend to have longer, stronger, and more muscular bones on the right side. (TPO12, R, S1, T1) 惯用右手的人一般身体右边的骨骼会更长、更强壮，肌肉更发达。

【派生】muscularity *n.* 力大；肌肉发达

Word List 14

myth[11] [mɪθ]

【释义】*n.* 神话，虚构的故事（legend, fable, fantacy）

【例句】The most widely accepted theory, championed by anthropologists in the late nineteenth and early twentieth centuries, envisions theater as emerging out of myth and ritual. (TPO1, R, S2, T1) 这一最广为接受的理论认为剧院产生于神话和宗教仪式，这一理论在19世纪末和20世纪早期受到了人类学家的拥护。

【派生】mythic (al) *a.* 神话的，传说的
mythology *n.* 神话，神话学，神话集

objective[11] [əb'dʒektɪv]

【释义】*a.* 客观的，无偏见的，真实的（impartial）*n.* 目标，目的（aim, goal）

【例句】Teachers rarely have the time or opportunities to view their own or the teaching of others in an objective manner. (TPO9, R, S2, T1) 教师们很少有机会和时间去客观地观察自己以及其他老师的教学。

【反义】subjective

【逆构】object *n.* 目标；物体

plastic[11] ['plæstɪk]

【释义】*n.* 塑料 *a.* 1. 可塑的，能适应的（changeable, flexible）2. 塑料的 3. 虚假的 4. [医]整形的

【例句】In particular, we talked about cotton fibers, which we said were very useful, not only in the textile industry, but also in the chemical industry, and in the production of many products, such as plastics, paper, explosives, and so on. (TPO2, L, S1, L2) 我们特别探讨了棉花纤维，它用途很广，不仅可用于纺织业、化学工业，还可用来制造很多物品，如塑料、纸张、炸药等等。

【搭配】plastic surgery 整容手术

promote[11] [prə'məʊt]

【释义】*v.* 1. 促进（boost, advance）2. 晋级，提升（elevate, raise）

【例句】Conditions that promote fossilization of soft-bodied animals include very rapid covering by sediments that create an environment that discourages decomposition. (TPO5, R, S2, T2) 促使软体动物化石化的条件包括被沉淀物迅速覆盖，从而创造一个防腐的环境。

【派生】promotion *n.* 促进，提升

recharge[11] ['riː'tʃɑːdʒ]

【释义】*v.* 1. 再装载 2. 充电 3. 休整

【例句】The recharge rate of the aquifer is decreasing. (TPO3, R, S1, T1) 蓄水层的补充率在下降。

retreat[11] [rɪ'triːt]

【释义】*v.* 撤退；退却（withdraw, secede）*n.* 隐退；消退

【例句】At the end of the Cretaceous, the geological record shows that these seaways retreated from the continents back into the major ocean basins. (TPO8, R, S2, T1) 在白垩纪结束的时候，地质记录显示这些航道从大陆退回到了主要的海洋盆地。

rite[11] [raɪt]

【释义】*n.* 仪式，典礼（ritual, ceremony）

【例句】Frequently the myths include representatives of those supernatural forces that the rites celebrate or hope to influence. (TPO1, R, S2, T1) 通常，神话中会包含那些超自然的力量，这些力量是那些仪式想要去赞美或施加影响的。

secure[11] [sɪ'kjʊə]

【释义】*a.* 安全的，可靠的，稳固的（safe, reliable）*v.* 1. 确保，保障 2. 获得（acquire）

【例句】The hard volcanic stone was a resource that had been in great demand for many years, at least since the rise of the Olmecs (a people who flourished between 1200 and 400 B.C.), and it apparently had a secure market.

(TPO8, R, S1, T1) 至少从奥尔梅克人(繁荣于公元前1200至402年的一个民族)的崛起开始,多年来坚硬的火山岩一直都是一种需求量巨大的资源,并且显然有着稳定的市场。

【反义】insecure

【派生】security *n.* 安全

【搭配】secure sth. to sth. 把…牢牢系在…上

session[11] [ˈseʃən]

【释义】*n.* 1.(进行某活动连续的)一段时间,一节 2.(尤指法庭、议会等)开庭,开会 3.学年

【例句】When the training session will be scheduled? (TPO3, L, S2, C1) 培训计划在什么时候进行?

【派生】sessional *a.* 开会的;开庭的

【搭配】in session 在开庭;在开会

severe[11] [sɪˈvɪə]

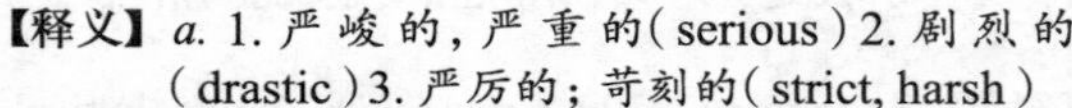

【释义】*a.* 1.严峻的,严重的(serious)2.剧烈的(drastic)3.严厉的;苛刻的(strict, harsh)

【例句】As periods of severe dryness have become more common, failures of a number of different crops have increased. (TPO2, R, Sl, T1, Q13) 随着严重干旱的现象越来越普遍,许多作物歉收的几率大大增加。

【反义】lenient, mild

【派生】severely *ad.* 严重地
severity *n.* 严重性

shelf[11] [ʃelf]

【释义】*n.* 1.架子,搁板 2.沙洲;暗礁;岩床

【例句】You've checked the shelves I assume. (TPO14, L, S1, C1) 我想你已经看过书架了。

【搭配】on the shelf 束之高阁,闲置的
shelf life 保存限期;闲置时间
off the shelf 现成的,不用定制的

slide[11] [slaɪd]

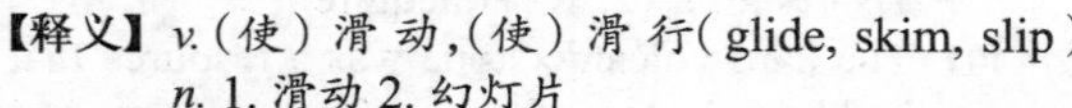

【释义】*v.*(使)滑动,(使)滑行(glide, skim, slip)*n.* 1.滑动 2.幻灯片

【例句】Shortly after the Cambrian explosion, mud slides rapidly buried thousands of marine animals under conditions that favored fossilization. (TPO5, R, S2, T2) 在寒武纪大爆炸发生后不久,土崩很快就将成千上万的海洋动物埋在有利于化石形成的环境中了。

【派生】slider *n.* 滑雪者;会滚动之物
slideway *n.* 滑道;滑斜面

【搭配】slide down 滑下
slide into 不知不觉陷入,不知不觉地染上

smooth[11] [smuːð]

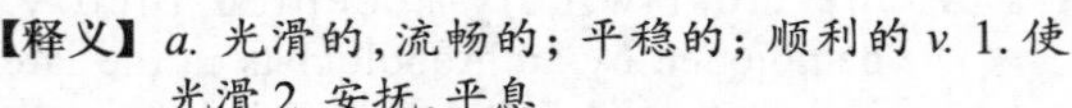

【释义】*a.* 光滑的,流畅的;平稳的;顺利的 *v.* 1.使光滑 2.安抚,平息

【例句】If it wants to have a smooth texture, it flattens out the papillae, so it can acquire a smooth texture to blend in with the sandy bottom of the sea. (TPO17, L, S2, L2) 如果想拥有平滑的肌理,它就会把乳突变平,这样就能拥有与海底沙地相融合的平滑肌理了。

【反义】rough

【派生】smoothen *v.* 使平滑
smoothly *ad.* 平稳地,顺利地
smoothness *n.* 平滑

【搭配】smooth over 消除,缓和,减轻
smooth out 消除;使平滑

station[11] [ˈsteɪʃən]

【释义】*v.* 配置,安置;驻扎 *n.* 1.车站,站台 2.岗位,位置 3.地位,身份

【例句】The physical bonds included the network of military garrisons, which were stationed in every province, and the network of stone-built roads that linked the provinces with Rome. (TPO7, R, S2, T1) 物质上的联结包括安置在各省的军事驻防网络以及连接各省与罗马的石筑公路网。

straight[11] [streɪt]

【释义】*ad.* 1.不断地 2.直接地,立即 3.坦率地 *a.* 1.笔直的 2.连续的 3.正直的

【例句】First, most students just cannot concentrate for three hours straight. (TPO7, S, Q3) 首先,大多数学生都不能连续3个小时一直集中精力。

【搭配】go straight 改邪归正

stretch[11] [stretʃ] 

【释义】*n.* 1. 一段连续的时间或空间 2. 伸展，拉紧 *v.* (使)伸展，(使)延长(extend)

【例句】It's been shaped by constraints over vast stretches of time, all of which comes down to the fact that the best foraging strategy for beavers isn't the one that yields the most food or wood. (TPO16, L, S2, L1) 这是由于经过很长时间的各种限制而形成的，这一切都归结于这样一个事实，就是对海狸来说，最好的觅食策略并不是得到最多的食物或木头。

【反义】shrink

【搭配】stretch oneself 伸懒腰；尽最大的努力
at a stretch 一口气地，不休息地

switch[11] [swɪtʃ] 

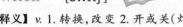

【释义】*v.* 1. 转换，改变 2. 开或关(灯等) *n.* 1. 开关 2. 改变，转变 3. 鞭子

【例句】Many have been attempting to conserve water by irrigating less frequently or by switching to crops that require less water. (TPO3, R, S1, T1) 很多人已经开始尝试通过降低灌溉频率或者改种需水较少的庄稼来节约水资源。

【搭配】switch on/off 开启 / 关闭

tendency[11] ['tendənsɪ] 

【释义】*n.* 1. 倾向，趋势(trend, propensity)

【例句】Further observation revealed the tendency of teachers to evaluate events rather than review the contributory factors in a considered manner by, in effect, standing outside the situation. (TPO9, R, S2, T1) 进一步的观察发现，教师们更倾向于评价事件，而不是站在事件之外以一种深思熟虑的方式洞察一个事件的促成因素。

【派生】tendentious *a.* 有倾向的，有偏见的

【逆构】tend *v.* 倾向，趋向，易于

thrive[11] [θraɪv] 

【释义】*v.* 茁壮成长；兴旺，繁荣(flourish, prosper)

【例句】This was an important innovation, because the camel's ability to thrive in harsh desert conditions and to carry large loads cheaply made it an effective and efficient means of transportation. (TPO7, R, S2, T2) 这是一次重要的创新，因为骆驼具有在严酷的沙漠环境中茁壮成长的本领，且能不费力地运送大批货物，这使其成为了一种高效的交通工具。

【搭配】First thrive and then wive. 先立业，后成家。

upset[11]

【释义】[ʌp'set] *v.* 1. 使心烦(distress) 2. 打乱(disturb) 3. 颠覆，推翻(overturn) *a.* 心烦意乱的(worried, concerned)；不适的 ['ʌpset] *n.* 困扰，麻烦，苦恼

【例句】I almost felt like screaming, but I didn't want to upset my daughter, so I said, "Don't worry, honey, it's nothing." (TPO4, S, Q4) 我差点都要叫出来了，但我不想吓到女儿，所以我说："别担心，宝贝，没事。"

【派生】upsetting *a.* 令人心烦的，令人苦恼的

【搭配】get upset 伤心；感到不安
upset the apple cart 美梦破灭

accompany[10] [ə'kʌmpənɪ] 

【释义】*v.* 陪伴，伴随

【例句】Performers may wear costumes and masks to represent the mythical charaters or supernatural forces in the rituals or in accompanying celebrations. (TPO1, R, S2, T1) 在这些仪式或伴随的庆祝活动中，表演者们会穿着各种服饰、戴着面具来代表神话中的人物或超自然的力量。

【派生】accompanying *a.* 陪伴的，伴随的
accompaniment *n.* 伴随

【搭配】accompany by 在…陪同下

amaze[10] [ə'meɪz]

【释义】*v.* 使大为惊奇，惊愕 *n.* 吃惊，好奇

【例句】It's been amazing, I mean, I'm just learning so much from just watching him. (TPO1, L, S2, C1) 真是令人惊奇，我是说，我只是通过看他上课就学习了这么多东西。

【同义】surprise, astound

【派生】amazed *a.* 感到惊奇的
amazing *a.* 使人惊奇的

返记菜单

stretch[11] switch[11] tendency[11] thrive[11] upset[11]
accompany[10] amaze[10]

award[10] [ə'wɔːd] 

【释义】*n.* 奖品，奖金（prize, reward）*v.* 授予，奖励；判给

【例句】I won an award from the Creative Writing Institute for a story I wrote. (TPO3, S, Q5) 我写的一个故事在创意写作研究中心获奖了。

【派生】awardee *n.* 获奖者

breed[10] [briːd] 

【释义】*v.* 生育，繁殖，孕育（raise, cultivate）*n.* 种，品种（species）

【例句】Now you know a humming bird is amazingly small, but even though it's really tiny, it migrates over very long distances, travels up and down the western hemisphere—the Americas, back and forth between where it breeds in the summer and the warmer climates where it spends the winter. (TPO3, L, S1, L1) 现在你知道了，蜂鸟非常得小，但纵使如此之小，它们迁徙的距离却非常长，它们往返于西半球——美洲，在夏天进行繁殖的地方和气候温暖的过冬的地方之间来来回回。

【派生】breeding *n.* 生育，繁殖
breeder *n.* 饲养动物的人，饲养员

circumstance[10] ['sɜːkəmstəns] 

【释义】*n.* 环境，条件，情况（condition, situation）

【例句】We can even do the photocopy for you because of the circumstances. (TPO9, L, S2, C1) 鉴于这种情况，我们甚至可以帮你复印。

【搭配】under/in no circumstances 决不，无论如何也不

clue[10] [kluː] 

【释义】*n.* 线索；提示（hint）*v.* 提示

【例句】This 700-million-year-old formation gives few clues to the origins of modern animals. (TPO5, R, S2, T2) 这个七亿年的地质构造并未给现代动物的起源提供什么有价值的线索。

【派生】clueless *a.* 无线索的；愚蠢的

collar[10] ['kɒlə] 

【释义】*n.* 1. 衣领 2.（狗等的）项圈 *v.* 1. 抓住 2. 给…戴上项圈

【例句】This species, which lives in the rain forests and scrublands of the east coast of Australia, has a brown-to-black plumage with bare, bright-red skin on the head and neck and a neck collar of orange-yellow loosely hanging skin. (TPO17, R, S2, T1) 这一物种生活在澳大利亚东海岸的雨林和灌木丛中，有着黑棕色的羽毛，光秃秃的头部和脖子上的皮肤是鲜亮的红色，脖子上还有一圈橙黄色的松垮的皮肤。

【派生】collared *a.* 有领圈的

collide[10] [kə'laɪd] 

【释义】*v.* 1. 碰撞（hit, bump）2. 冲突（conflict）

【例句】In view of these facts, scientists hypothesized that a single large asteroid, about 10 to 15 kilometers across, collided with Earth, and the resulting fallout created the boundary clay. (TPO8, R, S2,T1) 考虑到这些事实，科学家们假设有一颗10到15公里外的巨大小行星撞向地球，所产生的尘埃形成了界线粘土。

【逆构】collision *n.* 碰撞；冲突

communal[10] ['kɒmjʊnl] 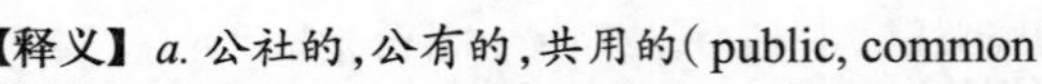

【释义】*a.* 公社的，公有的，共用的（public, common）

【例句】Communal online encyclopedias represent one of the latest resources to be found on the Internet. (TPO6, W, Q1) 公共在线百科全书代表了一种在互联网上发现的最新资源。

【派生】commune *n.* 公社

【搭配】communal property 公有财产

container[10] [kən'teɪnə]

【释义】*n.* 1. 容器 2. 集装箱

【例句】It may sound plausible that large empty rooms were used for storage, but excavations of the great houses have not uncovered many traces of maize or maize containers. (TPO5, W, Q1) 这些大而空的房间是作储藏之用的，这听起来很合理，但是对这些大房

子的发掘工作并没有揭露太多有关玉米或盛放玉米的容器的线索。
【逆构】contain *v.* 包含

continuous[10] [kən'tɪnjʊəs]

【释义】*a.* 继续的，连续不断的
【例句】China has one of the world's oldest continuous civilizations. (TPO10, R, S1, T1) 中国拥有世界上最为悠久而连续的文明。
【派生】continuity *n.* 连续性
【逆构】continue *v.* 持续，继续
【搭配】be continuous with 与…相连，是…的延续部分

conventional[10] [kən'venʃənl]

【释义】*a.* 传统的，惯例的，常规的（traditional, customary）
【例句】Dissatisfaction with conventional explanations for dinosaur extinctions led to a surprising observation that, in turn, has suggested a new hypothesis. (TPO8, R, S2, T1) 对有关恐龙灭绝的传统解释的不满引出了一个惊人的发现，而这一发现反过来又提出一个新的假说。

crack[10] [kræk]

【释义】*n.* 1. 裂缝，裂纹（crevice）2. 缺点 *v.*（使）爆裂；裂开（split, fracture）
【例句】It is reduced by cracks in the ice. (TPO7, L, S2, L2) 冰破裂使之减小。

criticize[10] ['krɪtɪsaɪz]

【释义】*v.* 1. 批评 2. 挑剔，非难 3. 评论
【例句】He criticizes that people of his time for abandoning their own minds and their own wills for the sake of conformity and consistency. (TPO4, L, S1, L2) 他批评他那个时代的人为了随大流而放弃自己的思想和愿望。
【反义】admire, praise
【派生】criticism *n.* 批评；评论
critical *a.* 批评的
【逆构】critic *n.* 批评家，评论家

dam[10] [dæm]

【释义】*n.* 坝，堤 *v.* 筑堤（坝）挡住
【例句】The filling of the Ataturk and other dams in Turkey has drastically reduced flows in the Euphrates, with potentially serious consequences for Syria and Iraq. (TPO12, R, S2, T2) 对土耳其的阿图塔克水坝和其他水坝的注水大幅度地减少了幼发拉底河的流量，这可能会对利比亚和伊拉克造成严重的影响。

deform[10] [diː'fɔːm]

【释义】*v.* 使变形（disfigure, distort）
【例句】The trees begin to become twisted and deformed. (TPO1, R, S1, T1) 树木开始变得扭曲变形。
【派生】deformed *a.* 变形的
deformation *n.* 变形，损坏

derive[10] [dɪ'raɪv]

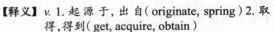

【释义】*v.* 1. 起源于，出自（originate, spring）2. 取得，得到（get, acquire, obtain）
【例句】Hydrogen can be derived from various plentiful sources, including natural gas and even water. (TPO9, W, Q1) 氢气可以通过多种丰富的来源获得，包括天然气，甚至是水。
【派生】derivative *n.* 派生，提取物
【搭配】derive from 源自…

dome[10] [dəʊm]

【释义】*n.* 圆屋顶，苍穹 *v.*（使）成圆顶状
【例句】But when the dome was rotated, the birds changed their direction to match the artificial sky. (TPO11, R, S2, T1) 但当圆屋顶被转动的时候，鸟儿们就会改变方向来适应这一人造天空。
【派生】domelike *a.* 穹顶状的
【搭配】dome structure 穹状构造

enlarge[10] [ɪn'lɑːdʒ]

【释义】*v.*（使）加大，（使）增大（broaden, expand, increase, magnify）
【例句】The skull is cetacean-like but its jawbones

lack the enlarged space that is filled with fat or oil and used for receiving underwater sound in modern whales. (TPO2, R, S2, T1) 这个头盖骨和鲸类动物的很像,但它的下颌骨和现代鲸类略有不同,现代鲸类动物的下颌骨中含有额外的空间储存脂肪或油脂,并用来接收水下的声音。
【派生】enlargement *n.* 扩大,扩展
【搭配】enlarge sb.'s knowledge 扩大某人的知识面

exaggerate[10] [ɪg'zædʒəreɪt]

【释义】*v.* 夸大,夸张(magnify, overstate)
【例句】Of course there are some negative consequences of selling fossils in the commercial market, but they have been greatly exaggerated. (TPO13, W, Q1) 当然,在商业市场上销售化石有一些负面后果,但这些后果却被大大夸大了。
【派生】exaggeration *n.* 夸张,夸大

expedition[10] [ˌekspɪ'dɪʃən]

【释义】*n.* 1. 远征 2. 探险队
【例句】An expedition to the Mediterranean answered some long-standing questions about the ocean's history. (TPO7, R, S1, T1) 对地中海的远征考察回答了一些有关这片海域历史的长期存在的问题。
【搭配】on an expedition 去考察

flaw[10] [flɔː]

【释义】*n.* 1. 缺点,瑕疵,缺陷(blemish) 2. 一阵狂风 *v.* 使有瑕疵
【例句】To be sure, their evaluation of the technical flaws in 1920's sound experiments was not so far off the mark, yet they neglected to take account important new forces in the motion picture field that, in a sense, would not take no for an answer. (TPO12, R, S2, T1) 诚然,他们对于20世纪20年代声音实验中存在的技术性缺陷的估计也不是完全没有道理,但是他们忘记把电影领域中的新力量考虑进去了,在某种意义上,那一领域是不会把"不能"作为答案的。
【派生】flawless *a.* 无暇的,完美的

flexible[10] ['fleksəbl]

【释义】*a.* 1. 柔韧的,易弯曲的(plastic, elastic) 2. 灵活的,可变通的(adaptable, adjustable)
【例句】They can easily be several feet in length and they're also very strong, very flexible. (TPO2, L, S1, L2) 它们很容易就能长到若干英尺高,茎杆很强壮,也很柔韧。
【派生】flexibility *n.* 柔韧性;灵活性
flexibly *ad.* 柔韧地;灵活地

flourish[10] ['flʌrɪʃ]

【释义】*v.* 1. 茂盛,繁荣(thrive, prosper) 2. 挥动 *n.* 1. 挥舞 2. 花样,夸张的行为或手势
【例句】Wildman and Niles were particularly interested in investigating the conditions under which reflection might flourish—a subject on which there is little guidance in the literature. (TPO9, R, S2, T1) 威尔德曼和纳尔斯尤其喜欢研究在哪种情况下反思可能大量出现——这是一个几乎没有任何文献指导的课题。
【反义】decay, decline
【派生】flourishing *a.* 繁茂的,欣欣向荣的

fluctuate[10] ['flʌktjʊeɪt]

【释义】*v.* 波动,涨落,起伏
【例句】The numbers of deer have fluctuated markedly since the entry of Europeans into Puget Sound country. (TPO4, R, S1, T1) 自从欧洲人进入皮吉特海峡后,鹿的数量出现了显著波动。
【派生】fluctuating *a.* 上下浮动的
fluctuation *n.* 波动,起伏
【搭配】fluctuate between hopes and fears 忽喜忽忧

fracture[10] ['fræktʃə]

【释义】*n.* 1. 破裂,裂痕 2. 骨折 *v.* (使)断裂,(使)破裂
【例句】Fractures and other cut marks are another source of evidence. (TPO12, R, S1, T1) 骨折和其他割痕是另一种证据来源。
【派生】fractured *a.* 断裂的
【搭配】fracture plane 破裂面

injury[10] [ˈɪndʒərɪ] 

【释义】*n.* 损害，伤害（harm, hurt）

【例句】Perhaps, like many contemporary peoples, Upper Paleolithic men and women believed that the drawing of a human image could cause death or injury, and if that were indeed their belief, it might explain why human figures are rarely depicted in cave art. (TPO4, R, S2, T1) 也许，跟很多同时代的人一样，旧石器时代的人们认为画人物像会带来伤亡，假如他们真这么认为，或许也就可以解释为什么在洞穴艺术中很少有人物画像了。

【逆构】injure *v.* 损害，伤害

inner[10] [ˈɪnə] 

【释义】*a.* 1. 内部的，内在的 *n.* 里面

【例句】But the Romance Poetry describes a lot of the inner feelings, the motivations, psychology you could say, of the knight trying to improve himself, to better himself, so he's worthy of love of a woman. (TPO13, L, S2, L1) 但是，浪漫主义诗歌描写了很多有关骑士为了提升和完善自己从而有资格赢得女士的爱的内在情感、动机和心理活动。

intellectual[10] [ˌɪntɪˈlektjʊəl] 

【释义】*a.* 1. 理智的，理性的 2. 知识的，智力的 *n.* 知识分子，脑力劳动者

【例句】In the end, Aristotle says that true happiness is the exercise of reason—a life of intellectual contemplation…of thinking. (TPO2, L, S2, L1) 最终，亚里士多德总结说，幸福就是对理性的实践——是对理性冥思的一生，是不断思考的一生。

【派生】intellectually *ad.* 理智地；智力地
intellectualism *n.* 理智主义

【逆构】intellect *n.* 智力

【搭配】intellectual property 知识产权

invertebrate[10] [ɪnˈvɜːtɪbrɪt] 

【释义】*a./n.* 无脊椎的（动物）（spineless）

【例句】One question was related to evidence that the invertebrate fauna (animals without spines) of the Mediterranean had changed abruptly about 6 million years ago. (TPO7, R, S1, T1) 问题之一是找到相关证据来证明地中海的无脊椎动物群体在约600万年前发生了突然的变化。

mast[10] [mɑːst] 

【释义】*n.* 船桅，桅杆；旗杆

【例句】It had a wider and deeper hull than the galley and hence could carry more cargo: increased stability made it possible to add multiple masts and sails. (TPO17, R, S1, T1) 这种船拥有比单层甲板船更加宽而深的船身，因此可以运送更多的货物：稳定性的提高使得船上可以增加多个桅杆和船帆。

【搭配】before the mast 作为普通水手

master[10] [ˈmɑːstə] 

【释义】*n.* 硕士；主人；大师 *v.* 控制；精通 *a.* 1. 熟练的 2. 主要的

【例句】Production was generally in the hands of skilled individual artisans doing piecework under the tutelage of a master. (TPO16, R, S1, T1) 通常都是熟练的工匠在大师的指导下进行生产的。

【搭配】master of 精通…的人
master degree 硕士学位

mislead[10] [misˈliːd] 

【释义】*v.* 误导，使误入歧途（misguide, deceive）

【例句】General concern about misleading tactics that advertisers employ is centered on the use of exaggeration. (TPO14, R, S1, T1) 对于广告商所使用的误导性策略的一般关注点集中在夸张的运用。

【派生】misleading *a.* 使误入歧途的，引起误解的

mobile[10] [ˈməʊbaɪl] 

【释义】*a.* 1. 可移动的（movable）2. 多变的（changeable）*n.* 风铃；（可随风摆动的）悬挂饰物

【例句】In other cases, the finer particles may be removed, while the sand-sized particles are accumulated to form mobile hills or ridges of sand. (TPO2, R, Sl, T1) 在另一些地区，细沙可能会被风吹走，而粗沙则逐渐堆积成小山状或山脊状的流沙。

返记菜单

injury[10] inner[10] intellectual[10] invertebrate[10] mast[10]
master[10] mislead[10] mobile[10]

【派生】 mobility *n.* 移动性
【搭配】 mobile phone 移动电话，手机

mode[10] [məʊd]

【释义】 *n.* 1. 方式，模式(form, manner) 2. 风格(style)
【例句】 This mode of craft production favored the growth of self-governing and ideologically egalitarian craft guilds everywhere in the Middle Eastern city. (TPO16, R, S1, T1) 这种工艺生产模式有利于中东城市中自治、意识上平等的工艺品行会的发展。
【搭配】 operation mode 操作方式
mode of thinking 思维方式

motif[10] [məʊ'tiːf]

【释义】 *n.* 1.（作品的）主题，主旨；装饰图案
【例句】 Ceramic products also include lead-glazed tomb models of the Han dynasty, three-color lead-glazed vessels and figures of the Tang dynasty, and Ming three-color temple ornaments, in which the motifs were outlined in a raised trail of slip—as well as the many burial ceramics produced in imitation of vessels made in materials of higher intrinsic value. (TPO10, R, S1, T1) 陶瓷制品还包括汉代的铅釉墓葬品、唐代的唐三彩铅釉器皿和塑像、以泥釉凸纹来展现图案轮廓的明代三彩庙饰以及模仿贵重材料器皿烧制而成的诸多入葬陶瓷品。

neonate[10] ['niːəneɪt]

【释义】 *n.* 新生儿，初生婴儿（尤指出生不满四周的）
【例句】 For example, if a uniformly moving pattern of some sort is passed across the visual field of a neonate (newborn), repetitive following movements of the eye occur. (TPO13, R, S2, T2) 例如，如果有某种均匀的移动形式通过过新生儿的视线范围，就会出现眼睛重复移动进行跟随的活动。
【搭配】 neonate psychology 新生儿心理学

ore[10] [ɔː(r)]

【释义】 *n.* 矿石，矿
【例句】 This has been so since ancient times, partly due to the geology of the area, which is mostly limestone and sandstone, with few deposits of metallic ore and other useful materials. (TPO16, R, S1, T1) 自古以来就是这样，部分原因在于该地的地质，这里的地质以石灰石、砂岩为主，只有少量金属矿藏和其他有用的原料。
【搭配】 iron ore 铁矿石
ore deposit 矿床，矿层

outflow[10] ['aʊtˌfləʊ]

【释义】 *n.* 流出，流出量
【例句】 Two types of flow features are seen: runoff channels and outflow channels. (TPO8, R, S2, T2) 我们可以看到两种类型的流动特征：径流通道和泄流通道。

parasite[10] ['pærəsaɪt]

【释义】 *n.* 寄生生物，寄生虫
【例句】 Parasitism is a kind of predator-prey relationship in which one organism, the parasite, derives its food at the expense of its symbiotic associate, the host. (TPO17, R, S2, T2) 寄生是捕食者与被食者之间的一种关系，其中一种生物，也就是寄生生物，通过掠夺其共生方，也就是宿主，来获取自身所需食物。
【派生】 parasitic *a.* 寄生的

Word List 15

peel[10] [piːl]

【释义】*v.* 剥皮，削皮，剥落 *n.* 皮，外皮

【例句】And if you peel birch bark in the winter, we call it "the winter bark", another layer, a tougher inner layer of the tree, adheres to the bark, producing a stronger material. (TPO7, L, S2, T1) 而且，如果你在冬天剥去白桦树的树皮，我们叫它"冬树皮"，那么另外一层，更加坚韧的紧贴树皮的树层就可以长出更强硬的材料。

【搭配】peel off 离开，分离

permanent[10] [ˈpɜːmənənt]

【释义】*a.* 永久的，持久的（everlasting, perpetual）

【例句】It's got peaks and valleys, vegetation, rocky areas, and some sea animals have developed permanent colors or shapes to resemble these environmental features. (TPO13, S, Q6)（海底）有山峰和山谷、植被、岩石，一些海洋动物已经具有了永久的颜色和形状来与这些环境特点保持相似。

【反义】temporary

【派生】permanence *n.* 永久，持久

pest[10] [pest]

【释义】*n.* 1. 害虫 2. 讨厌的人或物

【例句】To take an extreme example, farmlands dominated by a single crop are so unstable that one year of bad weather or the invasion of a single pest can destroy the entire crop. (TPO3, R, S1, T2) 举个极端的例子，单一作物的农田是极不稳定的，以至于一年的恶劣天气或一种害虫的入侵就可以摧毁所有作物。

popularity[10] [ˌpɒpjuˈlærɪtɪ]

【释义】*n.* 受大众欢迎，普及，流行

【例句】Though some early critics thought that sound film would fade, its popularity during the First World War proved that it was not simply a technical novelty. (TPO12, R, S2, T1) 虽然一些早期的评论家认为有声电影会逐渐消失，但其在一战期间的流行却证明这并不仅仅是一个技术上的新生事物。

【逆构】popular *a.* 流行的，受欢迎的

【搭配】gain in popularity 逐渐开始受欢迎

primitive[10] [ˈprɪmɪtɪv]

【释义】*a.* 1. 原始的，早期的（ancient, original）2. 简陋的 *n.* 原（始）人，原始事物

【例句】So are you saying there might be primitive life on the moon? (TPO5, L, S1, L2) 你是说月球上有原始生命喽？

【派生】primitiveness *n.* 原始，原始性

privilege[10] [ˈprɪvɪlɪdʒ]

【释义】*n.* 特权，优惠 v. 给予…特权，特免

【例句】So you signed up for extended borrowing privileges? (TPO9, L, S2, C1) 你续借了吗？

【派生】privileged *a.* 有特权的；荣幸的

【搭配】an exclusive privilege 专有特权

profound[10] [prəˈfaʊnd]

【释义】*a.* 1. 深刻的，深奥的，意义深远的（deep, thorough）

【例句】But the most profound reason for the restoration of high population numbers has been the fate of the forests. (TPO4, R, S1, T1) 但是（鹿群）能恢复到较高数量的最深层的原因是森林的命运。

【反义】shallow

【派生】profoundly *ad.* 深深地
profoundness *n.* 深度

【搭配】profound knowledge 渊博的知识
profound sympathy 深切的同情
a profound sleep 酣睡

proton[10] [ˈprəutɒn]

【释义】*n.* [物] 质子

【例句】The elements are arranged in order of increasing atomic number (the number of protons in the nucleus). (TPO16, R, S2, T1) 元素是按照原子序数（原子核内的质子数）的递增排列的。

返记菜单

peel[10] permanent[10] pest[10] popularity[10] primitive[10]
privilege[10] profound[10] proton[10]

questionable[10] [ˈkwestʃənəb (ə) l]

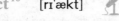

【释义】*a.* 可疑的，有疑问的（doubtful, uncertain）

【例句】The reading's arguments that the portrait is of Austen are questionable at best. (TPO12, W, Q1) 文章中有关这幅画画的是奥斯汀的有关论证无论如何是存在疑问的。

react[10] [rɪˈækt]

【释义】*v.* 1. 起反应 2. 反作用；影响 3. 背离，反抗

【例句】Babies just react to things that happen directly to them. (TPO10, S, Q6) 婴儿只对直接发生在他们身上的事做出反应。

【派生】reaction *n.* 反应，反作用（力）

【搭配】react on 起作用于；对…有影响
react against 反抗，反对；起反作用

rope[10] [rəʊp]

【释义】*n.* 绳索 *v.* 用绳捆

【例句】And this combination of characteristics—long, strong, flexible, resistant to salt water—makes Manila hemp a great material for ropes. (TPO2, L, S1, L2) 马拉加麻茎杆长、强壮、柔韧、抗盐水，这些特征综合在一起，使其成为制作绳子非常好的材料。

【搭配】be on the ropes 处于困境中
at the end of one's rope 一筹莫展，智穷力竭
throw someone a rope（在危难时）援助某人

seasonal[10] [ˈsiːzənl]

【释义】*a.* 季节的，季节性的

【例句】But the Maya homeland lies more than sixteen hundred kilometers from the equator, at latitudes 17 to 22 degrees north, in a habitat termed a "seasonal tropical forest." (TPO14, R, S2, T1) 但玛雅人的家园距离赤道 1600 多公里，位于北纬 17° 到 22° 之间一个被称为"季节性热带森林"的地方。

shade[10] [ʃeɪd]

【释义】*n.* 1. 遮光物，帘 2. 荫，阴凉处；阴影（shadow）
v. 1. 遮蔽 2. 画阴影于…之上，使变暗

【例句】It let him make these really intricate flowery designs for stained glass, which are used in lamp shades. (TPO16, L, S2, L2) 这让他为用来做灯罩的彩色玻璃设计了复杂绚丽的图案。

【派生】shady *a.* 多荫的；可疑的

【搭配】shades of［口语］令人想起…的
shade in 给…画阴影；逐渐变成

strip[10] [strɪp]

【释义】*n.* 条，带，条状物（band）*v.* 剥去，剥夺（peel, remove, deprive）

【例句】Mutoscope was a similar machine that reproduced motion by means of successive images on individual photographic cards instead of on strips of celluloid. (TPO2, R, S2, T2) Mutoscope 是与 Kinetoscope 相似的机器，它通过独立胶片上的连续影像来复制动态画面，而不是使用一条条的电影胶片。

【派生】stripper 脱衣舞女

trace[10] [treɪs]

【释义】*v.* 1. 发现；找到 2. 追踪，追溯 *n.* 1. 踪迹，痕迹 2. 极少量

【例句】Also beginning in the thirteenth century, there were new maps refined by precise calculations and the reports of sailors that made it possible to trace one's path with reasonable accuracy. (TPO17, R, S1, T1) 同样开始于 13 世纪，出现了经过精确测算的新地图和海员的报告，这使得较为准确的路线追踪变得可能。

【搭配】kick over the traces 挣脱羁绊，变得不服从

trail[10] [treɪl]

【释义】*n.* 1. 踪迹，痕迹（trace, track）2. 小径（path）
v. 1. 拖曳 2. 追踪

【例句】Ceramic products also include lead-glazed tomb models of the Han dynasty, three-color lead-glazed vessels and figures of the Tang dynasty, and Ming three-color temple ornaments, in which the motifs were outlined in a raised trail of slip—as well as the many burial ceramics produced in imitation of vessels made in materials of higher intrinsic value. (TPO10, R, S1, T1) 陶瓷制品还包括

汉代的铅釉墓葬品、唐代的唐三彩铅釉器皿和塑像、以泥釉凸纹来展现图案轮廓的明代三彩庙饰以及模仿贵重材料器皿烧制而成的诸多入葬陶瓷品。

【搭配】 on the trail 追踪，寻找

transition[10] [træn'zɪʃən] 

【释义】 *n.* 过渡，转变（change, transformation）

【例句】 The transition from forest to treeless tundra on a mountain slope is often a dramatic one. (TPO1, R, S1, T1) 从山坡上的树林转变为光秃秃的苔原的这一过程通常是显著而迅速的。

【派生】 transitional *a.* 转变的，变迁的

【搭配】 in the transition 在过渡阶段

troubadour[10] ['trubədɔr]

【释义】 *n.* 游吟诗人

【例句】 Another name for Romance Poetry that's often synonymous with it is troubadour poetry. (TPO13, L, S2, L1) 与浪漫主义诗歌有着相同意思的另外一个名称是吟游诗歌。

twist[10] [twɪst]

【释义】 *v.* 1. 搓，捻 2. 扭曲，使弯曲 3. 曲解…的意思 *n.* 1. 弯曲，拐弯处 2. 意想不到的转折

【例句】 And then you take that bundle of fibers and you twist it a little bit, because by twisting it, you increase its breaking strength even more. (TPO2, L, S1, L2) 然后，你拿起那束纤维并搓上几下，这样做是因为通过搓捻，纤维束的抗断能力会得到进一步加强。

【派生】 twisted *a.* 扭曲的；歪曲的
twisty *a.* 弯曲的，曲折的

【搭配】 twists and turns 迂回曲折之处；意想不到的转折
a twist in one's tongue 口齿不清

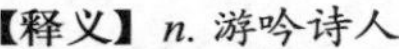

boring[9] ['bɔːrɪŋ]

【释义】 *a.* 无聊的，令人厌烦的，乏味的（tedious, tiresome）

【例句】 Honestly, I thought it was kind of slow and boring. (TPO4, L, S1, C1) 说实话，我觉得这有点拖沓沉闷。

【派生】 bored *a.* 无聊的，无趣的
boredom *n.* 烦恼，无聊

【逆构】 bore *v.* 使厌烦

adventure[9] [əd'ventʃə] 

【释义】 *n.* 冒险经历，奇遇（risk, venture）

【例句】 Thus by about 1400 the key elements were in place to enable Europe to begin its seaward adventure. (TPO17, R, S1, T1) 因此，到大约1400年，关键性因素已经成熟到可以让欧洲人开始海上冒险。

【派生】 adventureful *a.* 富于冒险事件的；奇遇的
adventurous *a.* 喜欢冒险的
adventurer *n.* 冒险家

budget[9] ['bʌdʒɪt]

【释义】 *n.* 预算 *v.* 为…编制预算 *a.* 合乎预算的，廉价的

【例句】 But they only succeeded in taking away about half the annual budget. (TPO4, L, S2, L2) 但他们只成功抽走了每年预算的一半。

【搭配】 budget for 为…作预算
on a budget 避免不必要的开支，节省费用

bundle[9] ['bʌndl] 

【释义】 *n.* (一)捆，(一)束（bunch, cluster）*v.* 1. 捆，扎 2. 把…匆匆送走

【例句】 Well, what you do is you extract these long fibers from the Manila hemp plant, and then you take several of these fibers, and you group them into a bundle. (TPO2, L, S1, L2) 你需要做的是将长纤维从马尼拉麻这种植物中提取出来，然后从中挑出几根长纤维，并将它们捆成一束。

【搭配】 a bundle of 一群；一包，一束，一捆

burrow[9] ['bʌrəʊ] 

【释义】 *n.* 地洞 *v.* 1. 挖掘(洞穴) 2. 翻寻

【例句】 Their burrows are easy to locate. (TPO1, L, S2, L2) 它们的洞非常容易找到。

【搭配】 burrow into 探查

cable[9] ['keɪbl] 

【释义】 *n.* 1. 缆绳 2. 电缆 3. 电报 *v.* 发电报

【例句】 In fact, by the early 1940's, even though

返记菜单

transition[10]	troubadour[10]	twist[10]	boring[9]	adventure[9]
budget[9]	bundle[9]	burrow[9]	cable[9]	

steel cables were available, most ships in the United States Navy were not moored with steel cables; they were moored with Manila hemp ropes. (TPO2, L, S1, L2) 事实上,在20世纪40年代早期,即使那时候已经有了钢丝绳,但是美国海军的大部分船只都不是用钢丝绳来停泊的,而是使用马尼拉麻绳。

cease[9] [siːs]

【释义】v. 停止,终止,结束(stop, end, terminate)
【例句】Without its stopping to feed and spread pollen from flower to flower, these plants would cease to exist. (TPO3, L, S1, L1) 如果没有它们停下来觅食并且将花粉在花朵之间传播开来,这些植物早就不存在了。
【搭配】without cease 不停地,不断地

classical[9] [ˈklæsɪkəl]

【释义】a. 古典的,经典的;传统的
【例句】Previously, large audiences had viewed spectacles at the theater, where vaudeville, popular dramas, musical and minstrel shows, classical plays, lectures, and slide-and-lantern shows had been presented to several hundred spectators at a time. (TPO2, R, S2, T2) 先前,大批观众在剧院观看表演,在那里,数百名观众可以同时观看轻歌舞剧、流行戏剧、音乐剧或歌唱表演、古典音乐、演讲和幻灯片放映。
【搭配】classical music 古典音乐

classify[9] [ˈklæsɪfaɪ]

【释义】v. 分类,归类(categorize, assort)
【例句】Now in a way, Painlevé's films conform to norms of the 20s and 30s, that is, they don't fit very neatly into the categories we use to classify films today. (TPO3, L, S1, L2) 现在从某种程度上来说,培乐威的电影与20年代和30年代的规范是一致的,也就是说,它们并不能被简单地归为我们用以划分当今电影的种类。
【派生】classification n. 分类,归类

copper[9] [ˈkɒpə]

【释义】n. 铜;铜币;紫铜色 v. 镀铜于
【例句】Most of Africa presents a curious case in which societies moved directly from a technology of stone to iron without passing through the intermediate stage of copper or bronze metallurgy, although some early copper-working sites have been found in West Africa. (TPO7, R, S2, T2) 非洲大部分地区都存在一种让人好奇的情况,就是其社会是从石器技术时代直接演化至铁器时代的,而没有经历青铜冶炼这一中间阶段,虽然人们曾在西非地区发现了早期炼铜厂的遗址。

cultivate[9] [ˈkʌltəveit]

【释义】v. 耕种,培养(farm, nurture, domesticate)
【例句】Whole villages began to cultivate fruit and vegetables. (TPO23, R, S2, T1) 整个村庄开始种植水果和蔬菜。
【派生】cultivation n. 耕种;培养

devise[9] [dɪˈvaɪz]

【释义】v. 设计,发明,策划(invent, make up)
【例句】In the absence of solid linguistic, archaeological, and biological data, many fanciful and mutually exclusive theories were devised. (TPO5, R, S2, T1) 由于没有确凿的语言学、考古学和生物学数据,所以人们想出了很多充满幻想、互相矛盾的理论。
【派生】deviser n. 设计者

dialect[9] [ˈdaɪəlekt]

【释义】n. 方言,土语
【例句】The section on dialects is the kind of thing that's always sort of intrigued me, you know? (TPO6, L, S2, C1) 方言的那一部分很是让我好奇,您知道吗?
【派生】dialectal a. 方言的,乡音的
【搭配】social dialect 社会方言

dinner[9] [ˈdɪnə]

【释义】n. 1. 正餐,主餐 2. 宴会
【例句】The university has announced that it will charge a small additional fee for these dinners in order to pay for the special gourmet food ingredients that will be required. (TPO5,

S, Q1) 学校已经宣布这些晚餐会收一点儿额外的费用，用以购买制作这些特殊的美味所需要的原材料。

【派生】 dinnerware *n.* 整套的餐具

discourage[9] [dɪsˈkʌrɪdʒ]

【释义】 *v.* 1. 阻碍，劝阻 2. 使气馁，使沮丧（depress）

【例句】 So I think most of us would be discouraged if we had to face challenges and difficulties like that. (TPO1, L, S1, L1) 所以我认为，假如面对那样的挑战和困难，我们大部分人都会气馁的。

distant[9] [ˈdɪstənt]

【释义】 *a.* 1. 远隔的，遥远的（faraway, remote）2. 疏远的，冷漠的

【例句】 In fact, many experts believe that the true subject of the portrait was one of those relatives, Marianne Kempian, who was a distant niece of Austen's. (TPO12, W, Q1) 实际上许多专家认为画中真正的主人公就是那些亲戚中的一个，Marianne Kempian，她是奥斯汀的一个远方侄女。

【派生】 distance *n.* 距离

dominate[9] [ˈdɒmɪneɪt]

【释义】 *v.* 1. 控制，支配（control, rule）2. 占优势，盛行（prevail）

【例句】 This capacity for increased expressiveness, in fact, was essential to the Romantic style that dominated 19th century music. (TPO16, L, S1, L2) 实际上对于主导着19世纪音乐的浪漫主义音乐来说，加强表现力是很重要的。

【派生】 dominant *a.* 支配的，首要的，占优势的
dominance *n.* 支配地位，优势

earthenware[9] [ˈɜːθənweə]

【释义】 *n.* 陶器

【例句】 The ceramics fall into three broad types—earthenware, stoneware, and porcelain—for vessels, architectural items such as roof tiles, and modeled objects and figures. (TPO10, R, S1, T1) 陶制瓷器从广义上可以被分为3大类：陶器、石器以及瓷器，比如容器、瓦片等建筑材料以及物体和人物模型。

elaborate[9]

【释义】 [ɪˈlæbərət] *a.* 复杂的；精心制作的（detailed, intricate）[iˈlæbəˌret] *v.* 详尽说明，详细制定（detail）

【例句】 So more space could be used for window openings allowing for large and quite elaborate window designs. (TPO16, L, S2, L2) 因此可以利用更多的空间来使窗户更大，设计更精致。

【派生】 elaboration *n.* 精心制作；详细阐述

【搭配】 elaborate on 详细说明…

empire[9] [ˈempaɪə]

【释义】 *n.* 帝国

【例句】 Horses were adopted by peoples of the West African savannah, and later their powerful cavalry forces allowed them to carve out large empires. (TPO7, R, S2, T2) 马匹被西非大草原居民所饲养，之后，居民们所拥有的强劲的骑兵使其得以开拓出大片疆域。

【搭配】 the Roman Empire 罗马帝国

employ[9] [ɪmˈplɔɪ]

【释义】 *v.* 雇用，使用，利用（hire）*n.* 雇用，受雇

【例句】 In order for the structure to achieve the size and strength necessary to meet its purpose, architecture employs methods of support that, because they are based on physical laws, have changed little since people first discovered them-even while building materials have changed dramatically. (TPO3, R, S1, T1) 建筑结构必须达到大小和强度的要求，以实现必要的建筑目的，因此建筑学上采用一些支撑的方法，这些方法都是以物理定律为基础的，尽管建筑材料已经发生了翻天覆地的变化，但是这些支撑方法自人们首次发现以来却鲜有变化。

【派生】 employee *n.* 受雇者，雇员
employer *n.* 雇主

enclose[9] [ɪnˈkləʊz]

【释义】 *v.* 1. 把…围起来，围绕 2. 把…装入封套，附入

返记菜单

discourage[9] distant[9] dominate[9] earthenware[9] elaborate[9]
empire[9] employ[9] enclose[9]

【例句】Architecture is the art and science of designing structures that organize and enclose space for practial and symbolic purposes. (TPO3, R, S1, T1) 建筑学是结构设计的艺术和科学，它以实用和象征为目的对空间予以组织和包围。
【派生】enclosure *n.* 围绕；围墙

enroll[9] [ɪn'rəʊl]

【释义】*v.* 登记，注册；招收，入伍（register, recruit）
【例句】Do you know how many people have to be enrolled in order to keep a class from being cancelled? (TPO3, L, S1, C1) 你知道需要有多少人报名才能保证一个班不被取消吗？
【派生】enrolment *n.* 登记，注册，入学
【搭配】enroll in 参加；选课

evaluate[9] [ɪ,væljueɪt]

【释义】*v.* 评价，评估（judge, appraise）
【例句】Further observation revealed the tendency of teachers to evaluate events rather than review the contributory factors in a considered manner by, in effect, standing outside the situation. (TPO9, R, S2, T1) 进一步的观察发现，教师们更倾向于评价事件，而不是站在事件之外以一种深思熟虑的方式洞察一个事件的促成因素。
【派生】evaluable *a.* 可估值的，可评估的
evaluation *n.* 评估，估价

extract[9] [ɪks'trækt]

【释义】*v.* 1. 提取，萃取 2. 摘录，节选 3. 抽出，拔出 *n.* 1. 摘录 2. 提取物
【例句】Well, what you do is you extract these long fibers from the Manila hemp plant. (TPO2, L, S1, L2) 你需要做的是将长纤维从马尼拉麻这种植物中提取出来。
【派生】extraction *n.* 抽取；萃取法

faculty[9] ['fækəltɪ]

【释义】*n.* 1.（高等院校中院、系的）全体教师（staff）2. 能力，才能（aptitude, ability）
【例句】He worked there before joining the university faculty. (TPO9, L, S1, C1) 在成为大学教师之前，他在那里工作。
【搭配】a retentive faculty 记忆力

fear[9] [fɪə]

【释义】*n./v.* 担心，害怕，恐惧
【例句】But the alligators grew to huge sizes and now strike fear into sewer workers. (TPO5, L, S1, L1) 但是现在鳄鱼的体型已经很大了，这让下水道工人感到非常害怕。
【派生】fearful *a.* 可怕的；严重的
fearless *a.* 无畏的，大胆的

gender[9] ['dʒendə]

【释义】*n.* 1. 性别 2.（语法中的）性
【例句】Inequalities of gender have also existed in pastoralist societies, but they seem to have been softened by the absence of steep hierarchies of wealth in most communities, and also by the requirement that women acquire most of the skills of men, including, often, their military skills. (TPO14, R, S2, T2) 性别不平等现象也同样存在于游牧社会，但是因为在大多数的群体中并不存在明显的财富分级，同时因为妇女也需要掌握大多数男人所拥有的技能，通常还包括军事技能，所以这种现象似乎被弱化了。

handle[9] ['hændl]

【释义】*v.* 1. 处理，应付（deal, treat）；拿，触，摸 *n.* 柄，把手
【例句】Now, for this group of people, business people, the company will have to show how efficient their phone is, how it can handle all business easily and maybe even save money. (TPO5, S, Q2) 现在，对于这些商人来说，手机公司将不得不向其展示他们的手机是多么有效，这手机是怎样轻松处理所有商业事务的，或许甚至还能省钱。
【搭配】handle with 处理

harvest[9] ['hɑːvɪst]

【释义】*n.* 收成，收获 *v.* 收获，收割
【例句】In modern agriculture, mineral depletion of soils is a major concern, since harvesting crops interrupts the recycling of nutrients back to the soil. (TPO5, R, S1, T1) 在现代农

业中,土壤中矿物质的消耗是一个值得担忧的问题,因为收割庄稼会扰乱土壤养分回归土壤的循环。

【派生】 harvestable *a.* 随时可收获的

hence[9] [hens] 

【释义】 *ad.* 1. 因此,所以(thus,as a result of) 2. 今后,从此

【例句】 Generally, the layering occurs on an annual basis, hence the observed changes in the records can be dated. (TPO10, R, S2, T1) 通常,分层堆积是每年发生的,因此记录中观察到的变化是可以确定日期的。

hind[9] [haɪnd] 

【释义】 *a.* 后部的,后面的(back, rear)

【例句】 Their streamlined bodies, the absence of hind legs, and the presence of a fluke and blowhole cannot disguise their affinities with land dwelling mammals. (TPO2, R, S2, T1) 它们的身体呈流线型,没有后腿,长有尾片和喷水孔,但这些都不能掩盖它们与陆生哺乳动物的相似性。

【反义】 front

honor[9] ['ɒnə] 

【释义】 *n.* 尊敬,敬意,荣誉(respect, fame, glory) *v.* 尊敬;给…以荣誉

【例句】 Well, it's a huge honor to win, and there's an award ceremony they've invited me to attend, which I'm so excited about, but…and here's what's frustrating: I've got a biology exam that's scheduled for the same time! (TPO3, S, Q5) 能获得胜利是一个很大的荣誉,而且他们已经邀请我参加颁奖典礼,我感到很兴奋,但是有一件事让我很纠结:颁奖典礼的同一时间我得参加一个生物考试。

【派生】 honorable *a.* 可敬的,光荣的

【搭配】 a sense of honor 荣誉感

ignore[9] [ɪg'nɔː] 

【释义】 *v.* 不顾,不理,忽视(disregard, overlook, neglect)

【例句】 And even though some members tried to warn the rest of the group that the project was moving in directions that might not work, they were basically ignored by other group members. (TPO2, W, Q1) 即使一些成员极力警告其他的成员,这一项目按目前的方式进行下去并不会很奏效,但其他成员均不予理睬。

【派生】 ignorant *a.* 无知的,愚昧的
ignorance *n.* 无知,愚昧

income[9] ['ɪnkəm] 

【释义】 *n.* 收入,所得,收益(earning)

【例句】 In Sweden, exports accounted for 18 percent of the national income in 1870, and in 1913, 22 percent of a much larger national income. (TPO18, R, S1, T1) 在1870年,瑞典的出口额占到了国民收入的18%,而到1913年,国民收入更多,而出口额更是占到了22%。

【搭配】 income tax 所得税
income gap 收入差距
disposable income 可支配收入

indirect[9] [ˌɪndɪ'rekt] 

【释义】 *a.* 间接的,迂回的,婉转的

【例句】 Because they cannot verbalize or fill out questionnaires, indirect techniques of naturalistic observation are used as the primary means of determining what infants can see, hear, feel, and so forth. (TPO13, R, S2, T2) 因为他们无法用言语表达或者填写问卷,所以自然观察这种间接技术就被用做确定婴儿看、听、感知等结果的主要手段。

【反义】 direct

【搭配】 an indirect route 迂回的路线

irrelevant[9] [ɪ'relɪvənt] 

【释义】 *a.* 不相干的,不恰当的(inconnected, unrelated)

【例句】 So, the displacement activity, the grooming, the straightening of its feathers, seems to be an irrelevant behavior. (TPO4, L, S1, L1) 所以,修饰整理自己的羽毛这一替换活动看起来是一种不相干的行为。

【逆构】 relevant *a.* 有关的

livestock[9] ['laɪvstɒk] 

【释义】 *n.* 家畜,牲畜(cattle)

【例句】The raising of livestock is a major economic activity in semiarid lands. (TPO2, R, Sl, T1) 饲养家畜是半干旱地区主要的一项经济活动。

lizard[9] ['lɪzəd]

【释义】*n.* 蜥蜴

【例句】But running is efficient only if an animal's legs are positioned underneath its body, not at the body's side, as they are for crocodiles and many lizards. (TPO4, W, Q1) 但是只有当动物的腿长在身体下面而不是身体两侧时才可以跑得快，就如鳄鱼和多种蜥蜴。

magnetic[9] [mæg'netɪk]

【释义】*a.* 1. 磁的，有磁性的 2. 有吸引力的（alluring, attractive）

【例句】Maybe the rocks are moved by a magnetic force. (TPO4, L, S2, L1) 也许岩石是在磁力作用下运动的。

【派生】agnetism *n.* 磁，磁力
magnetize *v.* 使磁化；吸引

【逆构】magnet *n.* 磁铁

【搭配】magnetic field 磁场

mantle[9] ['mæntl]

【释义】*n.* 1. 地幔 2. 覆盖物 *v.* 覆盖，笼罩

【例句】You know planetary researchers love studying deep craters until they learn about the impacts that created them, how they redistributed pieces of a planet's crust and in this case, we especially want to know if any of the mantle, the layer beneath the crust, was exposed by the impact. (TPO5, L, S1, L2) 你知道的，行星研究者们热衷于研究深火山口，直到了解形成火山的冲击力以及这些冲击力是如何对一颗行星的地壳进行重新分配的，在这样的情况下，我们尤其想知道是否有地幔（地壳下面的一层）在这种冲击之下暴露了出来。

【派生】mantled *a.* 披着斗篷的

mystery[9] ['mɪstəri:]

【释义】*n.* 迷，不可思议的事；秘密，神秘

【例句】Why and how these people spread out into central and southern Africa remains a mystery, but archaeologists believe that their iron weapons allowed them to conquer their hunting-gathering opponents, who still used stone implements. (TPO7, R, S2, T2) 这些人们为何以及是如何迁徙至非洲中南部的，至今仍是未解的谜题。不过考古学家们认为，他们的铁制武器使其能够战胜那些仍然使用石质工具、以狩猎为生的对手。

【逆构】mysterious *a.* 神秘的，不可思议的

occurrence[9] [ə'kʌrəns]

【释义】*n.* 发生；事件

【例句】It attributes both desirable and undesirable occurrences to supernatural or magical forces. (TPO1, R, S2, T1) 他们把尽如人意和不尽如人意的偶发事件都归因于超自然的或魔法的力量。

Word List 16

official[9] [ə'fɪʃəl] 

【释义】*n.* 官员，行政人员 *a.* 官方的，正式的

【例句】A university official announced plans to spend $2 million to build a new athletic stadium, commenting that a new stadium would help the university achieve its goal of attracting more top students. (TPO13, S, Q3) 一位大学官员宣布，计划花费200万美元修建一座新的体育场，他说新体育馆的建成将帮助学校达成吸引更多顶尖学生的目标。

【搭配】government officials 政府官员

overcome[9] [ˌəuvə'kʌm] 

【释义】*v.* 战胜，克服，解决(defeat, conquer)

【例句】It describes and comments on steps taken to overcome problems identified earlier in the passage. (TPO9, R, S2, T1) 它描述并且评论了之前在文中提到的解决问题的步骤。

【反义】submit, surrender

【搭配】overcome one's nervousness 克服紧张情绪

overtime[9] ['əuvətaɪm] 

【释义】*n.* 加班时间，(比赛)延长时间 *ad.* 超时地

【例句】Unlike building materials, the methods of support used in architecture have not changed overtime because they are based on physical laws. (TPO3, R, S1, T1) 与建筑材料不同，运用在建筑中的支撑方法并未随着时间发生变化，因为它们是以物理定律为依据的。

palimpsest[9] ['pælɪmpsest] 

【释义】*n.*(原有文字已擦去的)重写本

【例句】A manual script page that was written on, erased and then used again is called a palimpsest. (TPO15, L, S2, L1) 一张被写上字，然后被擦掉，然后又经重复利用的书页就叫做重写本。

passive[9] ['pæsɪv] 

【释义】*a.* 被动的，消极的

【例句】But we do have more complex systems that are used for space heating and they fall into two categories, passive and active heating systems. (TPO12, L, S2, L2) 但是我们的确拥有更复杂的用于空间加热的系统，它们分成两类，被动加热系统和主动加热系统。

【反义】active

【派生】passiveness *n.* 被动；顺从

peak[9] [piːk] 

【释义】*a.* 最高的；高峰的 *v.* 达到顶峰 *n.* 最高点，顶峰(top, summit)

【例句】Well, much of the soil is usually still frozen during peak run-off. (TPO9, L, S1, L2) 在融雪高峰期的时候，通常大部分的土壤仍处于冰冻状态。

【搭配】peak load 最大负荷

penetrate[9] ['penɪtreɪt] 

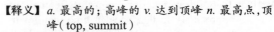

【释义】*v.* 穿过，穿透，渗透(pierce, permeate)

【例句】Knowledge of iron making penetrated into the forests and savannahs of West Africa at roughly the same time that iron making was reaching Europe. (TPO7, R, S2, T2) 冶铁知识传播到了西非的森林和热带草原地区，几乎与此同时，冶铁技术也传播到了欧洲。

【派生】penetrating *a.*(声音)响亮的，尖锐的，(气味)刺激的；敏锐的，有洞察力的

【搭配】penetrate into/through sth. 进入或穿过某物

personality[9] [ˌpɜːsə'nælɪtɪ] 

【释义】*n.* 1. 个性 2. 名人 3. 特色

【例句】After a minute, everyone was asked to describe the boy's personality. (TPO12, S, Q5) 一分钟后，每个人都被要求描述一下那个孩子的个性。

【逆构】personal *a.* 个人的

plentiful[9] ['plentɪful] 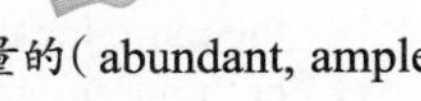

【释义】*a.* 丰富的，充足的，大量的(abundant, ample, sufficient, enough)

返记菜单

official[9] overcome[9] overtime[9] palimpsest[9] passive[9]
peak[9] penetrate[9] personality[9] plentiful[9]

【例句】In the 1930s, wells encountered plentiful water at a depth of about 15 meters; currently, they must be dug to depths of 45 to 60 meters or more. (TPO3, R, S1, T1) 在20世纪30年代,井下15米就有丰富的水资源,而现在,必须挖掘到45米到60米甚至更深的地方才行。

【反义】scarce, scant

【派生】plentifulness *n.* 大量,丰富

【逆构】plenty *n.* 充裕,大量

proxy[9] ['prɒksɪ]

【释义】*n.* 代理人;代理权;委托书

【例句】To build up a better picture of fluctuations appreciably further back in time requires us to use proxy records. (TPO10, R, S2, T1) 为了建立一个更好的关于过去的变化的描述,我们需要使用替代记录。

【搭配】proxy service 代理服务

pursue[9] [pə'sjuː]

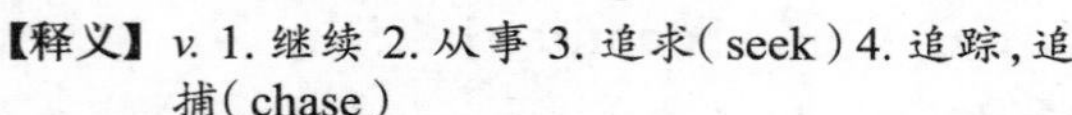

【释义】*v.* 1. 继续 2. 从事 3. 追求(seek)4. 追踪,追捕(chase)

【例句】I wanted to get my academic work settled before persuing my music here. (TPO5, L, S1, C1) 在这里继续我的音乐爱好之前,我想先完成好我的学习。

【派生】pursuit *n.* 追求;职业

relevant[9] ['relɪvənt]

【释义】*a.* 有关的,切题的,中肯的(related)

【例句】He thinks the topic is not relevant for a linguistics class. (TPO6, L, S2, C1) 他觉得这个课题和语言学无关。

【反义】irrelevant

【派生】relevance *n.* 相关

reward[9] [rɪ'wɔːd]

【释义】*n.* 报酬,报答,奖赏 *v.* 酬谢,奖赏(compensate)

【例句】As the number of visitors, eco-tourists who come to humming bird habitats to watch the birds, the more the number of visitors grows, the more local businesses' profit, so ecological tourism can bring financial rewards, all the more reason to value these beautiful little creatures in their habitat, right? (TPO3, L, S1, L1) 至于到蜂鸟栖息地观看这些鸟儿们的游客的数量,数量增长越多,为当地带来的商业利润也就越大,因此生态旅游业可以带来财政收益,这是保护这些漂亮的小生物更为重要的原因,是吧?

【派生】rewarding *a.* 报答的,值得的

row[9] [raʊ]

【释义】*n.* 1. 行,排 2. 划船 3. 吵闹 *v.* 1. 划船 2. 使…成排 3. 争吵

【例句】The series of elements was written so as to begin a new horizontal row with each alkali metal. (TPO16, R, S2, T1) 写下这一系列元素,从而以每个碱金属开始一个新的水平行列。

【搭配】in a row 连续,成一长行
front row 前排,头一排
row over 从容胜过,一路领先

score[9] [skɔː]

【释义】*n.* 1. 二十 2. 得分,比分 *v.* 1. 得(分)2. 刻痕于

【例句】It suddenly became public—an experience that the viewer shared with dozens, scores, and even hundreds of others. (TPO2, R, S2, T2) 电影一夜之间走向大众——观众能够和几十人、甚至上百人共同观看一部电影。

【搭配】scores of 几十个

seek[9] [siːk]

【释义】*v.* 试图;寻求,追求(pursue, search)

【例句】Ah, it's just a term that describes this situation, when people in the group seek to get the benefits of being in a group without contributing to the work. (TPO4, L, S2, C1) 嗯,就是这个词语,它描述了团队成员并未对团队工作作出贡献却试图从中获益的情形。

【搭配】seek for 寻找,追求;探索
seek out 找出,搜出
seek through 搜查遍
hide and seek 捉迷藏

semiarid[9] ['semɪ'ærɪd]

【释义】 *a.* 半干旱的

【例句】 Well, shrub expansion has occurred in other environments, like semiarid grassland, and tall grass prairies. (TPO9, L, S1, L2) 灌木扩张已经出现在其他环境中,比如半干旱草原地带和高草原地区。

senior[9] ['siːnjə]

【释义】 *a.* 1.(级别、地位等)较高的 2. 年长的 *n.* 1. 年长者(elder)2. 四年级学生

【例句】 A senior researcher, I think you know John Franklin, my assistant, is on site every day. (TPO3, L, S2, C1) 我想你应该知道我的助理约翰·富兰克林,一位资深的研究员,他每天都在。

【派生】 seniority *n.* 长辈,上级;资历

【搭配】 senior engineer 高级工程师

sheet[9] [ʃiːt]

【释义】 *n.* 1. 薄片,一大片 2. 纸张;薄板 3. 床单

【例句】 It's possible that rain on the desert floor could turn to thin sheets of ice when temperatures drop at night. (TPO4, L, S2, L1) 当夜间温度下降后,落到沙漠地面上的雨水有可能会变成薄冰层。

shelter[9] ['ʃeltə] 

【释义】 *v.* 掩蔽,庇护(hide, conceal)*n.* 掩蔽处;庇护所

【例句】 Humans instinctively seek structures that will shelter and enhance their way of life. (TPO3, R, S1, T1) 人类会本能地寻找可以庇护并改善其生活质量的建筑。

【派生】 sheltery *a.* 遮蔽的,庇护的

stimulate[9] ['stɪmjʊleɪt] 

【释义】 *v.* 刺激;激励,激发(motivate, encourage, spur, arouse)

【例句】 In the seventeenth century, the trading activities of the Dutch East India Company resulted in vast quantities of decorated Chinese porcelain being brought to Europe, which stimulated and influenced the work of a wide variety of wares, notably Delft. (TPO10, R, S1, T1) 17世纪时,荷兰东印度公司的贸易活动使得大量精致的中国瓷器流入欧洲,刺激和影响了很多器皿的制作,尤其是代尔夫特陶器。

【派生】 stimulation *n.* 刺激,鼓舞,激励
stimulus *n.* 刺激;刺激物
stimulant *n.* 刺激物,兴奋剂

【搭配】 stimulate economic growth 拉动经济增长

string[9] [strɪŋ]

【释义】 *n.* 1.(乐器的)弦 2. 线,绳,带子 3. 一串,一列

【例句】 There is a string quartet on campus, all students. (TPO5, L, S1, C1) 校园中将有一场弦乐四重奏,所有学生都会去看。

【派生】 stringer *n.* 拉线人;特约通讯员
on the string 在某人的彻底控制或影响下

substantial[9] [səb'stænʃəl] 

【释义】 *a.* 1. 大量的,可观的(considerable, significant)2. 坚固的;结实的(sturdy, solid, firm)3. 实质的(actual, authentic)

【例句】 Even in the areas that retain a soil cover, the reduction of vegetation typically results in the loss of the soil's ability to absorb substantial quantities of water. (TPO2, R, Sl, T1) 即使是在那些仍有土壤覆盖地表的地区,植被减少一般也会导致土壤无法吸收足够的水分。

【反义】 insubstantial

【派生】 substantially *ad.* 大量的
substantiality *n.* 实质性

systematic[9] [ˌsɪstɪ'mætɪk] 

【释义】 *a.* 成体系的,系统的

【例句】 Wildman and Niles observed that systematic reflection on teaching required a sound ability to understand classroom events in an objective manner. (TPO9, R, S2, T1) Wildman和Niles观察到,系统的教学反思需要具备一种可靠的能力,从而以一种客观的方式来理解教室中所发生的事。

【派生】 systermatically *ad.* 系统地

systemtize *v.* 使系统化
【逆构】 systerm *n.* 系统,体系

tough[9] [tʌf]

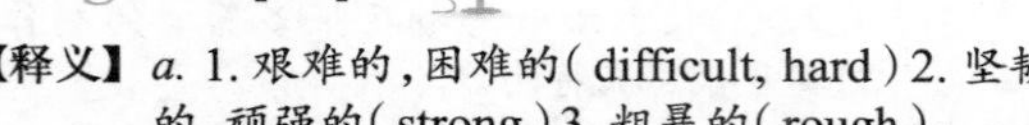

【释义】 *a.* 1. 艰难的,困难的(difficult, hard) 2. 坚韧的,顽强的(strong) 3. 粗暴的(rough)
【例句】 It's gotten really tough to find a space. (TPO2, S, Q3) 现在找个停车位真是太困难了。
【反义】 easy; tender
【派生】 toughen *v.* 使坚韧,使顽强
toughly *ad.* 顽强地
toughness *n.* 坚韧,顽强

unity[9] ['juːnɪtɪ]

【释义】 *n.* 1. 协调,统一 2. 团结一致,结合
【例句】 Effective designs create a delicate balance between two things; you need unity and you also need contrast which is essentially a break in unity. (TPO11, S, Q6) 有效的设计能够在两者达到一种微妙的平衡;你需要统一性,同时你还需要在统一中对比出哪一个实质上是打破平衡的。
【逆构】 unite *v.* 联合
【搭配】 live together in unity 和睦相处

universal[9] [ˌjuːnɪ'vɜːsəl]

【释义】 *a.* 普遍的,全体的,共同的;宇宙的,全世界的(common, general, cosmopolitan)
【例句】 If you could find such a thing, that would be the universal final good. (TPO2, L, S2, L1) 如果你可以找到那样的一件事物,那将会是所有人最终的福祉。
【搭配】 universal truth 普遍真理

vent[9] [vent]

【释义】 *n.* 通风口,排放口 *v.* 1. 从开口处排放 2. 表达,发泄
【例句】 It all began in 1977 with the exploration of hydrothermal vents on the ocean floor. (TPO15, L, S2, L2) 它是于1977年伴随着对海底热液喷口的勘测全面展开的。
【派生】 ventilate *v.* 使通风

abstract[8]

【释义】 ['æbstrækt] *a.* 抽象的 *n.* 1. 抽象派艺术作品 2. 摘要,梗概 [əb'strækt] *v.* 1. 提取,抽取 2. 做…的摘要
【例句】 The concepts of teacher reflection were so abstract that they could not be applied. (TPO9, R, S2, T1, Q5) 教师反思的概念如此抽象以至于不能得到应用。
【派生】 abstraction *n.* 抽象,抽象概念

adjacent[8] [ə'dʒeɪsənt]

【释义】 *a.* 邻近的,毗连的,接近的(adjoining, nearby, neighboring)
【例句】 Water or steam may be pumped down adjacent wells to help push the oil out. (TPO4, R, S2, T2) 为了将石油抽出来,可能会把水或蒸汽注入相邻的井里。
【派生】 adjacency *n.* 毗邻;四周
adjacently *ad.* 邻近地
【搭配】 adjacent to 与…相邻

appealing[8] [ə'piːlɪŋ]

【释义】 *a.* 1. 有魅力的,动人的,吸引人的(pleseant, charming)
【例句】 Architects seek to create buildings that are both visually appealing and well suited for human use. (TPO3, R, S1, T1) 建筑师们力求创造出既吸引人又适宜于人们使用的建筑。
【逆构】 appeal *v.* 有吸引力,有感染力

board[8] [bɔːd]

【释义】 *n.* 1. 板,木板 2. 委员会 *v.* 1. 上(飞机、车、船等) 2. 提供膳宿
【例句】 I'm going to start by writing some numbers on the board. (TPO2, L, S2, L2) 首先,我将会在黑板上写一些数字。
【派生】 boarding *n.* 木板
boarder *n.* 寄宿生
【搭配】 boarding school 寄宿学校
on board 在(船、车、飞机等)上
above board 光明正大地

brush[8] [brʌʃ] 

【释义】*n.* 1. 刷子；画笔 2. 轻拂，掠过 *v.* 1.（用刷子）刷，涂抹 2. 拭去，除去 3. 擦过，掠过

【例句】Right-handed artists try to avoid having the brush they are using interfere with the light source. (TPO12, R, S1, T1, Q4) 使用右手的艺术家尽量避免在使用画笔的时候让画笔挡住光源。

【派生】brushstroke *n.* 一笔

【搭配】brush away 刷去
brush past 擦过
brush up on 温习，复习

butter[8] ['bʌtə] 

【释义】*n.* 黄油 *v.* 涂黄油于…上

【例句】And an increase in the price of one means an increase in the demand for the other, like butter and margarine. (TPO12, S, Q6) 一种商品涨价意味着对另一种商品的需求增加，就像黄油和人造奶油。

【派生】buttered *a.* 涂奶油的，加奶油的

【搭配】butter up 谄媚，说好话

camouflage[8] ['kæmʊflɑːʒ] 

【释义】*v.* 伪装，掩饰（disguise）*n.* 1. 伪装，掩饰 2. 迷彩服

【例句】Many species of amphibians (frogs and toads) and reptiles (lizards and snakes) are able to change their color patterns to camouflage themselves. (TPO17, R, S2, T1) 很多两栖动物（青蛙、蟾蜍等）和爬行动物（蜥蜴、蛇等）都可以通过改变外表颜色来伪装自己。

【搭配】stratégic camouflage 战略伪装

cement[8] [sɪ'ment] 

【释义】*n.* 1. 水泥 2. 结合剂 *v.* 粘结，胶合

【例句】Like the stones of a Roman wall which were held together both by the regularity of the design and by that peculiarly powerful Roman cement, so the various parts of the Roman realm were bonded into a massive, monolithic entity by physical, organizational, and psychological controls. (TPO7, R, S2, T1) 如同罗马墙是通过规律的设计和独特有效的罗马水泥构筑而成一样，罗马王国的各个部分也是通过对物质、组织和心理层面的支配而联结成一个规模宏大、坚如磐石的统一体的。

compass[8] ['kʌmpəs] 

【释义】*n.* 1. 指南针，罗盘 2. 圆规 3. 范围

【例句】They seemed to be using the Sun as a compass to determine direction. (TPO11, R, S2, T1) 它们好像是以太阳作为指南针来确定方向。

【搭配】within the compass of 在…的范围内

complicated[8] ['kɒmplɪkeɪtɪd] 

【释义】*a.* 复杂的；难懂的，费解的（intricate, complex, sophisticated）

【例句】Well, here it gets a little more complicated for me. (TPO2, L, S2, L1) 好吧，讲到这儿对我来说就有点复杂了。

【反义】simple, easy

【逆构】complicate *v.* 使复杂，使难懂

contaminate[8] [kən'tæmɪneɪt] 

【释义】*v.* 弄脏，污染（pollute, infect）

【例句】Only recently have investigators considered using these plants to clean up soil and waste sites that have been contaminated by toxic levels of heavy metals. (TPO5, R, S1, T1) 只是近来研究者们才考虑利用这些植物来净化那些已经被有毒重金属污染过的土壤和废物处理场。

【派生】contaminated *a.* 受污染的；弄脏的
contamination *n.* 污染，污染物

convey[8] [kən'veɪ] 

【释义】*v.* 1. 表达，传达（communicate）2. 运输，转移（carry, deliver, transport）

【例句】As I said earlier, artists often combine elements to convey a message about the work. (TPO4, S, Q6) 如我之前所说，艺术家通常将不同的元素结合在一起来表达作品的信息。

返记菜单

brush[8] butter[8] camouflage[8] cement[8] compass[8]
complicated[8] contaminate[8] convey[8]

convincing[8] [kən'vɪnsɪŋ]

【释义】*a.* 令人相信的，有说服力的
【例句】Other effects, like waves, were also very convincing. (TPO9, L, S1, L1) 其他效果，例如波浪，也非常真实生动。
【派生】convinced *a.* 确信的，深信的
convincible *a.* 可说服的，可使信服的
【逆构】convince *v.* 使确信，使信服
【搭配】a convincing speech 令人信服的演讲

corporation[8] [ˌkɔːpə'reɪʃən]

【释义】*n.* 公司，法人（company, enterprise）
【例句】And by the mid 1970s, by 1974 I think, all fifty states had their own arts agencies, their own state arts councils that work with the federal government with corporations, artists, performers, you name it. (TPO4, L, S2, L2) 然后到20世纪70年代中期，我想是到1974年，全部的50个州都有了自己的艺术协会，与他们合作的有联邦政府、企业、艺术家、表演家，凡是你能说出来的。
【逆构】corporate *a.* 团体的，公司的

count[8] [kaʊnt]

【释义】*v.* 1. 计算，计数 2. 包含在内 *n.* 计算；总数
【例句】Count the birds that return to the same region every year. (TPO3, L, S1, L1) 计算一下每年回到同一地区的蜂鸟的数量。
【搭配】count on 依靠，指望

craft[8] [krɑːft]

【释义】*n.* 1. 工艺，手艺（art, skill）2. 容器 *v.*（尤指用手工）精心制作
【例句】The first water craft theory about this migration was that around 11,000-12,000 years ago there was an ice-free corridor stretching from eastern Beringia to the areas of North America south of the great northern glaciers. (TPO9, R, S1,T1) 关于此次迁徙的第一个水路理论是说大约在11000到12000年前，有一个不冻的走廊一直从白令海峡东部延伸到北美大北部冰河的南部。
【派生】craftsman *n.* 工匠，手艺精巧的人
craftsmanship *n.* 技能，技术
crafty *a.* 灵巧的，巧妙的
aircraft *n.* 航行器；飞机
spacecraft *n.* 太空船

crash[8] [kræʃ]

【释义】*v.* 1. 碰撞，撞击，坠毁 2. 破产，失败 *n.*（指公司、政府等）破产，垮台
【例句】We think meteors that crashed into the moon or tails of passing comets may have introduced water molecules. (TPO5, L, S1, L2) 我们认为撞进月球的流星或途经的彗星的尾巴有可能带去了水分子。
【派生】crashed *a.* 失事的
【搭配】crash down 朝下猛撞
crash into 闯入；撞到…上
crash out 撞毁；坠毁
crash and burn〈俚语〉彻底失败

cylinder[8] ['sɪlɪndə]

【释义】*n.* 1.（发动机的）汽缸 2. 圆柱体，圆筒
【例句】Early in the century, a pump had come into use in which expanding steam raised a piston in a cylinder, and atmospheric pressure brought it down again when the steam condensed inside the cylinder to form a vacuum. (TPO6, R, S1, T1) 在（19）世纪早期，泵曾被用于（发动机的）汽缸，在气缸中，膨胀的蒸汽推动活塞上升，而当汽缸内部的蒸汽被压缩形成真空环境时，气压又使得活塞下降。
【搭配】work on all cylinders（口语）竭尽全力地干

dairy[8] ['deərɪ]

【释义】*n.* 牛奶场；乳品店 *a.* 牛奶的，乳制品的
【例句】You know, there is a dairy not far from here in Chelsea. (TPO9, L, S1, C1) 你知道，在切尔西有一个牛奶场，离这儿不远。
【搭配】dairy products 奶制品

deficiency[8] [dɪ'fɪʃənsɪ]

【释义】*n.* 缺乏，不足（insufficiency, lack, scarcity）
【例句】Wildlife biologists have long been concerned that the loss of forests may create nutritional deficiencies for deer. (TPO4, R, S1, T1) 野生动物学家一直担心森林的减少

可能会引起鹿群的营养不足。
【反义】abundance, plenty
【派生】deficient *a.* 缺乏的，不足的

discipline[8] ['dɪsɪplɪn]

【释义】*n.* 1. 学科（field, subject）2. 纪律 3. 训练（training）*v.* 1. 训练（train）2. 惩罚（punish）
【例句】And it has applications in a lot of different disciplines. (TPO5, L, S2, L1) 它被应用在了很多不同的科目里。
【派生】disciplinal *a.* 惩罚的；训练的
disciplinary *a.* 训练的；规律的
【搭配】discipline sb. for sth. 因某事惩罚某人

disclaimer[8] [dɪs'kleɪmə(r)]

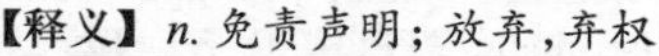

【释义】*n.* 免责声明；放弃，弃权
【例句】Advertisers sometimes offset or counterbalance an exaggerated claim with a disclaimer—a qualification or condition on the claim. (TPO14, R, S1, T1) 广告商有时会通过免责声明——对于广告所声称内容的一种限制和条件，来抵消和平衡夸张的广告词。
【逆构】disclaim *v.* 放弃，否认，弃权

diverse[8] [daɪ'vɜːs]

【释义】*a.* 不同的，多种多样的（different, various, varied）
【例句】Data from diverse sources, including geochemical evidence preserved in seafloor sediments, indicate that the Late Cretaceous climate was milder than today's. (TPO8, R, S2, T1) 各种来源的数据，包括保存在海底沉积物中的地球化学证据表明晚白垩世的气候比现在的要温和。
【派生】diversity *n.* 多样性

ecology[8] [ɪ(ː)'kɒlədʒɪ]

【释义】*n.* 生态；生态学
【例句】Because pastoralists are highly mobile, they tend to have few material possessions and can influence the culture, ecology, and language of very large areas. (TPO14, R, S2, T2) 因为牧民经常迁移，所以他们一般只有很少的物质财产，并且这会影响很广大地区的文化、生态和语言。

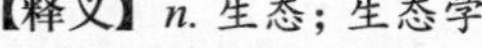

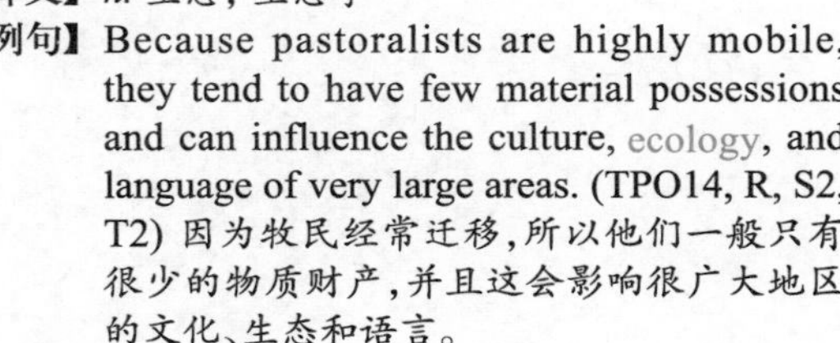

【派生】ecological *a.* 生态学的
ecologist *n.* 生态学家
【搭配】ecology environment 生态环境

emit[8] [ɪ'mɪt]

【释义】*v.* 发出，发射，放射（give off, send out）
【例句】The bats emit ultrasonic pulses, very high pitch sound waves that we cannot hear. (TPO7, L, S1, L2) 蝙蝠会发射出一种超声波脉冲，这是一种人类听不见的高音调声波。
【派生】emission *n.* 散发，发射

emotional[8] [ɪ'məʊʃənl]

【释义】*a.* 1. 感情的，情绪的 2. 易激动的，感动的
【例句】She had a variety of emotional reactions to the play. (TPO4, L, S1, C1) 她对这部话剧有着种种情绪反应。
【逆构】emotion *n.* 感情

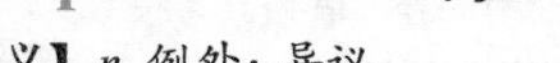

exception[8] [ɪk'sepʃən]

【释义】*n.* 例外；异议
【例句】Most crystalline rocks are much more solid; a common exception is basalt. (TPO1, R, S2, T2) 大部分结晶体岩石都非常坚硬，但也有例外，最常见的就是玄武岩。
【派生】exceptional *a.* 例外的；杰出的；异常的
【搭配】with the exception of 除了…以外
without/no exception 无一例外，一律
make an exception 破例

extension[8] [ɪks'tenʃən]

【释义】*n.* 延长，扩充，扩大（expansion）
【例句】Ok, um...now, let's touch briefly on extension and compression. (TPO7, L, S2, L2) 好，现在，我们来简要谈一下扩张和收缩。
【反义】compression

extrinsic[8] [eks'trɪnsɪk]

【释义】*a.* 外在的，外部的（external, outside）
【例句】Let me introduce a couple of technical terms: extrinsic value and intrinsic value. (TPO2, L, S2, L1) 我来给大家介绍两个术语：外在价值和内在价值。

返记菜单

discipline[8] disclaimer[8] diverse[8] ecology[8] emit[8]
emotional[8] exception[8] extension[8] extrinsic[8]

【反义】intrinsic
【派生】extrinsically *ad.* 外部地，外在地

fat[8] [fæt]

【释义】*n.* 1. 脂肪 2. 多余(物) *a.* 1. 肥胖的(plump) 2. 收益丰厚的
【例句】I mean, as it flies all the way across the Mexico Gulf, it uses up none of its body fat. (TPO3, L, S1, L1) 我指的是，当它飞越墨西哥海湾时，并没有耗掉身上的脂肪。
【搭配】the fat is in the fire 木已成舟；要出麻烦了

fence[8] [fens]

【释义】*n.* 栅栏，围墙 *v.* 用篱笆围住；防护
【例句】The fence of the foreground is blue. (TPO1, L, S1, L1) 前景部分的篱笆是蓝色的。
【派生】fenceless *a.* 没有围墙的，不设防的
【搭配】fence out 挡住；隔开

fiction[8] ['fɪkʃən]

【释义】*n.* 1. 小说 2. 虚构的事；假想之物
【例句】But when people think fiction, they may assume the characters come from the author's imagination. (TPO6, L, S2, L1) 当人们想到小说的时候，可能会认为其中的角色都源自作者的想象。
【派生】fictionist *n.* 小说家
fictional *a.* 虚构的，小说的

frequent[8] ['friːkwənt]

【释义】*a.* 经常(发生)的，常见的 *v.* 经常去，时常出入
【例句】Should the use of rewards fail, members can frequently win by rejecting or threatening to ostracize those who deviate from the primary group's norms. (TPO13, R, S1, T1) 如果没有有效利用奖励，成员就可以时常通过拒绝或威胁来排斥那些偏离主要群体行为规范的人，以此来达到目的。
【派生】frequently *ad.* 经常
frequency *n.* 频率，频次

funding[8] ['fʌndɪŋ]

【释义】*n.* 资金，基金；筹集资金，拨款
【例句】So, moving on, we don't actually see any real government involvement in the arts again until the early 1960s, when President Kennedy and other politicians started to push for major funding to support and promote the arts. (TPO4, L, S2, L2) 于是，往后，我们再没有见到政府真正参与任何艺术项目，直到20世纪60年代，肯尼迪总统和其他政治家开始奋力筹集资金来支持和推动艺术发展。
【逆构】fund *n.* 资金

gap[8] [gæp]

【释义】*n.* 1. 缺口，缝隙 2. 差距，空白 *v.* 使豁开
【例句】This is because the gaps among the original grains are often not totally plungged with cementing chemicals. (TPO1, R, S2, T2) 这是因为最初颗粒间的缝隙并没有被粘固的化学物质填满。
【派生】gaping *a.* 裂开的；敞开的
【搭配】generation gap 代沟

Word List 17

gift[8] [gɪft] 

【释义】*n.* 1. 天赋,天才(talent) 2. 礼物,赠品 *v.* 赋予,赠送

【例句】Another (answer), advanced in the twentieth century, suggests that humans have a gift for fantasy. (TPO1, R, S2, T1) 另一个在20世纪提出的答案表明人类拥有幻想的天赋。

【派生】gifted *a.* 天才的,有天赋的

【搭配】have a gift for 在…有天赋

govern[8] [ˈgʌvən] 

【释义】*v.* 1. 统治,治理,管理(rule, conduct) 2. 支配,控制(control)

【例句】The glacial system is governed by two basic climatic variables: precipitation and temperature. (TPO15, R, S1, T1) 冰川系统主要受两个基本的气候变量所控制:降雨和温度。

【派生】government *n.* 政府;管辖

harsh[8] [hɑːʃ] 

【释义】*a.* 1. 严酷的,恶劣的(severe) 2. 粗糙的(rough, coarse) 3. 刺耳的,刻薄的(acid)

【例句】What keeps the black-tailed deer alive in the harsher seasons of plant decay and dormancy? (TPO4, R, S1, T1) 是什么使得黑尾鹿在植物枯萎和休眠的最严酷的季节里生存了下来呢?

【反义】gentle, mild

【派生】harshly *ad.* 粗糙地;冷酷地
harshness *n.* 严酷,恶劣

adjust[8] [əˈdʒʌst] 

【释义】*v.* 调整,校准,调节;使适应(adapt, regulate)

【例句】If this hypothesis is true, then it follows that nestlings should adjust the intensity of their signals in relation to the signals produced by their nestmates, who are competing for parental attention. (TPO11, R, S2, T2) 如果这一假设成立,那接下来可以推测,雏鸟应该调整其信号的强度,这和与它们竞争父母注意力的同巢手足所发出的信号息息相关。

【派生】adjustment *n.* 调节,校正

【搭配】adjust and control 调控

intense[8] [ɪnˈtens] 

【释义】*a.* 强烈的,剧烈的(extreme, fierce)

【例句】Because of intense interest in developing and introducing sound in film, the general use of other technological innovations being developed in the 1920s was delayed. (TPO12, R, S2, T1) 由于对在电影中运用声音有强烈的兴趣,所以对于20世纪20年代发展起来的其他技术创新的普遍应用就推迟了。

【派生】intensity *n.* 强烈;强度

【搭配】intense emotion 激情

invest[8] [ɪnˈvest]

【释义】*v.* 1. 投资,投入 2. 授予,赋予

【例句】Finally, while a four-day workweek offers employees more free time to invest in their personal lives, it also presents some risks that could end up reducing quality of life. (TPO1, W, Q1) 最后,一周工作4天使得员工们有更多的闲暇时间用于个人生活的同时,它也带来了生活质量降低的风险。

【派生】invester *n.* 调查者
investee *n.* 投资对象

【搭配】invest in sth. 投资于

maize[8] [meɪz]

【释义】*n.* 玉米

【例句】One of the main crops of the Chaco people was grain maize, which could be stored for long periods of time without spoiling and could serve as a long-lasting supply of food. (TPO5, W, Q1) 查克峡谷人们的主要粮食作物之一是玉米,玉米能够长期存储且不变质,因此可以作为一种长期的食品供应。

【同义】corn

【派生】maizena *n.* 玉米粉,淀粉

manufacturer[8] [ˌmænjʊˈfæktʃərə]

【释义】 *n.* 制造商(producer)

【例句】 The thriving obsidian operation, for example, would necessitate more miners, additional manufacturers of obsidian tools, and additional traders to carry the goods to new markets. (TPO8, R, S1, T1) 例如,欣欣向荣的黑曜石生意将需要更多的矿工、额外的黑曜石工具制造商和其他商人来把这些货物带到新的市场。

【逆构】 manufacture *v.* 制造

meaningful[8] [ˈmiːnɪŋfʊl]

【释义】 *a.* 重要的,富有意义的,意味深长的(significant, important)

【例句】 I think this essay has the potential to be quite meaningful for all of you as young people who probably wonder about things like truth and where your lives are going—all sorts of profound questions. (TPO4, L, S1, L2) 我认为这篇文章对大家来说意义非凡,因为年轻人可能都会思考诸如真理和生命将何去何从这些意义深刻的问题。

【逆构】 meaning *n.* 意义

media[8] [ˈmiːdjə]

【释义】 *n.* 新闻媒介,媒体

【例句】 With financial assets considerably greater than those in the motion picture industry, and perhaps a wider vision of the relationships among entertainment and communications media, they revitalized research into recording sound for motion picture. (TPO12, R, S2, T1) 因为他们占有的资产要比电影产业多得多,又或许是因为对娱乐业和传播媒体之间的联系有着更广阔的愿景,所以他们复兴了对电影录音方面的研究。

【搭配】 mass media 大众传媒

monsoon[8] [mɒnˈsuːn]

【释义】 *n.* 季风,季风雨

【例句】 But there've been times in the past when monsoon rains soaked the Empty Quarter and turned it from a desert into grassland that was dotted with lakes and home to various animals. (TPO9, L, S2, L1) 过去,有时候季风雨浸润鲁卜哈利沙漠,使其从沙漠变成有许多湖的草地,成为许多动物的家。

【派生】 monsoonal *a.* 季风的

【搭配】 monsoon climate 季风气候

norms[8] [nɔːmz]

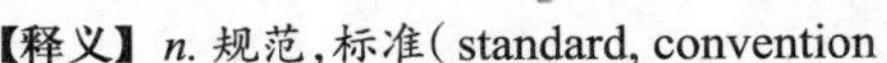

【释义】 *n.* 规范,标准(standard, convention)

【例句】 Now in a way, Painlevé's films conform to norms of the 20s and 30s, that is, they don't fit very neatly into the categories we use to classify films today. (TPO3, L, S1, L2) 现在从某种程度上来说,培乐威的电影与20年代和30年代的规范是一致的,也就是说,它们并不能被简单地归为我们用以划分当今电影的种类。

【派生】 normal *a.* 正常的,标准的
normally *ad.* 通常地

【搭配】 diplomatic norms 外交准则

nowadays[8] [ˈnaʊədeɪz]

【释义】 *ad.* 现今,现在(now, contemporarily)

【例句】 Reactions to the play are more positive nowadays than they were in the past. (TPO4, L, S1, C1) 这部话剧现今得到的反应比以前更加积极。

oral[8] [ˈɔːrəl]

【释义】 *a.* 1. 口头的,口述的(spoken, verbal) 2. 与口有关的

【例句】 They were put down orally within cultures from generation to generation, so they changed a lot over time. (TPO5, L, S2, L2) 它们在文化圈内一代一代口口相传,所以历经岁月已经改变了很多。

【派生】 orally *ad.* 口头地

【搭配】 oral language 口语

paleontologist[8] [ˌpæliɔnˈtɔlədʒist]

【释义】 *n.* 古生物学家

【例句】 Paleontologists continue to search the fossil record for answers to these questions. (TPO5, R, S2, T2) 古生物学家继续寻找可以为这些问题提供答案的化石标本。

panel[8] ['pænl] 

【释义】*n.* 1. 板，画板，镶板 2. 专门小组 *v.* 用板条装饰

【例句】For example, solar energy is gathered through large glass panels facing the sun. (TPO12, L, S2, L2) 比如说，太阳能是通过朝向太阳的大玻璃镶嵌板进行收集的。

peasant[8] ['pezənt]

【释义】*n.* 农民

【例句】In Denmark and Sweden agricultural reforms took place gradually from the late eighteenth century through the first half of the nineteenth, resulting in a new class of peasant landowners with a definite market orientation. (TPO18, R, S1, T1) 从18世纪末一直到19世纪上半叶，丹麦和瑞典逐渐进行了农业改革，从而导致了一个新的具有明确市场导向的农民地主阶层的出现。

【搭配】peasant household 庄户，农户

pepper[8] ['pepə]

【释义】*n.* 胡椒粉；辣椒 *v.* 在…上撒胡椒粉

【例句】And in the Middle Ages, Europeans were familiar with lots of different spices, the most import being pepper, cloves, ginger, cinnamon, maize and nutmeg. (TPO18, L, S2, L1) 在中世纪时期，欧洲人熟知许多种香料，其中引进最多的是胡椒、丁香、生姜、桂皮、玉米和肉豆蔻。

permission[8] [pə(ː)'mɪʃən] 

【释义】*n.* 允许，许可，准许

【例句】Well, I did have a problem with that but I disscussed it with one of your office staff, and she gave me permission. (TPO5, L, S1, L2) 嗯，我确实在那方面有问题，但是我和您的一个办公室职员就这事讨论了一下，她同意我这么做。

【反义】prohibition

pollute[8] [pə'luːt]

【释义】*v.* 污染；玷污（contaminate, defile）

【例句】So although the cars would not pollute, the factories that generated the hydrogen for the cars would pollute. (TPO9, W, Q1) 因此即使汽车不会产生污染，为汽车生产氢的工厂也会造成污染。

【派生】pollution *n.* 污染
pollutant *n.* 污染物

porous[8] ['pɔːrəs] 

【释义】*a.* 可渗透的，多孔的（permeable）

【例句】The result is that sandstone can be as porous as the loose sand from which it was formed. (TPO1, R, S2, T2) 结果，砂岩会变得像形成它的散沙一样多孔。

【派生】porousness *n.* 多孔性，孔隙率
porosity *n.* 有孔性，多孔性

pottery[8] ['pɒtərɪ] 

【释义】*n.* 陶器

【例句】To twentieth-century eyes, Chinese pottery may appear merely decorative, yet to the Chinese the form of each object and its adornment had meaning and significance. (TPO10, R, S1, T1) 在20世纪的人们眼中，中国陶器可能仅仅是装饰性的，但对于当时的中国人来说，每一个物品的形状及其装饰都有其意义和重要性。

principal[8] ['prɪnsəp(ə)l] 

【释义】*a.* 主要的，首要的（major, main, chief）*n.* 1. 本金，资本 2. 校长 3. 主角

【例句】Their principal function was to provide funds for the state. (TPO10, R, S2, T2) 它们的首要功能是为政府提供资金。

【派生】principally *ad.* 主要地

pronghorn[8] ['prɔːŋˌhɔːn] 

【释义】*n.* 叉角羚，麋鹿（生活在北美大平原西部）

【例句】So a good example of this, found right here in North America, is something an animal called the American pronghorn does. (TPO17, S, Q4) 在北美有一个极好的例子，就是一种叫做美国叉角羚的动物所做的事情。

返记菜单

panel[8] peasant[8] pepper[8] permission[8] pollute[8]
porous[8] pottery[8] principal[8] pronghorn[8]

protein[8] ['prəʊtiːn]

【释义】*n.* 蛋白质

【例句】The protein content of shade-grown vegetation, for example, was much lower than that for plants grown in clearings. (TPO4, R, S1, T1) 比如,在荫蔽处成熟的植物的蛋白质含量要远低于在空地上长熟的植物。

【搭配】protein content 蛋白质含量

puzzle[8] ['pʌzl]

【释义】*v.*(使)迷惑(confuse)*n.* 谜,难题(riddle, mystery)

【例句】This is a question that has puzzled scientists for ages. (TPO2, R, S2, T1) 这个问题已经困扰了科学家们很长时间了。

【派生】puzzled *a.* 感到困惑的
puzzling *a.* 令人困惑的
puzzlement *n.* 迷惑;令人困惑的事

【搭配】puzzle out 通过深思或研究而找出(解决问题的办法等)

reconstruct[8] ['riːkən'strʌkt]

【释义】*v.* 重建,重现(rebuild, restore)

【例句】Very exciting discoveries have finally allowed scientists to reconstruct the most likely origins of cetaceans. (TPO2, R, S2, T1) 一系列令人兴奋的发现终于使得科学家们能够重现鲸类动物几近真实的起源。

【派生】reconstruction *n.* 重建
reconstructive *a.* 重建的,复原的

recount[8] [rɪ'kaʊnt]

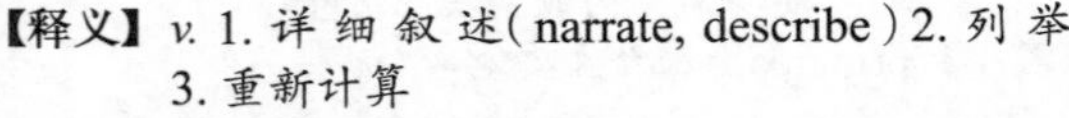

【释义】*v.* 1. 详细叙述(narrate, describe) 2. 列举 3. 重新计算

【例句】Toward the end of his life, the Chevalier de Seingalt (1725-1798) wrote a long memoir recounting his life and adventures. (TPO7, W, Q1) 在走向人生尽头的时候, Chevalier de Seingalt(1725-1798)写下了长长的回忆录,记载了他的人生和经历。

remarkable[8] [rɪ'mɑːkəbl]

【释义】*a.* 值得注意的,显著的,非凡的,卓越的(extraordinary, marvelous, notable)

【例句】The remarkable mobility and range of pastoral societies explain, in part, why so many linguists have argued that the Indo-European languages began their astonishing expansionist career not among farmers in Anatolia (present-day Turkey), but among early pastoralists from Inner Eurasia. (TPO14, R, S2, T2) 游牧社会显著的流动性和地域的广阔性在一定程度上解释了为何那么多语言学家认为印欧语系的惊人扩张并不是始于安纳托利亚(今天的土耳其)的农民,而是来自亚欧内陆的早期牧民。

【逆构】remark *v./n.* 谈论,评论

【搭配】remarkable development 显著发展

rent[8] [rent]

【释义】*v.* 出租,租借 *n.* 1. 租金 2. 出租

【例句】And I was supposed to rent a van for the trip. (TPO1, S, Q5) 这次旅行的时候我应该租一辆面包车。

【派生】rentable *a.* 可租用的
rental *a./n.* 租赁,租借

retrieve[8] [rɪ'triːv]

【释义】*v.* 重新得到,收回;挽回,补救(recall, regain)

【例句】And some people's information couldn't be retrieved. (TPO12, L, S2, C1) 而且一些人的信息找不回来了。

【搭配】retrieve data 检索数据

salvage[8] ['sælvɪdʒ]

【释义】*n.* 抢救(出的财产)*v.*(从火灾、海难等中)抢救,营救(rescue, save)

【例句】One way of dealing with the aftermath of these disasters is called salvage logging, which is the practice of removing dead trees from affected areas and using the wood for lumber, plywood, and other wood products. (TPO14, W, Q1) 对待这些灾难造成的后果的方法之一是抢救性砍伐,就是将受灾地区死掉的树木移除,将其制成木材、胶合板以及其他木制产品。

【派生】salvageable *a.* 可抢救的,可挽回的

salvager *n.* 拯救者,救援人员
【搭配】salvage charges 救援费
salvage value 残值,折余值

script[8] [skrɪpt] 

【释义】*n.*(戏剧、电影、广播、讲话等的)剧本,脚本,讲稿
【例句】Now in Europe in the Middle Ages before the invention of printing and the printing press, all books, all manual scripts were hand-made. (TPO15, L, S1, L2) 在中世纪的欧洲,在印刷术和印刷机出现之前,所有的书籍、手稿都是手工制作的。
【搭配】cuneiform script 楔形文字

shot[8] [ʃɒt]

【释义】*n.* 1. 射击;射门,投篮;发射;注射
【例句】And stuff like that will give them a better shot at getting a job after they graduate. (TPO12, S, Q5) 像那样的东西将会为他们在毕业后找工作提供一个很好的尝试机会。
【派生】shotgun *n.* 猎枪 *a.* 用猎枪的;强迫的;漫无目的的

sink[8] [sɪŋk]

【释义】*v.* 1. 下沉,沉没 2. 渗透 3. 低落,变低 *n.* 散热器,接收端
【例句】Well, since cold air sinks, and these spots are shaded, they are usually much cooler than the surrounding area. (TPO14, L, S1, L2) 因为冷空气下沉,而这些地方又处在荫蔽处,所以这些地方通常比周围的地方凉快得多。
【反义】float, rise
【派生】sinkable *a.* 易下沉的
sinkage *n.* 下沉
【搭配】sink in 渗入;完全被理解
sink into 陷入
sink down 沉落
sink or swim 成败全靠自己

slip[8] [slɪp] 

【释义】*n.* 1.(涂在陶器的)泥釉;粘土与水的混合物 2. 小过失,失误 3. 纸片 4. 溜,滑倒 *v.* 1. 滑动,滑行 2. 滑倒,滑落
【例句】Ceramic products also include lead-glazed tomb models of the Han dynasty, three-color lead-glazed vessels and figures of the Tang dynasty, and Ming three-color temple ornaments, in which the motifs were outlined in a raised trail of slip—as well as the many burial ceramics produced in imitation of vessels made in materials of higher intrinsic value. (TPO10, R, S1, T1) 陶瓷制品还包括汉代的铅釉墓葬品、唐代的唐三彩铅釉器皿和塑像、以泥釉凸纹来展现图案轮廓的明代三彩庙饰以及模仿贵重材料器皿烧制而成的诸多入葬陶瓷品。
【派生】slipper *n.* 拖鞋
slippery *a.*(指物体表面)滑的,光滑的
【搭配】let slip 错过;无意中吐露;放走
slip away 逃走;悄悄溜走
slip in 悄悄溜入
slip one's mind 忘记

slope[8] [sləʊp] 

【释义】*v.*(使)倾斜 *n.* 1. 斜坡,斜面(incline, slant) 2. 倾斜,斜度
【例句】Offshore drilling platforms extend the search for oil to the ocean's continental shelves—those gently sloping submarine regions at the edges of the continents. (TPO4, R, S2, T2) 寻找石油的近海钻井平台已经拓展到了大陆架——那些大陆边缘逐渐向海底倾斜的区域。
【派生】slopy *a.* 倾斜的
【搭配】slope stability 坡面稳定性
slope angle 斜角
slope failure 滑坡

specialized[8] ['speʃəlaɪzd] 

【释义】*a.* 专门的;专科的;专用的
【例句】Um, of course, you might think there might not be any areas where the tree could spread into, er…because…um…well, it's very specialized in terms of the habitat. (TPO6, L, S1, L2) 当然,你可能会认为这些树(的种子)无处传播,因为它们有着专门的生长地。
【派生】specialization *n.* 特殊化,专门化
【逆构】specialized knowledge 专门知识

返记菜单

script[8] shot[8] sink[8] slip[8] slope[8]
specialized[8]

squirrel[8] ['skwɪrəl]

【释义】*n.* 松鼠

【例句】This drift has been studied extensively in many animals and in biological activities ranging from the hatching of fruit fly eggs to wheel running by squirrels. (TPO13, R, S2, T1) 这种漂移在许多动物和生物活动中被广泛研究,从果蝇卵的孵化到松鼠的滚轮跑。

stick[8] [stɪk]

【释义】*v.* 1. 刺入,钉住 2. 粘贴 3. 坚持 *n.* 棍,棒;拐杖

【例句】It'd be sort of embarrassing, sticking my head into each lecture hall, asking if I was in the right place. (TPO4, S, Q5) 把头伸到每个讲堂里面,问我是不是应该在这儿,这有点儿尴尬。

【派生】sticker *n.* 不屈不挠的人,滞销物
sticky *a.* 粘的

【搭配】stick with/to 坚持
stick it out 坚持到底
stick together 团结一致
stick on 保持在…之上;贴上
stick around 逗留,徘徊
stick out 突出
stick up for 维护,支持
stick by 忠于
carrot and stick 软硬兼施的

stoneware[8] ['stəunˌweə]

【释义】*n.* 粗陶器,石器

【例句】The ceramics fall into three broad types—earthenware, stoneware, and porcelain—for vessels, architectural items such as roof tiles, and modeled objects and figures. (TPO10, R, S1, T1) 陶制瓷器从广义上可以被分为3大类:陶器、石器以及瓷器,比如容器、瓦片等建筑材料以及物体和人物模型。

surplus[8] ['sɜːpləs]

【释义】*a.* 过剩的,多余的(extra, additional, excess)
n. 过剩,剩余(物资)

【例句】Surplus snowfall is essential for a glacier to develop. (TPO15, R, S1, T1) 多余的降雪对冰山的形成是很重要的。

【反义】deficit

【派生】surplusage *n.* 剩余物;盈余额

【搭配】surplus value 剩余价值

survey[8] [sɜː'veɪ]

【释义】*n./v.* 调查

【例句】A survey of known hyperaccumulators indentified that 75 percent of them amassed nickel. (TPO5, R, S1, T1) 一份对已知重金属超富集植物的调查证实,它们之中的75%都富含镍元素。

【派生】surveyor *n.* 测量员

【搭配】survey feedback 调查反馈

tolerate[8] ['tɒləreɪt]

【释义】*v.* 忍受,容忍;容许(bear, endure, withstand)

【例句】In contrast, a complex climax community, such as a temperate forest, will tolerate considerable damage from weather or pests. (TPO3, R, S1, T2) 与此相反,一个复杂的顶级群落,比如温带森林,便可以承受由气候或害虫造成的诸多破坏。

【派生】tolerable *a.* 可容忍的
tolerant *a.* 容忍的,宽容的
tolerance *n.* 宽容,忍受

treat[8] [triːt]

【释义】*v.* 1. 处理;治疗 2. 对待,视为(consider, regard) 3. 招待

【例句】Steel cables can't take the salt air unless they're treated repeatedly with a zinc-based paint. (TPO2, L, S1, L2) 除非给钢丝绳反复地涂上锌漆,否则它很容易被空气中的盐分腐蚀。

【派生】treatment *n.* 对待;治疗

【搭配】treat sb. with respect 对某人尊敬有加
treat sb. like dirt 把某人看得一钱不值

tremendous[8] [trɪ'mendəs]

【释义】*a.* 极大的,巨大的,惊人的(enormous, huge)

【例句】The extreme seriousness of desertification results from the vast areas of land and the tremendous numbers of people affected. (TPO2, R, Sl, T1) 沙漠化的极端严重性在于

受其影响的地域之广、人口数量之多。

【反义】small, minute

【派生】tremendously *ad.* 巨大地
tremendousness *n.* 巨大

tuition[8] [tjuːˈɪʃən]

【释义】*n.* 1. 学费 2. 指导，教导

【例句】The university's poor financial condition led it to increase the price for campus housing and tuition by 15% this year. (TPO1, S, Q3) 学校困窘的财政状况使得今年的校园住宿费和学费上涨了15%。

【派生】tuitional *a.* 讲授的；学费的

variable[8] [ˈveərɪəbl]

【释义】*a.* 变化的，可变的，易变的(changeable) *n.* 可变因素，变量

【例句】Rainfall is not completely absent in desert areas, but it is highly variable. (TPO12, R, S2, T2) 在沙漠地区，降雨量不是完全没有的，但变化却相当大。

【派生】variably *ad.* 易变地，不定地
variation *n.* 变异；变种

【逆构】vary *v.* 变化

【搭配】variable zone 温带

withstand[8] [wɪðˈstænd]

【释义】*v.* 经受，承受(tolerate, endure, resist)

【例句】They are designed to withstand the forces of compression (pushing together), tension (pulling apart), bending, or a combination of these in different parts of the structure. (TPO3, R, S1, T1) 通过结构设计使建筑的不同部分能对抗压力、拉力、弯曲力或者以上各种压力的组合。

afford[7] [əˈfɔːd]

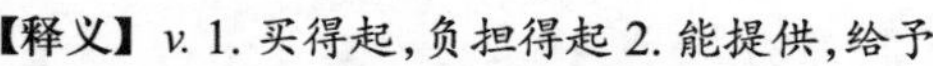

【释义】*v.* 1. 买得起，负担得起 2. 能提供，给予

【例句】So in some places, um, like ancient Greece for example, the wealthiest people with poor vision could have someone else read to them—easy solution if you could afford it. (TPO8, L, S2, L1) 因此，在一些地方，比如古希腊，那些视力不太好的富人们可以请人读给他们听——如果你能负担得起，这是一个很简单的方法。

【派生】affordable *a.* 负担得起的
affordability *n.* 可购性

anthropologist[7] [ˌænθrəˈpɒlədʒɪst]

【释义】*n.* 人类学家

【例句】The most widely accepted theory, championed by anthropologists in the late nineteenth and early twentieth centuries, envisions theater as emerging out of myth and ritual. (TPO1, R, S2, T1) 这一最广为接受的理论认为剧院产生于神话和宗教仪式，这一理论在19世纪末和20世纪早期受到了人类学家的拥护。

approve[7] [əˈpruːv]

【释义】*v.* 1. 赞成，同意(agree, endorse) 2. 批准，认可

【例句】She wants him to approve her plans for a term paper. (TPO6, L, S2, C1, Q1) 她希望他可以同意她的学期论文计划。

【派生】approval *n.* 赞成；批准

artisan[7] [ɑːtɪˈzæn]

【释义】*n.* 手艺人；技工(workman, craftsman)

【例句】Production was generally in the hands of skilled individual artisans doing piecework under the tutelage of a master. (TPO16, R, S1, T1) 生产通常都是由熟练的工匠在大师的指导下进行的。

【搭配】artisan industry 手工业，手工业生产

ash[7] [æʃ]

【释义】*n.* 1. 灰，灰烬 2. 骨灰，遗骸

【例句】There tends to be a lot of obsidian flakes and chips in the hearth ashes, but no chimney. (TPO1, L, S2, L1) 在炉灰里有很多黑曜石的剥片和碎屑，但没有烟囱。

【派生】ashen *a.* 灰色的；苍白的
ashtray *n.* 烟灰缸
ashy *a.* 灰色的；覆盖着灰的

assemble[7] [əˈsembl]

【释义】*v.* 1. 聚集，集合(gather, congregate) 2. 装配

返记菜单

tuition[8] variable[8] withstand[8] afford[7] anthropologist[7]
approve[7] artisan[7] ash[7] assemble[7]

【例句】But the movies differed significantly from these other forms of entertainment, which depended on either live performance or the active involvement of a master of ceremonies who assembled the final program. (TPO2, R, S2, T2) 但是电影与其他形式的娱乐活动有着很大的不同，电影无需依赖现场表演，也不需要串联全场节目的主持人的积极参与。

【派生】assembly *n.* 集合，装配

assist[7] [ə'sɪst]

【释义】*v.* 帮助，协助，援助(help, aid)

【例句】Some scientists believe that Torreya probably thrived in areas much further north in the distant past, so by relocating it now, in a process known as assisted migration, humans would simply be helping Torreya return to an environment that is more suited to its survival. (TPO17, W, Q1) 一些科学家认为榧实在早期可能繁盛地生长在更加靠北的地区，所以现在，通过一个叫做辅助迁徙的过程对其进行重植，人类就可以简单地帮助榧实回到更为适宜其生长的环境。

【派生】assistance *n.* 帮助，协助
assistant *a.* 助理的，辅助的

【搭配】assist sb. in doing sth. 帮助某人做某事

automatic[7] [ɔːtə'mætɪk]

【释义】*a.* 1.（人）无意识的，不自觉的 2.（尤指机器）自动的

【例句】The intention is for the positively perceived attributes of the celebrity to be transferred to the advertised product and for the two to become automatically linked in the audience's mind. (TPO14, R, S1, T1) 这样做的目的是把名人的正面感官特质转移到广告产品上去，并使两者能在观众头脑里自然联系起来。

【派生】automatical *a.* 自动的；无意识的
automatically *ad.* 自动地，无意识地

bare[7] [beə]

【释义】*a.* 1. 光秃的，赤裸的(bald, naked) 2. 仅有的
v. 露出，暴露

【例句】The paintings rest on bare walls, with no backdrops or environmental trappings. (TPO4, R, S2, T1) 这些画作以空白的墙面为依托，没有任何背景或环境装饰。

【派生】barely *ad.* 勉强；几乎不
bareness *n.* 裸露，赤裸

【搭配】lay bare 揭发，暴露，公开

barrier[7] ['bærɪə]

【释义】*n.* 1. 屏障，障碍(obstacle, hindrance) 2. 栅栏(hurdle)

【例句】The Wilmington field near Long Beach, California, has subsided nine meters in 50 years; protective barriers have had to be built to prevent seawater from flooding the area. (TPO4, R, S2, T2) 加州长滩附近的威灵顿油田在50年内下沉了9米；人们不得不在其周围设置保护性屏障以防止海水淹没该地区。

【搭配】trade barrier 贸易壁垒

Word List 18

belt[7] [belt] 

【释义】*n.* 1. 地带,地区(zone, area) 2. 带,皮带,腰带 *v.* 1. 用带扎牢(或系上)(fasten, tie)

【例句】Today I'm going to talk about how the asteroid belt was discovered. (TPO2, L, S2, L2) 今天,我将要讲解小行星带是如何被发现的。

【派生】belted *a.* (衣服)束带的,有腰带的

【搭配】give sb. a belt 狠揍某人
below the belt 不光明正大的

beneficial[7] [benɪ'fɪʃəl]

【释义】*a.* 有益的,有利的(advantageous, favorable)

【例句】Though beneficial in lower levels, high levels of salts, other minerals, and heavy metals can be harmful to plants. (TPO5, R, S1, T1) 尽管在低浓度时是有益的,但是过高水平的盐、其他矿物质以及重金属则是对植物有害的。

【派生】beneficially *ad.* 有利地,有用地

【搭配】be beneficial to 对…有益的

bloom[7] [bluːm]

【释义】*v.* 1. 使繁茂,使有活力 2. 开花 *n.* 1. 花,开花 2. 最盛期

【例句】Now astronomy didn't really bloom into the science it is today until the development of spectroscopy. (TPO3, L, S2, L2) 直到有了光谱学的发展,天文学在科学领域才真正占有一席之地。

bound[7] [baʊnd]

【释义】*a.* 1. 捆绑的,被束缚的(tied, held) 2. 有义务的 3. 准备去…的 *v.* 1. 划界,限制 2. 跳,跳跃 *n.* 1. 范围,限制(limit, constraint) 2. 跳跃

【例句】But with the printed and bound encyclopedia, the errors remain for decades. (TPO6, W, Q1) 但是对于早已印好成装的百科全书来说,其中的错误可能会存在几十年。

【派生】boundless *a.* 无限的,无边无际的
boundary *n.* 分界线,边界

【搭配】bound in leather 皮面装订

brand[7] [brænd] 

【释义】*n.* 1. 商标,品牌 2. 烙印 *v.* 1. 加污名于 2. 铭记,打烙印

【例句】By doing this, the company appeals to new consumers who weren't probably even interested in getting a computer, and, well of course, to existing consumers who might now be tempted to switch brands. (TPO8, S, Q6) 通过这样做,公司会吸引那些本来无意购买电脑的新顾客,而现有的消费者也可能会想要换个牌子。

【搭配】brand image 品牌形象

browse[7] [braʊz] 

【释义】*v.* 1. 吃草 2. 浏览

【例句】Browsing and grazing animals like the ibex may be another contributing factor. (TPO1, R, S1, T1) 像野山羊这样的食草动物可能是另外一个促成因素。

【派生】browser *n.* 食草动物;浏览者,浏览器

burial[7] ['beriəl] 

【释义】*n.* 葬,掩埋,葬礼(entombment)

【例句】The function and status of ceramics in China varied from dynasty to dynasty, so they may be utilitarian, burial, trade-collector's, or even ritual objects, accroding to their quality and the era in which they were made. (TPO10, R, S1, T1) 陶器在中国各个朝代的功能和地位是不同的,所以,根据其质量和制作的年代,有些可能是有实用意义的,有些可能是陪葬品,有些被作为艺术收藏品,有些甚至是宗教仪式上的法器。

【逆构】bury *v.* 埋葬

canvas[7] ['kænvəs] 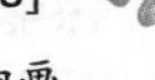

【释义】*n.* 帆布;帆布油画

【例句】First of all, you'll need to know the techniques Rembrandt used when he applied paint to canvas. (TPO5, L, S2, L1) 所以首先,你需要知道伦勃朗把颜料涂在画布上时所运用的

技巧。

【搭配】canvas shoes 帆布鞋

code[7] [kəʊd]

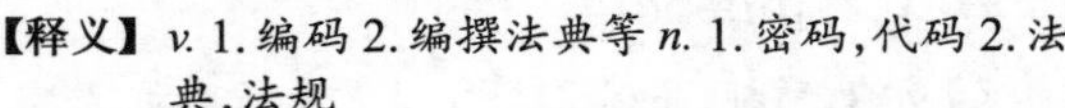

【释义】*v.* 1. 编码 2. 编撰法典等 *n.* 1. 密码，代码 2. 法典，法规

【例句】But if you took away all the DNA that codes for genes, you still have maybe 70% of the DNA left. (TPO12, L, S1, L1) 但是，如果你把为基因编码的全部 DNA 拿走的话，可能仍然能剩下 70% 的 DNA。

【派生】codebase *n.* 代码库

compact[7]

【释义】[kəm'pækt] *a.* 1. 紧密的，紧凑的(condensed) 2. 简洁的(concise) *v.* 压紧，压缩(tighten) ['kɔmpækt] *n.* 1. 粉盒 2. 小型汽车

【例句】This relatively low compact structure helps the house withstand the strong winds blowing off the ocean. (TPO11, L, S1, L2) 这种相对低矮紧密的结构有助于房子抵挡从海上吹来的强风。

【派生】compactness *n.* 密度；小巧；紧凑

complement[7] ['kɒmplɪmənt]

【释义】*v.* 补足，补充 *n.* 补充物，互为补充的东西(supplement)

【例句】Buildings contribute to human life when they provide shelter, enrich space, complement their site, suit the climate, and are economically feasible. (TPO3, R, S1, T1) 建筑物为人类的生活做出了贡献，给人们提供了庇护所，丰富了空间，完善了人们的居所，帮助人们适应气候的变化，同时，人们在经济上也是可以承受的。

【派生】complementary *a.* 补充的，互补的

【搭配】complement each other 相辅相成

compound[7]

【释义】['kɒmpaʊnd] *n.* 化合物(mixture, composite) *a.* 混合的 [kəm'paʊnd] *v.* 混合；和解；使增加

【例句】A harvest of the shoots would remove the toxic compounds off site to be burned or composted to recover the metal for industrial uses. (TPO5, R, S1, T1) 把这些幼苗收割之后就会带走场地中的有毒化合物，然后通过对这些幼苗进行焚烧或堆肥，使金属还原，以作工业之用。

【派生】compounded *a.* 复合的，化合的

confident[7] ['kɒnfɪdənt]

【释义】*a.* 1. 确信的，肯定的，有把握的(certain, convinced) 2. 有信心的，自信的

【例句】She is confident that people learned a valuable lesson from it. (TPO6, L, S1, L1) 她确信人们将会从中学到许多。

【派生】confidence *n.* 信心，把握

coordinate[7] [kəʊ'ɔːdɪnɪt]

【释义】*v.* (使)协调，(使)一致，配合(harmonize, integrate) *a.* 同等的 *n.* 同等的人或物；[数]坐标

【例句】Survival and successful reproduction usually require the activities of animals to be coordinated with predictable events around them. (TPO13, R, S2, T1) 生存并成功繁衍通常需要动物们的活动与周围可预知的事件保持协调一致。

【派生】coordinator *n.* 协调员

【搭配】coordinate sth. (with sth.) 使…协调

crucial[7] ['kruːʃɪəl]

【释义】*a.* 关键性的，至关重要的(important, essential)

【例句】The importance of the additional heat near the surface is crucial. (TPO1, R, S1, T1) 贴近地表的额外热量是至关重要的。

【派生】cruciality *n.* 临界点
crucially *ad.* 至关重要地

crust[7] [krʌst]

【释义】*n.* 1. 面包皮；糕饼等的酥皮 2. 外皮，壳；地壳

【例句】The water evaporates and the salts are left behind, creating a white crustal layer that prevents air and water from reaching the underlying soil. (TPO2, R, Sl, T1) 水分蒸发掉了，剩下的盐分则结成了一层白色外壳，使得空气和水分无法到达地表以下的土层。

【派生】crustal *a.* 外壳的，地壳的
crusted *a.* 有外壳的

crusty *a.* 有外壳的，易怒的
【搭配】earn one's crust 谋生，挣钱糊口

debris[7] [ˈdebriː] 

【释义】*n.* 碎片，残骸
【例句】Glaciers move slowly across the land with tremendous energy, carving into even the hardest rock formations and thereby reshaping the landscape as they engulf, push, drag, and finally deposit rock debris in places far from its original location. (TPO15, R, S1, T1) 冰川带着巨大的能量在陆地上缓慢地移动，甚至切碎最坚硬的岩层，在其吞噬、推动、拖拉直至最后将这些岩石碎片沉积到远离其原地的过程中，地貌被重新塑造。

defense[7] [dɪˈfens] 

【释义】*n.* 防御，防卫
【例句】But other plants protect themselves using chemical defenses, like the potato plant. (TPO9, S, Q6) 但是另外有些植物是利用化学防御来保护自己的，比如马铃薯。
【派生】defenseless *a.* 无防御的
defensive *a.* 防御的，保卫的
【搭配】defense against 对…的防御

desirable[7] [dɪˈzaɪərəbl] 

【释义】*a.* 值得拥有的；可取的，有利的
【例句】The political situation at home made emigration desirable. (TPO5, R, S2, T1) 国内的政治情况使得人们都想移民。
【派生】desirableness *n.* 满意，愿望
【逆构】desire *v.* 渴望

diameter[7] [daɪˈæmɪtə] 

【释义】*n.* 直径
【例句】The basin measures an amazing 2500km in diameter. (TPO5, L, S1, L2) 这一盆地的直径竟然有2500千米。

diet[7] [ˈdaɪət] 

【释义】*n.* 日常饮食 *v.* 节食，按规定饮食
【例句】That means that orcas have had to change their diet to survive. (TPO10, W, Q1) 这意味着虎鲸不得不改变它们的饮食才能生存。
【派生】dietary *a.* 饮食的，有关饮食的
dietician *n.* 营养学家
dieter *n.* 节食者
【搭配】be/go on a diet 节食，减肥

dig[7] [dɪg] 

【释义】*v.* 1. 挖，掘 2. 中意，了解，欣赏 *n.* 1. 戳，刺 2. 挖苦，讽刺
【例句】In the 1930s, wells encountered plentiful water at a depth of about 15 meters; currently, they must be dug to depths of 45 to 60 meters or more. (TPO3, R, S1, T1) 在20世纪30年代，井下15米就有丰富的水资源，而现在，则必须挖掘到45米到60米甚至更深的地方才行。
【搭配】dig a hole for oneself 使自己处于难堪的境地

drag[7] [dræg] 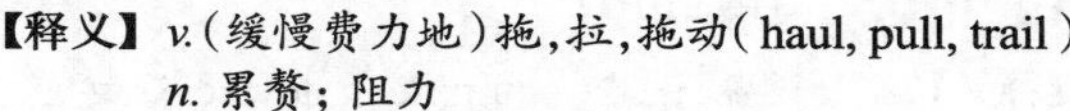

【释义】*v.*（缓慢费力地）拖，拉，拖动（haul, pull, trail）*n.* 累赘；阻力
【例句】On the other hand, plant products like Manila hemp, you can drag through the ocean for weeks on end. (TPO2, L, S1, L2) 另一方面，像由马尼拉麻这种植物制成的麻绳，你可以连续好几星期都用它在海里拖拽东西。
【搭配】drag one's feet 拖着脚步慢吞吞地走；故意拖拉
drag through（使）缓慢通过；挨过时光

exhaust[7] [ɪgˈzɔːst] 

【释义】*v.* 耗尽，使筋疲力尽 *n.* 排气装置，排气
【例句】A shorter drought in which they exhausted their stored food supplies might already have gotten them in deep trouble, because growing crops required rain rather than reservoirs. (TPO14, R, S2, T1) 在一次较短时间的干旱中，他们耗尽了储存的食物，这可能已经让他们深陷困境了，因为生长中的农作物更需要雨水而不是水库蓄水。

explicit[7] [ɪksˈplɪsɪt] 

【释义】*a.* 清楚的，明确的，显而易见的（clear, distinct）

返记菜单

debris[7]	defense[7]	desirable[7]	diameter[7]	diet[7]
dig[7]	drag[7]	exhaust[7]	explicit[7]	

【例句】The brain's level of physiological maturation may support these types of memories, but not ones requiring explicit verbal descriptions. (TPO6, R, S2, T2) 大脑的生理成熟程度可以支持对这些事件的记忆，但是不包括那些需要清晰语言描述的事件。

【反义】ambiguous, implicit, vague

exposure[7] [ɪks'pəʊʒə]

【释义】*v.* 暴露，揭露；曝光(disclosure, revelation)

【例句】Research shows that repeated exposure to a message, even something meaningless or untrue, is enough to make people accept it or see it in a positive light. (TPO3, S, Q6) 研究表明，一个信息的反复曝光，即使这一信息是无意义或不真实的，也足以让人们接受它或者以一种肯定的眼光来看待它。

【派生】exposed *a.* 易受攻击的，无保护的

【逆构】expose *v.* 暴露，使曝光

facility[7] [fə'sɪlɪtɪ] 

【释义】*n.* 1. 设备，设施(equipment, device) 2. 才能，资质

【例句】They are making a lot of money out of commercials and they are using it to offer more scholarships and to help fund projects to renovate the facilities of other programs. (TPO12, S, Q5) 他们在商业广告上赚了很多钱，并且正在用这些钱来提供更多的奖学金以及为其他项目的设备更新提供资金支持。

【派生】facilitate *v.* 促进，帮助

fascinate[7] ['fæsɪneɪt] 

【释义】*v.* 使…着迷，迷住(enchant, enthral, intrigue)

【例句】Artists were fascinated by photography because it offered a way of examining the world in much greater detail. (TPO22, R, S2, T1) 艺术家沉醉于摄影，因为摄影为他们提供了一种可以更加细致地审视这个世界的方法。

【派生】fascinating *a.* 迷人的，醉人的

fauna[7] ['fɔːnə] 

【释义】*n.* 动物群，(某地区或某时期的)所有动物

【例句】One question was related to evidence that the invertebrate fauna (animals without spines) of the Mediterranean had changed abruptly about 6 million years ago. (TPO7, R, S1, T1) 问题之一是找到相关证据来证明地中海的无脊椎动物群体在约 600 万年前发生了突然的变化。

flake[7] [fleɪk] 

【释义】*v.* 剥落，使成薄片(peel) *n.* 薄片，小片(slice, chip)

【例句】It flakes very nicely into really sharp points. (TPO1, L, S2, L1) 它恰好剥落成非常锐利的尖儿。

【派生】flaked *a.* 睡去的；精疲力竭的；失去知觉的

【搭配】flake away/off 剥落
flake out 入睡；昏倒

float[7] [fləʊt] 

【释义】*v.* (使)漂浮(drift) *n.* 筏子，救生用品

【例句】Spores light enough to float on the breezes were carried thousands of miles from more ancient lands and deposited at random across the bare mountain flanks. (TPO9, R, S2, T2) 孢子很轻，可以随着微风，从更古老的陆地飘过几千英里，然后被随意地撒播在荒芜的山腰上。

【搭配】float someone's boat 迎合；勾引，色诱

frustrate[7] ['frʌstreɪt] 

【释义】*v.* 1. 使沮丧，使灰心(discourage, depress) 2. 挫败，破坏(disconcert, thwart, baffle)

【例句】It was so frustrating. (TPO15, L, S2, C1) 我当时十分沮丧。

【派生】frustration *n.* 挫折，挫败

fry[7] [fraɪ] 

【释义】*v.* 油炸，油煎 *n.* 鱼苗；鱼秧子

【例句】But what about all those Italian tomato sauces, humgarengurush or my favorite, French fries? (TPO10, L, S1, L2) 但是所有那些意大利西红柿酱、汉堡包、或是我最爱的薯条怎么样呢？

【搭配】small fry 小人物，小事情

fundamental[7] [ˌfʌndəˈmentl]

【释义】 *a.* 基本的，基础的（basic, elementary, essential）
【例句】 In other words, if you want to know how a land formation was formed, the first thing you probably want to know is how old it is. It's fundamental. (TPO1, L, S1, L2) 换言之，如果你想要知道一个地质构造是怎样形成的，那么可能你首先要知道的就是它形成有多长时间了。这是最根本的。
【派生】 fundamentalism *n.* 原教旨主义
fundamentality *n.* 根本，基本性

germinate[7] [ˈdʒɜːmɪneɪt]

【释义】 *v.*（使）发芽，开始生长（sprout）
【例句】 You know, if the Nightcap Oak remains…if their seeds remain locked inside their shell, they will not germinate. (TPO6, L, S1, L2) 你知道，如果睡帽橡木的种子一直在壳里面，那么它便不会发芽。
【派生】 germination *n.* 发芽

graze[7] [greɪz]

【释义】 *v.* 1.（牛、羊等）吃草，放牧 2. 擦过，擦伤
【例句】 Browsing and grazing animals like the ibex may be another contributing factor. (TPO1, R, S1, T1) 像野山羊这样的食草动物可能是另外一个促成因素。
【派生】 grazer *n.* 吃草的动物；畜牧者
grazeable *a.* 适宜放牧的

guideline[7] [ˈgaidlain]

【释义】 *n.* 指导方针；准则
【例句】 In 1990, new rules and guidelines were adopted in the United Kingdom that have changed the whole field of Archaeology in that country. (TPO16, W, Q1) 1990年，英国实施了新的方针政策，这使得国家的整个考古领域都发生了改变。

hammer[7] [ˈhæmə]

【释义】 *v.* 锤击，反复敲打 *n.* 锤，榔头
【例句】 Elsewhere, you might have to hammer courses together on your own. (TPO 9, L, S1, C1) 另外，你可能需要自己将这些课结合在一起学习。
【派生】 hammerless *a.* 无锤的
【搭配】 under the hammer 被拍卖

hardy[7] [ˈhɑːdɪ]

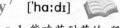

【释义】 *a.* 1. 能吃苦耐劳的，坚强的（robust, sturdy）2.（植物等）耐寒的
【例句】 Most of the older organisms were nearly wiped out, although a few hardy species survived. (TPO7, R, S1, T1) 大多数古老的生物都几近灭绝了，虽然有少数坚强的物种存活了下来。

herb[7] [hɜːb]

【释义】 *n.* 草本植物；药草
【例句】 They may be herbs, shrubs, or trees. (TPO5, R, S1, T1) 它们或许是草本植物、灌木或树木。
【派生】 herbal *a.* 草本的；草药的

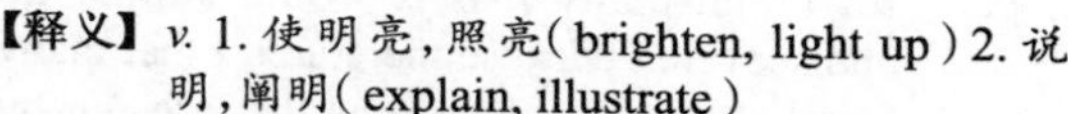

illuminate[7] [ɪˈljuːmɪneɪt]

【释义】 *v.* 1. 使明亮，照亮（brighten, light up）2. 说明，阐明（explain, illustrate）
【例句】 The face appears to be illuminated by light reflected onto it from below. (TPO3, W, Q1) 女人的脸似乎是被由下面反射到上面的光照亮的。
【派生】 illumination *n.* 照亮；阐明

inaccurate[7] [ɪnˈækjʊrɪt]

【释义】 *a.* 不准确的，错误的（incorrect, inexact）
【例句】 This view is inaccurate, and the reason proves to be important. (TPO14, R, S2, T1) 这一观点并不准确，而其中的原因非常重要。
【派生】 inaccurately *ad.* 不准确地

industrialization[7] [ɪnˌdʌstrɪəlaɪˈzeɪʃn]

【释义】 *n.* 工业化
【例句】 The exploitation of fossil fuels has brought planet wide developments: industrialization, construction, uh, mass transport. (TPO15, L, S1, L2) 化石燃料的开发为地球带来了很大的发展，如工业化、建筑以及大规模的交通

运输。

【逆构】 industrial *a.* 工业的，产业的
industrialize *v.*（使）工业化

inhibit[7] [ɪn'hɪbɪt]

【释义】 *v.* 抑制，阻止，使不能（curb, restrain, hinder）

【例句】 Where the forest inhibits the growth of grass and other meadow plants, the black-tailed deer browses on huckleberry, salal, dogwood, and almost any other shrub or herb. (TPO4, R, S1, T1) 在草和其它草地植物的生长受到森林抑制的地方，黑尾鹿就以越橘、沙巴叶、山茱萸以及几乎任何其他灌木或草本植物为食。

【派生】 inhibited *a.* 拘谨的，内向的
inhibition *n.* 禁止，阻止

【搭配】 inhibit sb. from doing sth. 阻止某人干某事

institution[7] [ˌɪnstɪ'tjuːʃən]

【释义】 *n.* 1. 机构 2. 制度，习俗

【例句】 Finally, whatever damage commercial fossil collectors sometimes do, if it weren't for them, many fossils would simply go undiscovered because there aren't that many fossil collecting operations that are run by universities and other scientific institutions. (TPO13, W, Q1) 最后，尽管商业化石收藏者有时候会（对化石）造成一些损害，但如果不是他们，很多化石就不能被发现，因为由大学及其他科学机构运营的化石收藏机构并不是那么多。

【派生】 institutional *a.* 制度上的

【逆构】 institute *n.* 组织

interior[7] [ɪn'tɪərɪə]

【释义】 *a./n.* 内部（的）（inside, inner, internal）

【例句】 Modern architectural forms generally have three separate components comparable to elements of the human body; a supporting skeleton or frame, an outer skin enclosing the interior spaces, and equipment, similar to the body's vital organs and systems. (TPO3, R, S1, T1) 与人类的身体结构类似，现代建筑通常包括三个独立的部分：支撑骨架或框架、覆盖内部空间的外壳以及类似于人体重要器官的设施。

【反义】 exterior

interrupt[7] [ˌɪntə'rʌpt]

【释义】 *v.* 1. 打断（讲话），插嘴（interfere）2. 暂停，使中断（impede, disconstinue）

【例句】 In modern agriculture, mineral depletion of soils is a major concern, since harvesting crops interrupts the recycling of nutrients back to the soil. (TPO5, R, S1, T1) 在现代农业中，土壤中矿物质的消耗是一个值得担忧的问题，因为收割庄稼会扰乱土壤养分回归土壤的循环。

【派生】 interruptable *a.* 可中断的
interruption *n.* 中断；干扰

【搭配】 interrupt sb./sth. with sth. 以…干扰某人或某物

intrigue[7] [ɪn'triːg]

【释义】 *v.* 1. 激起…的兴趣 2. 耍阴谋 *n.* 阴谋，密谋

【例句】 While these records provide broadly consistent indications that temperature variations can occur on a global scale, there are nonetheless some intriguing differences, which suggest that the pattern of temperature variations in regional climates can also differ significantly from each other. (TPO10, R, S2, T1) 虽然这些记录广泛而一致地表明温度变化可能在全球范围内发生，但仍然存在一些有趣的差异，这些差异表明对于不同地区的气候来说温度变化的形式也可能存在很大的不同。

joint[7] [dʒɔɪnt]

【释义】 *a.* 共同的，联合的 *n.* 1. 关节 2. 接头，接合处 3. 下流场所 *v.* 结合，联合

【例句】 Groundwater is stored in the pore spaces and joints of rocks and unconsolidated (unsolidified) sediments or in the openings widened through fractures and weathering. (TPO12, R, S2, T2) 地下水储存在空隙中、岩石的连接处、松散的沉积物中，或者是由于断裂及风化而形成的裂口中。

【派生】 jointer *n.* 接洽人；接合物

【搭配】 joint venture 合资企业

justify[7] ['dʒʌstɪfaɪ] 

【释义】v. 证明…有理；为…辩护(defend, prove)
【例句】This was justified by the view that reflective practice could help teachers to feel more intellectually involved in their role and work in teaching and enable them to cope with the paucity of scientific fact and the uncertainty of knowledge in the discipline of teaching. (TPO9, R, S2, T1) 有一种观点证明了这是合理的，那就是：反思实践可以帮助老师们更加理性地对待他们的角色和他们从事的事业，并能够让他们在教学中处理好科学事实缺乏和知识的不确定问题。
【派生】justification n.(做某事的)正当理由
【搭配】justify his action 是其所为

laryngeal[7] [lə'rɪndʒi:əl] 

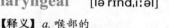

【释义】a. 喉部的
【例句】One kind of habit that he studied are laryngeal habits. (TPO2, L, S1, L1) 他研究的其中一种习惯是喉部习惯。

load[7] [ləʊd] 

【释义】n. 1. 负荷，负担，重任(weight) 2. 装载(量) v. 装载，使负担(burden)
【例句】Metal rails in roadbeds and wagons are capable of carrying heavy loads. (TPO6, R, S1, T1) 路基和货车之间的金属轨道是可以承受重物的。
【搭配】take a load off someone's mind 卸下心中的包袱

longevity[7] [lɒn'dʒevɪtɪ] 

【释义】n. 长寿；寿命
【例句】To be a successful replicator, there are three key characteristics: longevity, fecundity and fidelity. (TPO5, L, S1, L1) 要成为一个成功的复制基因，需要具备三个重要的特征：寿命长，繁殖力强，精确度高。
【搭配】longevity gene 长寿基因

manual[7] ['mænjʊəl]

【释义】a. 1. 用手的，手工的 2. 体力的 n. 指南，手册
【例句】They prefer to process checks manually. (TPO12, L, S2, C1) 他们倾向于用人工计算工资。
【派生】manually ad. 用手；手动地
【搭配】manual labor 体力劳动

millennium[7] [mɪ'lenɪəm] 

【释义】n. 1. 一千年 2. 盛世期
【例句】The other factor is the historical situation in and around the Valley of Mexico toward the end of the first millennium B. C. (TPO8, R, S1, T1) 另一个因素是公元前第一个千年末期时墨西哥山谷里面和周围的历史情况。
【搭配】Millennium Bug 千年虫

mimic[7] ['mɪmɪk] 

【释义】v. 模仿，模拟(imitate, copy) n. 模仿者；仿制品 a. 模仿的，假的
【例句】Well, they can no doubt create a lot with just those five colors, but you are right, maybe they can't mimic every color around them, so that's where the second kind of cell comes in. (TPO17, L, S2, L2) 它们肯定可以用那五种颜色创造出很多颜色，但你是对的，它们可能无法模仿周围的每一种颜色，所以才出现了第二种细胞。
【派生】mimical a. 模仿的
mimicry n. 模仿；拟态
【搭配】mimic warfare 模拟战争

molecule[7] ['mɒlɪkju:l]

【释义】n. 分子，微粒(particle, speck)
【例句】We think meteors that crashed into the moon or tails of passing comets may have introduced water molecules. (TPO5, L, S1, L2) 我们认为撞进月球的流星或途经的彗星的尾巴有可能带去了水分子。
【搭配】molecule weight 分子量

onion[7] ['ʌnjən]

【释义】n. 洋葱
【例句】He thought they were a kind of onion. (TPO6, L, S1, L1) 他以为它们是洋葱的一种。
【派生】oniony a. 洋葱似的，洋葱臭味的
【搭配】know one's onions 知识渊博的

返记菜单

justify[7] laryngeal[7] load[7] longevity[7] manual[7]
millennium[7] mimic[7] molecule[7] onion[7]

plaster[7] ['plɑːstə] 

【释义】*n.* 石膏,灰泥;膏药 *v.* 1. 涂以灰泥 2. 敷膏药 3. 张贴

【例句】You can still see the diagonal marks of the ladders in the plaster on the inside wall. (TPO1, L, S2, L1) 你仍然能够在屋内墙上的石灰上看到那些梯子斜斜的痕迹。

【派生】plastered *a.* 〈俚〉醉醺醺的;涂得厚厚的

plus[7] [plʌs] 

【释义】*conj.* 并且,再说 *prep.* 加,加上 *n.* 1. 好处 2. 加号,正数 *a.* 正的,超过的

【例句】I mean I really don't want to let the other three group members down. Plus the doctor said my wrist should be feeling better by then. (TPO5, S, Q2) 我的意思是,我真的不想让其他的三个组员失望。再说,医生说到那时我的手腕就会感觉好些了。

【反义】minus

portion[7] ['pɔːʃən] 

【释义】*n.* 一部分,一份(part, section, segment) *v.* 分配,划分

【例句】Their atmospheres make up only an infinitesimally small portion of their total mass. (TPO16, R, S2, T2) 空气只占其总质量的极小一部分。

【派生】apportion *v.* 分配,分摊

【搭配】portion sth. out 把…分成几份

pretend[7] [prɪ'tend]

【释义】*v.* 假装,装作

【例句】We would always watch the Action Hero program on television every week, and played games, pretending that we were as strong and powerful as he was. (TPO10, S, Q4) 我们每周都会在电视上看动作片、打游戏,假装我们像电视里的英雄一样强大、有力。

【派生】pretense *n.* 伪装,作假
pretender *n.* 伪装者,冒充者

proceed[7] [prə'siːd] 

【释义】*v.* 进行,继续下去(advance, progress, continue)

【例句】With questions such as these clearly before them, the scientists aboard the Glomar Challenger proceeded to the Mediterranean to search for the answers. (TPO7, R, S1, T1) 带着这些明确摆在眼前的问题,Glomar Challenger号上的科学家们朝着地中海的方向继续前行,寻找答案。

【派生】proceeds *n.* [*pl.*] 收益
proceeding *n.* 行动;进行

【搭配】proceed against 起诉,控诉
proceed from 从…出发

profession[7] [prə'feʃən] 

【释义】*n.* 1. 职业(job, occupation, vocation) 2. 声称,表明,宣布

【例句】She may change professions in order to earn more money. (TPO2, L, S2, L1) 为了多挣些钱,她可能会换个职业。

【派生】professional *a.* 职业的
professionalism *n.* 职业精神
professionalization *n.* 专业化,职业化

【搭配】by profession 就职业来说
enter/go into/join a profession 进入某一行业

Word List 19

promising[7] ['prɒmɪsɪŋ]

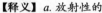

【释义】*a.* 有希望的，有前途的（hopeful, prospective）

【例句】Somewhat more promising have been recent experiments for releasing capillary water (water in the soil) above the water table by injecting compressed air into the ground. (TPO3, R, S1, T1) 最近一些更有希望获得成功的实验试图通过向土壤中注入压缩空气来释放地下水位线以上的毛管水（土壤中的水）。

【逆构】promise *v.* 许诺，答应

【搭配】a promising man 有前途的人

radioactive[7] ['reɪdɪəu'æktɪv]

【释义】*a.* 放射性的

【例句】Now element 43 would be called Masurium or Technetium is radioactive. (TPO8, L, S2, L2) 现在被称作锝的43号元素是具有放射性的。

restoration[7] ['restə'reɪʃən]

【释义】*n.* 1. 整修，修复 2.（遗失物等）归还原主

【例句】But the most profound reason for the restoration of high population numbers has been the fate of the forests. (TPO4, R, S1, T1) 但是鹿群能恢复到较高数量的最深层原因是森林的命运。

【逆构】restore *v.* 恢复，重建

restrict[7] [rɪs'trɪkt]

【释义】*v.* 约束，管束；限制，限定（数量、范围等）（bound, confine, limit, restrain）

【例句】Young toads and cane toad eggs are even easier to gather and destroy, since they are restricted to the water. (TPO15, W, Q1) 幼小的蟾蜍和海蟾蜍的蛋更容易被逮到和毁坏，因为它们只在水中活动。

【派生】restriction *n.* 限制

restricted *a.* 受限制的

restrictive *a.* 限制的

ridge[7] [rɪdʒ]

【释义】*n.* 脊，山脊，脊状突起

【例句】So, during the second rainy period, the dunes were kind of chopped up at the top, full of hollows and ridges, and these hollows would've captured the rain right there on the top. (TPO9, L, S2, L1) 因此，在第二个雨季的时候，沙丘的顶部已被风侵蚀，布满了洞穴和脊状突起，而沙丘顶部的这些洞穴会将雨水截住。

【派生】ridgy *a.* 有脊的

romance[7] [rəu'mæns]

【释义】*n.* 1. 传奇文学 2. 浪漫史，爱情故事 *v.* 1. 写传奇，虚构故事 2. 和…谈情说爱

【例句】People enjoy reading many different types of books such as mystery, biography, romance, etc, of all the different types of books that there are, what type do you most enjoy? (TPO14, S, Q1) 人们喜欢读各种类型的书，比如推理小说、自传、传奇文学等等，在这些不同种类的书中，你最喜欢哪一类？

【派生】romantic *a.* 浪漫的

sack[7] [sæk]

【释义】*n.* 1. 袋子，一袋（的量）2. 解雇 *v.* 1. 解雇 2. 把…装入袋子

【例句】Chromatophores consist of tiny sacks filled with color dye. (TPO17, L, S2, L2) 色素细胞是由充满染料的小袋子组成。

【派生】sackful *n.* 满袋

sackless *a.* 无害的，软弱无能的

【搭配】hit the sack 睡觉

sack paper 纸袋；制袋用纸

scarce[7] [skeəs]

【释义】*a.* 缺乏的，不足的；罕见的（deficient; rare）

【例句】But if you go down to the deepest parts of the ocean, it's cold and dark. And there's not a lot living down there. So food is very scarce. (TPO14, S,Q6) 如果你深入到海洋的最深处，会发现那里是黑暗而阴冷的，并没有太多的生物，所以食物是很匮乏的。

返记菜单

promising[7]	radioactive[7]	restoration[7]	restrict[7]	ridge[7]
romance[7]	sack[7]	scarce[7]		

【反义】 plentiful
【派生】 scarcity *n.* 缺乏，不足
scarsely *ad.* 几乎不，简直没有

scheme[7] [skiːm]

【释义】 *n.* 1. 计划，方案（design, plan）2. 阴谋，诡计（plot, intrigue）*v.* 策划，图谋
【例句】 Educators T. Wildman and J. Niles (1987) describe a scheme for developing reflective practice in experienced teachers. (TPO9, R, S2, T1) 教育家威尔德曼和奈尔斯 (1987) 描述了一个在资深教师中开展反思实践的方案。
【派生】 schemer *n.* 计划者，阴谋家
scheming *a.* 计划的，诡计多端的
【搭配】 propose a scheme 拟定计划

seal[7] [siːl]

【释义】 *v.* 1. 密封（stamp, fasten）2. 确定，使成定局 *n.* 1. 海豹 2. 印鉴，图章 3. 保证；信物
【例句】 The impact of raindrops on the loose soil tends to transfer fine clay particles into the tiniest soil space, sealing them and producing a surface that allows very little water penetration. (TPO2, R, Sl, T1) 雨滴落在松软的泥土表面，会把黏土微粒转移至土壤最小的缝隙之内，并把黏土微粒固定住，这样形成的地表是水分几乎无法渗透的。
【派生】 sealant *n.* 密封材料　　sealed *a.* 密封的
【搭配】 seal sb.'s fate 终结某人的命运
seal a deal/bargin/bussiness 完成交易
seal a victory/win/match 锁定胜利

sibling[7] ['sɪblɪŋ]

【释义】 *n.* 兄弟姐妹
【例句】 When experimentally deprived baby robins are placed in a nest with normally fed siblings, the hungry nestlings beg more loudly than usual. (TPO11, R, S2, T2) 实验时当把饥饿的知更鸟雏鸟与正常喂养的兄弟姐妹放在同一个巢中时，饥饿的雏鸟会发出比平常更大的乞食声。
【派生】 sibship *n.* 亲缘关系
【逆构】 sib *n.* 亲属，亲族 *a.* 亲属的
【搭配】 sibling rivalry 同胞争宠，手足之争

soak[7] [səʊk]

【释义】 *v.* 浸泡，使浸透，使湿透（saturate, drench）
【例句】 Ordinary meteoric water is water that has soaked into the ground from the surface, from precipitation and from lakes and streams. (TPO1, R, S2, T2) 一般的降水是指从地表渗入地下的水以及来自降雨、湖泊和溪流的水。
【派生】 soakage *n.* 浸泡，浸湿
【搭配】 soak into 浸入到
soak up the sun 沐日光浴

spoil[7] [spɔɪl]

【释义】 *v.* 1. 变质 2. 宠爱，溺爱 3. 损坏 *n.* 战利品
【例句】 One of the main crops of the Chaco people was grain maize, which could be stored for long periods of time without spoiling and could serve as a long-lasting supply of food. (TPO5, W, Q1) 查克峡谷人们的主要粮食作物之一是玉米，玉米能够长期存储且不变质，因此可以作为一种长期的食品供应。
【派生】 spoilage *n.* 损坏；掠夺
【搭配】 spoil for 渴望

starling[7] ['stɑːlɪŋ]

【释义】 *n.* 1. 欧掠鸟 2. 挡水木桩
【例句】 He then set up experiments with caged starlings and found that their orientation was in fact, in the proper migratory direction except when the sky was overcast, at which times there was no clear direction to their restless movements. (TPO11, R, S2, T1) 然后他把欧掠鸟关在笼中进行了实验，实验发现，它们的方向实际上与迁徙的方向是一样的，除了阴天的时候它们会因为没有明确的方向而焦躁不安。

strict[7] [strɪkt]

【释义】 *a.* 1. 严格的，严厉的，严谨的 2. 精确
【例句】 Advancing technology and strict laws, however, are helping control some of these adverse environmental effects.（TPO4, R, S2, T2）不过不管怎样，先进的技术和严格的法律正在协助控制这些对环境的不利影响。

【派生】strictness *n.* 严格，严谨

subsequent[7] ['sʌbsɪkwənt] 

【释义】*a.* 随后的，后来的（following, next, succeeding, persuant）

【例句】Desertification is accomplised primarily through the loss of stabilizing natural vegetation and the subsequent accelerated erosion of the soil by wind and water. (TPO2, R, Sl, T1) 由于加固土壤的自然植被消失，随后风力、流水对土壤的侵蚀速度加快，从而形成了沙漠化。

【反义】previous, preceding

【派生】subsequently *ad.* 随后地
subsequence *n.* 随后（发生的事）
subsequential *a.* 后来的

【搭配】subsequent to sth. 继…之后发生的

substitute[7] ['sʌbstɪtju:t] 

【释义】*n.* 代用品，代替者 *v.* 代替，用…替代（replace）

【例句】First, there are those products called substitute goods. (TPO12, S, Q6) 首先，有一些产品叫做代用品。

【派生】substitution *n.* 代替；置换
substitutable *a.* 可替换的

【搭配】substitute for 代替，取代

swallow[7] ['swɒləʊ] 

【释义】*n.* 1. 燕子 2. 吞咽 *v.* 吞下，咽下

【例句】In fact, when tapes of begging tree swallows were played at an artificial swallow nest containing an egg, the egg in that "noisy" nest was taken or destroyed by predators before the egg in a nearby quiet nest in 29 of 37 trials. (TPO11, R, S2, T2) 实际上，当我们把树燕乞食的录音放在装有鸟蛋的人工燕巢中播放时，在37次试验中，其中有29次的情况是该巢中的鸟蛋先于周围安静的鸟巢中的鸟蛋被食肉动物掠走或者破坏掉。

【派生】swallowtail *n.* 燕尾服

【搭配】swallow up 淹没；吞下去；耗尽

symbol[7] ['sɪmbəl] 

【释义】*n.* 1. 符号，记号（sign, signal）2. 象征，标志（emblem, representation）

【例句】Initially in parts of Europe and in China, glasses were a symbol of wisdom and intelligence. (TPO8, L, S2, L1) 起初，在欧洲的部分地区和中国，玻璃被视作智慧和智力的象征。

【派生】symbolic *a.* 象征的
symbolize *v.* 象征
symbology *n.* 符号学
symbolism *n.* 象征主义，符号论

tap[7] [tæp] 

【释义】*v.* 1. 开发，利用 2. 轻拍，轻击 *n.* 1. 龙头，塞子 2. 轻拍

【例句】In the Indus plain, the movement of saline (salty) groundwaters has still not reached equilibrium after 70 years of being tapped. (TPO12, R, S2, T2) 在印度河平原上，含盐的地下水在经过了70年的开发后还是没有达到平衡。

【搭配】tap dance 踢踏舞

territory[7] ['terɪtərɪ] 

【释义】*n.* 领土，领域；版图，范围（area, district, region）

【例句】As their numbers increased, they needed additional territory. (TPO5, R, S2, T1) 随着他们人口数量的增加，他们需要更多的领土。

【派生】territorial *a.* 领土的，领域的

textile[7] ['tekstaɪl] 

【释义】*n.* 纺织品（cloth, fabric）

【例句】In particular, we talked about cotton fibers, which we said were very useful, not only in the textile industry, but also in the chemical industry. (TPO2, L, S1, L2) 我们特别探讨了棉花纤维，它用途很广，不仅可用于纺织业，还可用于化学工业。

【搭配】textile industry 纺织业

thesis[7] ['θi:sɪs] 

【释义】*n.* 1. 毕业（或学位）论文（dissertation）2. 论题，论点

【例句】And I have to start writing my thesis. (TPO2, L, S2, C1) 另外，我得开始写论文了。

【搭配】graduate/master's/doctoral thesis 学士 / 硕士 / 博士论文

返记菜单

subsequent[7] substitute[7] swallow[7] symbol[7] tap[7]
territory[7] textile[7] thesis[7]

throat[7] [θrəʊt]

【释义】*n.* 咽喉，嗓子

【例句】When people are trying to solve a problem, they typically have increased muscular activity in the throat region. (TPO2, L, S1, L1) 当人们想解决一个问题的时候，他们通常会加强喉部的肌肉活动。

【派生】throaty *a.* 喉音的，嘶哑的

【搭配】clear one's throat（说话前）清清嗓子
cut one's own throat 自取灭亡
take by the throat 扼住咽喉，扼杀

title[7] ['taɪtl]

【释义】*n.* 1. 题目，标题（headline）2. 称号 3. 头衔 *v.* 加标题于；赋予…称号

【例句】If you want to search by title with the word "dream" for example, just type it in and all the article with "dream" will come up on the screen. (TPO1, L, S1, C1) 要是你想要通过题目来搜索，比如说，题目中含有"梦"这个字，那你就把这个词输进去，然后所有包含"梦"的文章就会在屏幕上出现了。

【派生】titled *a.* 有标题的，有头衔的
titleholder *n.* 冠军保持者

【搭配】title of honor 荣誉称号

trick[7] [trɪk]

【释义】*a.* 1. 特技的 2. 欺诈的 *n.* 1. 魔术，戏法 2. 诡计，花招，恶作剧 *v.* 欺骗，哄骗

【例句】What audiences came to see was the technological marvel of the movies: the lifelike reproduction of the commonplace motion of trains, of waves striking the shore, and of people walking in the street, and the magic made possible by trick photography and the manipulation of the camera. (TPO2, R, S2, T2) 观众所看到的是电影技术带来的奇迹，比如对平淡无奇的火车开动、海浪拍击海岸和人潮涌动栩栩如生的复述，以及通过特技摄影和操纵相机所制造出来的魔幻景象。

【搭配】try every trick in the book 用尽所有办法
trick out 装扮，打扮
not miss a trick 极其警觉

trigger[7] ['trɪgə]

【释义】*v.* 1. 引发，引起，触发（initiate, set off）*n.* 1. 扳机 2. 起因

【例句】Birds' migration is triggered by natural environmental cues, such as the position of the Sun. (TPO11, R, S2, T1) 鸟类的迁徙是由自然环境因素引发的，比如太阳的位置。

【搭配】pull the trigger 开枪
trigger off 引起；激起

underneath[7] [ˌʌndə'niːθ]

【释义】*prep.* 在…底下 *n.*（物体的）下部，底部 *ad.* 在下面

【例句】The large aquifer that lies underneath the High Plains was discovered by the Ogallala Sioux Indians. (TPO3, R, S1, T1) 位于北美大平原下面的巨大蓄水层是由奥加拉拉苏族印第安人发现的。

utilize[7] [juː'tɪlaɪz]

【释义】*v.* 利用，使用（apply, avail）

【例句】It utilizes space, mass, texture, line, light, and color. (TPO3, R, S1, T1) 它利用了空间、质量、纹理、线条、光线和颜色。

【派生】utilitarian *a.* 功利的，实利的
utility *n.* 效用
utilisation *n.* 利用

vital[7] ['vaɪtl]

【释义】*a.* 1. 至关重要的（important, crucial）2. 有活力的 3. 生死攸关的

【例句】In order to understand ancient Egyptian art, it is vital to know as much as possible of the elite Egyptians' view of the world and the functions and contexts of the art produced for them. (TPO11, R, S1, T1) 想要了解古埃及艺术，尽可能多地了解埃及上层人士的世界观和为他们所创造的艺术品的功能及背景是非常重要的。

【派生】vitality *n.* 活力，生命力
vitalize *v.* 激发，使有活力

wilderness[7] ['wɪldənɪs]

【释义】*n.* 荒野,荒地(wasteland)
【例句】Thing is this is a protective wilderness area. (TPO4, L, S2, L1) 情况是,这是一片受保护的荒野区。
【逆构】wild *a.* 荒凉的
【搭配】in the wilderness(政党)在野的; 在荒原中

administration[6] [ədmɪnɪs'treɪʃən]

【释义】*n.* 1. 管理,经营,施行(management, governing) 2. 政府,当局
【例句】The administration has plans to acquire a new sculpture for campus. (TPO1, S, Q3) 管理部门打算为校园设一座新的雕塑。
【派生】administrative *a.* 管理的; 行政的
administrator *n.* 管理者; 行政官
【逆构】administrate *v.* 管理,经营,实施

advisor[6] [əd'vaɪzə (r)]

【释义】*n.* 顾问,提供意见者
【例句】Why does the advisor discourage the student from transferring to another university? (TPO14, L, S2, C1) 为什么顾问不建议学生转到其它大学?
【派生】advisable *a.* 可取的,明智的
advisory *a.* 顾问的
【逆构】advise *v.* 建议,忠告

aesthetic[6] [iːs'θetɪk]

【释义】*a.* 美学的,审美的,美感的(artistic, pleasing)
【例句】When this occurs, the first step has been taken toward theater as an antonomous activity, and thereafter entertainment and aesthetic values may gradually replace the former mystical and socially efficacious concerns. (TPO1, R, S2, T1) 这时候,戏剧作为一种自发的活动迈出了自己的第一步,接着,戏剧的娱乐和审美价值开始渐渐取代先前的带有神话色彩的、在社会上灵验的关注。

agent[6] ['eɪdʒənt]

【释义】*n.* 1. 媒介,中介 2. 代理人,代理商 3. 特工
【例句】They are dispersed by some other agent, like the wind. (TPO8, L, S1, L1) 它们是靠一些其他的介质传播的,比如风。
【派生】agency *n.* 代理行,经销处;(政府等的)专业部门

aggressive[6] [ə'gresɪv]

【释义】*a.* 1. 侵略的,有进攻性的,好斗的(offensive, hostile) 2. 自信的,大胆的,有进取心的
【例句】Well, they are really territorial, and loners, and just so aggressive even with other Eastern marmots. (TPO1, L, S2, L2) 它们都相当具有领地意识,而且独来独往,所以即使是对其它的东部旱獭也极具攻击性。
【派生】aggressively *ad.* 侵略地; 攻击地
aggressiveness *n.* 侵略; 争斗
【逆构】aggress *v.* 攻击,侵略

alive[6] [ə'laɪv]

【释义】*a.* 1. 有活力的,活跃的,有生气的(vibrant, animated) 2. 活着的,存在的(existent, living)
【例句】And they look so real, so alive that it's very hard to imagine that they are so very old. (TPO3, L, S2, L1) 而且它们看起来如此真实、鲜活,以至于很难想象它们会这么古老。

architect[6] ['ɑːkɪtekt]

【释义】*n.* 建筑师,设计师,缔造者(designer, builder)
【例句】Then, well, the architect has to be very practical to think about the people who actually will be living in the house or working in the office building, whatever, so for the architect, it's all about users not about showing off how creative you can be. (TPO11, L, S1, L2) 那么,设计师需要从实用的角度出发,考虑到真正在这所房子里居住或在这座办公楼里工作的人们,不管怎样,对于设计师来说,这全都关乎使用者,而不是炫耀你多有创造力。
【派生】architecture *n.* 建筑,建筑学
architectural *a.* 建筑的,建筑学的

assess[6] [ə'ses] 

【释义】*v.* 估计,分析,评估(estimate, judge)
【例句】Occasionally one can determine whether stone tools were used in the right hand or the

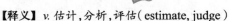

left, and it even possible to assess how far back this feature can be traced. (TPO12, R, S1, T1) 偶尔，人们能够判断出石质工具是用右手还是左手使用的，甚至还有可能估计出这种特征能追溯到多久之前。

【派生】 assessment *n.* 估价，评估
assessable *a.* 可估计的

astronaut[6] ['æstrənɔ:t]

【释义】 *n.* 宇航员

【例句】 There would be a very practical value for a future moon base for astronauts. (TPO5, L, S1, L2) 对宇航员来说，那对未来的月球基地是具有非常实际的好处的。

【派生】 astronautic *a.* 太空航行的，宇航员的
astronautics *n.* 航天学；宇宙航行

atmospheric[6] [ˌætməs'ferɪk]

【释义】 *a.* 1. 大气的 2. 有…气氛的

【例句】 Early in the century, a pump had come into use in which expanding steam raised a piston in a cylinder, and atmospheric pressure brought it down again when the steam condensed inside the cylinder to form a vacuum. (TPO6, R, S1, T1) 在(19)世纪早期，泵曾被用于(发动机的)汽缸，在气缸中，膨胀的蒸汽推动活塞上升，而当汽缸内部的蒸汽被压缩形成真空环境时，气压又使得活塞下降。

【逆构】 atmosphere *n.* 大气；气氛

【搭配】 atmospheric pressure 大气压力，大气压强

bearing[6] ['beərɪŋ]

【释义】 *n.* 1. 方向感，方位(direction) 2. 轴承 3. 举止，风度(manner)

【例句】 Birds' innate bearings keep them oriented in a direction that is within 15 degrees of the Suns direction. (TPO11, R, S2, T1) 鸟类天生的方向感使它们能保持在朝着太阳方位15度以内的方向飞行。

【逆构】 bear *v.* 忍受，支撑

【搭配】 bearing capacity 承载量

besides[6] [bɪ'saɪdz]

【释义】 *prep.* 除(某人/某事物)之外(还有)

【例句】 Now besides the bark, Native Americans also used the wood of the birch tree. (TPO7, L, S2, L1) 除了树皮，当地美洲人还充分利用了桦树的木材。

billboard[6] ['bɪlbɔ:d]

【释义】 *n.* 广告牌；布告板

【例句】 Obviously the major media are television, radio, newspapers, magazines, um, billboards, and so forth. (TPO11, L, S2, L2) 很明显，主要的媒体有电视、电台、报纸、杂志、广告牌等等。

bond[6] [bɒnd]

【释义】 *v.* 1. (使)结合(link, tie) 2. 为…作担保 *n.* 1. 联结，联系(connection) 2. 债券(securities, debenture)

【例句】 Like the stones of a Roman wall which were held together both by the regularity of the design and by that peculiarly powerful Roman cement, so the various parts of the Roman realm were bonded into a massive, monolithic entity by physical, organizational, and psychological controls. (TPO7, R, S2, T1) 如同罗马墙是通过规律的设计和独特有效的罗马水泥构筑而成一样，罗马王国的各个部分也是通过对物质、组织和心理层面的支配而联结成一个规模宏大、坚如磐石的统一体的。

border[6] ['bɔ:də]

【释义】 *n.* 边界，边境；边缘(boundary, edge) *v.* 与…接界，和…毗邻(abut, adjoin)

【例句】 The semiarid lands bordering the deserts exist in a delicate ecological balance. (TPO2, R, Sl, T1) 紧邻沙漠的半干旱地区处在一个十分脆弱的生态平衡状态。

【搭配】 border on 与…接壤/邻接

capability[6] [ˌkeɪpə'bɪlɪtɪ]

【释义】 *n.* 能力，才能；性能，容量(ability, capacity)

【例句】 Birds have some of the best vision capabilities in the animal kingdom. (TPO15, S, Q6) 在动物界中，鸟类拥有一些很好的视觉能力。

【逆构】 capable *a.* 能干的，能胜任的，有才华的

ceiling[6] ['siːlɪŋ] 

【释义】*n.* 1. 天花板 2. 最高限度，上限

【例句】A planetarium is essentially a theater with a domelike ceiling onto which a night sky can be projected for any night of the year. (TPO11, R, S2, T1) 天文馆实质上是一个有着穹顶天花板的剧院，在一年中的任何时候都能把夜晚的天空投射到天花板上。

【逆构】ceil *v.* 装天花板

【搭配】hit the ceiling 勃然大怒

centimeter[6] ['sentiˌmɪːtə] 

【释义】*n.* 厘米，公分

【例句】Scientists felt that they could get an idea of how long the extinctions took by determining how long it took to deposit this one centimeter of clay. (TPO8, R, S2, T1) 科学家们认为，他们可以根据这一厘米粘土的形成时间来确定其消失用了多长时间。

chaotic[6] [keɪ'ɒtɪk] 

【释义】*a.* 混乱的（confused）

【例句】Well, these elements together can convey a wilder, more chaotic emotion in the viewer than, say, a painting with tiny, smooth brush strokes and soft or pale colors. (TPO4, S, Q6) 与用细腻流畅的笔触和柔和苍白的色彩绘制而成的画作相比，这些元素组合在一起可以传递给观者一种更狂热、更混乱的情绪。

【逆构】chaos *n.* 混乱

cheep[6] [tʃip] 

【释义】*n.* 吱吱的叫声 *v.* 吱吱地叫

【例句】These loud cheeps and peeps might give the location of the nest away to a listening hawk or raccoon, resulting in the death of the defenseless nestlings. (TPO11, R, S2, T2) 这些吱吱的叫声会把其巢穴的位置暴露给正在全神聆听的老鹰或者浣熊，从而导致了毫无防备的雏鸟的死亡。

chip[6] [tʃiːp]

【释义】*n.* 1. 缺口 2. 碎片 3. 炸薯条 *v.* 削，凿，(使)切成碎片

【例句】You don't have to remove big chips of paint to do your analysis, which is what other methods require. (TPO5, L, S2, L1) 你不必像其他方法所要求的那样，从(作品)中切取大片的颜料来做分析。

【搭配】chip in 捐助；插嘴；下赌注

circadian[6] [sɜː'keɪdɪən] 

【释义】*a.* 生理节奏的，以 24 小时为周期的

【例句】Such a rhythm whose period is approximately—but not exactly—a day is called circadian. (TPO13, R, S2, T1) 这种和一天的循环周期很接近但不精确同步的循环叫做生理节奏。

【搭配】circadian rhythm 生理节奏，昼夜节律

circular[6] ['sɜːkjʊlə] 

【释义】*a.* 圆形的；循环的 *n.* 通知，通告

【例句】Modern irrigation devices, each capable of spraying 4.5 million liters of water a day, have produced a landscape dominated by geometric patterns of circular green islands of crops. (TPO3, R, S1, T1) 日喷水量达 450 万升的现代灌溉设备，形成了一个以圆形绿岛作物为主的景观。

【派生】circularity *n.* 环状

circularly *ad.* 圆地，循环地

【搭配】circular arch 圆拱

colleague[6] ['kɒliːg] 

【释义】*n.* 同事，同僚（co-worker, fellow worker, associate）

【例句】The exchanger would then send a bill of exchange to a colleague in Marseille. (TPO10, R, S2, T2) 那位兑换方其后会给他在马赛的同事寄去汇票。

commodity[6] [kə'mɒdɪtɪ] 

【释义】*n.* 商品，货物

【例句】Teotihuacán obsidian must have been

recognized as a valuable commodity for many centuries before the great city arose. (TPO8, R, S1, T1) 在这座伟大的城市崛起之前的几百年间,特奥蒂瓦坎黑曜石肯定已经被认为是一种宝贵的商品了。

concerning[6] [kən'sɜːnɪŋ]

【释义】 *prep.* 关于;就…而言(about, as for)

【例句】 In fact, a lack of understanding concerning the purposes of Egyptian art has often led it to be compared unfavorably with the art of other cultures. (TPO11, R, S1, T1) 事实上,因为对埃及艺术的目的缺乏理解,所以经常会把埃及艺术与其他文化中的艺术进行不利的比较。

【逆构】 concern *v.* 涉及;关心 *n.* 关心,忧虑

concrete[6] ['kɒnkriːt]

【释义】 *a.* 实在的,具体的(material, tangible)

【例句】 However, some modern architectural designs, such as those using folded plates of concrete or air-inflated structures, are again unifying skeleton and skin. (TPO2, R, Sl, T1, Q12) 但是,一些现代建筑设计,例如使用折板的实体结构或充气结构,再一次使骨架和表面成为一体。

【反义】 abstract

【派生】 concretely *ad.* 具体地

conform[6] [kən'fɔːm]

【释义】 *v.* 使一致,符合,遵从,顺从(fit, meet, assent, follow)

【例句】 Individual members of a group attempt to conform their opinions to what believe to be the group consensus even though the result may be negative. (TPO1, S, Q4) 群体里的每个成员都试图使自己的看法与集体的共识保持一致,即使这样做的结果可能并不好。

【派生】 conformable *a.* 一致的;顺从的;适合的
conformity *n.* 一致,符合

【搭配】 conform to 符合,遵照
conform with 符合,与…一致

conquest[6] ['kɒŋkwest]

【释义】 *n.* 征服,攻克

【例句】 While the Greek world had expanded along the Mediterranean sea lanes, the Roman world was assembled by territorial conquest. (TPO7, R, S2, T1) 希腊通过地中海海上航线完成了扩张,而罗马则是通过领土征服实现的。

【搭配】 the conquest of cancer 战胜癌症

correspond[6] [kɒrɪs'pɒnd]

【释义】 *v.* 1. 符合,一致 2. 通信,交流

【例句】 The purples and the blues in the middle correspond to low elevations. (TPO5, L, S1, L2) 中间的紫色和蓝色部分对应着低海拔地区。

【派生】 correspondence *n.* 通信,信件;符合,一致

【搭配】 correspond to 与…相对应

Word List 20

cortex[6] ['kɔːteks]

【释义】*n.* 外皮;(大脑)皮层

【例句】As the tool was made, the core was rotated clockwise, and the flakes, removed in sequence, had a little crescent of cortex on the side. (TPO12, R, S1, T1) 在制造工具时,岩芯按照顺时针方向旋转,其碎片就一点一点剥落,在一侧留下月牙状的表层(石芯的表面)。

court[6] [kɔːt]

【释义】*n.* 1. 庭院 2. 宫廷 3. 法院 4. 球场 *v.* 1. 献殷勤 2. 追求 3. 招致

【例句】In pillared courts, where they would be placed against or between pillars: their frontality worked perfectly within the architectural context. (TPO11, R, S1, T1) 在有柱子的院内,它们被安置在柱子中间或对着柱子:如此其正面描绘就与建筑环境完美融合了。

【派生】courtier *n.* 奉承者
courtship *n.* 求爱(时期)
courtyard *n.* 庭院

【搭配】out of court 不经法院;私了;被驳回
go to court 起诉;朝见君主
at court 当庭

crude[6] [kruːd]

【释义】*a.* 1. 粗糙的(rough, coarse)2. 天然的,未加工的(raw)3. 粗鲁的 *n.* 天然的物质(尤指原油)

【例句】We might expect that early artistic efforts would be crude, but the cave paintings of Spain and southern France show a marked degree of skill. (TPO4, R, S2, T1) 我们可能会认为早期的艺术成就会不够成熟,但西班牙和法国南部的洞穴壁画却显示出了高超的技巧。

【反义】refined

【搭配】crude oil [化] 原油

dealing[6] ['diːlɪŋ]

【释义】*n.* 交易,来往

【例句】Peripheral peoples therefore had a great advantage in their dealings with the center, making government authority insecure and anxious. (TPO16, R, S1, T1) 因此,周边地区的人们在和中心地区的人们交易时很有优势,这让政府机构感到焦虑不安。

【逆构】deal *v.* 交易;对待,处理 *n.* 交易;分量

【搭配】fair dealing 公平交易

decorate[6] ['dekəreɪt]

【释义】*v.* 装饰,装修(adorn, embellish)

【例句】You can see on the walls, which they plastered and decorated with paintings. (TPO1, L, S2, L1) 你可以看到,那些墙上涂着灰泥,并装饰着图画。

【派生】decoration *n.* 装饰,装饰品
decorative *a.* 装饰的,可作装饰的

defend[6] [dɪ'fend]

【释义】*v.* 1. 保卫,保护(protect, safeguard)2. 为…辩护,为(论文等)答辩

【例句】State and defend your opinion, analyze the issues, speculate about how things might have turned out differently. (TPO16, L, S2, C1) 表述并捍卫你的观点,分析问题,思考事情如何呈现出不同的结果。

【派生】defendant *n.* 保护;被告
defense *n.* 防御,保护;辩护
defensive *a.* 防御用的,防御性的

diffuse[6] [dɪ'fjuːz]

【释义】*v.* 散布,传播,扩散(spread)*a.* 散开的,弥漫的(dispersed, scattered)

【例句】Iron came from West Asia, although its routes of diffusion were somewhat different than those of agriculture. (TPO7, R, S2, T2) 铁器来自西亚,尽管其传播途径在某种程度上不同于农业。

【派生】diffusible *a.* 可扩散的

返记菜单

cortex[6] court[6] crude[6] dealing[6] decorate[6]
defend[6] diffuse[6]

discharge[6]

【释义】[dɪs'tʃɑːdʒ] v. 1. 排出(give off) 2. 释放(release) 3. 撤职，解雇 ['dɪstʃɑːdʒ] n. 1. 流出(emission, flow) 2. 放电

【例句】Today, river discharges are increasingly controlled by human intervention, creating a need for international river-basin agreement. (TPO12, R, S2, T2) 今天，河水的排放更多地受到人为干预的控制，这就需要人们在国际河流流域问题上达成一致。

【搭配】discharge from 解雇；释放
pollution discharge 排污
flood discharge 泄洪

disprove[6] [dɪs'pruːv]

【释义】v. 反驳，证明…是虚假的(confute, refute)

【例句】It cannot be completely proved or disproved. (TPO2, L, S1, L1) 这个理论无法被完全证实，也无法被彻底推翻。

【反义】prove, affirm

【派生】disproval n. 反证，反驳

disturb[6] [dɪs'tɜːb]

【释义】v. 1. 打扰(bother) 2. 扰乱，妨碍 3. 使不安，使烦恼(annoy)

【例句】So a microclimate can be something so small and so easily disturbed that even a tiny change can have a big impact. (TPO14, L, S1, L2) 所以微气候可以如此之小且特别容易受干扰，以至于即使是一点细微的变化也会有很大的影响。

【派生】disturbance n. 干扰，困扰
disturbing a. 令人不安的

encounter[6] [ɪn'kaʊntə]

【释义】v. 遇到，遭遇(meet, confront) n. 相遇，邂逅

【例句】In the 1930s, wells encountered plentiful water at a depth of about 15 meters; currently, they must be dug to depths of 45 to 60 meters or more. (TPO3, R, S1, T1) 在20世纪30年代，井下15米处就有丰富的水资源，而现在，必须挖掘到45米到60米甚至更深的地方才行。

【搭配】an unexpected encounter 不期而遇

endanger[6] [ɪn'deɪndʒə]

【释义】v. 危及，危害(imperil, threaten, jeopardize)

【例句】Second, other sea mammals such as seals and sea lions along the Alaskan coast were also declining, indicating that whatever had endangered the otters was affecting other sea mammals as well. (TPO10, W, Q1) 其次，其它海洋哺乳动物的数量也在下降，比如阿拉斯加海岸沿线的海豹和海狮，这表明，危及到了水獭的因素也在影响其它的海洋哺乳动物。

【反义】safeguard, protect

engrave[6] [ɪn'greɪv]

【释义】v. 雕刻，刻上(carve, cut)

【例句】Most engravings, for example, are best lit from the left, as befits the work of right-handed artists, who generally prefer to have the light source on the left so that the shadow of their hand does not fall on the tip of the engraving tool or brush. (TPO12, R, S1, T1) 例如，大多数的雕版都是左起的光照最好，这是为了配合惯用右手的工匠的工作。他们喜欢让光线从左面照过来，以便于他们手的影子不会落在雕版工具或是刷子的尖端。

【派生】engraved a. 被牢记的，被深深刻入的

equivalent[6] [ɪ'kwɪvələnt]

【释义】a. 相同的，相等的，等同的(equal, same) n. 相等物，等价物，对等词(substitute, match)

【例句】Watson makes the assumption that muscular activity is equivalent to thinking. (TPO2, L, S1, L1) 沃森猜测肌肉运动等同于思考活动。

【反义】different

【派生】equivalence n. 同等，等值

eruption[6] [ɪ'rʌpʃən]

【释义】n. 喷发，爆发(explosion, burst, outbreak)

【例句】The last factor is the impact of natural disasters, such as the volcanic eruptions of the late first millennium B. C. (TPO8, R, S1, T1) 最后一个因素是自然灾害的影响，如公元前一千年后期的火山喷发。

【逆构】 erupt *v.* 爆发

exotic[6] [ɪg'zɒtɪk] 

【释义】 *a.* 1. 外来的(foreign, alien)2. 奇异的(strange, unusual)

【例句】 Long-distance trade in obsidian probably gave the elite residents of Teotihuacán access to a wide variety of exotic goods, as well as a relatively prosperous life. (TPO8, R, S1, T1) 黑曜石的长途贸易使得特奥蒂瓦坎的上层居民们有机会接触到丰富多样的外来物品并过上相对繁荣的生活。

【反义】 indigenous, native

【派生】 exoticism *n.* 异国情调

export[6]

【释义】 [ɪk'spɔːt] *v.* 1. 出口 2. 传播,输出(思想或活动) ['ekspɔːt] *n.* 1. 输出,出口 2. 输出[出口]物

【例句】 The English made a major adjustment to opera and exported what they had done to opera back to Italy. (TPO12, L, S2, L1) 英国人在歌剧上做了一次重大的调整,并且把他们对歌剧所作出的改变又输送回意大利。

【反义】 import

【派生】 exportation *n.* 出口

extraordinary[6] [ɪk'strɔːdənəri] 

【释义】 *a.* 非常的,特别的,非凡的(exceptional, marvellous, remarkable, outstanding)

【例句】 Clara grew up to become a well-known and respected piano virtuoso, a performer of extraordinary skill who gave concerts across Europe. (TPO16, L, S1, L2) 克拉拉成长为了一个著名的、受人尊敬的钢琴演奏家,才华卓越,在欧洲各地巡回演出。

【反义】 ordinary, common, general

fame[6] [feɪm] 

【释义】 *n.* 名声,名望(reputation, renown)

【例句】 Many people value fame and seek fame. (TPO2, L, S2, L1) 许多人看重名声,并且追求名望。

【派生】 famous *a.* 著名的

fidelity[6] [fɪ'delɪtɪ] 

【释义】 *n.* 1. 准确性,保真度(accuracy)2. 忠实,忠诚(faith, loyalty)

【例句】 To be a successful replicator, there are three key charateristics: longevity, fecundity and fidelity. (TPO5, L, S1, L1) 要成为一个成功的复制基因,需要具备三个重要的特征:寿命长,繁殖力强,精确度高。

firn[6] [fɪən] 

【释义】 *n.* 粒雪,万年雪

【例句】 With further melting, refreezing, and increased weight from newer snowfall above, the snow reaches a granular recrystallized stage intermediate between flakes and ice known as firn. (TPO15, R, S1, T1) 随着进一步的融化、再结冰,以及承受着上方新的降雪的重量,这些积雪到了一种介于雪花和冰块之间颗粒再结晶阶段,这一阶段的雪被称为粒雪。

fold[6] [fəʊld]

【释义】 *v.* 折叠,对折 *n.* 折叠的部分,褶痕(crease, pleat)

【例句】 However, some modern architectural designs, such as those using folded plates of concrete or air-inflated structures, are again unifying skeleton and skin. (TPO2, R, Sl, T1) 但是,一些现代建筑设计,例如使用折板的实体结构或充气结构,再一次使骨架和表面成为一体。

【反义】 unfold

frame[6] [freɪm] 

【释义】 *n.* 框架,结构 2. 体形,身材,骨架 *v.* 1. 加外框 2. 提出,构造,制定

【例句】 Modern architectural forms generally have three separate components comparable to elements of the human body; a supporting skeleton or frame, an outer skin enclosing the interior spaces, and equipment, similar to the body's vital organs and systems. (TPO3, R, S1, T1) 与人类的身体结构类似,现代建筑通常包括三个独立的部分:支撑骨架或框

架、覆盖内部空间的外壳以及类似于人体重要器官的设施。

【派生】framework *n.* 框架,体系

【搭配】frame of mind 心绪,心情,心境

frost[6] [frɒst]

【释义】*n.* 霜,霜冻 *v.* 结霜(ice, freeze)

【例句】That's when it's not covered in snow and there is no frost covering the grass and, vegetative parts of a plant's herbs and the flowers the marmots like to eat. (TPO1, L, S2, L2) 那时候没有冰雪的覆盖,也没有霜冻覆盖着草地以及旱獭喜欢吃的植物的草本部分,比如叶子和花。

【派生】frostbite *n./v.* 冻伤

geomagnetic[6] [ˌdʒiomæg'nɛtɪk]

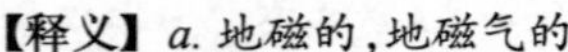

【释义】*a.* 地磁的,地磁气的

【例句】Well, geomagnetic activity, the natural variations in Earth's magnetic field, it fluctuates in 11-year cycles. (TPO18, L, S1, L1) 地磁活动,也就是地球磁场的自然变化,其波动周期是 11 年。

heliacal[6] [hɪ'laɪək(ə)l]

【释义】*a.* 太阳的,和太阳同时或几乎同时出没的

【例句】And this annual event is called a heliacal rising. (TPO17, L, S2, L1) 而这一年度大事被称为偕日升。

herd[6] [hɜːd]

【释义】*n.* 兽群,牧群;一群(flock)*v.* 1. 放牧 2.(使)成群

【例句】Cave art seems to have reached a peak toward the end of the Upper Paleolithic period, when the herds of game were decreasing. (TPO4, R, S2, T1) 石窟艺术似乎在旧石器时代即将结束时达到了顶峰,当时猎物的数量在下降。

【搭配】a herd of 一群(牛、鹿等)
herd behavior 羊群效应;从众行为
herd instinct [心] 群居本能,群体心理

hydrothermal[6] [ˌhaɪdrə'θɜml]

【释义】*a.* 水热作用的,热液的

【例句】It all began in 1977 with the exploration of hydrothermal vents on the ocean floor. (TPO15, L, S2, L2) 它是于 1977 年伴随着对海底热液喷口的勘测全面展开的。

immigrant[6] ['ɪmɪgrənt]

【释义】*n.* 移民

【例句】A local population that goes extinct is quickly replaced by immigrants from an adjacent community. (TPO3, R, S1, T2) 当地物种灭亡后,马上就会被相邻群落的移民所取代。

【派生】immigration *n.* 移民

【逆构】immigrate *v.*(从外国)移入,移民

【搭配】an illegal immigrant 非法移民

implicit[6] [ɪm'plɪsɪt]

【释义】*a.* 1. 含蓄的,不明确的(implied, tacit)2. 固有的 3. 无疑问的

【例句】Many older theories implicitly deprecated the navigational abilities and overall cultural creativity of the Pacific islanders. (TPO5, R, S2, T1) 许多古老的理论含蓄地否定了太平洋岛民的航海能力和总体文化创造力。

【派生】implicitly *ad.* 含蓄地;暗中地
implicity *n.* 不怀疑,不问原因

impose[6] [ɪm'pəʊz]

【释义】*v.* 1. 强加于 2. 施加影响 3. 征税 4. 欺骗,利用

【例句】Numerous controls imposed by Roman rulers held its territory together. (TPO7, R, S2, T1) 罗马统治者施加的多项控制政策确保了他们领土的完整。

【派生】imposing *a.* 印象深的

【搭配】impose a fine 处以罚款

incorporate[6] [ɪn'kɔːpəreɪt]

【释义】*v.* 合并,并入;包含(merge, unite, contain)*a.* 合并的,组成合法公司的

【例句】Ceramics produced during the Tang and

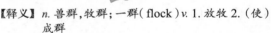

Ming dynasties sometimes incorporated multiple colors. (TPO10, R, S1, T1) 唐代和明代制造的陶器有时会融合多种色彩。

【搭配】incorporate with 合并；混合

incredible[6] [ɪn'kredəbl] 

【释义】*a.* 难以置信的(unbelievable)

【例句】At first thought it seems incredible that there can be enough space in the solid ground underfoot to hold all this water. (TPO1, R, S2, T2) 我们脚下坚实的土地中竟然有足够的空间容纳这么多水，这在一开始会让人感觉难以置信。

initiate[6] [ɪ'nɪʃɪeɪt] 

【释义】*v.* 1. 开始，着手(begin, start, originate) 2. 传授，使初步了解 3. 接纳新成员 *n.* 新入会的人

【例句】Kramer initiated important new kinds of research regarding how animals orient and navigate. (TPO11, R, S2, T1) Kramer 开创了有关动物如何确定方向和前行的重要的新研究。

【派生】initiation *n.* 开始；启蒙；入会
initial *a.* 开始的，最初的 *n.* 开头大写字母

interlock[6] [ˌɪntə'lɒk] 

【释义】*v.* (使)连结(connect, link)

【例句】Our ties with people often deepen as we interact with them and gradually evolve interlocking habits and interests. (TPO13, R, S1, T1) 当我们和人们进行长期的互动并且逐渐形成交织在一起的行为习惯和兴趣爱好时，我们之间的联系就加强了。

irrigate[6] ['ɪrɪgeɪt] 

【释义】*v.* 灌溉，浇灌

【例句】It is projected that the remaining Ogallala water will, by the year 2030, support only 35 to 40 percent of the irrigated acreage in Texas that it supported in 1980. (TPO3, R, S2, T1) 预计到 2030 年，奥加拉拉蓄水层剩余的水量将仅能维持其在 1980 年所覆盖的德克萨斯州土地灌溉面积的 35% 到 40%。

【派生】irrigation *n.* 灌溉
irrigational *a.* 灌溉的
irrigator *n.* 灌溉设备

lichen[6] ['laɪkən] 

【释义】*n.* 地衣，青苔

【例句】Lichens were probably the first successful flora. (TPO9, R, S2, T2) 地衣可能是第一批成功扎根的植物。

【派生】lichened *a.* 长满青苔的

lifestyle[6] ['laɪfstaɪl] 

【释义】*n.* 生活方式

【例句】Pastoralism is a lifestyle in which economic activity is based primarily on livestock. (TPO14, R, S2, T2) 畜牧生活是一种将经济活动主要基于牲畜的生活方式。

【搭配】healthy lifestyle 健康的生活方式

long-lasting[6] ['lɔːŋlaːstiŋ] 

【释义】*a.* 持续时间长的

【例句】However, intrinsic motivation is generally considered to be more long-lasting than the other. (TPO5, S, Q2) 但是，人们普遍认为内在动机比外在动机持续的时间更长。

lunar[6] ['luːnə] 

【释义】*a.* 月的，月球的

【例句】Consequently, the timing and rhythms of biological functions must closely match periodic events like the solar day, the tides, the lunar cycle, and the seasons. (TPO13, R, S2, T1) 因此，生物的计时与交替循环的机能也必须与像昼夜交替、潮涨潮落、月圆月缺和四季更迭这样的周期性事件保持一致。

【搭配】lunar calendar 阴历

maximum[6] ['mæksɪməm] 

【释义】*a.* 最大的，最高的，顶点的(greatest, uppermost) *n.* 最大量，最大限制，极大值

【例句】Even the kind of stability defined as simple lack of change is not always associated with maximum diversity. (TPO3, R, S1, T2) 即使是这种被定义为简单地缺乏变化的稳定性也并非总是与最大多样性联系起来。

【反义】minimum

返记菜单

incredible[6] initiate[6] interlock[6] irrigate[6] lichen[6]
lifestyle[6] long-lasting[6] lunar[6] maximum[6]

【派生】maximal *a.* 最大的，最高的
maximize *v.* 使(某事物)增至最大值
【搭配】maximum temperature 最高温度

---

meadow[6] ['medəu] 

【释义】*n.* 草地，牧场(grassland, pasture)
【例句】Where the forest inhibits the growth of grass and other meadow plants, the black-tailed deer browses on huckleberry, salal, dogwood, and almost any other shrub or herb. (TPO4, R, S1, T1) 在草和其它草地植物的生长受到森林抑制的地方，黑尾鹿便以越橘、沙巴叶、山茱萸和几乎任何其它灌木或草本植物为食。

---

mechanical[6] [mɪ'kænɪkl]

【释义】*a.* 1. 机械(制造)的 2. 力学的 3. 呆板的
【例句】No mechanical devices are used in passive heating systems. (TPO12, L, S2, L2) 在被动供热系统中不使用机械装置。
【派生】mechanically *ad.* 机械地；呆板地
【搭配】mechanical system 机械系统

---

merchandise[6] ['mɜːtʃəndaɪz] 

【释义】*n.* 商品，货物(goods) *v.* 买卖，销售
【例句】Well, for full refund: store policy is that you have to return merchandises 2 weeks from the time it was purchased. (TPO10, L, S2, C1) 对于全额退款，店里的政策是，你必须从购买之日起两周内返还商品。
【搭配】merchandise trade 商品贸易

---

mill[6] [mɪl] 

【释义】*n.* 1. 磨坊 2. 研磨机 *v.* 研磨，碾碎
【例句】Although waterpower abounded in Lancashire and Scotland and ran grain mills as well as textile mills, it had one great disadvantage. (TPO6, R, S1, T1) 尽管兰开夏和苏格兰地区丰富的水力资源可用于谷物作坊和纺织厂，但这种动力存在一个极大的缺陷。
【搭配】draw water to one's mill 事事为自己打算
go through the mill 历尽沧桑
in the mill 在制造中，在准备中

---

mission[6] ['mɪʃən]

【释义】*n.* 1. 使命，天职，任务(task, assignment, duty) 2. 代表团 *v.* 1. 派遣 2. 向…传教
【例句】Also, data from a later mission indicates significant concentrations of hydrogen and by inference water less than a meter underground at both poles. (TPO5, L, S1, L2) 同样，由最近的一个航天任务发回的数据表明，在月球的两极不到一米的地下聚集着大量的氢元素以及由此可能存在的水。
【派生】missionary *a.* 传教的 *n.* 传教士

---

modest[6] ['mɒdɪst] 

【释义】*a.* 1. 适量的，适度的(mild, moderate) 2. 谦虚的
【例句】In these shops differences of rank were blurred as artisans and masters labored side by side in the same modest establishment. (TPO16, R, S1, T1) 在这些商店里，由于工匠和大师在同样适中的设施下肩并肩地工作，所以等级的区分是模糊的。
【派生】modesty *n.* 谦逊，虚心

---

moss[6] [mɒs] 

【释义】*n.* 苔藓，藓类植物
【例句】Now, other forms of life could take hold: ferns and mosses (two of the most ancient types of land plants) that flourish even in rock crevices. (TPO9, R, S2, T2) 现在，另外两种生命形式也会在此扎根：蕨类和藓类植物(两种最古老的陆地植物)，这两种植物甚至能在岩石的缝隙中生长。
【搭配】A rolling stone gathers no moss. 滚石不生苔。

---

mound[6] [maund] 

【释义】*n.* 1. 土墩，土丘 2. 一堆 *v.* 用土石堆设
【例句】Close to one house, called Pueblo Alto, archaeologists identified an enormous mound formed by a pile of old material. (TPO5, W, Q1) 在一所叫做 Pueblo Altode 的房子附近，考古学家们发现了一个由一堆旧材料形成的大土堆。

niche6 [nɪtʃ] 

【释义】 *n.* 1. 壁龛,像壁龛样的一隅 2. 合适的职位 *v.* 把…放入壁龛

【例句】 Very often such statues were enclosed in rectangular shrines or wall niches whose only opening was at the front, making it natural for the statue to display frontality. (TPO11, R, S1, T1) 通常这些雕像都被封闭在只有前面有开口的矩形的神龛或者壁龛内,这样展示雕像的正面就显得很自然了。

off-campus6 [ˈɔfkæmpəs] 

【释义】 *a.* 在校园外的 *ad.* 在校园外地

【例句】 It's ridiculous that they haven't already changed the route—you know, so it goes where most off-campus students live now. (TPO2, S, Q3) 他们到现在都没有调整校车路线,这太可笑了——你也知道,应该将路线调整到大多数校外学生现在居住的地方。

【反义】 on-campus

opaque6 [əʊˈpeɪk]

【释义】 *a.* 1. 不透明的 2. 难理解的,晦涩的(dull, vague)

【例句】 That might be one reason that opaque bottles haven't really caught on. (TPO9, L, S1, C1) 那可能就是为什么没有采用不透明的瓶子的原因之一。

【派生】 opaquely *ad.* 不透明地,无光泽地

【搭配】 in an opaque manner 以难懂的方式

overcast6 [ˈəʊvəkɑːst] 

【释义】 *a.* 阴天的,阴暗的(cloudy, gloomy) *v.* 遮盖,使变暗

【例句】 He then set up experiments with caged starlings and found that their orientation was. in fact, in the proper migratory direction except when the sky was overcast, at which times there was no clear direction to their restless movements. (TPO11, R, S2, T1) 然后他把欧掠鸟关在笼中进行了实验,实验发现,它们的方向实际上与迁徙的方向是一样的,除了阴天的时候它们会因为没有明确的方向而焦躁不安。

【反义】 sunny, bright

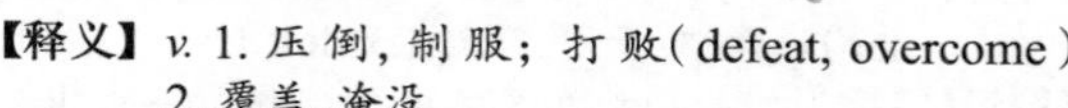

overwhelm6 [ˈəʊvəˈwelm]

【释义】 *v.* 1. 压倒,制服;打败(defeat, overcome) 2. 覆盖,淹没

【例句】 That's the problem. I'm overwhelmed. (TPO9, L, S1, C1) 那就是问题所在,我已为之所折服了。

【派生】 overwhelming *a.* 压倒性的,无法抵抗的

【搭配】 overwhelm people with one's power 以势压人

pack6 [pæk]

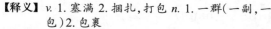

【释义】 *v.* 1. 塞满 2. 捆扎,打包 *n.* 1. 一群(一副,一包) 2. 包裹

【例句】 And it maybe this burial custom that explain why the houses were packed in so tightly without streets. (TPO1, L, S2, L1) 或许这种丧葬习惯可以解释为什么房屋建得满满当当的,连街道都没留。

【派生】 package *n.* 包裹 *a.* 一揽子的 *v.* 包装

【搭配】 pack into 挤进…里;塞进
pack with 塞满;挤满

partner6 [ˈpɑːtnə] 

【释义】 *n.* 1. 伙伴,搭档 2. 伴侣 3. 合伙人 *v.* 同…合作,做…的搭档

【例句】 In contrast to parasitism, in commensalism, one partner benefits without significantly affecting the other. (TPO17, R, S2, T2) 与寄生关系不同,在共生关系中,一方从另一方身上获益,却不会对其造成任何影响。

【派生】 partnership *n.* 合伙关系;合伙公司

peanut6 [ˈpiːnʌt]

【释义】 *n.* 1. 花生 2. [*pl.*] 很少的钱 *a.* [俚] 微不足道的,渺小的

【例句】 The Americas provide Europe and Asia with food like squash, beans, turkey, peanuts. (TPO10, L, S1, L2) 美洲向欧洲和亚洲提供南瓜、豆子、火鸡、花生等食品。

【搭配】 peanut oil 花生油

返记菜单

niche6	off-campus6	opaque6	overcast6	overwhelm6
pack6	partner6	peanut6		

pioneer[6] [ˌpaɪəˈnɪə] 

【释义】 *n.* 开拓者，先驱者，创始人(settler, forerunner) *v.* 开拓，开发，开创(exploit)

【例句】 The first community in a succession is called a pioneer community, while the long-lived community at the end of succession is called a climax community. (TPO3, R, S1, T2) 演替过程中的第一个群落被称作先锋群落，而处于演替过程最后的那个长期存在的群落被称为顶级群落。

【派生】 pioneering *a.* 开创性的

【搭配】 the pioneer spirit 拓荒精神

pipe[6] [paɪp] 

【释义】 *n.* 1. 管子，管道 2. 烟斗 3.[*pl.*] 管乐器 *v.* 用管道输送

【例句】 This same arrangement found in an old-fashioned stream radiator, in which the coiled pipes pass heat back and forth as water courses through them. (TPO15, R, S2, T1) 老式的蒸汽式暖气片上有着相同的构造，当水通过这些盘绕着的管子时热量就进行了交换。

【派生】 piped *a.* (服装)滚边的

piston[6] [ˈpɪstən] 

【释义】 *n.* 活塞

【例句】 Early in the century, a pump had come into use in which expanding steam raised a piston in a cylinder, and atmospheric pressure brought it down again when the steam condensed inside the cylinder to form a vacuum. (TPO6, R, S1, T1) 在(19)世纪早期，泵曾被用于(发动机的)汽缸，在气缸中，膨胀的蒸汽推动活塞上升，而当汽缸内部的蒸汽被压缩形成真空环境时，气压又使得活塞下降。

prosperity[6] [prɒsˈperɪtɪ] 

【释义】 *n.* 繁荣，兴旺

【例句】 Teotihuacán may have developed its own specific local religion as a result of the cultural advances made possible by the city's great prosperity. (TPO8, R, S1, T1) 由于城市的繁荣所带来的文化进步，特奥蒂瓦坎可能已经形成了自己独特的当地宗教。

【反义】 depression

【逆构】 prosper *v.* 繁荣，成功

purple[6] [ˈpɜːpl] 

【释义】 *a.* 1. 紫色的 2. 华而不实的 3. 贵族或皇室的 *n.* 紫色

【例句】 Some of the most priced tulips were white with purple stricks, or red with yellow stricks on the paddles, even a dark purple tulip that was very much priced. (TPO6, L, S1, L1) 一些很贵重的郁金香是有着紫条的白色花，或是有着黄条的红色花，甚至暗紫色的郁金香也是很值钱的。

【派生】 purplish *a.* 略带紫色的

【搭配】 born in/to the purple 出身王室

Word List 21

quarter[6] [ˈkwɔːtə] 

【释义】*n.* 1. 四分之一 2. 一刻钟 3. 一季 4. 区 *v.* 四等分

【例句】The introduction of new screen formats was put off for a quarter century, and color, though utilized over the next two decades for special productions, also did not become a norm until the 1950s. (TPO12, R, S2, T1) 新的屏幕形式的采用推迟了25年，而色彩，尽管在接下来的20年里被用作特殊生产，也是直到20世纪50年代才成为一种规范。

【派生】quarterly *ad.* 按季度 *a.* 季度的 *n.* 季刊
quartered *a.* 四等分的

race[6] [reɪs] 

【释义】*n.* 1. 比赛，竞争 2. 人种 *v.* 参赛；赛跑

【例句】I placed first in one race and third in another. (TPO15, L, S2, C1) 我在其中一场比赛中位列第一，另一场比赛中位列第三。

【搭配】race against 同…比赛

random[6] [ˈrændəm] 

【释义】*a.* 随意的，任意的，随机的

【例句】They may look like kind of randomly placed, but they actually form many distinct patterns. (TPO3, L, S2, L2) 它们看起来分的很随意，但实际上却形成了很多不同的模式。

【派生】randomly *ad.* 随意地

【搭配】random sampling 随机抽样

readily[6] [ˈredɪlɪ] 

【释义】*ad.* 1. 容易地，迅速地(easily) 2. 乐意地，欣然(willingly)

【例句】The author George Comstock suggested that less than a quarter of children between the ages of six and eight years old understood standard disclaimers used in many toy advertisements and that disclaimers are more readily comprehended when presented in both audio and visual formats. (TPO14, R, S1, T1) 作家乔治·康斯托克表示，在六到八岁的孩子中，只有不到四分之一的孩子能理解玩具广告中使用的标准的免责声明，如果那些免责声明能够以声音和图像的形式呈现出来，那么孩子们理解起来就会更容易些。

【搭配】readily accessible 易接近的，易达到的；可存取的

refine[6] [rɪˈfaɪn]

【释义】*v.* 精炼，精制

【例句】But mass production techniques were refined in the 19th century. (TPO16, L, S1, L2) 但是，在19世纪时大规模生产技术得到了改善。

【派生】refined *a.* 精制的；优雅的
refinment *n.* 文雅，精巧(尤指言谈、举止等)

【搭配】refine on 精于，改进

replicate[6] [ˈreplɪkɪt]

【释义】*v.* 复制(copy, duplicate)

【例句】A gene is a piece of biological information that gets copied or replicated, and the copy or replica is passed on to the new generation. (TPO5, L, S1, L1) 基因是一组可以被复制的生物信息，复制后的信息会遗传给下一代。

resist[6] [rɪˈzɪst] 

【释义】*v.* 1. 不受影响，抗，耐(withstand) 2. 抵抗，阻止(act against)

【例句】Apparently, genotypes (the genetic make-up of an organism) in the rabbit population were selected that were better able to resist the parasite. (TPO17, R, S2, T2) 显然，该兔群的遗传性状(生物体的基因结构)经过了自然选择之后，已经能够更好地抵抗粘液瘤病毒。

【反义】surrender, obey

【派生】resistance *n.* 抵抗；阻力
resistant *a.* 抵抗的，有阻力的

【搭配】resist heat 耐热
resist temptation 抵制诱惑

返记菜单

quarter[6] race[6] random[6] readily[6] refine[6]
replicate[6] resist[6]

rigid[6] ['rɪdʒɪd]

【释义】*a.* 1. 僵硬的，坚硬的（hard, stiff）2. 严格的（strict）3. 固执的，刻板的

【例句】When such statues are viewed in isolation, out of their original context and without knowledge of their function, it is easy to criticize them for their rigid attitudes that remained unchanged for three thousand years. (TPO11, R, S1, T1) 当脱离了其原来的环境而孤立地看这些雕像，且不了解其作用时，很容易会对其三千年来都保持不变的僵硬姿态提出批判。

【反义】pliable, yielding

【派生】rigidify *v.*（使）僵化
rigidity *n.* 坚硬，僵化

safety[6] ['seɪftɪ]

【释义】*n.* 安全；保险（security）

【例句】Further evidence for the costs of begging comes from a study of differences in the begging calls of warbler species that nest on the ground versus those that nest in the relative safety of trees. (TPO11, R, S2, T2) 更深层的有关乞食代价的证据来自于一项关于巢穴位于地面的鸣禽的乞食声和巢穴位于相对较安全的树上的那些鸣禽的乞食声之间的差异的研究。

【反义】danger

【逆构】safe *a.* 安全的

【搭配】in safety 安全地，平安地
with safety 放心地，安全地

sandy[6] ['sændɪ]

【释义】*a.* 含沙的；沙色的；沙质的

【例句】If it wants to have a smooth texture, it flattens out the papillae, so it can acquire a smooth texture to blend in with the sandy bottom of the sea. (TPO17, L, S2, L2) 如果想拥有平滑的肌理，它就会把乳突变平，这样就能拥有与海底沙地相融合的平滑肌理了。

【搭配】sandy soil 砂土，沙质土壤

scatter[6] ['skætə]

【释义】*v.*（使）散开，（使）分散（disperse, spread）

【例句】Now, the older lakes, about half the formations, the ones started forming 35000 years ago, the limestone formation we see, they're up to a kilometer long, but only a few meters wide, and they're scattered along the desert floor, in valleys between the dunes. (TPO9, L, S2, L1) 现在，久远一些的湖大约占到地层的一半，也就是我们所看到的35000年前开始形成的石灰岩层，它们有1000米长，但只有几米宽，并且在沙丘之间的山谷里沿着沙漠地面分散开来。

【反义】gather

【派生】scattered *a.* 离散的，分散的
scattershot *a.* 漫无目标的

【搭配】scatter litter 乱扔杂物

scrape[6] [skreɪp]

【释义】*n.* 1. 擦，刮 2. 刺耳的刮擦声 *v.* 1. 凑集 2. 摩擦，刮擦（rub, scratch）

【例句】These information wasn't particularly reliable because they were sometimes based on fictitious stories, great adventure or the scrape together from parts of the different poems. (TPO13, L, S2, L1) 这些信息不是特别可靠，因为它们有时是基于虚构的故事、大冒险或是不同诗歌的拼凑。

【派生】scraper *n.* 刮刀；铲土机

sheer[6] [ʃɪə]

【释义】*a.* 1. 十足的，绝对的，纯粹的（absolute, pure）2. 陡峭的（steep, abrupt）3. 极薄的 *ad.* 几乎垂直地；全然

【例句】By force of sheer numbers, however, the mosses and ferns reached Hawaii, survived, and multiplied. (TPO9, R, S2, T2) 然而，凭借着数量上的绝对优势，蕨类植物和地衣到达了夏威夷岛并在那里存活、繁衍开来。

【派生】sheerly *ad.* 完全地，全然地

shrine[6] [ʃraɪn]

【释义】*n.* 1. 圣地 2. 神龛 *v.* 1. 将…置于神龛内 2. 把…奉为圣

【例句】Teotihuacán had a religious significance as a shrine. (TPO8, R, S1, T1) 特奥蒂瓦坎作为一个宗教圣地,有着重要的宗教意义。

sight[6] [saɪt]

【释义】*n.* 1. 视力,视觉 2. 看见 3. 视野,预见 4. 景物 *v.* 瞄准; 看见,观测

【例句】Though it may be different to imagine from a later perspective, a strain of critical opinion in the 1920s predicted that sound film would be a technical novelty that would soon fade from sight, just as had many previous attempts, dating well back before the First World War, to link images with recorded sound. (TPO12, R, S2, T1) 尽管很难从以后的视角去想象,但20世纪20年代的一连串批评的观点预测说,有声电影作为一种技术上的新玩意儿,会很快淡出人们的视线,就像早在一战之前的那些将画面与录音连接在一起的尝试一样。

【派生】sightly *a.* 悦目的; 可眺望的

【搭配】Out of sight, out of mind. 眼不见,心不烦。

signature[6] ['sɪgnɪtʃə]

【释义】*n.* 1. 签名,署名,签字 2. 识别标志

【例句】We are talking about prehistory here, so obviously the artists didn't put a signature or a date on anything they did. (TPO17, L, S1, L1) 我们现在探讨的是史前历史,所以,很明显,艺术家们并没有在他们的作品上签署名字或日期。

【派生】signatory *n.* 签名人,签字者

【搭配】forged signature 伪造签字

span[6] [spæn]

【释义】*v.* 跨越(cover) *n.* 1. 跨度(distance, stretch) 2. 一段时间(duration)

【例句】As a method of spanning space, the arch can support greater weight than a horizontal beam. (TPO3, R, S1, T1) 作为跨越空间的一种方式,拱可以比水平横梁支撑更大的重量。

【派生】spanless *a.* 不可测量的

【搭配】average life span 平均寿命

spear[6] [spɪə]

【释义】*n.* 矛,梭镖,标枪 *v.* 刺,戳

【例句】This theory is suggested by evidence of chips in the painted figures, perhaps made by spears thrown at the drawings. (TPO4, R, S2, T1) 该理论的物证源于画上的碎屑,有可能是由于往画上投掷长矛造成的。

split[6] [splɪt]

【释义】*v.* 劈开,(使)裂开; 分开,分裂 *n.* 裂口; 分裂

【例句】It can be naturally generated from Uranium atom that has spontaneous split. (TPO8, L, S2, L2) 它可能是自然产生于自发分裂的铀原子。

stationary[6] ['steɪʃ(ə)nərɪ]

【释义】*a.* 固定的,静止不动的(fixed, immobile, static)

【例句】The boxes were stationary, and the one containing food was always at the same point of the compass. (TPO11, R, S2, T1) 盒子是固定不动的,而装有食物的盒子则总是处在指南针的同一个指向上。

steppe[6] [step]

【释义】*n.* (特指西伯利亚一带没有树木的)大草原,干草原

【例句】The forest passes into steppe or desert at its lower edge. (TPO1, R, S1, T1) 森林在它较低的边缘逐渐变成草原或沙漠。

stroke[6] [strəuk]

【释义】*n.* 1. (绘画的)一笔 2. 一击 3. 中风 *v.* 1. 击打 2. 划掉,取消

【例句】Take a painting that, say, uses a lot of strong colors like reds and oranges and uses brush strokes that are broad—wide, sweeping brush strokes that suggest a rough texture. (TPO4, S, Q6) 以一幅画为例,比如这幅,画中运用了大量强烈的色彩,如红色和橘色,还使用了很宽的笔触——这种宽大的扫笔表现了一种粗糙的肌理。

【搭配】on the stroke 准时地

返记菜单

sight[6] signature[6] span[6] spear[6] split[6]
stationary[6] steppe[6] stroke[6]

heat stroke 中暑
at one stroke 一举；一笔；马上
at a stroke 一下子

studio[6] ['stjuːdɪəʊ]

【释义】*n.* 1. 画室 2. 摄影室(棚)3. 播(录)音室 4. 电影公司

【例句】When this research resulted in the development of vastly improved sound techniques, film studios became convinced of the importance of converting to sound. (TPO12, R, S2, T1) 当这项研究引发了声音技术上的大发展时，电影制片厂对向有声电影转化的重要性就变得十分肯定了。

terrace[6] ['terəs]

【释义】*v.* 使成梯田 *n.* 1. 平台，阳台 2. 梯田

【例句】Proponents point to features such as the terraced "beaches" shown in one image, which could conceivably have been left behind as a lake or ocean evaporated and the shoreline receded. (TPO8, R, S2, T2) 支持者指出了一些特征，比如在一幅图中所展现的状如梯田的"海滩"，可以想象，这些"海滩"是在湖泊或海洋蒸发、海岸线退去后留下的。

terrain[6] ['tereɪn]

【释义】*n.* 地形，地势，地带

【例句】Boats could carry heavy weights, but canals could not cross hilly terrain: turnpikes could cross the hills, but the roadbeds could not stand up under great weights. (TPO6, R, S1, T1) 货船的确可以运载重物，但是运河无法穿过多山的地带，公路倒是可以穿过山区，但是地面的承载能力有限。

【搭配】a wavy terrain 起伏不平的地形

theme[6] [θiːm]

【释义】*n.* 1.（演讲、文章或艺术作品的）题目，主题，主旨(topic, subject) 2.（乐曲的）主旋律

【例句】Only when European decorative themes were introduced did these meanings become obscured or even lost. (TPO10, R, S1, T1) 当欧洲的装饰元素被引进后，这些元素也许慢慢的不再那么流行，甚至开始消失。

【搭配】theme park（游乐园中的）主题乐园

thereby[6] [ðɛr'baɪ]

【释义】*ad.* 因此，从而

【例句】Glaciers move slowly across the land with tremendous energy, carving into even the hardest rock formations and thereby reshaping the landscape as they engulf, push, drag, and finally deposit rock debris in places far from its original location. (TPO15, R, S1, T1）冰川带着巨大的能量在陆地上缓慢地移动，甚至切碎最坚硬的岩层，在其吞噬、推动、拖拉直至最后将这些岩石碎片沉积到远离其原地的过程中，地貌被重新塑造。

tide[6] [taɪd]

【释义】*n.* 1. 潮，潮汐 2. 潮流，趋势 *v.* 涨落

【例句】Consequently, the timing and rhythms of biological functions must closely match periodic events like the solar day, the tides, the lunar cycle, and the seasons. (TPO13, R, S2, T1) 因此，生物的计时与交替循环的机能也必须与像昼夜交替、潮涨潮落、月圆月缺和四季更迭这样的周期性事件保持一致。

【搭配】at high/low tide 在高 / 低潮时

tilt[6] [tɪlt]

【释义】*v.* 1.（使）倾斜 2. 攻击，抨击 *n.* 倾斜；斜面，斜坡(slant, lean)

【例句】Maybe the ground vibrates, or maybe the ground itself is shifting, tilting. (TPO4, L, S2, L1) 也许是地面在震动，或者地面本身在移动、倾斜。

【派生】tilted *a.* 倾斜的，翘起的

【搭配】at full tilt 全速地，全力以赴地

toddler[6] ['tɒdlə]

【释义】*n.* 学步的小孩；蹒跚行走的人

【例句】While such repression may occur, people cannot remember ordinary events from the infant and toddler periods, either. (TPO6, R, S2, T2) 虽然这种抑制可能会发生，但人们连孩提时代的普通事情也不记得。

【派生】toddlerhood *n.* 童年

【搭配】a fair-haired toddler 金发小孩

tomb[6] [tuːm] 

【释义】 *n.* 坟墓(grave),墓碑

【例句】 Many are made to be put in the tombs of the elite in order to serve the tomb owners in the afterlife. (TPO11, R, S1, T1) 许多都被放在上层人士的坟墓里,以便在阴间侍奉墓主。

【派生】 entomb *v.* 埋葬,作为…的坟墓

【搭配】 tomb stone 墓碑

tourism[6] ['tʊərɪz (ə) m] 

【释义】 *n.* 旅游,旅游业

【例句】 Promoting ecological tourism is another way to help save their habitat. (TPO3, L, S1, L1) 推进生态旅游业是挽救它们的栖息地的另一个方法。

trader[6] ['treɪdə] 

【释义】 *n.* 商人;商船

【例句】 Some people have argued that the Pacific was settled by traders who became lost while transporting domesticated plants and animals. (TPO5, R, S2, T1) 一些人认为是那些在运输家养动植物时迷失了方向的商人开辟了太平洋(岛国)。

trust[6] [trʌst] 

【释义】 *n.* 1. 信任,信赖,相信 2. 受托基金机构;受托团体 *v.* 1. 相信;信任 2. 相信;认为可靠 3. 想;希望;期望

【例句】 Young children are trusting of commercial advertisements in the media, and advertisers have sometimes been accused of taking advantage of this trusting outlook. (TPO14, R, S1, T1) 年轻的小孩容易相信媒体上的商业广告,而有些商家有时被指控利用这一信任。

【派生】 trustworthy *a.* 可信赖的,可靠的
trusty *a.* 可信任的

【搭配】 trust in 信任;依靠;存放
on trust 不加深究地,不加考察地;不凭证据
in trust 被托管

ultraviolet[6] ['ʌltrə'vaɪəlɪt] 

【释义】 *a.* 紫外线的 *n.* 紫外线

【例句】 The presence of increasing levels of ultraviolet light with elevation may play a role. (TPO1, R, S1, T1) 随着海拔上升而不断增强的紫外线可能也发挥着作用。

underlie[6] [ˌʌndə'laɪ] 

【释义】 *v.* 位于…之下;构成…的基础(或起因)

【例句】 The Ogallala aquifer is a sandstone formation that underlies some 583, 000 square kilometers of land extending from northwestern Texas to southern South Dakota. (TPO3, R, S1, T1) 奥加拉拉蓄水层属于砂岩结构,从德克萨斯州西北部到南达科塔州南部一直绵延了583000平方公里。

【派生】 underlying *a.* 在下面的;基础的,潜在的

van[6] [væn] 

【释义】 *n.* 1. 运货车,(载客的)面包车 2. 先锋,先驱

【例句】 And I was supposed to rent a van for the trip. (TPO1, S, Q5) 我本打算为这次旅行租一辆面包车的。

voyage[6] ['vɔɪɪdʒ] 

【释义】 *n./v.* 航行,旅行(cruise, sail)

【例句】 Just as important, the culture also possessed the basic foundation for an effective maritime adaptation, including outrigger canoes and a variety of fishing techniques that could be effective for overseas voyaging. (TPO5, R, S2, T1) 同样重要的是,该文化还拥有有效适应海洋生活的基础,包括桅杆船和各种适应出海航行的捕鱼技术。

【派生】 voyageable *a.* 能航行的,能航海的
voyager *n.* 航海者

weigh[6] [weɪ] 

【释义】 *v.* 1. 重量为… 2. 称重 3. 权衡,估量(assess, measure, estimate) 4. 有影响力

【例句】 So how do you take plant fibers that individually you could break with your hands and turn them into a rope that's strong

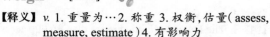

返记菜单

tomb[6]	tourism[6]	trader[6]	trust[6]	ultraviolet[6]
underlie[6]	van[6]	voyage[6]	weigh[6]	

enough to moor a ship that weighs thousands of tons? (TPO2, L, S1, L2) 你如何获取这些用手就可以将其一根根地单独折断的植物纤维，且把它们制成足够强韧、可以固定住上千吨的船只的麻绳呢？

【派生】weight *n.* 重量
weighted *a.* 加重的，负重的
weighty *a.* 重的；繁重的；重要的

【搭配】weigh against 1. 对…不利 2. 把两者权衡对比
weigh in sb./sth.'s favor 对某人 / 物有利

wheat[6] [wiːt]

【释义】*n.* 小麦

【例句】This region has a semiarid climate, and for 50 years after its settlement, it supported a low-intensity agricultural economy of cattle ranching and wheat farming. (TPO3, R, S1, T1) 这一区域属半干旱气候，在人们定居于此后的 50 年间，这里都是以畜牧业和小麦种植为主的低密度农业经济。

absolutely[5] [ˈæbsəluːtlɪ]

【释义】*ad.* 1. 当然，对极了 2. 完全地

【例句】Absolutely! Maybe you should do some preliminary research on that. (TPO9, L, S1, C1) 当然了！或许你应该提前做一些相关的研究。

acoustic[5] [əˈkuːstɪk]

【释义】*n.* 声音的；听觉的

【例句】Now, let's talk about the other and the acoustic spectrums, sound that is too high for humans to hear—ultrasounds. (TPO7, L, S1, L2) 现在，我们来谈一谈另一个声谱，这是一种因频率太高而不能被人耳所听见的声音——超声波。

【派生】acoustically *ad.* 听觉上地，声学上地

acre[5] [eɪkə]

【释义】*n.* 英亩

【例句】The Dutch reclaimed more than 36,000 acres from 1590 to 1615 alone. (TPO10, R, S2, T2) 仅在 1590 年到 1615 年间，荷兰就开垦了 36000 多英亩土地。

arid[5] [ˈærɪd]

【释义】*a.* 1. 贫瘠的（barren, infertile）2. 干旱的（dry）

【例句】Arid lands, surprisingly, contain some of the world's largest river systems, such as the Murray-Darling in Australia, the Rio Grande in North America, the Indus in Asia, and the Nile in the Arid zone. (TPO12, R, S2, T2) 令人惊奇的是，贫瘠的土地上倒是包含了世界上最大的几个河流系统，比如澳大利亚的墨累—达令河、北美的格兰德河、亚洲的印度河，以及位于干旱区的尼罗河。

【派生】aridity *n.* 干旱

【搭配】arid land 旱地

auditorium[5] [ˌɔːdɪˈtɔːrɪəm]

【释义】*n.* 礼堂，会堂，观众席

【例句】Like I explained on the phone we've always had our rehearsals in the Lincoln Auditorium every day at 3 o'clock. (TPO16, L, S1, C1) 和我在电话里说的一样，每天三点我们都会在林肯大教堂排练。

authority[5] [ɔːˈθɔrɪtɪ]

【释义】*n.* 1. 权力，权威（right, power）2. 权力机构，当局（official, government）

【例句】The psychological controls were built on fear and punishment—on the absolute certainty that anyone or anything that threatened the authority of Rome would be utterly destroyed. (TPO7, R, S2, T1) 心理上的控制建立在恐惧和惩罚的基础上，那就是不容任何质疑的原则：任何威胁到罗马统治的人或事物都将被彻底毁灭。

【派生】authoritative *a.* 权威性的，专断的，命令式的

barren[5] [ˈbærən]

【释义】*a.* 1. 贫瘠的，不毛的（unfertile）2. 不生育的，不结果的（sterile）

【例句】Then, as blazing sunshine alternated with drenching rains, the harsh, barren surfaces of the black rocks slowly began to soften. (TPO9, R, S2, T2) 然后，经过了炙热阳光和湿润雨水的交替作用之后，荒芜的黑色岩石表面慢慢开始变软。

【反义】rich, fertile
【派生】barrenness *n.* 不育症，不孕症
【搭配】a barren effort 无效的努力

bedrock[5] ['bedrɒk] 

【释义】*n.* 1. 基岩，岩床 2. 根底，基础
【例句】Basal slip or its sliding as it's often called, basically refers to the slipping or sliding of glacier across bedrock, actually across the thin layer of water, on top of the bedrock. (TPO7, L, S2, L2) 基面滑移或通常所说的滑行，实质上是指冰川滑过岩床，事实上是穿过基岩上的薄水层。

bias[5] ['baɪəs] 

【释义】*n.* 1. 偏见，偏心(prejudice) 2. 偏好(preference) *v.* 使倾向于，使有偏见
【例句】But the term "blind spot" has also taken on a more general meaning—it refers to people being unaware of a bias that may affect their judgment about the subject. (TPO14, L, S1, L1) 但"盲点"这个词还有更广泛的意思——指人们意识不到偏见可能会影响他们对于事物的判断。
【派生】biased *a.* 有偏见的
unbiased *a.* 无偏见的，公正的
【搭配】on the bias 倾斜地，歪斜地

bind[5] [baɪnd] 

【释义】*v.* 1. 捆绑，包扎 2. 使结(粘)合，装订 3. 约束
【例句】You'd have to know when he created his paintings, um, what pigments he used, in other words, what ingredients he used to make different colors of paint, 'coz the ingredients used in paints and binding agents plus varnishes have changed over time. (TPO5, L, S2, L1) 你需要了解他在作画时所使用的颜料，换句话说，就是他使用了哪些配料来调和出不同颜色的颜料，因为颜料中使用的配料、粘合剂和清漆都已经随着时间发生了变化。
【派生】binding *a.* 捆绑的；有约束力的
【搭配】binding agent 粘合剂

bite[5] [baɪt] 

【释义】*v.* 咬 *n.* 1. 咬 2. 一口 3. (被咬的)伤痕
【例句】The eggs "advertised" by the tree-nesters' begging calls were found bitten significantly more often than the eggs associated with the ground-nesters' calls. (TPO11, R, S2, T2) 由在树上筑巢的鸟儿的乞食声"做宣传"的蛋被咬的次数，明显比与在地面筑巢的鸟儿的乞食声联系在一起的蛋被咬的次数多。
【搭配】bite off 咬掉
grab a bite 随便吃几口
bite in 侵入；腐蚀
bite the dust 大败

blackcap[5] ['blækˌkæp] 

【释义】*n.* 莺类，白颊鸟类，黑色莓
【例句】We just call them blackcaps. (TPO8, L, S1, L1) 我们就叫它们莺鸟。

blanket[5] ['blæŋkɪt] 

【释义】*n.* 毯子，覆盖物 *v.* 用毯子裹，覆盖
【例句】The background of the painting is wrapped in a blanket of broad thick brushstokes. (TPO1, L, S1, L1) 这幅画的背景是一层宽而稠密的笔划。
【派生】blanketry *n.* 毛毯
blankety *a.* 可憎的，可恶的
【搭配】wet blanket 扫兴的人或事

bribe[5] [braɪb] 

【释义】*v./n.* 贿赂
【例句】Critics claim that while such a daring escape makes for enjoyable reading, it is more likely that the Chevalier's jailers were bribed to free him. (TPO7, W, Q1) 评论家声称，虽然这样英勇的逃脱带来了阅读上的享受，但更有可能的是看管谢瓦利埃的狱卒因为收到了贿赂，所以放了他。
【派生】bribery *n.* 受贿，行贿
【搭配】bribe a person with money 用钱收买某人

broadcast[5] ['brɔːdkɑːst] 

【释义】*v.* 广播；散布，撒播 *n.* 广播，广播节目

【例句】 Next semester university cafeterias will broadcast classical music during mealtimes. (TPO8, S, Q3) 下学期大学食堂将在就餐时间播放古典音乐。

bronze[5] [brɒnz]

【释义】 *n.* 青铜；青铜制品；青铜色

【例句】 Most of Africa presents a curious case in which societies moved directly from a technology of stone to iron without passing through the intermediate stage of copper or bronze metallurgy, although some early copper-working sites have been found in West Africa. (TPO7, R, S2, T2) 非洲大部分地区都存在一种让人好奇的情况，就是其社会是从石器技术时代直接演化至铁器时代的，而没有经历青铜冶炼这一中间阶段，虽然人们曾在西非地区发现了早期炼铜厂的遗址。

【搭配】 Bronze Age 青铜器时代
sun-bronzed 被太阳晒成古铜色的

bush[5] [bʊʃ]

【释义】 *n.* 灌木，灌木丛

【例句】 How about an animal that, um, instead of fighting its enemy or running away, attacks a plant or a bush? (TPO4, L, S1, L1) 那么，动物不攻击其敌人或逃跑而去攻击植物或灌木，该怎样解释？

【派生】 bushed *a.* 长满灌木的；疲倦的
bushy *a.* 浓密的

【搭配】 around the bush 拐弯抹角，说话绕圈子
beat about the bush 旁敲侧击

calculate[5] ['kælkjʊleɪt]

【释义】 *v.* 1. 计算，核算（compute）2. 估计（estimate）

【例句】 Ever since people had begun to catalog the strata in particular outcrops, there had been the hope that these could somehow be used to calculate geological time. (TPO6, R, S2, T1) 自从人们开始对某种露出地表的岩层进行分类起，人们就希望这些岩层某种方式上可以用来计算地质时间。

【派生】 calculation *n.* 计算，计算的结果
calculator *n.* 计算器

camel[5] ['kæməl]

【释义】 *n.* 骆驼

【例句】 Finally, the camel was introduced around the first century AD. (TPO7, R, S2, T2) 最后，骆驼于公元 1 世纪左右也被引进。

candidate[5] ['kændɪdɪt]

【释义】 *n.* 应试者；候选人

【例句】 Let's see, we have 4, all very good candidates, that we will be looking at over the next few weeks. (TPO11, L, S2, C1) 我们来看看，我们有四个应聘者，都非常优秀，在接下来的几周里我们将认真考察。

【派生】 candidacy *n.* 候选人的资格或身份

【搭配】 qualified candidate 合格的候选人

catalog[5] ['kætəlɒg]

【释义】 *n.* 目录，名单 *v.* 编制目录，分类

【例句】 For these reasons the painting was removed from the official catalog of Rembrandt's paintings in the 1930s. (TPO3, W, Q1) 由于以上原因，这幅画在 20 世纪 30 年代从伦勃朗的官方收录中摘出来了。

cavity[5] ['kævɪtɪ]

【释义】 *n.* 洞，穴（crater, hole, pit）；腔；龋洞

【例句】 This depends on the sizes of the individual cavities and the crevices linking them. (TPO1, R, S2, T2) 这取决于单个洞坑以及连接洞坑的裂缝的大小。

Word List 22

certify[5] ['sɜːtɪfaɪ]

【释义】*v.* 证明，证实，确认（attest, confirm, testify）

【例句】Thus ecologically-minded Americans are likely to react very favorably to wood products ecologically certified by an independent organization with an international reputation for trustworthiness. (TPO7, W, Q1) 因此，有生态学头脑的美国人很可能会对木质产品作出热切的回应，这些木质产品得到了一个因值得信赖而享有国际声誉的独立组织所做的生态学认证。

【派生】certification *n.* 证明，认证；证书

chain[5] [tʃeɪn]

【释义】*n.* 1. 链（条）2. [*pl.*]（一）连串，（一）系列（serial）*v.* 用铁链锁住，束缚

【例句】This disruption of food chain and climate would have eradicated the dinosaurs and other organisms in less than fifty years. (TPO8, R, S2, T1) 这种食物链和气候的破坏使得恐龙和其他生物在不到50年的时间里就灭绝了。

【搭配】chain reaction *n.* 连锁反应

chromosome[5] ['krəuməsəum]

【释义】*n.* 染色体

【例句】OK, you know that all of persons' genetic information is contained on very long pieces of DNA called Chromosomes. (TPO12, L, S1, L1) 你知道，人的所有遗传信息都包含在长长的DNA链条上，这些链条叫做染色体。

circulate[5] ['sɜːkjʊleɪt]

【释义】*v.*（使）循环，流通，（使）传播

【例句】This is the groundwater that circulates as part of the water cycle. (TPO1, R, S2, T2) 这是作为水循环的一部分而流通的地下水。

【派生】circulated *a.* 循环的，流通的

【搭配】circulate or exchange 通兑

coil[5] [kɔɪl]

【释义】*n.*（一）卷，线圈 *v.* 盘绕，卷成圈

【例句】Anyway, if we examine these ends of these coils of DNA, we will find a sequence of DNA at each end of every human Chromosome, called a telomere. (TPO12, L, S1, L1) 不管怎样，如果我们检查一下这些DNA链的末端，我们会发现每一条人类染色体的每一端都有一个DNA序列，叫做端粒。

【派生】coiled *a.* 盘绕的，卷成圈的

collapse[5] [kə'læps]

【释义】*v./n.* 倒塌，崩溃，瓦解（break down, crumble, fall）

【例句】Panic spread like wild fire and the tulip market collapsed totally. (TPO6, L, S1, L1) 惶恐如野火一般蔓延开来，郁金香市场完全崩溃。

【搭配】verge on collapse 濒于崩溃

column[5] ['kɒləm]

【释义】*n.* 圆柱，柱状物（pillar）；专栏（文章）

【例句】Elements of the same groups were automatically assembled in vertical columns in a periodic table of the elements. (TPO16, R, S2, T1) 同一族的元素在元素周期表中的同一列。

【派生】columnar *a.* 柱形的
columnist *n.* 专栏作家

conceal[5] [kən'siːl]

【释义】*v.* 隐藏，掩盖；隐瞒（hide, cover, veil）

【例句】It cannot conceal the fact that cetaceans are mammals. (TPO2, R, S2, T1) 这不能掩盖鲸类动物属于哺乳动物这一事实。

【反义】reveal, disclose

【派生】concealment *n.* 隐藏，隐藏的手段

condense[5] [kən'dens]

【释义】*v.*（使）凝结，（使）浓缩，（使）精简（compress, concentrate）

【例句】Early in the century, a pump had come into use in which expanding steam raised

返记菜单

certify[5]	chain[5]	chromosome[5]	circulate[5]	coil[5]
collapse[5]	column[5]	conceal[5]	condense[5]	

a piston in a cylinder, and atmospheric pressure brought it down again when the steam condensed inside the cylinder to form a vacuum. (TPO6, R, S1, T1) 在(19)世纪早期,泵曾被用于(发动机的)汽缸,在气缸中,膨胀的蒸汽推动活塞上升,而当汽缸内部的蒸汽被压缩形成真空环境时,气压又使得活塞下降。

【派生】condensation *n.* 浓缩,凝结

【搭配】condense…into… 把…压缩成…

conservation[5] [ˌkɒnsə (ː) ˈveɪʃ ən]

【释义】*n.* 保存,保护(preservation)

【例句】Eventually it ended up in an art auction where it was bought and then donated to an art museum in Baltimore, for conservation and study. (TPO15, L, S2, L1) 最终它在一场拍卖会上被买走,之后又被捐献给了巴尔的摩的一个博物馆,以供保存和研究。

【派生】conservationist *n.* 自然资源保护论者

conspicuous[5] [kənˈspɪkjʊəs]

【释义】*a.* 显著的,显眼的,显而易见的(obvious, prominent, noticeable)

【例句】What they do is they save their best performances, their most conspicuous and most risky displays for the time just before the baby birds become able to take care of themselves. (TPO11, L, S1, L1) 它们所做的是把其最引人注目、最冒险的表演保留到当它们的幼鸟开始能够照顾自己之前。

【派生】conspicuousness *n.* 显著,卓越

【搭配】conspicuous consumption 摆阔,挥霍

constitute[5] [ˈkɒnstɪtjuːt]

【释义】*v.* 1. 构成,组成(form) 2. 建立(政府)(found)

【例句】One of the most difficult aspects of deciding whether current climatic events reveal evidence of the impact of human activities is that it is hard to get a measure of what constitutes the natural variability of the climate. (TPO10, R, S2, T1) 要确定现在的气候事件是否是人类活动的影响,其中最大的困难之一在于很难找到一种测量方法来确定是什么构成了气候的自然可变性。

【搭配】constitute a crime 构成犯罪

contradictory[5] [ˌkɒntrəˈdɪktərɪ]

【释义】*a.* 矛盾的,抵触的

【例句】People experiencing cognitive dissonance often do not want to change the way they are acting, so they resolve the contradictory situation in another way, they change their interpretation of the situation in a way that minimizes the contradiction between what they are doing and what they believe should be doing. (TPO3, S, Q4) 人们在面对内心冲突时并不想改变他们正在做的事,因此他们会通过另一种方式来解决这种矛盾的处境,他们会换一种方式来解释这种情况,从而把他们所做的和应该做的之间的矛盾降到最小。

【派生】contradiction *n.* 矛盾性,对立性

【逆构】contradict *v.* 与…矛盾,违背

【搭配】contradictory elements 相互矛盾的因素

cord[5] [kɔːd]

【释义】*n.*(细)绳

【例句】The Native Americans would cut the bark and fold it into any shape they needed, then secure with cords until it dried. (TPO7, L, S2, L1) 美洲原住民会切开树皮,并且把它们折成各种需要的形状,然后再用绳子固定,直到其彻底干燥。

【派生】cordless *a.* 无线的

cousin[5] [ˈkʌzn]

【释义】*n.* 堂(或表)兄弟,堂(或表)姐妹

【例句】The black-tailed deer, a lowland, west-side cousin of the mule deer of eastern Washington, is now the most common. (TPO4, R, S1, T1) 目前最常见的一种鹿是华盛顿西部低地的黑尾鹿,是东华盛顿长耳鹿的表亲。

deciduous[5] [dɪˈsɪdʒʊəs]

【释义】*a.* 每年落叶的,非永久性的

【例句】These have some advantage over deciduous trees. (TPO1, R, S1, T1) 这些树比落叶树有优势。

declare[5] [dɪ'kleə]

【释义】 v. 1. 断言,宣称,声明(assert, proclaim) 2. 宣布,宣告,表明(announce)
【例句】 Well, I haven't declared a major yet, but I'm strongly considering accounting. (TPO6, L, S1, C1) 我还没确定要选哪个专业,但是我很看好会计。
【派生】 declaration n. 宣言,公告,声明
【搭配】 declare sb. guilty 宣布某人有罪

decomposition[5] [ˌdiːkɒmpə'zɪʃən]

【释义】 n. 腐烂,分解;崩溃
【例句】 Conditions that promote fossilization of soft-bodied animals include very rapid covering by sediments that create an environment that discourages decomposition. (TPO5, R, S2, T2) 促使软体动物化石化的条件包括被沉淀物迅速覆盖,从而创造一个防腐的环境。

deed[5] [diːd]

【释义】 n. 1. 事情,事迹;行为 2. [法] 契约,证书
【例句】 Chanson poem became popular in Europe, particularly in France, and the term is actually short for a longer French phrase that translates to a songs of deeds. (TPO13, L, S2, L1) 香颂诗在欧洲(尤其是在法国)流行了起来,这个术语实际上是一个较长的法语短语的简称,翻译为对事迹的颂歌。
【搭配】 deeds of heroism 英雄事迹

defeat[5] [dɪ'fiːt]

【释义】 n. 1. 失败,挫败 v. 1. 击败,战胜(win, conquer) 2. [法] 废除,作废
【例句】 Ask yourself questions, even if you don't use the details in your story, um…what does each character like to eat, what setting does each prefer, the mountains, the city, what about educational background, their reactions to success or defeat, write it all down. (TPO6, L, S2, L1) 问你自己一些问题,尽管在故事中不会涉及到这些细节,例如每个角色喜欢吃什么,喜欢什么样的场景,是山还是城市,他们的教育背景如何,以及他们面对成功和失败的反应是什么样的,把这些都写下来。
【反义】 victory

defect[5] [dɪ'fekt]

【释义】 n. 缺点,瑕疵,不足之处(fault, flaw, shortcoming)
【例句】 So product reliability means basically the absence of defects or problems that you weren't expecting. (TPO7, S, Q6) 因此,产品的可靠性基本上意味着产品没有你不期望出现的问题和瑕疵。
【派生】 defective a. 有缺陷的

delicate[5] ['delɪkɪt]

【释义】 a. 1. 易损的,易碎的;脆弱的(fragile, vulnerable) 2. 精美的,雅致的(ethereal, sensitive)
【例句】 The semiarid lands bordering the deserts exist in a delicate ecological balance. (TPO2, R, Sl, T1) 紧邻沙漠的半干旱地区处在一个十分脆弱的生态平衡中。
【反义】 coarse, crude, rough
【派生】 delicately ad. 微妙的
delicacy n. 微妙,精密

denouement[5] [deɪ'nuːmɒŋ]

【释义】 n.(尤指小说、戏剧等的)结局,结尾
【例句】 And that's followed by the final dramatic element—the denouement or the resolution, when all the lucent have to be tied up in the logical way. (TPO7, L, S1, L2) 这之后就是最终的戏剧元素——结局或解释,此时所有清楚明白的情节都要以一种符合逻辑的方式串联起来。

descend[5] [dɪ'send]

【释义】 v. 1. 传下,遗传 2. 下降(drop, fall)
【例句】 Today's Bantu-speaking peoples are descended from a technologically advanced people who spread throughout Africa. (TPO7, R, S2, T2) 现在说班图语的人们源于一个技术上领先、足迹遍布整个非洲的民族。
【反义】 ascend, rise
【派生】 descendant n. 子孙,后裔

返记菜单

declare[5] decomposition[5] deed[5] defeat[5] defect[5]
delicate[5] denouement[5] descend[5]

devastate[5] ['devəsteɪt]

【释义】 v. 彻底破坏,毁坏,摧毁(ruin, destroy)

【例句】 Spread rapidly by mosquitoes, the virus devastated the rabbit population. (TPO17, R, S2, T2) 通过蚊子,这种寄生虫在兔群中迅速传播开来,使兔子数量急剧减少。

【派生】 devastating a. 破坏性的,毁灭性的
devastation n. 毁坏

diminish[5] [dɪ'mɪnɪʃ]

【释义】 v.(使)变小,(使)减少(decrease, lessen, reduce)

【例句】 Discuss why the ability to recall memories diminishes as a person ages. (TPO10, L, S2, L2) 讨论一下为什么随着一个人年龄的增长记忆力会下降。

disaster[5] [dɪ'zɑːstə]

【释义】 n. 1. 灾害,灾难,不幸(catastrophe, misfortune, calamity) 2. [口]彻底的失败

【例句】 The last factor is the impact of natural disasters, such as the volcanic eruptions of the late first millennium B. C. (TPO8, R, S1, T1) 最后一个因素是自然灾害的影响,比如公元前一千年后期发生的火山喷发。

【派生】 disastrous a. 灾难性的

【搭配】 disaster relief 赈灾,救灾

divert[5] [dɪ'vɜːt]

【释义】 v. 使转向,转移(distract)

【例句】 It works in compression to divert the weight above it out to the sides, where the weight is borne by the vertical elements on either side of the arch. (TPO3, R, S1, T1) 它使得上面的压力转移到两侧,由拱两侧垂直的部分来承担压力。

【派生】 diversion n. 转向,转移;消遣,娱乐

【搭配】 divert one's attention 分散注意力

double[5] ['dʌbl]

【释义】 v.(使)翻倍 a. 双的,双倍的(twofold, dual) n. 1. 双倍 2. 双人房间

【例句】 I'm doubling the numbers, so 2 times 12 is 24. (TPO2, L, S2, L2) 我正在将数字翻一倍,所以 12 乘以 2 等于 24。

【反义】 single

【派生】 doubly ad. 双倍地

【搭配】 double layer 双层
double room/bed 双人房 / 床
on the double 快速地

downtown[5] ['daʊntaʊn]

【释义】 ad./a. 在市中心的,往市中心的

【例句】 Business owners in the city centers or the downtown areas have experienced some financial losses, because of the city movement of the people out of the city and then into suburbs. (TPO13, L, S1, L1) 城市居民从市区到郊区的迁移使得市中心的商家蒙受了一些经济损失。

【派生】 downtowner n. 闹市区的人

【搭配】 downtown Manhattan 曼哈顿商业区

duck[5] [dʌk]

【释义】 v. 1. 闪避 2. 忽地低下头(或弯腰) n. 鸭子,鸭肉

【例句】 Almost all animals have some way of regulating their body temperature; otherwise they wouldn't survive extreme hot or cold conditions—sweating, panting, swimming to cooler or warmer water, ducking into somewhere cool like a burrow or a hole under a rock; these are just a few. (TPO14, L, S1, L2) 几乎所有动物都有调节自己体温的方式,不然它们就无法在极热或者极冷的条件下生存——流汗、喘息、在凉爽或温暖的水中游泳、迅速躲到洞穴或岩洞等凉快的地方;这些只是一小部分。

【搭配】 lame duck 投机者;无用的人
sitting duck 易被击中的目标;易被欺骗的对象
dead duck 注定要完蛋的人;没有价值的人或事

dwell[5] [dwel]

【释义】 v. 居住,生活于(live, inhabit, reside)

【例句】 Their streamlined bodies, the absence of hind legs, and the presence of a fluke and

blowhole cannot disguise their affinities with land dwelling mammals. (TPO2, R, S2, T1) 它们的身体呈流线型，没有后腿，长有尾片和喷水孔，但这些都不能掩盖它们与陆生哺乳动物的相似性。

【派生】dweller *n.* 居住者
dwelling *n.* 住处，寓所

【搭配】dwell on/upon 详谈、细想某事（尤指令人不快的事）

economical[5] [ˌiːkəˈnɒmɪkəl] 

【释义】*a.* 经济的，合算的；节俭的（thrifty, saving）

【例句】And it would definitely be economical with everyone splitting the rent. (TPO14, S, Q5) 而且大家一起分摊房租绝对是比较经济划算的。

【反义】extravagant, uneconomical

【派生】economics *n.* 经济学
economist *n.* 经济学家
economy *n.* 经济
economize *v.* 节约

【逆构】economic *a.* 经济的，经济学的

eel[5] [iːl] 

【释义】*n.* 鳗鱼，鳝鱼

【例句】A good example, there's a species of eel that has an enormous mouth and a large stomach that's capable of expanding, and these unusual features allow this eel to eat prey larger than itself. (TPO14, S, Q6) 一个很好的例子，有一种鳗鱼有着巨大的嘴和能够扩展的超大的胃，这些不同寻常的特质使其能吃掉比自己更大的猎物。

【搭配】slippery as an eel（人）很狡猾；（物）很滑，抓不住

egalitarian[5] [ɪgælɪˈteərɪən] 

【释义】*a.* 平等主义的 *n.* 平等主义；平等主义者

【例句】This mode of craft production favored the growth of self-governing and ideologically egalitarian craft guilds everywhere in the Middle Eastern city. (TPO16, R, S1, T1) 这种工艺生产模式有利于遍布中东城市的自制、意识上平等的工艺品行会的发展。

【搭配】egalitarian society 平等社会

elective[5] [ɪˈlektɪv] 

【释义】*n.* 选修科目 *a.* 1. 选举的 2. 随意选择的（optional）

【例句】And as elective, you could take some Pre-Law classes like Constitution Law. (TPO14, L, S2, C1) 作为选修课，你可以选择一些法学入门课程，比如宪法。

【逆构】elect *v.* 选举

【搭配】elective course 选修课

engaging[5] [ɪnˈgeɪdʒɪŋ] 

【释义】*a.* 美丽动人的，有吸引力的（appealing, intriguing, attractive）

【例句】In this case, by doing something unexpected, something more engaging, you can tap in to their passive attention and it can last much longer than active attention. (TPO6, L, S, Q6) 在这种情形下，通过做一些意想不到的、更有趣的事情，你就能够调动他们的被动注意力，并且这比积极注意力持续的时间更长。

【派生】engagingly *ad.* 有吸引力地

【逆构】engage *v.* 吸引，占用

【搭配】an engaging smile 一个迷人的微笑

erase[5] [ɪˈreɪz]

【释义】*v.* 擦掉，抹去，清除

【例句】They simply erased the ink off the parchment. (TPO15, L, S2, L1) 他们只是简单地将羊皮纸上的墨迹擦去了。

【派生】eraser *n.* 橡皮

【搭配】erase from 抹去，划掉

excavate[5] [ˈekskəveɪt] 

【释义】*v.* 挖掘，挖开，发掘（burrow, dig）

【例句】So do the naturalistic paintings on slabs of stone excavated in southern Africa. (TPO4, R, S2, T1) 在非洲南部发掘出来的石板上的自然主义画作同样如此。

【搭配】to excavate a tunnel 挖隧道
to excavate an ancient city 发掘一座古城

exogenous[5] [ɛks'ɑdʒɪnəs] 

【释义】*a.* 外生的；外源的
【例句】These rivers and river systems are known as "exogenous" because their sources lie outside the arid zone. (TPO12, R, S2, T2) 这些河流和河流系统被认为是"外生的"，因为它们的源头都位于这片干旱带之外。
【派生】exogenously *ad.* 外因地

fertile[5] ['fɜːtaɪl] 

【释义】*a.*（指土地）肥沃的，富饶的（fruitful, productive）
【例句】In all probability it was the fertile plain of Latium, where the Latins who founded Rome originated, that created the habits and skills of landed settlement, landed property, landed economy, landed administration, and a land-based society. (TPO7, R, S2, L2) 很有可能，正是见证了创立罗马的拉丁人起源的肥沃的拉丁姆平原孕育了陆上定居的习惯和技能、土地财产、土地经济、土地管理和以土地为根基的社会。
【反义】infertile, barren, sterile
【派生】fertility *n.* 肥沃，丰饶

filter[5] ['fɪltə]

【释义】*v.* 过滤（液体、光等）（strain, purify）*n.* 过滤器
【例句】In fact, we kinds of assume that they were filtering a lot out. (TPO7, L, S1, L2) 事实上，我们总是假设它们会过滤出很多声音。
【派生】filtration *n.* 过滤
【搭配】filter tip *n.*（香烟的）过滤嘴；滤嘴香烟

flame[5] [fleɪm]

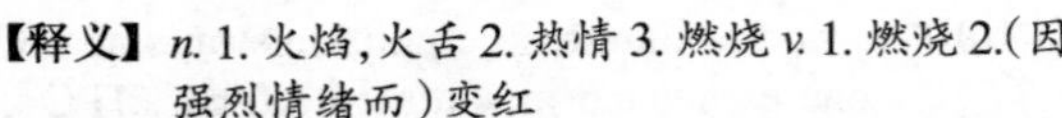

【释义】*n.* 1. 火焰，火舌 2. 热情 3. 燃烧 *v.* 1. 燃烧 2.（因强烈情绪而）变红
【例句】Well, a kind of spectroscopic library of elements was compiled using flame tests. (TPO3, L, S2, L2) 一种元素光谱对照表正在编制中，该项工作是以火焰实验为依据的。
【派生】flameless *a.* 无火焰的
【搭配】burst into flame(s) 突然开始熊熊燃烧

flatten[5] ['flætn] 

【释义】*v.*（使）变平
【例句】The circle is now stretched out, flattened into an oval. (TPO13, S, Q4) 圆现在变长变扁了，形成了一个卵形。
【搭配】flatten sth. (out) 使（某物）变平

fluid[5] ['flʊ(ː)ɪd] 

【释义】*n.* 液体，流体 *a.* 1. 易变的，不固定的 2. 流体的，流动的
【例句】The lungs of a fetus secrete a liquid that mixes with its mother's amniotic fluid. (TPO18, R, S2, T1) 胎儿的肺会分泌一种液体，这种液体会和母亲的羊水混合在一起。
【反义】solidity
【派生】fluidity *n.* 流动性，流质
【搭配】body fluid 体液

fragile[5] ['frædʒaɪl] 

【释义】*a.* 1. 易碎的，脆的（breakable）2. 虚弱的，脆弱的，不牢固的（weak, feeble）3. 纤巧的；精细的（delicate）
【例句】The central state, though often very rich and very populous, was intrinsically fragile, since the development of new international trade routes could undermine the monetary base and erode state power, as occurred when European seafarers circumvented Middle Eastern merchants after Vasco da Gama's voyage around Africa in the late fifteenth-century opened up a southern route. (TPO16, R, Sl, T1) 中心地区的国家虽然非常富足、人口稠密，但实质上却是很脆弱的，因为新的国际贸易路线的发展可能会削弱其金融基础、侵蚀其国家力量，正如当瓦斯科·达·伽马于15世纪末绕过非洲开辟了一条南部的航海路线之后，欧洲的船员们会避开中东的商人们一样。
【派生】fragility *n.* 脆弱
【搭配】fragile health 虚弱的体质

frontality[5] [frɔn'tɔliti] 

【释义】*n.*（绘画及雕塑中对人物、风景等的）正面描绘

【例句】The majority of three-dimensional representations, whether standing, seated, or kneeling, exhibit what is called frontality: they face straight ahead, neither twisting nor turning. (TPO11, R, S1, T1) 大多数这样的三维雕像，不论是站着的、坐着的或跪着的，都展现了什么叫正面描绘：他们都面朝前方，既不扭曲也不扭转。

frontier[5] ['frʌntjə] 

【释义】*n.* 边界，边境，边缘（border, outskirts）

【例句】Famous explorers of the North American frontier, Lewis and Clark arrived at the mouth of the Columbia River on November 14, 1805, in nearly starved circumstances. (TPO4, R, S1, T1) 北美边疆的著名探险家刘易斯和克拉克，在几乎饿死的情况下，于1805年11月14日抵达哥伦比亚河口。

giant[5] ['dʒaɪənt]

【释义】*a.* 巨大的，庞大的（enormous, huge, large, immense）*n.* 1. 巨人，巨大的怪物

【例句】So that's a giant step in the right direction. (TPO10, L, S1, L1) 所以这是朝着正确方向迈出的巨大一步。

【反义】diminutive, little, small

gravity[5] ['grævɪtɪ] 

【释义】*n.* 1. 万有引力，地心引力 2. 严肃，一本正经

【例句】Structures can be analyzed in terms of how they deal with downward forces created by gravity. (TPO3, R, S1, T1) 建筑师们在设计建筑结构的时候需要将重力对材料的影响考虑在内。

【派生】gravitation *n.* 引力，重力
gravitational *a.* 重力的，地心吸力的

habituation[5] [həˌbɪtʃuː'eɪʃən] 

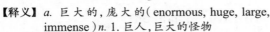

【释义】*n.* 习惯，熟习，习惯性

【例句】The first is the habituation-dishabituation technique, in which a single stimulus is presented repeatedly to the infant until there is a measurable decline (habituation) in whatever attending behavior is being observed. (TPO13, R, S2, T2) 第一个就是习惯与非习惯性技术，这种技术是通过重复地对婴儿施加某种单一刺激，直到婴儿对这一信号形成习惯并对信号的反应出现可测量的减弱（习惯性）。

【搭配】sensory habituation 感觉惯性

hatch[5] [hætʃ]

【释义】*n.* 1. 孵化 2. 舱口 *v.* 孵化（breed）

【例句】In that case, the parent will put on the most conspicuous distractions displays just before the babies' hatch because once the babies are hatched they can pretty much take care of themselves. (TPO11, L, S1, L1) 在那种情况下，父母会在雏鸟孵化之前上演最惹人注意的迷惑表演，因为雏鸟一孵化出来，它们差不多就能照顾自己。

【派生】hatchery *n.* 孵卵所

【搭配】hatch out 孵出；策划
escape hatch 安全舱口

hemisphere[5] ['hemɪsfɪə]

【释义】*n.* 半球

【例句】Now you know a humming bird is amazingly small, but even though it's really tiny, it migrates over very long distances, travels up and down the western hemisphere – the Americas, back and forth between where it breeds in the summer and the warmer climates where it spends the winter. (TPO3, L, S1, L1) 现在你知道了，蜂鸟非常得小，但纵使如此之小，它们迁徙的距离却非常长，它们往返于西半球——美洲，在夏天进行繁殖的地方和气候温暖的过冬的地方之间来来回回。

【派生】hemispheric *a.* 半球形的

【搭配】the Northern Hemisphere 北半球

hibernate[5] ['haɪbəneɪt]

【释义】*v.* 冬眠，蛰伏

【例句】And even though they spend the significant portion of the year hibernating, marmots are still considered excellent subjects for animal behavioral studies. (TPO1, L, S2, L2) 尽管旱獭把全年的大部分时间都花在冬眠上，但人们仍然把它们当做动物行为研究的绝佳

返记菜单

frontier[5] giant[5] gravity[5] habituation[5] hatch[5]
hemisphere[5] hibernate[5]

对象。

【派生】 hibernation *n.* 冬眠
hibernator *n.* 冬眠动物

hierarchy[5] ['haɪərɑːkɪ] 

【释义】 *n.* 等级制度,阶层

【例句】 Inequalities of wealth and rank certainly exist, and have probably existed in most pastoralist societies, but except in periods of military conquest, they are normally too slight to generate the stable, hereditary hierarchies that are usually implied by the use of the term class. (TPO14, R, S2, T2) 财富和地位的不平等现象肯定存在,并且有可能存在于大多数牧民社会,但是除了在军队征战时期,这些现象一般都太过微弱,不足以形成通常由"阶级"这个术语来表示的稳定的世袭等级制度。

【搭配】 social hierarchy 社会等级;社会阶层
knowledge hierarchy 知识体系

hint[5] [hɪnt] 

【释义】 *n.* 1. 提示,暗示,线索(clue, allusion) 2. 微量 *v.* 暗示,提示(imply, suggest)

【例句】 There's lots of orange, with little hints of an electric blue peeking out. (TPO1, L, S1, L1) (画上)有大量的橘黄色,中间有些微的铁蓝色隐隐露出。

【搭配】 hint window 提示窗口

impetus[5] ['ɪmpɪtəs] 

【释义】 *n.* 推动,刺激(stimulus, incentive);推动力(driving force)

【例句】 Because of the barrier of ice to the east, the Pacific Ocean to the west, and populated areas to the north, there may have been a greater impetus for people to move in a southerly direction. (TPO9, R, S1, T1) 由于东部是冰障,西部是太平洋,北部是移民区,所以有一股劲强大的力量促使人们往南方迁移。

【搭配】 give an impetus to trade 促进贸易

implement[5] ['ɪmplɪmənt]

【释义】 *v.* 使生效,履行,实施(execute, perform) *n.* 工具,器具(tool, instrument)

【例句】 Phytoremediation can be faster to implement. (TPO5, R, S1, T1) 植物修复法实施起来更快。

【派生】 implemental *a.* 器具的
implementary *a.* 实施的,执行的
implementation *n.* 履行,实现

incentive[5] [ɪn'sentɪv] 

【释义】 *n.* 刺激,诱因,动机(motive, stimulus)

【例句】 They might not support the arts unless the government made it attractive for them to do so, by offering corporations tax incentives to support the arts, that is, by letting corporations pay less in taxes if they were patrons of the arts. (TPO4, L, S2, L2) 除非政府通过提供税收刺激来支持艺术,也就是说,企业作为艺术的赞助商可以少缴税,这样才会让企业觉得有利可图,否则,他们可能不会支持艺术。

indicate[5] ['ɪndɪkeɪt] 

【释义】 *v.* 1. 指示,指出(show, reflect) 2. 象征,表明(imply)

【例句】 Changes in the electrical pattern of the brain indicate that the stimulus is getting through to the infant's central nervous system and eliciting some form of response. (TPO13, R, S2, T2) 脑电波的变化表明,这种刺激正通过婴儿的中枢神经系统,并诱发了一定形式的反应。

【派生】 indication *n.* 指出;迹象,象征
indicative *a.* 指示的,预示的

Word List 23

inflate⁵ [ɪnˈfleɪt] 

【释义】 *v.* 使充气，使膨胀（expand, fill with air or gas）

【例句】 During courtship and aggressive displays, the turkey enlarges its colored neck collar by inflating sacs in the neck region and then flings about a pendulous part of the colored signaling apparatus as it utters calls designed to attract or repel. (TPO17, R, S2, T1) 在求爱期和发起挑衅时，火鸡会使自己颈囊充气，从而张开艳丽的颈圈，当其发出吸引异性或驱逐敌人的叫声时，便晃动这个色彩绚烂的信号器官的下垂部分。

【反义】 deflate, shrink

【派生】 inflation *n.* 充气；通货膨胀

insulating⁵ [ˈɪnsjʊleɪtɪŋ] 

【释义】 *a.* 绝缘的

【例句】 It is not enough for whales, which supplement it with a thick layer of insulating blubber (fat). (TPO15, R, S2, T1) 对于通过厚厚的绝缘脂层来维持体温的鲸鱼来说这是不够的。

【逆构】 insulate *v.* 使绝缘，使隔热

【派生】 insulation *n.* 绝缘，隔离，孤立

intelligent⁵ [ɪnˈtelɪdʒənt] 

【释义】 *a.* 聪明的，有才智的（clever, bright, wise, ingenious）

【例句】 But with the monkeys he thought were less intelligent, he wasn't as enthusiastic. (TPO15, S, Q4) 但是对待那些他认为不那么聪明的猴子，他就没那么热情了。

【派生】 intelligently *ad.* 聪明地

【逆构】 intelligence *n.* 智力，智慧；情报

intentionally⁵ [inˈtenʃənli] 

【释义】 *ad.* 有意地，故意地（deliberately, purposely）

【例句】 The Independent Television Commission, regulator of television advertising in the United Kingdom, has criticized advertisers for "misleadingness"—creating a wrong impression either intentionally or unintentionally—in an effort to control advertisers' use of techniques that make it difficult for children to judge the true size, action, performance, or construction of a toy. (TPO14, R, S1, T1) 英国电视广告的管理者——独立电视委员会批评广告商为"误导"——总是有意或无意地制造一些假象——委员会试图通过此举来控制广告商滥用技术使得儿童无法判断玩具的真实大小、功能、性能以及构造。

【逆构】 intentional *a.* 故意的
intention *n.* 意图，目的

interval⁵ [ˈɪntəvəl] 

【释义】 *n.* 间隔，间歇，间隙

【例句】 What we do know is that as we include longer time intervals, the record shows increasing evidence of slow swings in climate between different regimes. (TPO10, R, S2, T1) 我们所知道的是，当我们包括的时间间隔越长，记录显示出不同国家之间气候缓慢变化的痕迹就越明显。

【搭配】 at intervals 时时，不时
in the interval 在这一期间；在间隔时

judgment⁵ [ˈdʒʌdʒmənt] 

【释义】 *n.* 1. 判断，评价（assessment, appraisal）2. 审判，判决（sentence）

【例句】 And in practice, the judgments of the group of academics that make these decisions don't reflect the great range of interests that people really have. (TPO6, W, Q1) 实际上，做出这些决定的学术研究者们的评价并不能反映人们内心真正的兴趣。

【逆构】 judge *n.* 法官；裁判员 *v.* 审判；评判

laden⁵ [ˈleɪdn] 

【释义】 *a.* 负重的，载满的

【例句】 In some industrial regions, heavily laden wagons, with flanged wheels, were being hauled by horses along metal rails; and the stationary steam engine was puffing in the factory and mine. (TPO6, R, S1, T1) 在一些工业地区,承载重物的四轮马车都配备有带凸的缘轮,并且是通过几匹马拉动而在铁轨上行驶的;而静止的蒸汽发动机则被用于工厂和矿井之中。

【搭配】 laden with grief 满怀忧伤

leafy[5] ['liːfɪ]

【释义】 *a.* 叶茂盛的,多叶的,叶状的

【例句】 Even with snow on the ground, the high bushy understory is exposed; also snow and wind bring down leafy branches of cedar, hemlock, red alder, and other arboreal fodder. (TPO4, R, S1, T1) 即便白雪覆盖了大地,高而浓密的林下叶层依然不会被掩盖;风雪也吹落了雪松、铁杉、赤阳木和其他树木的茂密枝叶。

【反义】 leafless

【逆构】 leaf *n.* 叶子

loyalty[5] ['lɔɪəltɪ]

【释义】 *n.* 忠诚,忠心

【例句】 Well, there's a hero, and a knight, who goes to battle, and he is inspired for his courage, bravery and loyalty, loyalty to the royalty serves, his country and his fellow warriors in the field. (TPO13, L, S2, L1) 有一位英雄,一个骑士,在勇气、勇敢、忠诚——对皇室、祖国和战场上的同胞勇士的忠诚的鼓舞下奔赴了战场。

【搭配】 customer loyalty 客户忠诚度

magnify[5] ['mægnɪfaɪ]

【释义】 *v.* 放大,扩大,夸大,增强(amplify, enlarge, exaggerate)

【例句】 Well, what happens if the sunlight's spectrum is magnified? (TPO3, L, S2, L2) 那么,光谱被放大之后会出现什么现象呢?

【反义】 diminish, minify

【派生】 magnification *n.* 扩大,放大

memorable[5] ['memərəbl]

【释义】 *a.* 难忘的,值得纪念的(rememberable)

【例句】 So these memes have longevity because they are memorable for one reason or another. (TPO5, L, S1, L1) 因为各种各样的原因,文化基因易于记忆,所以它们具有寿命长的特点。

【逆构】 memory *n.* 记忆

microbe[5] ['maɪkrəʊb]

【释义】 *n.* 微生物,细菌

【例句】 These microbes enable the soil to have more nitrogen, which plants need to live and they remain quite active during the winter. (TPO 9, L, S1, L2) 这些微生物能够使土壤中含有更多的氮,这是植物生长所需要的,并且这些微生物在冬天也能够保持活跃。

【派生】 microbial *a.* 微生物的,由细菌引起的

【搭配】 microbe warfare 细菌战

monitor[5] ['mɒnɪtə]

【释义】 *n.* 1. 监视器;显示器 2. 班长 *v.* 监控,监测(observe, watch)

【例句】 Film analysis of the infant's responses, heart and respiration rate monitors, and nonnutritive sucking devices are used as effective tools in understanding infant perception. (TPO13, R, S2, T2) 婴儿反应胶片分析、心脏和呼吸频率监听器以及与营养无关的吮吸装置是了解婴儿认知能力的有效工具。

【派生】 monitorship *n.* 班长职务

【搭配】 heart monitor 心脏监测器

moral[5] ['mɒrəl]

【释义】 *a.* 道德的,精神上的(ethical, mental) *n.* 寓意,格言

【例句】 And all of those actions are for the purpose of proving that he is an upright moral, well-mannered, well behaved individual. (TPO13, L, S2, L1) 所有这些行为都是为了证明他是一个为人正直、懂得礼数、行为得体的人。

【派生】 morality *n.* 道德,道义

neck[5] [nek]

【释义】 *n.* 1. 颈,脖子 2. 领圈,领口

【例句】 This species, which lives in the rain forests and scrublands of the east coast of Australia, has a brown-to-black plumage with bare, bright-red skin on the head and neck and a neck collar of orange-yellow loosely hanging skin. (TPO17, R, S2, T1) 这一物种生活在澳大利亚东海岸的雨林和灌木丛中，有着黑棕色的羽毛，光秃秃的头部和脖子上的皮肤是鲜亮的红色，脖子上还有一圈橙黄色的松垮的皮肤。

【派生】necked *a.* 收缩的，缩小的

【搭配】break one's neck 折断脖子

notable[5] ['nəʊtəbl] 

【释义】*a.* 著名的，显要的，显著的(noteworthy) *n.* 名人，显要人物

【例句】In the seventeenth century, the trading activities of the Dutch East India Company resulted in vast quantities of decorated Chinese porcelain being brought to Europe, which stimulated and influenced the work of a wide variety of wares, notably Delft. (TPO10, R, S1, T1) 17世纪时，荷兰东印度公司的贸易活动使得大量精致的中国瓷器流入欧洲，刺激和影响了很多器皿的制作，尤其是代尔夫特陶器。

【派生】notably *ad.* 显著地；特别地

occasional[5] [ə'keɪʒənəl] 

【释义】*a.* 偶然的；临时的(random, incidental)

【例句】China has one of the world's oldest continuous civilizations, despite invasions and occasional foreign rule. (TPO10, R, S1, T1) 尽管曾遭到侵略和偶尔受外国势力统治，但中国仍然是世界上最古老的源远流长的文明之一。

【逆构】occasion *n.* 场合，时机

【派生】occasionally *ad.* 偶然地，不经常地

odd[5] [ɒd] 

【释义】*a.* 1. 奇特的(bizarre, unusual, weird) 2. 临时的 3. 奇数的 4. 零头的，剩余的

【例句】The onrushing water arising from these flash floods likely also formed the odd teardrop-shaped "islands" (resembling the miniature versions seen in the wet sand of our beaches at low tide) that have been found on the plains close to the ends of the outflow channels. (TPO8, R, S2, T2) 这突如其来的洪水产生的急流可能也形成了这种奇特的泪滴形状的"岛屿"(类似于我们在落潮的沙滩湿地上看到的微型版本)，这些"岛屿"已经在靠近泄水渠末端的平原上被发现了。

【派生】odds *n.* 可能的机会，成败的可能性

【搭配】odd number 奇数
at odd 争执
odd one out 剔除一个；格格不入

optical[5] ['ɒptɪkəl] 

【释义】*a.* 1. 光学的，光的 2. 视觉的，视力的

【例句】So optical radiation is just visible light energy spreading out. (TPO3, L, S2, L2) 所以，光辐射也就是可见的光能传播开来。

【派生】optician *n.* 眼镜商；光学仪器制造商

【搭配】optical fibre 光导纤维

output[5] ['aʊtpʊt] 

【释义】*n.* 生产，产量，输出量(production, yield) *v.* 输出

【例句】They were working alone and their individual output were being measured. (TPO16, S, Q4) 他们独立工作，并且按个人的工作量进行衡量。

【反义】input

【搭配】output value 输出值，产值

pillar[5] ['pɪlə] 

【释义】*n.* 1. 柱，柱子(column, post) 2. 栋梁，支柱

【例句】From a practical aspect this protected the figures against breakage and psychologically gives the images a sense of strength and power, usually enhanced by a supporting back pillar. (TPO11, R, S1, T1) 从实用的方面来看，这样可以保护人像不受破坏，而且从心理上给人一种力量感，这种力量感通常会通过其后部的柱子得以强化。

【派生】pillared *a.* 有柱子的

【搭配】pillar industry 支柱产业，主要工业
from pillar to post 从一处到另一处，到处

pinpoint[5] ['pɪn,pɔɪnt] 

【释义】*v.* 1. 明确指出，准确地确定 2. 为…准确定位 *n.* 极小或尖的点；准确位置 *a.* 精确的；极小的

返记菜单

notable[5] occasional[5] odd[5] optical[5] output[5]
pillar[5] pinpoint[5]

【例句】The exact role of other factors is much more difficult to pinpoint. (TPO8, R, S1, T1) 其它因素的确切作用就更不容易准确地确定了。

planetarium[5] [plænɪ'teərɪəm]

【释义】*n.* 天文馆；天象仪；天体运转模型

【例句】To test the idea, caged night-migrating birds were placed on the floor of a planetarium during their migratory period. (TPO11, R, S2, T1) 为了证实这个观点，把夜间迁徙的鸟关在笼中，在其迁徙期时把它们放在天文馆的地上。

plover[5] ['plʌvə]

【释义】*n.* 千鸟

【例句】I just read about a short bird, the plover. (TPO8, L, S1, L1) 我刚读了一本关于一种名叫千鸟的小型鸟类的书。

plug[5] [plʌg]

【释义】*v.* 1. 插上插头 2. 塞住 *n.* 1. 插头，插座 2. 塞子 3. 栓

【例句】Jefferson City still got electricity, and there is a library there where you can plug in your laptop. (TPO10, S, Q5) 杰佛逊市依然有电，那里有一座图书馆，可以给你的笔记本电脑插上电源。

【搭配】plug in 插入；插上电源
plug into [口]把(电器)插头插入

pollen[5] ['pɒlɪn]

【释义】*n.* 花粉

【例句】Without its stopping to feed and spread pollen from flower to flower, these plants would cease to exist. (TPO3, L, S1, L1) 如果没有它们停下来觅食并且将花粉在花之间进行传播，这些植物早已不存在了。

【搭配】pollen granule 花粉粒

pond[5] [pɒnd]

【释义】*n.* 池塘

【例句】An ecologist who studies a pond today may well find it relatively unchanged in a year's time. (TPO3, R, S1, T2) 生态学家对现在的池塘进行研究就会发现池塘在一年当中相对而言并没有变化。

【搭配】fish pond 鱼塘

post[5] [pəʊst]

【释义】*v.* 1. 张贴，公布(告示、海报等)(publicize) 2. 邮递(mail) *n.* 柱，杆(pole)；邮件(mail)；岗位

【例句】It was posted on a bulletin board. (TPO7, L, S1, C1) 它被贴在了公告牌上。

【派生】poster *n.* 海报，招贴
postage *n.* 邮资
postal *a.* 邮政的，邮局的
postcard *n.* 明信片
postwar *a.* 战后的

precious[5] ['preʃəs]

【释义】*a.* 宝贵的，珍贵的(valued, valuable, costly)

【例句】The graves contained precious stones. (TPO1, L, S2, L1) 这座坟墓里有珍贵的石头。

【派生】preciously *ad.* 昂贵地，仔细地
preciousness *n.* 珍贵；过分讲究

prevalent[5] ['prevələnt]

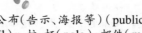

【释义】*a.* 流行的，普遍的(popular, prevaling)

【例句】Two species of deer have been prevalent in the Puget Sound area of Washington State in the Pacific Northwest of the United States. (TPO4, R, S1, T1) 在太平洋西北地区的美国华盛顿州皮吉特海湾，有两种鹿很常见。

【派生】prevalently *ad.* 流行地，普遍地

proof[5] [pru:f]

【释义】*n.* 证明，论证，证据(evidence) *a.* 1. 防…的；抗…的

【例句】Milankovitch didn't have any proof. (TPO17, L, S1, L2) 米兰科维奇没有任何证据。

【派生】proof-read *v.* 校对

【搭配】irrefutable proof 无可辩驳的论证，铁证如山

proper[5] ['prɒpə]

【释义】*a.* 1. 适合的，恰当的(appropriate, right) 2. 合乎体统的，得体的(suitable, decent)

【例句】 Properly speaking, tropical rainforests grow in high-rainfall equatorial areas that remain wet or humid all year round. (TPO14, R, S2, T1) 准确地说，热带雨林生长在降雨量较高的赤道地带，那里终年都是湿润的。
【反义】 improper
【派生】 properly *ad.* 恰当地
properness *n.* 恰当
propriety *n.* 恰当，得体

Proteus[5] ['prəʊtɪəs]

【释义】 *n.* 1. 普罗特斯(希腊海神) 2. [proteus] 变形杆菌
【例句】 Well, the octopus is the real world version of Proteus. (TPO17, L, S2, L2) 章鱼就是现实世界中的普罗特斯。

pulse[5] [pʌls]

【释义】 *n.* 脉搏，脉动，脉冲 *v.* 搏动，跳动
【例句】 The bats emit ultrasonic pulses, very high pitch sound waves that we cannot hear. (TPO7, L, S1, L2) 蝙蝠会发射出一种频率非常高而不能被人耳听见的超声波脉冲。
【派生】 pulsation *n.* 脉动，搏动，悸动
【搭配】 feel/take sb.'s pulse 诊脉，把脉
take the pulse of 判断意向

ratio[5] ['reɪʃɪəʊ]

【释义】 *n.* 比，比率，比例(proportion, percentage)
【例句】 The bigger the animal is, the lower its surface-to-volume ratio. (TPO15, R, S2, T1) 动物越大，表面和体积的比率越小。

realm[5] [relm]

【释义】 *n.* 王国；领域(kingdom, domain)
【例句】 Like the stones of a Roman wall which were held together both by the regularity of the design and by that peculiarly powerful Roman cement, so the various parts of the Roman realm were bonded into a massive, monolithic entity by physical, organizational, and psychological controls. (TPO7, R, S2, T1) 如同罗马墙是通过规律的设计和独特有效的罗马水泥构筑而成一样，罗马王国的各个部分也是通过对物质、组织和心理层面的支配而联结成一个规模宏大、坚如磐石的统一体的。
【搭配】 realm of necessity and realm of freedom 必然王国与自由王国

reclaim[5] [rɪ'kleɪm]

【释义】 *v.* 1. 开拓，开垦 2. 收回，回收再利用 3. 使改正
【例句】 The Dutch reclaimed more than 36,000 acres from 1590 to 1615 alone. (TPO10, R, S2, T2) 仅在1590年到1615年间，荷兰就开发利用了36000多英亩土地。
【派生】 reclaimable *a.* 可回收的；可教化的

relocate[5] ['riːləʊ'keɪt]

【释义】 *v.* 重新装置，重新配置
【例句】 Toxic minerals would first be absorbed by roots but later relocated to the stem and leaves. (TPO5, R, S1, T1) 有毒矿物质将会首先被根部吸收，然后再被输送到茎和叶。
【派生】 relocatee *n.* 迁到新地址的人

remote[5] [rɪ'məʊt]

【释义】 *a.* 遥远的，久远的，偏僻的(far, distant, isolated)
【例句】 Maybe your character loves the mountains and has lived in a remote area for years. (TPO6, L, S2, L1) 或许你(所描绘)的角色喜欢大山，并且已经在一个偏远的地方居住了很多年。
【反义】 close, near
【派生】 remoteness *n.* 远离，遥远
【搭配】 remote districts 偏远地区

reshape[5] ['riː'ʃeɪp]

【释义】 *v.* 再塑造，给…以新形式
【例句】 Glaciers move slowly across the land with tremendous energy, carving into even the hardest rock formations and thereby reshaping the landscape as they engulf, push, drag, and finally deposit rock debris in places far from its original location. (TPO15, R, S1, T1) 冰川带着巨大的能量在陆地上缓慢地移动，甚至切碎最坚硬的岩层，在其吞噬、推动、拖拉直至最后将这些岩石碎片沉积到远

返记菜单

Proteus[5] pulse[5] ratio[5] realm[5] reclaim[5]
relocate[5] remote[5] reshape[5]

离其原地的过程中，地貌被重新塑造。
【派生】reshaper *n.* 整形器，整形工具

resilience[5] [rɪˈzɪlɪəns]

【释义】*n.* 弹性，弹力；适应性
【例句】This kind of stability is also called resilience. (TPO3, R, S1, T2) 这种稳定性也被称作弹性。
【搭配】lacking resilience 缺少弹性

revolve[5] [rɪˈvɒlv]

【释义】*v.* (使)旋转；循环往复
【例句】However, its position with respect to the surroundings could be changed by revolving either the inner cage containing the birds or the outer walls, which served as the background. (TPO11, R, S2, T1) 然而，其相对于周围环境的位置却可以变动，只需旋转里面的装鸟的笼子或者充当背景的外墙即可。
【搭配】revolve around 围绕…转动，以…为中心

risky[5] [ˈrɪskɪ]

【释义】*a.* 冒险的，危险的(hazardous)
【例句】It's a little risky for me though. (TPO13, S, Q5) 但是这对于我来说有点冒险。
【派生】riskiness *n.* 冒险的事，危险

rotate[5] [rəʊˈteɪt]

【释义】*v.* 1. (使)旋转，(使)转动(spin, turn) 2. 轮流(alternate)
【例句】As the tool was made, the core was rotated clockwise, and the flakes, removed in sequence, had a little crescent of cortex on the side. (TPO12, R, S1, T1) 在制造工具时，岩芯按照顺时针方向旋转，其碎片就一点一点剥落，在一侧留下月牙状的表层(石芯的表面)。
【派生】rotation *n.* 旋转
rotative *a.* 回转的；循环的
【搭配】rotate about/around sth. 绕着…旋转

rush[5] [rʌʃ]

【释义】*v.* 1. 冲，奔 2. 仓促从事 3. 猛攻，突袭，急流 *n.* 冲，奔，蜂拥；匆忙；(感情等)一阵激动
【例句】Perhaps their rush to adulthood is driven by a simple need to keep warm. (TPO15, R, S2, T1) 它们(棱皮龟)或许是为了保暖才急于向成年过渡的。
【派生】rushed *a.* 匆忙的；贸然的
【搭配】rush about 奔波
rush hour 交通拥挤时间，上下班高峰时间

sharp[5] [ʃɑːp]

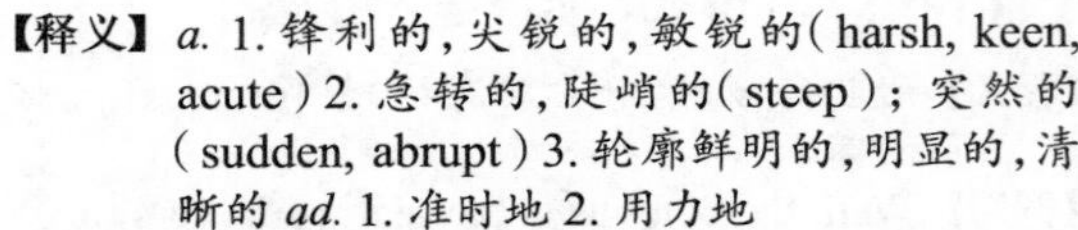

【释义】*a.* 1. 锋利的，尖锐的，敏锐的(harsh, keen, acute) 2. 急转的，陡峭的(steep)；突然的(sudden, abrupt) 3. 轮廓鲜明的，明显的，清晰的 *ad.* 1. 准时地 2. 用力地
【例句】While there has been a decline in book reading generally, the decline has been especially sharp for literature. (TPO11, W, Q1) 读书的人普遍减少，而文学作品读者数量的下降尤为明显。
【派生】sharpen *v.* 削尖；使敏锐，使敏捷
sharply *ad.* 突然地；猛烈地

skeletal[5] [ˈskelɪtl]

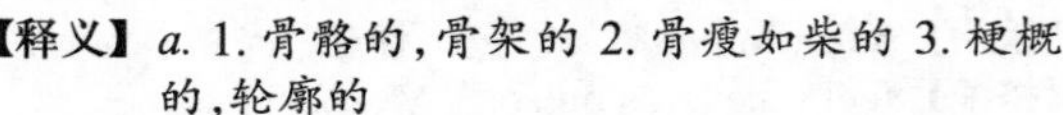

【释义】*a.* 1. 骨骼的，骨架的 2. 骨瘦如柴的 3. 梗概的，轮廓的
【例句】But, it also had a long skeletal structure. (TPO10, L, S1, L1) 但是，它也有一个很长的骨骼结构。
【搭配】skeletal system 骨骼系统

sleepy[5] [ˈsliːpɪ]

【释义】*a.* 欲睡的；困乏的；不活跃的(slumberous, inactive)
【例句】Much of the potential for European economic development lay in what at first glance would seem to have been only sleepy villages. (TPO10, R, S2, T2) 欧洲经济增长的巨大潜力存在于那些第一眼看去似乎一直沉睡着的乡村。
【反义】wakeful, awake

stadium[5] [ˈsteɪdɪəm]

【释义】*n.* 体育场，运动场
【例句】A university official announced plans to spend $2 million to build a new athletic

stadium, commenting that a new stadium would help the university achieve its goal of attracting more top students. (TPO13, S, Q3) 一位大学官员宣布，计划花费200万美元修建一座新的体育场，他说新体育馆的建成将帮助学校达成吸引更多顶尖学生的目标。

【搭配】athletic stadium 体育场

stony[5] ['stəʊnɪ] 

【释义】*a.* 1. 多石头的（rocky）2. 冷酷的，无情的

【例句】In some cases the loose soil is blown completely away, leaving a stony surface. (TPO2, R, Sl, T1) 在某些地区，松软的泥土已经全部被风吹走，只剩下了石头表面。

【派生】stonily *ad.* 铁石心肠地

strait[5] [streɪt] 

【释义】*n.* 1. 海峡 2. 困难，困境 *a.* 1. 狭窄的，紧身的 2. 困难的，窘迫的

【例句】It has long been accepted that the Americas were colonized by a migration of peoples from Asia, slowly traveling across a land bridge called Beringia (now the Bering Strait between northeastern Asia and Alaska) during the last Ice Age. (TPO9, R, S1, T1) 人们长久以来都认为：美洲被一群来自亚洲的移民殖民统治着，他们在上一个冰河时代慢慢地跨越了一个叫做白令的大陆桥（位于东北亚和阿拉斯加之间的现在的白令海峡）来到美洲。

【派生】straitness *n.* 狭窄，狭隘

【搭配】Dardanelles Strait 达达尼尔海峡

suck[5] [sʌk] 

【释义】*n.* 吮吸；卷入（absorb, take in）

【例句】Film analysis of the infant's responses, heart and respiration rate monitors, and nonnutritive sucking devices are used as effective tools in understanding infant perception. (TPO13, R, S2, T2) 婴儿反应胶片分析、心脏和呼吸频率监听器以及与营养无关的吮吸装置是了解婴儿认知能力的有效工具。

【搭配】suck up 奉承，拍马屁
suck in 吸收；吞没；欺骗
be sucked into 被卷入
sth. sucks（某事）糟糕透了

surge[5] [sɜːdʒ] 

【释义】*n./v.*（波涛）汹涌；激增

【例句】But sometimes, they experience surges, and during these surges, in some places, they can move its speeds as high as 7000 meters per year. (TPO7, L, S2, L2) 但有时它们会遇到汹涌的波浪，在一些地方，波涛汹涌时其（冰川）移动速度可高达每年7000米。

【派生】surgent *a.* 汹涌的，澎湃的

【搭配】a surge of anger/pity 一阵怒气 / 怜悯

suspend[5] [səs'pend] 

【释义】*v.* 1. 悬，挂，吊（hang）2. 延缓，推迟（delay, postpone）

【例句】Plants are suspended and the roots misted with a nutrient solution. (TPO5, R, S1, T1) 植物被悬挂着，根部喷洒着营养液。

【派生】suspendable *a.* 可中止的
suspended *a.* 悬浮的；暂停的

【搭配】suspend sb. from sth. 停职 / 停课
suspend production 停产

sustained[5] [səs'teɪnd]

【释义】*a.* 持久的，经久不衰的（continuing, lasting）

【例句】The physiology of endothermy allows sustained physical activity, such as running. (TPO4, W, Q1) 恒温动物的生理机能使其能进行持久的身体活动，比如奔跑。

【派生】sustainable *a.* 可持续的，可以支撑的

【逆构】sustain *v.* 保持，支撑，承受

【搭配】sustained growth 持续增长

返记菜单

stony[5] strait[5] suck[5] surge[5] suspend[5] sustained[5]

Word List 24

temporary[5] ['tempərərɪ]

【释义】*n.* 暂时的，临时的（impermanent, temporal）

【例句】Furthermore, jobs created by salvage logging are only temporary and are often filled by outsiders with more experience or training than local residents have. (TPO14, W, Q1) 此外，由抢救性砍伐创造的工作机会也只是暂时的，通常都由外来人员担任，他们比当地居民受到的训练多、经验丰富。

【反义】permanent

【搭配】temporary employment 临时工作

three-dimensional[5] ['θridaɪ'mɛnʃənəl]

【释义】*a.* 立体的，三维的

【例句】The majority of three-dimensional representations, whether standing, seated, or kneeling, exhibit what is called frontality: they face straight ahead, neither twisting nor turning. (TPO11, R, S1, T1) 大多数这样的三维雕像，不论是站着的、坐着的或跪着的，都展现了什么叫正面描绘：他们都面朝前方，既不扭曲也不扭转。

tip[5] [tɪp]

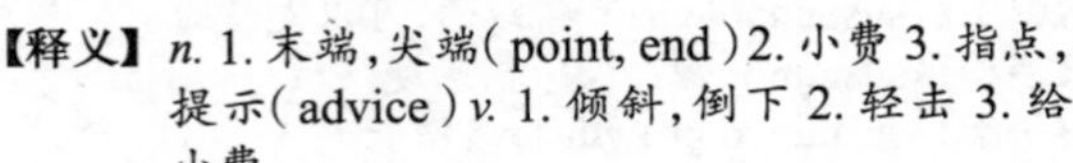

【释义】*n.* 1. 末端，尖端（point, end）2. 小费 3. 指点，提示（advice）*v.* 1. 倾斜，倒下 2. 轻击 3. 给小费

【例句】Most engravings, for example, are best lit from the left, as befits the work of right-handed artists, who generally prefer to have the light source on the left so that the shadow of their hand does not fall on the tip of the engraving tool or brush. (TPO12, R, S1, T1) 例如，大多数的雕版都是左起的光照最好，这是为了配合惯用右手的工匠的工作。他们喜欢让光线从左面照过来，以便于手的影子不会落在雕版工具或是刷子的尖端。

【派生】tipped *a.* 焊接在尖头上的
tippy *a.* 不安定的

tropic[5] ['trɒpɪk]

【释义】*n.* 回归线；热带 [Tropics] *a.* 热带的

【例句】The upper timberline is highest in the tropic. (TPO1, R, S1, T1) 上层林木线在热带地区是最高的。

【派生】tropical *a.* 热带的

turnpike[5] ['tɜːnpaɪk]

【释义】*n.* 收费公路

【例句】Steam also promised to eliminate a transportation problem not fully solved by either canal boats or turnpikes. (TPO6, R, S1, T1) 蒸汽动力也最终解决了运河及收费公路无法完全解决的交通问题。

ultrasound[5] ['ʌltrəˌsaʊnd]

【释义】*n.* 超声（波）

【例句】Now, let's talk about the other and the acoustic spectrums, sound that is too high for humans to hear— ultrasounds. (TPO7, L, S1, L2) 现在，我们来谈一谈另一个声谱，这是一种因频率太高而不能被人耳听见的声音——超声波。

【搭配】an ultrasound scan 超声波扫描检查

uncertainty[5] [ʌn'sɜːtntɪ]

【释义】*n.* 不确定，不可靠，易变

【例句】Generally, there is uncertainty as to whether very young children can distinguish between fantasy and reality in advertising. (TPO14, R, S1, T1) 总的来说，关于儿童是否能分辨广告中的幻想与现实还存在不确定性。

【逆构】uncertain *a.* 不确定的

uniform[5] ['juːnɪfɔːm]

【释义】*a.* 清一色的，一致的 *n.* 制服，校服（costume, outfit）

【例句】Many ecologists now think that the relative long-term stability of climax communities comes not from diversity but from the "patchiness" of the environment; an environment that varies from place to place supports more kinds of organisms than an

environment that is uniform. (TPO3, R, S1, T2) 现在的很多生态学家认为，顶级群落相对长期的稳定性并非源于多样性，而是来自环境的"不一致性"，随处变化的环境比统一的环境更有利于多种有机体的生存。

【反义】various

【派生】uniformly *ad.* 一致地，一律地；均匀地

unify[5] ['ju:nɪfaɪ] 

【释义】*v.* 使成一体，统一，使一致(combine, unite)

【例句】However, some modern architectural designs, such as those using folded plates of concrete or air-inflated structures, are again unifying skeleton and skin. (TPO2, R, Sl, T1, Q12) 但是，一些现代建筑设计，例如使用折板的实体结构或充气结构，再一次使骨架和表面成为一体。

【反义】disunify, devide

【派生】unified *a.* 统一的

unification *n.* 统一

unrealistic[5] ['ʌnrɪə'lɪstɪk] 

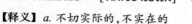

【释义】*a.* 不切实际的，不实在的

【例句】It is the melodious drama of ancient Greek theater, the term "melodious drama" being shortened eventually to "melodrama" because operas frequently are melodramatic, not to say unrealistic. (TPO12, L, S2, L1) 它是古希腊剧场里悦耳的戏剧，"melodious drama (悠扬的戏剧)"这一术语最终被缩改成"melodrama (音乐戏剧)"，是因为戏剧不切实际不说，还经常情节夸张。

【派生】unrealistically *ad.* 不切实际地，不现实地

upcoming[5] ['ʌpˌkʌmɪŋ] 

【释义】*a.* 即将来到的，即将出现的

【例句】In the face of the upcoming water supply crisis, a number of grandiose schemes have been developed to transport vast quantities of water by canal or pipeline from the Mississippi, the Missouri, or the Arkansas rivers. (TPO3, R, S1, T1) 在即将到来的水资源供应危机面前，人们提出了一些宏伟的计划，比如将密西西比河、密苏里河或者阿肯色河的水通过运河或管道输送到需要用水的地方。

【搭配】the upcoming concert 即将上演的音乐会

vacation[5] [və'keɪʃən] 

【释义】*n.* 假期(holiday, leave)

【例句】In fact, we were on vacation in New York. (TPO4, L, S1, C1) 事实上，那时我们正在纽约度假。

【逆构】vacate *v.* 休假；搬出；辞去(职务)

vehicle[5] ['viːɪkl] 

【释义】*n.* 1. 交通工具，车辆(carriage) 2. 传播媒介，手段(medium)

【例句】Now it may not be a very fast car, er…it could even be an inexpensive vehicle with a low performance rating, but if a popular race car driver is shown driving it, and saying "I like my cars fast", then people will believe the car is impressive for its speed. (TPO3, S, Q6) 可能这辆车并不快，甚至是一个速度很慢且很便宜的交通工具，但如果配合赛车手出现在屏幕中，并且伴随"我喜欢我的车跑得快"的广告语，那么人们就会对车的速度留下很深的印象。

【派生】vehicular *a.* 车的，用车运载的

vein[5] [veɪn] 

【释义】*n.* 1. 静脉，血管 2. 叶脉；纹理 3. 方式，风格

【例句】Iron deficiency is characterized by chlorosis between veins in young leaves. (TPO5, R, S1, T1) 铁缺乏主要表现为嫩叶叶脉的萎黄病。

【派生】veinal *a.* 静脉的

veiny *a.* 有静脉的；多脉纹的

verify[5] ['verɪfaɪ] 

【释义】*v.* 验证，核实，查证(confirm, prove, validate)

【例句】While a person could describe his thoughts, no one else can see or hear them to verify the accuracy of his report. (TPO2, L, S1, L1) 一个人可以描述自己的思想活动，但是其他人无法证实其描述的准确性，因为他们无法看到或听到这些思想活动。

【派生】verifiable *a.* 可被证实的

verification *n.* 证实；证据

返记菜单

unify[5] unrealistic[5] upcoming[5] vacation[5] vehicle[5]
vein[5] verify[5]

vertical[5] ['vɜːtɪkəl]

【释义】*a.* 垂直的，竖直的，纵向的（upright, erect）*n.* 垂直物，垂直的位置

【例句】If it's sitting on a vertical branch, it'll groom its breast feathers. (TPO4, L, S1, L1) 如果它站在纵向的树枝上，它就会梳理自己胸前的羽毛。

【反义】horizontal

【派生】vertically *ad.* 垂直地

【搭配】out of the vertical 不垂直的

violent[5] ['vaɪələnt]

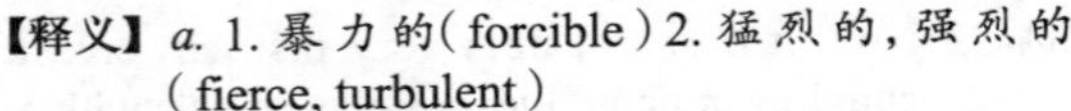

【释义】*a.* 1. 暴力的（forcible）2. 猛烈的，强烈的（fierce, turbulent）

【例句】There is yet another aspect of the harsh environment that they have to adapt to, the force of the tides and occasional violent storms. (TPO19, L, S2, L1) 他们需要适应恶劣环境的另外一个方面：来自潮汐和偶尔发生的暴风雨的力量。

【派生】violence *n.* 暴力
violently *ad.* 暴力地；猛烈地

vulnerable[5] ['vʌlnərəb(ə)l]

【释义】*a.* 易受攻击的，易受伤害的，脆弱的（liable, prone, susceptible）

【例句】Excessive numbers of cattle and the need for firewood for fuel have reduced grasses and trees leaving the land unprotected and vulnerable. (TPO2, R, Sl, T1, Q13) 过度放牧以及对木柴的需求使得草地和树木不断减少，进而使得土地缺乏植被保护，易受侵蚀。

【反义】defensive, immune

【搭配】be vulnerable to 易受…影响

warrior[5] ['wɒrɪə]

【释义】*n.*（尤指旧时）武士，勇士

【例句】Iron hoes, which made the land more productive, and iron weapons, which made the warrior more powerful, had symbolic meaning in a number of West African societies. (TPO7, R, S2, T2) 增强了土地生产力的铁锄以及使士兵变得更强的铁制武器，在西部非洲的诸多社会群体中都具有象征意义。

zenith[5] ['zenɪθ]

【释义】*n.* 顶点，最高点，巅峰（top, peak, pinnacle）

【例句】One important way the Polynesians had for orienting themselves was by using zenith stars. (TPO14, L, S2, L1) 玻利尼西亚人确定方向的一个重要方法就是利用天顶星。

abrupt[4] [ə'brʌpt]

【释义】*a.* 突然的，意外的（sudden, unexpected）

【例句】One question was related to evidence that the invertebrate fauna (animals without spines) of the Mediterranean had changed abruptly about 6 million years ago. (TPO7, R, S1, T1) 问题之一是找到相关证据来证明地中海的无脊椎动物群体在约600万年前发生了突然的变化。

【派生】abruptly *ad.* 突然地，莽撞地

accelerate[4] [æk'seləreɪt]

【释义】*v.*（使）加快，（使）增速（hasten, speed up, quicken）

【例句】Desertification is accomplised primarily through the loss of stabilizing natural vegetation and the subsequent accelerated erosion of the soil by wind and water. (TPO2, R, Sl, T1) 由于加固土壤的自然植被消失，随后使得风力、流水对土壤的侵蚀速度加快，从而形成了沙漠化。

【派生】acceleration *n.* 加速
accelerator *n.* 油门
accelerative *a.* 加速的
acceleratory *a.* 加速的

acupuncture[4] ['ækjʊpʌŋktʃə(r)]

【释义】*n.* 针刺疗法，针灸

【例句】So lots of people in the U.S. have realized that acupuncture is effective. (TPO17, S, Q6) 因此，很多美国人认识到针灸是有效的。

altogether[4] [ˌɔːltə'geðə]

【释义】*ad.* 1. 完全 2. 全部，合计 3. 总而言之

返记菜单

vertical[5] violent[5] vulnerable[5] warrior[5] zenith[5]
abrupt[4] accelerate[4] acupuncture[4] altogether[4]

【例句】The empirical evidence, such as it is, suggests an altogether different function for yawning—namely, that yawning prepares us for a change in activity level. (TPO18, R, S2, T1) 实验证据，尽管不怎么好，却表明了打呵欠的一个完全不同的功能——即，打呵欠是在为我们活动的变化做准备。

analogy⁴ [ə'nælədʒɪ]

【释义】*n.* 1. 类比，类推 2. 类似物
【例句】Well, the whole point of defining this familiar process as transmission of memes is so that we can explore its analogy with the transmission of genes. (TPO5, L, S1, L1) 把这一熟悉的过程定义为文化基因的传播的整个用意就在于我们可以用基因传播来与其做类比。
【搭配】analogy analysis 类比分析

approximate⁴ [ə'prɒksɪmeɪt]

【释义】*a.* 近似的，大约的（rough）*v.* 近似，接近（approach）
【例句】The deserts, which already occupy approximately a fourth of the Earth's land surface, have in recent decades been increasing at an alarming pace. (TPO2, R, Sl, T1) 沙漠已经占据地球表面约四分之一的面积，近几十年仍在以惊人的速度扩张。
【反义】exact, precise
【派生】approximately *ad.* 大约地
【搭配】approximate value 近似值

aquatic⁴ [ə'kwætɪk]

【释义】*a.* 水生的，水产的，水栖的
【例句】Painlevé was a pioneer in underwater filmmaking, and a lot of his short films focused on the aquatic animal world. (TPO3, L, S1, L2) 培乐威是水下电影的先驱人物，他的很多电影短片描述的都是水中生物世界。
【派生】aquacultue *n.* 水产养殖
aquarium *n.* 水族馆
【搭配】aquatic plants 水生植物

arrival⁴ [ə'raɪvəl]

【释义】*n.* 1. 到达 2. 到达者
【例句】The arrival of sound film technology in the United States forces smaller producers in the motion picture industry out of business. (TPO12, R, S2, T1) 在美国，有声电影技术的出现使得电影产业中的一些小生产商退出了这个行业。
【反义】departure
【逆构】arrive *v.* 到达

aside⁴ [ə'saɪd]

【释义】*ad.* 在旁边，到（或向）一边；另外 *n.* 旁白，题外话
【例句】Also, large blocks thrown aside by the impact would form secondary craters surrounding the main crater. (TPO15, R, S2, T2) 在撞击中被抛到一边的大石块也会在主要陨石坑周围形成次级陨石坑。
【搭配】aside from 除…以外

attain⁴ [ə'teɪn]

【释义】*v.* 实现，获得，达到（achieve, accomplish）
【例句】Trees trend to attain greater heights on ridges. (TPO1, R, S1, T1) 生长在山脊上的树趋向于长得更高。
【派生】attainable *a.* 可达到的，可获得的
attainment *n.* 成就

audio⁴ ['ɔːdɪəu]

【释义】*a.* 1. 听觉的，声音的（vocal）2. 音频的（acoustic）*n.* 音频；音响设备
【例句】The author George Comstock suggested that less than a quarter of children between the ages of six and eight years old understood standard disclaimers used in many toy advertisements and that disclaimers are more readily comprehended when presented in both audio and visual formats. (TPO14, R, S1, T1) 作家乔治·康斯托克表示，在六到八岁的孩子中，只有不到四分之一的孩子能理解玩具广告中使用的标准的免责声明，如果那些免责声明能够以声音和图像的形式呈现出来，那么孩子们理解起来就会更容易些。
【搭配】digital audio 数字音频
audio signal 声频信号
audio frequency 音频；成音频率

autonomous[4] [ɔːˈtɔnəməs]

【释义】*a.* 自治的，独立自主的

【例句】Another condition that contributes to the development of autonomous theater is the emergence of the aesthetic sense. (TPO1, R, S2, T1) 另一个导致戏剧独立的条件是审美意识的出现。

【派生】autonomously *ad.* 独立地，自主地

bar[4] [bɑː(r)]

【释义】*n.* 1. 棒，条 2. 横木，栅栏 3. 酒吧 *v.* 关闭；阻挠

【例句】If you leave, for example, a bar of ice supported only at one end, the unsupported end will deform under its own way due. (TPO7, L, S2, L2) 比如，如果你放置一根冰条，并将其一端固定，那么没有固定的一端将会发生变形。

barely[4] [ˈbeəlɪ]

【释义】*ad.* 1. 仅仅，只不过（just, only）2. 几乎不（hardly）

【例句】They look like low-lying, white or grey builds, long, narrow hills with flat tops, barely a meter high. (TPO9, L, S2, L1) 它们看起来如同低矮的白色或灰色的建筑，又如同又长又窄的平顶山，仅一米之高。

【逆构】bare *a.* 赤裸的，没有保护的

battle[4] [ˈbætl]

【释义】*n.* 战争，战斗，竞争 *v.* 和…作战，和…斗争

【例句】In Berlin, for the premiere performance of *The* Battleship *Potemkin*, film director Sergei Eisenstein worked with Austrian composer Edmund Meisel on a musical score matching sound to image. (TPO12, R, S2, T1) 在柏林，为了电影《战舰波将金号》的首映，导演谢尔盖·爱森斯坦与奥地利作曲家埃德蒙·梅赛奥合作创作与电影相匹配的音效。

beam[4] [biːm]

【释义】*n.* 1. 梁，横梁 2.（光线的）束，柱

【例句】As a method of spanning space, the arch can support greater weight than a horizontal beam. (TPO3, R, S1, T1) 作为跨越空间的一种方式，拱可以比水平横梁支撑更大的重量。

【派生】beaming *a.* 照耀的，光亮的，喜气洋洋的
beamy *a.* 放射光线的，光亮的

【搭配】a beam in one's eye 与他人相比自身特别重大的缺点

bend[4] [bend]

【释义】*v.*（使）弯曲；屈身 *n.* 1.（尤指道路或河流的）拐弯，弯道 2. 弯身，弯腰

【例句】Unlike formal statues that are limited to static poses of standing, sitting, and kneeling, these figures depict a wide range of actions, such as grinding grain, baking bread, producing pots, and making music, and they are shown in appropriate poses, bending and squatting as they carry out their tasks. (TPO11, R, S1, T1) 这些雕像不像正规雕像那样只有静止的站立、坐和跪的姿态，而是表现了各种不同的动作，比如磨谷物、烤面包、造壶罐，还有奏乐，而且进行这些活动时的姿态都很恰当，或弯腰，或蹲坐着。

【搭配】bend in 把…往里弯
bend over 俯身；折转
on the bend 用不正当的手段
bend over backwards 拼命
bend down 蹲下，弯腰

blame[4] [bleɪm]

【释义】*v.* 指责，责怪，归咎于（condemn, rebuke）*n.* 过失，责备

【例句】He'll probably blame the interviewers or bad luck rather than look at himself and try to figure out what he could have done better. (TPO16, S, Q6) 他可能会责备面试官或是霉运，而不是审查并思考自己有什么地方可以改进。

【搭配】blame for 责备；因…责备
put the blame on 归咎于…

blowhole[4] [ˈbləʊˌhəʊl]

【释义】*n.* 呼吸孔，鼻孔（nostril）

【例句】Their streamlined bodies, the absence of hind legs, and the presence of a fluke and

返记菜单

autonomous[4] bar[4] barely[4] battle[4] beam[4]
bend[4] blame[4] blowhole[4]

blowhole cannot disguise their affinities with land dwelling mammals. (TPO2, R, S2, T1) 它们的身体呈流线型,没有后腿,长有尾片和喷水孔,但这些都不能掩盖它们与陆生哺乳动物的相似性。

blubber[4] ['blʌbə] 

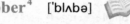

【释义】*n.* 1. 鲸脂 2. 肥胖 3. 痛苦流涕

【例句】It is not enough for whales, which supplement it with a thick layer of insulating blubber (fat). (TPO15, R, S2, T1) 对于通过厚厚的绝缘脂层来维持体温的鲸鱼来说这是不够的。

【派生】blubbery *a.* 鲸脂的

【搭配】blubber oil 鲸脂油

bud[4] [bʌd] 

【释义】*n.* 嫩芽,花蕾 *v.* 发芽,萌芽(sprout)

【例句】Tree shoots and buds cannot mature sufficiently to survive the winter months. (TPO1, R, S1, T1) 树木的嫩枝和嫩芽还没有成熟到可以熬过数月的严冬。

bulk[4] [bʌlk] 

【释义】*n.* 1. 容积,体积,大小(mass, volume) 2. 大块,大量,主体(majority, main part)

【例句】But even high-priced commodities like spices had to be transported in large bulk in order to justify the expense and trouble of sailing around the African continent all the way to India and China. (TPO17, R, S1, T1) 但是即使是像香料这样的高价日用品也不得不大量运输,以便平衡要航行绕过非洲大陆到达中国和印度所花费的巨大成本和期间的麻烦。

【派生】bulky *a.* 庞大的;笨重的

【搭配】sell in bulk 整批出售

campaign[4] [kæm'peɪn] 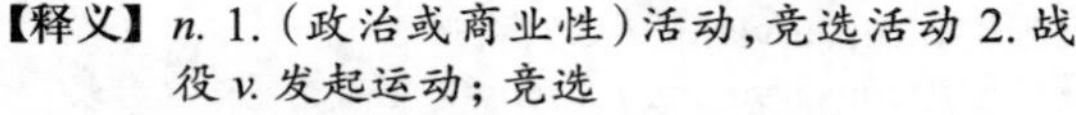

【释义】*n.* 1. (政治或商业性)活动,竞选活动 2. 战役 *v.* 发起运动;竞选

【例句】If the Australian government were to organize a campaign among Australian citizens to join forces to destroy the toads, the collective effort might stop the toad from spreading. (TPO15, W, Q1) 如果澳大利亚政府在市民中组织一个活动,联合起各方力量消除蟾蜍,那么,蟾蜍的扩散可能会被阻止。

cargo[4] ['kɑːɡəʊ] 

【释义】*n.* (船、飞机等装载的)货物

【例句】Spillage from huge oil-carrying cargo ships, called tankers, involved in collisions or accidental groundings (such as the one off Alaska in 1989) can create oil slicks at sea. (TPO4, R, S2, T2) 大型的运油货船——也叫油轮——因撞击或搁浅(比如1989年发生在阿拉斯加的事件)引发的石油泄漏会造成海面浮油。

【搭配】bulk cargo 散装货
cargo clauses 货物保险条款

cascade[4] [kæs'keɪd] 

【释义】*v.* 如瀑布般落下 *n.* 瀑布(waterfall)

【例句】As a result of crustal adjustments and faulting, the Strait of Gibraltar, where the Mediterranean now connects to the Atlantic, opened, and water cascaded spectacularly back into the Mediterranean. (TPO7, R, S1, T1) 由于地壳运动发生断层现象,致使现在连接地中海和大西洋的直布罗陀海峡裂开,海水如瀑布般地流回地中海,十分壮观。

categorize[4] ['kætɪɡəraɪz] 

【释义】*v.* 分类(classify, sort)

【例句】The second hypothesis is that, yes, we do perceive everything, but the brain categorizes the information, and whatever is not relevant to what we are concentrating on gets treated as low priority. (TPO15, L, S1, L1) 第二种假设是,是的,我们的确会察觉到一切事物,但是大脑会将信息分类,任何与我们所关注的事物不相干的东西都会被作为次优先考虑的事情对待。

【派生】category *n.* 种类,范畴

celebrate[4] ['selɪbreɪt] 

【释义】*v.* 庆祝;颂扬(commemorate)

【例句】Frequently the myths include representatives

of those supernatural forces that the rites celebrate or hope to influence. (TPO1, R, S2, T1) 通常,神话中会包含那些超自然的力量,这些力量是那些仪式想要去赞美或施加影响的。

【派生】 celebration *n.* 庆祝活动

chair[4] [tʃeə]

【释义】 *n.* 1.(会议)主席(chairperson, chairman) 2.椅子 *v.* 担任主席

【例句】 You have to meet with your department chair to outline a plan for the rest of your time here. (TPO8, L, S1, C1) 你必须见见你们系主任,然后大概规划出一个你在这里的剩余时间的计划。

charcoal[4] ['tʃɑːkəʊl]

【释义】 *n.* 1.炭,木炭 2.炭画笔 3.炭黑色

【例句】 There are charcoal marks from their torches on the cave walls clearly dating from thousands of years after the paintings were made. (TPO3, L, S2, L1) 在画壁形成的几千年之后,在洞穴的墙上能很清晰地看到火把的木炭痕迹。

【搭配】 a charcoal burner 烧炭工人

coach[4] [kəʊtʃ]

【释义】 *v.* 指导,训练(teach, train, tutor) *n.* 1.教练 2.经济舱,客车车厢 3.四轮马车

【例句】 He also coaches the swim team. (TPO11, L, S1, C1) 他也指导游泳队。

【搭配】 head coach 主教练;总教练
assistant coach 助理教练

coloration[4] [ˌkʌlə'reɪʃən]

【释义】 *n.* 着色,染色;色泽,色调

【例句】 Many animals use coloration to protect themselves from predators. (TPO8, S, Q4) 许多动物利用色彩来保护自己不受天敌的侵害。

【逆构】 color *n.* 颜色;颜料;情调 *v.* 给…着(染)色

compression[4] [kəm'preʃ(ə)n]

【释义】 *n.* 浓缩,压缩,压力

【例句】 They are designed to withstand the forces of compression (pushing together), tension (pulling apart), bending, or a combination of these in different parts of the structure. (TPO3, R, S1, T1) 通过结构设计使建筑的不同部分能对抗压力、拉力、弯曲力或者以上各种压力的综合。

【逆构】 compress *v.* 压缩,浓缩

【搭配】 tension and compression 拉伸和压缩

compromise[4] ['kɒmprəmaɪz]

【释义】 *n./v.* 妥协,折中

【例句】 Even those artists who were most dependent on photography became reluctant to admit that they made use of it, in case this compromised their professional standing. (TPO22, R, S2, T1) 即使是那些对摄影术最为依赖的艺术家也不愿意承认他们使用过摄影术,害怕这会影响到他们的专业地位。

【派生】 compromised *a.* 妥协的,折中的

【搭配】 compromise with 与…妥协

consensus[4] [kən'sensəs]

【释义】 *n.*(意见等)一致,同意,共识(agreement, unanimity)

【例句】 People can govern themselves by shared consensus while minimizing distinctions of wealth and power. (TPO16, R, S1, T1) 人们可以通过分享共识、同时使财富和权力的区分最小化来管理自己。

【反义】 disagreement, difference

【搭配】 reach a consensus 达成共识

conserve[4] [kən'sɜːv]

【释义】 *v.* 保护,保藏(keep, preserve) *n.* 果酱,蜜饯

【例句】 Many have been attempting to conserve water by irrigating less frequently or by switching to crops that require less water. (TPO3, R, S1, T1) 很多人已经开始尝试通过降低灌溉频率或者改种需水较少的庄稼来节约水资源。

【派生】 conservation *n.* 保存,保护

【搭配】 conserve one's strength 保存力量,留后劲

controversial[4] [ˌkɒntrə'vɜːʃəl]

【释义】 *a.* 有争议的,引起争论的(disputed)

【例句】It's so controversial. (TPO4, L, S1, C1) 它饱含争议。
【派生】controversialism *n.* 争论精神
controversialist *n.* 争论者
controversially *ad.* 引起争议地
【逆构】controversy *n.* 争论，辩论

cooperate[4] [kəʊ'ɒpəreɪt] 

【释义】*v.* 合作，协力，配合(collaborate)
【例句】More often, we simply cooperate with others to reach some end without endowing the relationship with any larger significance. (TPO13, R, S1, T1) 更多时候，我们只是与他人合作来达成某种目标，而并不赋予这种关系以更多的意义。
【派生】cooperation *n.* 合作，协作
cooperative *a.* 合作的 *n.* 合作机构，合作社

cope[4] [kəʊp] 

【释义】*v.* 1. 处理，应付 2. 笼罩 *n.* 长袍，斗篷状覆盖物
【例句】This was justified by the view that reflective practice could help teachers to feel more intellectually involved in their role and work in teaching and enable them to cope with the paucity of scientific fact and the uncertainty of knowledge in the discipline of teaching. (TPO9, R, S2, T1) 有一种观点证明了这是合理的，那就是：反思实践可以帮助老师们更加理性地对待他们的角色和他们从事的事业，并能够让他们在教学中处理好科学事实缺乏和知识的不确定问题。
【搭配】cope with 处理，应对

costly[4] ['kɒstlɪ] 

【释义】*a.* 代价高的，昂贵的(expensive)
【例句】Given that predators can make it costly to beg for food, what benefit do begging nestlings derive from their communications? (TPO11, R, S2, T2) 既然食肉动物会让雏鸟乞食付出巨大代价，那么这些乞食的雏鸟又能从这种交流中获得什么益处呢？
【反义】cheap

currency[4] ['kʌrənsɪ] 

【释义】*n.* 1. 通货，货币 2. 流通，通用，流行
【例句】The exchanger would then send a bill of exchange to a colleague in Marseille, authorizing the colleague to pay the Marseille merchant in the merchant's own currency after the actual exchange of goods had taken place. (TPO10, R, S2, T2) 然后兑换人会把一张汇票寄给在马赛的同事，并授权该同事在货物交易完成后，以商人本国的货币形式支付给在马赛的商人相应的钱。
【搭配】foreign currency 外币

damaging[4] ['dæmɪdʒɪŋ] 

【释义】*a.* 有害的，损害的(harmful)
【例句】Many signals that animals make seem to impose on the signallers costs that are overly damaging. (TPO11, R, S2, T2) 动物发出的许多信号似乎给它们带来了毁灭性的损害。
【逆构】damage *v.* 损害

deceive[4] [dɪ'siːv] 

【释义】*v.* 欺骗，蒙蔽(fool, trick, hoax)
【例句】Two percent may be a deceiving figure, however, 80 percent of the world's fresh water is locked up as ice in glaciers, with the majority of it in Antarctica. (TPO15, R, S1, T1) 但是，2% 可能是一个欺骗性的数字，因为地球上 80% 的淡水都以冰的形式存在于冰川中，而其中绝大多数都在南极洲。
【派生】deceivable *a.* 可骗的
【搭配】deceive sb. into doing sth. 欺骗某人做某事

definite[4] ['defɪnɪt] 

【释义】*a.* 1. 肯定的，一定的(certain, sure) 2. 明确的，确切的(clear, obvious, distinct)
【例句】— I was wondering if I should also include the notes from the research journal you suggested I keep.
— Yes, definitely. (TPO2, L, S1, C1)
——我在考虑要不要把您建议我做的研究日志写进去。
——当然应该写进去。
【反义】indefinite, obscure, vague
【派生】definitely *ad.* 肯定地；明确地

返记菜单

cooperate[4] cope[4] costly[4] currency[4] damaging[4]
deceive[4] definite[4]

Word List 25

deprive[4] [dɪ'praɪv]

【释义】*v.* 剥夺，使失去（deny, take away）

【例句】When experimentally deprived baby robins are placed in a nest with normally fed siblings, the hungry nestlings beg more loudly than usual. (TPO11, R, S2, T2) 实验时当把饥饿的知更鸟雏鸟与正常喂养的兄弟姐妹放在同一个巢中时，饥饿的雏鸟会发出比平常更大的乞食声。

【派生】deprivation *n.* 缺乏；剥夺

【搭配】be deprived of 被剥夺，被夺去

destination[4] [ˌdestɪ'neɪʃən]

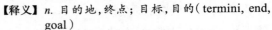

【释义】*n.* 目的地，终点；目标，目的（termini, end, goal）

【例句】The path a person takes can only be seen clearly after the destination has been reached. (TPO4, L, S1, L2) 一个人所选择的路只有在其到达终点后才会清晰地呈现出来。

dimension[4] [dɪ'menʃən]

【释义】*n.* 尺寸，大小，尺度（measurement, size）

【例句】At the same time, the image that the spectator looked at expanded from the minuscule peepshow dimensions of 1 or 2 inches (in height) to the life-size proportions of 6 or 9 feet. (TPO2, R, S2, T2) 与此同时，观众所看到的图像大小也从狭小的1至2英寸扩展到与实物契合的6至9英尺。

【派生】dimensional *a.* 尺寸的，…维的

dishabituation[4] ['dishəˌbitju'eiʃən]

【例句】The first is the habituation-dishabituation technique, in which a single stimulus is presented repeatedly to the infant until there is a measurable decline (habituation) in whatever attending behavior is being observed. (TPO13, R, S2, T2) 第一个就是习惯与非习惯性技术，这种技术是通过重复地对婴儿施加某种单一刺激，直到婴儿对这一信号形成习惯并对信号的反应出现可测量的减弱（习惯性）。

dismiss[4] [dɪs'mɪs]

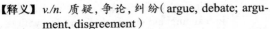

【释义】*v.* 1. 摒除（思想、感情等）（eliminate）2. 解雇，撤职；驳回（fire, disband）3. 解散（send away）

【例句】It takes geniuses, people like, say, Shakespeare, who're unique because when they have a glimpse at this truth, this universal truth, they pay attention to it and express it and don't just dismiss it like most people do. (TPO4, L, S1, L2) 这需要天赋，像莎士比亚这样的人是独一无二的，因为他们只需瞥一眼这普遍的真理，就会对其予以关注并将其表达出来，而不像大多数人那样把它忽略掉。

【搭配】dismiss from 解雇，开除

dispute[4] [dɪs'pjuːt]

【释义】*v./n.* 质疑，争论，纠纷（argue, debate; argument, disgreement）

【例句】One strategy they started using is to put the crucial facts in the articles that nobody disputes in a read-only format, which is a format that no one can make changes to. (TPO6, W, Q1) 他们开始使用的一个策略是将关键事实写到只有可读模式的文章里，这样的话就没有人来质疑、改变它们了。

【派生】disputed *a.* 有争议的

disputable *a.* 有讨论余地的，值得商榷的

【搭配】beyond dispute 毫无争议的（地）

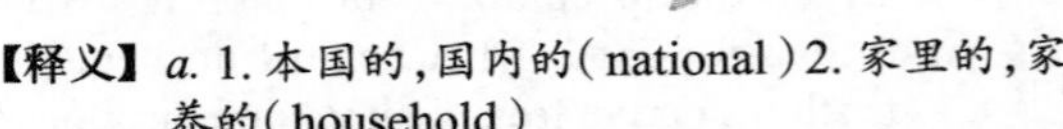

domestic[4] [də'mestɪk]

【释义】*a.* 1. 本国的，国内的（national）2. 家里的，家养的（household）

【例句】If American companies are slow capturing those customers, you can be sure that foreign companies will soon start crowding into the American market, offering eco-certified wood that domestic companies don't. (TPO7, W, Q1) 如果美国公司慢慢抓住这部分消费者，可以肯定外国公司会很快涌进美国市

场,提供国内公司不提供的经过环保认证的木材。

【派生】domesticity *n.* (喜欢)家庭生活,顾家
domesticate *v.* 驯化
domesticated *a.* 驯化的,驯养的

【搭配】domestic water/gas 家庭用水 / 气

drastic[4] ['dræstɪk] 

【释义】*a.* 极端的,严厉的,剧烈的(fierce, intense, extreme)

【例句】But still, they are being drastic. (TPO7, S, Q3) 但是,他们正在变得很极端。

【反义】mild

【派生】drastically *ad.* 大幅度地,彻底地

【搭配】a drastic emetic 烈性催吐药

drum[4] [drʌm] 

【释义】*n.* 鼓,鼓声 *v.* 击鼓

【例句】If you make a constant noise inside the chamber, maybe by steadily beating drum at certain rate, a particular frequency of sound will resonate. (TPO14, L, S2, L2) 如果你在室内持续制造噪音,可能是以一定的频率不断地敲鼓,那么噪音的某种特定的频率便会形成共振。

【搭配】drum up 招徕
drum for 鼓吹

durable[4] ['djʊərəbl] 

【释义】*a.* 耐用持久的(permanent, enduring) *n.* [常 *pl.*]耐用品

【例句】They'll definitely make the project more durable. (TPO1, L, S1, C1) 它们肯定会使项目更加持久。

【派生】durableness *n.* 耐久性

【搭配】durable consumer goods 耐久消费品

dye[4] [daɪ] 

【释义】*n.* 染料,染色 *v.* 染,染色

【例句】Petrochemicals such as dyes, fertilizer, and plastic are also manufactured from the petroleum. (TPO4, R, S2, T2) 诸如染料、肥料和塑料之类的石油化工产品也是从石油中生产出来的。

【派生】dyestuff *n.* 染料

【搭配】reactive dye 活性染料
hair dye 染发剂

dynamic[4] [daɪ'næmɪk] 

【释义】*a.* 1. 动力的,动态的,有活力的(vigorous, animate)

【例句】These expeditions were likely driven by population growth and political dynamics on the home islands, as well as the challenge and excitement of exploring unknown waters. (TPO5, R, S2, T1) 很有可能是母岛上人口的增长和政治动态,还有开发未知水域的挑战和兴奋驱动了这些冒险。

【派生】dynamics *n.* 动力学
dynamical *a.* 动力学的;有生气的

ease[4] [iːz] 

【释义】*n.* 1. 容易,不费劲 2. 舒适,自在(comfort, relax) *v.* 减轻,舒缓

【例句】Enormous changes in materials and techniques of construction within the last few generations have made it possible to enclose space with much greater ease and speed and with a minimum of material. (TPO3, R, S1, T1) 近几代建筑材料和建筑技术的巨大变化使得包围空间变得更加简单、快速,且用料更少。

【派生】easiness *n.* 容易,舒适,从容

【搭配】ease someone's mind 宽慰某人

elliptical[4] [ɪ'lɪptɪkəl] 

【释义】*a.* 1. 椭圆的 2. 省略的(omissive)

【例句】Under the control of the sun's gravitational force, each planet maintains an elliptical orbit. (TPO16, R, S2, T2) 由于太阳引力的作用,所有行星都在椭圆轨道上运行。

【搭配】elliptical orbit 卫星椭圆轨道,椭圆轨迹

engulf[4] [ɪn'gʌlf] 

【释义】*v.* 吞没,吞噬(devour, swallow)

【例句】Glaciers move slowly across the land with tremendous energy, carving into even the hardest rock formations and thereby reshaping the landscape as they engulf, push, drag, and finally deposit rock debris in places far from its original location. (TPO15, R, S1, T1) 冰川带着巨大的能量在陆地上缓慢地移动，甚至切碎最坚硬的岩层，在其吞噬、推动、拖拉直至最后将这些岩石碎片沉积到远离其原地的过程中，地貌被重新塑造。

【逆构】 gulf *v.* 吞没 *n.* 深渊，鸿沟

enrich[4] [ɪn'rɪtʃ]

【释义】 *v.* 使肥沃；使充实，使富足

【例句】 Animal dung enriches the soil by providing nutrients for plant growth. (TPO2, R, Sl, T1) 动物粪便使土壤更加肥沃，为植物生长提供养分。

【派生】 enriched *a.* 丰富的
enrichment *n.* 丰富，充实

entity[4] ['entɪtɪ]

【释义】 *n.* 实体

【例句】 Like the stones of a Roman wall which were held together both by the regularity of the design and by that peculiarly powerful Roman cement, so the various parts of the Roman realm were bonded into a massive, monolithic entity by physical, organizational, and psychological controls. (TPO7, R, S2, T1) 如同罗马墙是通过规律的设计和独特有效的罗马水泥构筑而成一样，罗马王国的各个部分也是通过对物质、组织和心理层面的支配而联结成一个规模宏大、坚如磐石的统一体的。

【搭配】 a separate political entity 独立的政治实体

entry[4] ['entrɪ]

【释义】 *n.* 1. 进入，进入权，入口(entrance, admission, admittance) 2. 条目

【例句】 The numbers of deer have fluctuated markedly since the entry of Europeans into Puget Sound country. (TPO4, R, S1, T1) 自从欧洲人进入皮吉特海峡后，鹿的数量出现了显著波动。

【反义】 exit

evenly[4] ['iːvənlɪ]

【释义】 *ad.* 1. 均匀地，平衡地，平坦地

【例句】 Despite the fact that wealth is relatively evenly distributed in pastoral societies, gender inequality still exists because only men can acquire military skills and social status. (TPO14, R, S2, T2) 尽管在游牧社会财富分配相对均衡，但因为只有男人才能掌握军事技能和拥有社会地位，所以性别不平等现象仍然存在。

【逆构】 even *a.* 平坦的，相等的

evergreen[4] ['evəgriːn]

【释义】 *n.* 常绿树，常绿植物 *a.* 常绿的

【例句】 Timeberline trees are normally evergreen. (TPO1, R, S1, T1) 正常情况下，林木线上的树木是常绿植物。

evoke[4] [ɪ'vəʊk]

【释义】 *v.* 使人想起，唤起，引起(summon, arouse)

【例句】 An artist chooses certain colors to evoke a particular mood and make powerful statements. (TPO4, S, Q6) 艺术家会选择某些颜色来唤起人们一种特定的情绪，做出有力的表达。

excess[4] [ɪk'ses]

【释义】 *a.* 超量的，超额的，附加的(additional, extra, spare, suplus) *n.* 1. 过度，过分，过量，超过 2. 放肆行为；越轨行为

【例句】 Excess water from irrigation sinks down into the water table. (TPO2, R, Sl, T1) 灌溉的多余用水将会渗入到地下水层。

【反义】 insufficient, short of, lack

【派生】 excessive *a.* 过多的

【搭配】 in excess of 超过，多于

excessive[4] [ɪk'sesɪv]

【释义】 *a.* 过多的，过度的，过分的(extravagant, extreme, unreasonable)

【例句】 The consequences of an excessive number of livestock grazing in an area are the reduction of the vegetation cover and the trampling and pulverization of the soil. (TPO2, R, Sl, T1) 在某一地区放牧过多家畜的后果就是：植被减少，土壤被牲畜践踏、破坏。

【反义】 moderate, reasonable

【派生】 excessively *ad.* 过多地

exposition[4] [ˌekspəˈzɪʃən] 

【释义】*n.* 1. 阐述，说明 2. 展览会，博览会（exhibition）
【例句】Well, the first is logical exposition. (TPO7, L, S1, L1) 首先是逻辑叙述。

expressive[4] [ɪksˈpresɪv] 

【释义】*a.* 意味深长的，富于表情的
【例句】People are bound within relationships by two types of bonds: expressive ties and instrumental ties. (TPO13, R, S1, T1) 人们通过两种形式的关系联系到一起：情感联系和实用联系。

fade[4] [feɪd] 

【释义】*v.* 1. 逐渐消失（disappear, die out）2. 褪色，枯萎（lose color）
【例句】Though it may be difficult to imagine from a later perspective, a strain of critical opinion in the 1920s predicted that sound film would be a technical novelty that would soon fade from sight, just as had many previous attempts, dating well back before the First World War, to link images with recorded sound. (TPO12, R, S2, T1) 尽管可能很难从后来的视角去想象，但20世纪20年代的一连串批评观点预测说，有声电影作为一种技术上的新玩意儿，不久就会淡出人们的视线，就像早在一战之前的那些将画面与录音结合在一起的尝试一样。
【派生】faded *a.* 已褪色的
【搭配】fade away 逐渐消失

feat[4] [fiːt] 

【释义】*n.* 功绩，壮举（accomplishment, achievement）
【例句】Contrary to the arguments of some that much of the Pacific was settled by Polynesians accidentally marooned after being lost and adrift, it seems reasonable that this feat was accomplished by deliberate colonization expeditions that set out fully stocked with food and domesticated plants and animals. (TPO5, R, S2, T1) 一些人认为在太平洋大部分地区定居的是意外迷路而流亡的波利尼西亚人，但与此相反的另一种理论看似更加合理，该理论认为这一壮举是由有意的殖民远征活动创造的，他们在出发时准备了充足的食物及驯化的动植物。

fetus[4] [ˈfiːtəs] 

【释义】*n.* 胎，胎儿
【例句】It has been suggested that yawning and hiccupping might serve to clear out the fetus's airways. (TPO18, R, S2, T1) 有人曾提出，打呵欠和打嗝所起的作用可能是清理胎儿的气道。
【搭配】fetus period 胎儿期

figurine[4] [ˈfɪgjʊriːn] 

【释义】*n.* 小雕像，小塑像（statuette）
【例句】In addition to other artworks, figurines representing the human female in exaggerated form have also been found at Upper Paleolithic sites. (TPO4, R, S2, T1) 除了其他艺术品外，形式夸张的女性形象的雕像也在旧石器时代的遗址中被发掘出来。
【搭配】clay figurine *n.* 泥人；泥塑

firm[4] [fɜːm]

【释义】*n.* 公司，商行 *a.* 1. 结实的，牢固的（hard, fixed）2. 坚定的，坚决的（steadfast）*v.*（使）坚固
【例句】What do you want to know about working for an accounting firm? (TPO6, L, S1, C1) 对于在一个会计公司工作，你想了解些什么？
【反义】fragile, loose, weak
【搭配】be on firm ground 理直气壮

flora[4] [ˈflɔːrə] 

【释义】*n.*（某地区、环境或时期的）植物群（vegetation）
【例句】Lichens were probably the first successful flora. (TPO9, R, S2, T2) 地衣可能就是第一批成功安家的植物。
【搭配】alpine flora 高山植物群

fluke[4] [fluːk] 

【释义】*n.* 1. 鲸尾叶突 2.［航海］锚爪 3. 侥幸；偶然；意外（非正式用语）

返记菜单

exposition[4]	expressive[4]	fade[4]	feat[4]	fetus[4]
figurine[4]	firm[4]	flora[4]	fluke[4]	

【例句】Their streamlined bodies, the absence of hind legs, and the presence of a fluke and blowhole cannot disguise their affinities with land dwelling mammals. (TPO2, R, S2, T1) 它们的身体呈流线型，没有后腿，长有尾片和喷水孔，但这些都不能掩盖它们与陆生哺乳动物的相似性。

foodstuff[4] ['fu:dstʌf]

【释义】n. 食品，食料

【例句】The people of the Netherlands, with a long tradition of fisheries and mercantile shipping, had difficulty in developing good harbors suitable for steamships: eventually they did so at Rotterdam and Amsterdam, with exceptional results for transit trade with Germany and central Europe and for the processing of overseas foodstuffs and raw materials(sugar, tobacco, chocolate, grain, and eventually oil). (TPO18, R, S1, T1) 有着悠久的渔业和商业船运业传统的荷兰人在发展适宜于大轮船的优良港口方面遇到了困难，但他们最终在鹿特丹和阿姆斯特丹做到了，并在与德国和中欧国家进行的转口贸易以及海外食品和原材料(糖、烟草、巧克力、谷物以及油)加工方面取得了杰出的成果。

fragment[4] ['frægmənt]

【释义】n.(某物的)碎片(fraction, piece, segment) v.(使某物)破碎或分裂

【例句】The sample consisted of pebbles of hardened sediment that had once been soft, deep-sea mud, as well as granules of gypsum and fragments of volcanic rock. (TPO7, R, S1, T1) 样本中包含由曾经柔软的深海泥浆硬化沉积而成的卵石以及石膏微粒和火山岩碎片。

【派生】fragmentary a. 零碎的，片段的，不完全的

friction[4] ['frɪkʃən]

【释义】n. 1. 摩擦，摩擦力 2. 矛盾，冲突(clash, conflict)

【例句】This layer of water reduces friction, like a lubricant. (TPO7, L, S2, L2) 这层水层就像润滑剂一样减少了摩擦。

gear[4] [gɪə]

【释义】n. 齿轮；传动装置 v. 使适合，使一致

【例句】The semester is in gear. (TPO10, L, S2, C1) 新学期就要开始了。

【搭配】gear box 齿轮箱

genius[4] ['dʒi:njəs]

【释义】n. 天才，天赋(talent, gift)

【例句】From this arose the Roman genius for military organization and orderly government. (TPO7, R, S2, T1) 由此形成了罗马人卓越的军事组织才能和有序管理政府的才能。

genre[4] [ʒɑ:ŋr]

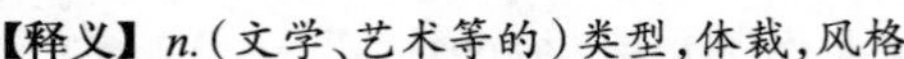

【释义】n.(文学、艺术等的)类型，体裁，风格

【例句】Now we can't really talk about fairy tales without first talking about folk tales because there's a strong connection between these two genres, these two types of stories. (TPO5, L, S2, L2) 现在我们在真正谈论童话故事的时候不能不首先谈论民间故事，因为这两种体裁、这两种形式的故事之间有着强烈的联系。

grant[4] [grɑ:nt]

【释义】v. 1. 同意，准许 2. 答应给予，授予 n. 补助金；授予物

【例句】You don't think he'd grant an extension in this case? (TPO10, S, Q5) 你认为他不会准予延长这个案子吗？

【搭配】take for granted 认为…理所当然

guarantee[4] [ˌgærən'ti:]

【释义】v. 保证，担保 n. 1. 保证，保证书 2. 担保，担保人，抵押品

【例句】It is hoped that this change will decrease the number of students enrolled in day classes and thus guarantee individual access to computers for all students in computer classes. (TPO4, S, Q3) 希望此举有助于减少白日班的学生人数，从而保证每个学生在电脑课上都有电脑可用。

hawk[4] [hɔːk] 

【释义】*n.* 1. 鹰(eagle) 2. 鹰派人物；主战派 *v.* 1. 像鹰一样俯冲攻击 2. 叫卖

【例句】These loud cheeps and peeps might give the location of the nest away to a listening hawk or raccoon, resulting in the death of the defenseless nestlings. (TPO11, R, S2, T2) 这些吱吱的叫声会把其巢穴的位置暴露给正在全神聆听的老鹰或者浣熊，从而导致了毫无防备的雏鸟的死亡。

hectare[4] [ˈhektɑː] 

【释义】*n.* 公顷

【例句】The actual rainforest is much larger than the few hectares where the Nightcap Oak grows. (TPO6, L, S1, L2) 真正的雨林要比睡帽橡树所生长的那几公顷大的地儿大得多。

horn[4] [hɔːn] 

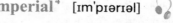

【释义】*n.* 1. (牛等的)角 2. 号角，喇叭(trumpet) 3. 角状物

【例句】In addition, the paintings mostly portray animals that the painters may have feared the most because of their size, speed, natural weapons such as tusks and horns, and the unpredictability of their behavior. (TPO4, R, S2, T1) 此外，绘画里描绘得最多的是绘画人可能最畏惧的那些动物，通常是由于这些动物的体型、速度、诸如獠牙和角这样的天然武器，及其不可预测的行为。

【搭配】horn in 闯入，侵入

identical[4] [aɪˈdentɪkəl] 

【释义】*a.* 同样的，完全相同的(same, alike)

【例句】So, for Watson, thinking is identical with the activity of muscles. (TPO2, L, S1, L1) 所以，对于Waston来说，思考与肌肉运动是等同的。

【反义】different

【派生】identically *ad.* 完全一致地

【逆构】identify *v.* 认为…等同于

illusion[4] [ɪˈluːʒən] 

【释义】*n.* 1. 幻觉，错觉 2. 错误的信仰(或观念)

【例句】The way an artist paints certain areas of the painting can create the illusion of texture, an object's smoothness or roughness or softness. (TPO4, S, Q6) 艺术家作画时在局部调色上所用的手法能制造出一种纹理的视觉效果，也就是物体的平滑、粗糙或柔软。

【派生】illusive *a.* 迷惑人的，错觉的

imperial[4] [ɪmˈpɪərɪəl] 

【释义】*a.* 1. 帝国的，皇家的(sovereign, royal) 2. 特大的 3. (度量衡)英制的

【例句】They were supposed to communicate specific ideas about the emperor and the imperial family and to help inhabitants of the conquered areas become familiar with the Roman way of life. (TPO18, L, S1, L2) 他们是用来传达皇帝和皇室的具体旨意，并帮助被征服地区的居民了解和熟悉罗马的生活方式。

【派生】imperially *ad.* 帝王般地
imperialism *n.* 帝国主义
imperialist *n.* 帝国主义者
imperialistic *a.* 帝国主义的

impersonal[4] [ɪmˈpɜːsənl]

【释义】*a.* 1. 不受个人感情影响的，客观的；冷淡的(detached, objective)

【例句】And their mating ritual is just so impersonal. (TPO1, L, S2, L2) 它们的交配仪式非常没有人情味。

【派生】impersonality *n.* 无人情味；冷静

【逆构】personal *a.* 个人的，私人的

implication[4] [ˌɪmplɪˈkeɪʃən] 

【释义】*n.* 1. 含意，暗示(significance, meaning, hint) 2. 卷入，牵连(involvement)

【例句】She was concerned about its implications. (TPO12, L, S1, L1) 她关心的是其含意。

【派生】implicational *a.* 启发的，启示的

返记菜单

hawk[4] hectare[4] horn[4] identical[4] illusion[4]
imperial[4] impersonal[4] implication[4]

inadequate[4] [ɪnˈædɪkwɪt]

【释义】*a.* 不充足的，不适当的（short, deficient）

【例句】When people first started to build, the structural methods used to provide strength and size were inadequate because they were not based on physical laws. (TPO3, R, S1, T1, Q4) 当人们一开始建房时，用于保证强度和尺寸的建筑方法是不合适的，因为这些方法并没有以物理定律为依据。

【反义】adequate, sufficient

【派生】inadequacy *n.* 不充分，不足，不胜任

【搭配】inadequate resources 资源不足

incident[4] [ˈɪnsɪdənt]

【释义】*n.* 事变，事件，发生的事（常指小事）（event, occurrence）

【例句】The next key elements of the well-made play refer to as the inciting incidents. (TPO7, L, S1, L1) 佳构剧的另一个关键元素叫做煽动事件。

【派生】incidental *a.* 偶然的；附带的

incomplete[4] [ˌɪnkəmˈpliːt]

【释义】*a.* 不完全的，不完整的，未完成的（imperfect, unfinished）

【例句】Many incomplete skeletons were found but they included, for the first time in an archaeocyte, a complete hind leg that features a foot with three tiny toes. (TPO2, R, S2, T1) 尽管发现的这些骨骼并不完整，但这是专家们第一次在原始动物身上发现完整的后肢，其主要特征是有三个小脚趾的足部。

【派生】incompletely *ad.* 不完全地，不彻底地

infection[4] [ɪnˈfekʃən]

【释义】*n.* 传染，传播；传染病（contamination）

【例句】Water samples from the area revealed increased levels of chemicals that could decrease the otters' resistance to life-threatening infections and thus could indirectly cause their deaths. (TPO10, W, Q1) 这个区域的水样显示，水中含有的不断增加的化学物质会降低水獭对致命感染的抵抗能力，从而间接导致它们的死亡。

【逆构】infect *v.* 传染，感染
infectious *a.* 传染性的，易传染的

intact[4] [ɪnˈtækt]

【释义】*a.* 完整无缺的，未经触动的（complete, unchanged）

【例句】Even if the new population is of a different species, it can approximately fill the niche vacated by the extinct population and keep the food web intact. (TPO3, R, S1, T2) 即使这一新种群是一种完全不同的物种，它们也大致可以填补由于物种灭绝造成的空缺，并保持食物网的完整性。

【派生】intactness *n.* 完整无缺，未受损伤

【搭配】keep the scene intact 保护现场

interconnect[4] [ˌɪntə(ː)kəˈnekt]

【释义】*v.* 互相连接，互相联系

【例句】Since the northeastern region of North America was interconnected by many streams and waterways, water transportation by vessels like a canoe was most essential. (TPO7, L, S2, T1) 由于北美的东北部地区处在河流航道交汇的地带，所以通过独木舟这样的船舶开展的水上运输是非常重要的。

【反义】disconnect

lane[4] [leɪn]

【释义】*n.* 1.（船或飞机预定或定期的）航道，航线 2. 小路，小巷

【例句】While the Greek world had expanded along the Mediterranean sea lanes, the Roman world was assembled by territorial conquest. (TPO7, R, S2, T1) 希腊通过地中海海上航线完成了扩张，而罗马则是通过领土征服实现的。

【搭配】ocean lanes 远洋航线

Word List 26

lately[4] ['leɪtlɪ] 

【释义】*ad.* 近来,不久前(recently)

【例句】And lately her favorite toy is a cute little baby doll with a big round face and lots of curly hair named Rosa. (TPO10, S, Q4) 最近,她喜欢上了一个名叫罗莎的圆脸、卷发、可爱的小玩具娃娃。

liberal[4] ['lɪbərəl] 

【释义】*a.* 1. 自由主义的 2. 开明的 3. 慷慨的,大方的 *n.* 自由主义者,开明的人

【例句】As small countries dependent on foreign markets, they followed a liberal trade policy in the main, though a protectionist movement developed in Sweden. (TPO18, R, S1, T1) 因为小国家都依赖国外市场,所以尽管瑞典正在开展一场贸易保护运动,但是基本上还是会采用自由贸易政策。

【反义】conservative

【派生】liberty *n.* 自由,独立自主
liberally *ad.* 随意地,不受限制地
liberation *n.* 解放,释放

【搭配】liberal education 普通教育; 文科教育
liberal studies 人文学科

literate[4] ['lɪtərɪt] 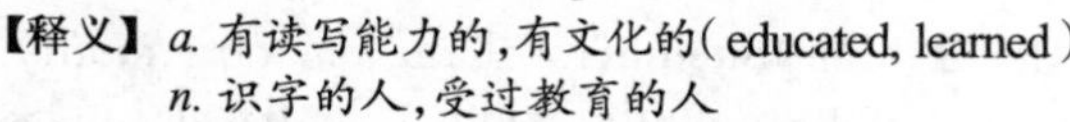

【释义】*a.* 有读写能力的,有文化的(educated, learned) *n.* 识字的人,受过教育的人

【例句】And, what did people with poor vision do, I mean, especially those few people who were actually literate? (TPO8, L, S2, L1) 那么,视力不好的人做什么呢,我是说,尤其是少数实际上有文化的人?

【派生】literacy *n.* 读写能力,识字

localize[4] ['ləʊkəlaɪz] 

【释义】*v.* 使地方化,使局部化

【例句】A microclimate is a group of climate conditions that affect the localized area, weather features like temperature, wind, moisture and so on. (TPO14, L, S1, L2) 微气候是一系列影响局部地区的气候条件以及诸如温度、风、湿度等等的天气特征。

maritime[4] ['mærɪtaɪm] 

【释义】*a.* 1. 海的,海事的,海运的

【例句】Just as important, the culture also possessed the basic foundation for an effective maritime adaptation, including outrigger canoes and a variety of fishing techniques that could be effective for overseas voyaging. (TPO5, R, S2, T1) 同样重要的是,该文化还有着能够有效适应海洋生活的基础,包括桅杆船以及各种有效适应出海航行的捕鱼技术。

meager[4] ['mi:gə(r)] 

【释义】*a.* 1. 贫乏的,不足的(poor, scanty) 2. 瘦的

【例句】Members of poor peasant families spun or wove cloth and linens at home for scant remuneration in an attempt to supplement meager family income. (TPO10, R, S2, T2) 为了补贴本已经微薄的家庭收入,贫困潦倒的农民们通过在家纺织衣料或亚麻来换取少量的报酬。

【反义】ample, plentiful; plump

【搭配】meager profit 微利

measurable[4] ['meʒərəbl] 

【释义】*a.* 1. 可测量的 2. 重要的,重大的(important, crucial)

【例句】There is a growing body of opinion that both these physical variations have a measurable impact on the climate. (TPO10, R, S2, T1) 有越来越多的观点认为这两种物理变化都对气候有着重要的影响。

【反义】immeasurable

millennia[4] [mɪ'lenɪə] 

【释义】*n.* (millennium 的复数)千年,千年期

【例句】Archaeological evidence suggests that by 3000 B. C., and perhaps even earlier, there had emerged on the steppes of Inner Eurasia the distinctive types of pastoralism that were to dominate the region's history for several

返记菜单

lately[4] liberal[4] literate[4] localize[4] maritime[4]
meager[4] measurable[4] millennia[4]

millennia. (TPO14, R, S2, T2) 考古学的证据表明，到公元前3000年甚或更早时，在亚欧大陆内陆的大草原上就已经出现了形式独特的畜牧主义，并一直主宰着该地区的历史达数千年。

【搭配】over millennia 数千年来

minimize⁴ ['mɪnɪmaɪz]

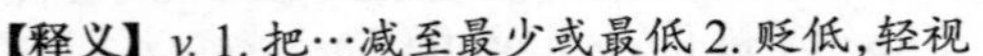

【释义】v. 1. 把…减至最少或最低 2. 贬低，轻视

【例句】People can govern themselves by shared consensus while minimizing distinctions of wealth and power. (TPO16, R, S1, T1) 人们可以通过分享共识、同时使财富和权力的区分最小化来管理自己。

【派生】minimum n. 最少量，最小值

【搭配】minimize button 最小化按钮

mirror⁴ ['mɪrə]

【释义】n. 1. 镜子 2. 写照 v. 反映，反射，映照

【例句】To test this idea, he blocked their view of the Sun and used mirrors to change its apparent position. (TPO11, R, S2, T1) 为了测试这一观点，他挡住了他们看太阳的视线，并且用镜子改变太阳表面上的位置。

molten⁴ ['məʊltən]

【释义】a. 熔化的，熔融的(melted, fused)

【例句】Lichens helped to speed the decomposition of the hard rock surfaces, preparing a soft bed of soil that was abundantly supplied with minerals that had been carried in the molten rock from the bowels of Earth. (TPO9, R, S2, T2) 地衣有利于加速坚硬的岩石表面的分解，并产生一层柔软的土壤，这些土壤可以提供丰富的来自地球内部的熔融岩石所含有的矿物质。

【逆构】melt v. 熔化，融化，溶解

【搭配】a molten image 一尊铸像

monument⁴ ['mɒnjumənt]

【释义】n. 1. 纪念碑 2. 历史遗迹 3. 不朽作品

【例句】Were these just monuments to honor the dead buried there or were they designed to be used somehow by the living? (TPO14, L, S2, L2) 这仅仅是为了纪念埋葬在这里的死者的纪念碑，还是设计出来供活着的人使用的？

【派生】monumental a. 杰出的，不朽的

mood⁴ [muːd]

【释义】n. 1. 心情，情绪 2. 气氛，氛围

【例句】It depends on what mood they are in, and you know, luck. (TPO16, S, Q6) 这取决于他们的情绪，以及如你所知的，运气。

【搭配】in the mood 兴致勃勃

motive⁴ ['məʊtɪv]

【释义】n. 动机，目的 v. 促使 a. 运动的；使成为动机的

【例句】In addition to exploring the possible antecedents of theater, scholars have also theorized about the motives that led people to develop theater. (TPO1, R, S2, T1) 除了探索戏剧可能的起源外，学者们还提出了关于人们发展戏剧的动机的理论。

multiply⁴ ['mʌltɪplɪ]

【释义】v. 1. 乘，使相乘 2. (使)增加(increase, soar) 3. 使繁殖(breed, reproduce)

【例句】Multiplying by 2? (TPO2, L, S2, L2) 是将数字乘以2吗？

【派生】multiple a. 多重的；多倍的

mustard⁴ ['mʌstəd]

【释义】n. 1. 十字花科的一种 2. 芥末，芥菜 3. 中棕黄色

【例句】Many members of the mustard family, spurge family, legume family and grass family are top hyperaccumulators. (TPO5, R, S1, T1) 很多十字花科、牧草科、豆科和禾本科植物都是顶级的重金属超富集植物。

naturalistic⁴ [ˌnætʃərə'lɪstɪk]

【释义】a. 自然的，自然主义的

【例句】So do the naturalistic paintings on slabs of stone excavated in southern Africa. (TPO4, R, S2, T1) 在非洲南部发掘出来的石板上的自然主义画作同样如此。

【逆构】natural a. 自然的

neighborhood[4] ['neɪbəhʊd] 

【释义】*n.* 1. 邻近地区，附近(surroundings, vicinity) 2. 邻里关系

【例句】It only goes through the neighborhoods that've gotten too expensive for students to live in. (TPO2, S, Q3)(校车)只从学校附近的地段经过，可是那些地段都太贵了，学生们根本住不起。

【逆构】neighbor *n.* 邻居

【搭配】in the neighbourhood of 在…的附近

nomad[4] ['nɒməd] 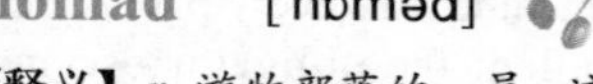

【释义】*n.* 游牧部落的一员；流浪者

【例句】It was Turkish nomads who first discovered tulips and spread them slowly westward. (TPO6, L, S1, L1) 是土耳其的游牧民最先发现了郁金香，并且慢慢将其西传的。

【派生】nomadic *a.* 游牧的；流浪的

【搭配】a wandering nomad 游牧的人

obstacle[4] ['ɒbstəkl] 

【释义】*n.* 1. 障碍(物)，妨碍，绊脚石(impediment, obstruction)

【例句】There are numerous obstacles to implementing reflection in schools and insufficient understanding of why teachers might want to reflect. (TPO9, R, S2, T1) 在学校中施行反思有很多障碍，而且对于为何教师们可能想进行反思的理解也很不足。

【反义】help, assistence

【搭配】pose an obstacle to 成为…的障碍

old-fashioned[4] ['əuld'fæʃənd] 

【释义】*a.* 老式的，老派的，守旧的(antique, outmoded) *n.* 古典鸡尾酒

【例句】Our technology was advanced, but the outside design lookes really old-fashioned. (TPO1, S, Q4) 我们的技术是先进的，但是外在的设计看起来相当过时。

ooze[4] [u:z]

【释义】*n.* 渗出物 *v.*(使)渗出，泄漏

【例句】Soon layers of oceanic ooze began to accumulate above the old hard layer. (TPO7, R, S1, T1) 不久，海水渗出物便开始堆积在原来的硬层上。

【搭配】ooze from/out of sth. 从…中渗出，缓慢流出

overcrowd[4] [ˌəuvə'kraud] 

【释义】*v.*(使)过度拥挤

【例句】The proposal to add the classes is a response to student complaints that daytime computer classes have become increasingly overcrowded and there are no longer enough computers available. (TPO4, S, Q3) 增班的建议是对学生抱怨白天的电脑班越来越挤而且电脑不够用所做的回应。

【派生】overcrowded *a.* 过度拥挤的

pace[4] [peɪs] 

【释义】*n.* 1. 速度(speed) 2. 步伐，(一)步(step) *v.* 踱步(walk, tread)

【例句】The deserts, which already occupy approximately a fourth of the Earth's land surface, have in recent decades been increasing at an alarming pace. (TPO2, R, Sl, T1) 沙漠已经占据地球表面约四分之一的面积，近几十年仍在以惊人的速度扩张。

【派生】pacer *n.* 慢行者；步测者

【搭配】at a…pace 以…的速度
keep pace with sth./sb. 与某物/某人并驾齐驱

palm[4] [pɑ:m] 

【释义】*n.* 1. 手掌 2. 棕榈树 *v.* 把…藏于手中

【例句】One also has to make the assumption that the dominant hand were stencilled palm downward. (TPO12, R, S1, T1) 人们也要做出这样的假设，即，那只惯用手在被塑模下来的时候是掌心向下的。

partial[4] ['pɑ:ʃəl] 

【释义】*a.* 1. 部分的，不完全的(fractional, incomplete) 2. 偏袒的，偏爱的

【例句】Genetic engineering also may provide a partial solution, as new strains of drought-resistant crops continue to be developed. (TPO3, R, S1, T1) 基因工程也会通过继续研发抗旱的新品种作物来帮助解决部分难

返记菜单

neighborhood[4] nomad[4] obstacle[4] old-fashioned[4] ooze[4]
overcrowd[4] pace[4] palm[4] partial[4]

题。

【反义】whole, total

【派生】partially *ad.* 部分地
impartially *ad.* 公平地，无私地

【搭配】partial crisis 局部危机

pave[4] [peɪv]

【释义】*v.* 铺路，铺设；安排

【例句】I think these trails should be paved with cement. (TPO15, S, Q3) 我认为这些小路应该用水泥来铺。

【派生】pavement *n.* 人行道

【搭配】pave the way 为…做准备，为…铺平道路

persist[4] [pə(:)'sɪst]

【释义】*v.* 坚持不懈；继续(continue, insist, persevere)

【例句】We can gain some insight about how they spread, persist or change. (TPO5, L, S1, L1) 我们可以得到一些关于它们是如何扩散、持续或者改变的见解。

【派生】persistance *n.* 持久性；持续
persistent *a.* 坚持不懈的

【搭配】persist in 坚持，固执于

phonograph[4] ['fəunəgrɑ:f]

【释义】*n.* 留声机

【例句】The Kinetoscope arcades were modeled on phonograph parlors. (TPO2, R, S2, T2) 这些电影播放厅是仿照留声机播放厅设计的。

【派生】phonographic *a.* 留声机的；表音速记法的

pitch[4] [pɪtʃ]

【释义】*n.* 音高

【例句】The bats emit ultrasonic pulses, very high pitch sound waves that we cannot hear. (TPO7, L, S1, L2) 蝙蝠会发射出一种超声波脉冲，这是一种人类听不见的高音调声波。

【搭配】give the pitch 定出音高

plausible[4] ['plɔ:zəbl]

【释义】*a.* 1. 看似真实的，貌似正确的 2. 花言巧语的

【例句】It may sound plausible that large empty rooms were used for storage, but excavations of the great houses have not uncovered many traces of maize or maize containers. (TPO5, W, Q1) 巨大的空屋子是用来存储(玉米)的，这听起来似乎是合理的，但是通过对屋子的发掘却并没有找到很多与玉米或玉米容器有关的痕迹。

【派生】plausibility *n.* 似乎有理；善辩

【搭配】a plausible excuse 看似有理的借口

playwright[4] ['pleɪraɪt]

【释义】*n.* 剧作家(dramatist)

【例句】This became so popular that the playwright almost had to include it in every play which is why it is called: the obligatory scene. (TPO7, L, S1, L1) 这变得非常流行，以至于剧作家几乎在每一部戏剧中都要包含这样的场景，这也是它为何叫做"必要场景"的缘故。

poisonous[4] ['pɔɪznəs]

【释义】*a.* 1. 有毒的(toxic, noxious, venomous) 2. 恶毒的，恶意的(vicious)

【例句】So it's no wonder that people once considered potatoes and tomatoes to be inedible too, even poisonous. (TPO10, L, S1, L2) 难怪人们曾经认为马铃薯和西红柿不可食用的，甚至是有毒的。

【搭配】poisonous gas 毒气，有毒气体

portable[4] ['pɔ:təbl]

【释义】*a.* 便于携带的，手提式的(luggable, hand-held) *n.* 轻便易携物

【例句】Now portable drilling machines are set up and are then dismantled and removed. (TPO4, R, S2, T2) 现在便携式的钻井器械可以安装，然后再拆卸移走。

【搭配】portable equipment 便携设备，手提设备
portable system 可移植系统

precipitate[4] [prɪ'sɪpɪteɪt]

【释义】*v.* 1. (使)沉淀 2. 促成，加速 3. 使…突然降临，猛然落下

【例句】As evaporation continued, the remaining brine (salt water) became so dense that the calcium sulfate of the hard layer was

precipitated. (TPO7, R, S1, T1) 随着继续蒸发，剩下的盐水变得很浓，从而使得硬层中的硫酸钙被沉淀下来。

【派生】 precipitation *n.* 降水，降水量

precision[4] [prɪ'sɪʒən]

【释义】 *n.* 精确(性)，精密(度)(exactness, accuracy)

【例句】 A particular animal typically maintains its own characteristic cycle duration with great precision for many days. (TPO13, R, S2, T1) 某一种动物通常会精确地保持其特有的循环周期很多天。

predominant[4] [prɪ'dɒmɪnənt]

【释义】 *a.* 占主导地位的，主要的(principal, chief, dominant)

【例句】 The archaeological evidence clearly indicates, though, that Teotihuacán was the center that did arise as the predominant force in the area by the first century *AD*. (TPO8, R, S1, T1) 不过，考古证据清楚地表明，公元一世纪时，特奥蒂瓦坎就作为该地区的主导力量中心出现了。

【派生】 predominance *n.* 优势

predominate[4] [prɪ'dɒmɪneɪt]

【释义】 *v.* 统治，成为主流

【例句】 Light has a predominating influence in setting the clock. (TPO13, R, S2, T1) 在调节生物钟的过程中，光起着主导性的影响。

【搭配】 ~ over sb./sth. 支配，统治，左右某人 / 某事物

prep[4] [prep]

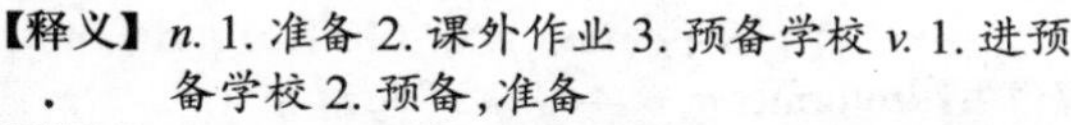

【释义】 *n.* 1. 准备 2. 课外作业 3. 预备学校 *v.* 1. 进预备学校 2. 预备，准备

【例句】 If you don't mind working in the kitchen, we've got some pretty flexible hours for students doing food prep work, anything from early morning to late afternoon. (TPO17, L, S2, C1) 如果你不介意在厨房工作的话，我们有灵活的时间让学生们做一些食物准备工作，从清早到傍晚都行。

【搭配】 prep school 预备学校(私立)；预科

prestige[4] [pres'tiːʒ]

【释义】 *n.* 威信，威望，声望(fame, reputation, credit)

【例句】 Here, the horse was already becoming the animal of prestige in many regions, though sheep, goats, and cattle could also play a vital role. (TPO14, R, S2, T2) 在这里，尽管绵羊、山羊和牛也起到了至关重要的作用，但是马已经成为很多地区有口皆碑的动物了。

【派生】 prestigious *a.* 有名望的，有威信的

presumably[4] [prɪ'zjuːməbəlɪ]

【释义】 *ad.* 大概，据推测，可能(probably, assumedly)

【例句】 The ancient Maya were presumably more experienced and did better, but nevertheless they too must have faced risks of crop failures from droughts and hurricanes. (TPO14, R, S2, T1) 古玛雅人可能经验更丰富，做得也更好，但他们也一定会面临因干旱和飓风所带来的农作物减产的风险。

prime[4] [praɪm]

【释义】 *a.* 主要的，首要的(primary, principal, main) *n.* 鼎盛时期

【例句】 So the results of the study suggests that when the number of the competitors in the prime habitat reaches a certain point, the second random habitat becomes just as successful as the prime habitat, just because there are fewer members of the same species living there. (TPO8, L, S1, L1) 研究结果表明，当主要栖息地内的竞争者达到一定的数量之后，第二个任意的栖息地就会变得和主要栖息地一样成功，只是因为生活在那里的同一物种的数量更少。

【搭配】 prime number 素数，质数

priority[4] [praɪ'ɒrɪtɪ]

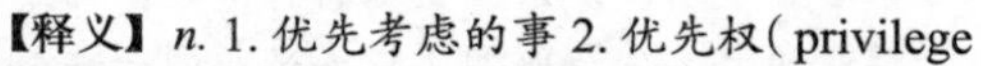

【释义】 *n.* 1. 优先考虑的事 2. 优先权(privilege)

【例句】 Furthermore, changing government priorities brought about periodic reductions in funding. (TPO16, W, Q1) 此外，改变政府的优先考虑导致了基金的周期性减少。

【逆构】 prior *a.* 优先的，在前的

【搭配】give priority to 优先考虑…

propagate[4] ['prɒpəgeɪt]

【释义】v. 1. 繁衍，增殖（raise, reproduce）2. 传播，散布（spread, disperse）

【例句】These plants propagate by producing spores—tiny fertilized cells that contain all the instructions for making a new plant—but the spore are unprotected by any outer coating and carry no supply of nutrient. (TPO9, R, S2, T2) 这些植物通过产生孢子来繁殖，孢子是一些有营养的细胞，它们携带了一株新的植物生长所需要的所有遗传物质，但它没有任何外部表皮的保护，也没携带任何供应营养的组织。

【派生】propagation n. 繁殖；传播

【搭配】propagate scientific knowledge 普及科学知识

questionnaire[4] [ˌkwestʃə'neə]

【释义】n. 问卷，调查表

【例句】Because they cannot verbalize or fill out questionnaires, indirect techniques of naturalistic observation are used as the primary means of determining what infants can see, hear, feel, and so forth. (TPO13, R, S2, T2) 因为他们无法用言语回答也不能填写问卷，所以自然观察的非直接性技术被用作确定婴儿看、听、感知等的结果的主要手段。

recruit[4] [rɪ'kruːt]

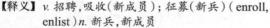

【释义】v. 招聘，吸收（新成员）；征募（新兵）（enroll, enlist）n. 新兵，新成员

【例句】Well, as you know, the career fair is generally an opportunity for local businesses to recruit new employees, and for soon-to-be graduates to have interviews with several companies they might be interested in working for. (TPO6, L, S1, C1) 你知道，人才招聘会主要是为当地企业招聘新员工和为即将毕业的大学生与他们比较感兴趣的一些公司进行面试提供机会。

【派生】recruiter n. 招聘人员；征兵人员

【搭配】an inexperienced recruit 没经验的新手

rectangular[4] [rek'tæŋgjʊlə]

【释义】a. 长方形的，矩形的

【例句】Very often such statues were enclosed in rectangular shrines or wall niches whose only opening was at the front, making it natural for the statue to display frontality. (TPO11, R, S1, T1) 通常这些雕像都被封闭在只有前面有开口的矩形的神龛或者壁龛内，这这样雕像展示正面就显得很自然了。

【派生】rectangularity n. 成直角，呈长方形
rectangularly ad. 矩形地

recur[4] [rɪ'kɜː]

【释义】v. 再次发生，重现

【例句】It is important for animals' daily activities to be coordinated with recurring events in their environment. (TPO13, R, S2, T1) 动物的日常活动与周围反复发生的事件保持协调很重要。

【派生】recurrence n. 再发生，循环，重现

【搭配】recur to sb./sth.（指想法、事情等）在头脑中重现

reform[4] [rɪ'fɔːm]

【释义】n./v. 改革，革新，改良，改造

【例句】In Denmark and Sweden agricultural reforms took place gradually from the late eighteenth century through the first half of the nineteenth, resulting in a new class of peasant landowners with a definite market orientation. (TPO18, R, S1, T1) 从18世纪末一直到19世纪上半叶，丹麦和瑞典逐渐进行了农业改革，从而导致了一个新的具有明确市场导向的农民地主阶层的出现。

【派生】reformer n. 改革家，改革运动者

【搭配】reform and opening-up 改革开放

repetition[4] [ˌrepɪ'tɪʃən]

【释义】n. 重复，反复，重复的事

【例句】In a lot of ads, repetition is a key strategy. (TPO3, S, Q6) 在很多广告中，重复是主要策略。

【派生】repetitive a. 重复的，反复性的

【逆构】repeat v. 重复，复述

replant[4] ['riː'plɑːnt] 

【释义】 *v.* 再植,改种,移植

【例句】 And one of the concrete ways people have been doing this is by cleaning up polluted habitat areas and then replanting flowers, um, replanting native flowers that humming birds feed on. (TPO3, L, S1, L1) 其中一个具体的方法就是清理受污染的栖息地,然后重新种植上蜂鸟以之为生的花。

resolve[4] [rɪ'zɒlv] 

【释义】 *v.* 1. 解决(settle) 2. 决定(decide, determine) *n.* 决意,决定

【例句】 People experiencing cognitive dissonance often do not want to change the way they are acting, so they resolve the contradictory situation in another way, they change their interpretation of the situation in a way that minimizes the contradiction between what they are doing and what they believe should be doing. (TPO3, S, Q4) 人们在面对内心冲突时并不想改变他们正在做的事,因此他们会通过另一种方式来解决这种矛盾的处境,他们会换一种方式来解释这种情况,从而把他们所做的和应该做的之间的矛盾降到最小。

【派生】 resolved *a.* 下定决心的,断然的

restore[4] [rɪs'tɔː]

【释义】 *v.* 1. 恢复,复原(repair, renew) 2. 归还

【例句】 After several years of cultivation and reburial, the site would be restored at a cost much lower than the price of excavation and reburial, the standard practice for remediation of contaminated soil. (TPO5, R, S1, T1) 经过几年的耕种和再掩埋,这块地就会恢复原貌,比起挖掘和重埋这种标准的整治受污染土地的方法,这种方法的花费要少得多。

【派生】 restoration *n.* 恢复,归还

resume[4]

【释义】 ['rezjuːmeɪ] *n.* 1. 简历,履历 2. 摘要 [rɪ'zjuːm] *v.* 重新开始,再继续(continue, restart)

【例句】 You could put it on your resume. (TPO11, L, S2, C1) 你可以把它加到你的简历中。

【派生】 resumption *n.* 重新开始,恢复

【搭配】 personal resume 个人简历

rival[4] ['raɪvəl] 

【释义】 *n.* 竞争对手,敌手(competitor) *v.* 1. 与…竞争 2. 与…匹敌,比得上

【例句】 Recent evidence favors a rival to the long-standing theory that the Americas were colonized 11,000-12,000 years ago by people migrating south from Beringia along a midcontinental ice-free corridor. (TPO9, R, S1, T1) 有一个长久以来的理论认为,美洲早在 11000 到 12000 年前就成为了从白令陆桥沿大陆间的无冰走廊向南迁徙而来到这里的人们的殖民地,但最近出现了与这一理论相悖的证据。

【派生】 rivalry *n.* 竞争,敌对状态

【搭配】 a rival in love 情敌

satisfactory[4] [ˌsætɪs'fæktərɪ] 

【释义】 *a.* 令人满意的

【例句】 He does not consider it satisfactory preparation for the class he teaches. (TPO5, L, S2, C1) 他认为为所教课程所做的准备并不令人满意。

【反义】 unsatisfactory

【逆构】 satisfy *v.* 令人满意,满足

saving[4] ['seɪvɪŋ] 

【释义】 *n.* 储蓄,存款

【例句】 Third, there won't necessarily be any cost savings when you consider how expensive it is to manufacture the fuel-cell engine. (TPO9, W, Q1) 当你知道生产燃料电池发动机的成本有多高时,就不会觉得它有多经济了。

scribe[4] [skraɪb] 

【释义】 *n.* 抄写员,书记员

【例句】 So it wasn't uncommon for the scribes or monks who produce the manual scripts . (TPO15, L, S2, L1) 所以,这对抄记手稿的书记员或僧侣来说是十分平常的。

【派生】 scriber *n.* 画线器

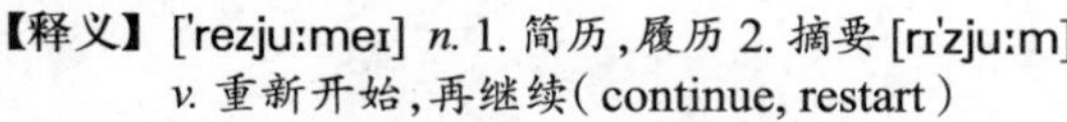

replant[4] resolve[4] restore[4] resume[4] rival[4]
satisfactory[4] saving[4] scribe[4]

secrete[4] [sɪ'kriːt] 

【释义】 *v.* 1. 分泌 2. 隐匿，隐藏

【例句】 The ants live in large, hollow thorns and eat sugar secreted by the tree. (TPO17, R, S2, T2) 这些蚂蚁住在宽敞、凹陷的荆棘丛中，汲取（金合欢）树分泌出来的糖分。

【派生】 secretion *n.* 分泌，分泌物
secretin *n.* 分泌素，分泌腺

seemingly[4] ['siːmɪŋlɪ]

【释义】 *ad.* 表面上，似乎（apparently）

【例句】 It is responsible for the appearance of seemingly irrelevant behavior. (TPO4, L, S1, L1) 它主要是指外表上看来不相干的行为。

shoot[4] [ʃuːt]

【释义】 *v.* 1. 拍摄 2. 射击，射门 3. 疾驰 *n.* 1. 幼苗，嫩芽 2. 拍摄，摄影 3. 射击；狩猎

【例句】 The audiences of the 1920s and 1930s were not used to films shot underwater. (TPO3, L, S1, L2) 二十世纪二三十年代的观众不太习惯在水底拍摄的电影。

【搭配】 shoot the breeze 吹牛，闲扯
trouble shoot 故障查找
shoot for 争取，为…而努力

skeptical[4] ['skeptɪkəl] 

【释义】 *a.* 怀疑的；多疑的（suspicious, doubtful）

【例句】 Critics are also skeptical about the accuracy of the conversations that the Chevalier records in the memoir between himself and the famous writer Voltaire. (TPO7, W, Q1) 评论者也对他在回忆录中记载的有关他和著名作家伏尔泰的对话的真实性表示怀疑。

【派生】 skeptic *n.* 怀疑论者；怀疑者；无神论者
scepticism *n.* 怀疑论；怀疑态度

solidify[4] [sə'lɪdɪfaɪ] 

【释义】 *v.* 变固体，凝固，使牢固

【例句】 A common exception is basalt, a form of solidified volcanic lava. (TPO1, R, S2, T2) 最常见的例外情况就是玄武岩，一种固化的火山熔岩。

【派生】 solidification *n.* 固化，凝固

specimen[4] ['spesəmɪn] 

【释义】 *n.* 标本，样本（example, sample）

【例句】 The same was found for brains of specimens from Neanderthal, Gibalter, and La Quina. (TPO12, R, S1, T1) 同样的现象也在 Neanderthal, Gibalter 以及 La Quina 人的脑标本上发现过。

spectacular[4] [spek'tækjʊlə] 

【释义】 *a.* 壮观的；精彩的（sensational, grand, fascinating）*n.* 精彩的节目或表演；壮观的场面

【例句】 As a result of crustal adjustments and faulting, the Strait of Gibraltar, where the Mediterranean now connects to the Atlantic, opened, and water cascaded spectacularly back into the Mediterranean. (TPO7, R, S1, T1) 由于地壳运动发生断层现象，致使现在连接地中海和大西洋的直布罗陀海峡裂开，海水如瀑布般地流回地中海，十分壮观。

【搭配】 a spectacular display of fireworks 焰火奇观

Word List 27

spectator[4] [spek'teɪtə]

【释义】*n.* 观众,旁观者(audience, watcher)
【例句】Previously, large audiences had viewed spectacles at the theater, where vaudeville, popular dramas, musical and minstrel shows, classical plays, lectures, and slide-and-lantern shows had been presented to several hundred spectators at a time. (TPO2, R, S2, T2) 先前,大批观众在剧院观看表演,在那里,数百名观众可以同时观看轻歌舞剧、流行戏剧、音乐剧或歌唱表演、古典音乐、演讲和幻灯片放映。
【逆构】spectate *v.* 观看

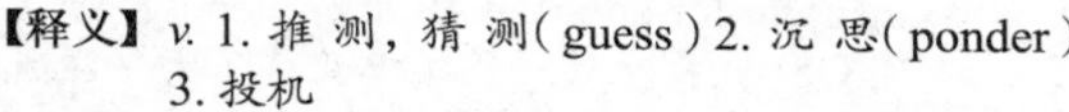

speculate[4] ['spekjʊˌleɪt]

【释义】*v.* 1. 推测,猜测(guess) 2. 沉思(ponder) 3. 投机
【例句】We'll never really know of course, though it's interesting to speculate. (TPO3, L, S2, L1) 当然我们永远也不可能真正知道,虽然推测起来也充满乐趣。
【派生】speculation *n.* 思考;推测;投机买卖
speculator *n.* 投机者
【搭配】speculate in stocks 股票投机

sphere[4] [sfɪə]

【释义】*n.* (某人的兴趣、活动、影响等的)范围,领域(field)
【例句】The Roman genius was projected into new spheres—especially into those of law, military organization, administration, and engineering. (TPO7, R, S2, T1) 罗马人把才能投入到了新的领域,特别是法律、军事组织、管理和工程方面。
【派生】spherical *a.* 球的,球面的,球状的

spill[4] [spɪl]

【释义】*n.* 溢出,溅出 *v.* (使)溅出,(使)溢出
【例句】Pipelines carrying oil can be broken by faults or landslides, causing serious oil spills. (TPO4, R, S2, T2) 输油管道可能会因断层或滑坡而受损,从而引发严重的漏油事件。
【派生】spillage *n.* 溢出;溢出量
【搭配】spill over 溢出
spill the beans 泄密,说漏嘴
spill out (使)溢出,(使)溅出;突然涌出;说出(真相、内情)
spill into 涌进

spoon[4] [spuːn]

【释义】*n.* 匙,调羹 *v.* 用匙舀
【例句】Long-handed Neolithic spoons of yew wood preserved in Alpine villages dating to 3000 BC have survived. (TPO12, R, S1, T1) 可追溯到公元前3000年、保存于阿尔卑斯山村庄中的新石器时代的紫衫木长柄勺子保存了下来。
【派生】spoonful *n.* 一匙

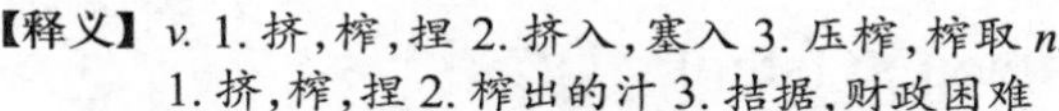

squeeze[4] [skwiːz]

【释义】*v.* 1. 挤,榨,捏 2. 挤入,塞入 3. 压榨,榨取 *n.* 1. 挤,榨,捏 2. 榨出的汁 3. 拮据,财政困难
【例句】And as it goes along it makes a little squeezing noises. (TPO11, L, S1, L1) 它一边跑还一边发出轻微的声响。
【搭配】squeeze out 挤出;榨出;排出
squeeze in/into 榨出;挤入,硬塞进…
put the squeeze on 对…施加压力
squeeze through 挤过;勉强通过
credit squeeze 贷款紧缩,银根紧缩

stake[4] [steɪk]

【释义】*n.* 1. 桩,柱 2. 赌注 3. 股份 4. 利害关系 *v.* 以…打赌,拿…冒险
【例句】The only thing at stake is your grade. (TPO10, L, S1, C1) 唯一危险的是你的分数。
【搭配】at stake 处于危险中,在紧要关头
have a stake in 与…利害攸关

starve[4] [stɑːv]

【释义】*v.* 挨饿,饿死(hunger)
【例句】Indeed, if you take baby tree swallows out of a nest for an hour feeding half the set and starving the other half, when the birds are

返记菜单

spectator[4] speculate[4] sphere[4] spill[4] spoon[4]
squeeze[4] stake[4] starve[4]

replaced in the nest, the starved youngsters beg more loudly than the fed birds, and the parent birds feed the active beggars more than those who beg less vigorously. (TPO11, R, S2, T2) 确实,如果你把树燕幼鸟从巢中拿出来一小时,其中一半的鸟喂食,而另一半饿着,那么当把它们放回巢中时,挨饿的幼鸟的乞食声就比喂过的鸟大,而相比求食不够活跃的幼鸟,父母会更多地喂食给积极求食的幼鸟们。

【派生】starvation *n.* 饥饿,饿死

【搭配】starve to death 饿死
starve for 渴望,急需

steady[4] ['stedɪ]

【释义】*a.* 稳定的,牢固的(stable)*v.* 使稳固,使坚定

【例句】So glasses were a steady symbol in some parts of the world. (TPO8, L, S2, L1) 所以,在世界上的部分地区,眼镜是一个稳固的象征。

【派生】steadily *ad.* 稳定地,稳固地
steadiness *n.* 稳健,稳固

steep[4] [stiːp]

【释义】*a.* 1. 险峻的,陡峭的(sharp, abrupt)2.(价格等)过高的,不合理的 *v.* 浸泡,沉浸(immerse, absorb)

【例句】Inequalities of gender have also existed in pastoralist societies, but they seem to have been softened by the absence of steep hierarchies of wealth in most communities, and also by the requirement that women acquire most of the skills of men, including, often, their military skills. (TPO14, R, S2, T2) 性别不平等现象也同样存在于游牧社会,但是因为在大多数的群体中并不存在明显的财富分级,同时因为妇女也需要掌握大多数男人所拥有的技能,通常还包括军事技能,所以这种现象似乎被弱化了。

strain[4] [streɪn]

【释义】*n.* 1.(动、植物的)品系,品种 2. 过度疲劳,紧张(tension, pressure)*v.* 1. 拉紧 2. 使(stress)

【例句】Genetic engineering also may provide a partial solution, as new strains of drought-resistant crops continue to be developed. (TPO3, R, S1, T1) 基因工程也会通过继续研发抗旱的新品种作物来帮助解决部分难题。

stunt[4] [stʌnt]

【释义】*v.* 阻碍…生长(hinder, bar)*n.* 特技,绝技,花招

【例句】Phosphorus-deficient plants are often stunted, with leaves turning a characteristic dark green, often with the accumulation of anthocyanin. (TPO5, R, S1, T1) 缺乏磷的植物通常会发育受阻,表现为叶子呈现典型的暗绿色,并经常伴有花青素的积聚。

【派生】stunted *a.* 成长受妨碍的;发育不良的

【搭配】stunt man 特技替身演员

submit[4] [səb'mɪt]

【释义】*v.* 1. 呈送,提交(present)2.(使)顺从,(使)屈服(comply, obey, surrender, yield)

【例句】I won an award from the Pacific Journalism institute for an article I submitted. (TPO12, S, Q5) 我提交的一篇文章获得了太平洋新闻学院所颁发的一个奖项。

【派生】submission *n.* 投降,屈服;提交物
submissive *a.* 顺从的,谦卑的

【搭配】submit an application 提交申请

subtle[4] ['sʌtl]

【释义】*a.* 微妙的,细微的,巧妙的(delicate)

【例句】The strategies they use can be subtle, uh…friendly forms of persuasion that are sometimes hard to recognize. (TPO3, S, Q6) 他们运用的策略非常巧妙,是一种有时候很难被识别出来的友好的说服方式。

【派生】subtlety *n.* 微妙,精明

successive[4] [sək'sesɪv]

【释义】*a.* 连续的,依次的(consecutive, sequential)

【例句】For the price of 25 cents (or 5 cents per machine), customers moved from machine to machine to watch five different films (or, in the case of famous prizefight, successive rounds of a single fight). (TPO2, R, S2, T2) 观众花 25 美分(或者每台播放器的观看价格是 5 美分),便可以从一个播放器换到下

一个播放器，依次观看5场不同的影片（例如观看著名的职业拳击赛时，观众可以连续观看同一场比赛的几轮战况）。

【派生】successively *ad.* 连续地

【逆构】succeed *v.* 继续，接着发生

superior[4] [sjuːˈpɪəriə] 

【释义】*a.* 1. 上好的 2. 上级的 3. 高傲的 *n.* 上级，长官

【例句】Smaller European producers believed that silent films with music accompaniment were aesthetically superior to sound films. (TPO12, R, S2, T1) 欧洲的一些小制片人认为有音乐伴奏的无声电影在审美上要优于有声电影。

【反义】inferior

【派生】superiority *n.* 优越性

【搭配】superior to sb./sth. 比起…来更好、更具优越性

supplement[4] 

【释义】[ˈsʌplɪment] *v.* 补充，增补（add, complement）
[ˈsʌpləmənt] *n.* 补充，增补（addition）

【例句】Members of poor peasant families spun or wove cloth and linens at home for scant remuneration in an attempt to supplement meager family income. (TPO10, R, S2, T2) 为了补贴本已经微薄的家庭收入，贫困潦倒的农民们通过在家纺织衣料或亚麻来换取少量的报酬。

【搭配】food supplement 保健品

suppress[4] [səˈpres] 

【释义】*v.* 镇压，抑制，禁止（check, restrain, control）

【例句】The high costs of converting to sound and the early limitations of sound technology were among the factors that suppressed innovations or retarded advancement in these other areas. (TPO12, R, S2, T1) 转化成有声影像的高花费和早期声音技术的局限性都是制约创新或妨碍这些领域进步的因素。

【派生】suppression *n.* 抑制，镇压

【搭配】suppress inflation 遏制通货膨胀

symbiosis[4] [sɪmbaɪˈəʊsɪs] 

【释义】*n.* 1.（通常互利的）共生（现象）2.（人与人之间的）互利关系

【例句】It is significant that the earliest living thing that built communities on these islands are examples of symbiosis, a phenomenon that depends upon the close cooperation of two or more forms of life and a principle that is very important in island communities. (TPO9, R, S2, T2) 岛屿上最早的生物群落以共生的方式存在是非常重要的。共生是一种依赖于两种或两种以上的生物紧密合作的现象，也是对于岛屿上的生物群落来说非常重要的一项原则。

【派生】symbiotic *a.* 共生的

【搭配】mutualistic symbiosis 互惠共生

symptom[4] [ˈsɪmptəm] 

【释义】*n.* 症状，征兆（implication, indication）

【例句】Mineral deficiencies can often be detected by specific symptoms such as chlorosis (loss of chlorophyll resulting in yellow or white leaf tissue), necrosis (isolated dead patches), anthocyanin formation (development of deep red pigmentation of leaves or stem), stunted growth, and development of woody tissue in an herbaceous plant. (TPO5, R, S1, T1) 矿物质的缺乏通常可以通过一些特别的症状表现出来，比如萎黄病（水溶性叶绿素的缺乏导致的黄色或白色的叶片组织）、坏死（分离的枯死的叶片）、花色素甙生成（叶子或枝干上深红色色素的扩散），生长萎缩以及草本植物中木质组织的发展。

【派生】symptomatic *a.* 症候的，有症状的
symptomize *v.* 是…的症候；表明

【搭配】symptom complex 症候群

synthesize[4] [ˈsɪnθɪsaɪz] 

【释义】*v.* 综合，合成

【例句】In this, he synthesized all his tricks from Drury Lane: mechanical motions, sound, light, other special effects to create, if you will, an early multimedia production. (TPO9, L, S1, L1) 在“Eidophusikon”中，他运用了在朱瑞巷剧院里的所有技巧：机械运动、声

音、灯光以及其他特效，如果你愿意承认，那便是早期的多媒体产品。

【搭配】synthesize various opinions 综合各方面的意见

talent[4] ['tælənt]

【释义】*n.* 1. 才能，天资(gift) 2. 人才(genius)

【例句】If you rely on yourself and trust your own talents, your own interest, don't worry, your path will make sense in the end. (TPO4, L, S1, L2) 如果你依靠自己，相信自己的才能和兴趣，不必担心，你最终必将有所收获。

【派生】talented *a.* 有天才的，有才干的
talentless *a.* 无能的

tone[4] [təʊn]

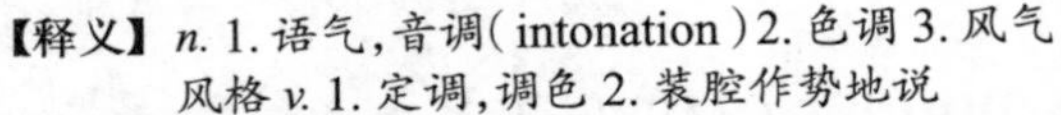

【释义】*n.* 1. 语气，音调(intonation) 2. 色调 3. 风气，风格 *v.* 1. 定调，调色 2. 装腔作势地说

【例句】When we speak with other people face-to-face, the nonverbal signals we give—our facial expressions, hand gestures, body movements, and tone of voice—often communicate as much as, or more than, the words we utter. (TPO4, S, Q4) 当我们和人面对面交流时，我们所使用的非语言信号——面部表情、手势、肢体动作和声调——所传达的信息通常跟我们说的话一样多，甚至更多。

【派生】toneless *a.* 缺乏声调的，沉闷的

【搭配】tone of voice 语调，声调，口吻
set the tone 定调子
tone up 增强，提高(声调等)

truck[4] [trʌk]

【释义】*n.* 1. 交易，商品 2. 卡车，敞篷火车 *v.* 1. 用火车运载 2. 交易，交换

【例句】If you need to get hold of a book that is not in our library, there is a truck that runs between our library and a few public and university libraries in this area. (TPO7, L, S2, C1) 如果在我们图书馆里找不到你需要的书，在我们的图书馆和其他一些大学和公共图书馆之间有往返的卡车。

【搭配】have no truck with sb./sth. 拒不与某人打交道；不容忍或不考虑某事物

ultimate[4] ['ʌltɪmɪt]

【释义】*a.* 最后的，最终的(final, last) *n.* 最终的观点或结论；极限

【例句】These kinds of implicit pressures to conform to lead group members ultimately make dicisions that each, by himself or herself, might normally not make. (TPO1, S, Q4) 这种需顺从群内领导成员的隐式压力使得最终做出的决定是群内某个个体成员一般情况下不会做出的。

【派生】ultimately *ad.* 最后；根本上
ultimateness *n.* 结论；终结

【搭配】ultimate concern 终极关怀

unaware[4] [ˌʌnə'weə]

【释义】*a.* 没有意识到的，不知道的

【例句】She is frustrated that most of her students are unaware of the phenomenon. (TPO10, L, S2, L1) 令她沮丧的是，她的大部分学生都没有意识到这种现象。

【逆构】aware *a.* 知道的，意识到的

【派生】awareness *n.* 认识，察觉，意识

unconsolidated[4] [ˌʌnkən'sɑlɪˌdetɪd]

【释义】*a.* 松散的

【例句】Groundwater is stored in the pore spaces and joints of rocks and unconsolidated (unsolidified) sediments or in the openings widened through fractures and weathering. (TPO12, R, S2, T2) 地下水储存在空隙中、岩石的连接处、松散的沉积物中，或者是由于断裂及风化而形成的裂口中。

uncover[4] [ʌn'kʌvə]

【释义】*v.* 揭开，揭露(disclose, expose, reveal)

【例句】Then if we want to undo some bad restoration attempts, we can determine what kind of process we can use to remove them to dissolve the paint and uncover the original. (TPO5, L, S2, L1) 那么，如果我们想要取消一些糟糕的修复结果，我们可以决定通过怎样的过程将其去除，将油漆溶解，从而复原本相。

【派生】uncovered *a.* 无盖的；未保险的

undergo[4] [ˌʌndəˈɡəʊ] 

【释义】*v.* 经历,遭受(encounter, experience)

【例句】We know that over the past millennia the climate has undergone major changes without any significant human intervention. (TPO10, R, S2, T1) 我们知道,在过去的几千年里,气候在没有重大人类干预的情况下也已经经历了一些显著的变化。

unreliable[4] [ˈʌnrɪˈlaɪəbl] 

【释义】*a.* 不可靠的,靠不住的

【例句】First, the observation may be unreliable in that two or more observers may not agree that the particular response occurred, or to what degree it occurred. (TPO13, R, S2, T2) 首先,这种观察可能是不可靠的,因为两个甚至更多的观察者也许不会察觉到特殊反应的发生或者反应发生到什么程度。

【搭配】an unreliable source of information 不可靠的消息来源

urge[4] [ɜːdʒ] 

【释义】*n.* 强烈的欲望,冲动 *v.* 1. 驱策,鼓励 2. 强烈要求,力劝

【例句】Displacement occurs because the animal's got two conflicting drives – two competing urges, in this case, fear and hunger. (TPO4, L, S1, L1) 替换的出现是因为动物有两种相矛盾的驱动力——两种相抵触的欲望,在这一案例中是恐惧和饥饿。

【搭配】urge…into doing/to do 催促 / 怂恿…做
urge on/onward 推进;驱策
urge sth. on /upon sb. 向某人极力陈述某事

utensil[4] [jʊ(ː)ˈtensl] 

【释义】*n.* 用具,器皿(尤指家庭日用的)

【例句】And this waterproof quality of the bark made it useful for making things like cooking containers and a variety of utensils. (TPO7, L, S2, L1) 树皮的这种防水特性使得这种树木可以用来制作烹饪器具以及各种各样的器皿。

【搭配】writing utensils 书写用具

utter[4] [ˈʌtə] 

【释义】*v.* 说,发出,表达(speak, express) *a.* 完全的,全然的,绝对的(absolute, complete)

【例句】When we speak with other people face-to-face, the nonverbal signals we give—our facial expressions, hand gestures, body movements, and tone of voice—often communicate as much as, or more than, the words we utter. (TPO4, S, Q4) 当我们和人面对面交流时,我们所使用的非语言信号——面部表情、手势、肢体动作和声调——所传达的信息通常跟我们说的话一样多,甚至更多。

【派生】utterance *n.* 发声,说话方式
utterly *ad.* 完全地,绝对地

vanish[4] [ˈvænɪʃ] 

【释义】*v.* 消失,灭绝(disappear, die out)

【例句】Left over from an earlier time, the behavior remains as a relict, or remnant, long after the environmental circumstance that influenced its evolution has vanished. (TPO18, S, Q4) 这种行为从很早的时候就作为遗迹遗留下来,甚至在影响它们进化的环境消失之前。

【搭配】vanish away 消失

varnish[4] [ˈvɑːnɪʃ] 

【释义】*n.* 清漆 *v.* 涂清漆,修饰

【例句】You'd have to know when he created his paintings, um, what pigments he used, in other words, what ingredients he used to make different colors of paint, 'cos the ingredients used in paints and binding agents plus varnishes have changed over time. (TPO5, L, S2, L1) 你需要了解他在作画时所使用的颜料,换句话说,就是他使用了哪些配料来调和出不同颜色的颜料,因为颜料中使用的配料、粘合剂和清漆都已经随着时间发生了变化。

【派生】varnished *a.* 涂漆的;浸渍过的

versus[4] [ˈvɜːsəs] 

【释义】*prep.* 1. 对抗 2. 与…相对

【例句】For him, it's sculpture versus convenience. (TPO1, S, Q3) 对他来说,是雕塑影响了他的便利。

返记菜单

undergo[4] unreliable[4] urge[4] utensil[4] utter[4]
vanish[4] varnish[4] versus[4]

vigorous[4] ['vɪgərəs]

【释义】*a.* 精力充沛的，有力的，强壮的（active, energetic, strong, robust）

【例句】If parent birds use begging intensity to direct food to healthy offspring capable of vigorous begging, then parents should make food delivery decisions on the basis of their offsprings' calls. (TPO11, R, S2, T2) 如果鸟儿的父母是凭借乞食声的强度来把食物分给能发出有力叫声的健康幼鸟，那么它们应该基于幼鸟的叫声来做食物分配决定。

【逆构】vigor *n.* 精力，活力

wagon[4] ['wægən]

【释义】*n.* 四轮的运货马车（carriage, van）

【例句】In some industrial regions, heavily laden wagons, with flanged wheels, were being hauled by horses along metal rails; and the stationary steam engine was puffing in the factory and mine. (TPO6, R, S1, T1) 在一些工业地区，承载重物的四轮马车都配备有带凸的缘轮，并且是通过几匹马拉动而在铁轨上行驶的；而静止的蒸汽发动机则被用于工厂和矿井之中。

【搭配】on the wagon 〈俚〉戒酒

wander[4] ['wɒndə]

【释义】*v./n.* 漫步，闲逛，徘徊（drift, meander）

【例句】I want to describe a very simple method of researching customer preference, and it is becoming increasingly common, it's called MBWA—which stands for managing by wandering around. (TPO12, L, S1, L2) 我想描述一种用来调查顾客喜好的非常简单的方法，这种方法正变得越来越普遍，叫做MBWA，代表的意思就是"走动管理"。

【派生】wanderer *n.* 流浪者

【搭配】wander about 徘徊，漫步；流浪
wander from 离题
wander off 漫步，漫游

wire[4] ['waɪə]

【释义】*v.* 1. 安装电线 2. 发电报 *n.* 1. 金属丝 2. 电缆，电线 3. 电报

【例句】In 1929 the United States motion picture industry released more than 300 sound films—a rough figure, since a number were silent films with music tracks, or films prepared in dual versions, to take account of the many cinemas not yet wired for sound. (TPO12, R, S2, T1) 1929年，美国电影业推出了300多部有声电影——这是一个粗略的数值，因为有一些电影只是带有音乐的无声电影，或者是有两个版本的电影，那是考虑到很多影院还没有安装音响设备。

【派生】wireless *a.* 无线的 *n.* 无线电
wiring *n.* 线路；配线
wireman *n.* 电线工人

【搭配】wire up 用电线连接

workshop[4] ['wɜːkʃɒp]

【释义】*n.* 1. 专题讨论会，讲习班 2. 车间，工场，作坊

【例句】And if you plan on attending future career fairs, I recommend you sign up for one of our interview workshops. (TPO6, L, S1, C1) 如果你计划参加即将举行的人才招聘会，我推荐你先报名参加一个我们的面试专题讨论会。

【搭配】workshop director 车间主任

wrist[4] [rɪst]

【释义】*n.* 腕，腕关节

【例句】That's my wrist actually, I hurt it last weekend. (TPO5, S, Q2) 实际上是我的手腕，上周末的时候扭伤了。

【派生】wristwatch *n.* 手表

aboard[3] [ə'bɔːd]

【释义】*prep.* 在（船、飞机、公共汽车、火车等）上；上（船、飞机、公共汽车、火车等）

【例句】In 1970 geologists Kenneth J. Hsu and William B. F. Ryan were collecting research data while aboard the oceanographic research vessel Glomar Challenger. (TPO7, R, S1, T1) 1970年，地质学家Kenneth J. Hsu和William B. F. Ryan在航船Glomar Challenger号上进行海洋研究时收集了科研数据。

accidental[3] [ˌæksɪ'dentl]

【释义】*a.* 意外的，偶然的（unexpected, unforeseen）

返记菜单

vigorous[4] wagon[4] wander[4] wire[4] workshop[4]
wrist[4] aboard[3] accidental[3]

【例句】Spillage from huge oil-carrying cargo ships, called tankers, involved in collisions or accidental groundings (such as the one off Alaska in 1989) can create oil slicks at sea. (TPO4, R, S2, T2) 大型的运油货船——也叫油轮——因撞击或搁浅(比如 1989 年发生在阿拉斯加的事件)引发的石油泄漏会造成海面浮油。
【反义】intentional, planned
【逆构】accident *n.* 事故,意外

accommodation[3] [əˌkɒmə'deɪʃən] 

【释义】*n.* 1. 调和,适应 2. 住处(尤指仅供短期使用的),膳宿
【例句】So then I read the part about dialect accommodation. (TPO6, L, S2, C1) 然后我读到了关于方言互融的部分。
【逆构】accommodate *v.* 容纳;提供住宿;适应,调节
【搭配】unprincipled accommodation 无原则的迁就

adept[3] ['ædept]

【释义】*a.* 熟练的,老练的(proficient, skillful) *n.* 名手,专家(expert)
【例句】Children have strong imaginations and the use of fantasy brings their ideas to life, but children may not be adept enough to realize that what they are viewing is unreal. (TPO14, R, S1, T1) 孩子们具有丰富的想象力,而且幻想的使用能激活他们的想法,但是小孩却不够老练,从而无法意识到他们所见的并非是真实的。
【搭配】adept at 熟练于…
adept in 善于

adverse[3] ['ædvɜːs]

【释义】*a.* 1. 不利的,有害的(harmful, detrimental) 2. 相反的,敌对的(opposite, hostile)
【例句】Several current studies are looking at these effects and I really do hope we can find the way to deal with this issue before these ecosystems are adversely affected. (TPO10, L, S2, L1) 当前有几个研究正在探讨这些影响,而我真的希望我们能在这些生态系统受到不利影响之前找到解决这个问题的方法。
【反义】favorable
【搭配】adverse effect 不利影响,副作用

afterwards[3] ['ɑːftəwədz] 

【释义】*ad.* 以后,后来
【例句】But, sometimes students like to watch with classmates, so they can review the material with each other afterwards. (TPO13, L, S2, C1) 但是,有时学生愿意和同学一起看,这样,之后他们就可以一起就这些资料进行复习。

alongside[3] [ə'lɒŋ'saɪd] 

【释义】*ad.* 在旁边 *prep.* 在…旁边,和…一起
【例句】In many instances, spectators in the era before recorded sound experienced elaborate aural presentations alongside movies' visual images, from the Japanese benshi (narrators) crafting multivoiced dialogue narratives to original musical compositions performed by symphony-size orchestras in Europe and the United States. (TPO12, R, S2, T1) 在很多情况下,在有声电影出现以前的观众们在观看影像的同时也能欣赏到精心制作的音效,从日本的多人对话式叙事到欧美交响乐团的原声乐,无不体现着这一点。
【搭配】alongside of 与…并肩;在旁边

alternate[3] 

【释义】['ɔːltəneɪt] *v.* 交替,轮流(rotate, turn)
[ɔː'tɜːnɪt] *a.* 1. 轮流的,交替的 2. 替代的(alternative) *n.* 代替者;代理人
【例句】Then, as blazing sunshine alternated with drenching rains, the harsh, barren surfaces of the black rocks slowly began to soften. (TPO9, R, S2, T2) 然后,经过了炙热阳光和湿润雨水的交替作用之后,荒芜的黑色岩石表面慢慢开始变软。
【派生】alternation *n.* 交替,轮流
alternately *ad.* 交替地
【搭配】alternate between…and… 在…与…间交替

amateur[3] ['æmətə(ː)] 

【释义】*a.* 业余的,非专业的(inexpert) *n.* 业余爱好者,外行(nonprofessional, layman)

【例句】Like most amateur musicians, I only play because, well, I just enjoy it. (TPO2, L, S2, L1) 像很多业余音乐爱好者一样，我玩乐器只是因为我享受这种感觉。

【派生】amateurish *a.* 业余的，外行的
amateurism *n.* 业余办法；业余身份

ambitious[3] [æm'bɪʃəs]

【释义】*a.* 1. 有抱负的，雄心勃勃的（aspiring, enterprising）

【例句】It's just too ambitious for the scope of the assignment. (TPO12, L, S1, C1) 这项作业的范畴实在过于宏大了。

【派生】ambitiously *ad.* 雄心勃勃地；劲头十足地

【逆构】ambition *n.* 野心；抱负

analogous[3] [ə'næləgəs]

【释义】*a.* 相似的，类似的

【例句】Well, the solar system also has two analogous classes of objects, smaller than planets—namely, asteroids and comets. (TPO13, L, S2, L2) 太阳系也有两个相似类别的物体，比行星小——即：小行星和彗星。

【反义】different

【派生】analogously *ad.* 类似地，近似地

【搭配】analogous to/with 与…相似

anecdotal[3] [ˌænek'dəʊtl]

【释义】*a.* 轶事的，趣闻的

【例句】This accords with anecdotal evidence that people often yawn in situations where they are neither tired nor bored, but are preparing for impending mental and physical activity. (TPO18, R, S2, T1) 有轶事证据表明通常人们打呵欠的时候既不是因为疲倦，也不是因为无聊，而是在为即将进行的精神和身体活动做准备。这与该说法是一致的。

【逆构】anecdote *n.* 轶事

【搭配】anecdotal evidence 轶事证据

antifreeze[3] ['æntɪ'fri:z]

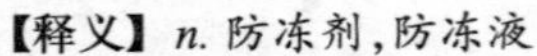

【释义】*n.* 防冻剂，防冻液

【例句】Slower and slower but…and in those last few hours before it freezes, it distributes glucose, a blood sugar throughout its body, its circulatory system, sort of acts like an antifreeze. (TPO18, L, S2, L2) 心跳越来越慢…但是就在它冻结前的最后几个小时中，它会释放出葡萄糖，这是一种存在于身体血液循环中的糖分，其作用就像防冻液。

aristocratic[3] [ˌærɪstə'krætɪk]

【释义】*a.* 贵族的；贵族气派的，高贵的

【例句】Someone probably wanted to increase the value of the painting by making it look like a formal portrait of an aristocratic lady. (TPO3, W, Q1) 可能会有人想通过使其看上去更像一幅贵族夫人的正式画像来增加画作的价值。

【派生】aristocratically *ad.* 贵族地

【搭配】of an aristocratic cast 具有贵族气质

astonishing[3] [əs'tɒnɪʃɪŋ]

【释义】*a.* 惊人的，令人惊讶的（amazing, striking）

【例句】The remarkable mobility and range of pastoral societies explain, in part, why so many linguists have argued that the Indo-European languages began their astonishing expansionist career not among farmers in Anatolia (present-day Turkey), but among early pastoralists from Inner Eurasia. (TPO14, R, S2, T2) 游牧社会显著的流动性和地域的广阔性一定程度上解释了为何那么多语言学家认为印欧语系的惊人扩张并不是始于安纳托利亚（今天的土耳其）的农民，而是来自亚欧内陆的早期牧民。

【逆构】astonish *v.* 使惊讶

auditory[3] ['ɔ:dɪtərɪ]

【释义】*a.* 听觉的，听觉器官的

【例句】Humans are constantly perceiving visual and auditory stimuli. (TPO12, S, Q5). 人类正不断地感受到视觉和听觉上的刺激。

【搭配】auditory organ 听觉器官

Word List 28

await[3] [ə'weɪt]

【释义】*v.* 1. 等候,期待 2. 即将来临

【例句】Perhaps another ancient fossil bed of soft-bodied animals from 600-million-year-old seas is awaiting discovery. (TPO5, R, S2, T2) 或许另一个含有6亿年前的海洋软体动物的古化石层正亟待发现。

barter[3] ['bɑːtə]

【释义】*v./n.* 物物交换,物物交易(exchange, trade)

【例句】Some societies make use of a barter system. (TPO2, S, Q6) 一些社会很好地利用了物物交换体制。

【派生】barter *n.* 交易商

【搭配】barter sth. for sth. 以某物交换另一事物
barter trade 实物交易

biotic[3] [bai'ɔtik]

【释义】*a.* 生物的,有关生命的

【例句】Wildlife zoologist Helmut Buechner (1953), in reviewing the nature of biotic changes in Washington through recorded time, says that "since the early 1940s, the state has had more deer than at any other time in its history, the winter population fluctuating around approximately 320,000 deer (mule and black-tailed deer), which will yield about 65,000 of either sex and any age annually for an indefinite period." (TPO4, R, S1, T1) 野生动物学家Helmut Buechner (1953)在回顾自有史记载以来华盛顿生物变化的本质时说:"自20世纪40年代以来,该州鹿群的数量达到最高峰,冬天时的数量大约在32万头左右(包括骡和黑尾鹿),这样每年一段时期将会产出65,000头小鹿,不论性别和年龄。

【搭配】biotic community 生物群落;生物共同体

breakthrough[3] ['breɪk'θruː]

【释义】*n.* 突破,突破性进展,重大成就(progress, discovery)

【例句】The arch is among the many important structural breakthroughs that have characterized architecture throughout the centuries. (TPO3, R, S1, T1) 而拱只是近百年来众多重要建筑结构的突破之一。

【搭配】a medical breakthrough 医学上的突破

brilliant[3] ['brɪljənt]

【释义】*a.* 1. 杰出的,卓越的(excellent, outstanding) 2. 闪光的,明亮的(bright)

【例句】Are people wasting their time when they listen to a brilliant song or watch a good movie? (TPO11, W, Q1) 当人们听一首非常好的歌曲或者欣赏一部很好的电影时,是否是在浪费时间?

【派生】brilliance *n.* (指人)聪明;(指物体)辉煌

brittle[3] ['brɪtl]

【释义】*a.* 易碎的,脆弱的(fragile, frail)

【例句】You've already known that the ice is brittle, if you heat it with hammer, it will shatter like glass. (TPO7, L, S2, L2) 大家都知道冰很脆,如果用锤子去敲它的话,它就会像玻璃一样碎掉。

【搭配】as brittle as thin glass 如薄玻璃一样容易破碎

built-in[3] [ˌbɪlt'ɪn]

【释义】*a.* 嵌入的,内置的

【例句】Yet despite this synchronization of the period of the internal cycle, the animal's timer itself continues to have its own genetically built-in period close to, but different from, 24 hours. (TPO13, R, S2, T1) 但是尽管存在这种内部循环的同步性,动物的时间控制机制本身会继续保持有其天生固有的节律,接近但不是24小时。

【搭配】a built-in cabinet 嵌入的橱柜

返记菜单

await[3] barter[3] biotic[3] breakthrough[3] brilliant[3]
brittle[3] built-in[3]

by-product[3] ['baɪˌprɔdʌkt]

【释义】*n.* 副产品,副作用

【例句】An unavoidable by-product of burning oil is carbon dioxide, and carbon dioxide harms the environment. (TPO9, W, Q1) 油燃烧之后不可避免的产物是二氧化碳,而二氧化碳会破坏环境。

capillary[3] [kə'pɪlərɪ]

【释义】*n.* 毛细管 *a.* 毛状的,小内径的

【例句】Somewhat more promising have been recent experiments for releasing capillary water (water in the soil) above the water table by injecting compressed air into the ground. (TPO3, R, S1, T1) 最近一些更有希望获得成功的实验试图通过向土壤中注入压缩空气来释放地下水位线以上的毛管水(土壤中的水)。

【搭配】capillary condensation 毛细管凝聚

chant[3] [tʃɑ:nt]

【释义】*v.* 1. 吟唱,颂扬 2. 叫喊 *n.* 1. 圣歌,赞美诗 2. 叫喊声

【例句】When religious leaders started chanting with echoes bounced off the stonewalls over and over again, it must seem like a whole chorus of other voices, spirits of God maybe join in. (TPO14, L, S2, L2) 当宗教领袖开始吟唱时,回声会从石墙上不断反射回来,这听上去就像一整个合唱团在吟唱,上帝的神灵也许也加入其中了。

chief[3] [tʃi:f]

【释义】*a.* 1. 主要的(primary) 2. 首席的 *n.* 1. 首领(leader, head) 2. 族长,酋长

【例句】The chief problem was technological: How were the Europeans to reach the East? (TPO17, R, S1, T1) 最主要的问题其实还是技术:欧洲人怎样到达东方呢?

【派生】chiefdom *n.* 首领的地位,首领的权威

【搭配】chief engineer 总工程师

chimney[3] ['tʃɪmnɪ]

【释义】*n.* 烟囱

【例句】There tends to be a lot of obsidian flakes and chips in the hearth ashes, but no chimney. (TPO1, L, S2, L1) 在炉灰里有很多黑曜石的剥片和碎屑,但是没有烟囱。

client[3] ['klaɪənt]

【释义】*n.* 委托人,当事人,客户,顾客

【例句】The client who pays for the building and defines its function is an important member of the architectural team. (TPO3, R, S1, T1) 那些支付建设费用并且限定建筑的功能的客户是建筑团队中的重要成员。

【派生】clientele *n.* (总称)顾客,委托人

clip[3] [klɪp]

【释义】*n.* 1. 剪报,电影片段 2. 夹子,别针 *v.* 1. 修剪,剪下 2. 夹住,扣住

【例句】He might take a clip of a mollusk going up and down in the water and set it to music. (TPO3, L, S1, L2) 他可能会给一个软体动物在水中上下窜动的镜头,并且为之配上音乐。

【搭配】at a clip 每次,一次;同时
clip off 缩短,削减
clip sb's wings 限制某人的自由或权力

coating[3] ['kəʊtɪŋ]

【释义】*n.* 1. 涂层,(薄的)覆盖层 2. 上衣布料

【例句】These plants propagate by producing spores – tiny fertilized cells that contain all the instructions for making a new plant – but the spore are unprotected by any outer coating and carry no supply of nutrient. (TPO9, R, S2, T2) 这些植物通过产生孢子来繁殖,孢子是一些有营养的细胞,它们携带了一株新的植物生长所需要的所有遗传物质,但它没有任何外部表皮的保护,也没携带任何供应营养的组织。

【搭配】metallic coating 金属涂层

collaboration[3] [kəˌlæbə'reɪʃən]

【释义】*n.* 1. 合作,协作(cooperation) 2. 勾结

【例句】 Their competition and collaboration were creating the broadcasting industry in the United States. (TPO12, R, S2, T1) 他们之间的竞争和合作创造了美国的广播产业。
【逆构】 collaborate *v.* 合作；勾结
【搭配】 in collaboration with 与…合作

comedy[3] ['kɒmɪdɪ] 

【释义】 *n.* 喜剧；幽默事件
【例句】 Comedy requires sufficient detachment to view some deviations from social norms as ridiculous rather than as serious threats to the welfare of the entire group. (TPO1, R, S2, T1) 喜剧要求人们充分地从痛苦中脱离，并将一些与社会准则相背离的表现看作是可笑的，而不是将其视为对群体利益的巨大威胁。
【反义】 tragedy

commensalism[3] [kə'mensəˌlɪzəm] 

【释义】 *n.* 共栖
【例句】 There are three main types of symbiotic relationships: parasitism, commensalism, and mutualism. (TPO17, R, S2, T2) 共生关系共有三种类型：寄生、共栖和共生。

commit[3] [kə'mɪt] 

【释义】 *v.* 1. 委托，交付 2. 承诺，担保 3. 犯(错误)，干(坏事)
【例句】 Expressive ties are social links formed when we emotionally invest ourselves in and commit ourselves to other people. (TPO13, R, S1, T1) 情感联系是当我们投入情感并把自己交付于他人时所发生的社会联系。
【派生】 commitment *n.* 信奉，支持；许诺，承担义务
【搭配】 commit suicide 自杀

companion[3] [kəm'pænjən] 

【释义】 *n.* 同伴 2. 成双成对的物品之一
【例句】 The possibility that mass extinctions may recur periodically has given rise to such hypotheses as that of a companion star with a long-period orbit deflecting other bodies from their normal orbits, making some of them fall to Earth as meteors and causing widespread devastation upon impact. (TPO15, R, S2, T2) 大规模物种灭绝可能会周期性发生的可能性引发了这样的假想：一个在长周期轨道上运行的伴星从其正常的轨道偏向其他天体，从而造成某些天体以流星的形式坠落到地球上，而这种撞击就造成了大范围的破坏。
【派生】 companionable *a.* 好交往的；友善的；适于做朋友的

compel[3] [kəm'pel] 

【释义】 *v.* 强迫，迫使(force, require)
【例句】 But there are compelling reasons in favor of another Moon landing too, um, not the least of which is trying to pinpoint the moon's age. (TPO5, L, S1, L2) 但是也有一些不可抗拒的理由来支持另一次登月活动，嗯，其中最重要的理由是设法准确测定月球的年龄。
【反义】 free, liberate
【派生】 compelling *a.* 强制的；引人注目的
【搭配】 compell sb. to do sth. 强迫某人做某事

compensate[3] ['kɒmpənseɪt] 

【释义】 *v.* 弥补，赔偿，抵消(make up for)
【例句】 In other words, they were able to compensate for the sun's movement. (TPO11, R, S2, T1) 换言之，他们可以抵消太阳运动。

complain[3] [kəm'pleɪn] 

【释义】 *v.* 抱怨，发牢骚
【例句】 The proposal to add the classes is a response to student complaints that daytime computer classes have become increasingly overcrowded and there are no longer enough computers available. (TPO4, S, Q3) 增班的建议是对学生抱怨白天的电脑班越来越挤而且电脑不够用所做的回应。

confront[3] [kən'frʌnt]

【释义】 *v.* 面对；遭遇；对抗(encounter, face)
【例句】 An animal eats some food when confronted by its enemy. (TPO4, L, S1, L1) 动物在遇到敌人时会吃东西。
【反义】 avoid
【派生】 confrontation *n.* 面对，对抗

返记菜单

comedy[3] commensalism[3] commit[3] companion[3] compel[3]
compensate[3] complain[3] confront[3]

【搭配】confront with 使面临…

conquer[3] ['kɒŋkə]

【释义】*v.* 战胜,征服;克服(overcome)

【例句】You see, in the late 4th century B. C., the Romans began a campaign to expand the Roman Empire, and in 300 years they had conquered most of the Mediterranean area and parts of Europe. (TPO18, L, S1, L2) 你们知道,在公元前四世纪晚期,罗马人就开始了扩张罗马帝国的活动,在300年间,他们已经征服了地中海的大部分地区以及欧洲的部分地区。

【派生】conquerable *a.* 可征服的
conqueror *n.* 征服者

【搭配】divide and conquer 分而治之;各个击破

consult[3] [kən'sʌlt]

【释义】*v.* 1. 请教,咨询,征求意见(confer, counsel, advise)

【例句】Witnesses who lived with Chevalier in his later life confirmed that he regularly consulted notes and journals when composing the memoir. (TPO8, W, Q1) 在谢瓦利埃晚年时与其一起生活的目击者证实,在撰写回忆录的时候,他经常会查阅笔记和期刊等。

【搭配】consult with 商量,协商

contract[3]

【释义】[kən'trækt] *v.* 1. 收缩(shrink, constrict) 2. 订契约,立合同 3. 招致,感染(疾病)
['kɒntrækt] *n.* 合同,契约(agreement)

【例句】But if the muscles contract, then the sack expands, and you can see the colors. (TPO17, L, S2, L2) 但如果肌肉收缩,那袋子就会膨胀,这样你就能看见颜色了。

【派生】contractive *a.* 收缩的
contraction *n.* 缩短,收缩
contractor *n.* 订约人

【搭配】contract with 承包;与…订有合约
contract in 保证承担义务

converse[3] [kən'vɜːs]

【释义】*v.* 交谈,谈话 *a.* 逆向的,颠倒的 *n.* 相反的事物

【例句】No one doubts that the Chevalier and Voltaire met and conversed. (TPO7, W, Q1) 没有人怀疑谢瓦利埃和伏尔泰曾经相遇并且交谈过。

correlation[3] [ˌkɒrɪ'leɪʃən]

【释义】*n.* 关联,相互关系(relationship, relevance)

【例句】There appears to be a correlation between the positions of these planets and their sizes. (TPO16, R, S2, T2) 这些行星的位置分布和其大小之间似乎有关联。

【逆构】correlate *v.* 使…相互关联,使相互影响

【搭配】positive correlation 正相关
negative correlation 负相关

couch[3] [kaʊtʃ]

【释义】*n.* 长沙发,睡椅 *v.* 1. 表达 2. (使)躺卧 3. 隐蔽,埋伏

【例句】They don't have an extra bedroom, but they said it'd be OK for me to sleep on their living room couch. (TPO9, S, Q5) 他们没有多余的房间,但他们说我可以睡在客厅的沙发上。

【派生】on the couch 在沙发上;[美口]接受精神分析

council[3] ['kaʊnsɪl]

【释义】*n.* 1. 委员会,地方议会,理事会(committee) 2. 会议(conference)

【例句】And then individual states throughout the country started to establish their own state arts councils to help support the arts. (TPO4, L, S2, L2) 之后全国各州相继开始建立起本州的艺术委员会来支持艺术。

【搭配】state council 国务院
security council (联合国)安全理事会
city council 市议会

coverage[3] ['kʌvərɪdʒ]

【释义】*n.* 1. 覆盖范围 2. 新闻报道(reportage)

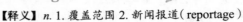

【例句】They may also be passed over for promotions because companies might prefer to have five-day employees in management positions to ensure continuous coverage and consistent supervision for the entire workweek. (TPO1, W, Q1) 他们可能会在职位晋升中被刷下去，因为公司可能更喜欢让那些一周工作五天的人来担当行政职位，以确保在整个的工作周内都有不断的职责覆盖和持续的督导。

coworker[3] ['kəuˌwəːkə] 

【释义】 *n.* 合作者

【例句】 So one day, a coworker and I suggested we should give our computers a design makeover, make them look more up-to-date. (TPO1, S, Q4) 所以有一天，我和同事建议，我们应该给我们的电脑做一个设计上的大转变，使它们看上去更加新潮。

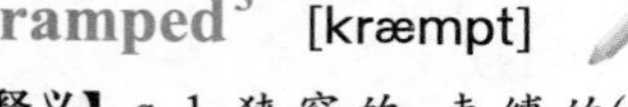

cramped[3] [kræmpt]

【释义】 *a.* 1. 狭窄的，束缚的(confining, jammed, stuffed) 2. 难认的

【例句】 If the trees are not removed, they will take years to decompose; in the meantime, no new trees can grow in the cramped spaces. (TPO14, W, Q1) 如果不把这些树移走，它们得需要很多年才会腐烂；而在此期间，新的树木也无法在狭窄的空间里生长。

【逆构】 cramp *v.* 束缚

craze[3] [kreɪz]

【释义】 *n.* 狂热；风尚(passion, trend) *v.* 使发狂

【例句】 What happened then was a craze for these specialized tulips. (TPO6, L, S1, L1) 接下来发生的便是对这种特殊品种的郁金香的狂热。

cubicle[3] ['kjuːbɪkəl] 

【释义】 *n.* (大房间中隔出的)小室

【例句】 This summer, the tables will be exchanged for new personal study cubicles—small, one-person desks enclosed by walls. (TPO17, S, Q3) 今年夏天，这些课桌将换成崭新的个人小书房——用墙围起来的单人小书桌。

【逆构】 a shower cubicle 淋浴间

curious[3] ['kjʊərɪəs] 

【释义】 *a.* 1. 新奇的，古怪的 2. 好奇的(inquisitive)

【例句】 Most of Africa presents a curious case in which societies moved directly from a technology of stone to iron without passing through the intermediate stage of copper or bronze metallurgy, although some early copper-working sites have been found in West Africa. (TPO7, R, S2, T2) 非洲大部地区都呈现出一种奇特的情况：其社会是直接从石器时代过渡到铁器时代的，而没有经历青铜冶炼的中间阶段，虽然人们曾在西非地区发现炼铜厂的旧址。

【派生】 curiosity *n.* 好奇心

cushion[3] ['kuʃən] 

【释义】 *n.* 垫子 *v.* 1. 为…装垫子 2. 以垫子覆盖 3. 保护，缓冲

【例句】 This explains how, for example, alpine cushion plants have been found growing at an altitude of 6,180 meters. (TPO1, R, S1, T1) 例如，这解释了高山垫状植物是如何在海拔 6180 米的地方生长的。

damp[3] [dæmp]

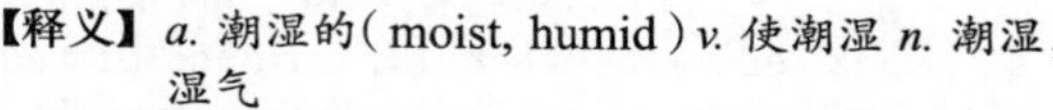

【释义】 *a.* 潮湿的(moist, humid) *v.* 使潮湿 *n.* 潮湿，湿气

【例句】 Scientists have been working to plant Torreya seeds in the coolest, dampest areas of the microclimate. (TPO17, W, Q1) 科学家一直致力于将榧树的种子种植在最为凉爽、潮湿的微气候中。

【派生】 dampish *a.* 含湿气的，稍湿的
dampen *v.* 使潮湿

【搭配】 damp off (因过于潮湿而)枯萎，腐败

daring[3] ['deərɪŋ] 

【释义】 *a.* 勇敢的，英勇的(bold)

【例句】 Critics claim that while such a daring escape makes for enjoyable reading, it is more likely that the Chevaliers jailers were bribed to free him. (TPO7, W, Q1) 评论家声称，虽然这样英勇的逃脱带来了阅读上的享受，但更有可能的是看管谢瓦利埃的狱卒因为收到了贿赂，所以放了他。

返记菜单

coworker[3] cramped[3] craze[3] cubicle[3] curious[3]
cushion[3] damp[3] daring[3]

decipher[3] [dɪ'saɪfə]

【释义】v. 破译，解读

【例句】In fact, it might reappear to the extent that scholars could make out and even decipher the original text. (TPO15, L, S2, L1) 事实上，它可能会重新显现，其清晰程度足以使学者辨认出甚至破译原始的文本。

deforest[3] [diː'fɔːrɪst]

【释义】v. 砍伐森林

【例句】Great tracts of lowland country deforested by logging, fire, or both have become ideal feeding grounds for deer. (TPO4, R, S1, T1) 低地的森林被大面积砍伐、焚烧，已经变成了鹿群理想的进食场所。

【派生】deforestation n. 砍伐森林

delta[3] ['deltə]

【释义】n.（河流的）三角洲

【例句】A 2004 Mars Global Surveyor image shows what mission specialists think may be a delta—a fan-shaped network of channels and sediments where a river once flowed into a larger body of water in this case a lake filling a crater in the southern highlands. (TPO8, R, S2, T2) 2004年的一张火星环球探测照片显示，任务专家所想的可能是一个三角洲——这是一个由河槽和沉积物构成的扇形区域，曾经有河流从这里流入更大的水体，在这种情况下，湖泊填补了南部高原的火山口。

【派生】deltaic a. 三角形的（三棱的，扁方形的）

deplete[3] [dɪ'pliːt]

【释义】v. 耗尽，使空竭（consume, exhaust）

【例句】But such plants are of little use for recycling nutrients back into depleted soils. (TPO5, R, S1, T1) 但是这种植物在使养分重新回到贫瘠的土壤中所发挥的作用是很小的。

【派生】depleted a. 废弃的；贫化的
depletion n. 消耗，用尽

depress[3] [dɪ'pres]

【释义】v. 1. 按下，压下（lower）2. 使沮丧，使消沉（discourage）

【例句】But detractors maintain that the terraces could also have been created by geological activity, perhaps related to the geologic forces that depressed the Northern Hemisphere far below the level of the south, in which case they have nothing whatever to do with Martian water. (TPO8, R, S2, T2) 但是诽谤者坚持认为，梯田也可能是由地质活动造成的，或许与造成北半球低于南半球的地质力量有关，在这种情况下，它们就和火星上的水体没有任何关系了。

【派生】depression n. 沮丧，萧条；压低
depressed a. 沮丧的

deserve[3] [dɪ'zɜːv]

【释义】v. 应得，值得（be worthy of, merit）

【例句】I know the award was well deserved. (TPO16, L, S2, C1) 我知道该奖是当之无愧的。

【派生】deserving a. 应得的，值得的

deterioration[3] [dɪˌtɪərɪə'reɪʃən]

【释义】n. 恶化，变质，退化，衰退（degeneration, decadence, decline）

【例句】The gradual drying of the soil caused by its diminished ability to absorb water results in the further loss of vegetation, so that a cycle of progressive surface deterioration is established. (TPO2, R, Sl, T1) 土壤吸收水分的能力降低会导致土壤越来越贫瘠，进而加剧了植被的消失，这样就造成了土壤不断退化这一恶性循环。

【反义】amelioration, improvement

【逆构】deteriorate v. 恶化，退化

differentiate[3] [ˌdɪfə'renʃɪeɪt]

【释义】v. 区分，区别（distinguish）

【例句】For example, we can differentiate between: "A large coyote moves fast." and say "Move the large coyote fast." or "Move fast, large coyote.", and I truly doubt whether anyone

返记菜单

decipher[3] deforest[3] delta[3] deplete[3] depress[3]
deserve[3] deterioration[3] differentiate[3]

has ever uttered either of these sentences before. (TPO9, L, S2, L2) 例如，我们能够区分开“一只大狼在很快地移动”或者说“很快地移动这只大狼”，或者“快点动，大狼”，我的确怀疑以前是否有人真地说过其中的任何一个句子。

【派生】differentiation *n.* 区别
undifferentiated *a.* 无差别的；无明显特征的

【搭配】differentiate between good and evil 分清善恶

dirt[3] [dɜːt]

【释义】*n.* 1. 污垢，泥土，灰尘 2. 污秽的言行；卑鄙的人

【例句】Well, with wetlands, it's like there is more standing water, more Stillwater around, and that water is a lot cleaner than swiftly flowing water, because the dirt and settlement and stuff has the chance to sink to the bottom. (TPO13, L, S1, L2) 有了湿地，周围就有了更多的静水，这些水比快速流动的水要清澈得多，因为污垢、悬浮物、聚集物等有机会沉淀到底部。

【派生】dirty *a.* 脏的；肮脏的

discern[3] [dɪ'sɜːn]

【释义】*v.* 辨别，看出，察觉到(distinguish, detect, perceive)

【例句】So it was easier to discern the order in the sky than farther north or farther south, where everything would seem more chaotic. (TPO14, L, S2, L1) 所以，相比看起来一切都更加无序的靠北和靠南的地方，(赤道)这里更容易辨认出天空中的秩序。

【派生】discerning *a.* 有洞察力的
discernment *n.* 辨别(力)，眼力
discernible *a.* 可识别的

discontinue[3] ['dɪskən'tɪnjʊ(ː)]

【释义】*v.* 中止，停止(stop, cease)

【例句】The university has decided to discontinue its free bus service for students. (TPO2, S, Q3) 学校决定停止为学生提供的免费校车服务。

【反义】continue

【派生】discontinuation *n.* 中止，停止

disorient[3] [dɪs'ɔːrɪent]

【释义】*v.* 使…失去方向感，使…迷惑

【例句】On overcast days, however, the birds were disoriented and had trouble locating their food box. (TPO11, R, S2, T1) 然而，在阴天的时候，这些鸟就会迷失方向而难以找到装有食物的盒子。

【派生】disoriented *a.* 分不清方向的

【逆构】orient *v.* 确定方向；朝(向)东 *n./a.* 东方(的)

disrupt[3] [dɪs'rʌpt]

【释义】*v.* 使中断，打乱，扰乱(break up, interrupt)

【例句】Contrast serves to disrupt or break up the unity in places, but in a careful intentional way. (TPO11, S, Q6) 对比的作用在于在一些地方打破和扰乱统一性，而这是经过精心策划的。

【派生】disruption *n.* 中断，破坏

dissonance[3] ['dɪsənəns]

【释义】*n.* 不和谐的音调；不一致(disagreement)

【例句】These contradictions can cause a kind of mental discomfort known as cognitive dissonance. (TPO3, S, Q4) 这些矛盾可能会引起一种被称为“认知失调”的心理不适感。

【反义】consonance

【搭配】cognitive dissonance theory 认知失调理论

donor[3] ['dəʊnə]

【释义】*n.* 捐赠人，施主，供者

【例句】I'd like to shake the donor's hand and say “Thank you.” (TPO1, S, Q3) 我想同捐赠者握手并说声“谢谢”。

dormant[3] ['dɔːmənt]

【释义】*a.* 静止的，休眠的(inactive, sleeping)

【例句】And Lechuguilla is pretty much dormant now. (TPO16, L, S1, L1) 现在雷修古拉几乎处于休眠状态。

【反义】active

【派生】dormancy *n.* 睡眠，休眠

【搭配】dormant volcano 休眠火山
dormant period 潜伏期

返记菜单

dirt[3] discern[3] discontinue[3] disorient[3] disrupt[3]
dissonance[3] donor[3] dormant[3]

dormitory[3] ['dɔːmɪtrɪ] 

【释义】n. 集体宿舍

【例句】Over the last ten years, the number of Central College students living on campus in dormitories has decreased by twenty percent. (TPO11, S, Q3) 在过去十年中，住在校内宿舍的中央学院的学生数量下降了百分之二十。

dot[3] [dɒt] 

【释义】v. 点缀，标记 n. 1. 点 2. 少量 3. [数]小数点

【例句】The deer which once picturesquely dotted the meadows around the fort were gone (in 1832), hunted to extermination in order to protect the crops. (TPO4, R, S1, T1) 曾把城堡周围的草原装点地如画般美丽的鹿群消失了（在 1832 年），为了保护农作物而几乎被人们猎杀殆尽。

【派生】dotted a. 有点的；星罗棋布的；点线的

【搭配】on/at the dot 准时

droplet[3] ['drɒplɪt] 

【释义】n. 小滴，微滴

【例句】As muddy sediments are pressed together, the gas and small droplets of oil may be squeezed out of the mud and may move into sandy layers nearby. (TPO4, R, S2, T2) 随着泥泞的沉积物被挤压在一起，天然气和油滴就可能被从泥土中挤压出来，并流到周围的沙层上面。

edit[3] ['edɪt] 

【释义】v. 编辑，校订，剪辑

【例句】To be honest, the articles got a lot of editing. (TPO14, L, S2, C1) 说实话，那篇文章有很多地方被编辑过。

【派生】edition n. 版，版本
editor n. 编辑，编者
editorial a. 编辑的

elk[3] [elk] 

【释义】n. 麋，驼鹿

【例句】They had experienced great difficulty finding game west of the Rockies and not until the second of December did they kill their first elk. (TPO4, R, S1, T1) 他们历经艰难才在落基山以西找到猎物，而且直到 12 月 2 日他们才杀死了第一头驼鹿。

embarrass[3] [ɪm'bærəs] 

【释义】v. 1. 使窘迫，使尴尬(shame, humiliate) 2. 使困惑

【例句】She was embarrassed because she gave an incorrect answer. (TPO5, L, S1, C1) 她因为给出了错误的答案而感到尴尬。

【派生】embarrassment n. 窘迫，尴尬
embarrassed a. 尴尬的，窘迫的

embed[3] [ɪm'bed] 

【释义】v. 使…嵌入(埋入)；使铭记于心

【例句】Pakicetus was found embedded in rocks formed from river deposits that were 52 million years old. (TPO2, R, S2, T1) 这块化石是在一条河的沉积岩中发现的，这条河里的沉积物有 5200 万年的历史。

【搭配】be embedded in sth. 嵌在 / 埋在某物中

endogenous[3] [en'dɔdʒinəs] 

【释义】a. 内生的，内成的

【例句】Regularly flowing rivers and streams that originate within arid lands are known as “endogenous”. (TPO12, R, S2, T2) 起源于旱地中的、有规律流动的河流和小溪被认为是“内生的”。

enforce[3] [ɪn'fɔːs] 

【释义】v. 1. 强迫，强制(compel) 2. 实施，执行

【例句】The organizational bonds were based on the common principles of law and administration and on the universal army of officials who enforced common standards of conduct. (TPO7, R, S2, T1) 组织联系是基于法律和行政上的共同准则以及强制实施共同行为标准的全体官员。

【派生】enforcement n. 执行；强制

【搭配】enforce obedience to an order 强迫服从命令

Word List 29

ensemble[3] [ɜːn'sɑːmbl] 

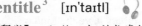

【释义】*n.* 1. 剧团或文工团（band, orchestra）2. 合奏（唱）曲 3. 全体，整体

【例句】We switched with the jazz ensemble. (TPO16, L, S1, C1) 我们与爵士乐队交换了一下场地。

enthusiastic[3] [ɪnˌθjuːzɪ'æstɪk] 

【释义】*a.* 热心的，热情的，热烈的

【例句】But with the monkeys he thought were less intelligent, he wasn't as enthusiastic. (TPO15, S, Q4) 但是对于那些他认为不是那么聪明的猴子来说，他就没那么热情了。

【派生】enthusiastically *ad.* 热心地，满腔热忱地

entitle[3] [ɪn'taɪtl]

【释义】*v.* 1. 给…权利或资格（authorize, empower）2. 给…提名或命名（name）

【例句】The district courts decide in if the university entitle to any of our professors' profits. (TPO14, L, S2, C1) 地方法院决定大学是否有权给予教授红利。

【派生】entitlement *n.* 权利；命名

entrance[3] [ɪn'trɑːns] 

【释义】*n.* 1. 入口 2. 进入，登场 3. 进入权 *v.* 使入迷，使陶醉

【例句】Other statues were designed to be placed within an architectural setting, for instance, in front of the monumental entrance gateways to temples known as pylons. (TPO11, R, S1, T1) 其他雕像被放置在建筑群中，比如，在庙宇的纪念性入口塔门的前方。

【反义】exit

exclusive[3] [ɪks'kluːsɪv] 

【释义】*a.* 1. 排外的 2. 单独的，唯一的，独家的（single, solo, only）

【例句】In the absence of solid linguistic, archaeological, and biological data, many fanciful and mutually exclusive theories were devised. (TPO5, R, S2, T1) 由于没有确凿的语言学、考古学和生物学数据，人们想出了很多充满幻想、互相矛盾的理论。

【反义】inclusive

【派生】exclusively *ad.* 专有地；排外地
exclusiveness *n.* 排外性，排他性

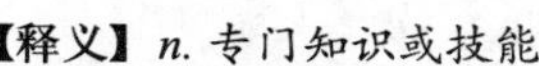

expertise[3] [ˌekspə'tiːz]

【释义】*n.* 专门知识或技能

【例句】First of all, a group of people has a wider range of knowledge, expertise, and skills than any single individual is likely to possess. (TPO2, W, Q1) 首先，一个团队较单独个体来说可能拥有更广泛的知识和专业技能。

exterior[3] [eks'tɪərɪə] 

【释义】*a.* 外部的，外来的，对外的（external, outside）*n.* 外部，外表

【例句】Exactly, now see how the house has very little exterior decoration, that's also typical of early Cape Cod houses. (TPO11, L, S1, L2) 没错，现在看看房子的外部装饰是多么地少，那也是早期科德角房屋的典型特征之一。

【反义】interior

facial[3] ['feɪʃəl] 

【释义】*a.* 脸部的，面部的；表面的 *n.* 美容，脸部按摩

【例句】When we speak with other people face-to-face the nonverbal signals we give—our facial expressions, hand gestures, body movements, and tone of voice—often communicate as much as, or more than, the words we utter. (TPO4, S, Q4) 当我们和人面对面交流时，我们所使用的非语言信号——面部表情、手势、肢体动作和声调——所传达的信息通常跟我们说的话一样多，甚至更多。

【逆构】face *n.* 脸

【搭配】facial expression 面部表情
facial nerve 面部神经

faint[3] [feɪnt]

【释义】*a.* 1. 微弱的；模糊的(vague, dim) 2. 无力的(weak, feeble)

【例句】Those produced a large number of faint reflection in which what's we called as: a smooth of echo. (TPO7, L, S1, L2) 它们产生出大量微弱的反射波，我们称之为柔和回声。

【派生】faintness *n.* 衰弱，眩晕

【搭配】in a (dead) faint (完全)失去知觉

fan[3] [fæn]

【释义】*n.* 1. (风)扇，扇形物 2. 迷，狂热爱好者 *v.* 1. 扇 2. 成扇形 3. 煽动，激起(stir, arouse)

【例句】Then you use pumps and fans to move heat from the collectors through a plumbing system to a tank. (TPO12, L, S2, L2) 然后你使用泵和风扇把热量从收集器中经由一个管道系统输入到一个罐中。

fancy[3] ['fænsɪ]

【释义】*a.* 新奇的，精美的，别致的(fanciful, elegant) *n.* 想像力，幻想力 *v.* 想要，喜欢(like, love)

【例句】And Cousteau's adventures were high-tech, with lots of fancy equipment, whereas Painlevé kind of patched the equipment together as he needed it. (TPO3, L, S1, L2) 库斯托的冒险电影是高科技的，有很多奇幻装置，而培乐威只是在需要的时候把装置拼合在一起。

【派生】fancily *ad.* 爱幻想地，做作地

【搭配】take/catch someone's fancy 讨某人喜欢，迎合某人的口味

fate[3] [feɪt]

【释义】*n.* 命运，宿命(destiny, fortune)

【例句】Recall the fate of the Columbian white-tailed deer, now in a protected status. (TPO4, R, S1, T1) 回想一下哥伦比亚白尾鹿的命运，它们现在处于被保护的状态。

【搭配】a twist/quirk of fate 命运无常

fecundity[3] [fɪ'kʌndətɪ]

【释义】*n.* 1. 多产，富饶，肥沃 2. 繁殖力

【例句】To be a successful replicator, there are three key charateristics: longevity, fecundity and fidelity. (TPO5, L, S1, L1) 要成为一个成功的复制基因，需要具备三个重要的特征：寿命长，繁殖力强，精确度高。

federal[3] ['fedərəl]

【释义】*a.* 联邦(制)的，联邦政府的

【例句】The idea was that there be a federal subsidy…um…uh…financial assistance to artists and artistic or cultural institutions. (TPO4, L, S2, L2) 这一意见是设立联邦津贴，为艺术家及艺术文化机构提供财政支持。

file[3] [faɪl]

【释义】*v.* 1. 把…归档 *n.* 1. 档案(document) 2. 纵队，行列

【例句】Like my elder brothers have the kind of jobs they are talking about and typically you are just there to do basic tasks like typing or filing stuff, nothing very meaningful. (TPO9, S, Q3) 比如我哥就做过他们说的那些工作，基本上你就是在那儿做一些基本的工作，比如打字、将东西归档，不是很有意义。

【派生】filer *n.* 文件编档员

【搭配】file number 档案号

finance[3] [faɪ'næns]

【释义】*v.* 为…供给资金，资助(subsidize, fund) *n.* 财政，金融

【例句】This capital financed the production of goods, storage, trade, and even credit across Europe and overseas. (TPO10, R, S2, T2) 这些资本资助了商品的生产、存储、交易，甚至全欧洲乃至海外的贷款。

【派生】financial *a.* 财政的
financing *n.* 筹措资金

finite[3] ['faɪnaɪt]

【释义】*a.* 1. 有限的，有限度的 2. 〈语〉限定的

【例句】This unprecedented development of a finite groundwater resource with an almost negligible natural recharge rate—that is, virtually no natural water source to replenish the water supply— has caused water tables in the region to fall drastically. (TPO3, R, S1, T1) 考虑到几乎没有补充率(实质上没有自然水资源进行补充),这种有限的地下水资源的前所未有的发展已经造成了该地区地下水位的急剧下降。
【派生】finiteness *n.* 有限性

fireplace3 [ˈfaɪəpleɪs] 

【释义】*n.* 壁炉
【例句】If hundreds of people were living in the great houses, then there would have to be many fireplaces, where each family did its daily cooking, but there are very few fireplaces. (TPO5, W, Q1) 如果成百上千的人住在那些大房子里的话,那么那里就应该有很多壁炉,每个家庭每天都会用它来做饭,但是那里的壁炉却很少。

flavor3 [ˈfleɪvə]

【释义】*n.* 1. 味道,风味(taste) *v.* 1. 给…调味
【例句】Yeah, and I read a study that showed how light can give milk a funny flavor and decrease the nutritional value. (TPO9, L, S1, C1) 是的,并且我看了一个研究,说明光是如何给予牛奶一种奇怪的口味并减低它的营养价值的。
【派生】flavoring *n.* 调味品,调料

flee3 [fliː]

【释义】*v.* 逃走,逃跑;逃避
【例句】Their migration may have been set in motion by an increase in population caused by a movement of peoples fleeing the desiccation, or drying up, of the Sahara. (TPO7, R, S2, T2) 其迁徙可能是由逃离撒哈拉地区干旱气候的原住民人口激增导致的。
【搭配】flee from sb./sth. 逃离,逃避

forever3 [fəˈɛvə] 

【释义】*ad.* 永远地(always, eternally)
【例句】Fame does not last forever. (TPO2, L, S2, L1) 名声不能永恒。
【搭配】last forever 持续到永远

foster3 [ˈfɒstə] 

【释义】*v.* 1. 养育,培养(nurture, raise, cultivate) 2. 鼓励,促进(encourage, promote) *a.* (被)收养的
【例句】Music will foster a more relaxed atmosphere. (TPO8, S, Q3) 音乐可以营造一个更加轻松的氛围。

fungus3 [ˈfʌŋgəs] 

【释义】*n.* 真菌,霉菌
【例句】These are not single individual plants; each one is a symbiotic combination of an alga and a fungus. (TPO9, R, S2, T2) 它们不是单一的一种植物;每一个都是海藻和真菌的共生体。
【搭配】honey fungus 蜜环菌

furnace3 [ˈfɜːnɪs] 

【释义】*n.* 熔炉(oven, stove)
【例句】Unlike in the Americas, where metallurgy was a very late and limited development, Africans had iron from a relatively early date, developing ingenious furnaces to produce the high heat needed for production and to control the amount of air that reached the carbon and iron ore necessary for making iron. (TPO7, R, S2, T2) 美洲的冶金业起步晚,发展也极为缓慢,而与此不同的是,非洲在相对很早的时候就出现了铁,并发明了精妙的熔炉,来提供冶铁所需要的热量,并对冶铁过程中作用于碳和铁矿的空气量进行控制。

galley3 [ˈgælɪ] 

【释义】*n.* 1. 单层甲板大帆船,远洋轮船 2. (船或飞机上的)厨房
【例句】The principal seagoing ship used throughout the Middle Ages was the galley, a long, low ship fitted with sails but driven primarily by oars. (TPO17, R, S1, T1) 中世纪最为主要的海船是单层甲板帆船,其低矮狭长的船体装

返记菜单

fireplace3 flavor3 flee3 forever3 foster3
fungus3 furnace3 galley3

配着船帆，但主要还是靠船桨来操控。
【搭配】a galley in a ship 船上的厨房

glaze[3] [gleɪz]

【释义】v. 1. 装玻璃 2. 上釉，使光亮 n. 釉，釉料
【例句】As early as the fifteenth century B. C., high-temperature stonewares were being made with glazed surfaces. (TPO10, R, S1, T1) 早在公元前15世纪的时候，粗陶器会在高温下进行表面上釉。
【派生】glazed a. 上过釉的，表面光滑的
【搭配】glazed brick 釉面砖

glue[3] [gluː]

【释义】v. 胶合，粘合（paste）n. 胶，胶水
【例句】Finally, examination of the back of the painting reveals that it was painted on a panel made of several pieces of wood glued together. (TPO3, W, Q1) 最后，查看一下画作的背面，你会发现，这幅画是画在一块由胶水将几块木头粘合在一起而组成的木板上的。
【派生】gluey a. 胶的，粘着的

grand[3] [grænd]

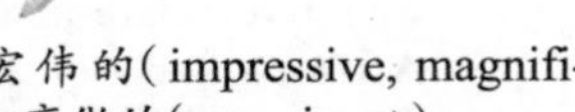

【释义】a. 1. 壮丽的，宏伟的（impressive, magnificent）2. 显赫的，高傲的（prominent）
【例句】It turns out that when the fur collar was added, the wood panel was also enlarged with extra wood pieces glued to the sides and the top to make the painting more grand and more valuable. (TPO3, W, Q1) 结果是，当（画中女人的衣服上）加上毛领时，木板也需要加大，并在木板的两面和顶部粘上额外的木片，以便使得画作更加宏大、更有价值。
【派生】grandeur n. 庄严，伟大
【搭配】a grand banquet 盛大的宴会

guild[3] [gɪld]

【释义】n. 行会，协会（union, institute）
【例句】They were usually members of the same guild and religious sect. (TPO16, R, S1, T1) 他们通常是同一行会或宗教的成员。

hollow[3] ['hɒləʊ]

【释义】n. 洞，坑，凹地，山谷 a. 1. 空的，空心的（empty, vacant）2. 空洞的（void, vain）v. 挖洞，挖坑
【例句】So, during the second rainy period, the dunes were kind of chopped up at the top, full of hollows and ridges, and these hollows would've captured the rain right there on the top. (TPO9, L, S2, L1) 因此，在第二个雨季的时候，沙丘的顶部已被风侵蚀，布满了洞穴和脊状突起，而沙丘顶部的这些洞穴会将雨水截住。
【派生】hollowly ad. 凹陷地；不诚实地
【搭配】beat someone hollow 完全击败某人

horizon[3] [hə'raɪzn]

【释义】n. 1. 地平线 2. 眼界，视野
【例句】Small boats moved more quickly across the foreground than larger ones did that were closer to the horizon. (TPO 9, L, S1, L1) 小船比靠近地平线的大船更快地划过前景。
【派生】horizontal a. 与地平线平行的，水平的
【搭配】on the horizon 即将来临，开始显现

immaturity[3] [imə'tjuəriti]

【释义】n. 不成熟
【例句】Rational appeals in advertising are certainly limited by children's emotional immaturity and the indirect nature of their associations. (TPO14, R, S1, T1) 广告中理性的吸引力必定因为儿童感情的不成熟和联想的间接性而受到限制。
【反义】maturity
【逆构】immature a. 不成熟的

immobile[3] [ɪ'məʊbaɪl]

【释义】a. 不动的，不变的，静止的
【例句】Water does not remain immobile in an aquifer but can seep out as springs or leak into other aquifers. (TPO12, R, S2, T2) 蓄水层中的水并不是静止不动的，而是能够以泉水的形式渗出，或是渗透到其它蓄水层中去。
【反义】mobile
【派生】immobility n. 不动，固定

【逆构】mobile *a.* 移动的，易变的

inaccessible[3] [ˌɪnæk'sesəbl] 

【释义】*a.* 达不到的，不可及的（unreachable, unapproachable）

【例句】What inspired the Paleolithic artists to make such beautiful art in such inaccessible places? (TPO3, L, S2, L1) 是什么启发了旧石器时代的艺术家们，使他们能在如此密不透光的地方创造出如此精美的艺术品？

【反义】accessible

【派生】inaccessibility *n.* 不易接近，难达到

【逆构】access *n.* 入口，进口

inadvertently[3] [ˌɪnəd'vɜːtəntlɪ] 

【释义】*ad.* 无意地，不经意地

【例句】Commensal associations sometimes involve one species' obtaining food that is inadvertently exposed by another. (TPO17, R, S2, T2) 共生关系有时候表现为这样一种方式，即：一个物种寻觅食物会经由另外一个物种不经意地暴露出来。

【逆构】inadvertent *a.* 粗心大意的，疏忽的

inconclusive[3] [ˌɪnkən'kluːsɪv] 

【释义】*a.* 非决定性的，不确定的，无说服力的

【例句】When researchers fail to make generalizations from their studies, their observed data is often inconclusive. (TPO13, R, S2, T2) 当研究人员不能从研究中做出归纳时，他们的观察数据常常是非决定性的。

【反义】conclusive

【派生】inconclusiveness *n.* 不确定

inefficient[3] [ˌɪnɪ'fɪʃənt] 

【释义】*a.* 效率低的，无效的，不称职的（incompetent, inexpert）

【例句】He thereby transformed an inefficient pump of limited use into a steam engine of a thousand uses. (TPO6, R, S1, T1) 这样，他就把原本效率低下、使用范围有限的活塞式结构转变成了得到广泛应用的蒸汽机。

【反义】efficient

【派生】inefficiency *n.* 效率低下
inefficiently *ad.* 低效率地

inevitable[3] [ɪn'evɪtəbl] 

【释义】*a.* 不可避免的，必然（发生）的（certain, sure, unavoidable）

【例句】These include the desire to be liked, fear of losing a job, or even not wanting to be the one employee delaying a decision that seems inevitable. (TPO1, S, Q4) 这其中的原因包括：想要讨人欢心，害怕丢掉工作，甚至是不想成为那个拖延一个似乎已成必然的决定的人。

【反义】avoidable

inhospitable[3] [ɪn'hɒspɪtəbl] 

【释义】*a.* 1. 不适于居住的 2. 不好客的，不友好的（ungracious, unfriendly）

【例句】This is the time period in which most scientists formerly believed the area to be inhospitable for humans. (TPO9, R, S1, T1) 在这一时期，大部分科学家此前都认为该地区不适合人类居住。

【反义】hospitable

【派生】inhospitality *n.* 冷淡，冷漠，不和气

【搭配】inhospitable desert areas 荒漠地带

instinct[3] ['ɪnstɪŋkt] 

【释义】*n.* 本能，直觉，天性（intuition, nature）

【例句】But neither the human imitative instinct nor a penchant for fantasy by itself leads to an autonomous theater. (TPO1, R, S2, T1) 但是，人类的模仿本能或对幻想的嗜好本身都不能使戏剧发展成为一门独立的艺术形式。

【派生】instinctive *a.* 本能的，直觉的，天生的

【搭配】instinct for 有…的天赋

instruction[3] [ɪn'strʌkʃən] 

【释义】*n.* 1. 指令，说明（command, direction）2. 教学，教诲（teaching）

【例句】An employee in the department did not follow instructions. (TPO5, L, S2, C1) 这个部门的一个职员没有按照指示去做。

【派生】instructional *n.* 指导的；教育的

【搭配】instruction after class 课外指导

返记菜单

inaccessible[3]	inadvertently[3]	inconclusive[3]	inefficient[3]	inevitable[3]
inhospitable[3]	instinct[3]	instruction[3]		

insufficient[3] [ˌɪnsəˈfɪʃənt]

【释义】a. 不足的(deficient, inadequate)

【例句】Although initially appealing, the hypothesis of a simple climatic change related to sea levels is insufficient to explain all the data. (TPO8, R, S2, T1) 虽然最初听起来很有吸引力,但一个简单的与海平面相关的气候变化的假设并不足以解释所有的数据。

【反义】sufficient

integral[3] [ˈɪntɪgrəl]

【释义】a. 构成整体所必需的(essential);整体的(complete, full)

【例句】Materials and methods of construction are integral parts of the design of architectural structures. (TPO3, R, S1, T1) 材料和建筑方法是建筑结构设计中不可或缺的组成部分。

【派生】integration n. 综合,整体
integrity n. 完整;正直,诚实

interplay[3] [ˈɪntə(:)ˈpleɪ]

【释义】n. 相互影响

【例句】Its development illustrates the essential interplay between observation, prediction, and testing required for scientific progress. (TPO16, R, S2, T1) 它的发展阐述了科学进步所需要的观察、预测和检验三者之间的基本的相互影响。

invade[3] [ɪnˈveɪd]

【释义】v. 侵犯,侵入,侵略(intrude)

【例句】An abandoned field, for instance, will be invaded successively by herbaceous plants (plants with little or no woody tissue), shrubs, and trees, eventually becoming a forest. (TPO19, R, S2, T1) 一块儿废弃的土地,在相继被草本植物(有极少或者没有木质组织的植物)、灌木、树木入侵之后,会变为一片森林。

【派生】invader n. 侵略者
invasion n. 入侵

ion[3] [ˈaɪən]

【释义】n.〈物〉离子

【例句】Quartz is quartz—a silicon ion surrounded by four oxygen ions—there's no difference at all between two-million-year-old Pleistocene quartz and Cambrian quartz created over 500 million years ago. (TPO6, R, S2, T1) 石英是一种由四个氧离子包围一个硅离子的化合物。两百万年前的更新世石英和五亿年前形成的寒武纪石英并无差别。

【搭配】ion pair 离子对

irrational[3] [ɪˈræʃənəl]

【释义】a. 无理性的,不合理的

【例句】One process by which groups may make bad or irrational decisions is known as groupthink. (TPO1, S, Q4) 某些集体可能会做出错误的或不理智的决定,这一过程被成为集体审议。

【派生】irratioanality n. 不合理,无理性
irrationalize v. 使不合理

【逆构】rational a. 理性的,理智的

【搭配】irrational fear 非理性恐惧(症)

isotope[3] [ˈaɪsəˌtəup]

【释义】n. 同位素

【例句】Such anomalies are due to the relative abundance of the "isotopes" or varieties of each element. (TPO16, R, S2, T1) 这种异常的产生是由于"同位素"的相对丰盛度或每种元素的多样性。

【搭配】radioactive isotope 放射性同位素

jewelry[3] [ˈdʒuːəlrɪ]

【释义】(同 jewellery) n. 珠宝,珠宝类

【例句】Such rules limit variations in accumulated material goods between pastoralist households (though they may also encourage a taste for portable goods of high value such as silks or jewelry). (TPO14, R, S2, T2) 这些规则限制了牧民家庭之间积聚的货物的变更(尽管他们也支持对丝绸或珠宝等价值高昂的轻便商品的追求)。

【派生】jeweler n. 珠宝商,钟表商

返记菜单

insufficient[3] integral[3] interplay[3] invade[3] ion[3]
irrational[3] isotope[3] jewelry[3]

【搭配】costume jewelry（用作服饰的）人造珠宝

kneel[3] [niːl]

【释义】*v.* 跪

【例句】The majority of three-dimensional representations, whether standing, seated, or kneeling, exhibit what is called frontality: they face straight ahead, neither twisting nor turning. (TPO11, R, S1, T1) 大多数这样的三维雕像，不论是站着的、坐着的或跪着的，都展现了什么叫正面描绘：他们都面朝前方，既不扭曲也不扭转。

【搭配】kneel down 下跪，跪倒

lava[3] ['lɑːvə]

【释义】*n.* 熔岩

【例句】A volcano emits smoke, lava and ashes. (TPO1, R, S2, T2) 火山在喷发时会释放出烟雾、熔岩和火山灰。

limb[3] [lɪm]

【释义】*n.* 1. 肢；臂；腿；翼；翅膀（arm, leg）2. 大树枝（branch）

【例句】However, unlike the cases of sea otters and pinnipeds (seals, sea lions, and walruses, whose limbs are functional both on land and at sea) , it is not easy to envision what the first whales looked like. (TPO2, R, S2, T1) 然而，想知道世上第一只鲸长什么样并非易事，不像还原海獭及鳍足类动物（四肢水陆两用，如海豹、海狮、海象）的原貌那么简单。

【搭配】out on a limb 处于危险境地，处于孤立无援状态

literally[3] ['lɪtərəlɪ]

【释义】*ad.* 1. 确实地，真正地（actually, exactly）2. 逐字地，照字面意义地

【例句】In other words, tulips were literally worth their weight in gold. (TPO6, L, S1, L1) 换句话说，郁金香和黄金一样按重量称值。

【派生】literal *a.* 照字面的，原义的

【搭配】translate literally 照字面翻译，直译

livable[3] ['lɪvəbl]

【释义】*a.* 适于居住的，（人）可相处的

【例句】These animals are at the mercy of the climate to maintain a livable body temperature. (TPO8, R, S2, T1) 这些动物依靠气候来保持适宜生存的体温。

【逆构】live *v.* 居住

loaf[3] [ləʊf]

【释义】*v.* 1. 游手好闲，虚掷光阴 *n.*（一条）面包，块

【例句】While it is not a deliberate behavior, the consequence of social loafing is less personal efficiency when working in groups than when working on one's own. (TPO16, S, Q4) 尽管它不是一种蓄意的行为，但社会惰化还是会导致个人在小组工作时，相对于单独工作而言，更为低下的效率。

【搭配】use one's loaf［俚］动脑筋想想
on the loaf 闲荡，混日子

long-standing[3] ['lɔːŋ'stændɪŋ]

【释义】*a.* 长久的，经久不衰的

【例句】They solve a long-standing mystery involving fossil evidence. (TPO10, L, S1, L1) 他们解决了一个长久以来的涉及化石证据的谜团。

loop[3] [luːp]

【释义】*n.* 圈，环，环状物 *v.* 把…圈成环；缠绕（circle, ring）

【例句】It's a circle, a loop. (TPO 9, L, S1, L2) 这是一个循环，一个圈。

【搭配】in the loop 在消息圈内，在决策圈内

lyric[3] ['lɪrɪk]

【释义】*n.* 抒情诗；歌词

【例句】Someone might walk out on the stage and say: "lyric quotation" . (TPO7, L, S1, L1) 有些演员会走上舞台，说那些抒情的台词。

【派生】lyricist *n.* 抒情诗人
lyrically *ad.* 抒情地

返记菜单

kneel[3]	lava[3]	limb[3]	literally[3]	livable[3]
loaf[3]	long-standing[3]	loop[3]	lyric[3]	

Word List 30

margarine[3] [mɑːdʒə'riːn]

【释义】*n.* 人造黄油

【例句】And an increase in the price of one means an increase in the demand for the other, like butter and margarine. (TPO12, S, Q6) 一种商品价格的上涨意味着另一种商品需求的增长，比如黄油和人造奶油。

marshy[3] ['mɑːʃɪ]

【释义】*a.* 沼泽般的，湿软的(swampy, muddy)

【例句】Wetlands are areas of marshy, swampy land, areas where water covers the soil, or is present either at or near the surface of the soil for large part of the year. (TPO11, L, S2, L1) 湿地是多沼泽、湿软的地带，在一年中的大部分时候，这些地区要么被水淹没，要么是水位处于或接近地表面。

【逆构】marsh *n.* 湿地，沼泽

masterpiece[3] ['mɑːstəpiːs]

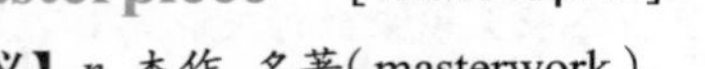

【释义】*n.* 杰作，名著(masterwork)

【例句】They are masterpieces. (TPO3, L, S2, L1) 它们是杰作。

【搭配】an exquisite masterpiece 精美的杰作

measurement[3] ['meʒəmənt]

【释义】*n.* 1. 测量，衡量 2. (量得的)尺寸

【例句】Instrumental records do not go back far enough to provide us with reliable measurements of global climatic variability on timescales longer than a century. (TPO10, R, S2, T1) 仪器记录不能追溯到那么久远，因而无法给我们提供长达百年之久的全球气候变化的可靠测量记录。

【搭配】measurement system 测量系统

medical[3] ['medɪkəl]

【释义】*a.* 医学的，医疗的，医术的

【例句】Adding new workers means putting much more money into providing training and medical benefits. (TPO1, W, Q1) 增加新员工意味着要把更多的钱投入到培训和医疗福利上。

【派生】medically *ad.* 医学上地；医药上地

【逆构】medicine *n.* 医学，药品

mercantile[3] ['mɜːkəntaɪl]

【释义】*a.* 商业的，贸易的(commercial)

【例句】The mercantile economy was also characterized by a peculiar moral stance. (TPO16, R, S1, T1) 有独特的道德立场也是商业经济的特点之一。

【搭配】mercantile system 重商主义

metabolism[3] [me'tæbəlɪzəm]

【释义】*n.* 新陈代谢

【例句】Leatherbacks apparently do not generate internal heat the way we do, or the way birds do, as a by-product of cellular metabolism. (TPO15, R, S2, T1) 棱皮龟产生内部热量的方式显然与我们或者鸟类产生内部热量的方式不一样，我们或者鸟类产生的热量是细胞新陈代谢的副产品。

micro[3] ['maɪkrəʊ]

【释义】*a.* 微小的 *pref.* 小的，微的

【例句】Some soils are notoriously deficient in micro nutrients and are therefore unable to support most plant life. (TPO5, R, S1, T1) 有些土壤极其缺乏微量元素，因而，无法为植物生长提供营养。

【反义】macro

microorganism[3] [maɪkrəʊ'ɔːgənɪz(ə)m]

【释义】*n.* 微生物

【例句】It turns out that certain microorganisms are chemosynthetic—they don't need sunlight because they take their energy from chemical reactions. (TPO15, L, S2, L2) 结果表明，某些微生物是化学合成的——它们不需要阳光，因为它们是从化学反应中获取能量的。

microscope[3] ['maɪkrəskəʊp] 

【释义】*n.* 显微镜

【例句】Well, we put an infrared microscope—a spectroscope—on tiny bits of paint. (TPO5, L, S2, L1) 我们把一些颜料的微粒放在一台红外显微镜——一台分光镜下。

【搭配】electron microscope 电子显微镜

miniature[3] ['mɪnjətʃə]

【释义】*a.* 小型的，小规模的(small, tiny) *n.* 缩图，缩影，小模型

【例句】The onrushing water arising from these flash floods likely also formed the odd teardrop-shaped "islands" (resembling the miniature versions seen in the wet sand of our beaches at low tide) that have been found on the plains close to the ends of the outflow channels. (TPO8, R, S2, T2) 这突如其来的洪水产生的急流可能也形成了这种奇特的泪滴形状的"岛屿"(类似于我们在落潮的沙滩湿地上看到的微型版本)，这些"岛屿"已经在靠近泄水渠末端的平原上被发现了。

【反义】large

【搭配】in miniature 小规模，小型

mist[3] [mɪst] 

【释义】*v.* (使)蒙上薄雾，(使)模糊 *n.* 薄雾

【例句】Plants are suspended and the roots misted with a nutrient solution. (TPO5, R, S1, T1) 植物被悬挂着，根部喷洒着营养液。

【派生】misty *a.* 有薄雾的，朦胧的

moor[3] [mʊə] 

【释义】*v.* 停泊，系泊(船只)(anchor, dock, tie) *n.* 荒野，旷野

【例句】In fact, by the early 1940's, even though steel cables were available, most ships in the United States Navy were not moored with steel cables; they were moored with Manila hemp ropes. (TPO2, L, S1, L2) 事实上，在20世纪40年代早期，即使那时候已经有了钢丝绳，但是美国海军的大部分船只都不是用钢丝绳来停泊的，而是使用马尼拉麻绳。

【派生】mooring *n.* 停泊区；系泊设备

mouse[3] [maʊs] 

【释义】*n.* 1. 老鼠 2. 鼠标

【例句】Hawks have such good eyesight that they can spot a tiny mouse in the field from high up in the air. (TPO15, S, Q6) 鹰的视力非常好，它们能够从高空中看见田地里的一只小老鼠。

【搭配】mouse trap 捕鼠器；鼠笼式打捞器

mule[3] [mjuːl] 

【释义】*n.* 骡子

【例句】The black-tailed deer, a lowland, west-side cousin of the mule deer of eastern Washington, is now the most common. (TPO4, R, S1, T1) 目前最常见的一种鹿是华盛顿西部低地的黑尾鹿，是东华盛顿长耳鹿的表亲。

mutual[3] ['mjuːtjʊəl] 

【释义】*a.* 1. 相互的，彼此的 2. 共同的，共有的

【例句】In the absence of solid linguistic, archaeological, and biological data, many fanciful and mutually exclusive theories were devised. (TPO5, R, S2, T1) 由于没有确凿的语言学、考古学和生物学数据，人们想出了很多充满幻想、互相矛盾的理论。

【派生】mutually *ad.* 相互地

【搭配】mutual benefit 互惠互利

necessitate[3] [nɪ'sesɪteɪt] 

【释义】*v.* 使…成为必要，需要(demand, need, require)

【例句】The thriving obsidian operation, for example, would necessitate more miners, additional manufacturers of obsidian tools, and additional traders to carry the goods to new markets. (TPO8, R, S1, T1) 例如，欣欣向荣的黑曜石生意将需要更多的矿工、额外的黑曜石工具制造商和其他商人来把这些货物带到新的市场。

【派生】necessity *n.* 必要性；必需品

negotiate[3] [nɪ'gəʊʃɪeɪt] 

【释义】*v.* 谈判，协商，交涉(discuss, mediate)

【例句】The continued proliferation of banks made

返记菜单

microscope[3]	miniature[3]	mist[3]	moor[3]	mouse[3]
mule[3]	mutual[3]	necessitate[3]	negotiate[3]	

it easier for those without cash to negotiate loans in paper money. (TPO20, R, S1, T1) 银行的不断发展使得那些没有现金的人贷款变得容易了。

【派生】 negotiation *n.* 谈判,洽谈

【搭配】 negotiate about 就…进行协商

nonverbal[3] ['nɒn'vɜːbəl]

【释义】 *a.* 非言语的,不用语言的

【例句】 When we speak with other people face-to-face the nonverbal signals we give—our facial expressions, hand gestures, body movements, and tone of voice—often communicate as much as, or more than, the words we utter. (TPO4, S, Q4) 当我们和人面对面交流时,我们所使用的非语言信号——面部表情、手势、肢体动作和声调——所传达的信息通常跟我们说的话一样多,甚至更多。

【搭配】 nonverbal communication 非言语交际;非语言沟通

notorious[3] [nəʊ'tɔːrɪəs]

【释义】 *a.* 恶名昭彰的,声名狼藉的(infamous)

【例句】 Some soils are notoriously deficient in micro nutrients and are therefore unable to support most plant life. (TPO5, R, S1, T1) 有些土壤极其缺乏微量元素,因而,无法为植物生长提供营养。

offset[3] ['ɔːfset]

【释义】 *v.* 1. 抵消,补偿(compensate, counteract) 2. 平版印刷

【例句】 Advertisers sometimes offset or counterbalance an exaggerated claim with a disclaimer—a qualification or condition on the claim. (TPO14, R, S1, T1) 广告商有时会通过免责声明——对于广告所声称内容的一种限制和条件,来抵消和平衡夸张的广告词。

【搭配】 offset printing 胶印,平版印刷

opposing[3] [ə'pəʊzɪŋ]

【释义】 *a.* 相反的,对立的,反作用的(contradictory, conflicting)

【例句】 The opposing points of view about bird migration are clarified through the study of contrasting experiments. (TPO11, R, S2, T1) 通过对比实验研究,关于鸟类迁徙的对立观点得以阐明。

【逆构】 oppose *v.* 反对

【派生】 opposed *a.* 反对的,相对的
opposition *n.* 反对,敌对

optimistic[3] [ˌɒptɪ'mɪstɪk]

【释义】 *a.* 乐观的,乐观主义的(hopeful, positive)

【例句】 He is optimistic that he will learn to appreciate the play he is researching. (TPO4, L, S1, C1) 他乐观地认为他能够欣赏自己正在研究的话剧。

【逆构】 optimist *n.* 乐观主义者

orchestra[3] ['ɔːkɪstrə]

【释义】 *n.* 管弦乐队

【例句】 At home I was the youngest member of our community orchestra. (TPO5, L, S1, C1) 我是我们社区管弦乐队里最年轻的成员。

【派生】 orchestrator *n.* 管弦乐演奏家
orchestral *a.* 管弦乐的,管弦乐队的

【搭配】 orchestra box 乐池

ornament[3] ['ɔːnəmənt]

【释义】 *n.* 装饰,装饰物(adornment, decoration) *v.* 装饰

【例句】 It embraces the old custom of earthenware burial ceramics with later religious images and architectural ornament. (TPO10, R, S1, T1) 它将土质陪葬陶器的古老传统与后来的宗教图案和建筑装饰进行了融合。

【派生】 ornamentation *n.* 装饰,装饰品
ornamental *a.* 装饰的

outcome[3] ['aʊtkʌm]

【释义】 *n.* 结果,后果(result, effect)

【例句】 The experimenter effect occurs when a researcher's expectations affect the outcome of the experiment. (TPO15, S, Q4) 当实验者的预期影响到实验的结果时,实验者效应就出现了。

oval[3] ['əʊvəl]

【释义】*a.* 卵形的，椭圆的(elliptic)

【例句】The circle is now stretched out, flattened into an oval. (TPO13, S, Q4) 圆现在变长变扁了，形成了一个卵形。

【搭配】an oval-shaped face 鸭蛋脸

overlie[3] [ˌəʊvə'laɪ]

【释义】*v.* 躺在…的上面

【例句】Later, under the weight of overlying sediments, this salt flowed plastically upward to form salt domes. (TPO7, R, S1, T1) 之后，在上层沉积物的压力下，这些盐被迫向上塑性流动，形成盐丘。

【派生】overlying *a.* 躺在上面的，叠加的

overly[3] ['əʊvəlɪ]

【释义】*ad.* 过度地，极度地

【例句】Many signals that animals make seem to impose on the signaler's costs that are overly damaging. (TPO11, R, S2, T2) 动物发出的许多信号似乎给它们带来了毁灭性的损害。

pale[3] [peɪl]

【释义】*v.* (使)变得苍白，变得暗淡，相形见绌 *a.* 苍白的；暗淡的；微弱的

【例句】The destruction caused by the volcanic explosion of Mount St Helens, in the northwestern United States, for example, pales in comparison to the destruction caused by humans. (TPO3, R, S1, T2) 比如，美国西北部圣海伦火山的喷发所造成的破坏与人类活动所造成的破坏相比也是相形见绌的。

【派生】paleness *n.* 苍白，暗淡

【搭配】pale yellow 浅黄

pan[3] [pæn]

【释义】*n.* 1. (不透水的)硬土层 2. 平底锅，盘子 *v.* 1. 严厉批评(戏剧、电影等) 2. (用淘盘)淘金

【例句】And wherever these particles settled, they formed a pan, a layer that water couldn't penetrate. (TPO9, L, S2, L1) 这些颗粒在哪里沉淀下来，哪里就会形成一个水都难以渗入的硬土层。

【派生】panful *n.* 一满锅

【搭配】go down the pan 毫无用处
pan out 结果好，成功

papilla[3] [pə'pɪlə]

【释义】*n.* 乳突，乳头状突起

【例句】The projections are called papillae. (TPO17, L, S2, L2) 这种凸起叫做乳突。

patron[3] ['peɪtrən]

【释义】*n.* 1. 赞助人，资助人(benefactor) 2. 老主顾，顾客(customer, client)

【例句】They were employed in the services of a specific patron. (TPO16, L, S1, L2) 他们为一个特定的赞助人工作。

【派生】patronizing *a.* 摆出恩惠态度的，要人领情的
patronage *n.* 赞助；惠顾

peach[3] [piːtʃ]

【释义】*n.* 1. 桃子，桃树，桃红色 2. 受欢迎的人或物

【例句】Some are soft and tempting, like a peach or a cherry. (TPO9, R, S2, T2) 有一些则很软，很诱人，比如桃子或樱桃。

peculiar[3] [pɪ'kjuːljə]

【释义】*a.* 1. 特有的，独有的(special, distinctive) 2. 奇怪的，异常的(odd, strange, unusual)

【例句】Like the stones of a Roman wall which were held together both by the regularity of the design and by that peculiarly powerful Roman cement, so the various parts of the Roman realm were bonded into a massive, monolithic entity by physical, organizational, and psychological controls. (TPO7, R, S2, T1) 如同罗马墙是通过规律的设计和独特有效的罗马水泥构筑而成一样，罗马王国的各个部分也是通过对物质、组织和心理层面的支配而联结成一个规模宏大、坚如磐石的统一体的。

【反义】common

【派生】peculiarity *n.* 特性，怪癖

peninsula[3] [pɪ'nɪnsjʊlə]

【释义】*n.* 半岛

返记菜单

oval[3]	overlie[3]	overly[3]	pale[3]	pan[3]
papilla[3]	patron[3]	peach[3]	peculiar[3]	peninsula[3]

【例句】For those of you who don't know the northeast coastal region, Cape Cod is a peninsula, a narrow strip of land that jets out into the Atlantic, and so many houses in this particular style were built on Cape Cod, that the name of the place became the name of the style. (TPO11, L, S1, L2) 对于你们这些不了解东北部海岸地区的人来说,科德角是一个半岛,一块突入到大西洋中的狭长陆地,科德角上建有许多风格独特的房子,而这种风格的房子也是以该地命名的。

perfume[3] ['pɜːfjuːm] 

【释义】*n.* 1 香水；香味 *v.* 使充满香气；喷香水于…

【例句】Spices not only dramatically improved the taste of the European diet but also were used to manufacture perfumes and certain medicines. (TPO17, R, S1, T1) 香料不仅显著提高了欧洲菜肴的口感,而且也被应用于生产香水和一些特定的药品。

【搭配】natural perfume 天然香料

perish[3] ['perɪʃ] 

【释义】*v.* 丧生；毁灭,消亡；腐烂(die, decease, decay)

【例句】The Permian event has attracted much less attention than other mass extinctions because mostly unfamiliar species perished at that time. (TPO15, R, S2, T2) 由于当时灭绝的物种大部分是人们不熟悉的,所以人们对二叠纪时期的这次物种灭绝所给予的关注远远不如其它几次大规模物种灭绝。

【反义】survive

【派生】perishable *a.* 易腐坏的；易毁灭的

【搭配】perish the thought 打消念头

permeable[3] ['pɜːmɪəbl]

【释义】*a.* 可渗透的,可穿透的

【例句】Increases in average winter temperatures have made permafrost permeable to water. (TPO9, L, S1, L2) 冬天平均气温的升高使水可以渗进永久冻土层。

【逆构】permeate *v.* 渗透；弥漫

perplex[3] [pə'pleks] 

【释义】*v.*(使)困惑,(使)糊涂,(使)复杂化(bewilder, puzzle, baffle, confuse)

【例句】The question perplexed people for years, until, in the 1950s, a German scientist named Gustave Kramer provided some answers and, in the process, raised new questions. (TPO11, R, S2, T1) 这个问题困扰了人们很多年,直到20世纪50年代,一位名叫Gustave Kramer的德国科学家才提供了一些答案,而在此过程中,又出现了新的问题。

【派生】perplexed *a.* 困惑的,不知所措的
perplexity *n.* 困惑,混乱
perplexing *a.* 令人费解的

pile[3] [paɪl] 

【释义】*v.* 堆起,堆叠 *v.* 蜂拥,拥,挤 *n.* 1. 一堆,一叠 2. 大厦,建筑群

【例句】In the past, whole cities grew from the arduous task of cutting and piling stone upon stone. (TPO3, R, S1, T1) 在过去,整个城市的建筑物都是辛辛苦苦地由一块块石头经过切割和堆砌而建成的。

【派生】piling *n.* 打桩工程

【搭配】make a/one'spile 赚钱,发财

platform[3] ['plætfɔːm] 

【释义】*n.* 1. 平台 2. 论坛,讲台 3. 月台,站台 4. 纲领

【例句】Offshore platforms may also lose oil, creating oil slicks that drift ashore and foul the beaches, harming the environment. (TPO4, R, S2, T2) 海上钻井平台也会漏油,从而导致浮油漂向海岸,污染海滩,破坏环境。

【搭配】service platform 工作台,操作平台

platinum[3] ['plætɪnəm] 

【释义】*n.* 铂；白金

【例句】Without the platinum components in the engine, the hydrogen doesn't undergo the chemical reaction that produces the electricity to power the automobile. (TPO9, W, Q1) 如果发动机的内部不是白金构造,那么氢将

不会发生化学反应，从而无法产生电力来发动汽车。
【搭配】go platinum（唱片等）达到白金销量

pole[3] [pəul] 

【释义】*n.* 1. 柱，杆 2. 地极 3. 磁极，电极
【例句】Any water molecules that found their way to the floors of craters near the moon's poles, the water would be perpetually frozen, because the floors of those craters are always in shadow. (TPO5, L, S1, L2) 任何落在靠近月球极地的火山底的水分子都将永远冻结，因为那些火山的底部永远处于阴影之中。
【派生】polestar *n.* 北极星；指导原则
ploeward *a.* 向极的；向南极的

pollinate[3] ['pɒlɪneɪt] 

【释义】*v.* 给…传授花粉
【例句】There are some flowers that can only be pollinated by the humming birds. (TPO3, L, S1, L1) 有一些花只能靠蜂鸟来为之授粉。
【派生】pollination *n.* 授粉

pop[3] [pɒp]

【释义】*v.* 1. 突然出现 2. 发出砰的响声 3. 开枪 4. 爆裂 *n.* 1. 流行音乐 2. 砰的一声 *ad.* 1. 突然地 2. 砰一声地 *a.* 流行的，通俗的
【例句】But its back wings, which are usually closed and hidden, have these bright colorful spots on them and when the peanut bug's attacked, it suddenly opens its back wings and out pop these big bright colors. (TPO8, S, Q4) 但其翅膀通常是闭合的、隐藏的，上面还有明亮的斑点。当提灯虫遭受攻击时，它会突然打开翅膀，亮出这些大的鲜艳的色彩。
【搭配】pop off [informal] 突然离开；突然死亡

practitioner[3] [præk'tɪʃənə] 

【释义】*n.* 从业者，执业者，实践者
【例句】They have often failed in their attempts to become reflective practitioners. (TPO9, R, S2, T1) 他们成为反思实践者的尝试经常以失败告终。
【搭配】a general practitioner 全科医生

precede[3] [prɪ(:)'siːd]

【释义】*v.* 在…之前，先于（come before, antecede）
【例句】Extreme changes in daily and seasonal climates preceded the retreat of the seas back into the major ocean basins. (TPO8, R, S2, T1) 日常及季节性气候的剧烈变化是在海洋退回到主要的海洋盆地之前发生的。
【派生】precedent *n.* 先例，前例

predatory[3] ['predətərɪ] 

【释义】*a.* 1. 食肉的 2. 掠夺性的
【例句】As an example, plants make chemicals toxic to fungal and bacterial parasites, along with ones toxic to predatory animals (sometimes they are the same chemicals). (TPO17, R, S2, T2) 比如说，植物可以产生某些对真菌和细菌类寄生物有害的化学毒剂以及一些对食肉动物有害的化学毒剂（有时候是同一种化学物）。
【逆构】predator *n.* 食肉动物，捕食者
【搭配】a predatory war 掠夺性战争

premiere[3] ['premieə] 

【释义】*n.*（电影、戏剧的）首次公演，首映
【例句】In Berlin, for the premiere performance of *The Battleship Potemkin*, film director Sergei Eisenstein worked with Austrian composer Edmund Meisel on a musical score matching sound to image. (TPO12, R, S2, T1) 在柏林，为了电影《战舰波将金号》的首映，导演谢尔盖·爱森斯坦与奥地利作曲家埃德蒙·梅赛奥合作创作与电影相匹配的音效。

prevailing[3] [prɪ'veɪlɪŋ]

【释义】*a.* 普遍的，盛行的，流行的（dominant, fashionable, widespread）
【例句】The prevailing winds became stronger. (TPO6, L, S2, L2) 盛行风刮得更厉害了。
【逆构】prevail *v.* 流行，盛行，占主导地位
【搭配】a prevailing practice 流行惯例

probability[3] [ˌprɒbə'bɪlɪtɪ] 

【释义】*n.* 可能性，几率

返记菜单

pole[3] pollinate[3] pop[3] practitioner[3] precede[3]
predatory[3] premiere[3] prevailing[3] probability[3]

【例句】And third, the probability that we will develop primary group bonds increases as we have frequent and continuous contact. (TPO13, R, S1, T1) 第三，如果我们保持频繁不断的联系，那么发展主要群体的联系的可能性就会增加。
【搭配】in all probability 极有可能

procedure[3] [prə'siːdʒə]

【释义】n. 程序，步骤，手续(course, process)
【例句】The man is not familiar with the procedures used at the language lab. (TPO13, L, S2, C1) 这个人对语音室的使用程序不太熟悉。

prolong[3] [prə'lɒŋ]

【释义】v. 拖长，延长(extend, lengthen)
【例句】Remarkably resistant to the vicissitudes of ocean travel, they can survive prolonged immersion in saltwater; when they come to rest on warm beaches and the conditions are favorable, the seed coats soften. (TPO9, R, S2, T2) 它们对洋流变动有着极强的抵抗力，因此可以在长时间的海水浸泡中存活下来。当它们停歇在温暖的海滩上且条件适宜时，种子的外皮就会变软。
【派生】prolonged a. 持续很多的，长期的
【搭配】prolong the agony 延长痛苦

prone[3] [prəʊn]

【释义】a. 有…倾向的，易于…的(likely, inclined)
【例句】They (valleys) are less prone to dry out. (TPO1, R, S1, T1) 它们(山谷)不易干涸。
【派生】proneness n. 倾向
【搭配】prone to 有…倾向的

propulsion[3] [prə'pʌlʃən]

【释义】n. 推进，推进力
【例句】The large hind legs were used for propulsion in water. (TPO2, R, S2, T1) 强大的后肢用来为水中前行提供推动力。
【派生】propulsive a. 推进的

prosperous[3] ['prɒspərəs]

【释义】a. 成功的，繁荣的，兴旺的(flourishing, thriving, successful)
【例句】Trade between the West and the settled and prosperous Chinese dynasties introduced new forms and different technologies. (TPO10, R, S1, T1) 西方国家和繁荣稳定的中国王朝之间的贸易带来了(瓷器制造方面的)新方法和新技术。
【反义】unprosperous
【逆构】prosper v. 繁荣，成功
【派生】prosperity n. 繁荣，兴旺
【搭配】thriving and prosperous 繁荣昌盛

pumpkin[3] ['pʌmpkɪn]

【释义】n. 南瓜，南瓜藤
【例句】The other painting I really want you to look at is of a young woman surrounded by pumpkins. (TPO1, L, S1, L1) 我特别想让你们看另外一幅画，画的是一个身边满是南瓜的年轻女人。
【搭配】pumpkin pie 南瓜派

pyramid[3] ['pɪrəmɪd]

【释义】n. 1. 金字塔 2. 三角锥(体) v. 成金字塔形状
【例句】When we think of large monumental structures built by early societies and Egyptian pyramid probably comes to mind. (TPO14, L, S2, L2) 当我们想到早期的社会所建造的大型纪念性建筑时，埃及金字塔就会出现在我们脑海中。
【搭配】pyramid selling scheme 层压式推销

qualified[3] ['kwɒlɪfaɪd]

【释义】a. 有资格的，合格的，胜任的(competent, certified, eligible)
【例句】Well, Bill, we have several qualified applicants for serious about and this part of this interview process we have to meet with the committee of the professors and students in our department. (TPO11, L, S2, C1) 比尔，我们有几个合格的申请人值得认真考虑，而这个面试流程的这部分必须要会见由学部的教授和学生组成的委员会。
【反义】disqualified
【派生】qualification n. 资格
【逆构】qualify v. (使)具有资格，(使)合格
【搭配】qualified for 有担任…的资格

Word List 31

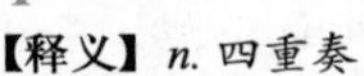

quartet[3] [kwɔːˈtet]

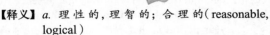

【释义】*n.* 四重奏
【例句】There is a string quartet on campus, all students. (TPO5, L, S1, C1) 学校将有一场弦乐四重奏,所有学生都可以去看。
【派生】quartette (=quarter) *n.* 四个一组; 四重奏, 四重唱

quit[3] [kwɪt]

【释义】*v.* 1. 离开,辞职 2. 停止,放弃(give up, abandon) 3. 离开某地(leave, depart)
【例句】I would have to quit my job in a couple of weeks 'cause it'll be just too much. (TPO2, L, S2, C1) 几周后我可能会辞职,因为要做的事情太多了。
【派生】quitter *n.* 轻易放弃的人
【搭配】quit doing sth. 放弃做某事

quiz[3] [kwɪz]

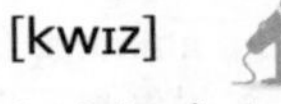

【释义】*n.* 小测验; 智力竞赛 *v.* 1. 盘问,询问 2. 测验
【例句】And, you know, not all of us did very well on your last quiz. (TPO6, S, Q5) 而且,您也知道,在上次的测试中并不是所有人都表现良好的。
【派生】quizzer *n.* 提问者; 测验节目

radical[3] [ˈrædɪkəl]

【释义】*a.* 1. 激进的(drastic, extreme) 2. 基本的,根本的 *n.* 激进分子
【例句】I'm sure you will be surprised that anyone ever found it radical. (TPO4, L, S1, C1) 我肯定你一定会惊讶于居然有人曾经认为它很偏激。
【派生】radicalism *n.* 激进主义
radically *ad.* 彻底地; 以激进的方式
radicalization *n.* 激进
radicalize *v.* 使…激进
【搭配】radical change 彻底的改变
radical errors 基本错误
a radical speech 激进的演讲

ranch[3] [ræntʃ]

【释义】*n.* 大农场,大牧场(farm) *v.* 经营牧场,在牧场工作
【例句】I bet it is the ranch-style house. (TPO11, L, S1, L2) 我打赌这是牧场式的房子。
【搭配】ranch house 低矮的平房
dude ranch 度假牧场; 观光牧场或农场

rank[3] [ræŋk]

【释义】*n.* 1. 等级,阶层 2. 排,列 *v.* 1. 排列 2. 分等级 *a.* 1. 繁茂的 2. 恶臭的,讨厌的
【例句】In these shops differences of rank were blurred as artisans and masters labored side by side in the same modest establishment. (TPO16, R, S1, T1) 在这些商店里,由于工匠和大师在同样适中的设施下肩并肩地工作,所以等级的区分是模糊的。
【搭配】first rank 一流的
in rank 成行列,成队列
rank first 名列第一

rational[3] [ˈræʃənl]

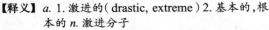

【释义】*a.* 理性的,理智的; 合理的(reasonable, logical)
【例句】Certainly, rational appeals in advertising aimed at children are limited, as most advertisements use emotional and indirect appeals to psychological states or associations. (TPO14, R, S1, T1) 当然,广告中针对儿童的理性吸引是有限的,因为大多数广告都会利用情感的和间接的吸引来影响儿童的心理状态和思想。
【派生】rationalize *v.* 使合理
【搭配】rational design 合理的设计
rational choice 理性选择,理性抉择

reasoning[3] [ˈriːzənɪŋ]

【释义】*n.* 推论,推理,论证(argument, inference)
【例句】So for example, reasoning is a cognitive process, so it's perception. (TPO14, L, S1, L1) 那么,举个例子,论证是一个认知过程,所以它是知觉。
【逆构】reason *v.* 推论,推理 *n.* 原因

返记菜单

quartet[3] quit[3] quiz[3] radical[3] ranch[3]
rank[3] rational[3] reasoning[3]

【搭配】 inductive reasoning 归纳推理,归纳法

recrystallize[3] [riː'kristəlaiz]

【释义】 v.(使)再结晶

【例句】 With further melting, refreezing, and increased weight from newer snowfall above, the snow reaches a granular recrystallized stage intermediate between flakes and ice known as firn. (TPO15, R, S1, T1) 随着进一步的融化、再结冰,以及承受着上方新的降雪的重量,这些积雪到了一种介于雪花和冰块之间颗粒再结晶阶段,这一阶段的雪被称为粒雪。

【逆构】 crystal n. 水晶;晶体
crystallize v. 结晶

redirect[3] ['riːdɪ'rekt]

【释义】 v. 改变方向,改变线路

【例句】 But that's called "redirecting". (TPO4, L, S1, L1) 但那被称为"改变方向"。

regarding[3] [rɪ'gɑːdɪŋ]

【释义】 prep. 关于,至于

【例句】 One interpretation regarding the absence of fossils during this important 100-million-year period is that early animals were soft bodied and simply did not fossilized. (TPO5, R, S2, T2) 对于在这重要的一亿年中却无化石这一现象的一种解释是,早期动物都是软体的,所以未能变成化石。

【逆构】 regard v. 尊敬;看待

rehearse[3] [rɪ'hɜːs]

【释义】 v. 1. 预演,排练(drill, exercise, practice) 2. 详述,复述

【例句】 We have less than a week left to rehearse for the concert. (TPO5, S, Q5) 我们只剩下不到一周的时间来为音乐会排练。

【派生】 rehearsal n. 排演,预演

reinforce[3] [ˌriːɪn'fɔːs]

【释义】 v. 加强,增强(strengthen, enhance, intensify)

【例句】 The supply of raw materials has been greatly reinforced. 原料的供应量已大大增加。

【反义】 weaken

【派生】 reinforcement n. 增援,加固

【搭配】 reinforce the management 加强管理

relic[3] ['relɪk]

【释义】 n. 遗迹,遗物

【例句】 Outflow channels are probably relics of catastrophic flooding on Mars long ago. (TPO8, R, S2, T2) 流出渠道可能是很久以前火星上发生的灾难性洪水的遗迹。

reluctant[3] [rɪ'lʌktənt]

【释义】 a. 不情愿的,勉强的(unwilling)

【例句】 Obviously, we are reluctant to do that in some cases. (TPO17, L, S1, L1) 很显然,有些情况下我们不愿那么做。

【反义】 willing

【派生】 reluctance n. 不愿,勉强

【搭配】 a reluctant answer 勉强的答复

remnant[3] ['remnənt]

【释义】 n. 残留部分(leftover, remains)

【例句】 Holocene sediments contain remnants of more recent plants and animals. (TPO15, L, S1, L2) 新世代的沉积物中含有更多近期动植物的遗骸。

renovate[3] ['renəuveɪt]

【释义】 v. 整修,修复,革新(renew, repair)

【例句】 In an effort to counteract the trend, the college has announced a plan to renovate its on-campus housing. (TPO11, S, Q3) 为了抵制这一倾向,校方宣布了一项整修校园内房屋的计划。

【派生】 renovation n. 修复,整修

reptilian[3] [rep'tɪlɪən]

【释义】 a. 1. 爬虫类的,爬行动物的 2. 卑下的

【例句】 When it comes to physiology the leatherback turtle is, in some ways, more like a reptilian whale than a turtle. (TPO15, R, S2, T1) 从生理学角度来说,棱皮龟在某些方面更像是一种爬行类的鲸鱼,而不是海龟。

reputation[3] [ˌrepju(ː)ˈteɪʃən]

【释义】*n.* 名声，名誉，名气（fame）

【例句】Thus ecologically-minded Americans are likely to react very favorably to wood products ecologically certified by an independent organization with an international reputation for trustworthiness. (TPO7, W, Q1) 因此，有生态学头脑的美国人很可能会对木质产品作出热切的回应，这些木质产品得到了一个因值得信赖而享有国际声誉的独立组织所做的生态学认证。

【搭配】a school with an excellent reputation 享有盛誉的学校

resemblance[3] [rɪˈzembləns]

【释义】*n.* 相似，形似（likeness, sameness）

【例句】Second, the portrait could very well be that of a relative of Austen's, a fact that would explain the resemblance between its subject and that of Cassandra's sketch. (TPO12, W, Q1) 其次，画像很可能画的是奥斯汀的一个亲戚，这个事实可以解释画中的人物和Cassandra的素描中的人物的相似性。

【逆构】resemble *v.* 像，类似于

reset[3] [ˈriːset] 

【释义】*v.* 重置，重放；清零

【例句】Even a fifteen-minute burst of light in otherwise sustained darkness can reset an animal's circadian rhythm. (TPO13, R, S2, T1) 在黑暗中，即使是15分钟的强光，也可以改变动物的生理节奏。

【派生】resettable *a.* 可重放的

reside[3] [rɪˈzaɪd]

【释义】*v.* 居住（live, dwell, inhabit）

【例句】They reside throughout the eastern region of North America where is a temperate climate, where the growing season lasts for at least five months of the year, which is when they do all their mating, playing and eating. (TPO1, L, S2, L2) 它们在北美洲东部的各处栖息，那里气候温和，生长期至少有五个月，在那期间，它们完成全部交配、嬉戏和觅食活动。

【派生】residence *n.* 居住；住宅，住处
resident *n.* 居民
residential *a.* 住宅的，与居住有关的
residency *n.* 住处；住院医生实习期

【搭配】resident population 常驻人口

resonate[3] [ˈrezəneɪt]

【释义】*v.* 产生回声、共鸣或共振

【例句】Or it is the physics might put it, each bottle resonates at a particular frequency. (TPO14, L, S2, L2) 或者是由于物理作用使得每个瓶子都产生特定频率的共鸣。

【派生】resonant *a.* 引起共鸣的
resonance *n.* 共鸣

ridiculous[3] [rɪˈdɪkjʊləs] 

【释义】*a.* 荒谬的，可笑的（absurd, foolish）

【例句】It's ridiculous that they haven't already-changed the route. (TPO2, S, Q3) 他们到现在都没有调整校车路线，这太可笑了。

【反义】logical, rational

【派生】ridiculously *ad.* 荒谬地

【逆构】ridicule *v./n.* 嘲笑，奚落

ruin[3] [rʊɪn] 

【释义】*v.* 破坏，毁掉（damage, destory）

【例句】Some of the world's finest stone architecture can be seen in the ruins of the ancient Inca city of Machu Picchu high in the eastern Andes Mountains of Peru. (TPO3, R, S1, T1) 在秘鲁安第斯山脉东部的马丘比丘印加古城遗址中，可以看到世界上最棒的石质建筑。

【反义】repair, restore

【派生】ruins *n.* 废墟，遗迹
ruinous *a.* 带来巨大损失的

【搭配】in ruins 被毁灭的，毁坏了的

sacrifice[3] [ˈsækrɪfaɪs] 

【释义】*v.* 1. 牺牲，献出 2. 以…做祭献 *n.* 1. 牺牲 2. 祭品

【例句】He's a skilled fighter, willing to face the most extreme dangers, sacrificial, willing that sacrifice anything and everything to

返记菜单

reputation[3]	resemblance[3]	reset[3]	reside[3]	resonate[3]
ridiculous[3]	ruin[3]	sacrifice[3]		

protect his king and country. (TPO13, L, S2, L1) 他是一个技艺精湛的斗士，面对艰险愿意牺牲自己，愿意为保卫国王和祖国牺牲一切。

【派生】sacrificial *a.* 牺牲的；献祭的

【搭配】sacrifice sth. (to sb./sth.) 为…牺牲某事物

saline[3] ['seɪlaɪn]

【释义】*a.* 含盐的；咸的

【例句】In the Indus plain, the movement of saline (salty) groundwaters has still not reached equilibrium after 70 years of being tapped. (TPO12, R, S2, T2) 在印度河平原上，含盐的地下水在经过了70年的开发后还是没有达到平衡。

【派生】salineness *n.* 含盐度

【搭配】saline soil 盐碱土

savannah[3] [sə'vænə]

【释义】*n.* 大草原，热带草原

【例句】Knowledge of iron making penetrated into the forests and savannahs of West Africa at roughly the same time that iron making was reaching Europe. (TPO7, R, S2, T2) 冶铁知识传播到了西非的森林和热带草原地区，几乎与此同时，冶铁技术也传播到了欧洲。

security[3] [sɪ'kjʊərɪtɪ]

【释义】*n.* 安全(protection, safety)

【例句】Through association with people who are meaningful to us, we achieve a sense of security, love, acceptance, companionship, and personal worth. (TPO13, R, S1, T1) 通过与对我们有意义的人来往，我们获得了安全感、爱、认可、伙伴关系和自我价值。

【反义】danger

selective[3] [sɪ'lektɪv]

【释义】*a.* 1. 选择的，选择性的 2. 精挑细选的

【例句】This technique allows researchers to create solutions that selectively omit certain nutrients. (TPO5, R, S1, T1) 这种技术容许研究者们制作一些溶液，溶液里有选择性地除去了特定的养分。

【派生】selectively *ad.* 有选择性地

sensitive[3] ['sensɪtɪv]

【释义】*a.* 1. 易受伤害的，敏感的(susceptible, vulnerable) 2. 灵敏的(delicate)

【例句】Besides, in powerful windstorms, sensitive camera equipment would be destroyed. (TPO4, L, S2, L1) 而且，在强劲的暴风下，脆弱的摄影机可能会被毁掉。

【派生】sensitivity *n.* 敏感

shellfish[3] ['ʃelfɪʃ]

【释义】*n.* 甲壳类动物，贝类

【例句】The plover lives by the ocean and feeds on small shellfish insects in plants. (TPO8, L, S1, L1) 这种千鸟生活在海边，以植物上的小型甲壳类昆虫为食。

shiny[3] ['ʃaɪnɪ]

【释义】*a.* 闪亮的，闪光的(lustrous, radiant)

【例句】As they drilled into the central and deepest part of the Mediterranean basin, the scientists took solid, shiny, crystalline salt from the core barrel. (TPO7, R, S1, T1) 当钻探到地中海海床的最中心最深处时，科学家从钻管中得到了坚硬闪光的晶体盐类。

【逆构】shine *v.* 照耀，发光

【搭配】a shiny red apple 一个红得发亮的苹果

shipping[3] ['ʃɪpɪŋ]

【释义】*n.* 1. 船舶(总称) 2. 船运

【例句】Mr. Brown has held 500 shares in the shipping company. 布朗先生持有该船运公司500股的股份。

【搭配】shipping company 航运公司；船舶公司

shoelace[3] ['ʃuːleɪs]

【释义】*n.* 鞋带

【例句】It is sort of like the plastic tip on each end of shoelace. (TPO12, L, S1, L1) 它有点儿像鞋带每一个头儿上的塑料端。

silicon[3] ['sɪlɪkən]

【释义】*n.*〈化〉硅，矽

【例句】Quartz is quartz—a silicon ion surrounded by four oxygen ions—there's no difference at all between two-million-year-old Pleistocene quartz and Cambrian quartz created over 500 million years ago. (TPO6, R, S2, T1) 石英是一种由四个氧离子包围一个硅离子的化合物。两百万年前的更新世石英和五亿年前形成的寒武纪石英并无差别。

【搭配】silicon transistor 硅晶体管

simultaneous[3] [ˌsɪməlˈteɪnjəs] 

【释义】*a.* 同步的，同时存在的，同时发生的(coincident, concurrent)

【例句】Some hypotheses fail to account for simultaneous extinctions on land and in the seas. (TPO15, R, S2, T2) 一些假设很难解释那些同时发生在陆上和大洋中的灭绝现象。

【派生】simultaneously *ad.* 同时地

【搭配】simultaneous interpretation 同声传译

slab[3] [slæb] 

【释义】*n.*(石、木等坚硬物质的)厚板，平板，厚片

【例句】So do the naturalistic paintings on slabs of stone excavated in southern Africa. (TPO4, R, S2, T1) 在非洲南部发掘出来的石板上的自然主义画作同样如此。

slight[3] [slaɪt]

【释义】*a.* 轻微的，微小的，微不足道的(subtle, small, tiny) *v.* 轻视，忽略 *n.* 轻蔑，怠慢

【例句】When researchers measured the heart rate, muscle tension and skin conductance of people before, during and after yawning, they did detect some changes in skin conductance following yawning, indicating a slight increase in physiological activity. (TPO18, R, S2, T1) 当研究人员对人在打呵欠前、打呵欠时和打呵欠之后的心率、肌肉紧张度及皮肤的电传导进行测试后，他们发现，在打呵欠之后皮肤的电传导发生了一些变化，这表明人的生理活跃度有轻微的提高。

【派生】slightly *ad.* 轻微地，有一点

【搭配】slight fever 微热，低烧
slight illness 小病，不适

snack[3] [snæk]

【释义】*n.* 快餐，小吃，点心 *v.* 吃快餐

【例句】Oh, and we usually serve lunch and snacks depending on what time the talk is. (TPO11, L, S2, C1) 对了，我们通常会根据谈话的时间来供应午餐和小吃。

【搭配】snack bar 小吃店；快餐柜
snack street 小吃街

solidarity[3] [ˌsɒlɪˈdærɪtɪ] 

【释义】*n.* 团结，团结一致(unity, accord)

【例句】Sociologists view primary groups as bridges between individuals and the larger society because they transmit, mediate, and interpret a society's cultural patterns and provide the sense of oneness so critical for social solidarity. (TPO13, R, S1, T1) 社会学家认为主要群体是个体和社会之间的桥梁，因为这些群体会传递、调整、诠释社会的文化形态并提供对促进社会团结极为关键的整体感。

【搭配】national solidarity in the face of danger 危难当头举国团结一致

soot[3] [sʊt]

【释义】*n.* 煤烟，烟尘 *v.* 熏以煤灰

【例句】They (the walls) ended up with a layer of black soot on them, and so did people's lungs. (TPO1, L, S2, L1) 最终这些墙被一层黑色的烟尘覆盖，人们的肺也是如此。

【派生】sootblower *n.* 吹灰器

spell[3] [spel]

【释义】*n.* 1. 一段时间(period) 2. 轮班 3. 咒语，魔力 *v.* 1. 拼写 2. 导致 3. 轮班，交替工作

【例句】A bad barrier of cold weather, a long spell of frosts could ruin a farm and the entire crop, anyway, before these citric growers moved south, much of the land in south Florida, was what we called wetlands. (TPO11, L, S2, L1) 严寒天气的严重阻碍、长时间的霜冻期会毁掉一个农场和全部庄稼，不管怎样，在这些柠檬的种植者南迁之前，佛罗里达州南部的大部分土地都是我们所称的湿地地

返记菜单

simultaneous[3] slab[3] slight[3] snack[3] solidarity[3]
soot[3] spell[3]

带。

【派生】 spelling *n.* 拼写，拼法

【搭配】 spell out 讲清楚
under a spell 被迷住；被符咒镇住
cold spell 春寒期
spell over 读懂；清楚地说明

spin[3] [spɪn]

【释义】 *v.* 1. 旋转(twirl, whirl) 2. 纺织(reel) 3. (用洗衣机)甩干衣服

【例句】 Members of poor peasant families spun or wove cloth and linens at home for scant remuneration in an attempt to supplement meager family income. (TPO10, R, S2, T2) 为了补贴本已经微薄的家庭收入，贫困潦倒的农民们通过在家纺织衣料或亚麻来换取少量的报酬。

【搭配】 spin out 消磨，拖延时间
spin in 上床，睡午觉
in a flat spin 晕头转向，急得团团转

spray[3] [spreɪ]

【释义】 *v.* 喷，向…喷洒(splash, sprinkle) *n.* 浪花，喷雾，飞沫

【例句】 Modern irrigation devices, each capable of spraying 4.5 million liters of water a day, have produced a landscape dominated by geometric patterns of circular green islands of crops. (TPO3, R, S1, T1) 日喷水量达450万升的现代灌溉设备，形成了一个以圆形绿岛作物为主的景观。

【派生】 sprayer *n.* 喷雾，喷雾器

【搭配】 sea spray 浪花

spur[3] [spɜː]

【释义】 *v.* 鞭策，激励，刺激(provoke, urge) *n.* 1. 马刺 2. 鞭策，激励

【例句】 So what happened in the 1970s was oil and natural gas became expensive very quickly, and that spurred people to start looking into alternative forms of energy, solar energy probably being the most popular. (TPO12, L, S2, L2) 20世纪70年代，石油和天然气非常迅速地变得昂贵起来，这就促使人们开始找寻可替代性能源，太阳能或许是最普遍的选择。

stare[3] [steə(r)]

【释义】 *n.* 盯着看，凝视(gaze)

【例句】 And we know that when a baby is surprised by something, a loud noise, or an unexpected flash of light maybe, it stares at where the noise or light is coming from. (TPO1, S, Q5) 我们知道，当婴儿被某种东西惊到的时候，比如一声巨响或是一道突如其来的闪光，他就会凝视着那声音或是光束投来的方向。

【搭配】 stare into/at 凝视
stare down 盯得某人不敢对视

static[3] ['stætɪk]

【释义】 *a.* 静态的，静止的，稳定的(still, inactive) *n.* 静电，静电干扰

【例句】 Unlike formal statues that are limited to static poses of standing, sitting, and kneeling, these figures depict a wide range of actions, such as grinding grain, baking bread, producing pots, and making music, and they are shown in appropriate poses, bending and squatting as they carry out their tasks. (TPO11, R, S1, T1) 这些雕像不像正规雕像那样只有静止的站立、坐和跪的姿态，而是表现了各种不同的动作，比如磨谷物、烤面包、造壶罐，还有奏乐，而且进行这些活动时的姿态都很恰当，或弯腰，或蹲坐着。

【反义】 dynamic

【搭配】 static electricity 静电

statistical[3] [stə'tɪstɪkəl]

【释义】 *a.* 统计的，统计学的

【例句】 I used different methods for analyzing the data, like certain statistical tests. (TPO2, L, S1, C1) 我使用了多种不同的方法来分析数据，例如某些统计学测试。

【派生】 statistically *ad.* 统计(学)地

【逆构】 statistics *n.* 统计，统计学

stereotype[3] ['stɪərɪəʊtaɪp]

【释义】 *n.* 老套，陈规，典型 *v.* 把…模式化，使成陈规

【例句】 Don't make your character into a stereotype.

(TPO6, L, S2, L1) 不要让小说中的人物太模式化。
【派生】stereotypical *a.* 老套的,陈规的
【搭配】dynamic stereotype 〈生〉动力定型

stratum[3] ['streɪtəm] 

【释义】*n.* 1. 地层 2. 阶层
【例句】Ever since people had begun to catalog the strata in particular outcrops, there had been the hope that these could somehow be used to calculate geological time. (TPO6, R, S2, T1) 自从人们开始对某种露出地表的岩层进行分类起,人们就希望这些岩层某种方式上可以用来计算地质时间。
【搭配】social stratum 社会阶层

submerge[3] [səb'mɜːdʒ] 

【释义】*v.*(使)沉没,淹没(immerse, sink)
【例句】It had been assumed that the ice extended westward from the Alaskan/Canadian mountains to the very edge of the continental shelf, the flat, submerged part of the continent that extends into the ocean. (TPO9, R, S1, T1) 人们猜测,冰从阿拉斯加/加拿大山脉向西延伸到大陆架的边缘,也就是大陆延伸到海洋中而被淹没的平坦的部分。
【派生】submergence *n.* 浸没,淹没

subside[3] [səb'saɪd] 

【释义】*v.* 1. 下沉,塌陷(decline, decrease)2. 平息,消退(appease, mitigate)
【例句】Sometimes, the ground at an oil field may subside as oil is removed. (TPO4, R, S2, T2) 有时,随着油被抽空,原油所在的地面会塌陷。
【反义】rise
【派生】subsidence *n.* 下沉

suburb[3] ['sʌbɜːb] 

【释义】*n.* 郊区(outskirt)
【例句】Business owners in the city centers or the downtown areas have experienced some financial losses, because of the city movement of the people out of the city and then into suburbs. (TPO13, L, S1, L1) 城市居民从市区到郊区的迁移使得市中心的商家蒙受了一些经济损失。
【派生】suburban *a.* 郊外的,偏远的
【搭配】an industrial suburb 城郊工业区

succeeding[3] [sək'siːdɪŋ]

【释义】*a.* 接连的;随后的(following, subsequent)
【例句】Programs to replant flowers native to humming bird habitats are not succeeding. (TPO3, L, S1, L1) 重新种植蜂鸟栖息地的本土花类的项目没有继续进行。

super[3] ['sjuːpə]

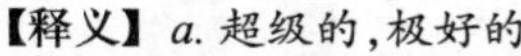

【释义】*a.* 超级的,极好的
【例句】To get more people to stop in, well, like you said, better equipments, maybe a super fast internet connection, not just a good variety of books but also like nice and comfortable areas where people can read and do research. (TPO8, L, S2, C1) 想让更多的人驻足,就像你说的,需要有更好的设施,可能是超级快速的网络,不只是各种各样的书,还要有一个舒服惬意的环境供人们读书或做研究。
【搭配】super hero 大英雄

susceptible[3] [sə'septəbl] 

【释义】*a.* 1. 易受影响的(vulnerable, liable)2. 易动感情的,感情丰富的(responsive)3. 容许…的,可以…的
【例句】Since the raising of most crops necessiates the prior removal of the natural vegetation, crop failures leave extensive tracts of land devoid of a plant cover and susceptible to wind and water erosion. (TPO2, R, Sl, T1) 由于耕种作物的需要,人们必须将土地原有的自然植被清除,所以当庄稼歉收时,大片土地就会没有任何植被覆盖,从而更易于受到风力和流水的侵蚀。
【派生】susceptibility *n.* 易受影响性
susceptibleness *n.* 易受影响性
susceptibly *ad.* 易受影响的
【搭配】susceptible to 易受…感动的,易受…影响的
susceptible of 容许…的,能…的

返记菜单

stratum[3] submerge[3] subside[3] suburb[3] succeeding[3]
super[3] susceptible[3]

Word List 32

tactic[3] ['tæktɪk] 

【释义】*n.* 策略，战略，手段(strategy, maneuver)

【例句】General concern about misleading tactics that advertisers employ is centered on the use of exaggeration. (TPO14, R, S1, T1) 对于广告商所使用的误导性策略的一般关注点集中在夸张的运用。

【派生】tactical *a.* 战术上的

temple[3] ['templ] 

【释义】*n.* 1. 寺院，庙宇，神殿 2. 太阳穴 3. 眼镜腿

【例句】Other statues were designed to be placed within an architectural setting, for instance, in front of the monumental entrance gateways to temples known as pylons. (TPO11, R, S1, T1) 其他雕像被放置在建筑群中，比如，在庙宇的纪念性入口塔门的前方。

【搭配】Temple of Heaven 天坛
temple fair 庙会

tempt[3] [tempt] 

【释义】*v.* 诱惑，怂恿，引诱，吸引(appeal, attract)

【例句】By doing this, the company appeals to new consumers who weren't probably even interested in getting a computer, and, well of course, to existing consumers who might now be tempted to switch brands. (TPO8, S, Q6) 通过这样做，公司会吸引那些本来无意购买电脑的新顾客，而现有的消费者也可能会想要换个牌子。

theatrical[3] [θɪ'ætrɪkəl] 

【释义】*a.* 1. 剧场的 2. 夸张的，矫揉造作的

【例句】Despite all the highly visible technological developments in theatrical and home delivery of the moving image that have occurred over the decades since then, no single innovation has come close to being regarded as a similar kind of watershed. (TPO12, R, S2, T1) 尽管在那之后的几十年中，电影在剧场和家庭传输方面都有很显著的技术性发展，但是没有哪项单独的创新能与电影界的这一分水岭相提并论。

【派生】theatricality *n.* 戏剧风格；夸张

【逆构】theater *n.* 剧场

【搭配】theatrical performance 戏剧表演

thorough[3] ['θʌrə] 

【释义】*a.* 1. 完全的，彻底的(exhaustive, complete, profound) 3. 全面的，详尽的

【例句】Everything you just read about "Portrait of an Elderly Woman in a White Bonnet" is true, and yet after a thorough re-examination of the painting, a panel of experts has recently concluded that it's indeed a work by Rembrandt. (TPO3, W, Q1) 你刚看过的《一个戴白帽子的老女人的肖像》都是真实的，但是经过再次仔细观察，专家组最近认为这幅作品的确为伦勃朗所作。

【派生】thoroughgoing *a.* 全面的，细致的

theoretical[3] [θɪə'retɪkəl] 

【释义】*a.* 理论的，理论上的

【例句】Now, for a customer base, the most obvious example would be a large office building since the employees could theoretically go shopping after work or during their lunch hour, right? (TPO13, L, S1, L1) 现在，对于顾客群来说，最明显的例子就是大型的办公楼，因为工作人员理论上可以在下班以后或午饭期间去购物，对吗？

【反义】empirical

【逆构】theory *n.* 理论，原理

【搭配】theoretical physicist 理论物理学家

thrill[3] [θrɪl] 

【释义】*n.* 兴奋；引起兴奋或激动的事物 *v.* (使)兴奋，(使)激动

【例句】That would mean less studying time for me, which I'm not thrilled about. (TPO12, S, Q6) 那对于我来说就意味着学习的时间更少了，这我可激动不起来。

【派生】thrilled *a.* 非常兴奋的，极为激动的

thrush[3] [θrʌʃ]

【释义】*n.* 画眉鸟

【例句】For example, there's a bird, the "wood thrush", anyway, when the "wood thrush" is in an attack-escape conflict, that is, it's caught between the two urges to escape from or to attack an enemy, if it's sitting on a horizontal branch, it'll wipe its beak on its perch. (TPO4, L, S1, L1) 比如,有一种鸟,"鸫科鸣鸟",当它在处在攻击还是逃跑的矛盾中时,也就是说,它陷入了逃跑还是攻击敌人的两种想法中,如果它位于水平的树枝上,它会用鸟喙啄其所栖息的树枝。

tight[3] [taɪt]

【释义】*a.* 1. 密集的,紧凑的 2. 牢固的 3. 紧(身)的 *ad.* 紧紧地

【例句】And it may be this burial custom that explain why the houses were packed in so tightly without streets. (TPO1, L, S2, L1) 或许这种丧葬习惯可以解释为什么房屋建得满满当当的,连街道都没留。

【反义】loose

【派生】tighten *v.* (使)变紧

【搭配】tight corner 紧要关头

timber[3] ['tɪmbə]

【释义】*n.* 木材,木料(lumber, wood)

【例句】They traded grain for raw materials, such as timber and stones, as well as for metals and gems. (TPO16, R, S1, T1) 他们用谷物交换原材料,比如木料和石头,以及金属和宝石等物品。

【派生】timbering *n.* 木材,建筑用材

【搭配】timber structure 木结构,木构造

torch[3] [tɔːtʃ]

【释义】*n.* 1. 手电筒 2. 火把,火炬 *v.* 放火烧,纵火烧(建筑物或汽车)

【例句】And each time you'd have to bring along torches to light your way. (TPO3, L, S2, L1) 而且每次你都要带上火把照明。

【搭配】flash a torch 打手电

tract[3] [trækt]

【释义】*n.* 1. 大片土地(area, region) 2. (体内的)道,束 3. 传单,小册子

【例句】Since the raising of most crops necessiates the prior removal of the natural vegetation, crop failures leave extensive tracts of land devoid of a plant cover and susceptible to wind and water erosion. (TPO2, R, Sl, T1) 由于耕种作物的需要,人们必须将土地原有的自然植被清除,所以当庄稼歉收时,大片土地就会没有任何植被覆盖,从而更易于受到风力和流水的侵蚀。

【搭配】tract house [建筑工程](设计相同的)地区性住宅

trait[3] [treɪt]

【释义】*n.* 特点,特征,特性(characteristic, feature)

【例句】By communal, we mean they reflect the traits and the concerns of a particular community at a particular time. (TPO5, L, S2, L2) 说它是社会性的,我们是说它们反映了特定时期特定社会团体的特征和关注点。

【搭配】traits of character 性格特征

transmit[3] [trænz'mɪt]

【释义】*v.* 传播,传送,传递(forward, transfer, convey)

【例句】Second, when an orally transmitted story is written down, an authoritative version with a recognized author is created. (TPO5, L, S2, L2) 第二,当一个经口头传播的故事被写下来的时候,一个由公认的作者写成的权威版本就诞生了。

【派生】transmittal *n.* 传输,传送
transmitter *n.* 转送者,发送器

【搭配】transmit sth. to 把…传递到…

trash[3] [træʃ]

【释义】垃圾,废物

【例句】The pots in the pile could be regular trash too, leftover from the meals of the construction workers. (TPO5, W, Q1) 土堆里的罐子可能也就是些普通的垃圾,是建筑工人用餐之后留下的。

返记菜单

thrush[3]	tight[3]	timber[3]	torch[3]	tract[3]
trait[3]	transmit[3]	trash[3]		

turkey³ ['tɜːkɪ] 

【释义】*n.* 1. 火鸡；火鸡肉 2. 失败 3. 笨蛋，傻瓜

【例句】The Americas provide Europe and Asia with food like squash, beans, turkey, peanuts. (TPO10, L, S1, L2) 美洲向欧洲和亚洲提供南瓜、豆子、火鸡、花生等食品。

【搭配】go cold turkey 快速戒掉坏习惯

underlying³ [ˈʌndəˈlaɪɪŋ] 

【释义】*a.* 1. 含蓄的，潜在的，隐含的（implicit）2. 表面下的；下层的

【例句】The water evaporates and the salts are left behind, creating a white crustal layer that prevents air and water from reaching the underlying soil. (TPO2, R, Sl, T1) 水分蒸发掉了，剩下的盐分则结成了一层白色外壳，使得空气和水分无法到达地表以下的土层。

【反义】superficial; explicit

【逆构】underlie *v.* 位于…的下面

【搭配】underlying cause/problem 潜在原因 / 问题

undesirable³ [ˈʌndɪˈzaɪərəbl] 

【释义】*a.* 令人不悦的，不合意的，讨厌的（unsuitable, unacceptable）*n.* 不受欢迎的人

【例句】The disadvantage of using waterpower is that streams do not necessarily flow in places that are the most suitable for factories, which explains why so many water-powered grain and textile mills were located in undesirable places. (TPO6, R, S1, T1) 使用水力的一个缺点就是，水流不一定会从最适合工厂的地方流过，这也可以解释为什么那么多以水力为动力的粮场和纺织厂会坐落在一些不如人意的地方。

【反义】desirable

【派生】undesirability *n.* 不受欢迎

【搭配】undesirable tendencies 不良倾向

unemployment³ [ˈʌnɪmˈplɔɪmənt] 

【释义】*n.* 失业率；失业；失业人数

【例句】But then when the United States became involved in the Second World War, unemployment was down and it seems that these programs weren't really necessary any longer. (TPO4, L, S2, L2) 但当美国被卷入二战之后，失业率下降了，这些项目似乎也不再必要了。

【逆构】employment *n.* 雇佣；职业

unite³ [jʊ(ː)ˈnaɪt] 

【释义】*v.* 联合，合并，统一，团结

【例句】Romans built walls to unite the various parts of their realm into a single entity, which was controlled by powerful laws. (TPO7, R, S2, T1) 罗马人建造城墙是为了将国家的各个部分统一为一个整体，并受强大的法律控制。

【反义】disunite, divide

unstable³ [ˈʌnˈsteɪbl] 

【释义】*a.* 不稳固的，不结实的，易变的（changeable, unsteady）

【例句】Since they had relatively shallow hulls, they were unstable when driven by sail or when on rough water: hence they were unsuitable for the voyage to the East. (TPO17, R, S1, T1) 由于船身相对来说比较浅，所以这些船在靠帆航行或在大浪中航行时是不稳定的，因此不适合向东航行。

【反义】stable

【派生】unstability *n.* 不安定性

【搭配】unstable situation 不安定的局面

updraft³ [ˈʌpdrɑːft] 

【释义】*n.* 上升气流

【例句】Then updraft wind currents carry the light, positively charged ice crystals up to the top of the cloud. (TPO18, R, S2, T2) 然后上升气流负载着光、带正电荷的冰晶体上升到云层顶端。

utilitarian³ [ˌjuːtɪlɪˈteərɪən]

【释义】*a.* 功利的，实用的 *n.* 功利主义者

【例句】The function and status of ceramics in China varied from dynasty to dynasty, so they may be utilitarian, burial, trade-collector's, or even ritual objects, accroding to their quality and the era in which they were made. (TPO10, R, S1, T1) 陶器在中国各个朝代的功能和地位是不同的，所以，根据其质量和

制作的年代，有些可能是有实用意义的，有些可能是陪葬品，有些被作为艺术收藏品，有些甚至是宗教仪式上的法器。

【逆构】utility *n.* 效用，有用
utilize *v.* 利用，使用

valid[3] ['vælɪd] 

【释义】*a.* 1. 有根据的，正确的（well-grounded, sound, true）2.（法律上）有效的（legal, lawful, effective）

【例句】It is the most valid theory of thinking at the present time. (TPO2, L, S1, L1, Q11) 目前，这是关于思考活动最有理有据的理论了。

【反义】invalid

【派生】validate *v.* 使具有法律效力
validation *n.* 有效性
validity *n.*（法律上）有效；确实

warfare[3] ['wɔːfeə] 

【释义】*n.* 战争，冲突，斗争

【例句】It is the use of horses for transportation and warfare that explains why Inner Eurasian pastoralism proved the most mobile and the most militaristic of all major forms of pastoralism. (TPO14, R, S2, T2) 马匹在交通和战争中的使用说明了为什么亚欧内陆的畜牧主义在畜牧主义的所有主要形式中是公认的最具机动性和军事性的。

【逆构】war *n./v.* 战争，作战

【搭配】psychological warfare 心理战
positional warfare 阵地战

waterproof[3] ['wɔːtəpruːf] 

【释义】*a.* 防水的，耐水的 *n.* 防水材料 *v.* 使防水

【例句】Yes. The birch tree has white bark, and this tough protective outer layer of the tree, this white bark, is waterproof. (TPO7, L, S2, L1) 是的，桦树有着白色的树皮，这种坚硬的保护外皮，这种白色的树皮，是防水的。

windmill[3] ['wɪndmɪl] 

【释义】*n.* 风车

【例句】There were three sources of power: animal or human muscles; the wind, operating on sail or windmill; and running water. (TPO6, R, S1, T1) 当时的驱动力仅限于三种：动物或人力、用于航行或推动风车的风力以及流水产生的动力。

wisdom[3] ['wɪzdəm] 

【释义】*n.* 1. 智慧，明智 2. 至理名言

【例句】That's been the conventional wisdom among geologists for quite some time. (TPO1, L, S1, L2) 这是长久以来地理学家们的传统智慧。

【搭配】Wisdom of Solomon 所罗门智慧书

woody[3] ['wudi]

【释义】*a.* 1. 木质的，木材的 2. 多树木的

【例句】An abandoned field, for instance, will be invaded successively by herbaceous plants (plants with little or no woody tissue), shrubs, and trees, eventually becoming a forest. (TPO19, R, S2, T1) 一块儿废弃的土地，在相继被草本植物（有极少或者没有木质组织的植物）、灌木、树木入侵之后，会变为一片森林。

【派生】woodiness *n.* 木质

【搭配】woody plant 木本植物

worthwhile[3] [ˌwɜːθ'waɪl] 

【释义】*a.* 值得做的，值得花时间的

【例句】One possibility is that a noisy baby bird provides accurate signals of its real hunger and good health, making it worthwhile for the listening parent to give it food in a nest where several other offspring are usually available to be fed. (TPO11, R, S2, T2) 一种可能是，一只叽叽喳喳的雏鸟能发出精确的信号，表示它真的饿了并且身体健康，这使其父母觉得在巢中还有其它几只幼鸟需要喂养的情况下把食物给它是值得的。

wrap[3] [ræp]

【释义】*v.* 1. 包，裹 2. 覆盖，隐藏 *n.* 1. 围巾，披肩 2. 包装材料

【例句】By contrast, wooden statues were carved from several pieces of wood that were pegged together to form the finished work, and metal statues were either made by wrapping sheet

返记菜单

valid[3] warfare[3] waterproof[3] windmill[3] wisdom[3]
woody[3] worthwhile[3] wrap[3]

metal around a wooden core or cast by the lost wax process. (TPO11, R, S1, T1) 相比之下，木雕是由钉在一起的几块木头雕刻而成的，而金属雕塑要么是金属片包裹着一块木质核心，要么是用脱蜡铸造法铸成的。

【派生】wrapped *a.* 有包装的
wrapper *n.* 包装纸，包装材料

【搭配】wrap up 包裹起来；多穿衣服；〈美口〉使圆满完成
under wraps 不公开的，秘密的

zigzag[3] ['zɪgzæg]

【释义】*a.* 之字形的，曲折的 *n.* 曲折，之字形 *v.*（使）曲折行进

【例句】He talks about a ship's voyage and this is one of the most famous bits of the essay—how the best voyage is made up of zigzag lines. (TPO4, L, S1, L2) 他谈到了一艘船的航行，而这是他全文中最著名的一段——最好的航程是如何由之字路线组成的。

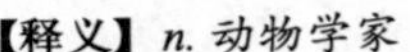

zoologist[3] [zəʊ'ɒlədʒɪst]

【释义】*n.* 动物学家

【例句】Wildlife zoologist Helmut Buechner (1953), in reviewing the nature of biotic changes in Washington through recorded time, says that "since the early 1940s, the state has had more deer than at any other time in its history, the winter population fluctuating around approximately 320, 000 deer (mule and black-tailed deer) , which will yield about 65, 000 of either sex and any age annually for an indefinite period. " (TPO4, R, S1, T1) 野生动物学家 Helmut Buechner (1953) 在回顾自有史记载以来华盛顿生物变化的本质时说："自 20 世纪 40 年代以来，该州鹿群的数量达到最高峰，冬天时的数量大约在 32 万头左右(包括骡和黑尾鹿)，这样每年一段时期将会产出 65,000 头小鹿，不论性别和年龄。

abolish[2] [ə'bɒlɪʃ]

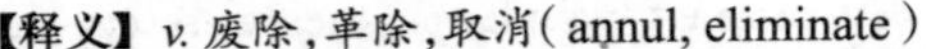

【释义】*v.* 废除，革除，取消（annul, eliminate）

【例句】In 1857, in return for a payment of 63 million kronor from other commercial nations, Denmark abolished the Sound toll dues, the fees it had collected since 1497 for the use of the Sound. (TPO18, R, S1, T1) 1857 年，作为来自其他商业国家 6300 万克朗的付款的交换，丹麦废除了松德海峡的通行税，这笔费用是从 1497 年开始征收并用于松德海峡的。

【派生】abolition *n.* 废除，废止
abolitionist *n.* 废奴主义者

accordingly[2] [ə'kɔːdɪŋlɪ]

【释义】*ad.* 1. 因此，于是（therefore, thus）2. 相应地（consequently）

【例句】Now they had a much hardier crop that could be grown easily in more northerly climates and centers of power began to shift accordingly. (TPO10, L, S1, L2) 现在他们有了一种更加顽强的作物，可以很容易地在更偏北方的气候里生长，力量中心因而也开始转移。

activate[2] ['æktɪveɪt]

【释义】*v.* 激活，使活动，起动（spark, stimulate, encourage）

【例句】The visual cortex is activated during the sensation of movement. (TPO15, L, S1, L1) 大脑皮层的视觉中枢区在感知到运动时会被激活。

【派生】activated *a.* 活性化的；活泼的

adobe[2] [ə'dəubi]

【释义】*n.* 泥砖，土坯（clay, brick）

【例句】Of course in early architecture—such as igloos and adobe structures—there was no such equipment, and the skeleton and skin were often one. (TPO3, R, S1, T1) 当然，在早期的建筑中，比如雪块砌成的圆顶小屋和土坯建筑，并没有这样的设施，支撑架和外壳也往往是合在一起的。

【搭配】an adobe house 土坯屋

afield[2] [ə'fiːld]

【释义】*ad.* 远离（尤指家乡），在远方

【例句】Sometimes they are carried farther afield by water or by wind. (TPO9, R, S2, T2) 有时候它们会被流水和风带到更远的地方。

【搭配】go too far afield 走入歧途

alert[2] [ə'lɜːt]

【释义】*a.* 警觉的，机敏的（wary, vigilant）*v.* 使意识到，警惕（warn, alarm）*n.* 警戒，警报

【例句】The shortened workweek would increase company profits because employees would feel more rested and alert. (TPO1, W, Q1) 缩短工作周将提高公司的利润，因为职员们将会感到更放松、更机敏。

【派生】alterly *ad.* 留意地；警觉地
alertness *n.* 警戒，机敏

【搭配】be on full alert 保持高度戒备状态

ambient[2] ['æmbɪənt]

【释义】*a.* 周围的，包围着的

【例句】Over long periods of time, substances whose physical and chemical properties change with the ambient climate at the time can be deposited in a systematic way. (TPO10, R, S2, T1) 经过很长一段时间，那些会随着当时周围的气候变化改变其物理和化学特性的物质将会以系统的方式沉淀下来。

【派生】ambience *n.* 周围环境，气氛

【搭配】ambient temperature/pressure 周围的温度/压力

amplification[2] [ˌæmplɪfɪ'keɪʃən]

【释义】*n.* 扩大，放大

【例句】These critics were making a common assumption—that the technological inadequacies of earlier efforts (poor synchronization, weak sound amplification, fragile sound recordings) would invariably occur again. (TPO12, R, S2, T1) 这些评论家门做了一个共同的假设，即，先前的努力中存在的技术上的不足（同步性差、扩音微弱、录音差）将一定会再次出现。

【逆构】amplify *v.* 扩大，放大，增强

anchor[2] ['æŋkə]

【释义】*n.* 1. 锚 2. 给人安全感的人（或物）*v.* 1. 抛锚，停泊 2. 使稳固，系牢（attach, fasten）

【例句】If you wanna tie your anchor to it and drop it right into the ocean, that's no problem, because plant fibers can stand up for months, even years, in direct contact with salt water. (TPO2, L, S1, L2) 如果你想用它系住锚、然后直接扔到海里，那也没有问题，因为植物纤维可以直接与盐水接触，好几个月甚至好几年都不会被腐蚀。

【派生】anchorage *n.* 锚地，泊地；泊船费

【搭配】at anchor（船）抛锚，停泊着

animated[2] ['ænɪmeɪtɪd]

【释义】*a.* 动画（片）的；栩栩如生的；活泼生动的（lively, vigorous, vivacious）

【例句】In children's advertising, the "celebrities" are often animated figures from popular cartoons. (TPO14, R, S1, T1) 在儿童广告中，"名人"通常是流行动画片里的卡通人物。

【逆构】animate *v.* 使活泼，使有生气

anomaly[2] [ə'nɒməlɪ]

【释义】*n.* 异常，不规则，反常的事物（abnormality）

【例句】Such anomalies are due to the relative abundance of the "isotopes" or varieties of each element. (TPO16, R, S2, T1) 这种异常的产生是由于"同位素"的相对丰盛度或每种元素的多样性。

【反义】normality

【派生】anomalous *a.* 异常的，反常的，不规则的

【搭配】congenital anomaly 先天性异常

apparatus[2] [ˌæpə'reɪtəs]

【释义】*n.* 1. 设备，仪器，用具（equipment, appliance, device）2. 机制

【例句】They devised an apparatus that connected a baby's pacifier to a counting device. (TPO13, R, S2, T2) 他们设计出了一个将婴儿奶嘴连接到计数器上的设备。

【搭配】laboratory apparatus 实验室设备

apprentice[2] [ə'prentɪs]

【释义】*n.* 学徒，徒弟；见习生（beginner, novice）*v.* 令人当学徒

【例句】When he grew older, William Smith taught himself surveying from books he bought with his small savings, and at the age of eighteen he was apprenticed to a surveyor of the local

返记菜单

alert[2] ambient[2] amplification[2] anchor[2] animated[2]
anomaly[2] apparatus[2] apprentice[2]

parish. (TPO6, R, S2, T1) 长大后，威廉·史密斯开始用微薄的积蓄买书自学测量，18 岁的时候，他成为了当地教区测量员的学徒。

【反义】 old-hand, veteran

arcade[2] [ɑːˈkeɪd]

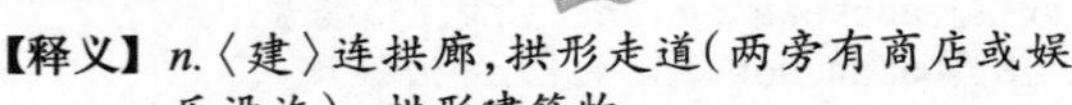

【释义】 n.〈建〉连拱廊，拱形走道（两旁有商店或娱乐设施）；拱形建筑物

【例句】 It was designed for use in Kinetoscope parlors or arcades. (TPO2, R, S2, T2) 这种放映机仅适用于活动电影放映室或电影娱乐城。

archaeocyte[2]

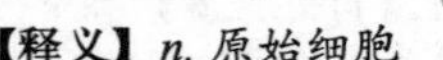

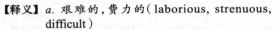

【释义】 n. 原始细胞

【例句】 The fossil consists of a complete skull of archaeocyte. (TPO2, R, S2, T1) 这块化石包含一个完整的原始动物的头盖骨。

arduous[2] [ˈɑːdjuəs]

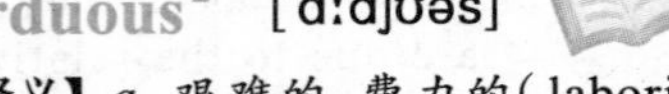

【释义】 a. 艰难的，费力的（laborious, strenuous, difficult）

【例句】 In the past, whole cities grew from the arduous task of cutting and piling stone upon stone. (TPO3, R, S1, T1) 在过去，整个城市的建筑物都是辛辛苦苦地由一块块石头经过切割和堆砌而建成的。

【搭配】 an arduous winter 严冬

asset[2] [ˈæset]

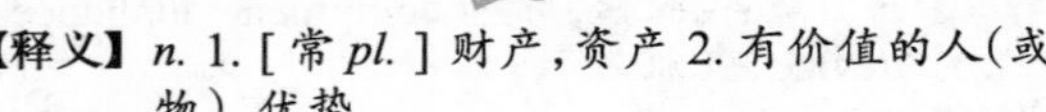

【释义】 n. 1. [常 pl.] 财产，资产 2. 有价值的人（或物），优势

【例句】 With financial assets considerably greater than those in the motion picture industry, and perhaps a wider vision of the relationships among entertainment and communications media, they revitalized research into recording sound for motion picture. (TPO12, R, S2, T1) 因为他们的资产比电影产业的多得多，又或许是因为看到了娱乐业和传播媒体之间的联系，他们重新开始了对电影录音的研究。

【搭配】 asset income 资产收益

assortment[2] [əˈsɔːtmənt]

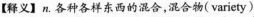

【释义】 n. 各种各样东西的混合，混合物（variety）

【例句】 Instead, students will be offered a wide assortment of cold breakfast items in the morning. (TPO3, S, Q3) 相反，（餐厅）将在每天早上为学生们供应各种各样的冷早餐。

【派生】 assorted a. 各式各样的

【搭配】 a mixed assortment of sweets 什锦糖果

athletic[2] [æθˈletɪk]

【释义】 a. 运动的；健壮的

【例句】 A university official announced plans to spend $2 million to build a new athletic stadium, commenting that a new stadium would help the university achieve its goal of attracting more top students. (TPO13, S, Q3) 一位大学官员宣布，计划花费 200 万美元修建一座新的体育场，他说新体育馆的建成将帮助学校达成吸引更多顶尖学生的目标。

【搭配】 athletic sports 体育运动

attach[2] [əˈtætʃ]

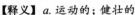

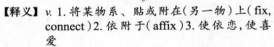

【释义】 v. 1. 将某物系、贴或附在（另一物）上（fix, connect）2. 依附于（affix）3. 使依恋，使喜爱

【例句】 In turn, a deep attachment to the land, and to the stability which rural life engenders, fostered the Roman virtues: gravitas, a sense of responsibility, pietas, a sense of devotion to family and country, and justitia, a sense of the natural order. (TPO7, R, S2, T1) 反之，对土地和平稳的乡村生活的深深依恋孕育了罗马人的美德：庄重，一种责任感；敬重，对祖国和家庭奉献的使命感；正义，对自然秩序的遵循。

【反义】 detach

【派生】 attachment n. 依恋，爱慕；附属物，连接物

auction[2] [ˈɔːkʃən]

【释义】 n./v. 拍卖（vendue）

【例句】 But in 1998, a book of prayers from the Middle Ages sold in an art auction for a lot of money. (TPO15, L, S2, L1) 但是在 1998 年，一本源自中世纪的祷告书在一个艺术品

拍卖会上以高价售出。
【派生】auctioneer *n.* 拍卖商

audition[2] [ɔːˈdɪʃən]

【释义】*n.*（面试时）试听，试演，试唱 *v.* 试演；试唱；试听
【例句】Would you be interested in auditioning? (TPO5, L, S1, C1) 你有兴趣来试音吗？
【逆构】audit *v.* 旁听；审计
【派生】auditory *a.* 听觉的

authorize[2] [ˈɔːθəraɪz] 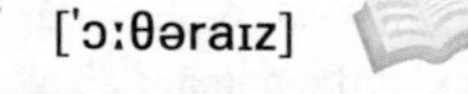

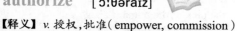

【释义】*v.* 授权，批准(empower, commission)
【例句】The exchanger would then send a bill of exchange to a colleague in Marseille, authorizing the colleague to pay the Marseille merchant in the merchant's own currency after the actual exchange of goods had taken place. (TPO10, R, S2, T2) 然后兑换人会把一张汇票寄给在马赛的同事，并授权该同事在货物交易完成后，以商人本国的货币形式支付给在马赛的商人相应的钱。
【派生】authorized *a.* 权威认可的，经授权的
authorization *n.* 授权，认可
authority *n.* 权力，权威；当局

avenue[2] [ˈævɪnjuː] 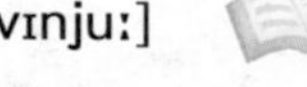

【释义】*n.* 1. 途径，手段 2. 大街
【例句】They were interested in all forms of sound technology and all potential avenues for commercial exploitation. (TPO12, R, S2, T1) 他们对所有形式的声音技术和所有潜在的商业开发途径都很感兴趣。
【搭配】avenue of appeal 上诉途径

axis[2] [ˈæksɪs]

【释义】*n.* 轴，轴线，轴心(shaft, pivot)
【例句】Precession basically is the change in the direction of Earth's axis of rotation. (TPO17, L, S1, L2) 岁差从根本上讲就是地轴转动方向的改变。
【搭配】the earth's axis 地轴

bake[2] [beɪk] 

【释义】*v.* 烤，烘焙，烘干
【例句】Unlike formal statues that are limited to static poses of standing, sitting, and kneeling, these figures depict a wide range of actions, such as grinding grain, baking bread, producing pots, and making music, and they are shown in appropriate poses, bending and squatting as they carry out their tasks. (TPO11, R, S1, T1) 这些雕像不像正规雕像那样只有静止的站立、坐和跪的姿态，而是表现了各种不同的动作，比如磨谷物、烤面包、造壶罐，还有奏乐，而且进行这些活动时的姿态都很恰当，或弯腰，或蹲坐着。

bison[2] [ˈbaɪsn] 

【释义】*n.* 野牛
【例句】Horses are most common overall with deer and bison pretty common too, probably animals they hunted. (TPO3, L, S2, L1) 总的来说，马是画中最常出现的动物，鹿和野牛也是经常出现的，可能这些动物是他们捕获到的。

blacksmith[2] [ˈblæksmɪθ] 

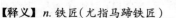

【释义】*n.* 铁匠(尤指马蹄铁匠)
【例句】In West Africa the blacksmith who made tools and weapons had an important place in society, often with special religious powers and functions. (TPO7, R, S2, T2) 在西非地区，制造铁具和武器的铁匠具有重要的社会地位，他们通常都拥有特殊的宗教权利和职责。

bleak[2] [bliːk]

【释义】*a.* 1. 萧瑟的，阴郁的(chill, gloomy) 2. 没有希望的，令人沮丧的
【例句】It (a painting) 's an outdoor scene. It's kind of bleak, which you can really see those broad brushstrokes and the blurry lines. (TPO1, L, S1, L1) 这是一幅有关室外风景的画。这幅画(的基调)有些凄凉，这一点你可以从那些粗犷的笔触和模糊的线条上看

出来。

【派生】bleakly *ad.* 荒凉地，阴郁地
bleakness *n.* 阴郁；惨淡无望

blink[2] [blɪŋk] 

【释义】*v./n.* 1. 眨眼(wink) 2.(灯光)闪烁

【例句】The occurrence of these eye movements provides evidence that the moving pattern is perceived at some level by the newborn. Similarly, changes in the infant's general level of motor activity —turning the head, blinking the eyes, crying, and so forth— have been used by researchers as visual indicators of the infant's perceptual abilities. (TPO13, R, S2, T2) 眼球运动的发生证明移动的物体在一定程度上会引起的新生儿的注意。同样，新生儿运动行为整体水平的变化，比如摆头、眨眼、哭泣等，已经被研究人员用做婴儿认知能力的视觉表现。

【搭配】blink the fact (that…) 不考虑，不顾及
the blink of an eye 一眨眼工夫，瞬间
on the blink 失灵，出毛病

bombard[2] ['bɒmbɑːd] 

【释义】*v.* 1. 炮轰，轰击 2. 连珠炮似地质问

【例句】Even today, microscopic meteorites continually bombard Earth, falling on both land and sea. (TPO8, R, S2, T1) 即使在今天，小型的陨石也在不断地撞击地球，落到陆地上和海洋中。

【派生】bombardment *n.* 炮轰，轰炸
bombardier *n.*(飞机上的)轰炸员，投弹手

bovine[2] ['bəuvaɪn] 

【释义】*n.* 牛科动物 *a.* 1.(似)牛的 2. 迟钝的

【例句】That is, mammoths, bovines, and horses are portrayed more often than deer and reindeer. (TPO4, R, S2, T1) 就是说，猛犸象、牛和马比鹿和驯鹿被描绘得更多。

【搭配】bovine spongiform encephalopathy 疯牛病

bulldozer[2] ['bʊldəuzə] 

【释义】*n.* 推土机

【例句】I mean, we keep the windows down and everything, but once those bulldozers get going. (TPO16, L, S1, C1) 我是说，推土机开始工作时，我们得关上窗子，关上一切能关上的。

bunch[2] [bʌntʃ] 

【释义】*n.* 1. 束，串 2. 群，伙 *v.*(使)…成束

【例句】I'm supposed to be driving a bunch of them to the zoo tomorrow. (TPO1, S, Q5) 我明天应该载着他们一大群去动物园。

【派生】bunched *a.* 成束的
bunchiness *n.* 成串，束状

【搭配】a bunch of 一群，一束，一堆
the pick of the bunch 佼佼者
bunch together/up 聚成堆

Word List 33

burst[2] [bɜːst] 

【释义】 v. 1. 爆炸,爆裂,爆发(explode, break) 2. 突然出现 n. 爆裂,裂口

【例句】 I think some of the pipes burst or wore out or something. (TPO9, S, Q5) 我觉得有一些管子爆裂或者用坏了之类的。

【搭配】 burst someone's bubble 打碎某人的梦想
full to bursting(吃得)太饱
burst into tears 突然放声大哭

calve[2] [kɑːv] 

【释义】 v. 1.(使冰山)崩解 2. 生小牛崽

【例句】 For a glacier to grow or maintain its mass, there must be sufficient snowfall to match or exceed the annual loss through melting, evaporation, and calving, which occurs when the glacier loses solid chunks as icebergs to the sea or large lakes. (TPO15, R, S1, T1) 为了保持或增加一个冰川的体积,就必须要有足够多的降雪量,这些降雪量需要能够抵销或者超过每年因融雪、蒸发或者因冰川以冰山的形式飘向海洋或湖泊而形成的裂冰损失的量。

caravan[2] ['kærəvæn] 

【释义】 n. 1. 旅行拖车,大篷车 2.(穿越沙漠等的)旅行队

【例句】 Trade was the mainstay of the urban economy in the Middle East, as caravans negotiated the surrounding desert, restricted only by access to water and by mountain ranges. (TPO16, R, S1, T1) 贸易是中东城市经济的中流砥柱,尽管受到水源缺乏以及山岭的阻挡,商队还是能够成功地穿越沙漠。

caravel[2] ['kærəˌvel] 

【释义】 n. 小帆船

【例句】 Shipbuilders began developing a new type of vessel properly designed to operate in rough, open water: the caravel. (TPO17, R, S1, T1) 造船工匠们开始研制一种适用于水流较急的开放水域的新型船只——小型帆船。

carnivore[2] ['kɑːnɪvɔː] 

【释义】 n. 食肉动物

【例句】 The reduced level of photosynthesis led to a massive decline in plant life of all kinds, and this caused massive starvation first of herbivores and subsequently of carnivores. (TPO15, R, S2, T2) 光合作用的减弱导致了各种植物的大规模减少,而这首先会造成大量食草动物被饿死,随后就是食肉动物被饿死。

castle[2] ['kɑːsl] 

【释义】 n. 城堡 v. 置于城堡中

【例句】 The poems were song performed by a minstrel, a singer who travelled from castle to castle, singing to its local lord and its knights. (TPO13, L, S2, L1) 诗歌是由游吟诗人所唱的歌,他会穿梭于各个城堡之间,为当地的君王和骑士吟唱。

cellular[2] ['seljʊlə] 

【释义】 a. 细胞的

【例句】 Leatherbacks apparently do not generate internal heat the way we do, or the way birds do, as a by-product of cellular metabolism. (TPO15, R, S2, T1) 棱皮龟产生内部热量的方式显然与我们或者鸟类产生内部热量的方式不一样,我们或者鸟类产生的热量是细胞新陈代谢的副产品。

【派生】 cellularity n. 细胞性

certificate[2] [səˈtɪfɪkɪt] 

【释义】 n. 证明,证书

【例句】 It'd be kind of fun plus participants get a 50-dollar gift certificate. (TPO18, L, S2, C1) 这会比较有趣,加上参与者还能得到50美元的礼券。

【派生】 certification n. 证明,被证明的状态
certificated a. 授予证明书的,合格的

cessation[2] [səˈseɪʃən]

【释义】 *n.* 休止，停止(close, end)

【例句】 There should be such a dramatic cessation of tree growth at the upper timberline. (TPO1, R, S1, T1) 林木线上的树木竟然会这样突然地停止生长。

champion[2] [ˈtʃæmpjən]

【释义】 *v.* 拥护，保卫，为…斗争 *n.* 冠军；拥护者

【例句】 The most widely accepted theory, championed by anthropologists in the late nineteenth and early twentieth centuries, envisions theater as emerging out of myth and ritual. (TPO1, R, S2, T1) 这一最广为接受的理论认为剧院产生于神话和宗教仪式，这一理论在19世纪末和20世纪早期受到了人类学家的拥护。

【派生】 championship *n.* 锦标赛；冠军称呼

chariot[2] [ˈtʃærɪət]

【释义】 *n.*(古代用于战争或竞赛的)双轮战车

【例句】 Rock paintings in the Sahara indicate that horses and chariots were used to traverse the desert and that by 300-200 B. C., there were trade routes across the Sahara. (TPO7, R, S2, T2) 撒哈拉地区的岩画表明，马匹和战车被用来穿越沙漠地带，并且在公元前300至200年间，该地区已出现商贸通道。

chase[2] [tʃeɪs]

【释义】 *v.* 1. 追逐，追赶 2. 试图赢得，追求 *n.* 追捕，追逐

【例句】 Well, it turns out that quite a long time ago—I'm talking tens of thousands of years—things on the grassy plains used to be very different for the pronghorns, because back then, lions used to live on the plains, chasing and preying upon the pronghorns. (TPO17, S, Q4) 结果是，在很久以前——我说的是在大约几百万年前——生活在草原上的叉角羚的境况是完全不同于现在的，因为那个时候草原上生活着狮子，它们追逐并捕获叉角羚为食。

chemosynthetic[2]

【释义】 *a.* 化能合成的

【例句】 You see, it turns out that certain microorganisms are chemosynthetic. (TPO15, L, S2, L2) 你看，结果显示某些微生物是化能合成的。

cherry[2] [ˈtʃerɪ]

【释义】 *n.* 樱桃，樱桃树，樱桃色

【例句】 Some are soft and tempting, like a peach or a cherry. (TPO9, R, S2, T2) 有一些则很软，很诱人，比如桃子或樱桃。

chivalry[2] [ˈʃɪvəlrɪ]

【释义】 *n.* 骑士精神，骑士制度

【例句】 The French said you really cannot talk about real people who lived in opera and they relied on mythology to give them their characters and their plots, mythology, the past old traditions, the novels of chivalry or the epics of chivalry out of the middle ages. (TPO12, L, S2, L1) 法国人说你无法讨论那些真实存在于歌剧中的人，因此他们通过神话学来给予他们性格和特征。神话，就是那些过去的老传统，那些有关于中世纪骑士精神的小说或是史诗。

chromatophore[2] [krəuˈmætəˌfɔː]

【释义】 *n.* 色素细胞，色素体

【例句】 The color changes are executed by two different kinds of cells in the octopus' skin, mainly by color cells on the skin's surface called chromatophores. (TPO17, L, S2, L2) 颜色变化是由章鱼皮肤上两种不同的细胞完成的，主要由皮肤表面上叫做色素细胞的颜色细胞完成。

cinnamon[2] [ˈsɪnəmən]

【释义】 *n.* 肉桂皮，桂皮香料

【例句】 Spices can come from tree bark like cinnamon, plant roots like ginger, flower buds like cloves. (TPO18, L, S2, L1) 香料可能是树皮做成的，例如桂皮，也可能是植物的根，

例如生姜，再或者是花蕾，比如丁香。

citric[2] ['sɪtrɪk]

【释义】*a.* 柠檬的，柠檬酸的
【例句】Florida has long had a great citric industry, large growth of oranges, lemons and the like. (TPO11, L, S2, L1) 佛罗里达州一直有庞大的柠檬酸产业，大批地种植橘子、柠檬和类似的东西。
【搭配】citric acid 柠檬酸

clove[2] [kləʊv]

【释义】*n.* 丁香
【例句】Spices can come from tree bark like cinnamon, plant roots like ginger, flower buds like cloves. (TPO18, L, S2, L1) 香料可能是树皮做成的，例如桂皮，也可能是植物的根，例如生姜，再或者是花蕾，比如丁香。

clutter[2] ['klʌtə]

【释义】*v.* 乱堆，塞满，充满 *n.* 一堆杂乱的东西
【例句】Darger's picture looks more cluttered, more crowded with details than the pictures of other artists because its entire surface's painted and there are no spaces left empty. (TPO11, S, Q4) Darger 的画比其他画家的画看起来更凌乱，挤满了更多的细节，因为整个画面都被画满了，没有留下一点空间。
【搭配】clutter up 乱堆，塞满
in a clutter 杂乱无章，乱七八糟

coastline[2] ['kəʊstlaɪn]

【释义】*n.* 海岸线
【例句】Other areas under investigation include magnetism, landmarks, coastlines, sonar, and even smells. (TPO11, R, S2, T1) 其它正在研究的领域包括磁性、地标、海岸线、声纳，甚至还有气味。

coerce[2] [kəʊ'ɜːs]

【释义】*v.* 强制，威胁（compel, force）
【例句】The growing power of the elite, who controlled the economy, would give them the means to physically coerce people to move to Teotihuacán and serve as additions to the labor force. (TPO8, R, S1, T1) 那些控制着经济的上层人士权力的增长使得他们有办法强迫人们迁移到特奥蒂瓦坎，从而作为劳动力的补充。
【派生】coercion *n.* 强迫，逼迫
coercive *a.* 强制的，强迫的
【搭配】coerce sb. into doing sth. 强迫某人干某事

coexist[2] [kəʊɪg'zɪst]

【释义】*v.* 共存，共处
【例句】Prior to 200 B. C. , a number of relatively small centers coexisted in and near the Valley of Mexico. (TPO8, R, S1, T1) 公元前200年前，在墨西哥山谷及山谷附近共存着一些相对较小的中心。
【派生】coexistence *n.* 共存
coexistent *a.* 同时共存的
【逆构】exist *v.* 存在
【搭配】coexist with 与…共处

cognition[2] [kɒg'nɪʃən]

【释义】*n.* 认识，认知
【例句】We've said that the term "Cognition" refers to mental states like: knowing and believing, and to mental processes that we use to arrive at those states. (TPO14, L, S1, L1) 我们所说的术语"认知"指的是这样的心理状态：知道且相信，以及达到这种心理状态的心理过程。
【逆构】cognitive *a.* 认识的，认知的
【搭配】social cognition 社会认知
cognition process 认知过程

cohesion[2] [kəʊ'hiːʒən]

【释义】*n.* 团结，凝聚力（unity）
【例句】The source of the Roman obsession with unity and cohesion may well have lain in the pattern of Rome's early development. (TPO7, R, S2, T1) 罗马人对于团结统一和凝聚力的沉迷或许在罗马早期发展的模式中就已经存在了。
【派生】cohesive *a.* 黏着的；紧凑的
【搭配】a lack of cohesion 缺乏凝聚力

返记菜单

citric[2] clove[2] clutter[2] coastline[2] coerce[2]
coexist[2] cognition[2] cohesion[2]

combat[2] ['kɒmbət]

【释义】 *n.* 战斗，斗争（battle, war）*v.* 战斗，与…斗争（fight）

【例句】 Such yawning is often referred to as "incongruous" because it seems out of place, at least on the tiredness view: soldiers yawning before combat, musicians yawning before performing, and athletes yawning before competing. (TPO18, R, S2, T1) 这种打呵欠的行为通常被称为是"不合适"的，因为这看起来很不得体，至少从疲倦论的观点来看是这样的：士兵在战斗前打呵欠，音乐家在表演前打呵欠，运动员在竞赛前打呵欠。

【派生】 combatant *n.* 战士
combative *a.* 好斗的
combativeness *n.* 斗志

【搭配】 combat with 与…战斗
combat for 为…奋斗
hand-to-hand combat 肉搏战，白刃战

command[2] [kə'mɑːnd]

【释义】 *n./v.* 1. 命令，指挥（order, instruct）2. 控制，支配（control, dominate）

【例句】 A maritime code known as the *Consulate of the Sea* which originated in the western Mediterranean region in the fourteenth century, won acceptance by a majority of sea goers as the normative code for maritime conduct; it defined such matters as the authority of a ship's officers, protocols of command, pay structures, the rights of sailors, and the rules of engagement when ships met one another on the sea-lanes. (TPO17, R, S1, T1) 14世纪时起源于西地中海地区的一部叫作《康索拉度海法》的海运法典赢得了大多数航海人的认可，并把它作为海上行为的规范指南。法典规定了船长的职权范围、指令的礼节、工资结构、水手们的权利以及船与船在海上相遇时的交战方式。

【派生】 commanding *a.* 指挥的，发号施令的
commandment *n.* 命令，指挥

【搭配】 obey command 服从命令

commerce[2] ['kɒmə(ː)s]

【释义】 *n.* 贸易，商业，商务

【例句】 Because people made large investments in sea commerce between East and West, they expected to make immense profits. (TPO17, R, S1, T1) 因为人们对东西方的海上贸易进行了大量投资，所以他们期望可以从中获得巨大利润。

commonplace[2] ['kɒmənpleɪs]

【释义】 *a.* 平常的，平凡的（common, ordinary, usual）*n.* 1. 陈词滥调 2. 寻常的事物

【例句】 What audiences came to see was the technological marvel of the movies: the lifelike reproduction of the commonplace motion of trains, of waves striking the shore, and of people walking in the street, and the magic made possible by trick photography and the manipulation of the camera. (TPO2, R, S2, T2) 观众所看到的是电影技术带来的奇迹，比如对平淡无奇的火车开动、海浪拍击海岸和人潮涌动栩栩如生的复述，以及通过特技摄影和操纵相机所制造出来的魔幻景象。

comprehend[2] [ˌkɒmprɪ'hend]

【释义】 *v.* 理解，领会（understand, grasp）

【例句】 The author George Comstock suggested that less than a quarter of children between the ages of six and eight years old understood standard disclaimers used in many toy advertisements and that disclaimers are more readily comprehended when presented in both audio and visual formats. (TPO14, R, S1, T1) 作家乔治·康斯托克表示，在六到八岁的孩子中，只有不到四分之一的孩子能理解玩具广告中使用的标准的免责声明，如果那些免责声明能够以声音和图像的形式呈现出来，那么孩子们理解起来就会更容易些。

【派生】 comprehension *n.* 理解（力）
comprehensive *a.* 广泛的；易理解的
comprehensible *a.* 可理解的，易懂的

conclusive[2] [kən'kluːsɪv]

【释义】 *a.* 令人确信的，毫无疑问的，决定性的（definitive, decisive）

【例句】 Wildman and Niles proved conclusively that

reflection, though difficult, benefits both teachers and students. (TPO9, R, S2, T1, Q12) Wildman和Niles确定地证明，反思虽然难，但对学生和老师都有益。

【派生】inconclusive *a.* 非决定性的
conclusion *n.* 结论，推论

【逆构】conclude *v.* 推断出，推论出

【搭配】conclusive evidence 确凿的证据

---

constraint[2] [kən'streɪnt]

【释义】*n.* 限制，约束，强制（bound, limitation, restraint）

【例句】The "Eidophusikon" was Loutherbourg's attempt to release painting from the constraints of the picture frame. (TPO9, L, S1, L1) "Eidophusikon"是鲁斯伯格想要把绘画从画框的局限中解放出来的尝试。

【反义】freedom

【派生】constrain *v.* 约束，抑制
constrained *a.* 被约束的，被迫的

【搭配】under constraint 被迫（地）

---

contrary[2] ['kɒntrərɪ]

【释义】*a.* 相反的，相对的，对抗的（opposite）*n.* 对立方，相反，反面

【例句】Contrary to what many people believe today, folk tales were originally intended for adults, not for children. (TPO5, L, S2, L2) 与很多人今天所认为的相反，民间故事最初是针对成年人而不是儿童的。

【派生】contrariwise *ad.* 反之，相反地

【搭配】on the contrary 正相反，恰恰相反
to the contrary 相反的（地），完全不同的（地）

---

controversy[2] ['kɒntrəvɜːsɪ]

【释义】*n.* 争论，辩论（contention, argument）

【例句】And more research might just raise more questions and create more controversies. (TPO10, L, S1, L1) 更多的研究可能只会引出更多的问题并制造更多的争论。

【派生】controversial *a.* 引起或可能引起争论的

---

convenience[2] [kən'viːnjəns]

【释义】*n.* 1. 便利，舒适，适宜 2. 便利设施，方便的时间

【例句】Yeah. For him, it's sculpture versus convenience. (TPO1, S, Q3) 是啊，对他来说，是雕塑影响了他的便利。

【逆构】convenient *a.* 舒适的，便利的

【搭配】convenience store 便利商店
for convenience 为了方便起见
at one's convenience 在某人方便之时

---

conversion[2] [kən'vɜːʃən]

【释义】*n.* 转变；改变信仰（change, transformation）

【例句】At the production level, in the United States the conversion was virtually completed by 1930. (TPO12, R, S2, T1) 在生产的层面，美国实际上在1930年才完成这种转变。

【逆构】converse *a.* 相反的，逆向的

---

conviction[2] [kən'vɪkʃən]

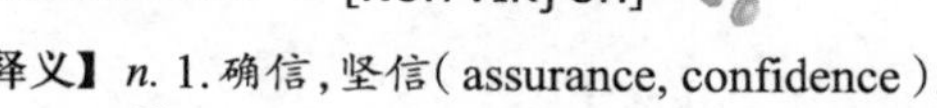

【释义】*n.* 1. 确信，坚信（assurance, confidence）2. 定罪

【例句】It's a bit abstract but he's very into…ah…into each person believing his or her own thought, believing in yourself, the thought or conviction that's true for you. (TPO4, L, S1, L2) 这有些抽象，但是他深信，嗯，深信每个人都有自己的想法，相信自己，相信你认为正确的想法及信念。

【逆构】convict *v.* 证明…有罪，宣判…有罪

---

cottage[2] ['kɒtɪdʒ]

【释义】*n.* 小屋；村舍

【例句】Woollens and textile manufacturers, in particular, utilized rural cottage (in-home) production, which took advantage of cheap and plentiful rural labor. (TPO10, R, S2, T2) 尤其是羊毛和纺织制造商们，他们利用农村大量的廉价劳动力来进行家庭式生产。

【搭配】cottage industry 家庭手工业

---

credible[2] ['kredəbl]

【释义】*a.* 可信的，可靠的（believable, reliable）

【例句】Researcher Charles Atkin found that children believe that the characters used to advertise breakfast cereals are knowledgeable about cereals, and children accept such characters as credible sources of nutritional information. (TPO14, R, S1, T1) 研究员

Charles Atkin 发现,孩子们认为那些广告中做谷物早餐广告的人有着丰富的谷物知识,所以孩子们会把这些人物作为营养信息的可靠来源。

【派生】 credibility *n.* 可靠性,可信度

crevice[2] ['krevɪs] 

【释义】 *n.*(尤指岩石的)裂缝,缺口(gap, crack)

【例句】 Now, other forms of life could take hold: ferns and mosses (two of the most ancient types of land plants) that flourish even in rock crevices. (TPO9, R, S2, T2) 现在,另外两种生命形式也会在此扎根:蕨类和藓类植物(两种最古老的陆地植物),这两种植物甚至能在岩石的缝隙中生长。

【搭配】 a crevice in a wall 墙上的裂缝

critique[2] [krɪ'tiːk]

【释义】 *n.*(文艺等的)批评,评论(review, commentary)

【例句】 The critiques really tore the play to pieces when it opened. (TPO4, L, S1, C1) 那部话剧开演后被批评得体无完肤。

cure[2] [kjʊə] 

【释义】 *v.* 1. 治愈,治疗 2. 解决(问题)*n.* 1. 治愈,疗法 2. 对策

【例句】 Mineral deficiencies in many plants can be cured by misting their roots with a nutrient solution or by transferring the plants to a soilless nutrient solution. (TPO5, R, S1, T1) 很多植物的矿物质缺乏问题可以通过用营养液的雾气熏蒸其根部或是把它们移植到一种无土的营养液中来治愈。

curly[2] ['kɜːlɪ]

【释义】 *a.* 卷曲的(frizzy)

【例句】 Those curly lines are supposed to be cracks in the rock. (TPO16, L, S1, L1) 那些卷曲的线条应该是岩石上的裂缝。

【搭配】 curly hair 卷发

cyclotron[2] ['saiklətrɔn]

【释义】 *n.* 回旋加速器

【例句】 But then, 12 years later in 1937, a different team became the first to synthesize the element using a cyclotron. (TPO8, L, S2, L2) 但在12年后的1937年,另一支队伍成为了第一个使用回旋加速器将元素合成的队伍。

dawn[2] [dɔːn]

【释义】 *n.* 1. 开端,萌芽(outset) 2. 黎明,拂晓 *v.* 1. 破晓,(天)刚亮 2. 逐渐明白

【例句】 But be that as it may, whatever the exact date, whether it's 15,000, 20,000 or 30,000 years ago, the Chauvet paintings are from the dawn of art. (TPO3, L, S2, L1) 尽管如此,无论是多么确切的日期,15000或20000或30000年前,肖韦洞窟的壁画都是艺术的渊源。

【搭配】 at dawn 拂晓时

decimal[2] ['desɪməl] 

【释义】 *n.* 小数 *a.* 十进制的(tenfold)

【例句】 Putting in a decimal? (TPO2, L, S2, L2) 将这些数字转换成小数?

【搭配】 decimal point 小数点
decimal system 十进制

decisive[2] [dɪ'saɪsɪv] 

【释义】 *a.* 1. 决定性的 2. 果断的,确定的

【例句】 Their results were decisive. (TPO4, L, S2, L1) 他们的结果是决定性的。

【派生】 decisiveness *n.* 果断,决断

【逆构】 decision *n.* 决定,决心

deglaciation[2] [diːgleiʃi'eiʃən] 

【释义】 *n.* 冰川的消失,冰消作用

【例句】 More recent geologic studies documented deglaciation and the existence of ice-free areas throughout major coastal areas of British Columbia, Canada, by 13,000 years ago. (TPO9, R, S1, T1) 更多最近的地质研究证明13000年前英属哥伦比亚、加拿大的主要海岸地区发生过冰川的消失并存在无冰区域。

返记菜单

crevice[2] critique[2] cure[2] curly[2] cyclotron[2]
dawn[2] decimal[2] decisive[2] deglaciation[2]

dehydrate[2] [diːˈhaɪdreɪt]

【释义】*v.* 脱水，去水（dry, desiccate）
【例句】They dehydrate. (TPO14, L, S1, L2) 它们会脱水。
【派生】dehydration *n.* 脱水，干燥
dehydrated *a.* 脱水的，干燥的

deliberate[2] [dɪˈlɪbəreɪt]

【释义】*a.* 1. 有意的，蓄意的（intentional, planned）2. 沉着的，从容不迫的 *v.* 仔细考虑
【例句】Contrary to the arguments of some that much of the Pacific was settled by Polynesians accidentally marooned after being lost and adrift, it seems reasonable that this feat was accomplished by deliberate colonization expeditions that set out fully stocked with food and domesticated plants and animals. (TPO5, R, S2, T1) 一些人认为在太平洋大部分地区定居的是意外迷路而流亡的波利尼西亚人，但与此相反的另一种理论看似更加合理，该理论认为这一壮举是由有意的殖民远征活动创造的，他们在出发时准备了充足的食物及驯化的动植物。
【派生】deliberately *ad.* 故意地；慎重地
deliberation *n.* 仔细考虑，商议
deliberative *a.* 审议的，商议的

deliver[2] [dɪˈlɪvə]

【释义】*v.* 1. 递送，交付（transfer, send）2. 发言（express）3. 给…接生 4. 解救，拯救
【例句】Merchants were able to avoid the risk of carrying large amounts of gold and silver by waiting to pay for goods until the goods had been delivered. (TPO10, R, S2, T2) 通过等到货物被交付以后再支付货款，商人们就能避免携带大量金银的风险。
【派生】delivery *n.* 投递，传送；讲话方式，风度
deliverable *a.* 可交付的 *n.* [常 *pl.*] 备送货物
【搭配】deliver up 交出，放弃
deliver from 从…处释放出来

depart[2] [dɪˈpɑːt]

【释义】*v.* 离开，出发（leave, take off）
【例句】He had driven me to a place in the desert where I would depart from his territory. 他开车送我去沙漠里一个地方，从那儿，我将离开他的领地。
【派生】departure *n.* 离开，离去

detach[2] [dɪˈtætʃ]

【释义】*v.* 拆卸，使分开，使分离（seperate）
【例句】One necessary condition seems to be a somewhat detached view of human problems. (TPO1, R, S2, T1)（戏剧发展的）一个必要条件似乎是有点超脱地看待人类的问题。
【反义】attach
【派生】detachable *a.* 可拆卸的
detached *a.* 分开的，独立的；超然的，客观的
detachment *n.* 分遣队，独立小分队；冷静，超然
【搭配】detach from 从…分离
detach yourself 使自己少卷入…

deviate[2] [ˈdiːvɪeɪt]

【释义】*v.* 背离，偏离（diverge, divert）
【例句】Should the use of rewards fail, members can frequently win by rejecting or threatening to ostracize those who deviate from the primary group's norms. (TPO13, R, S1, T1) 如果没有有效利用奖励，成员就可以时常通过拒绝或威胁来排斥那些偏离主要群体行为规范的人，以此来达到目的。
【派生】deviation *n.* 背离
【搭配】deviate from the rules 背离规则

devoid[2] [dɪˈvɔɪd]

【释义】*a.* 毫无，完全没有的（lacking, empty, vacant）
【例句】Since the raising of most crops necessiates the prior removal of the natural vegetation, crop failures leave extensive tracts of land devoid of a plant cover and susceptible to wind and water erosion. (TPO2, R, Sl, T1) 由于耕种作物的需要，人们必须将土地原有的自然植被清除，所以当庄稼歉收时，大片土地就会没有任何植被覆盖，从而更易于受到风力和流水的侵蚀。
【搭配】be devoid of sth. 完全没有某物

返记菜单

dehydrate[2] deliberate[2] deliver[2] depart[2] detach[2]
deviate[2] devoid[2]

digest[2] [dɪ'dʒest]

【释义】*v.* 1. 消化 2. 领会，领悟 *n.* 摘要，概要

【例句】It often takes a long time to digest new ideas. 领会新的思想通常要花很长时间。

【派生】digestive *a.* 消化的，有消化力的
digestion *n.* 消化力；领悟

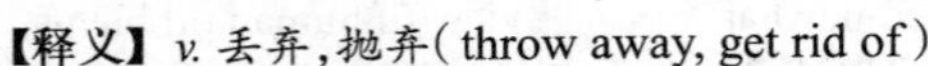

discard[2] [dɪs'kɑːd]

【释义】*v.* 丢弃，抛弃（throw away, get rid of）

【例句】At the ceremonies, they ate festive meals and then discarded the pots in which the meals had been prepared or served. (TPO5, W, Q1) 在仪式期间，他们吃掉节日大餐，然后把用来准备或盛放食物的锅锅罐罐丢掉。

【派生】discardable *a.* 可丢弃的

discoloration[2] [dɪsˌkʌlə'reiʃən]

【释义】*n.* 变色，变色点，污渍

【例句】Anthocyanin discoloration occurs on stems, petioles, and low leaf surfaces. (TPO5, R, S1, T1) 花青素变色会出现在枝干、叶柄和低处的叶子的表面。

【逆构】discolor *v.* 使褪色，使变色

discriminate[2] [dɪs'krɪmɪneɪt]

【释义】*v.* 1. 区别，辨别（distinguish）2. 不公正地对待，歧视

【例句】Each of the preceding techniques provides the researcher with evidence that the infant can detect or discriminate between stimuli. (TPO13, R, S2, T2) 之前的每一种技术都向研究者提供了证据，证明婴儿能够对刺激进行探知或区别。

【派生】discrimination *n.* 辨别（力），区别；歧视

【搭配】discriminate from 区分

disguise[2] [dɪs'gaɪz]

【释义】*v./n.* 1. 掩饰，掩盖（conceal）2. 伪装，假装（camouflage）

【例句】Their streamlined bodies, the absence of hind legs, and the presence of a fluke and blowhole cannot disguise their affinities with land dwelling mammals. (TPO2, R, S2, T1) 它们的身体呈流线型，没有后腿，长有尾片和喷水孔，但这些都不能掩盖它们与陆生哺乳动物的相似性。

【派生】disguiser *n.* 伪装者

【搭配】in disguise 伪装的，乔装的

disinhibition[2] [ˌdɪsɪnhə'bɪʃən]

【释义】*n.* [心] 抑制解除

【例句】And what happens is, they inhibit each other, they cancel each other out in a way, and a third seemingly irrelevant behavior surfaces through a process that we call "Disinhibition". (TPO4, L, S1, L1) 而出现的情况是，他们互相抑制，在某种程度上相互抵消，于是一种似乎不相干的第三种行为通过一个我们称之为"抑制解除"的过程浮出水面。

【搭配】disinhibition theory 抑制解除说
disinhibition effect 松绑效应

dislike[2] [dɪs'laɪk]

【释义】*n./v.* 不喜欢，厌恶

【例句】The likes and dislikes of that patron would've had an effect on what was being composed and performed. (TPO16, L, S1, L2) 对赞助人的好恶会影响所谱写和演奏的曲子。

disposal[2] [dɪs'pəuzəl]

【释义】*n.* 1. 清除，处理，处置 2.（企业、财产等的）变卖，让与

【例句】But I can imagine that…for instance, seed disposal might be a factor. (TPO6, L, S1, L2) 但是我可以想象，例如，种子的处理可能是一个因素。

【派生】dispose *v.* 处理，处置
disposed *a.* 有…倾向的

【搭配】at one's disposal 由某人随意使用

Word List 34

distort[2] [dɪs'tɔːt] 

【释义】v. 使(某物)变形;歪曲(deform, twist)
【例句】They claim that the Chevalier distorted or invented many events in the memoir to make his life seem more exciting and glamorous than it really was. (TPO7, W, Q1) 他们断言,Chevalier 在回忆录中扭曲或杜撰了许多事件,想以此来让他的生活看起来更加刺激和充满吸引力。
【派生】distortion n. 扭曲,变形,曲解

dive[2] ['daɪv] 

【释义】v./n. 跳水,潜水;俯冲,扑
【例句】The skull also lacks a blowhole, another cetacean adaption for diving. (TPO2, R, S2, T1) 头盖骨也没有呼吸孔,呼吸孔是鲸类为适应水下环境的一种适应性表现。

divorce[2] [dɪ'vɔːs] 

【释义】v./n. 离婚,分离,脱离
【例句】The myths may even come to be acted out under conditions divorced from these rites. (TPO1, R, S2, T1) 神话甚至可以在脱离宗教仪式的情况下产生。
【搭配】divorce from 从…分离出来

donate[2] [dəʊ'neɪt] 

【释义】v. 捐赠,赠送
【例句】Eventually it ended up in an art auction where it was bought and then donated to an art museum in Baltimore. (TPO15, L, S2, L1) 最终,它在一场艺术品拍卖会上被买走,之后又被捐献给了巴尔的摩的一个博物馆。
【派生】donation n. 捐献

drawback[2] ['drɔːbæk]

【释义】n. 缺点,毛病,不利因素(flaw, disadvantage, shortcoming)
【例句】That is the biggest drawback to solar energy. (TPO13, L, S2, L2) 这是太阳能的最大缺点。

egocentric[2] [iːgəʊ'sentrɪk] 

【释义】a. 自我中心的,利己主义的
【例句】In addition, her thinking would be primarily egocentric. (TPO13, L, S1, C1) 另外,她的思想主要以自我为中心。
【搭配】egocentric thinking 自我中心思维

elicit[2] [ɪ'lɪsɪt] 

【释义】v. 套出(信息);引出(某人的反应)(arouse, educe, evoke)
【例句】By providing us with definitions of situations, they elicit from us behavior that conforms to group-devised meanings. (TPO13, R, S1, T1) 通过对我们进行形势的说明,他们引导我们作出符合群体意义的行为。
【派生】elicitation n. 引出,启发
【搭配】elicit sth. from sb. 从某人处探出

embrace[2] [ɪm'breɪs] 

【释义】v. 1. 拥抱 2. 包含,涉及(include, involve) 3. 欣然接受,采纳 n. 拥抱
【例句】It embraces the old custom of earthenware burial ceramics with later religious images and architectural ornament. (TPO10, R, S1, T1) 它将土质陪葬陶器的古老传统与后来的宗教图案和建筑装饰进行了融合。
【搭配】warm embrace 温暖的拥抱

empirical[2] [em'pɪrɪkəl] 

【释义】a. 经验主义的;以观察或实验为根据的
【例句】The empirical evidence, such as it is, suggests an altogether different function for yawning—namely, that yawning prepares us for a change in activity level. (TPO18, R, S2, T1) 实验证据,尽管不怎么好,却表明了打呵欠的一个完全不同的功能——即,打呵欠是在为我们活动的变化做准备。

endorse[2] [ɪn'dɔːs]

【释义】v. 1. 赞同,认可(accept, confirm) 2. (在支票背面)签名,背书

【例句】So, for over a century now, the Austen's family itself has endorsed the claim that the girl in the portrait is Jane Austen. (TPO12, W, Q1) 所以，一个多世纪以来，奥斯汀家族本身已经认可了这一说法，即画像中的女孩就是简·奥斯汀。

【派生】endorsement *n.* 认可，支持；背书

endow[2] [ɪn'daʊ]

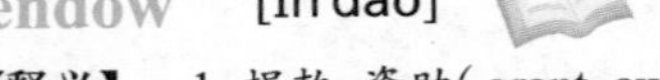

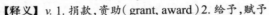

【释义】*v.* 1. 捐款，资助(grant, award) 2. 给予，赋予

【例句】More often, we simply cooperate with others to reach some end without endowing the relationship with any larger significance. (TPO13, R, S1, T1) 更多时候，我们只是与他人合作来达成某种目标，而并不赋予这种关系以更多的意义。

【派生】endowment *n.* 禀赋；捐款

【搭配】endow sb. with sth. 天生赋有

engender[2] [ɪn'dʒendə]

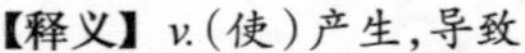

【释义】*v.* (使)产生，导致

【例句】In turn, a deep attachment to the land, and to the stability which rural life engenders, fostered the Roman virtues: gravitas, a sense of responsibility, pietas, a sense of devotion to family and country, and justitia, a sense of the natural order. (TPO7, R, S2, T1) 反之，对土地和平稳的乡村生活的深深依恋孕育了罗马人的美德：庄重，一种责任感；敬重，对祖国和家庭奉献的使命感；正义，对自然秩序的遵循。

ensuing[2] [ɪn'sjuːɪŋ]

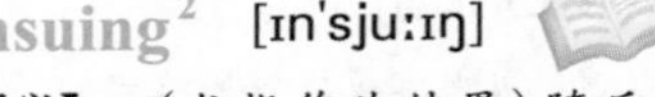

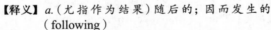

【释义】*a.* (尤指作为结果)随后的；因而发生的(following)

【例句】The ensuing rapid expansion of irrigation agriculture, especially from the 1950s onward, transformed the economy of the region. (TPO3, R, S1, T1) 随后发生的灌溉农业的迅速扩张，特别是20世纪50年代之后，改变了这一地区的经济。

【逆构】ensue *v.* 因而发生，继而发生

entail[2] [ɪn'teɪl]

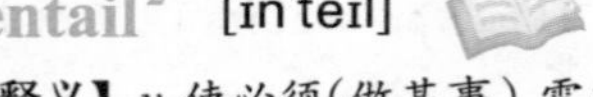

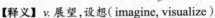

【释义】*v.* 使必须(做某事)，需要

【例句】A secondary group entails two or more people who are involved in an impersonal relationship and have come together for a specific, practical purpose. (TPO13, R, S1, T1) 次要群体需要两个或两个以上的人，他们应该不牵涉私人关系，而是为了一个具体的实际目的走到一起。

【派生】entailment *n.* 需要

envision[2] [ɪn'vɪʒən]

【释义】*v.* 展望，设想(imagine, visualize)

【例句】The most widely accepted theory, championed by anthropologists in the late nineteenth and early twentieth centuries, envisions theater as emerging out of myth and ritual. (TPO1, R, S2, T1) 这一最广为接受的理论认为剧院产生于神话和宗教仪式，这一理论在19世纪末和20世纪早期受到了人类学家的拥护。

equilibrium[2] [ˌiːkwɪ'lɪbrɪəm]

【释义】*n.* 平衡(balance, stability)

【例句】In the Indus plain, the movement of saline (salty) groundwaters has still not reached equilibrium after 70 years of being tapped. (TPO12, R, S2, T2) 在印度河平原上，含盐的地下水在经过了70年的开发后还是没有达到平衡。

erect[2] [ɪ'rekt]

【释义】*v.* 1. 建立，创立 2. 使直立，竖起 *a.* 直立的，垂直的，挺立的(straight, upright)

【例句】This used to be an agricultural area and we already know that where the main lecture hall now stands, there once were farm house and barn that were erected in the late 1700s. (TPO3, L, S2, C1) 这里过去是一片农场，我们已经知道，现在主讲厅所在的地方曾经是18世纪后期时建立起来的农舍和仓库。

【派生】erection *n.* 直立，竖起；建筑物

erode[2] [ɪ'rəʊd]

【释义】*v.* 1. (风雨等)腐蚀，侵蚀(corrode, wash away) 2. 逐步削弱(权力或信心等)

【例句】The development of new international trade routes could undermine the monetary base

and erode state power. (TPO16, R, S1, T1) 新国际贸易路线的开发可能会削弱货币基础,并侵蚀国家政权。

【派生】erosion *n.* 腐蚀,侵蚀

ethic² [ˈeθɪk]

【释义】*n.* 伦理,道德体系

【例句】They favor an egalitarian ethic of the open market. (TPO16, R, S1, T1) 他们崇尚自由市场的平等伦理规范。

【派生】ethical *a.* 伦理的,合乎道德的
ethics *n.* 道德规范,道德标准

【搭配】professional ethics 职业道德
a code of ethics 道德准则

exceed² [ɪkˈsiːd]

【释义】*v.* 超过,超出(surpass)

【例句】For a glacier to grow or maintain its mass, there must be sufficient snowfall to match or exceed the annual loss through melting, evaporation, and calving, which occurs when the glacier loses solid chunks as icebergs to the sea or large lakes. (TPO15, R, S1, T1) 为了保持或增加一个冰川的体积,就必须要有足够多的降雪量,这些降雪量需要能够抵销或者超过每年因融雪、蒸发或者因冰川以冰山的形式飘向海洋或湖泊而形成的裂冰损失的量。

【派生】exceeded *a.* 超过的,超出的

【搭配】exceed in 在…方面超过

expanse² [ɪksˈpæns]

【释义】*n.* 宽阔的区域(patch)

【例句】Other researchers go even further, suggesting that the data provide evidence for large open expanses of water on the early Martian surface. (TPO8, R, S2, T2) 其他研究人员通过更进一步的研究表明,这些数据提供了早期火星表面上存在大片水域的证据。

【逆构】expand *v.* 扩展

expend² [ɪksˈpend]

【释义】*v.* 1. 急剧扩大,激增 2. 爆炸,爆发(burst, erupt, blow up)

【例句】Should they go out during the daytime when it's hotter outside and they have to expend more energy? (TPO16, L, S2, L1) 他们应该在白天外面较热的时候出去,然后不得不消耗更多的能量吗?

【搭配】expend sth. in/on doing sth. 在做某事上花费(时间、金钱或精力等)

explode² [ɪkˈspləʊd]

【释义】*n.* 1. 激增,急剧膨胀 2. 爆炸 3. 爆发

【例句】And finally, you have an unregulated market place, no government constrains, where price could explode. (TPO6, L, S1, L1) 最后,市场极为不规律,没有政府的限制,价格激增。

【派生】explosion *n.* 爆炸,爆发;激增

extermination² [ekˈstəːmiˈneiʃən]

【释义】*n.* 根绝,灭绝(extinction)

【例句】The deer which once picturesquely dotted the meadows around the fort were gone [in 1832], hunted to extermination in order to protect the crops. (TPO4, R, S1, T1) 曾把堡垒周围的草原装点得如画般美丽的鹿群消失了(在1832年)——人们为了保护农作物而将其猎杀殆尽。

【逆构】exterminate *v.* 根除,灭绝

eyesight² [ˈaɪsaɪt]

【释义】*n.* 视力

【例句】Hawks have such good eyesight that they can spot a tiny mouse in the field from high up in the air. (TPO15, S, Q6) 鹰的视力非常好,它们能够从高空中看见田地里的一只小老鼠。

factual² [ˈfæktjʊəl]

【释义】*a.* 基于事实的,真实的,实在的(real, actual)

【例句】The real point is that it's easy for errors in factual material to be corrected in an online encyclopedia. (TPO6, W, Q1) 真正的要点是,实际材料中所存在的错误很容易在在线百科全书中得到修正。

【派生】factualistic *a.* 求实的,尊重事实的

【搭配】factual proof 〈法〉事实证明

返记菜单

ethic² exceed² expanse² expend² explode²
extermination² eyesight² factual²

feasible[2] ['fi:zəbl]

【释义】*a.* 可行的，行得通的（practicable, possible）

【例句】Buildings contribute to human life when they provide shelter enrich space, complement their site, suit the climate, and are economically feasible. (TPO3, R, S1, T1) 建筑物为人类的生活做出了贡献，给人们提供了庇护所，丰富了空间，完善了人们的居所，帮助人们适应气候的变化，同时人们在经济上也是可以承受的。

【派生】feasibility *n.* 可行性，可能性

【搭配】a feasible plan 可行的计划

federation[2] [ˌfedə'reɪʃən]

【释义】*n.* 1. 联合会，联盟（confederation, union）2. 联邦政府，联邦共和国

【例句】Having an efficient means of transportation, well, that helps the Iroquois to form a federation linked by natural waterways. (TPO7, L, S2, L1) 有了如此便利的交通运输工具，易洛魁人就可以通过自然航道形成联盟。

【搭配】All-China Women's Federation 中华妇女联合会

fishery[2] ['fɪʃərɪ]

【释义】*n.* 渔业；渔场

【例句】The people of the Netherlands, with a long tradition of fisheries and mercantile shipping, had difficulty in developing good harbors suitable for steamships. (TPO18, R, S1, T1) 有着悠久的渔业和商业船运业传统的荷兰人在发展适宜于大轮船的优良港口方面遇到了困难。

fissure[2] ['fɪʃə]

【释义】*n.*（岩石或土地的）裂缝，裂隙（crack, break）

【例句】He does not agree that it causes fissures in glaciers. (TPO7, L, S2, L2) 他不同意这会引起冰山裂缝的观点。

【搭配】a narrow fissure in rock 岩石上的狭窄的裂缝

flange[2] [flændʒ]

【释义】*n.*（机械等的）凸缘，（火车的）轮缘

【例句】In some industrial regions, heavily laden wagons, with flanged wheels, were being hauled by horses along metal rails; and the stationary steam engine was puffing in the factory and mine. (TPO6, R, S1, T1) 在一些工业地区，承载重物的四轮马车都配备有带凸的缘轮，并且是通过几匹马拉动而在铁轨上行驶的；而静止的蒸汽发动机则被用于工厂和矿井之中。

【派生】flangeless *a.* 无凸缘的

flutter[2] ['flʌtə]

【释义】*v.* 1. 振翼，拍打翅膀 2. 飘动 3.（因激动或紧张使心脏）怦怦跳 *n.* 1. 拍动，振颤 2. 不安，激动 3.（赛马时）下一笔小赌注

【例句】Furthermore, he noticed that as they fluttered around in the cage, they often launched themselves in the direction of their normal migratory route. (TPO11, R, S2, T1) 此外，他注意到，每当它们在笼子里扇动翅膀时，它们总是让自己朝向其平常迁徙的路线。

【搭配】have a flutter（在证券交易市场或赛马场）参加小赌

fodder[2] ['fɒdə]

【释义】*n.* 饲料，草料（forage）

【例句】Even with snow on the ground, the high bushy understory is exposed; also snow and wind bring down leafy branches of cedar, hemlock, red alder, and other arboreal fodder. (TPO4, R, S1, T1) 即便白雪覆盖了大地，高而浓密的林下叶层依然不会被掩盖；风雪也吹落了雪松、铁杉、赤阳木和其他树木的茂密枝叶。

foreground[2] ['fɔ:graʊnd]

【释义】*n.* 1.（图片或照片的）前景

【例句】Small boats moved more quickly across the foreground than larger ones did that were closer to the horizon. (TPO9, L, S1, L1) 小船比靠近地平线的大船更快地划过前景。

【搭配】be in the foreground 处于重要地位

forerunner[2] ['fɔːˌrʌnə] 

【释义】*n.* 1. 先驱,前身(predecessor) 2. 前兆,预兆(herald)

【例句】This table was the forerunner of the modern table. (TPO16, R, S2, T1) 此元素周期表是现代元素周期表的前身。

formula[2] ['fɔːmjʊlə] 

【释义】*n.* 公式,规则

【例句】But the formula for well-made play required certain elements being included, in a particular order, and most importantly, that everything in the plays be logically connected. (TPO7, L, S1, L1) 但是佳构剧的规则需要包含一些按特定顺序排列的元素,并且最重要的是,剧中的每一情节都要在逻辑上紧密相连。

【派生】formulate *v.* 系统地阐述或表达

formulate[2] ['fɔːmjʊleɪt] 

【释义】*v.* 系统地阐述或表达;用公式表示

【例句】The time had come to formulate a hypothesis. (TPO7, R, S1, T1) 到了该提出假说的时候了。

【派生】formulation *n.* 公式化;规划,构想

foul[2] [faʊl] 

【释义】*v.* 1. 弄脏,玷污,败坏 2. 妨碍,犯规 *a.* 1. 污秽的,肮脏的 2. 恶劣的,不道德的 3. 犯规的 *n.* 犯规

【例句】Offshore platforms may also lose oil, creating oil slicks that drift ashore and foul the beaches, harming the environment. (TPO4, R, S2, T2) 海上钻井平台也会漏油,从而导致浮油漂向海岸,污染海滩,破坏环境。

【派生】foulness *n.* 纠缠,卑鄙

【搭配】technical foul 技术犯规

founder[2] ['faʊndə] 

【释义】*n.* 创立者,创始人(establisher,originator) *v.* 摔倒;失败;沉没;坍塌

【例句】Its founder Rudolph Julian was a canny business man. (TPO8, L, S1, L2) 其创始人鲁道夫·朱利安是一个精明的商人。

【逆构】found *v.* 创立,建立

fraction[2] ['frækʃən] 

【释义】*n.* 1. 小部分,少量(segment, fragment) 2. 分数

【例句】When researchers look really carefully at the DNA in Chromosomes though, they were amazed, we all were, to find that only a fraction of it, maybe 20-30%, converts into meaningful genetic information. (TPO12, L, S1, L1) 然而,当研究人员对染色体中的DNA进行仔细观察后,他们惊奇地发现,我们都很惊奇,只有其中一小部分,大约20-30%,转变成了有意义的基因信息。

【派生】fractional *a.* 部分的;分数的

【搭配】fraction defective 不合格率;废品率

fuse[2] [fjuːz] 

【释义】*v.* 熔化,熔合(combine, blend) *n.* 保险丝,熔丝

【例句】He had a special way of fusing, or some people might say confusing, science and fiction. (TPO3, L, S1, L2) 他有一种特别的方式来把科学和小说融合在一起,或者一些人可能会说是混淆在一起。

【派生】fusion *n.* 熔合;核聚变

【搭配】safety fuse 保险丝

garrison[2] ['gærɪsn] 

【释义】*n.* 驻地;守备部队 *v.* 派兵驻防于(军事驻地)

【例句】The physical bonds included the network of military garrisons, which were stationed in every province, and the network of stone-built roads that linked the provinces with Rome. (TPO7, R, S2, T1) 物质上的联结包括安置在各省的军事驻防网络以及连接各省与罗马的石筑公路网。

【搭配】garrison duty 守备任务

gaseous[2] ['gæsɪəs] 

【释义】*a.* 气体的,气态的

【例句】It was therefore quite surprising when John William Strutt, Lord Rayleigh, discovered a gaseous element in 1894 that did not fit into

返记菜单

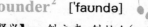

forerunner[2]	formula[2]	formulate[2]	foul[2]	founder[2]
fraction[2]	fuse[2]	garrison[2]	gaseous[2]	

the previous classification scheme. (TPO16, R, S2, T1) 因此，当1894年约翰·威廉·斯特拉特，也就是瑞利勋爵，发现了一种不属于之前类别中的气态元素时，这是相当惊人的。

【搭配】 gaseous fuel 气体燃料

gateway[2] ['geɪtweɪ]

【释义】 *n.* 入口，通道，途径(entry, opening)

【例句】 Other statues were designed to be placed within an architectural setting, for instance, in front of the monumental entrance gateways to temples known as pylons. (TPO11, R, S1, T1) 其他雕像被放置在建筑群中，比如，在庙宇的纪念性入口塔门的前方。

ginger[2] ['dʒɪndʒə]

【释义】 *n.* 1. 姜，生姜 2. [非正式] 精力，活力

【例句】 Spices can come from tree bark like cinnamon, plant roots like ginger, flower buds like cloves. (TPO18, L, S2, L1) 香料可能是树皮做成的，例如桂皮，也可能是植物的根，例如生姜，再或者是花蕾，比如丁香。

【派生】 gingery *a.* 姜味的

【搭配】 ginger up 使充满活力

gist[2] [dʒɪst]

【释义】 *n.* 要点，主旨(essence, theme)

【例句】 Through hearing stories with a clear beginning, middle, and ending, children may learn to extract the gist of events in ways that they will be able to describe many years later. (TPO6, R, S2, T2) 听故事的时候有个清晰的开头、情节和结尾，孩子们就可能学会提取事件的要点，这样他们在过了很多年以后仍可以描述这些事情。

glamorous[2] ['glæmərəs]

【释义】 *n.* 充满魅力的，迷人的(attractive, charming, enchanting)

【例句】 They claim that the Chevalier distorted or invented many events in the memoir to make his life seem more exciting and glamorous than it really was. (TPO7, W, Q1) 他们断言，Chevalier 在回忆录中扭曲或杜撰了许多事件，想以此来让他的生活看起来更加刺激和充满吸引力。

glance[2] [glɑːns]

【释义】 *n.* 一瞥，扫视 *v.* 1. 一瞥，扫视(glimpse) 2. 浏览，粗略地看(skim)

【例句】 After all, even the most action filled exciting painting can represent only one moment in time; and any illusion of movement is gone after the first glance. (TPO9, L, S1, L1) 毕竟，再动感的画面也只能持续一时，关于运动的任何假象在一眼扫过之后都消失不见。

【反义】 stare, gaze

【搭配】 at a glance 看一眼就…；马上

gloomy[2] ['gluːmɪ]

【释义】 *a.* 1. 阴暗的(bleak) 2. 令人沮丧的，忧郁的(melancholy, depressing) 3. 前景黯淡的

【例句】 The other thing I noticed right away from this first image, just when the scene started, was that the city seemed gloomy. (TPO9, S, Q4) 在电影刚刚开始时，除了这个定场镜头，我还注意到城市看起来很灰暗。

【派生】 gollmily *ad.* 阴暗地，阴沉地

gorilla[2] [gə'rɪlə]

【释义】 *n.* 大猩猩

【例句】 Today, I'd like to look at some communication systems found in mammals, particularly in primates, such as orangutans, chimpanzees, gorillas. (TPO9, L, S2, L2) 今天我们将研究哺乳动物的一些交流系统，尤其是灵长目动物，比如猩猩、黑猩猩、大猩猩等。

gossip[2] ['gɒsɪp]

【释义】 *v.* 传播或散布流言蜚语 *n.* 流言蜚语，小道新闻(rumor)

【例句】 So, for example, you might have two servants gossiping as they are cleaning the house. (TPO7, L, S1, L1) 比如，你可能会看见两个佣人一边收拾房子一边说闲话。

【派生】 gossipy *a.* 闲聊式的，喜饶舌的

【搭配】 the gossip column（报纸上的）漫谈专栏

grandiose[2] ['grændɪəʊs] 

【释义】*a.* 庄严的，壮观的，浮夸的（magnificent, exaggerated）

【例句】In the face of the upcoming water supply crisis, a number of grandiose schemes have been developed to transport vast quantities of water by canal or pipeline from the Mississippi, the Missouri, or the Arkansas rivers. (TPO3, R, S1, T1) 在即将到来的水资源供应危机面前，人们提出了一些宏伟的计划，比如将密西西比河、密苏里河或者阿肯色河的水通过运河或管道输送到需要用水的地方。

【派生】grandiosity *n.* 宏伟，壮观

【逆构】grand *a.* 壮丽的，宏伟的

【搭配】a grandiose writing style 浮夸的写作风格

granule[2] ['grænjuːl] 

【释义】*n.* 小粒，微粒

【例句】With additional time, pressure, and refrozen meltwater from above, the small firn granules become larger, interlocked crystals of blue glacial ice. (TPO15, R, S1, T1) 有了额外的时间、压力以及那些位于上方的融雪重新结冰，那些较小的积雪颗粒就会变成更大的、互相连结的蓝色冰川晶体。

【派生】granular *a.* 颗粒状的

graph[2] [grɑːf]

【释义】*n.* 图表，图解（chart, diagram）

【例句】I've got all my data, so I'm starting to summarize it now, preparing graphs and stuff. (TPO2, L, S1, C1) 我已经收集好了所有需要的数据，所以我现在要开始对数据进行总结，准备图表和文字内容。

【派生】graphic *a.* 图表的；生动的
graphics *n.* 制图法，制图学
photograph *n.* 照片
telegraph *n.* 电报；电报机

grateful[2] ['greɪtfʊl]

【释义】*a.* 感激的，感谢的（thankful, appreciative）

【例句】We'd be grateful for any quiet place. (TPO16, L, S1, C1) 有一个安静的地方我们就感激不尽了。

gravitation[2] [ˌgrævɪ'teɪʃən] 

【释义】*n.* 万有引力，重力，引力作用（gravity）

【例句】It isn't really a scientific law, not in the sense of predicting gravitation mathematically or something. (TPO2, L, S2, L2) 它实际上并不是一条科学定律，至少从估算重力数值或者类似的方面来说不是。

【派生】gravitational *a.* 万有引力的

groat[2] [grəut]

【释义】*n.* 1. 昔日英国的四便士银币 2. 些许，少许的金钱

【例句】It's always worked just groat. (TPO16, L, S1, C1) 花费总是很少。

【搭配】not care a groat 毫不在意
not worth a groat 毫无价值

gull[2] [gʌl] 

【释义】*n.* 海鸥 *v.* 欺骗

【例句】Gulls have a countercurrent exchange in their legs. (TPO15, R, S2, T1) 海鸥的腿部有一个逆流交换循环系统。

【派生】gullery *n.* 鸥的繁殖地
gullible *a.* 易受骗的

【搭配】gull wing （飞机的）鸥翼

gusher[2] ['gʌʃə(r)] 

【释义】*n.* 1. 自喷井 2. 说话滔滔不绝的人

【例句】Although this rise of oil is almost always carefully controlled today, spouts of oil, or gushers, were common in the past. (TPO4, R, S2, T2) 虽然这种原油上浮现在几乎总是被小心地控制着，可在过去喷油管或自喷井却是很常见的。

【逆构】gush *v.* 喷涌，涌流

hacker[2] ['hækə]

【释义】*n.* 黑客，电脑高手

【例句】Second, even if the original entry in the online encyclopedia is correct, the communal nature of these online encyclopedias gives unscrupulous users and vandals or

返记菜单

grandiose[2] granule[2] graph[2] grateful[2] gravitation[2]
groat[2] gull[2] gusher[2] hacker[2]

hackers the opportunity to fabricate, delete, and corrupt information in the encyclopedia. (TPO6, W, Q1) 其次，即使在线百科全书的原始录入是正确的，但其公共性也会给那些无道德的用户、破坏者以及黑客们提供一些伪造、删除或更改百科全书中的信息的机会。

handicraft[2] ['hændɪkrɑːft]

【释义】*n.* 手工艺，手工艺品

【例句】Population growth generated an expansion of small-scale manufacturing, particularly of handicrafts, textiles, and metal production in England. (TPO10, R, S2, T2) 在英国，人口的增长促进了小规模制造业的发展，尤其是手工艺品、纺织品和金属制品。

【搭配】handicraft industry 手工业

harmony[2] ['hɑːmənɪ]

【释义】*n.* 一致，和谐，融洽

【例句】Individuals could interact with one another within a community of harmony. (TPO16, R, S1, T1) 在和谐的社区内个体可以相互影响。

【派生】harmonious *a.* 和谐的，融洽的
harmonize *v.*（使）协调，（使）和谐

【搭配】in harmony with 与…相协调
live in harmony 和睦相处

harness[2] ['hɑːnɪs]

【释义】*v.* 1. 利用…以产生动力 2. 套（马），给…上挽具 *n.*（全套）马具

【例句】In Britain one of the most dramatic changes of the Industrial Revolution was the harnessing of power. (TPO6, R, S1, T1) 在英国，工业革命带来的最大的变化之一就是动力的使用。

【搭配】in harness 在职，在工作中

hatchway[2] ['hætʃˌweɪ]

【释义】*n.* 舱口，天窗；地窖口

【例句】People walked around on the roofs and entered the house through a hatchway on the roof, down a wooden ladder. (TPO1, L, S2, L1) 人们可以在屋顶上来回走动，而且可以通过屋顶上的天窗，爬下梯子进入房子里。

haul[2] [hɔːl]

【释义】*v.* 拖，拉（pull）*n.* 1. 搬运物，搬运一次的量

【例句】In some industrial regions, heavily laden wagons, with flanged wheels, were being hauled by horses along metal rails; and the stationary steam engine was puffing in the factory and mine. (TPO6, R, S1, T1) 在一些工业地区，承载重物的四轮马车都配备有带凸的缘轮，并且是通过几匹马拉动而在铁轨上行驶的；而静止的蒸汽发动机则被用于工厂和矿井之中。

【反义】push

【派生】haulage *n.* 运输；运费
overhaul *n.* 全面检查，全面修订

【搭配】haul up 停止
haul off 退却，撤退

Word List 35

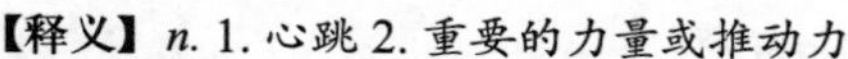

headquarters[2] ['hed,kwɔːtəz]

【释义】*n.* 总部，指挥部
【例句】Later on in the early years of the nineteenth century, when Fort Vancouver became the headquarters for the Hudson's Bay Company, deer populations continued to fluctuate. (TPO4, R, S1, T1) 后来，在19世纪早期，当温哥华成了哈德逊湾公司的总部所在地时，鹿群数量持续波动。
【逆构】headquarter *v.* 设立总部

heartbeat[2] ['hɑːtbiːt]

【释义】*n.* 1. 心跳 2. 重要的力量或推动力
【例句】Heart and respiration monitors provide the investigator with the number of heartbeats or breaths taken when a new stimulus is presented. (TPO13, R, S2, T2) 心脏和呼吸监测仪可以为观察者提供(婴儿)在受到新的刺激时的心跳和呼吸频率。
【搭配】in a heartbeat 立刻，马上

hearth[2] [hɑːθ]

【释义】*n.* 炉床，灶台
【例句】The main room had the hearths, for cooking and for heat. (TPO1, L, S2, L1) 主室里有灶台，供烹饪和取暖之用。
【派生】hearthside *n.* 炉边

heighten[2] ['haɪtn]

【释义】*v.* 提高，升高，加强
【例句】Numerical increases are used as quantifiable indicators of heightened interest in the new stimulus. (TPO13, R, S2, T2) 数值的增加被作为对新刺激的兴趣提升的量化指示。
【逆构】height *n.* 高处，高度，顶点

helpdesk[2] ['helpdesk]

【释义】*n.* 帮助平台
【例句】The technology support department needs people to work at its helpdesk. (TPO18, L, S1, C1) 技术支持部门需要人在帮助平台工作。

hesitate[2] ['hezɪteɪt]

【释义】*v.* 犹豫，踌躇，不情愿
【例句】I hesitate to mention it. (TPO7, L, S1, C1) 我本不想说。
【派生】hesitation *n.* 犹豫，踌躇

hiccup[2] ['hɪkʌp]

【释义】*v.* 打嗝 *n.* 1. 打嗝 2. 暂时性的小问题
【例句】It has been suggested that yawning and hiccupping might serve to clear out the fetus's airways. (TPO18, R, S2, T1) 有人曾提出，打呵欠和打嗝所起的作用可能是清理胎儿的气道。

hinder[2] ['hɪndə]

【释义】*v.* 阻碍，妨碍(inhibit, hamper, inpede, retard)
【例句】The Nile's periodic flooding hinders the growth of some crops. (TPO12, R, S2, T2) 尼罗河周期性的洪水爆发妨碍了一些庄稼的生长。

hormone[2] ['hɔːməʊn]

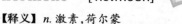

【释义】*n.* 激素，荷尔蒙
【例句】Normally, the constantly changing levels of an animal's activity—sleeping, feeding, moving, reproducing, metabolizing, and producing enzymes and hormones, for example—are well coordinated with environmental rhythms. (TPO13, R, S2, T1) 通常意义上讲，动物活动的经常性变化——例如，睡觉、进食、活动、繁殖、新陈代谢以及产生酶和荷尔蒙——都是与环境的节奏同步的。
【派生】hormonal *a.* 荷尔蒙的，激素的
【搭配】hormone deficiency/imbalance 激素缺乏/失调

hub[2] [hʌb]

【释义】*n.* 1. 活动中心(center, heart) 2. 轮轴
【例句】So that's where access to the public

返记菜单

headquarters[2]	heartbeat[2]	hearth[2]	heighten[2]	helpdesk[2]
hesitate[2]	hiccup[2]	hinder[2]	hormone[2]	hub[2]

transportation comes in, if...if the designer planed to locate the malls in central transportation hub, like bus terminal, a major train, subway station or they work with city officials to create sufficient parking areas, not too far from the mall, which make sense because people can drive into the mall area or then they need easy access to it. (TPO13, L, S1, L1) 因此，这就涉及到使用公共交通了，如果设计者计划将这些步行街建在主要的交通中心附近，比如公交车终点站、主要地铁站或者与官方交涉在离步行街不远的地方建立足够大的停车场，这是很明智的选择，因为这样人们就能把车开到步行街区域或者很容易就能到达。

hull² [hʌl]

【释义】*n.* 1. 船体，船身 2. 外壳 *v.* 去(谷物、豆等的)壳

【例句】Since they had relatively shallow hulls, they were unstable when driven by sail or when on rough water: hence they were unsuitable for the voyage to the East. (TPO17, R, S1, T1) 由于船身相对来说比较浅，所以这些船在靠帆航行或在大浪中航行时是不稳定的，因此不适合向东航行。

【派生】hulled *a.* 有壳的；有船身的

humanness² ['hjuːmənnis]

【释义】*n.* 为人，为人的资格，人性

【例句】Our humanness arises out of these relationships in the course of social interaction. (TPO13, R, S1, T1) 我们的人性源于在社会互动过程中所发生的这些关系中。

humiliate² [hjʊ(ː)'mɪlɪeɪt]

【释义】*v.* 羞辱，使丢脸(embarrass, disgrace, shame)

【例句】And then your round, your main character who loves success and loves to show off, comes and boasts about succeeding and jokes about the flat character's defeat in front of others, humiliates the other guy. (TPO6, L, S2, L1) 然后是圆形人物——喜欢成功和炫耀的主要人物——出场，他吹嘘成功，在别人面前嘲笑扁平角色的失败，并对其进行羞辱。

【派生】humiliation *n.* 羞辱，耻辱
humility *n.* 谦卑

hybrid² ['haɪbrɪd]

【释义】*n.* 1. 混合物，合成物 2. 杂种

【例句】We said that by today's standards, many of the films of the 20s and 30s would be considered hybrids, that is, a mixture of styles that wouldn't exactly fit into any of today's categories, and in that context. (TPO3, L, S1, L2) 我们说过，依据现在的标准，20年代和30年代的许多电影都将被看成混杂物，也就是一种既不确切符合任何一种当今的分类也不符合当时的背景的混合风格。

【派生】hybridism *n.* 杂种，杂交

【搭配】culture hybrid 文化融合

igloo² ['ɪgluː]

【释义】*n.* 雪块砌成的圆顶小屋

【例句】Of course in early architecture—such as igloos and adobe structures—there was no such equipment, and the skeleton and skin were often one. (TPO3, R, S1, T1) 当然，在早期的建筑中，比如雪块砌成的圆顶小屋和土坯建筑，并没有这样的设施，支撑架和外壳也往往是合在一起的。

imaginary² [ɪ'mædʒɪnərɪ]

【释义】*a.* 想像中的，假想的，虚构的

【例句】The second movement involved in the Hypothesis has to do with axial tilt, the tilt of Earth's axis, that imaginary pole that runs through the center of the Earth. (TPO17, L, S1, L2) 假说中提到的第二种运动是关于地轴倾斜的，即一条围绕地心运动的假定线。

immense² [ɪ'mens]

【释义】*a.* 巨大的，广大的，无边无际的(huge, colossal, enormous, vast)

【例句】Leatherbacks reach their immense size in a much shorter time than it takes other sea turtles to grow. (TPO15, R, S2, T1) 棱皮龟长到其巨大的体型所花费的时间比其它海龟短得多。

【派生】immensity *n.* 广大,无限,浩瀚

immortal[2] [ɪ'mɔːtl]

【释义】*a.* 不朽的,永世的(eternal, everlasting)*n.* 1. 不朽的人物 2. 神
【例句】And in the future we may have virtually immortal nerve cells and immortal skin cells of whatever. (TPO12, L, S1, L1) 而且将来我们也许能拥有近乎不朽的神经细胞以及不朽的皮肤细胞和其他任何细胞的永生。
【派生】immortality *n.* 不朽,永生
【逆构】mortal *n.* 凡人 *a.* 凡人的,终有一死的

inactivity[2] [ˌɪnæk'tɪvɪti]

【释义】*n.* 不活动,静止(stability)
【例句】She has bouts of hard work followed by long periods of inactivity. 她总是努力干上一阵,然后一待就是很长时间。
【逆构】active *a.* 积极的,活动的

inappropriate[2] [ˌɪnə'prəuprɪɪt]

【释义】*a.* 不适当的,不合宜的(unfitting, unsuitable)
【例句】But that's not an irrelevant or inappropriate behavior. (TPO4, L, S1, L1) 但这不是一种不相关或不适当的行为。
【逆构】appropriate *a.* 适当的
【搭配】be inappropriate for 不适当的,不合适的

incite[2] [ɪn'saɪt]

【释义】*v.* 煽动,刺激,激励(agitate, instigate, provoke)
【例句】The next key elements of the well-made play refer to as the inciting incidents. (TPO7, L, S1, L1) 佳构剧的另一个关键元素叫做煽动事件。
【派生】incitement *n.* 煽动,刺激,激励物

inclination[2] [ˌɪnklɪ'neɪʃən]

【释义】*n.* 1. 倾向,嗜好(tendency, preference)2. 斜坡,倾斜度
【例句】Prairie dogs may be able to tell you about a hawk at circling over head right now, but they never show any inclination to describe the one they saw last week. (TPO9, L, S2, L2)草原犬鼠可能会告诉你有一只鹰正在头顶上盘旋,但他们永远不会愿意去描述他们上周看到的那只。
【逆构】incline *v.* 倾向于

indefinite[2] [ɪn'defɪnɪt]

【释义】*a.* 1. 模糊的(unclear, vague)2. 不确定的(uncertain)
【例句】Wildlife zoologist Helmut Buechner (1953), in reviewing the nature of biotic changes in Washington through recorded time, says that "since the early 1940s, the state has had more deer than at any other time in its history, the winter population fluctuating around approximately 320, 000 deer (mule and black-tailed deer) , which will yield about 65, 000 of either sex and any age annually for an indefinite period. " (TPO4, R, S1, T1) 野生动物学家 Helmut Buechner (1953) 在回顾自有史记载以来华盛顿生物变化的本质时说:"自 20 世纪 40 年代以来,该州鹿群的数量达到最高峰,冬天时的数量大约在 32 万头左右(包括骡和黑尾鹿),这样每年一段时期将会产出 65,000 头小鹿,不论性别和年龄。
【反义】definite
【派生】indefinitely *ad.* 不确定地;无穷尽地
【逆构】definite *a.* 明确的,一定的,有把握的
【搭配】indefinite equation 不定方程式

infinite[2] ['ɪnfɪnɪt]

【释义】*a.* 无限的,无穷的
【例句】Modern attitudes to Roman civilization range from the infinitely impressed to the thoroughly disgusted. (TPO7, R, S2, T1) 现代人对罗马文明的态度各有不同,从无限的感动到彻底的厌恶。

innovative[2] ['ɪnəuveɪtɪv]

【释义】*a.* 革新的,创新的
【例句】This approach works very well with innovative high-tech products. (TPO8, S, Q6) 这种方法非常适用于创新性的高科技产品。
【派生】innovation *n.* 创新,革新

返记菜单

immortal[2] inactivity[2] inappropriate[2] incite[2] inclination[2]
indefinite[2] infinite[2] innovative[2]

install² [ɪn'stɔːl]

【释义】v. 1. 安装，安置（set up, fix）2. 任命

【例句】Install a new program on her home computer. (TPO1, L, S1, C1) 在她家的电脑上安装一个新程序。

【派生】installation n. 安装，安置；就职
instalment n. 分期付款；安装
installed a. 已安装的

instigate² ['ɪnstɪgeɪt]

【释义】v. 煽动，唆使，鼓动（incite, inspire, stir up）

【例句】So admired were these pieces that they encouraged the development of earthenware made in imitation of porcelain and instigated research into the method of their manufacture. (TPO10, R, S1, T1) 这些瓷器受到了极高的评价，这不仅促进了模仿瓷器制作的土质瓷器的发展，也促进了关于土质瓷器制作技术的研究的开展和进行。

【派生】instigation n. 教唆，鼓动，煽动

institute² ['ɪnstɪtjuːt]

【释义】v. 开始，实行；制定（establish, start）n. 协会，学会；学院，研究院（association, organization）

【例句】The work of Wildman and Niles suggests the importance of recognizing some of the difficulties of instituting reflective practice. (TPO9, R, S2, T1) Wildman 和 Niles 的工作表明了认识到进行反思实践的某些困难的重要性。

【派生】institution n. 公共机构，协会，制度
institutional a. 制度上的

【搭配】research institute 研究所

interplanetary² [ˌɪntə(ː)'plænɪtərɪ]

【释义】a. 行星间的

【例句】Uh... the thing is what's especially interesting about meteoroids is that they come from interplanetary space, but they consist of the same chemical elements that are in matter originated on earth, just in different proportions. (TPO13, L, S2, L2) 嗯……流星体特别令人感兴趣的地方在于它们来自于星际空间，但是却包含与源于地球上的物质相同的化学元素，只是比例不同。

intervention² [ˌɪntə(ː)'venʃən]

【释义】n. 介入，干涉，干预（interference, influence）

【例句】Today, river discharges are increasingly controlled by human intervention, creating a need for international river-basin agreement. (TPO12, R, S2, T2) 今天，河水的排放因为人类的介入而逐渐受到控制，这就需要人们在国际流域问题上达成一致。

【派生】interventional a. 介入性的

【逆构】intervene v. 干涉

【搭配】intervention by government 政府干预

inventory² ['ɪnvəntrɪ]

【释义】n. 详细目录，存货清单（check list）v. 编制目录，盘存

【例句】The culture of that time, based on archaeology and linguistic reconstruction, is assumed to have had a broad inventory of cultivated plants including taro, yams, banana, sugarcane, breadfruit, coconut, sago, and rice. (TPO5, R, S2, T1) 那时基于考古学和语言重建的文化被假定为有着广泛的栽培植物，包括芋头、山药、香蕉、甘蔗、面包果、椰子、西谷米和大米。

invoke² [ɪn'vəʊk]

【释义】v. 1. 调用，借助 2. 恳求，祈求 3. 唤起

【例句】They cannot be invoked to explain the rapid warming in recent decades. (TPO10, R, S2, T1) 这不能用来解释最近几十年来迅速变暖的情况。

irony² ['aɪərənɪ]

【释义】n. 反讽，讽刺（sarcasm）

【例句】And you know here's an incredible irony, Ida Tack, led the chemist of that Musurium team, and were she the first to suggest that Uranium could break up into small pieces but she didn't know that that was the defense of her own discovery of element 43. (TPO8, L, S2, L2) 你知道，这是一个令人难以置信的讽刺，Ida Tack，锝元素小组的领头化学

家，她首先提出了铀可以裂变成小的分子，但她却不知道那是对她自己发现的 43 号元素的辩护。

【派生】ironic *a.* 挖苦的，讽刺的

irregular[2] [ɪ'regjʊlə]

【释义】*a.* 1. 不规则的，不整齐的（erratic, uneven）2. 不合法的，不合规矩的 *n.* 不合格品；非正规军

【例句】They are willing to work irregular hours. (TPO18, L, S1, C1) 他们愿意按没有规律的时间工作。

【派生】irregularity *n.* 不规则，无规律
irregularly *ad.* 不整齐地，不规则地

【搭配】irregular verb 不规则动词

ivory[2] ['aɪvərɪ]

【释义】*n.* 1. 象牙 2. 象牙制品 3. 象牙色，乳白色

【例句】This sculpture is called *The Lady with The Hood*, and it was carved from ivory, probably a mammoth's tusk. (TPO17, L, S1, L1) 这部雕刻作品叫作“夫人与头巾”，是由象牙雕刻而成的，可能是一只猛犸象的长牙。

【搭配】ivory carving 象牙雕刻

jailer[2] ['dʒeɪlə (r)]

【释义】*n.* 狱卒，负责看管囚犯的人

【例句】Critics claim that while such a daring escape makes for enjoyable reading, it is more likely that the Chevaliers jailers were bribed to free him. (TPO7, W, Q1) 评论家声称，虽然这样英勇的逃脱带来了阅读上的享受，但更有可能的是看管谢瓦利埃的狱卒因为收到了贿赂，所以放了他。

jungle[2] ['dʒʌŋgl]

【释义】*n.* 1.（热带）丛林，密林 2. 混乱的一堆

【例句】To understand the ancient Mayan people who lived in the area that is today southern Mexico and Central America and the ecological difficulties they faced, one must first consider their environment, which we think of as “jungle” or “tropical rainforest.” (TPO14, R, S2, T1) 要了解居住在现今墨西哥南部和中美洲地区的古代玛雅人以及他们所面临的生态困难，就一定要先了解他们的居住环境，也就是我们所认为的“丛林”或者“热带雨林”。

junior[2] ['dʒuːnjə]

【释义】*a.* 1. 地位较低的，资历较浅的 2. 年少的 *n.* 年少者，晚辈

【例句】Yet it would be wrong to suggest that Rome was somehow a junior partner in Greco-Roman civilization. (TPO7, R, S2, T1) 然而，认为罗马在某种程度上只是希腊罗马文明中的一个小角色也是错误的。

【反义】senior

junk[2] [dʒʌŋk]

【释义】*n.* 废旧物品，破烂，垃圾（trash, litter）*v.* 丢弃，废弃

【例句】That's the so-called JUNK DNA. (TPO12, L, S1, L1) 那就是所谓的垃圾基因。

【派生】junked *a.* 报废的

【搭配】junk food 垃圾食品，无营养的速食

kiln[2] [kɪln]

【释义】*n.* 窑 *v.* 在窑中烧

【例句】During the Six Dynasties period (AD 265-589), kilns in north China were producing high-fired ceramics of good quality. (TPO10, R, S1, T1) 在六朝时期（公元 265 至 589 年），中国北方的窑就出产经高温烧制而成的高质量的瓷器。

【搭配】a brick kiln 砖窑

kingdom[2] ['kɪŋdəm]

【释义】*n.* 1. 界，领域 2. 王国

【例句】Birds have some of the best vision capabilities in the animal kingdom. (TPO15, S, Q6) 在动物界中，鸟类拥有很好的视觉能力。

knap[2] [næp]

【释义】*v.* 敲碎，叩击

【例句】Toth's knapping produced 56 percent flakes with the cortex on the right, and 44 percent left-oriented flakes. (TPO12, R, S1, T1) Toth 的敲打所产生的碎片，56% 的碎痕在右，

返记菜单

irregular[2]	ivory[2]	jailer[2]	jungle[2]	junior[2]
junk[2]	kiln[2]	kingdom[2]	knap[2]	

44%的碎痕有向左的倾向。

【派生】knapper *n.* 碎石器

knapsack *n.* 背包

label[2] ['leɪbl]

【释义】*v.* 1. 贴标签于，标记(mark) 2. 把…归类 3. 把…称为 *n.* 1. 标签，标记(tag) 2. 称号

【例句】The band is labelled with tracking number, and there is a phone number on the band for people to call for free, to report a banded bird to be found or recaptured. (TPO3, L, S1, L1) 带子上标有追踪号码，还有一个供人们免费拨打的电话，以便于人们在发现或抓获绑有这种带子的鸟儿时可以上报。

【搭配】noise label 噪声指标

ladder[2] ['lædə]

【释义】*n.* 1. 梯子，阶梯，体状物 2.(袜子)抽丝 *v.* 抽丝

【例句】People walked around on the roofs and entered the house through a hatchway on the roof, down a wooden ladder. (TPO1, L, S2, L1) 人们可以在屋顶上来回走动，而且可以通过屋顶上的天窗，爬下梯子进入到房子里。

【派生】laddered *a.* 有规则的，设有梯子的

ladderman *n.* 云梯消防员

leaflet[2] ['li:flɪt]

【释义】*n.* 1. 小叶 2. 传单，散页印刷品 *v.* 散发传单

【例句】The ants also eat yellow structures at the tip of leaflets: these are protein rich and seem to have no function for the tree except to attract ants. (TPO17, R, S2, T2) 蚂蚁也会吃小嫩叶末端的黄色组织，这个部分富含蛋白质，但是除了吸引蚂蚁，似乎对树木本身没有任何功能。

【搭配】a terminal leaflet 顶生小叶

leak[2] [li:k]

【释义】*v.* 1. 渗出，漏出 2. 使泄露 *n.* 1. 漏洞，裂缝 2. 泄漏，漏出量 3. 泄露

【例句】The explanation is that the Maya excavated depressions, or modified natural depressions, and then plugged up leaks in the karst by plastering the bottoms of the depressions in order to create reservoirs, which collected rain from large plastered catchment basins and stored it for use in the dry season. (TPO14, R, S2, T1) 可以这样解释：玛雅人挖掘出洼地或者改造了天然的洼地，并将洼地的底部涂上水泥来堵住喀斯特地形漏水处，这样便建造出了水库，从而可以利用涂抹了水泥的大集水盆地来收集雨水以备旱季使用。

legitimate[2] [lɪ'dʒɪtɪmɪt]

【释义】*a.* 1. 合法的(legal, lawful) 2. 合理的，正当的 *v.* 使合法(legalize, legitimize)

【例句】These early projection devices were used in vaudeville theaters, legitimate theaters, local town halls, makeshift storefront theaters, fairgrounds, and amusement parks to show films to a mass audience. (TPO2, R, S2, T2) 这些早期的投影机可以在众多场合为广大观众播放电影，如：杂技剧团、正式影院、当地礼堂、临时店面影院、露天游乐场和游乐园等。

【反义】illegitimate

【派生】legitimacy *n.* 合法性

legitimately *ad.* 合法地

legitimize *v.* 使合法

lifespan[2] ['laɪfspæn]

【释义】*n.*(人或动物的)寿命

【例句】So when a banded bird is recaptured and reported, we learn about its migration route, its growth, and how long it has been alive, its lifespan. (TPO3, L, S1, L1) 因此当一只被做了标记的鸟儿被重新捕获并汇报时，我们就可以知道它的迁徙路线、它的成长、它已经生存了多久以及它的寿命。

lift[2] [lɪft]

【释义】*v.* 1. 举起，提升 2. 空运 3. 清偿，付清 *n.* 1. 电梯 2. 举起 3. 搭便车

【例句】In the late sixteenth century and into the seventeenth, Europe continued the growth that had lifted it out of the relatively less prosperous medieval period. (TPO10, R, S2, T2) 从十六世纪末到十七世纪，欧洲经济继

续增长，已经摆脱了中世纪相对低迷的形势。

【搭配】 lift up 举起；激励
lift from 从…提起

likewise[2] ['laɪkˌwaɪz]

【释义】 *ad.* 同样地，照样地，也，又（as well, too, similarly）

【例句】 Mathematical models of ecosystems likewise suggest that diversity does not guarantee ecosystem stability—just the opposite, in fact. (TPO3, R, S1, T2) 生态系统的数学模型同样表明多样性本身并不能保证生态系统的稳定性，而实际上正好相反。

【搭配】 go and do likewise 去照样做

linen[2] ['lɪnɪn]

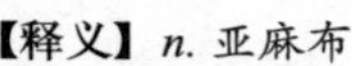

【释义】 *n.* 亚麻布

【例句】 She is wearing a white linen cap of a kind that only servants would wear—yet the coat she is wearing has a luxurious fur collar that no servant could afford. (TPO3, W, Q1) 她戴着一项白色亚麻布的帽子，这种帽子只有仆人才会戴，但她穿的上衣却有着华丽的毛领，而这是任何一个仆人都买不起的。

【搭配】 linen articles 亚麻织品

lumber[2] ['lʌmbə]

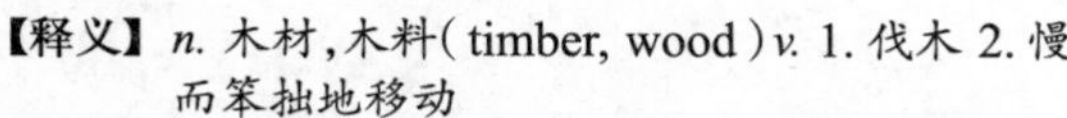

【释义】 *n.* 木材，木料（timber, wood）*v.* 1. 伐木 2. 慢而笨拙地移动

【例句】 One way of dealing with the aftermath of these disasters is called salvage logging, which is the practice of removing dead trees from affected areas and using the wood for lumber, plywood, and other wood products. (TPO14, W, Q1) 对待这些灾难造成的后果的方法之一是抢救性砍伐，就是将受灾地区死掉的树木移除，将其制成木材、胶合板以及其他木制产品。

【派生】 lumbering *n.* 采伐林木

maintenance[2] ['meɪntɪnəns]

【释义】 *n.* 1. 维持，保持，维护 2. 保养；维修

【例句】 Maintenance of PC is in my element. 我对电脑的维修保养很在行。

【逆构】 maintain *v.* 保持，维持；保养

【搭配】 maintenance of equipment 设备养护

malicious[2] [mə'lɪʃəs]

【释义】 *a.* 恶意的，恶毒的（vicious, hateful）

【例句】 Online encyclopedias have recognized the importance of protecting their articles from malicious hackers. (TPO6, W, Q1) 在线百科全书已经意识到了保护文章不受恶意黑客侵害的重要性。

【逆构】 malice *n.* 恶意

【搭配】 malicious act 恶意行为

manipulate[2] [mə'nɪpjuleɪt]

【释义】 *v.* 1. 操作（maneuver）2. 利用，操纵，控制（control）

【例句】 Artists combine and manipulate these visual elements to express a message or to create a mood. (TPO4, S, Q6) 艺术家把这些视觉元素结合起来并利用它们来表达一种信息或是创造一种意境。

【派生】 manipulation *n.* 操作，操纵

margin[2] ['mɑːdʒɪn]

【释义】 *n.* 1. 边缘（edge, border, rim）2. 余地（room）

【例句】 During the dry periods that are common phenomena along the desert magins, though, the pressure on the land is often far in excess of its diminished capacity, and desertification results. (TPO2, R, Sl, T1) 尽管对于沙漠边缘地带来说，干旱是一个很普遍的现象，但是干旱期土地面临的压力仍然远远超过其日渐式微的抗旱能力，干旱的破坏作用也远高于沙漠化带来的结果。

【搭配】 margin of error 误差界限
on the margins 处在（社会的）边缘

maroon[2] [mə'ruːn]

【释义】 *v.* 放逐；使孤立无援 *n.* 1. 褐紫色 2. 被放逐者

【例句】 Contrary to the arguments of some that much of the Pacific was settled by Polynesians accidentally marooned after being lost and adrift, it seems reasonable that this feat was accomplished by deliberate colonization expeditions that set out fully stocked with food and domesticated plants and animals. (TPO5, R, S2, T1) 一些人认为在太平洋大部分地区定居的是意外迷路而流亡的波利尼西亚人，但与此相反的另一种理论看似更加合理，该理论认为这一壮举是由有意的殖民远征活动创造的，他们在出发时准备了充足的食物及驯化的动植物。

【派生】 marooned *a.* 陷于孤立无援困境的

marvel[2] [ˈmɑːvəl]

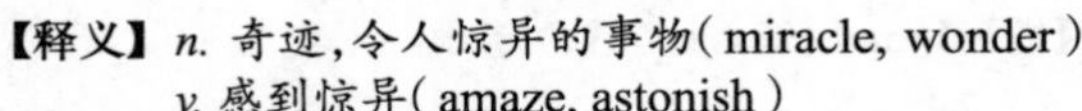

【释义】 *n.* 奇迹，令人惊异的事物（miracle, wonder）*v.* 感到惊异（amaze, astonish）

【例句】 What audiences came to see was the technological marvel of the movies. (TPO2, R, S2, T2) 观众所看到的是电影技术带来的奇迹。

【派生】 marvelous *a.* 不可思议的，奇迹般的

【搭配】 marvel at 对…感到惊异

mask[2] [mɑːsk]

【释义】 *n.* 面具，面罩 *v.* 带面具；掩饰

【例句】 Performers may wear costumes and masks to represent the mythical characters or supernatural forces in the rituals or in accompanying celebrations. (TPO1, R, S2, T1) 在这些仪式或伴随的庆祝活动中，表演者们会穿着各种服饰、戴着面具来代表神话中的人物或超自然的力量。

【派生】 masker *n.* 戴面具的人

maturation[2] [ˌmætʃəˈreɪʃən]

【释义】 *n.* 化脓；成熟

【例句】 Maturation of the frontal lobes of the brain continues throughout early childhood, and this part of the brain may be critical for remembering particular episodes in ways that can be retrieved later. (TPO6, R, S2, T2) 在孩子们早期的童年时代中，脑前叶不断地成熟，大脑的该区域对于记忆特定的事件并在日后还能回想起来（这一活动中）可能起着至关重要的作用。

【逆构】 mature *a.* 成熟的，考虑周到的
maturity *n.* 成熟，完备

mediocre[2] [ˌmiːdɪˈəʊkə]

【释义】 *a.* 普通的，平庸的，平凡的（moderate, ordinary）

【例句】 The mediocre design of many contemporary buildings can be traced to both clients and architects. (TPO3, R, S1, T1) 许多当代建筑设计平庸的根源在于客户和建筑师。

【反义】 extraordinary

【搭配】 mediocre work 平庸的作品

Word List 36

melodious[2] [mɪ'ləudiəs] 

【释义】 *a.* 悦耳的,旋律美妙的

【例句】 It is the melodious drama of ancient Greek theater, the term "melodious drama" being shortened eventually to "melodrama" because operas frequently are melodramatic, not to say unrealistic. (TPO12, L, S2, L1) 它是古希腊剧场里悦耳的戏剧,"melodious drama(悠扬的戏剧)"这一术语最终被缩改成"melodrama(音乐戏剧)",是因为戏剧不切实际不说,还经常情节夸张。

【派生】 melodiously *ad.* 悦耳地,旋律优美地

【逆构】 melody *n.* 旋律;歌曲
melodic *a.* 有旋律的,调子优美的

merge[2] [mɜːdʒ] 

【释义】 *v.*(使)合并,(使)融合(combine, mingle)

【例句】 These flow features are extensive systems—sometimes hundreds of kilometers in total length—of interconnecting, twisting channels that seem to merge into larger, wider channels. (TPO8, R, S2, T2) 这些流动特征就是广泛的相互联系、相互交错的水道系统——有时总长可达上万米——似乎要汇入更加宽大的水道。

metropolis[2] [mɪ'trɒpəlɪs] 

【释义】 *n.* 大都市,主要中心

【例句】 Clearly, much planning and central control were involved in the expansion and ordering of this great metropolis. (TPO8, R, S1, T1) 显然,这座大都市的扩张和布置中涉及到诸多规划和集中控制。

【派生】 metropolitan *a.* 大都市的 *n.* 大城市人

militaristic[2] [ˌmɪlətə'rɪstɪk] 

【释义】 *a.* 军国主义的

【例句】 It is the use of horses for transportation and warfare that explains why Inner Eurasian pastoralism proved the most mobile and the most militaristic of all major forms of pastoralism. (TPO14, R, S2, T2) 马匹在交通和战争中的使用说明了为什么亚欧内陆的畜牧主义在畜牧主义的所有主要形式中是公认的最具机动性和军事性的。

miscalculate[2] [mɪs'kælkjʊleɪt] 

【释义】 *v.* 错误地计算或估计

【例句】 I think my professor really miscalculated. (TPO10, L, S2, C1) 我认为教授确实估算错了。

misconception[2] ['mɪskən'sepʃən] 

【释义】 *n.* 误解,错误想法(misunderstanding, misinterpretation)

【例句】 This is a well-known misconception about reptiles. 这是一个关于爬行动物的非常著名的误解。

mismatch[2] ['mɪs'mætʃ] 

【释义】 *n.* 配错,不匹配,不协调

【例句】 The disorienting effects of this mismatch between external time cues and internal schedules may persist, like our jet lag, for several days or weeks until certain cues such as the daylight/darkness cycle reset the organism's clock to synchronize with the daily rhythm of the new environment. (TPO13, R, S2, T1) 外部时间与内在循环的这种不协调所产生的令人困惑的影响就像我们的时差综合症,可能会持续几天或者几个星期,直到诸如白昼和黑夜的循环之类的特定信号重新设定生物体的生物钟,使其与新环境的昼夜节律同步。

mistaken[2] [mɪs'teɪkən]

【释义】 *a.* 误解的,错误的(false, misguided)

【例句】 Students sometimes mistakenly assume that the section contains literature books. (TPO7, L, S2, C1) 学生有时会误认为这个部门有文学类图书。

【派生】 mistakenly *ad.* 错误地,曲解地

【搭配】 be mistaken about 对…有所误会,误解

返记菜单

melodious[2] merge[2] metropolis[2] militaristic[2] miscalculate[2]
misconception[2] mismatch[2] mistaken[2]

mollusk[2] ['mɒləsk]

【释义】*n.*〈动〉软体动物

【例句】He might take a clip of a mollusk going up and down in the water and set it to music. (TPO3, L, S1, L2) 他可能会给一个软体动物在水中上下窜动的镜头，并且为之配上音乐。

monk[2] [mʌŋk]

【释义】*n.* 僧侣，修道士

【例句】So it wasn't uncommon for the scribes or monks who produce the manual scripts. (TPO15, L, S2, L1) 所以，这对抄记手稿的书记员或僧侣来说是十分平常的。

【派生】monkish *a.* 僧侣的；苦行僧般的

mount[2] [maʊnt]

【释义】*v.* 1. 登上，爬上 2. 骑上，跨上 3. 发起，发动 4. 上升，增加

【例句】As the ice that is close to the mounting points, in fact, it is not too different from... the weight oil is, thicker at the lower temperature. (TPO7, L, S2, L2) 当冰接近临界点时，与…并没有什么不同，温度越低，油脂越厚。

【派生】mountain *n.* 山，山峰

【搭配】be mounted to/on 被固定在…上
mount up（规模或数量）逐渐增加

multicellular[2] [mʌltɪ'seljʊlə]

【释义】*a.* 多细胞的

【例句】The origin of multicellular forms of life seems a relatively simple step compared to the origin of life itself. (TPO5, R, S2, T2) 多细胞生命形式的起源相比生命本身的起源来说是一个相对简单的步骤。

【派生】multicellularity *n.* 多细胞

【搭配】multicellular organism 多细胞生物

mute[2] [mjuːt]

【释义】*a.* 缄默的；哑的 *n.*（乐器上的）弱音器；哑巴 *v.* 使（声音）减弱；使（乐器声音）弱化

【例句】In nearly every language, however the words are phrased, the most basic division in cinema history lies between films that are mute and films that speak. (TPO12, R, S2, T1) 在几乎所有的语言中，无论是以哪种方式被描述，电影最基本的分水岭都是在无声和有声电影之间。

【派生】muted *a.*（声音）减弱的，变低声的；（颜色）柔和的，不耀眼的

【搭配】deaf mute 聋哑人；聋哑的

neglect[2] [nɪ'glekt]

【释义】*v./n.* 疏忽，忽视，忽略，忘记（disregard, ignore）

【例句】To be sure, their evaluation of the technical flaws in 1920's sound experiments was not so far off the mark, yet they neglected to take account important new forces in the motion picture field that, in a sense, would not take no for an answer. (TPO12, R, S2, T1) 诚然，他们对于20世纪20年代的声音实验中存在的技术性缺陷的估计也不是完全没有道理，但是他们忘记把电影领域中的新力量考虑进去了，在某种意义上，那一领域是不会把"不能"作为答案的。

【派生】neglectable *a.* 可忽略不计的
neglectful *a.* 疏忽的，不注意的

【搭配】neglect to do sth. 没有做某事

nickel[2] ['nɪkl]

【释义】*n.* 1. 镍 2.（美国和加拿大的）五分钱

【例句】A survey of known hyperaccumulators indentified that 75 percent of them amassed nickel. (TPO5, R, S1, T1) 一份对已知超富集植物的调查证实它们之中的75%都富含镍。

【派生】nickelage *n.* 镀镍

notion[2] ['nəʊʃən]

【释义】*n.* 概念，观念，看法（conception）

【例句】He confused his audience in the way he portrayed the animals he filmed, mixing up on notions of the categories of humans and animals. (TPO3, L, S1, L2) 他在电影中描述动物的方式混淆了人类和动物范畴的概念，这种方式让观众感到迷惑。

【派生】notional *a.* 概念的，想象的

【搭配】an outmoded notion 陈旧的观念

nourish[2] [ˈnʌrɪʃ] 

【释义】*v.* 养育，滋养，培养（feed, nurture）
【例句】The fungi absorb moisture and mineral salts from the rocks, passing these on in waste products that nourish algae. (TPO9, R, S2, T2) 真菌从岩石中吸收水分和矿物盐，并传递到代谢废物中，从而滋养海藻。
【派生】nourishment *n.* 食物，营养品；养料
【搭配】nourish a hope 保持希望

nucleus[2] [ˈnjuːklɪəs] 

【释义】*n.* 核，核心，原子核
【例句】The elements are arranged in order of increasing atomic number (the number of protons in the nucleus). (TPO16, R, S2, T1) 元素是按照原子序数（原子核内的质子数）的递增排列的。
【派生】nuclear *a.* 原子核的，原子能的

obscure[2] [əbˈskjʊə] 

【释义】*a.* 1. 不引人注意的，身份卑微的 2. 朦胧的，模糊的（unclear, dim）3. 晦涩的，费解的（vague, indefinite）*v.* 使…模糊，隐藏（conceal, veil）
【例句】Only when European decorative themes were introduced did these meanings become obscured or even lost. (TPO10, R, S1, T1) 当欧洲的装饰元素被引进后，这些元素也许慢慢的不再那么流行，甚至开始消失。
【搭配】obscure glass 毛玻璃

obsession[2] [əbˈseʃən] 

【释义】*n.* 着魔，入迷；困扰人的想法
【例句】The source of the Roman obsession with unity and cohesion may well have lain in the pattern of Rome's early development. (TPO7, R, S2, T1) 罗马人对于团结统一和凝聚力的沉迷或许在罗马早期发展的模式中就已经存在了。
【派生】obsessed *a.* 心神不宁的
obsessive *a.* 着迷的；（在某方面）过分的
【逆构】obsess *v.* 使着迷，使心神不宁
【搭配】obsession with/about 沉迷于

offend[2] [əˈfend] 

【释义】*v.* 冒犯，得罪，使…不愉快
【例句】I don't want to offend him. (TPO17, S, Q5) 我不想冒犯他。
【派生】offensive *a.* 讨厌的，无礼的；攻击（性）的
inoffensive *a.* 无害的，无恶意的
【搭配】offend against 触犯，冒犯

olfactory[2] [ɒlˈfæktərɪ] 

【释义】*a.* 嗅觉的
【例句】The habituation-dishabituation paradigm has been used most extensively with studies of auditory and olfactory perception in infants. (TPO13, R, S2, T2) 这种习惯与非习惯的实验模式被广泛应用于婴儿的听觉与嗅觉的认知研究上。
【派生】olfactorily *ad.* 嗅觉地
【搭配】olfactory nerve 嗅觉神经

omelet[2] [ˈɒmlɪt] 

【释义】*n.* 煎蛋饼，煎蛋卷
【例句】Sure it is, but they are saying yogurt's better for you than an omelet or than hot cereal? (TPO3, S, Q3) 的确是这样，但是他们说酸奶比煎鸡蛋或热麦片粥更好？

omit[2] [əʊˈmɪt] 

【释义】*v.* 省略，省去，忽略（neglect, bypass, exclude）
【例句】This technique allows researchers to create solutions that selectively omit certain nutrients. (TPO5, R, S1, T1) 这种技术容许研究者们制作一些溶液，溶液里有选择性地除去了特定的养分。
【派生】omittance *n.* 遗漏
omitted *a.* 省略了的，省去的
【搭配】omit form 从…中漏掉，从…中删掉

ongoing[2] [ˈɒngəʊɪŋ] 

【释义】*a.* 不断发展的，进行中的（continuous, existing）
【例句】This has been an ongoing theme in our discussion, and we will be getting back to it just a moment. (TPO11, L, S1, L2) 这一直

返记菜单

nourish[2]	nucleus[2]	obscure[2]	obsession[2]	offending[2]
olfactory[2]	omelet[2]	omit[2]	ongoing[2]	

都是我们讨论的话题，稍后我们将再回到这上面来。

opportunist[2] ['ɒpətju:nɪst]

【释义】 n. 机会主义者；投机取巧者
【例句】 You need to be a bit of opportunists. (TPO10, L, S1, C1) 你需要一点儿投机心理。
【派生】 opportunity n. 机会
opportunism n. 机会主义

outcrop[2] ['aʊtkrɒp]

【释义】 n. 露出地面的岩层 v.(岩石等)露出地表
【例句】 This job gave Smith an opportunity to study the fresh rock outcrops created by the newly dug canal. (TPO6, R, S2, T1) 这项工作使得史密斯有机会对那些因为运河开掘而露出地面的新鲜岩层进行研究。

outdated[2] [aʊt'deɪtɪd]

【释义】 a. 过时的，旧式的(antique, out-fashioned)
【例句】 Like the science laboratories having such old outdated equipment, and the library needing more books, and the student center being so small…I think that the two million could be spent in better places if the university is really serious about achieving its goal. (TPO13, S, Q3) 比如，科学实验室里的设备太过时了，图书馆也需要更多的书，还有学生中心太小了…我认为，如果学校真的很想达成目标的话，这200万应该花在更好的地方。
【反义】 modern, fashionable
【逆构】 outdate v. 使过时，使落伍

outstanding[2] [aʊt'stændɪŋ]

【释义】 a. 1. 突(杰)出的，显著的(remarkable, distinguished) 2. 未解决的
【例句】 Julian possessed outstanding business skills. (TPO8, L, S1, L2, Q13) 朱利安有杰出的商业技能。
【反义】 commonplace
【逆构】 outstand v. 突出

outwash[2] ['aʊtˌwɔ:ʃ]

【释义】 n. 冰水沉积
【例句】 The water was always laden with pebbles, gravel, and sand, known as glacial outwash, that deposited as the flow slowed down. (TPO1, R, S2, T2) 水里总会携带些石子、砾石和沙子，也就是所谓的冰水沉积，这些颗粒会随水流的减缓而沉淀下来。
【搭配】 outwash plain 冰川冲积平原

outweigh[2] [aʊt'weɪ]

【释义】 v. 比…重要，比…有价值
【例句】 The benefits of commercial fossil trade greatly outweigh the disadvantages. (TPO13, W, Q1) 商业化石交易的益处远远大于其缺点。

overgeneralize[2] ['əʊvə'dʒɛnərəlˌaɪz]

【释义】 v. 过分概括，说话过于笼统
【例句】 Therefore, when observational assessment is used as a technique for studying infant perceptual abilities, care must be taken not to overgeneralize from the data or to rely on one or two studies as conclusive evidence of a particular perceptual ability of the infant. (TPO13, R, S2, T2) 因此，当把观察评估用作研究婴儿认知能力的技术手段时，必须要注意，不能过于笼统地对数据进行概括或者仅仅把一两个具体的研究得出的结论作为婴儿某项特定认知能力的决定性证据。

overhead[2] ['əʊvəhed]

【释义】 ad. 在头顶上 a. 高架的，在头上的 n. 经常开支，普通用费
【例句】 So the Polynesians could estimate their latitude just by looking straight up, by observing whether a certain zenith star passed directly overhead at night, they'd know if they have reached the same latitude as a particular island they were trying to get to. (TPO14, L, S2, L1) 所以，玻利尼西亚人只需要抬头看看就能估计出他们的纬度，通过观察晚上的时候是否有某颗天顶星正好从他们头顶经过，他们就能知道是否已经到

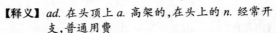

达所要前往的岛屿的纬度上了。

【搭配】 overhead light 顶灯，高架照明灯
overhead expense 营业费用
no overhead 不准超车

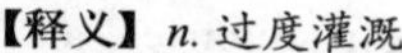

overirrigation[2] ['əuvəˌɪrə'geʃən]

【释义】 *n.* 过度灌溉

【例句】 Four specific activities have been identified as major contributions to the desertification process: overcultivation, overgrazing, firewood gathering, and overirrigation. (TPO2, R, Sl, T1) 四种特定活动被确定为促进沙漠化进程的罪魁祸首：过度耕种、过度放牧、伐木做柴以及过度灌溉。

【逆构】 overirrigate *v.* 过度灌溉

overlook[2] [ˌəuvə'luk]

【释义】 *v.* 1. 忽视，忽略（neglect）2. 俯视，远眺

【例句】 He believes that Jean Painleve's films have been unfairly overlooked. (TPO3, L, S1, L2, Q17) 他认为培乐威的电影受到了不公平的忽视。

【搭配】 overlook a fault 宽容过失

overshadow[2] [ˌəuvə'ʃædəu]

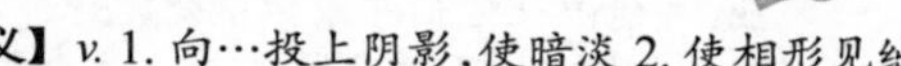

【释义】 *v.* 1. 向…投上阴影，使暗淡 2. 使相形见绌

【例句】 Beyond that, the triumph of recorded sound has overshadowed the rich diversity of technological and aesthetic experiments with the visual image that were going forward simultaneously in the 1920s. (TPO12, R, S2, T1) 除此之外，录音的成功使得在20世纪20年代同时发展起来的丰富多样的视觉技术和审美实验显得暗淡无光了。

overwork[2] ['əuvə'wɜːk]

【释义】 *n.* 过度操劳，过度工作 *v.* 工作过度，把…做过头

【例句】 In the end, the companies would have fewer overworked and error-prone employees for the same money. (TPO1, W, Q1) 最后，这些公司将在支付相同工资的情况下，少一些劳累过度且易于出错的员工。

【派生】 overworked *a.* 工作过度的，劳累过度的

pad[2] [pæd]

【释义】 *n.* 1. 便条簿（notebook）2. 衬垫（cushion）*v.* 1.（用软物）填塞，包裹（staff）2.（放轻脚步）走

【例句】 I carry a little pad with me all the time. (TPO2, L, S1, C1) 我总是随身携带一个小便签簿。

【派生】 padded *a.* 填充的
padding *n.* 填充物

【搭配】 pad A with B 用B来填充A

pant[2] [pænt]

【释义】 *v.* 1. 喘息 2. 渴望 3. 气喘吁吁地说

【例句】 Almost all animals have some way of regulating their body temperature; otherwise they wouldn't survive extreme hot or cold conditions—sweating, panting, swimming to cooler or warmer water; ducking into somewhere cool like a burrow or a hole under a rock; these are just a few. (TPO14, L, S1, L2) 差不多所有动物都有调节自己体温的方式，不然它们无法在极热或者极冷的条件下生存——流汗、喘息、在较冷或较温暖的水中游泳、迅速躲到诸如洞穴或岩石下面的洞之类凉快的地方；这些只是一小部分。

【搭配】 pant for 渴望…，迫切想要…

papyrus[2] [pə'paɪərəs]

【释义】 *n.* 莎草纸

【例句】 Archimedes' writings were originally done on papyrus scrolls. (TPO15, L, S2, L1) 阿基米德的作品最初是写在莎草纸的卷宗上的。

paradigm[2] ['pærədaɪm]

【释义】 *n.* 示例，范例，样式

【例句】 The habituation-dishabituation paradigm has been used most extensively with studies of auditory and olfactory perception in infants. (TPO13, R, S2, T2) 这种习惯与非习惯的实验模式被广泛应用于婴儿的听觉与嗅觉的认知研究上。

【派生】 paradigmatic *a.* 范式的；词形变化的

返记菜单

overirrigation[2] overlook[2] overshadow[2] overwork[2] pad[2]
pant[2] papyrus[2] paradigm[2]

paradise[2] [ˈpærədaɪz]

【释义】 *n.* 天堂，乐园，乐土（heaven）

【例句】 A male bird of paradise may put himself in the limelight by displaying his spectacular plumage in the best stage setting to attract a female. (TPO17, R, S2, T1) 雄性极乐鸟会让自己置身于聚光灯下，在最佳的舞台背景下展现自己缤纷绚烂的羽翼，以吸引雌鸟的注意。

【派生】 paradisaical *a.* 天堂的，乐园的

【搭配】 paradise of the adventurers 冒险家的乐园

paradox[2] [ˈpærədɒks]

【释义】 *n.* 悖论，似是而非的论点，自相矛盾的话

【例句】 Yet this most fundamental standard of historical periodization conceals a host of paradoxes. (TPO12, R, S2, T1) 但是历史分期这一最根本的标准隐含着大量悖论。

【派生】 paradoxical *a.* 矛盾的，悖论的

participant[2] [pɑːˈtɪsɪpənt]

【释义】 *n.* 参加者，参与者

【例句】 That expectation causes the researcher to act in ways that influence the behavior of the experiment participants. (TPO15, S, Q4) 那一预期使得研究者的做法影响到了实验参与者的行为。

【逆构】 participate *v.* 参与，参加

patch[2] [pætʃ]

【释义】 *n.* 1. 片，块 2. 补丁 *v.* 1. 补，修补 2. 拼凑

【例句】 Mineral deficiencies can often be detected by specific symptoms such as chlorosis (loss of chlorophyll resulting in yellow or white leaf tissue), necrosis (isolated dead patches), anthocyanin formation (development of deep red pigmentation of leaves or stem), stunted growth, and development of woody tissue in an herbaceous plant. (TPO5, R, S1, T1) 矿物质的缺乏通常可以通过一些特别的症状表现出来，比如萎黄病（水溶性叶绿素的缺乏导致的黄色或白色的叶片组织）、坏死（分离的枯死的叶片）、花色素甙生成（叶子或枝干上深红色色素的扩散），生长萎缩以及草本植物中木质组织的发展。

patriotic[2] [ˌpætrɪˈɒtɪk]

【释义】 *a.* 爱国的

【例句】 Hearing the songs probably made them feel more patriotic, made them feel like a good noble thing to serve their countries, and whatever way they could. (TPO13, L, S2, L1) 听到这些歌曲可能会使他们感到更有爱国热情，让他们感觉尽其所能服务祖国是高尚的事业。

【逆构】 patriot *n.* 爱国者

【搭配】 patriotic songs 爱国歌曲

paucity[2] [ˈpɔːsɪtɪ]

【释义】 *n.* 少量，缺乏，不足（insufficience, scarcity）

【例句】 This was justified by the view that reflective practice could help teachers to feel more intellectually involved in their role and work in teaching and enable them to cope with the paucity of scientific fact and the uncertainty of knowledge in the discipline of teaching. (TPO9, R, S2, T1) 有一种观点证明了这是合理的，那就是：反思实践可以帮助老师们更加理性地对待他们的角色和他们从事的事业，并能够让他们在教学中处理好科学事实缺乏和知识的不确定问题。

【搭配】 a paucity of natural resources 缺乏自然资源

paycheck[2] [ˈpeɪtʃek]

【释义】 *n.* 1. 薪水支票 2. 工资（salary, wage）

【例句】 I'm fine; except I have a question about my paycheck. (TPO12, L, S2, C1) 我很好；除了在薪水方面我有个疑问。

peddler[2] [ˈpedlə]

【释义】 *n.* 小贩

【例句】 People could purchase them easily from a traveling peddler. (TPO8, L, S2, L1) 人们能够很容易地从流动小贩那里买到。

penchant[2] [ˈpɒnʃɒn]

【释义】 *n.* 爱好，嗜好（liking, inclination, preperence）

【例句】 But neither the human imitative instinct nor

返记菜单

a penchant for fantasy by itself leads to an autonomous theater. (TPO1, R, S2, T1) 但是,人类的模仿本能或对幻想的嗜好本身都不能使戏剧发展成为一门独立的艺术形式。

percussion[2] [pɜːˈkʌʃən]

【释义】*n.* 1. 打击乐器 2. 打击,振动

【例句】The piano is a percussion instrument. (TPO16, L, S1, L2) 钢琴是一种打击乐器。

【逆构】percuss *v.* 有力地敲击;叩诊

persuade[2] [pəˈsweɪd]

【释义】*v.* 说服,劝说,使相信(convince)

【例句】In advertising, um…various strategies are used to persuade people to buy products. (TPO3, S, Q6) 在广告业中,广告商会运用各种各样的策略来说服顾客购买产品。

【派生】persuasion *n.* 说服,说服力

persuasive *a.* 善于说服的,有说服力的

【搭配】gently persuade 婉言相劝

plane[2] [pleɪn]

【释义】*n.* 1. 平面 2. 飞机 3. 刨子 *v.* 1. 刨平,刨掉 2.(飞机)滑翔 *a.* 平坦的

【例句】Death valley is this desert plane, a dry lake bed in California surrounded by mountains and on the desert floor these huge rocks, some of them hundreds of pounds. (TPO4, L, S2, L1) 死亡谷是这样一片沙地,位于加利福尼亚的一处干涸的湖床,周围群山环绕,而这片沙地上的巨石有的重达几百磅。

【搭配】by plane 乘飞机

planetary[2] [ˈplænɪtrɪ]

【释义】*a.* 行星的,有轨道的

【例句】You know planetary researchers love studying deep craters until learn about the impacts that created them, how they redistributed pieces of a planet's crust and in this case, we especially want to know if any of the mantle, the layer beneath the crust, was exposed by the impact. (TPO5, L, S1, L2) 你知道的,行星研究者们热衷于研究深火山口,直到他们了解了那些创造了火山的冲击力,以及这些冲击力是如何对一颗行星的地壳进行了重新分配,在这样的情况下,我们尤其想知道是否有地幔——地壳下面的一层——在该冲击力的作用下暴露了出来。

【搭配】planetary orbit 行星轨道

pleasing[2] [ˈpliːzɪŋ]

【释义】*a.* 使人满意的,令人愉快的(delightful)

【例句】Although I would be the first to admit those things are aesthetically appealing, however, visually pleasing sights are not a part of the pedestrian mall's design that matter the most. (TPO13, L, S1, L1) 尽管我承认那些东西很美观,但视觉上的美并不是步行商业街设计最看重的部分。

【搭配】a pleasing piece of news 一则令人高兴的消息

Word List 37

pluck[2] [plʌk]

【释义】*v.* 1. 拨(弦) 2. 采,摘,拔 3. 突然地拉,扯 4. 开除 *n.* 勇气,胆量

【例句】Pressing a key of a harpsichord causes a tiny quill that's connected to the key to pluck the strings that are inside the instrument. (TPO16, L, S1, L2) 按下大键琴的一个键,就会使得连接该琴键的微小琴拨拉动大键琴内部的琴弦。

【搭配】pluck up (the) courage 振作精神,鼓起勇气
pluck sth. out of the air (未经仔细考虑)随口说出

plumage[2] ['plu:mɪdʒ]

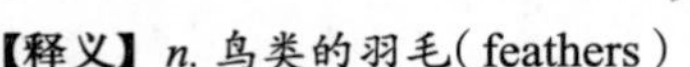

【释义】*n.* 鸟类的羽毛(feathers)

【例句】A male bird of paradise may put himself in the limelight by displaying his spectacular plumage in the best stage setting to attract a female. (TPO17, R, S2, T1) 雄性极乐鸟会让自己置身于聚光灯下,在最佳的舞台背景下展现自己缤纷绚烂的羽翼,以吸引雌鸟的注意。

plumbing[2] ['plʌmɪŋ]

【释义】*n.* 管道工程,管道工行业

【例句】Then you use pumps and fans to move heat from the collectors through a plumbing system to a tank. (TPO12, L, S2, L2) 然后你使用泵和风扇把热量从收集器中经由一个管道系统输入到一个罐中。

【逆构】plumb *n.* 铅锤 *a.* 垂直的 *ad.* 垂直地;直接地 *v.* 测量;使垂直

【搭配】plumbing system 管道系统;水暖设备系统

porpoise[2] ['pɔ:pəs]

【释义】*n.* 鼠海豚

【例句】It should be obvious that cetaceans—whales, porpoises, and dolphins—are mammals. (TPO2, R, S2, T1) 显然,鲸类动物——鲸、鼠海豚、海豚——都是哺乳动物。

possession[2] [pə'zeʃən]

【释义】*n.* 1. 财产(estate, belongings,property) 2. 拥有,占有(ownership) 3. 殖民地

【例句】Because pastoralists are highly mobile, they tend to have few material possessions and can influence the culture, ecology, and language of very large areas. (TPO14, R, S2, T2) 因为牧民经常迁移,所以他们一般只有很少的物质财产,并且这会影响很广大地区的文化、生态和语言。

【逆构】possess *v.* 拥有,占有

【搭配】in possession of 拥有,占有(某物)
take possession of 拥有或占有(某物),拿到某物
come into sb.'s possession 为某人所得到或占有,落入某人手中

postulate[2] ['pɒstjʊleɪt]

【释义】*v.* 假定,要求(assume, presume) *n.* 基本条件,假定

【例句】Rayleigh and Ramsay postulated the existence of a new group of elements. (TPO16, R, S2, T1) 瑞利和拉姆齐假设存在一组新的元素。

【派生】postulation *n.* 假定,要求

posture[2] ['pɒstʃə]

【释义】*n.* 1. 姿势,姿态 2. 看法,态度 *v.* 1. 摆出某种姿势 2. 装模作样

【例句】It gave her an understanding of body movements and actions, how humans move and stand still, what their postures were like, too. (TPO1, L, S1, L1) 这让她理解了身体的运动和动作:人是怎样移动和静立的,还有他们的姿势是什么样的。

【派生】posturer *n.* 杂技演员;装腔作势的人

【搭配】posture map 态势地图

potent[2] ['pəʊtənt]

【释义】*a.* 有效力的,有影响力的,强有力的(mighty, powerful, strong)

【例句】The third, and most potent, limitation is that it is not possible to be certain that the

infant's response was due to the stimulus presented or to a change from no stimulus to a stimulus. (TPO13, R, S2, T2) 第三点局限性,也是最有影响力的一点,就是不可能非常明确地说婴儿的反应是由现在的刺激引起的,还是由于从没有刺激到产生刺激的变化导致的。

【派生】potence *n.* 力量,潜能
potential *n.* 潜力,潜能,潜在性 *a.* 潜在的,可能的

prehistory[2] [priː'hɪstəriː]

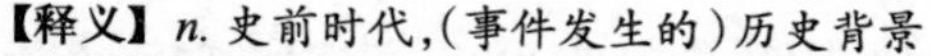

【释义】*n.* 史前时代,(事件发生的)历史背景
【例句】Can one trace this same pattern far back in prehistory? (TPO12, R, S1, T1) 有人能将这种相同的性状追溯到遥远的史前时期吗?
【派生】prehistorical *a.* 史前的

premier[2] ['premjə]

【释义】*a.* 最早的,最先的;首位的,首要的 *n.* 首相,总理
【例句】So that was the year premier, great, but eh, newspaper from back then weren't online, so, how do I…(TPO4, L, S1, C1) 那这是很早的年头了,很好,但当时的报纸没有网络版,那我怎么…?
【派生】premier league 超级联赛

preposterous[2] [prɪ'pɒstərəs]

【释义】*a.* 荒谬的,可笑的(absurd, ridiculous)
【例句】At the time, this idea seemed preposterous. How could a bird navigate by the Sun when some of us lose our way with road maps? (TPO11, R, S2, T1) 在那时,这一观点让人觉得相当荒谬。当我们有些人拿着地图都会迷路的时候,一只鸟儿怎么可能凭着太阳进行导航呢?

prerequisite[2] ['priː'rekwɪzɪt]

【释义】*n.* 先决条件,前提
【例句】It is now generally believed that these prerequisites originated with people speaking Austronesian languages. (TPO5, R, S2, T1) 现在普遍认为这些先决条件起源于那些说南岛语的人。
【搭配】prerequisite course 先修科目,预修课程

profile[2] ['prəʊfaɪl]

【释义】*n.* 1. 简介,传略 2. 侧面,侧影 3. 轮廓,外形 4. 态度,姿态 *v.* 描绘…的轮廓,给…画侧面图
【例句】Yeah…the first article I wrote was profile of the chemistry professor. (TPO14, L, S2, C1) 对,我写的第一篇文章是关于这位化学教授的简介。
【搭配】keep a low profile 保持低姿态,低调

prohibit[2] [prə'hɪbɪt]

【释义】*v.* 禁止;阻止(ban, bar)
【例句】Currently, there is a university-wide policy that prohibits eating in the classroom. (TPO14, S, Q2) 目前,有一条全校通行的政策,禁止在教室内吃饭。
【反义】allow, permit
【派生】prohibition *n.* 禁止,阻止
prohibitive *a.* 禁止的,抑制的;(价格等)过高的
prohibitory *a.* 阻止的,禁止(性)的
【搭配】prohibit sb. from doing sth. 禁止某人做某事

prospective[2] [prəs'pektɪv]

【释义】*a.* 预期的,未来的,可能的
【例句】I think I told you that we ask prospective reporters to turn in some outlines for possible articles. (TPO15, L, S1, C1) 我想我告诉过你,我们要求可能成为记者的人为可能的文章提交一些提纲。
【逆构】prospect *n.* 前景,预期;可能性,机会

protectionist[2] [prə'tɛkʃənɪst]

【释义】*a.* 贸易保护论的 *n.* 贸易保护论者
【例句】As small countries dependent on foreign markets, they followed a liberal trade policy in the main, though a protectionist movement developed in Sweden. (TPO18, R, S1, T1) 因为小国家都依赖国外市场,所以尽管瑞典正在开展一场贸易保护运动,但是基本上还是会采用自由贸易政策。
【逆构】protection *n.* 保护
protectionism *n.* 贸易保护主义

返记菜单

prehistory[2] premier[2] preposterous[2] prerequisite[2] profile[2]
prohibit[2] prospective[2] protectionist[2]

proximity[2] [prɒk'sɪmɪtɪ]

【释义】*n.*（距离或时间的）接近，临近；邻近（closeness, propinquity）

【例句】Seeing and talking with one another in close physical proximity makes possible a subtle exchange of ideas and feelings. (TPO13, R, S1, T1) 彼此之间近距离的对视和交谈使双方能够进行细微的思想和情感交流。

【派生】proximate *a.* 最接近的；直接的

【搭配】in close proximity 非常靠近的，紧挨的

puddle[2] ['pʌdl]

【释义】*n.* 水坑（尤指道路上的雨水坑）

【例句】That first of all starts drawing water away from the center of its body, so the middle part of the frog, its internal organs, its heart, lungs, liver, these start getting drier and drier while the water that's being pulled away is forming a puddle around the organs just underneath the skin. (TPO18, L, S2, L2) 首先把水从身体中抽出，这样当抽出的水在皮肤下面的器官周围形成一个小水坑时，林蛙的中心内脏部位，包括心脏、肺、肝脏，就会变得越来越干。

【搭配】mud puddle 泥坑

purify[2] ['pjʊərɪfaɪ]

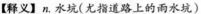

【释义】*v.* 使纯净，净化（cleanse, decontaminate）

【例句】From the Middle East the Chinese acquired a blue pigment—a purified form of cobalt oxide unobtainable at that time in China—that contained only a low level of manganese. (TPO10, R, S1, T1) 中国人从中东地区得到了一种蓝色的颜料，这种颜料在当时的中国还没有，是氧化钴经过提纯后的一种成分，只含有少量的锰。

【派生】purification *n.* 净化；提纯

pushy[2] ['pʊʃɪ]

【释义】*a.* 咄咄逼人的（aggressive）

【例句】I am hoping you were done to get been too pushy. (TPO10, L, S2, C1) 我希望你不要太过于爱出风头。

quotation[2] [kwəʊ'teɪʃən]

【释义】*n.* 1. 引文，引语，语录（citation, reference）2. 报价

【例句】Someone might walk out on the stage and say: "lyric quotation". (TPO7, L, S1, L1) 有些演员会走上舞台，说那些抒情的台词。

【逆构】quote *v.* 引用，引证

raft[2] [rɑːft]

【释义】*n.* 1. 木排（筏）2. 救生圈 *v.* 制成筏，用筏子渡河

【例句】In 1947 Norwegian adventurer Thor Heyerdahl drifted on a balsa-log raft westward with the winds and currents across the Pacific from South America to prove his theory that Pacific islanders were Native Americans (also called American Indians). (TPO5, R, S2, T1) 1947 年，挪威冒险家 Thor Heyerdahl 为了证明他的关于太平洋岛民是美洲土著人（也称作美洲印第安人）的理论，乘木筏随着风和水流向西漂流，从南美洲穿过太平洋。

rarity[2] ['reərɪtɪ]

【释义】*n.* 1. 稀有，罕见 2. 稀有物，珍品

【例句】The rarity of commensal relationships stems from the difficulty to finding relationships that benefit one species without affecting the other. (TPO17, R, S2, T2, Q13) 共生关系的珍贵之处在于：很难找到一种关系，可以使一个物种获益并且不影响另一个物种。

ravage[2] ['rævɪdʒ]

【释义】*n./v.* 毁坏，破坏，蹂躏（destroy, damage, devastate）

【例句】In the German states, the ravages of the Thirty Years' War (1618-1648) further moved textile production into the countryside. (TPO10, R, S2, T2) 在德国，由于"三十年战争（1618-1648）"所造成的破坏进一步促使纺织业向乡村迁移。

【反义】preserve

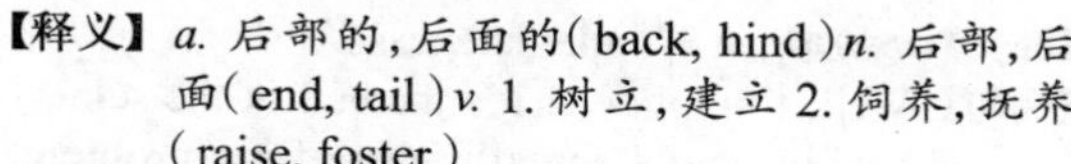

rear[2] [rɪə]

【释义】*a.* 后部的，后面的（back, hind）*n.* 后部，后面（end, tail）*v.* 1. 树立，建立 2. 饲养，抚养（raise, foster）

【例句】Ambulocetus swam like modern whales by moving the rear portion of its body up and down. (TPO2, R, S2, T1) 陆行鲸和现代鲸鱼一样，通过上下摆动身体的尾部来移动。

【反义】front, head

【搭配】at the rear of sth. 在某物的尾部

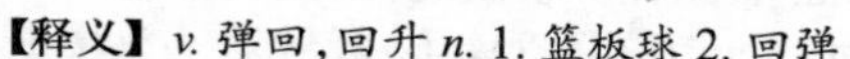

rebound[2] [rɪ'baʊnd]

【释义】*v.* 弹回，回升 *n.* 1. 篮板球 2. 回弹

【例句】The causes of this population rebound are consequences of other human actions. (TPO4, R, S1, T1) 这次数量反弹的原因是其他人类活动的结果。

【派生】rebounder *n.* 善于篮板球之球员

【搭配】on the rebound 在弹回时；在失望、沮丧之际

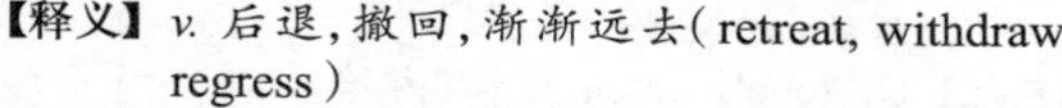

recede[2] [rɪ'siːd]

【释义】*v.* 后退，撤回，渐渐远去（retreat, withdraw, regress）

【例句】Proponents point to features such as the terraced "beaches" shown in one image, which could conceivably have been left behind as a lake or ocean evaporated and the shoreline receded. (TPO8, R, S2, T2) 支持者指出了一些特征，比如在一幅图中所展现的状如梯田的"海滩"，可以想象，这些"海滩"是在湖泊或海洋蒸发、海岸线退去后留下的。

【反义】proceed

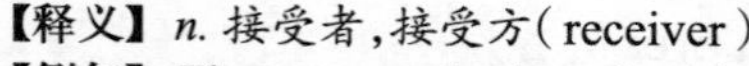

recipient[2] [rɪ'sɪpɪənt]

【释义】*n.* 接受者，接受方（receiver）

【例句】They were designed to be put in places where these beings could manifest themselves in order to be the recipients of ritual actions. (TPO11, R, S1, T1) 它们被放置在特定的位置上，使那些神灵和人物得以显现，通过仪式活动来接受人们的膜拜。

recollection[2] [ˌrekə'lekʃən]

【释义】*n.* 记忆力；回忆（remembrance, reminiscence）

【例句】An explicit memory is a conscious or intentional recollection, usually of facts, names, events, or other things that a person can state or declare. (TPO7, S, Q4) 外显记忆通常是对事实、名称、事件或其它可以清楚描述或说明的事物的一种有意识或有目的的回忆。

【逆构】recollect *v.* 回忆，记起

refreeze[2] [riː'friːz]

【释义】*v.* 再结冰，重新冻结，再制冷

【例句】With further melting, refreezing, and increased weight from newer snowfall above, the snow reaches a granular recrystallized stage intermediate between flakes and ice known as firn. (TPO15, R, S1, T1) 随着进一步的融化、再结冰，以及承受着上方新的降雪的重量，这些积雪到了一种介于雪花和冰块之间颗粒再结晶阶段，这一阶段的雪被称为粒雪。

【逆构】freeze *v.* 使结冰，冻结；僵硬

refreshing[2] [rɪ'freʃɪŋ]

【释义】*a.* 1. 耳目一新的，新颖的；使人精神焕发的（invigorating）

【例句】They were concerned that many would be "drawn to these new, refreshing" conceptions of teaching only to find that the void between the abstractions and the realities of teacher reflection is too great to bridge. (TPO9, R, S2, T1) 他们担心很多人会沉浸在这种全新的教育理念中，结果却发现，教师反思的抽象概念和现实之间的鸿沟太大而无法逾越。

【逆构】refresh *v.* 使恢复精神，使清新

【搭配】a refreshing change 别开生面的变化

regardless[2] [rɪ'gɑːdlɪs]

【释义】*ad./a.* 不顾后果地（的），不顾（的）（despite, notwithstanding）

【例句】Other some cells just seem to keep on dividing regardless which mean not be always a good thing if it gets out of control. (TPO12,

返记菜单

rear[2] rebound[2] recede[2] recipient[2] recollection[2]
refreeze[2] refreshing[2] regardless[2]

L, S1, L1) 其他细胞看起来可以不停地分裂下去，尽管如果失去控制这未必是件好事。

【派生】regardlessly *ad.* 毫无价值地；不受注意地
regardlessness *n.* 不重视，不顾一切

【逆构】regard *v.* 注意，重视，尊敬

【搭配】regardless of 不管，无论

register[2] ['redʒɪstə]

【释义】*v./n.* 登记，注册

【例句】Did you register already for your classes next semester? (TPO2, L, S2, C1) 你已经注册下学期的课了吗？

reign[2] [reɪn]

【释义】*n./v.* 1.（君主）统治（时期）2. 支配，主宰（rule）

【例句】Until the reign of George III (1760-1820), available sources of power for work and travel had not increased since the Middle Ages. (TPO6, R, S1, T1) 从中世纪直到乔治三世统治时期（1760-1820），可用于劳作和行驶的动力一直没有得到发展。

【派生】reigning *a.* 统治的，在位的

【搭配】reign supreme 主宰，称雄，盛行

relict[2] ['relɪkt]

【释义】*n.* 遗物，残留物 *a.* 残存的

【例句】Left over from an earlier time, the behavior remains as a relict, or remnant, long after the environmental circumstance that influenced its evolution has vanished. (TPO18, S, Q4) 这种行为是早期遗留下来的，在影响其进化的环境已经消失了很久以后依然作为一种遗留物存在着。

relief[2] [rɪ'liːf]

【释义】*n.* 1. 宽慰 2.（痛苦等）缓解，减轻 3. 救济，救援物品

【例句】Oh, good, that's a relief. (TPO3, L, S2, C1) 啊，太好了，那我就放心了。

【搭配】social relief 社会救济
on relief 接受公共救济的

relieve[2] [rɪ'liːv]

【释义】*v.* 减轻，缓解（alleviate, ease）

【例句】Well, I'm relieved it's the end of the semester but, that's actually part of my problem. (TPO7, S, Q5) 啊，期末了，我可以放松了，但那实际上只是我的部分问题。

【搭配】relieve oneself 排泄（解小便或大便）

remark[2] [rɪ'mɑːk]

【释义】*n.* 评论，备注，注释（comment）*v.* 1. 评论，谈及（comment, mention）2. 注意到，觉察

【例句】Other students should comment on the man's remark. (TPO4, L, S2, L2) 其他学生应该对这个人的话做出评论。

【派生】remarkable *a.* 非凡的，显著的

repel[2] [rɪ'pel]

【释义】*v.* 驱逐，击退，排斥（repulse, resist）

【例句】It repels water. (TPO7, L, S2, L1) 这是防水的。

【派生】repellent *n.* 驱虫剂，防水剂；讨厌的人 *a.* 击退的；讨人嫌的

【搭配】Oil repels water. 油水不相溶。

replica[2] ['replɪkə]

【释义】*n.* 复制品（copy, duplicate）

【例句】A gene is a piece of biological information that gets copied or replicated, and the copy or replica is passed on to the new generation. (TPO5, L, S1, L1) 基因是一组可以被复制的生物信息，复制后的信息会遗传给下一代。

【派生】replicate *v.* 复制；折叠

repress[2] [rɪ'pres]

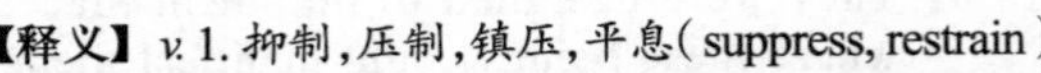

【释义】*v.* 1. 抑制，压制，镇压，平息（suppress, restrain）

【例句】Well, once a popular explanation was that child memories are always repressed. (TPO10, L, S2, L2) 曾经一度流行的一种解释是儿童的记忆总是受到压制。

【反义】incite

【派生】repression *n.* 镇压，抑制

repudiate² [rɪ'pjuːdɪeɪt] 

【释义】v. 否认，批判，驳斥，拒绝(deny, reject, renounce)

【例句】The worker was bound to the master by a mutual contract that either one could repudiate, and the relationship was conceptualized as one of partnership. (TPO16, R, S1, T1) 员工和雇主双方通过签订的合同互为约束，任何一方都可以否认，他们之间是合作伙伴的关系。

【派生】repudiation n. 批判，驳斥

reschedule² [riːʃedjuːl] 

【释义】v. 重订时间表，重新计划(replan)

【例句】I'm assuming you've tried to reschedule your rehearsals. (TPO16, L, S1, C1) 我以为你已经尽力重新安排排练时间了。

resin² ['rezɪn]

【释义】n. 树脂，树脂制品

【例句】The bark was stretched over frames made from tree branches, stitched together and sealed with resin. (TPO7, L, S2, T1) 树皮依照用树枝做好的框架进行延展，然后缝合在一起，并用树脂密封好。

【派生】resinous a. 树脂的，树脂质的

respiration² [ˌrespɪ'reɪʃən] 

【释义】n. 呼吸，呼吸作用

【例句】Film analysis of the infant's responses, heart and respiration rate monitors, and nonnutritive sucking devices are used as effective tools in understanding infant perception. (TPO13, R, S2, T2) 婴儿反应胶片分析、心跳和呼吸频率监测器以及与营养无关的吮吸装置都是了解婴儿认知能力的有效工具。

【搭配】artificial respiration 人工呼吸

retail² ['riːteɪl]

【释义】n. 零售

【例句】In the last 15 years or so, many American cities have had difficulties in maintaining a successful retail environment. (TPO13, L, S1, L1) 在过去的约15年中，美国的许多城市都没能保持良好的零售环境。

【反义】wholesale

【派生】retailer n. 零售商

【搭配】retail businesses 零售生意

retire² [rɪ'taɪə] 

【释义】v. 退休，退役，引退

【例句】To honor an important professor who retired recently. (TPO22, L, S1, C1) 为了纪念一位刚刚退休的教授。

【派生】retiree n. 退休人员
retirement n. 退休

rhinoceros² [raɪ'nɒsərəs] 

【释义】n. 犀牛

【例句】The piercing cries of the rhinoceros hornbill characterize the Southeast Asian rain forest, as do the unmistakable calls of the gibbons. (TPO17, R, S2, T1) 马来犀鸟的尖锐叫声是东南亚雨林的代表性特色，长臂猿那确凿无误的叫声也一样。

【派生】rhinocerotic a. 犀牛的，像犀牛的

【搭配】rhinoceros horn ware 犀角器

rib² [rɪb]

【释义】n. 肋骨，肋状物 v. 1. 装肋于 2. 嘲笑，开玩笑

【例句】The bones found in the graves show a layer of soot on the inside of the ribs. (TPO1, L, S2, L1) 从坟墓里发现的骨头来看，在肋骨的内侧有一层灰。

rig² [rɪg]

【释义】v. 1. (用不正当手段)操纵 2. 装配，装扮 n. 1.【船】 帆装 2. 装备，设备

【例句】The first reason why pollution seemed the more likely cause was that there were known sources of it along the Alaskan coast, such as oil rigs and other sources of industrial chemical pollution. (TPO10, W, Q1) 之所以污染似乎是更可能的原因，首先在于阿拉斯加海岸沿线有已知的污染源，比如石油钻机，以及其它工业化学污染源。

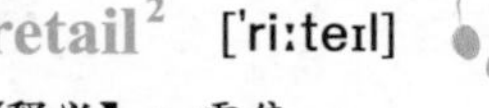

repudiate²	reschedule²	resin²	respiration²	retail²
retire²	rhinoceros²	rib²	rig²	

rigor[2] ['rɪgə]

【释义】*n.* 严酷，严格，严厉（harshness, hardship, strictness）

【例句】This enables them to avoid the worst rigors of high winds. (TPO1, R, S1, T1) 这使得它们能够避免狂风最猛烈的肆虐。

【派生】rigorous *a.* 严厉的，严酷的

rot[2] [rɒt]

【释义】*v.*（使）腐烂，（使）腐朽（decay）*n.* 腐烂，腐朽

【例句】So by removing rotting wood, salvage logging helps minimize the dangers of insect infestation, thus contributing to the health of the forest. (TPO14, W, Q1) 所以通过移除腐烂的树木，抢救性砍伐可以把森林遭受虫害的危险降到最低，因而有利于森林的健康生长。

routinely[2] [ruː'tiːnlɪ]

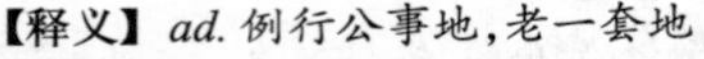

【释义】*ad.* 例行公事地，老一套地

【例句】Commercial fossil hunting makes a lot of fossils available for purchase, and as a result, even low-level public institutions like public schools and libraries can now routinely buy interesting fossils and display them for the public. (TPO13, W, Q1) 化石搜寻的商业化使得许多化石都可以被交易，因此，即使是低水平的公共机构，比如公立学校和图书馆，现在都可以很平常地购买他们感兴趣的化石并将其展示给公众。

royalty[2] ['rɔɪəltɪ]

【释义】*n.* 1. 皇家 2. 版税

【例句】Oh, that's another common element, royalty—a prince or princess. (TPO5, L, S2, L2) 哦，那是另外一个元素，皇室成员——一位王子或是公主。

【逆构】royal *a.* 皇家的 *n.* 王室成员

rudimentary[2] [ruːdɪ'mentərɪ]

【释义】*a.* 基本的，初步的，发展未完全的（primitive, undeveloped）

【例句】He received rudimentary village schooling, but mostly he roamed his uncle's farm collecting the fossils that were so abundant in the rocks of the Cotswold hills. (TPO6, R, S2, T1) 他只在村里接受了最基本的教育，而大部分的时间都是在他叔叔的农场里搜寻化石，这些化石大量存在于科茨沃尔德山的岩石中。

【逆构】rudiment *n.*［常 *pl.*］初步，初级，基本原理

【搭配】in the rudimentary stage 处于萌芽时期

rye[2] [raɪ]

【释义】*n.* 黑麦，黑麦粒

【例句】English and Dutch ships carrying rye from the Baltic states reached Spain and Portugal. (TPO10, R, S2, T2) 英国和荷兰的商船装载着从波罗的海各国带回的黑麦到达了西班牙和葡萄牙。

【搭配】rye bread 黑面包

sac[2] [sæk]

【释义】*n.*（动植物组织中的）液囊

【例句】During courtship and aggressive displays, the turkey enlarges its colored neck collar by inflating sacs in the neck region and then flings about a pendulous part of the colored signaling apparatus as it utters calls designed to attract or repel. (TPO17, R, S2, T1) 在求爱期和发起挑衅时，火鸡会使自己颈囊充气，从而张开艳丽的颈圈，当其发出吸引异性或驱逐敌人的叫声时，便晃动这个色彩绚烂的信号器官的下垂部分。

【搭配】renal sac 肾囊

Word List 38

salt-tolerant[2] [sɔlt'tɑlərənt] 

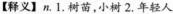

【释义】*a.* 耐盐的

【例句】Research continues to focus on developing salt-tolerant varieties of agricutural crops. (TPO5, R, S1, T1) 研究会继续聚焦在对耐盐农作物种类的开发上。

sapling[2] ['sæplɪŋ] 

【释义】*n.* 1. 树苗，小树 2. 年轻人

【例句】Torreya seeds and saplings have been successfully planted and grown in forests further north, where the temperature is significantly cooler. (TPO17, W, Q1) 榧实的种子和幼苗已经被成功地种植在更北部的森林中，那里的温度低得多。

【搭配】tending in sapling stage 幼林抚育

scan[2] [skæn]

【释义】*v.* 细看，审视；扫描；浏览(survey, scrutinize) *n.* 扫描

【例句】This time she used brain scanning equipment to monitor activity in a certain part of the brain, the area called V5, which is part of the visual cortex, the part of our brains that processes visual stimuli. (TPO15, L, S1, L1) 这次，她使用了大脑扫描仪来监控大脑某一区域的活动，该区域叫做V5，是视觉皮层的一部分，是大脑中用来处理视觉刺激的部分。

【派生】scanning *n.* 扫描

scannable *a.* 能扫描的；可校验的

scenario[2] [sɪ'nɑːrɪəʊ] 

【释义】*n.* 1. 剧本 2. 情节梗概

【例句】This scenario begins with the planting of hyperaccumulating species in the area such as an abandoned mine or an irrigation pond contaminated by runoff. (TPO5, R, S1, T1) 这种方法始于在诸如废弃的煤矿或被污染的灌溉水池等区域种植超富集植物。

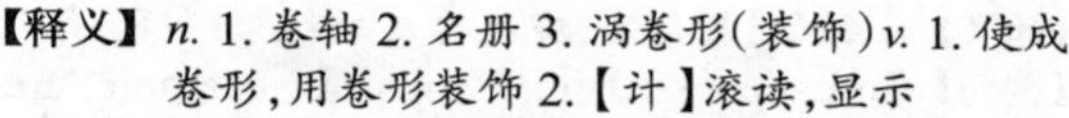

scroll[2] [skrəʊl]

【释义】*n.* 1. 卷轴 2. 名册 3. 涡卷形(装饰) *v.* 1. 使成卷形，用卷形装饰 2.【计】滚读，显示

【例句】Archimedes' writings were originally done on papyrus scrolls. (TPO15, L, S2, L1) 阿基米德的作品最初是写在莎草纸的卷宗上的。

【派生】scrollable *a.* 可卷动的

【搭配】scroll up 向上滚动

scroll down 向下滚动

seafarer[2] ['siːˌfeərə] 

【释义】*n.* 船员；航海家(shipman, navigator)

【例句】European seafarers circumvented Middle Eastern merchants. (TPO16, R, S1, T1) 欧洲海员绕过了中东客商。

secular[2] ['sekjʊlə] 

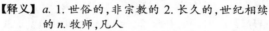

【释义】*a.* 1. 世俗的，非宗教的 2. 长久的，世纪相续的 *n.* 牧师，凡人

【例句】From early times pots were used in both religious and secular contexts. (TPO10, R, S1, T1) 从早期起，壶罐就被用于宗教和日常的生活中。

【搭配】secular trend 长期趋势

self-sustain[2] [ˌself'sə'stein] 

【释义】*a.* 自立的，自谋生路的

【例句】So water ice could enable the creation of a self-sustaining moon base someday, a mining camp perhaps or a departure point for further space exploration. (TPO5, L, S1, L2) 所以也许某一天，固态水可能创造出一个自给自足的月球基地、一个采矿营地或是一个未来空间开发的起点。

sensation[2] [sen'seɪʃən] 

【释义】*n.* 1. 感觉，知觉，感觉能力 2. 兴奋，激动，轰动一时的人(或事物)

【例句】V5 is the area of the visual cortex that's responsible for the sensation of movement. (TPO15, L, S1, L1) V5是视觉皮层区，负责对运动的感知。

【派生】sensational *a.* 极好的，绝妙的；引起轰动的

返记菜单

salt-tolerant[2]	sapling[2]	scan[2]	scenario[2]	scroll[2]
seafarer[2]	secular[2]	self-sustain[2]	sensation[2]	

serpentine[2] ['sɜːpəntaɪn] 

【释义】*a.* 蛇的，蛇形的，蜿蜒的 *n.* 蛇纹岩

【例句】So-called serpentine soils, for example, are deficient in calcium, and only plants able to tolerate low levels of this mineral can survive. (TPO5, R, S1, T1) 比如，所谓的蛇纹岩土中缺乏钙质，因而只有那些对这种矿物质的含量要求不高的植物才能在此土壤中存活。

setup[2] ['setʌp] 

【释义】*n.* 1.（事物的）组织，结构 2. 计划，方案

【例句】If you still have to help out, any chance you could get the museum setup done before then? (TPO2, S, Q5) 如果你仍然需要去帮忙，有可能在那个时间之前安排好博物馆展览吗？

shaft[2] [ʃɑːft] 

【释义】*n.* 杆，柄，杆状物，轴（axes, spindle）*v.* 1. 装柄 2. 苛刻地对待

【例句】Many shafts of spears and similar objects were decorated with figures of animals. (TPO4, R, S2, T1) 很多矛柄和类似的工具上面都装饰有动物图案。

【搭配】main shaft 主轴，总轴
air shaft 通风井

shrink[2] [ʃrɪŋk] 

【释义】*v.* 起皱，收缩，缩小（contract）

【例句】Some populations may shrink, but others will grow. (TPO17, W, Q1) 一些种类（的鸟儿）会减少，而另一些则会增多。

【反义】expand, stretch

【派生】shrinkable *a.* 会收缩的
shrinkage *n.* 收缩

【逆构】shrink from sth./doing sth. 不愿做某事

shun[2] [ʃʌn] 

【释义】*v.* 避开，避免，回避

【例句】For instance, some social groups employ shunning (a person can remain in the community, but others are forbidden to interact with the person) as a device to bring into line individuals whose behavior goes beyond that allowed by the particular group. (TPO13, R, S1, T1) 例如，某些社会群体把回避（一个人可以留在群体中，但其他人被禁止与其接触）作为一种手段，来使那些行为上超出了某个特定群体所允许的范围的个人与（整个群体）保持一致。

sizable[2] ['saɪzəbl] 

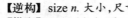

【释义】*a.* 相当大的，颇大的（significant, large, bulky）

【例句】Research now indicates that sizable areas of southeastern Alaska along the inner continental shelf were not covered by ice toward the end of the last Ice Age. (TPO9, R, S1, T1) 现在研究表明，直到上个冰河时代末期，沿内陆架的阿拉斯加东南部的大部分地区并没有被冰层覆盖。

【逆构】size *n.* 大小，尺寸

【搭配】a sizable battle 一场大仗

skip[2] [skɪp] 

【释义】*v.* 1. 跳过，略过（escape, omit）2. 跳，跳跃（jump, leap）

【例句】But I kind of have to skip the one after Mars for now. (TPO2, L, S2, L2) 但是现在我可能得跳过火星之后的那个了。

【派生】skippable *a.* 可跳过的

【搭配】skip rope 跳绳

skyscraper[2] ['skaɪskreɪpə(r)] 

【释义】*n.* 摩天大楼

【例句】There were lots of buildings, tall ones, skyscrapers. (TPO9, S, Q4) 那里有很多高的建筑，摩天大楼。

slick[2] [slɪk] 

【释义】*n.* 海面浮油 *a.* 1. 光滑的（smooth）2.（指人）圆滑的（crafty）*v.* 使平滑

【例句】Spillage from huge oil-carrying cargo ships, called tankers, involved in collisions or accidental groundings (such as the one off Alaska in 1989) can create oil slicks at sea. (TPO4, R, S2, T2) 大型的运油货船——也叫油轮——因撞击或搁浅（比如 1989 年发生在阿拉斯加的事件）引发的石油泄漏会造

成海面浮油。

【派生】slickly *ad.* 平滑地
slickness *n.* 光滑，光滑度

smelt[2] [smelt] 

【释义】*v.* 熔炼，熔解

【例句】Only iron smelting and mining required marshaling a significant amount of capital. (TPO10, R, S2, T2) 只有冶铁和采矿需要投入大量的资金。

smoky[2] ['sməʊkɪ] 

【释义】(= smokey) *a.* 冒烟的，烟雾弥漫的

【例句】You and I would have found it a bit too smoky in there. (TPO1, L, S2, L1) 我和你本来会发现那里有点儿烟雾弥漫的。

【逆构】smoke *n.* 烟，烟雾

【搭配】somky eyes 烟熏眼妆

smother[2] ['smʌðə] 

【释义】*v.* 1. (使)窒息，闷死(choke, suffocate) 2. 覆盖

【例句】Too much snow can smother the trees. (TPO1, R, S1, T1) 积雪过多可能会导致树木窒息死亡。

【派生】smothery *a.* 令人窒息的

so-called[2] [səʊ'kɔld] 

【释义】*a.* 所谓的(supposed, alleged)

【例句】That's the so-called JUNK DNA. (TPO12, L, S1, L1) 那就是所谓的垃圾基因。

solo[2] ['səʊləʊ]

【释义】*n.* 独奏，独唱，独舞 *a.* 单独的(alone, unaccompanied)

【例句】It revolved mainly around solo pieces. (TPO12, L, S2, L1) 它主要是围绕着独奏曲目。

【派生】soloist *n.* 独唱者，独奏者

【搭配】solo concert 个人演唱会

soluble[2] ['sɒljʊbl] 

【释义】*a.* 可溶的

【例句】In the central deeper part of the basin, the last of the brine evaporated to precipitate more soluble sodium chloride (salt). (TPO7, R, S1, T1) 在地中海中部更深处，最后的盐水也蒸发了，从而沉淀出水溶性更好的氯化钠(食盐)。

【反义】insoluble

【派生】solubility *n.* 可溶性，溶度

sorghum[2] ['sɔ:gəm] 

【释义】*n.* 高粱

【例句】Agriculture seems to have reached these people from the Near East, since the first domesticated crops were millets and sorghums whose origins are not African but West Asian. (TPO7, R, S2, T2) 非洲农业很可能来源于近东地区，因为非洲最初种植的农作物是小米和高粱，它们都是源于西亚，而不是非洲。

specify[2] ['spesɪfaɪ] 

【释义】*v.* 明确说明，具体指定(detail, designate)

【例句】With fairy tales, however, the location is generally unspecified. (TPO5, L, S2, L2) 但是在童话故事里，地点往往不那么明确。

【派生】specific *a.* 特殊的；明确的
specification *n.* 规格，说明书
specified *a.* 具体的，特指的

spectacle[2] ['spektəkl] 

【释义】*n.* 1. 演出(performance, display, show) 2. 景色，奇观(sight) 3. 眼镜

【例句】Previously, large audiences had viewed spectacles at the theater, where vaudeville, popular dramas, musical and minstrel shows, classical plays, lectures, and slide-and-lantern shows had been presented to several hundred spectators at a time. (TPO2, R, S2, T2) 先前，大批观众在剧院观看表演，在那里，数百名观众可以同时观看轻歌舞剧、流行戏剧、音乐剧或歌唱表演、古典音乐、演讲和幻灯片放映。

【派生】spectacular *a.* 壮观的

【搭配】make a spectacle of yourself 当场出丑

返记菜单

smelt[2] smoky[2] smother[2] so-called[2] solo[2]
soluble[2] sorghum[2] specify[2] spectacle[2]

spine[2] [spaɪn]

【释义】*n.* 1. 脊柱，脊椎（backbone, vertebrate）2. 书脊 3. 刺（thorn）

【例句】One question was related to evidence that the invertebrate fauna (animals without spines) of the Mediterranean had changed abruptly about 6 million years ago. (TPO7, R, S1, T1) 问题之一是找到相关证据来证明地中海的无脊椎动物群体在约 600 万年前发生了突然的变化。

【反义】spineless

【派生】spinal *a.* 脊骨的，脊髓的
spiny *a.* 多刺的，刺状的

【搭配】spinal cord 脊髓

sponge[2] [spʌndʒ]

【释义】*n.* 海绵 *v.* 用海绵擦拭

【例句】Think of wetlands as, Umm, like a giant sponge, the earth soaks up a lot of this water that's continually flooding the surface, which increases the amount of water below. (TPO13, L, S1, L2) 将湿地想象成，呃，一个巨大的海绵，土壤会吸收大量不断淹没地表的水，这就增加了地下水的含量。

sponsor[2] ['spɒnsə]

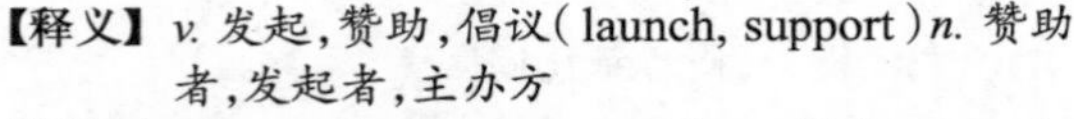

【释义】*v.* 发起，赞助，倡议（launch, support）*n.* 赞助者，发起者，主办方

【例句】The study is sponsored by a TV network. (TPO18, L, S2, C1) 这个研究是由一个电视网赞助的。

【派生】sponsorial *a.* 保证人的；主办者的；教父的

spontaneous[2] [spɒn'teɪnjəs]

【释义】*a.* 自发的，自然产生的（instinctive, natural）

【例句】It can be naturally generated from Uranium atom that has spontaneous split. (TPO8, L, S2, L2) 它可以自然产生于自发分裂的铀原子。

【反义】compulsory

【派生】spontaneity *n.* 自然，自发

spout[2] [spaʊt]

【释义】*n.* 喷口；水管，水柱 *v.* 1.（使）喷出，（使）流出 2. 滔滔不绝地讲

【例句】The Chinese themselves adapted many specific vessel forms from the West, such as bottles with long spouts, and designed a range of decorative patterns especially for the European market. (TPO10, R, S1, T1) 中国人采纳了很多源于西方的独特的器皿形式，比如有着长的喷水口的瓶子，并设计出了一系列专门适应欧洲市场的装饰性器皿。

【搭配】up the spout 无可挽回；落空；在困难中
down spout 下水管

sprain[2] [spreɪn]

【释义】*v./n.* 扭伤

【例句】That's my wrist actually, I sprained it last weekend. (TPO5, S, Q2) 实际上是我的手腕，上周末的时候扭伤了。

stack[2] [stæk]

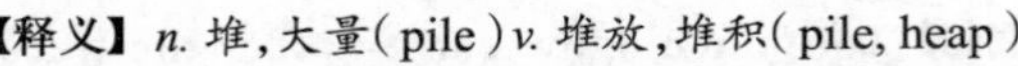

【释义】*n.* 堆，大量（pile）*v.* 堆放，堆积（pile, heap）

【例句】You will find them in the reference stacks in the back. (TPO4, L, S1, C1) 你可以在后面的参考书目中找到它们。

【搭配】a stack of 一堆，一摞
stack up 堆积；累计，加起
stack room 书库
stack up against 争胜负，较量

startle[2] ['stɑːtl]

【释义】*v.* 使惊吓，使吃惊（frighten, shock, surprise）

【例句】This unexpected display of color startles or confuses the predator and provides the would-be prey with an opportunity to escape. (TPO8, S, Q4) 这种出人意料的颜色展示会吓到或迷惑捕食者，从而给可能的猎物提供了一个逃脱的机会。

strick[2] [strik]

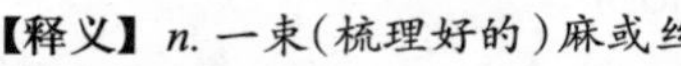

【释义】*n.* 一束（梳理好的）麻或丝

【例句】Some of the most priced tulips were white with purple stricks, or red with yellow

stricks on the paddles, even a dark purple tulip that was very much priced. (TPO6, L, S1, L1) 一些很贵重的郁金香是有着紫条的白色花，或是有着黄条的红色花，甚至暗紫色的郁金香也是很值钱的。

subliminal² [sʌb'lɪmɪnl] 

【释义】*a.* 下意识的，潜意识的

【例句】This phenomenon—the perception of a stimulus just below the threshold of conscious awareness—is called subliminal perception. (TPO12, S, Q5) 这种现象——对意识知觉阈限以下的刺激的感知——叫做阈下知觉。

【派生】subliminally *ad.* 下意识地，潜意识地

substantiate² [sʌbs'tænʃɪeɪt] 

【释义】*n.* 证明，证实，加强(prove, verify, testify)

【例句】Theories that are not substantiated by evidence should generally be considered unreliable. (TPO6, R, S2, T2, Q1) 未被证据证明的理论通常应被认为是不可靠的。

【派生】unsubstantiated *a.* 未被证实的
substantive *a.* 真实的，实质的

【搭配】substantiate one's argument 充实论据

supervise² [ˌsuːpəvaɪz]

【释义】*v.* 监督，管理，指导 (administer, direct)

【例句】She thought all sports activities were supervised by coaches. (TPO11, L, S1, C1) 她原以为所有的体育活动都会由教练监督。

【派生】supervision *n.* 监督，管理
supervisor *n.* 主管，管理人

surmise² [sə'maɪz] 

【释义】*v.* 猜测，推测，认为(guess, presume) *n.* 推测，猜测

【例句】Kramer surmised, therefore, that they were orienting according to the position of the Sun. (TPO11, R, S2, T1) Kramer 由此推测，它们是根据太阳的位置来确定方向的。

suspicious² [səs'pɪʃəs]

【释义】*a.* 可疑的；表示怀疑的，持怀疑态度的 (doubtful, questionable, skeptical)

【例句】It gives him films an uncanny feature: the familiar made unfamiliar, the normal made suspicious. (TPO3, L, S1, L2) 这赋予了他的电影一种奇异的特点：熟悉的东西让人感觉不熟悉，正常的东西让人怀疑。

【派生】suspectable *a.* 可疑的，有嫌疑的
suspicion *n.* 猜疑，怀疑

【搭配】be suspicious of 对…起疑

swamp² [swɒmp] 

【释义】*v.* 1. 淹没 2. 使陷于困境，使忙于应付 *n.* 沼泽，湿地(marsh, bog)

【例句】I'm really swamped. (TPO12, L, S1, C1) 我真是忙不过来了。

【派生】swamped *a.* 泥沼状的
swampy *a.* 沼泽的，湿地的

【搭配】swamp gas 沼气

swift² [swɪft] 

【释义】*a.* 快的，迅速的，敏捷的(quick, fast, rapid) *n.* 1. 雨燕 2. 线轴

【例句】The triumph of sound cinema was swift, complete, and enormously popular. (TPO12, R, S2, T1) 有声电影的成功迅速、彻底，而且非常受欢迎。

【反义】slow

【派生】swiftly *ad.* 很快地；即刻

【搭配】swift growth 快速增长

swing² [swɪŋ] 

【释义】*v.* (使) 摇摆，(使) 旋转(dangle, fluctuate, hang) *n.* 1. 摆动，摇摆 2. 秋千

【例句】What we do know is that as we include longer time intervals, the record shows increasing evidence of slow swings in climate between different regimes. (TPO10, R, S2, T1) 我们所知道的是，当我们包括的时间间隔越长，记录显示出不同国家之间气候缓慢变化的痕迹就越明显。

【搭配】in full swing 活跃；正在全力进行中

synonym² ['sɪnənɪm] 

【释义】*n.* 同义词

【例句】He is searching for a synonym for the term.

返记菜单

subliminal²	substantiate²	supervise²	surmise²	suspicious²
swamp²	swift²	swing²	synonym²	

(TPO5, L, S2, L1) 他在为这个术语寻找同义词。

【反义】antonym

【派生】synonymous *a.* 同义的

---

tabletop[2] ['teibl,tɔp]

【释义】*n.* 桌面 *a.* 台式的

【例句】Paper was scarce and expensive, so typically they drew the design onto a white tabletop. (TPO16, L, S2, L2) 纸张稀少且昂贵，所以他们通常把设计画在一个白色的台面上。

---

tank[2] [tæŋk]

【释义】*n.* 1. 油(或水)箱，罐，槽 2. 坦克 *v.* 把…储于槽中

【例句】The heat is then stored in water-filled tanks or concrete. (TPO12, L, S2, L2) 然后热量被储存在注水的罐子中或是混凝土中。

【派生】tankage *n.* 桶槽容量
tanked *a.* 喝醉的；放在槽中的

【搭配】tank capacity 油罐容量

---

temporal[2] ['tempərəl]

【释义】*a.* 1. 时间的 2. 世俗的 3. 短暂的

【例句】By following the fossils, Smith was able to put all the strata of England's earth into relative temporal sequence. (TPO6, R, S2, T1) 通过追踪化石，史密斯对英国范围内所有的地层以时间先后顺序进行了排序。

【反义】eternal; spiritual

【搭配】a temporal clause 时间从句

---

terminology[2] [,tɜːmɪ'nɒlədʒɪ]

【释义】*n.* 专门用语，术语；术语学

【例句】Okay, now, I'll throw out a little terminology. (TPO6, L, S2, L1) 好了，现在我要讲几个术语。

【派生】terminological *a.* 术语学的

【搭配】medical terminology 医学术语

---

thereafter[2] [ðeər'ɑːftə]

【释义】*ad.* 在那之后

【例句】When this occurs, the first step has been taken toward theater as an antonomous activity, and thereafter entertainment and aesthetic values may gradually replace the former mystical and socially efficacious concerns. (TPO1, R, S2, T1) 这时候，戏剧作为一种自发的活动迈出了自己的第一步，接着，戏剧的娱乐和审美价值开始渐渐取代先前的带有神话色彩的、在社会上灵验的关注。

---

thread[2] [θred]

【释义】*n.* 1. 线 2. 线(索) 3. 思路 *v.* 穿(过)，通过

【例句】It means not help you tie your shoe but that little plastic tip keeps the rest of the shoelace, the shoe string from unraveling into weak and useless threads. (TPO12, L, S1, L1) 它并不意味着能帮你系住你的鞋，但是那个小小的塑料末端却能使鞋带剩余的部分免于松散成不结实且无用的线。

【派生】threadbare *a.* 磨破的，衣衫褴褛的

---

tiring[2] ['taɪərɪŋ] 

【释义】*a.* 累人的，令人疲倦的(tedious, exhausting)

【例句】I myself have taken these three-hour seminars and found them tiring and sometimes boring. (TPO6, L, S, Q3) 我自己参加过这些长达3小时的研讨会，感觉很累人，有时候也很无聊。

【派生】tired *a.* 疲倦的，困倦的

---

toe[2] [təʊ]

【释义】*n.* 脚趾，足尖 *v.* 踮着脚尖走

【例句】Many incomplete skeletons were found but they included, for the first time in an archaeocyte, a complete hind leg that features a foot with three tiny toes. (TPO2, R, S2, T1) 尽管发现的这些骨骼并不完整，但这是专家们第一次在原始动物身上发现完整的后肢，其主要特征是有三个小脚趾的足部。

【搭配】from tip to toe 从头到脚，彻头彻尾

---

topographical[2] [,tɒpə'græfɪkəl] 

【释义】*a.* 地形学的，地质的

【例句】Its orbits enable it to send back data to create this topographical map. (TPO5, L, S1, L2) 它的运行范围使其能够发送回数据，从而制

成这幅地形图。

【派生】topographically *ad.* 从地形上，在地形构造方面

【搭配】topographical map 地形图
topographical features 地貌

tower[2] ['taʊə]

【释义】*n.* 塔，高楼 *v.* 高耸，超出

【例句】The stream of positive particles that meets the surge of electrons from the cloud often arises from a tall pointed structure such as a metal flagpole or a tower. (TPO18, R, S2, T2) 正电粒子流与来自云层的电流相遇通常是由一个高而突出的建筑引发的，比如金属旗杆或者高塔。

【派生】towery *a.* 高耸的；有塔的

【搭配】tower above/over 远远胜过，大大高出

trial[2] ['traɪəl]

【释义】*n.* 1. 审判，审理 2. 测试，试验，考验

【例句】For example, in field trials, the plant alpine pennycress removed zinc and cadmium from soils near a zinc smelter, and Indian mustard, native to Pakistan and India, has been effective in reducing levels of selenium salts by 50 percent in contaminated soils. (TPO5, R, S1, T1) 比如，在现场实验中，阿尔卑斯菥蓂就从靠近一个锌冶炼厂的土壤里清除了锌和镉，而巴基斯坦和印度的本土植物印度芥菜则有效地将被污染的土壤中的硒的含量降低了50%。

【搭配】trial and error 反复试验；试错法
on trial 在试用中；在受审中
trial by fire 考验某人的能力

triumph[2] ['traɪəmf]

【释义】*n./v.* 胜利，成功

【例句】Beyond that, the triumph of recorded sound has overshadowed the rich diversity of technological and aesthetic experiments with the visual image that were going forward simultaneously in the 1920s. (TPO12, R, S2, T1) 除此之外，录音的成功使得在20世纪20年代同时发展起来的丰富多样的视觉技术和审美实验显得暗淡无光了。

【派生】triumphant *a.* 成功的；得意的
triumphal *a.* 凯旋的

【搭配】triumph over 击败，获胜

trivial[2] ['trɪvɪəl]

【释义】*a.* 不重要的，琐碎的（insignificant, trifling）

【例句】Clearly, diverting time previously spent in reading literature to trivial forms of entertainment has lowered the level of culture in general. (TPO11, W, Q1) 很明显，人们把从前用来阅读文学作品的时间转而用来进行一些浅薄的娱乐活动，这从整体上降低了文化的程度。

【逆构】trivia *n.* 琐事，无价值之物

【搭配】trivial matters 无关重要的事情

tusk[2] [tʌsk]

【释义】*n.* 长牙，獠牙

【例句】In addition, the paintings mostly portray animals that the painters may have feared the most because of their size, speed, natural weapons such as tusks and horns, and the unpredictability of their behavior. (TPO4, R, S2, T1) 此外，绘画里描绘得最多的是绘画人可能最畏惧的那些动物，通常是由于这些动物的体型、速度、诸如獠牙和角这样的天然武器，及其不可预测的行为。

typify[2] ['tɪpɪfaɪ]

【释义】*v.* 代表，作为…的典型（characterize, represent, symbolize）

【例句】The discovery and use of the arch typifies the way in which architecture advances by developing more efficient types of structures. (TPO3, R, S1, T1) 拱的发明和使用，使更多有效的建筑类型发展起来，而这也成为了建筑业进步的典型。

【派生】typical *a.* 典型的，象征性的
typicality *n.* 典型性，特征
prototypical *a.* 原型的

unaffected[2] [ˌʌnə'fektɪd]

【释义】*a.* 1. 不受影响的，没有改变的 2. 自然的，不矫揉造作的

【例句】Few cases of absolute commensalism

返记菜单

tower[2] trial[2] triumph[2] trivial[2] tusk[2]
typify[2] unaffected[2]

probably exist, because it is unlikely that one of the partners will be completely unaffected. (TPO17, R, S2, T2) 纯粹的共生关系可能几乎不存在，因为其中一方很难完全不受影响。

【派生】 unaffectedly *ad.* 自然地，真挚地

【搭配】 unaffected by time 无始无终的，永恒的

unavoidable[2] ['ʌnə'vɔɪdəbl]

【释义】 *a.* 不可避免的（inevitable, inescapable）

【例句】 An unavoidable by-product of burning oil is carbon dioxide, and carbon dioxide harms the environment. (TPO9, W, Q1) 油燃烧之后不可避免的产物是二氧化碳，而二氧化碳会破坏环境。

【反义】 avoidable

【派生】 unavoidably *ad.* 不可避免地

【搭配】 an unavoidable accident 一次不可避免的事故

unconsciously[2] [ʌn'kɒnʃəslɪ]

【释义】 *ad.* 无意识地，不知不觉地（senselessly）

【例句】 When our nonverbal signals, which we often produce unconsciously, agree with our verbal message, the verbal message is enhanced and supported, made more convincing. (TPO4, S, Q4) 非语言信号通常在我们不经意间产生，当其与我们的语言信息一致时，语言信息得以强化和证实，从而变得更有说服力。

【逆构】 unconscious *a.* 无意识的
consciously *ad.* 有意识地

unconventional[2] ['ʌnkən'venʃənəl]

【释义】 *a.* 非传统的，不合惯例的，非常规的（unorthodoxy, nontraditional）

【例句】 As a result of the unconventional methods that Outsider Artists often use, their work can look strange and not at all like traditional art to the observer. (TPO11, S, Q4) 由于流外艺术家常常使用非传统的方法，所以他们的作品在观者看来可能会觉得很奇怪，一点都不像传统的艺术。

【反义】 conventional, traditional

【逆构】 conventional *a.* 传统的

undermine[2] [ˌʌndə'maɪn]

【释义】 *v.* 逐渐削弱，暗中破坏（weaken, impair）

【例句】 The development of new international trade routes could undermine the monetary base and erode state power. (TPO16, R, S1, T1) 新国际贸易路线的开发可能会削弱货币基础，并侵蚀国家政权。

undertake[2] [ˌʌndə'teɪk]

【释义】 *v.* 1. 担任，承揽，从事，负责（take on, engage）
2. 承诺，答应（promise）

【例句】 Sometimes these creative solutions come about because a group is more likely to make risky decisions that an individual might not undertake. (TPO2, W, Q1) 由于团队比个人更容易作出具有风险的决定，因此有时会产生具有创造性的解决方案。

【派生】 undertaker *n.* 承办者，承担者
undertaking *n.* 事业；承诺

Word List 39

unfair[2] ['ʌn'feə]

【释义】*a.* 不公平的,(商业上)不正当的(unjust)
【例句】You know, reserving book seems a bit unfair. (TPO14, L, S1, C1) 你知道,保留图书似乎有点不公平。
【搭配】unfair competition 不公平竞争
unfair treatment 不公平待遇

unified[2] ['juːnɪfaɪd]

【释义】*a.* 统一的,一体的
【例句】The way he brought together design and lighting and sound as a unified feature of the stage, can easily be seen in English theater's subsequent emphasis on lighting and motion. (TPO9, L, S1, L1) 他将设计、灯光和声音结合在一起作为舞台的统一特色的方式在英国剧院后来对灯光和动作的重视方面有着明显的体现。
【派生】unify *v.* 统一,使成一体
【搭配】national unified price 全国统一价

unintentionally[2] ['ʌnɪn'tenʃənlɪ]

【释义】*ad.* 非故意地(inadvertently)
【例句】The Independent Television Commission, regulator of television advertising in the United Kingdom, has criticized advertisers for "misleadingness"—creating a wrong impression either intentionally or unintentionally—in an effort to control advertisers' use of techniques that make it difficult for children to judge the true size, action, performance, or construction of a toy. (TPO14, R, S1, T1) 英国电视广告的管理者——独立电视委员会批评广告商为"误导"——总是有意或无意地制造一些假象——委员会试图通过此举来控制广告商滥用技术使得儿童无法判断玩具的真实大小、功能、性能以及构造。
【反义】intentionally, deliberately, purposely
【逆构】intentionally *ad.* 故意地

update[2] [ʌp'deɪt]

【释义】*v.* 更新,升级 *n.* 更新
【例句】I don't care if you look updates and that kind of thing. (TPO16, L, S2, C1) 我不在乎你看一些新鲜的事。
【派生】updated *a.* 最新的,现代化的
【搭配】update information 更新信息

upright[2] ['ʌp'raɪt]

【释义】*a.* 1. 直立的,垂直的(erect, vertical) 2. 正直的,诚实的 *ad.* 笔直,竖立着 *n.* 竖立,直立的东西
【例句】And all of those actions are for the purpose of proving that he is an upright moral, well-mannered, well behaved individual. (TPO13, L, S2, L1) 所有这些行为都是为了证明他是一个为人正直、懂得礼数、行为得体的人。
【搭配】an upright citizen 正直的公民

vague[2] [veɪg] 

【释义】*a.* 模糊的,含糊的(dim, faint, obscure, indistinct)
【例句】Such programs are much needed because in many arid lands there is only a vague idea of the extent of groundwater resources. (TPO12, R, S2, T2) 这样的项目是非常必要的,因为在许多干旱地区,对于地下水资源的分布情况都只有一个模糊的概念。
【反义】clear, distinct
【派生】vaguely *ad.* 暧昧地;含糊地
vagueness *n.* 模糊;含糊
【搭配】vague attitude 暧昧的态度

vaudeville[2] ['vəʊdəvɪl] 

【释义】*n.* 滑稽剧,杂耍
【例句】Previously, large audiences had viewed spectacles at the theater, where vaudeville, popular dramas, musical and minstrel shows, classical plays, lectures, and slide-and-lantern shows had been presented to several hundred spectators at a time. (TPO2, R, S2, T2) 先前,大批观众在剧院观看表演,在那里,数百名观众可以同时观看轻歌舞剧、流行戏剧、音乐剧或歌唱表演、古典音乐、演讲

返记菜单

unfair[2] unified[2] unintentionally[2] update[2] upright[2]
vague[2] vaudeville[2]

和幻灯片放映。

venture[2] ['ventʃə]

【释义】*n.* 冒险(事业),投机活动(adventure) *v.* 敢于,冒险

【例句】Opera was commonplace in Italy for almost thousands of years before it became commercial as a venture. (TPO12, L, S2, L1) 歌剧在变得像风险投资一样具有商业性之前,几千年来在意大利一直是司空见惯的。

【派生】venturer *n.* 冒险者;投机者
adventure *n.* 冒险,冒险经历

【搭配】venture on 冒险;鼓起勇气前进
venture out 探险

vertebrate[2] ['vɜːtɪbrɪt]

【释义】*n.* 脊椎动物

【例句】In recent years, however, the sale of fossils, particularly of dinosaurs and other large vertebrates, has grown into a big business. (TPO13, W, Q1) 然而,近些年来,化石交易——特别是恐龙和其它大型脊椎动物的化石——已经发展成为一个大的产业。

via[2] ['vaɪə]

【释义】*prep.* 经由,通过

【例句】Perception is the faculty that allows us to process information in the present as we take it via our senses. (TPO14, L, S1, L1) 感知是一种让我们能够处理通过感觉获取到的信息的能力。

vocal[2] ['vəʊkl]

【释义】*a.* 1. 口头的,发音的 2. 大声的,直言不讳的

【例句】After they've been frozen and thawed of course, they don't seem quite as vocal. (TPO18, L, S2, L2) 当然,在它们被冻结又融化之后,声带不再像从前一样好了。

【派生】vocality *n.* 声乐,声音

void[2] [vɔɪd]

【释义】*n.* 1. 空隙,空处,空白(space) 2. 空虚(emptiness) *a.* 1. 空的,空虚的(vacant) 2. 无效的(invalid) *v.* 1. 使无效 2. 使空出,排放

【例句】They were concerned that many would be "drawn to these new, refreshing" conceptions of teaching only to find that the void between the abstractions and the realities of teacher reflection is too great to bridge. (TPO9, R, S2, T1) 他们担心很多人会沉浸在这种全新的教育理念中,结果却发现,教师反思的抽象概念和现实之间的鸿沟太大而无法逾越。

【派生】voidable *a.* 可以作废的,可被取消的

【搭配】void marriage 无效婚姻

vote[2] [vəʊt]

【释义】*n./v.* 1. 投票,选举,表决

【例句】As more people sided with senior management, I started to feel like I was the only one holding up the vote everyone else seemed to think change wasn't necessary, so I voted against my own idea in the end. (TPO1, S, Q4) 由于越来越多的人都站在了高级管理层的那一边,我开始觉得我是唯一一个还坚持着别人都认为没必要改变的那一票的人,所以最终我还是投了违背自己意愿的一票。

【派生】voter *n.* 选举人,投票人

【搭配】vote against 投票反对

wedded[2] ['wedɪd]

【释义】*a.* 1. 热爱的或献身的 2. 已婚的

【例句】The Greeks were wedded to the sea: the Romans, to the land. (TPO7, R, S2, T1) 希腊注重海上,而罗马注重陆上。

weird[2] [wɪəd]

【释义】*a.* 离奇的,古怪的(strange, uncanny, odd) *n.* 厄运,宿命

【例句】This may sound a bit weird. (TPO14, L, S1, C1) 这听起来有点儿怪。

welfare[2] ['welfeə]

【释义】*n.* 福利,福利救济(benefit)

【例句】Since comedy requires sufficient detachment to view some deviations from social norms as ridiculous rather than as serious threats to the welfare of the entire group. (TPO1, R, S2, T1) 喜剧要求人们充分地从痛苦中脱离,

返记菜单

venture[2] vertebrate[2] via[2] vocal[2] void[2]
vote[2] wedded[2] weird[2] welfare[2]

并将一些与社会准则相背离的表现看作是可笑的，而不是将其视为对群体利益的巨大威胁。

【搭配】welfare system 福利体系
welfare lottery 福利彩票

whereby[2] [weə'baɪ]

【释义】*conj.* 与…一致；通过…，凭借

【例句】Diffusion is the process whereby something cultural like a custom, a type of food or an invention is spread from one group to another or from one society to another. (TPO17, S, Q6) 文化传播是某种文化的东西，比如一种风俗、一种食物或一项发明，从一个群体传到另一个群体或者从一个社会传到另一个社会的过程。

would-be[2] ['wudˌbiː]

【释义】*a.* 想要成为的

【例句】They were positioned as if they were heading in the direction of the points on the sea horizon where certain stars would appear and young would-be navigators set by the stones at night and turned in different directions to memorize the constellations they saw, so they could recognize them and navigate by them later on when they went out to sea. (TPO14, L, S2, L1) 它们被放置成好像要朝向海平面的样子，那里会有固定的星座出现，而想要成为航海家的年轻人夜晚时会留些石头在那里并变换不同的方向，以此来记录他们所看见的星座，这样他们日后出海时就可以认出这些星座并凭借它们进行导航。

yogurt[2] ['jɒgət]

【释义】*n.* 酸奶，酸乳酪

【例句】These cold breakfast foods, such as breads, fruit, and yogurt, are healthier than many of the hot breakfast items that we will stop serving, so health-conscious students should welcome this change. (TPO3, S, Q3) 这些冷早餐，比如面包、水果和酸奶，比很多即将停止供应的热早餐更加健康，因此这一改变应该会受到对健康比较关注的学生的欢迎。

abound[1] [ə'baʊnd]

【释义】*v.*（物产或资源）丰富，富于（be full of, be abundant）

【例句】Although waterpower abounded in Lancashire and Scotland and ran grain mills as well as textile mills, it had one great disadvantage. (TPO6, R, S1, T1) 尽管兰开夏和苏格兰地区丰富的水力资源可用于谷物作坊和纺织厂，但这种动力存在一个极大的缺陷。

【反义】lack

【派生】abounding *a.* 丰富的，大量的

【搭配】abound in/with 充满，富于

abrasive[1] [ə'breɪsɪv]

【释义】*n.* 磨料 *a.* 1. 有研磨作用的 2. 粗糙的，粗暴的

【例句】In the late Middle Ages, it was customary to scrape away the surface of the parchment with an abrasive. (TPO15, L, S2, L1) 在中世纪晚期，用研磨料来擦去羊皮纸的表层是一种惯常的方法。

【派生】abrasively *ad.* 研磨地；粗暴地

adhere[1] [əd'hɪə]

【释义】v. 1. 粘着，粘附 2. 坚持，遵守

【例句】And if you peel birch bark in the winter, we call it "the winter bark", another layer, a tougher inner layer of the tree adheres to the bark, producing a stronger material. (TPO7, L, S2, T1) 而且，如果你在冬天剥去白桦树的树皮，我们叫它"冬树皮"，那么另外一层，更加坚韧的紧贴树皮的树层就可以长出更强硬的材料。

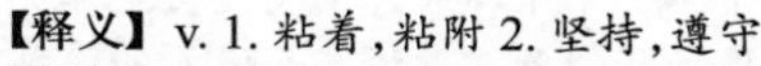

admission[1] [əd'mɪʃən]

【释义】*n.* 1. 准许进入，进入权 2. 承认，供认 3. 入场费，入场券，门票费

【例句】Exhibitors, however, wanted to maximize their profits, which they could do more readily by projecting a handful of films to hundreds of customers at a time (rather than one at a time) and by charging 25 to 50 cents admission. (TPO2, R, S2, T2) 然而，影院老

板希望将收益最大化。要想更容易地做到这一点，他们可以一次性向数百名观众放映几部电影（而不是一次一位观众），每位观众的入场费是25到50美分。

【逆构】admit *v.* 承认

adorn[1] [ə'dɔːn] 

【释义】*v.* 装饰，使生色（decorate, garnish）

【例句】Some scientists speculate that Mars may have enjoyed an extended early period during which rivers, lakes, and perhaps even oceans adorned its surface. (TPO8, R, S2, T2) 一些科学家推测，火星可能经历了一个很长的早期发展阶段，在这期间，河流、湖泊甚或海洋点缀着火星的表面。

【派生】adornment *n.* 装饰，装点；装饰物

adrift[1] [ə'drɪft] 

【释义】*a.* 漂泊的，漫无目的的

【例句】Contrary to the arguments of some that much of the Pacific was settled by Polynesians accidentally marooned after being lost and adrift, it seems reasonable that this feat was accomplished by deliberate colonization expeditions that set out fully stocked with food and domesticated plants and animals. (TPO5, R, S2, T1) 一些人认为在太平洋大部分地区定居的是意外迷路而流亡的波利尼西亚人，但与此相反的另一种理论看似更加合理，该理论认为这一壮举是由有意的殖民远征活动创造的，他们在出发时准备了充足的食物及驯化的动植物。

affinity[1] [ə'fɪnɪtɪ] 

【释义】*n.* 1.（生性）喜爱，（本性）倾向 2. 密切关系，连接关系

【例句】Their streamlined bodies, the absence of hind legs, and the presence of a fluke and blowhole cannot disguise their affinities with land dwelling mammals. (TPO2, R, S2, T1) 它们的身体呈流线型，没有后腿，长有尾片和喷水孔，但这些都不能掩盖它们与陆生哺乳动物的相似性。

【反义】dissimilarity

affluence[1] ['æfluəns] 

【释义】*n.* 富裕

【例句】So in addition to intelligence, they also symbolize affluence, um, wealth. (TPO8, L, S2, L1) 所以，除了知识，它们还象征着富裕，嗯，财富。

【反义】effluence

【逆构】affluent *a.* 富裕的，大量的

afloat[1] [ə'fləʊt] 

【释义】*a.* 浮在水面（的）（adrift, floating）

【例句】The ship was tilting badly but still kept afloat. 船倾侧地厉害，但却仍然漂浮着。

aftermath[1] ['ɑːftəmæθ]

【释义】*n.* 后果，余波

【例句】One way of dealing with the aftermath of these disasters is called salvage logging, which is the practice of removing dead trees from affected areas and using the wood for lumber, plywood, and other wood products. (TPO14, W, Q1) 对待这些灾难造成的后果的方法之一是抢救性砍伐，就是将受灾地区死掉的树木移除，将其制成木材、胶合板以及其他木制产品。

agitate[1] ['ædʒɪteɪt] 

【释义】*v.* 1. 煽动（instigate, stir）2. 搅动 3. 焦虑

【例句】We are mysteriously agitated by a…but it is not a sound our ears can hear. (TPO14, L, S2, L2) 某种声音让我们莫名地焦虑难安，但这种声音不是我们的耳朵可以听见的。

【反义】calm

【派生】agitation *n.* 焦虑，不安

agitated *a.* 激动不安的，焦虑的

【搭配】agitate for 鼓动

ailment[1] ['eɪlmənt] 

【释义】*n.* 小病，疾病（illness）

【例句】The situation at the health center is unacceptable: you sit in a crowded waiting room for hours waiting to get treatment for minor ailments. (TPO16, S, Q3) 医务室的情况是

返记菜单

adorn[1] adrift[1] affinity[1] affluence[1] afloat[1]
aftermath[1] agitate[1] ailment[1]

很难让人接受的：你坐在拥挤的候诊室里数小时，只为等待治疗一个小病。

【逆构】 ail *v.* 有病，生病

alarming[1] [ə'lɑːmɪŋ] 

【释义】 *a.* 惊人的，令人忧虑的

【例句】 The deserts, which already occupy approximately a fourth of the Earth's land surface, have in recent decades been increasing at an alarming pace. (TPO2, R, Sl, T1) 沙漠已经占据地球表面约四分之一的面积，近几十年仍在以惊人的速度扩张。

【派生】 alarmingly *ad.* 惊人地

【逆构】 alarm *v.* 使警觉 *n.* 警报

【搭配】 at an alarming rate 以惊人的速度

alliance[1] [ə'laɪəns] 

【释义】 *n.* 联姻；联盟；联合（alignment, confederation）

【例句】 Well, if they could travel so easily over such a large area, they could trade with people from other areas which I guess would lead them to form alliances? (TPO7, L, S2, L1) 啊，如果他们可以轻而易举地穿过这么广阔的区域，那么他们就可以和其他部落的人进行贸易，并且我认为这会使他们结盟吧？

【搭配】 in alliance (with sb./sth.) 与…联合，与…结合

altruistic[1] [ˌæltrʊ'ɪstɪk] 

【释义】 *a.* 利他主义的，无私的（selfless）

【例句】 Well, you see, corporations aren't always altruistic. (TPO4, L, S2, L2) 你明白，企业是总是那么无私的。

【反义】 egoistic

【派生】 altruist *n.* 利他主义者
altruism *n.* 利他主义

amass[1] [ə'mæs] 

【释义】 *v.* 积累，积聚（accumulate, assemble）

【例句】 A survey of known hyperaccumulators indentified that 75 percent of them amassed nickel. (TPO5, R, S1, T1) 一份对已知超富集植物的调查证实它们之中的75%都富含镍。

【派生】 amassment *n.* 继续；聚积

ambassador[1] [æm'bæsədə] 

【释义】 *n.* 大使，使节

【例句】 By the Middle Ages, spices were regarded as so important and expensive that they were used in diplomacy, as gifts by heads of state and ambassadors. (TPO18, L, S2, L1) 到中世纪时，香料被视为非常重要且昂贵的东西，因而被各国元首和大使们用作外交中的礼物。

【派生】 ambassadorial *a.* 大使的，使节的
ambasadress *n.* 大使夫人

【搭配】 an ambassador extraordinary 特派大使

ambition[1] [æm'bɪʃən] 

【释义】 *n.* 雄心，野心，抱负

【例句】 His ambition was consummated when he received his doctor's degree from Cambridge. 当他从剑桥大学获得了博士学位时，他的抱负实现了。

【派生】 ambitious *a.* 有雄心的，有抱负的

annoying[1] [ə'nɔɪɪŋ] 

【释义】 *a.* 恼人的，讨厌的（bothersome, troublesome, irritating）

【例句】 Consider why they're unique or annoying. (TPO6, L, S2, L1) 思考一下他们为什么是特别的或令人讨厌的。

【逆构】 annoy *v.* 使恼怒；打扰

anonymous[1] [ə'nɒnɪməs] 

【释义】 *a.* 1. 匿名的 2. 无名的 3. 没特色的

【例句】 An anonymous donor is paying the bill for most the sculpture. (TPO1, S, Q3) 一个不愿透露姓名的捐赠者为雕塑的大部分费用买单。

【派生】 anonymously *ad.* 不具名地；化名地

【逆构】 anonym *n.* 匿名者；假名

【搭配】 anonymous donation 不记名捐款

antecedent[1] [ˌæntɪ'siːdənt] 

【释义】 *n.* 1. 前情 2. 祖先 3. 先行词 *a.* 先前的，在先的

【例句】 In addition to exploring the possible

antecedents of theater, scholars have also theorized about the motives that led people to develop theater. (TPO1, R, S2, T1) 除了探索戏剧的起源外，一些学者还就人类发展戏剧的动机提出了一些理论。

【反义】subsequent

【派生】antecedently *ad.* 先前，在先

anticipate[1] [æn'tɪsɪpeɪt] 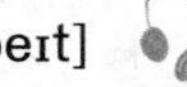

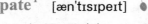

【释义】*v.* 1. 期望，预期(expect, foresee, predict) 2. 先于…做，早于…行动

【例句】Imagination is a faculty that some people use to anticipate future events in their lives. (TPO14, L, S1, L1) 想象力是人们用来预料其生活中未来将发生的事情的一种机能。

【派生】anticipation *n.* 预期，期望，预料

anxious[1] ['æŋkʃəs] 

【释义】*a.* 1. 渴望的，急切的(keen, eager) 2. 担忧的，焦虑的(worried)

【例句】Peripheral peoples therefore had a great advantage in their dealings with the center, making government authority insecure and anxious. (TPO16, R, S1, T1) 因此，周边人民在和中心地区的人交易时很有优势，这让政府机构感到焦虑不安。

【派生】anxiously *ad.* 急切地
anxiousness *n.* 焦虑

【搭配】anxious for/about 为…而焦虑
anxious to do sth. 急于做…

arboreal[1] [ɑː'bɔːrɪəl] 

【释义】*a.* 树木的，栖于树木的

【例句】Even with snow on the ground, the high bushy understory is exposed; also snow and wind bring down leafy branches of cedar, hemlock, red alder, and other arboreal fodder. (TPO4, R, S1, T1) 即便白雪覆盖了大地，高而浓密的林下叶层依然不会被掩盖；风雪也吹落了雪松、铁杉、赤阳木和其他树木的茂密枝叶。

archway[1] ['ɑːtʃweɪ]

【释义】*n.* 拱门，拱道

【例句】In architecture, a keystone in an archway or doorway is the stone that holds the whole thing together, and keeps it from collapsing. (TPO13, L, S1, L2) 在建筑中，拱顶石是用于拱道或者门中，可以将所有的东西连接起来，防止其倒塌。

aria[1] ['ɑːrɪə]

【释义】*n.* 咏叹调，唱腔

【例句】And so the music was secondary to the way the rhythm of language was used to add drama and of course as a result instead of arias or solos. (TPO12, L, S2, L1) 所以，比起语言中的节奏运用在戏剧中(而非独唱或独奏中)的方式来说，音乐是第二位的。

aromatic[1] [ˌærəʊ'mætɪk] 

【释义】*a.* 芳香的，有香味的(fragrant)

【例句】Technically speaking, a spice is part of an aromatic plant that is not a leaf or herb. (TPO18, L, S2, L1) 严格地讲，香料是芳香植物的一部分，不是叶子或草本植物。

【逆构】aroma *n.* 香气，芳香

【搭配】aromatic compounds 芳香族化合物

arouse[1] [ə'raʊz] 

【释义】*v.* 唤醒；激起(awaken, stimulate, excite)

【例句】Artists use these visual effects and the senses they arouse to give meaning to their work. (TPO4, S, Q6) 艺术家用这些视觉效果和他们所唤起的感觉来赋予其作品含义。

【搭配】arouse the enthusiasm of 调动积极性
arouse from 从…中唤醒

artistically[1] [ɑː'tɪstɪklɪ]

【释义】*ad.* 在艺术上，富有艺术地

【例句】Now artistically for both composers and performers this was a major turning point. (TPO16, L, S1, L2) 现在从艺术上来说，这对创作家和表演者来说都是一个重大的转折点。

artsy[1] ['ɑːtsi]

【释义】*a.* 懂(搞)艺术的

【例句】Everyone's into sports and I'm more artsy,

you know, into music. (TPO5, L, S1, C1) 每个人都喜欢运动，而我，你知道的，更有艺术天分，喜欢音乐。

ascribe[1] [əs'kraɪb] 

【释义】*v.* 归因于
【例句】He ascribed his failure to bad luck. 他把自己的失败归因于运气不好。
【搭配】ascribe to 把…归因于

aspiration[1] [ˌæspə'reɪʃən] 

【释义】*n.* 强烈的愿望，志向，抱负(ambition, intention)
【例句】Because architecture grows out of human needs and aspirations, it clearly communicates cultural values. (TPO3, R, S1, T1) 因为建筑源于人类的需求和愿望，同样也可以清楚地传达文化价值。
【派生】aspiring *a.* 有志气的，有抱负的
【逆构】aspire *v.* 渴求，追求，有志于

assert[1] [ə'sɜːt] 

【释义】*v.* 断言，维护，坚持，主张(affirm, declare)
【例句】So the family members who asserted that the painting was Jane had never actually seen her themselves. (TPO12, W, Q1) 所以，那些断言画上的人就是Jane的家庭成员们实际上连他们自己都没见过她。
【派生】assertion *n.* 断言，声明
【搭配】assert oneself 坚持自己的权利或意见

astrolabe[1] ['æstrəleɪb] 

【释义】*n.* 星盘
【例句】The astrolabe had long been the primary instrument for navigation, having been introduced in the eleventh century. (TPO17, R, S1, T1) 自从11世纪星象盘引入欧洲以来，已经成为了航海的基础工具之一。

asymmetrical[1] [ˌeisi'metrikl] 

【释义】*a.* 不对称的，不均匀的
【例句】The finding above suggest that the human brain was already asymmetrical in its structure and function. (TPO12, R, S1, T1) 以上的发现表明人类大脑早已在其结构和功能上不对称了。
【反义】symmetrical
【派生】asymmetrically *ad.* 不对称地

aural[1] ['ɔːrəl] 

【释义】*a.* 听觉的
【例句】In many instances, spectators in the era before recorded sound experienced elaborate aural presentations alongside movies' visual images, from the Japanses benshi (narrators) crafting multivoiced dialogue narratives to original musical compositions performed by symphony-size orchestras in Europe and the United States. (TPO12, R, S2, T1) 很多情况下，那些处在还没有录音音效时代的观众们都在观看电影影像的同时经历着旁边复杂的音效呈现：从日本的benshi(口技)的多点音效的对话演绎到欧洲和美国的由管弦交响乐乐队演奏的原创音乐曲谱。
【派生】aurally *ad.* 听觉上；听起来
【搭配】aural signal 音频信号

authentic[1] [ɔː'θentɪk] 

【释义】*a.* 1. 真的，真正的(genuine, true) 2. 可靠的，可信的
【例句】How do you determine whether the painting is authentic? (TPO5, L, S2, L1) 你怎么判断这幅画是不是真的呢？
【反义】false, fictitious
【派生】authentically *ad.* 真正地，确实地
authenticate *v.* 鉴定
【搭配】authentic interpretation 权威解释

avalanche[1] ['ævəlɑːnʃ] 

【释义】*n.* 雪崩
【例句】Avalanches and snow creep can damage or destroy them. (TPO1, R, S1, T1) 雪崩和雪的缓慢推进可能会伤害或是摧毁它们。

awesome[1] ['ɔːsəm] 

【释义】*a.* 了不起的，精彩的，绝妙的(amazing, awful)
【例句】The total amount of ice is even more awesome if we estimate the water released upon the hypothetical melting of the world's

glaciers. (TPO15, R, S1, T1) 如果我们对理论上全球冰川融化后所释放的水量进行估计，那么冰块的总量会更加令人叹为观止。

【派生】awesomely *a.* 赫然；惊叹地

backdrop[1] ['bækdrɒp]

【释义】*n.* 背景幕，背景

【例句】The paintings rest on bare walls, with no backdrops or environmental trappings. (TPO4, R, S2, T1) 画作以空白的墙面为依托，没有任何背景或环境装饰。

barley[1] ['bɑːlɪ]

【释义】*n.* 大麦

【例句】And finally the time of the year would arrive when the valley would produce crops, such as wheat, barley, fruit, all ready to harvest. (TPO17, L, S2, L1) 最后全年中的黄金时期到来了，此时该流域内会产出各种农作物，如小麦、大麦、水果，全都只等着丰收了。

【派生】barleycorn *n.* 大麦粒

【搭配】highland barley 青稞
barley malt 大麦芽
barley wine 大麦酒

barn[1] [bɑːn]

【释义】*n.* 1. 仓房 2. 简陋的大建筑物 3.（公共汽车、卡车等的）车库

【例句】This used to be an agricultural area and we already know that where the main lecture hall now stands, there once were farm house and barn that were erected in the late 1700s. (TPO3, L, S2, C1) 这里过去是一片农场，我们已经知道，现在主讲厅所在的地方曾经是18世纪后期时建立起来的农舍和仓库。

【搭配】grain barn 粮食仓库

barrel[1] ['bærəl]

【释义】*n.* 1.（物体某部的）金属管（尤指枪管或笔管）2. 桶

【例句】As they drilled into the central and deepest part of the Mediterranean basin, the scientists took solid, shiny, crystalline salt from the core barrel. (TPO7, R, S1, T1) 当钻探到地中海海床的最中心最深处时，科学家从钻管中得到了坚硬闪光的晶体盐类。

basement[1] ['beɪsmənt]

【释义】*n.* 地下室（cellar）

【例句】Well, we have copies of all the newspapers in the basement, and all the major papers publish reference guides to their articles reviews, etc. (TPO4, L, S1, C1) 我们地下室有全部的报纸，还有各大报纸发行的关于其文章评论的索引。

bask[1] [bɑːsk]

【释义】*v.* 坐着或躺着取暖，沐浴在阳光下

【例句】A leatherback may be able to pick up some body heat by basking at the surface; its dark, almost black body color may help it to absorb solar radiation. (TPO15, R, S2, T1) 一只棱皮龟也许可以通过晒太阳来收集身体所需的热量，它的它深色的近乎黑色的体色可能会帮助其吸收太阳光的辐射。

【搭配】bask in sth. 沐浴在…

battery[1] ['bætərɪ]

【释义】*n.* 1.（蓄）电池（组）2. 一系列 3. 排炮，列炮

【例句】I have a history paper due tomorrow, and I've been writing it on my laptop computer and the battery is running low. (TPO10, S, Q5) 我有一个历史论文明天要交，我一直在笔记本电脑上写，但是电池的电量已经不足了。

【搭配】battery of 一组，一套
in battery （炮）准备发射的状态

Word List 40

bead[1] [bi:d]

【释义】*n.* 1. 珠子(pearl) 2. 滴(drop) *v.* 1. 形成珠状,起泡 2. 用珠装饰

【例句】The earliest discovered traces of art are beads and carvings, and then paintings, from sites dating back to the Upper Paleolithic period. (TPO4, R, S2, T1) 最早发现的艺术遗迹是从可以追溯到旧石器时代的遗址中发现的珠子和雕刻品,然后才是画。

beak[1] [bi:k]

【释义】*n.* 1. 鸟喙;鸟嘴状物体 2. 鹰钩鼻 3. 男教师

【例句】For example, there's a bird, the 'wood thrush', anyway, when the 'wood thrush' is in an attack-escape conflict, that is, it's caught between the two urges to escape from or to attack an enemy, if it's sitting on a horizontal branch, it'll wipe its beak on its perch. (TPO4, L, S1, L1) 比如,有一种鸟,"鸫科鸣鸟",当它在处在攻击还是逃跑的矛盾中时,也就是说,它陷入了逃跑还是攻击敌人的两种想法中,如果它位于水平的树枝上,它会用鸟喙啄其所栖息的树枝。

bean[1] [bi:n]

【释义】*n.* 豆,豆科植物

【例句】The Americas provide Europe and Asia with food like squash, beans, turkey, peanuts. (TPO10, L, S1, L2) 美洲向欧洲和亚洲提供诸如南瓜、豆子、火鸡、花生之类的食物。

【搭配】bean curd 豆腐
full of beans 精力旺盛;严重的错误
spill the beans 泄密

befit[1] [bɪ'fɪt]

【释义】*v.* 适合(于),适宜(suit)

【例句】Most engravings, for example, are best lit from the left, as befits the work of right-handed artists, who generally prefer to have the light source on the left so that the shadow of their hand does not fall on the tip of the engraving tool or brush. (TPO12, R, S1, T1) 例如,大多数的雕版都是左起的光照最好,这是为了配合惯用右手的工匠的工作。他们喜欢让光线从左面照过来,以便于他们手的影子不会落在雕版工具或是刷子的尖端。

【派生】befitting *a.* 适合的

beforehand[1] [bɪ'fɔ:hænd]

【释义】*ad.* 预先,事先(ahead, in advance)

【例句】Familiarize himself with certain business beforehand is a good way for the student to prepare for speaking to companies representatives. (TPO6, L, S1, C1, Q4) 学生事先熟悉一些公司将有助于其和公司代表的谈话。

【反义】afterwards

【搭配】be beforehand with 防止

bellow[1] ['beləu]

【释义】*n.* 风箱

【例句】Iron manufacturers, which had starved for fuel while depending on charcoal, also benefited from ever-increasing supplies of coal: blast furnaces with steam-powered bellows turned out more iron and steel for the new machinery. (TPO6, R, S1, T1) 依赖于木炭供应的铁匠们亟需燃料,他们也受益于越来越多的煤炭供应。配备有蒸汽动力的鼓风炉使得越来越多的钢铁供应成为可能。

【搭配】pump the bellows 拉风箱

bemoan[1] [bɪ'məun]

【释义】*v.* 悲叹;为…惋惜(sigh, lament)

【例句】The early explorers and settlers told of abundant deer in the early 1800s and yet almost in the same breath bemoaned the lack of this succulent game animal. (TPO4, R, S1, T1) 19世纪初期的探险家和移民们描述有大量的鹿群,而几乎与此同时又哀叹这种肉质鲜嫩的猎物的不足。

返记菜单

bead[1] beak[1] bean[1] befit[1] beforehand[1]
bellow[1] bemoan[1]

beverage[1] ['bevərɪdʒ]

【释义】*n.* 饮料(drink, bevvy)

【例句】Also, if food were allowed in classrooms, it would be possible for us to have in-class parties on the last day of class—with snack foods and beverages—to celebrate the end of each semester. (TPO14, S, Q3) 另外,如果可以带食物进教室,我们就能够在上课的最后一天在教室中举办聚会——有食物和饮料——来庆祝每学期的结束。

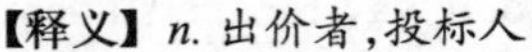

bidder[1] ['bɪdə]

【释义】*n.* 出价者,投标人

【例句】And bust it did, when one cold February morning in 1637, a group of bulb traders got together and discovered that suddenly there were no bidders. (TPO6, L, S1, L1) 最后市场崩溃了,那是1637年一个寒冷的二月的早晨,一群郁金香的交易者聚在了一起,却突然发现没有了投标人。

【逆构】bid *v.* 出价,投标

【派生】bidding *n.* 投标

bingo[1] ['bɪŋgəʊ]

【释义】*int.* 看吧!瞧!(因出乎意料的成功而表示兴奋的叫声)

【例句】Wow! So just add a chemical to a gas, and bingo, you've got a food supply? (TPO15, L, S2, L2) 喔!所以就仅仅是给气体中加入一种化学成分,然后,瞧,你就得到食品供应了吗?

biography[1] [baɪ'ɒgrəfɪ]

【释义】*n.* 传记,传记文学

【例句】People enjoy reading many different types of books such as mystery, biography, romance, etc, of all the different types of books that there are, what type do you most enjoy? (TPO14, S, Q1) 人们喜欢读各种类型的书,比如推理小说、传记,传奇文学等等,在这些不同种类的书中,你最喜欢哪一类?

【派生】biographer *n.* 传记作家

bitter[1] ['bɪtə]

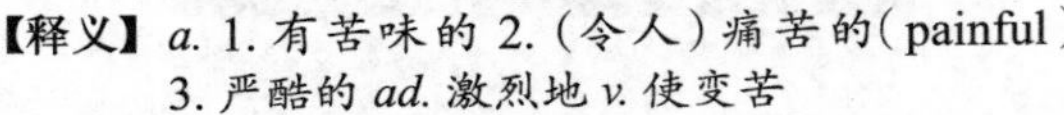

【释义】*a.* 1. 有苦味的 2. (令人)痛苦的(painful) 3. 严酷的 *ad.* 激烈地 *v.* 使变苦

【例句】And that green of skin can make the potatoes tastes bitter. (TPO10, L, S1, L2) 土豆绿色的表层吃起来很苦。

【派生】bitterness *n.* 苦味;辛酸,苦难

【搭配】bitter cold 严寒

bizarre[1] [bɪ'zɑː]

【释义】*a.* 奇异的,怪诞的(eccentric)

【例句】That seems so bizarre. (TPO1, L, S2, L2) 那看起来还真是古怪。

【派生】bizarrely *ad.* 奇形怪状地,怪诞地

blade[1] [bleɪd]

【释义】*n.* 1. 刀刃,刀锋 2. 桨叶 3. 叶片

【例句】Because the flippers are comparatively thin and blade like, they are the one part of the leatherback that is likely to become chilled. (TPO15, R, S2, T1) 因为棱皮龟的鳍相对较薄且像刀片,所以这是棱皮龟身上比较容易被冻坏的部位之一。

【逆构】bladed *a.* 有叶片的;有刀刃的

bland[1] [blænd]

【释义】*a.* 1. (食物)清淡的 2. 平和的,温和的,沉稳的

【例句】The diet then was relatively bland, compared to today's. (TPO18, L, S2, L1) 那个时候的饮食相对现在而言是比较清淡无味的。

【派生】blandly *ad.* 温和地;殷勤地

【搭配】a bland diet 清淡的饮食

blast[1] [blɑːst]

【释义】*n.* 1. 爆炸 2. 一阵(疾风等),一股(强烈的气流) 3. 严厉的批评 *v.* 1. 炸毁 2. 发出刺耳的高音

【例句】Iron manufacturers, which had starved for fuel while depending on charcoal, also benefited from ever-increasing supplies of coal: blast furnaces with steam-powered bellows turned out more iron and steel for

the new machinery. (TPO6, R, S1, T1) 依赖于木炭供应的铁匠们亟需燃料，他们也受益于越来越多的煤炭供应。配备有蒸汽动力的鼓风炉使得越来越多的钢铁供应成为可能。

【派生】blaster *n.* 爆破工

【搭配】(at) full blast 全力地，开足马力地

blazing[1] ['bleɪzɪŋ] 

【释义】*a.* 1. 酷热的，炽热的 2. 极其愤怒的；感情强烈的

【例句】Then, as blazing sunshine alternated with drenching rains, the harsh, barren surfaces of the black rocks slowly began to soften. (TPO9, R, S2, T2) 然后，经过了炙热阳光和湿润雨水的交替作用之后，荒芜的黑色岩石表面慢慢开始变软。

【逆构】blaze *n.* 火焰，烈火

【搭配】blazing with colour 五彩缤纷

bleed[1] [bliːd] 

【释义】*v.* 1. 出血，流血 2. 榨取，勒索

【例句】So we've got a spectrum of a beam of sunlight and it looks like the colors bleed into each other. (TPO3, L, S2, L2) 我们现在有一束阳光，它看起来像融在一起的颜色。

【搭配】bleed someone dry/white 使耗尽财富

blemish[1] ['blemɪʃ] 

【释义】*n.* 瑕疵，污点，缺点(defect, stain, flaw) *v.* 玷污，损害

【例句】That's because of their belief at the time that the heavenly bodies, the Sun, moon, stars and planets, were perfect, without any flaws or blemishes, so the opinion was the spots were actually something else, like shadows of planets crossing the Sun's face. (TPO18, L, S1, L1) 那是因为当时他们的认为太阳、月亮、行星这些天体是完美的，没有任何瑕疵和污点，所以他们的观点是那些斑点实际上是其他东西，比如划过太阳表面的行星的投影。

【派生】blemished *a.* 有瑕疵的，有污点的

bliss[1] [blɪs] 

【释义】*n.* 幸福，极乐(happiness)

【例句】Mandarin ducks stood for wedded bliss. (TPO10, R, S1, T1) 鸳鸯代表了婚姻的幸福美满。

blur[1] [blɜː] 

【释义】*v.* 使…模糊不清；使暗淡 *n.* 污迹；模糊不清的事物

【例句】In these shops differences of rank were blurred as artisans and masters labored side by side in the same modest establishment. (TPO16, R, S1, T1) 在这些商店里，由于工匠和大师在同样适中的设施下肩并肩地工作，所以等级的区分是模糊的。

【派生】blurred *a.* 模糊的

botanical[1] [bə'tænɪk(ə)l] 

【释义】*a.* 植物学的，植物的

【例句】David Douglas, Scottish botanical explorer of the 1830s, found a disturbing change in the animal life around the fort during the period between his first visit in 1825 and his final contact with the fort in 1832.(TPO4, R, S1, T1) 19 世纪 30 年代的苏格兰植物学探险家大卫·道格拉斯，在其 1825 年首次探访这一要塞到其 1832 年最后一次访问要塞期间，发现了要塞周围动物生活的一个令人不安的变化。

【派生】botanically *ad.* 植物学地

【逆构】botanic *a.* 植物的，植物学的

bravery[1] ['breɪvərɪ] 

【释义】*n.* 勇敢

【例句】Well, there's a hero, and a knight, who goes to battle, and he is inspired for his courage, bravery and loyalty, loyalty to the royalty serves, his country and his fellow warriors in the field. (TPO13, L, S2, L1) 有一位英雄，一个骑士，在勇气、勇敢、忠诚——对皇室、祖国和战场上的同胞勇士的忠诚的鼓舞下奔赴了战场。

【反义】cowardice

返记菜单

blazing[1] bleed[1] blemish[1] bliss[1] blur[1]
botanical[1] bravery[1]

breakage[1] ['breikidʒ]

【释义】*n.* 破损，破坏(damage, destruction)

【例句】From a practical aspect this protected the figures against breakage and psychologically gives the images a sense of strength and power, usually enhanced by a supporting back pillar. (TPO11, R, S1, T1) 从实用的方面来看，这样可以保护人像不受破坏，而且从心理上给人一种力量感，这种力量感通常会通过其后部的柱子得以强化。

【逆构】break *v.* 打破

【搭配】risk of breakage 破损险

breast[1] [brest]

【释义】*n.* 胸脯，乳房 *v.* 以胸对着；坚毅地面对

【例句】If it's sitting on a vertical branch, it'll groom its breast feathers. (TPO4, L, S1, L1) 如果它站在纵向的树枝上，它就会梳理自己胸前的羽毛。

【搭配】at the breast(婴儿在)吃奶的

breathable[1] ['bri:ðəbl]

【释义】*a.* 可以呼吸的

【例句】Water ice could be processed to provide breathable air for astronauts. (TPO5, L, S1, L2) 固态水经过加工后可以为宇航员们提供适宜呼吸的空气。

【逆构】breathe *v.* 呼吸

breeze[1] [bri:z]

【释义】*n.* 1. 微风，轻风 2. 轻而易举的事 *v.* 轻盈而自信地走

【例句】Spores light enough to float on the breezes were carried thousands of miles from more ancient lands and deposited at random across the bare mountain flanks. (TPO9, R, S2, T2) 孢子很轻，可以随着微风，从更古老的陆地飘过几千英里，然后被随意地撒播在荒芜的山腰上。

【搭配】shoot the breeze 闲聊

buffer[1] ['bʌfə]

【释义】*v.* 缓冲 *n.* 起缓冲作用的人(或物)；减震器

【例句】The shallow seas on the continents probably buffered the temperature of the nearby air, keeping it relatively constant. (TPO8, R, S2, T1) 大陆的浅海可能缓冲了附近空气的温度，使之保持相对恒定。

【搭配】buffer area/zone 缓冲地区

buoyant[1] ['bɔɪənt]

【释义】*a.* 1. 有浮力的 2. 轻松愉快的，开朗的，容易复原的 3. 上涨的

【例句】Plants with large, buoyant seeds—like coconuts—drift on ocean currents and are washed up on the shores. (TPO9, R, S2, T2) 一些拥有硕大的、可以浮于水面的种子的植物，比如椰子，会随着洋流被冲上海岸。

【派生】buoyantly *ad.* 有浮力地

【搭配】in a buoyant mood 轻松的心情

bureaucratic[1] [ˌbjʊərəʊ'krætɪk]

【释义】*a.* 官僚的，官僚政治的

【例句】Over time, the calendar got out of step with seasons and the flooding of the Nile, but for bureaucratic purposes, they didn't mind. (TPO17, L, S2, L1) 随着时间的流逝，这种历法渐渐与季节和尼罗河的汛期不同步了，但出于官僚政治的目的，他们并不在乎。

【派生】bureaucratically *ad.* 官僚主义地

【逆构】bureaucrat *n.* 官僚
bureaucracy *n.* 官僚制度，官僚作风

bustle[1] ['bʌsl]

【释义】*v.* 1. 喧闹 2. 忙乱

【例句】So I am sure you can see how heavy an area that off-limits to automobile traffic would be ideal for a heavily populated city where, well, the streets will otherwise be bustling with noise, unpleasant traffic congestion. (TPO13, L, S1, L1) 所以我相信你会看到，在拥挤的城市中，限制机动车辆通行，没有了不断的噪声和交通阻塞，是多么理想啊。

【搭配】bustling streets 熙熙攘攘的街道

byline[1] ['baiˌlain]

【释义】*n.* 标题下署名的一行 *v.* 署名

【例句】When I saw my name, I mean my byline in

print, I was hooked. (TPO14, L, S2, C1) 当我看见我的名字时，我是说看见我的署名印在上面时，我着迷了。

cabin[1] ['kæbɪn] 

【释义】*n.* 1. 小木屋（cottage, hut）2. 机舱，船舱

【例句】So you get more details about the characters, about where the action takes place, what people's houses were like, ur, whether they're small cabins or grand palaces. (TPO5, L, S2, L2) 所以你可以得到更多的信息：关于人物，关于事情发生的地点，关于人们的房子是什么样的，是小木屋还是大宫殿。

【派生】cabined *a.* 拘束的；狭窄的

【搭配】cabin boy 船上的侍者
log cabin 小木屋

caliber[1] ['kælɪbə(r)] 

【释义】*n.* 品质，质量；才干

【例句】It was no accident that many leading Roman soldiers and statesmen were writers of high caliber. (TPO7, R, S2, T1) 许多罗马士兵和政治家都是有才华的作家，这种现象不是偶然的。

canny[1] ['kænɪ] 

【释义】*a.* 1. 精明的，狡诈的 2. 谨慎的，节俭的

【例句】Its founder Rudolph Julian was a canny business man. (TPO8, L, S1, L2) 其创始人 Rudolph Julian 是一个精明的商人。

canopy[1] ['kænəpɪ]

【释义】*n.* 1. 树冠层 2.（宝座或床等上面的）华盖，罩篷 3.（飞行器上的）座舱罩

【例句】Very little light filters through the canopy of leaves and branches in a rain forest to reach ground level—or close to the ground——and at those levels the yellow-to-green wavelengths predominate. (TPO17, R, S2, T1) 很少有光能够从热带雨林的树冠层穿透到地面或靠近地面的地方，而在这些能够到达的地方，黄绿光波占了主要地位。

【搭配】a thick canopy of branches 芸芸如华盖的树枝

canyon[1] ['kænjən] 

【释义】*n.* 峡谷

【例句】Now, we geologists thought we had a pretty good idea of how the Grand Canyon in the southwestern United States was formed. (TPO1, L, S1, L2) 现在，我们地质学家认为，关于美国西南部的大峡谷的形成，我们有一个非常好的想法。

carnival[1] ['kɑːnɪvəl] 

【释义】*n.* 狂欢节；嘉年华会

【例句】Some chameleon species can change from a rather dull appearance to a full riot of carnival colors in seconds. (TPO17, R, S2, T1) 有些变色龙物种可以在几秒钟之内就将其暗淡的外表变得灿烂夺目。

【派生】carnivalesque *a.* 好像过节的，快乐的

【搭配】a book carnival 图书展览会

catalyst[1] ['kætəlɪst] 

【释义】*n.* 1.<化>催化剂 2. 促进因素

【例句】In the first case, the plants provide the bacteria with carbohydrates and other organic compounds, and the bacteria have enzymes that act as catalysts that eventually add nitrogen to the soil, enriching it. (TPO17, R, S2, T2) 在前者关系中，植物可以为细菌提供其生存所需的碳水化合物以及其他一些有机化合物，而这些细菌则能产生一种酶，作为催化剂来增加土壤中的氮元素从而滋养植物。

【逆构】catalyze *v.* 促使，激励

【搭配】catalyst industry 催化剂工业

catastrophic[1] [ˌkætə'strɒfɪk] 

【释义】*a.* 灾难的，灾难性的

【例句】Outflow channels are probably relics of catastrophic flooding on Mars long ago. (TPO8, R, S2, T2) 流出渠道可能是很久以前火星上发生的灾难性洪水的遗迹。

【逆构】catastrophe *n.* 灾难

返记菜单

cabin[1] caliber[1] canny[1] canopy[1] canyon[1]
carnival[1] catalyst[1] catastrophic[1]

causal[1] ['kɔːzəl]

【释义】*a.* 原因的，关于因果的

【例句】As people become more sophisticated, its conceptions of supernatural forces and causal relationships may change. (TPO1, R, S2, T1) 随着人们变得更加世故老练，其对于超自然力量和因果关系的认识也许会改变。

【派生】causality *n.* 因果关系

【搭配】causal chain 因果链

caution[1] ['kɔːʃən]

【释义】*n.* 谨慎，警告 *v.* 劝…小心，警告(remind, warn)

【例句】The professor discusses the presence of zinc in paint pigments to stress the need for caution when attempting to restore old artworks. (TPO5, L, S2, L1) 教授讨论颜料中锌的存在是为了使学生在恢复旧艺术品时倍加谨慎。

【派生】cautionary *a.* 警告的，劝诫的

cavalry[1] ['kævəlrɪ]

【释义】*n.* 骑兵

【例句】Horses were adopted by peoples of the West African savannah, and later their powerful cavalry forces allowed them to carve out large empires. (TPO7, R, S2, T2) 马匹被西非大草原居民所饲养，之后，居民们拥有的强劲的骑兵使其得以开拓出大片疆域。

cautious[1] ['kɔːʃəs]

【释义】*a.* 谨慎的，十分小心的(careful)

【例句】Some people enjoy taking risks and trying new things. Others are not adventurous: they are cautious and prefer to avoid danger. (TPO8, S, Q2) 一些人喜欢冒险，尝试新事物，另外一些就不爱冒险，他们很谨慎，倾向于避免危险。

cellist[1] ['tʃelɪst]

【释义】*n.* 大提琴演奏者

【例句】And it so happened that the cellist graduated last year. (TPO5, L, S1, C1) 而且恰巧大提琴手去年毕业了。

【逆构】cello *n.* 大提琴

cerebral[1] ['serɪbrəl]

【释义】*a.* 1. 大脑的 2. 理智的(intellectual)

【例句】The part of the brain responsible for fine control and movement is located in the left cerebral hemisphere. (TPO12, R, S1, T1) 大脑中负责精细控制和运动的部分位于大脑左半球上。

chef[1] [ʃef]

【释义】*n.* 厨师，主厨

【例句】Then you'll think you are a bad chef, right? (TPO5, S, Q1) 那么，你会觉得你是个糟糕的厨师，对吗？

chick[1] [tʃɪk]

【释义】*n.* 1. 小鸡(鸟) 2. 少妇

【例句】It suggests that the choice of where to nest does have impact on the number of chicks they have. (TPO8, L, S1, L1) 这就暗示着，选择到哪儿筑巢确实对它们会有几个幼仔有影响。

chill[1] [tʃɪl]

【释义】*v.* 使变冷(冷冻) *n.* 寒冷(气)

【例句】Because the flippers are comparatively thin and blade like, they are the one part of the leatherback that is likely to become chilled. (TPO15, R, S2, T1) 因为棱皮龟的鳍相对较薄且像刀片，所以这是棱皮龟身上比较容易被冻坏的部位之一。

【反义】heat, warm

【派生】chilly *a.* 寒冷的

choked[1] [tʃəʊkt]

【释义】*a.* 1. 堵塞的 2. 生气的，恼怒的

【例句】First, after a devastating fire, forests are choked with dead trees. (TPO14, W, Q1) 首先，经过一场破坏性极大的火灾后，森林被死去的树木所阻塞。

【逆构】choke *v.* 堵塞，阻塞

chorus[1] ['kɔːrəs] 

【释义】*n.* 1. 合唱队 2. 副歌部分 *v.* 合唱，一齐说

【例句】When religious leaders started chanting with echoes bounced off the stonewalls over and over again, it must seem like a whole chorus of other voices, spirits of God maybe join in. (TPO14, L, S2, L2) 当宗教领袖开始吟唱时，回声会从石墙上不断反射回来，这听上去就像一整个合唱团在吟唱，上帝的神灵也许也加入其中了。

【派生】choral *a.* 合唱的，唱诗班的

【搭配】in chorus 一齐，一致，异口同声

chunk[1] [tʃʌŋk]

【释义】*n.* 1. 厚片，大块（bulk）2. 相当大的部分（数量）（mass）

【例句】For a glacier to grow or maintain its mass, there must be sufficient snowfall to match or exceed the annual loss through melting, evaporation, and calving, which occurs when the glacier loses solid chunks as icebergs to the sea or large lakes. (TPO15, R, S1, T1) 为了保持或增加一个冰川的体积，就必须要有足够多的降雪量，这些降雪量需要能够抵销或者超过每年因融雪、蒸发或者因冰川以冰山的形式飘向海洋或湖泊而形成的裂冰损失的量。

【派生】chunked *a.* 长条块的

circumvent[1] [ˌsɜːkəm'vent] 

【释义】*v.* 1. 围绕，包围（besiege, surround）2. 规避（evade）

【例句】European seafarers circumvented Middle Eastern merchants. (TPO16, R, S1, T1) 欧洲海员绕过中东客商。

clergy[1] ['klɜːdʒɪ]

【释义】*n.* 神职人员

【例句】But the language of everyday life was evolving in Europe and at a certain point in the middle ages it was really only merchants, Socratics and clergy who can deal with Latin. (TPO12, L, S2, L1) 但是，在欧洲日常生活中的语言正在演变，而在中世纪的某个时期，只有商人、苏格拉底派哲学家和神职人员能够使用拉丁语。

【派生】clergyman *n.* 牧师，教士

clockwise[1] ['klɒkwaɪz] 

【释义】*a.* 顺时针方向的

【例句】As the tool was made, the core was rotated clockwise, and the flakes, removed in sequence, had a little crescent of cortex on the side. (TPO12, R, S1, T1) 在制造工具时，岩芯按照顺时针方向旋转，其碎片就一点一点剥落，在一侧留下月牙状的表层（石芯的表面）。

【反义】anti-clockwise

【搭配】clockwise direction 顺时针方向

clog[1] [klɒg]

【释义】*v.*（使）阻碍，妨碍（block, obstruct）*n.* 木底鞋；木屐

【例句】This could cause a rapid growth of water plants in the river, which can lead to the water waste getting clogged with organisms. (TPO10, L, S2, L1) 这会引起河流中水生植物的快速繁殖，导致水中的废物被有机物堵塞。

coarse[1] [kɔːs] 

【释义】*a.* 1. 粗糙的，粗劣的（crude, rough）2. 粗俗的

【例句】They are found wherever fast rivers carrying loads of coarse sediment once flowed. (TPO1, R, S2, T2) 在携带着大量粗泥沙的湍急的河流冲刷过的地方可以发现它们。

【反义】delicate, fine

【派生】coarsen *v.* 使变粗糙
coarseness *n.* 粗糙

coincidence[1] [kəʊ'ɪnsɪdəns] 

【释义】*n.* 巧合，一致，同时发生

【例句】But it really was quite a coincidence. (TPO16, L, S1, C1) 这纯属巧合。

【逆构】coincide *v.* 同时发生，相符，一致

【搭配】by coincidence 碰巧

返记菜单

chorus[1] chunk[1] circumvent[1] clergy[1] clockwise[1]
clog[1] coarse[1] coincidence[1]

comic[1] ['kɒmɪk]

【释义】*a.* 喜剧的，滑稽的，有趣的

【例句】For example, one sign of this condition is the appearance of the comic vision. (TPO1, R, S2, T1) 比如，这种情况的一个标志是喜剧观点的诞生。

【反义】tragic

【派生】comical *a.* 滑稽的，可笑的

【搭配】comic books 连环画

commemorate[1] [kə'meməreɪt]

【释义】*v.* 纪念，庆祝(honor, celebrate)

【例句】We've already looked at portrait sculpture which are busts created to commemorate people who had died, and we've looked at relief sculpture, or sculpting on walls. (TPO18, L, S1, L2) 我们已经看过用来纪念死者的半身肖像雕塑了，而且我们还看了浮雕和壁雕。

【派生】commemoration *n.* 纪念，纪念仪式

commend[1] [kə'mend]

【释义】*v.* 1. 表扬，称赞 2. 推荐，委托

【例句】To commend and reward the behavior of the other members of the group. (TPO13, R, S1, T1, Q11) 为了表扬和奖励群体内其他成员的行为。

【派生】commendable *a.* 值得表扬的

【搭配】commend sb. on/for sth. 就某事表扬某人

commission[1] [kə'mɪʃən]

【释义】*n.* 1. 委员会 2. 佣金，回扣 3. 犯(罪、错误) *v.* 委任，委托

【例句】The imperial court commissioned work and in the Yuan dynasty (A. D. 1279-1368) an imperial ceramic factory was established at Jingdezhen. (TPO10, R, S1, T1) 元朝(公元 1279-1369 年) 时期，在景德镇设立了一座官窑来替朝廷制作陶瓷。

【搭配】military commission 特别军事法庭

commute[1] [kə'mjuːt]

【释义】*v.* 1. 通勤，乘车上下班 2. 折换，改变，交换 3. 减刑 *n.* 乘车上下班

【例句】So I thought I could drive and commute to campus every day. (TPO11, S, Q5) 所以我想我能每天开车通勤到学校。

【派生】commuter *n.* 通勤者

compensation[1] [kɒmpen'seɪʃən]

【释义】*n.* 补偿，赔偿

【例句】One compensation for not hibernating is the built-in urge to migrate. (TPO4, R, S1, T1) 对不冬眠的弥补则是一种内在的迁徙的欲望。

【逆构】compensate *v.* 补偿，弥补，抵消

【搭配】compensation for/on 补偿，弥补

compile[1] [kəm'paɪl]

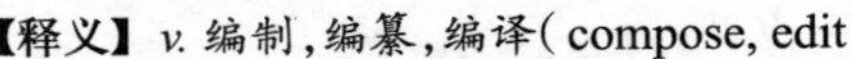

【释义】*v.* 编制，编纂，编译(compose, edit)

【例句】Well, a kind of spectroscopic library of elements was compiled using flame tests. (TPO3, L, S2, L2) 一种元素光谱对照表正在编制中，该项工作是以火焰实验为依据的。

【派生】compiler *n.* 编辑者，编译器

【搭配】compile an index 编索引

Word List 41

compliment[1] ['kɒmplɪmənt]

【释义】*n./v.* 称赞，恭维

【例句】Her guests complimented her on her cooking. 客人们对她的烹饪技艺大加赞扬。

compost[1] ['kɒmpɒst] 

【释义】*n.* 混合肥料，堆肥 *v.* 使成堆肥

【例句】A harvest of the shoots would remove the toxic compounds off site to be burned or composted to recover the metal for industrial uses. (TPO5, R, S1, T1) 把这些幼苗收割之后就会带走场地中的有毒化合物，然后通过对这些幼苗进行焚烧或堆肥，使金属还原，以作工业之用。

comprehensive[1] [ˌkɒmprɪ'hensɪv]

【释义】*a.* 全面的，广泛的，综合的（universal, inclusive）

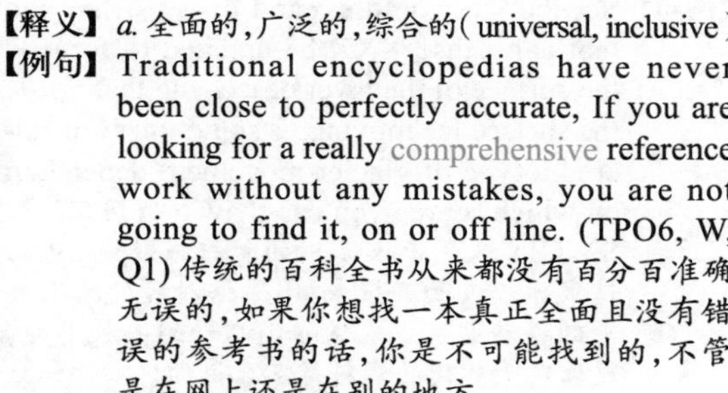

【例句】Traditional encyclopedias have never been close to perfectly accurate, If you are looking for a really comprehensive reference work without any mistakes, you are not going to find it, on or off line. (TPO6, W, Q1) 传统的百科全书从来都没有百分百准确无误的，如果你想找一本真正全面且没有错误的参考书的话，你是不可能找到的，不管是在网上还是在别的地方。

【派生】comprehensively *ad.* 包括地，全面地

【搭配】comprehensive university 综合性大学

comprise[1] [kəm'praɪz] 

【释义】*v.* 构成，由…组成，包含（consist of, contain）

【例句】The author call the Mayan homeland both a "seasonal tropical forest" and "seasonal desert" to emphasize the vast size of the area that comprised the Mayan homeland in ancient times.（TPO14, R, S2, T1）作者将玛雅家园称作"季节性热带森林"和"季节性沙漠"，主要是为了强调构成古代玛雅人家园的区域的辽阔。

【搭配】be comprised of 由…组成

confederacy[1] [kən'fedərəsɪ] 

【释义】*n.* 联盟，联邦（alliance, union, association）

【例句】The shepherds of tribal confederacies were left alone by their leaders. (TPO16, R, S1, T1) 放牧部落联盟不是由他们的头来管理。

【逆构】confederate *v.*（使）联盟，（使）联合

conflate[1] [kən'fleɪt] 

【释义】*v.* 合并（merge, coalesce）

【例句】In the recent past, the role of celebrities in advertising to children has often been conflated with the concept of host selling. (TPO14, R, S1, T1) 前不久，在针对儿童的广告中，人们常常将名人的角色和主持人销售的概念合并在一起。

【派生】conflation *n.* 合并

congenital[1] [kɒn'dʒenɪtl] 

【释义】*a.* 天生的，先天的（inborn, innate）

【例句】Babies with congenital blockages that prevent this fluid from escaping from their lungs are sometimes born with deformed lungs. (TPO18, R, S2, T1) 婴儿有先天阻塞会妨碍这种液体流出其肺部，有时他们的肺生下来就是畸形的。

【搭配】congenital heart disease 先天性心脏病
congenital malformation 先天畸形

congestion[1] [kən'dʒestʃən] 

【释义】*n.* 阻塞，拥挤；充血

【例句】So I am sure you can see how heavy an area that off-limits to automobile traffic would be ideal for a heavily populated city where, well, the streets will otherwise be bustling with noise, unpleasant traffic congestion. (TPO13, L, S1, L1) 所以我相信你会看到，在拥挤的城市中，限制机动车辆通行，没有了不断的噪声和交通阻塞，是多么理想啊。

【逆构】congest *v.*（使）充满，（使）拥塞

【搭配】traffic congestion 交通拥塞

conglomerate[1] [kɒn'glɒmərɪt]

【释义】*n.* 1. 砾岩 2. 混合物 3. 联合大企业 *a.* 聚成一团的，成簇的

【例句】Because they are porous, sedimentary rocks, such as sandstones and conglomerates, are important potential sources of groundwater. (TPO12, R, S2, T2) 因为它们是多孔的，所以沉积岩，比如砂岩和砾岩，都是地下水重要的潜在来源。

【派生】conglomeratic *a.* 砾岩状的

【搭配】conglomerate merger 混合并购

conjure[1] ['kʌndʒə]

【释义】*v.* 1. 祈求，恳求 2. 变戏法

【例句】The color red, for example, is a strong color and can conjure up strong emotions, such as extreme joy or excitement or even anger. (TPO4, S, Q6) 比如，红色是一种很强烈的色彩，能唤起人强烈的情感，比如强烈的欢喜、兴奋甚或愤怒。

【搭配】conjure up 想起；(用魔法)唤起

consecutive[1] [kən'sekjʊtɪv]

【释义】*a.* 连续的，连贯的(continuous, following)

【例句】You know that studying six consecutive hours is not equivalent to studying one hour a day for six days. (TPO15, L, S2, C1) 你知道的，连续学习六个小时并不等同于六天每天学习一小时。

【派生】consecutively *ad.* 连续地
consecutiveness *n.* 顺序，连续

consolidate[1] [kən'sɒlɪdeɪt]

【释义】*v.* 巩固，加强(concentrate, condense)

【例句】The commonest spaces are those among the particles—sand grains and tiny pebbles—of loose, unconsolidated sand and gravel. (TPO1, R, S2, T2) 松散的沙子和砾石间有许多沙粒和小石子，它们之间的空隙是最常见的储存地下水的空间。

【派生】consolidated *a.* 巩固的，统一的

constellation[1] [kɒnstə'leɪʃən]

【释义】*n.* 星座，星群

【例句】They were positioned as if they were heading in the direction of the points on the sea horizon where certain stars would appear and young would-be navigators set by the stones at night and turned in different directions to memorize the constellations they saw, so they could recognize them and navigate by them later on when they went out to sea. (TPO14, L, S2, L1) 它们被放置成好像要朝向海平面的样子，那里会有固定的星座出现，而想要成为航海家的年轻人夜晚时会留些石头在那里并变换不同的方向，以此来记录他们所看见的星座，这样他们日后出海时就可以认出这些星座并凭借它们进行导航。

constrict[1] [kən'strɪkt]

【释义】*v.* 使(某事物)缩紧，压缩(compress, tighten, constringe)

【例句】So, the ice would expand or constrict, and that can cause XXX be cracked to form in the surface of the layer of ice, and that brittle the surface ice moving, is sometimes considered a type of glacier movement depending on which source you can thaw to. (TPO7, L, S2, C1) 这会带来冰川的扩张或收缩，从而造成冰山表面开裂或垮塌，这种脆的冰山表面的移动也可以看做冰山移动的一种类型，这取决于你读的资料是怎么说的。

【派生】constriction *n.* 压缩，收缩

contemplation[1] [ˌkɒntem'pleɪʃən]

【释义】*n.* 1. 沉思，冥想(reflecion) 2. 凝视，凝望

【例句】In the end, Aristotle says that true happiness is the exercise of reason—a life of intellectual contemplation…of thinking. (TPO2, L, S2, L1) 最终，亚里士多德总结说，幸福就是对理性的实践——是对理性冥思的一生，是不断思考的一生。

【派生】contemplative *a.* 沉思的

【逆构】contemplate *v.* 沉思，冥想

contend[1] [kən'tend]

【释义】*v.* 声称，主张(argue) *v.* 竞争；搏斗(fight, struggle)

【例句】A second theory contends that the Chaco structures were used to store food supplies. (TPO5, W, Q1) 第二个理论主张查克建筑是用来贮藏粮食的。

【派生】contender *n.* 竞争者

【搭配】contend with 对付；与…作斗争

continuation[1] [kənˌtɪnjʊ'eɪʃən] 

【释义】*n.* 继续，延续；续集

【例句】The continuation of biological rhythms in an organism without external cues attests to its having an internal clock. (TPO13, R, S2, T1) 这种在没有外界信号的时候生物体的生物节律的延续性证明生物是具有内在生物钟的。

【搭配】a continuation class 补习班

contort[1] [kən'tɔːt] 

【释义】*v.* (使)扭曲，曲解(deform, distort)

【例句】Meanwhile, I was shaking my hand as if that would stop my thumb from hurting, and my face was contorted in pain. (TPO4, S, Q4) 与此同时，我使劲摇着自己的手，好像这样可以让我的拇指不再疼似的，而我的脸则因疼痛而扭曲。

【派生】contortion *n.* 扭曲

coral[1] ['kɒrəl] 

【释义】*n.* 珊瑚 *a.* 珊瑚的，珊瑚色的

【例句】But when it wants to blend in with its environment to hide from its enemies, it can take on the color of its immediate surroundings: the ocean floor, a rock, a piece of coral, whatever. (TPO17, L, S2, L2) 但当它要融入周围环境来躲避敌人时，它就能变为其周围环境的颜色：海底、岩石、一片珊瑚，无论什么。

【派生】coralline *n.* 珊瑚状构造
corallaceous *a.* 似珊瑚的
coralliferous *a.* 含珊瑚的

correlate[1] ['kɒrəleɪt]

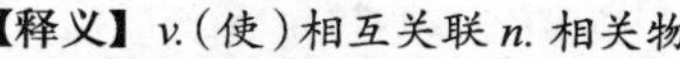

【释义】*v.* (使)相互关联 *n.* 相关物

【例句】But preferred environment doesn't always seem to correlate with greater reproductive success. (TPO8, L, S1, L1) 但是更受喜欢的环境不总是和更成功的生产有关系。

【搭配】correlate with 与…有关联

corrupt[1] [kə'rʌpt]

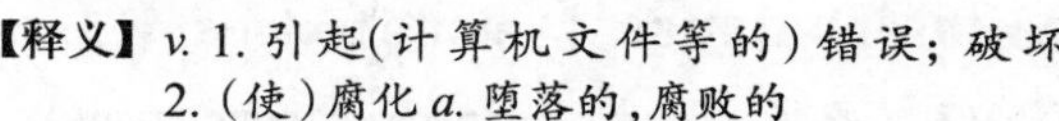

【释义】*v.* 1. 引起(计算机文件等的)错误；破坏 2. (使)腐化 *a.* 堕落的，腐败的

【例句】Second, even if the original entry in the online encyclopedia is correct, the communal nature of these online encyclopedias gives unscrupulous users and vandals or hackers the opportunity to fabricate, delete, and corrupt information in the encyclopedia. (TPO6, W, Q1) 其次，即使在线百科全书的原始录入是正确的，但其公共性也会给那些无道德的用户、破坏者以及黑客们提供一些伪造、删除或更改百科全书中的信息的机会。

【派生】corruption *n.* 贪污，腐败

【搭配】corrupt and incompetent 腐败无能

cost-effective[1] ['kɒstə'fɛktɪv] 

【释义】*a.* 有成本效益的，划算的

【例句】The department has decided that despite some added expense, the most cost-effective way of addressing this problem is by adding computer classes in the evening. (TPO4, S, Q3) 部门决定尽管要增加开支，但是解决该问题最划算的方式是增开夜间电脑课。

costume[1] ['kɒstjuːm] 

【释义】*n.* (流行的)服装，戏装，特定场合的套装(dress, suit, outlit)

【例句】Performers may wear costumes and masks to represent the mythical charaters or supernatural forces in the rituals or in accompanying celebrations. (TPO1, R, S2, T1) 在这些仪式或伴随的庆祝活动中，表演者们会穿着各种服饰、戴着面具来代表神话中的人物或超自然的力量。

【搭配】costume ball 化妆舞会

counteract[1] [ˌkaʊntə'rækt]

【释义】v. 抵消,中和,对抗(offset)

【例句】In an effort to counteract the trend, the college has announced a plan to renovate its on-campus housing. (TPO11, S, Q3) 为了抵制这一倾向,校方宣布了一项整修校园内房屋的计划。

counterbalance[1] [ˌkaʊntə'bæləns]

【释义】v. 抵销,使平衡(compensate, countervail) n. 平衡,平衡力

【例句】Advertisers sometimes offset or counterbalance an exaggerated claim with a disclaimer—a qualification or condition on the claim. (TPO14, R, S1, T1) 广告商有时会通过免责声明——对于广告所声称内容的一种限制和条件,来抵消和平衡夸张的广告词。

covert[1] ['kʌvət]

【释义】a. 隐蔽的,暗地的(covered, hidden)

【例句】As the individual matures, that overt talking to oneself becomes covert talking to oneself. (TPO2, L, S1, L1) 当个体逐渐成熟起来后,这种公开的自我对话就转变为秘密的自我交谈。

【反义】overt

【派生】covertly ad. 隐蔽地

credential[1] [krɪ'denʃəl]

【释义】n. 外交使节所递的国书,信任状

【例句】First, contributors to a communal online encyclopedia often lack academic credentials, thereby making their contributions partially informed at best and downright inaccurate in many cases. (TPO6, W, Q1) 在线百科全书的编撰者经常缺乏学术可信度,因此使他们的成果只有一部分比较好,而大部分都是完全不准确的。

creep[1] [kriːp]

【释义】n. 爬行,蠕动 v. 蹑手蹑脚地走;爬行

【例句】Avalanches and snow creep can damage or destroy them. (TPO1, R, S1, T1) 雪崩和雪的缓慢推进可能会伤害或是摧毁它们。

【派生】creeper n. 爬行物,匍匐植物
creepy a. 令人毛骨悚然的

crescent[1] ['kresnt]

【释义】n. 新月(形),月牙(形)(crescent-shaped, lunate)

【例句】As the tool was made, the core was rotated clockwise, and the flakes, removed in sequence, had a little crescent of cortex on the side. (TPO12, R, S5) 在制造工具时,岩芯按照顺时针方向旋转,其碎片就一点一点剥落,在一侧留下月牙状的表层(石芯的表面)。

【派生】crescentic a. 新月形的

【搭配】crescent moon 新月

crevasse[1] [krɪ'væs]

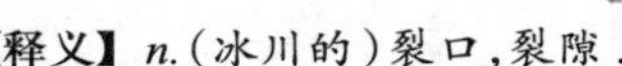

【释义】n.(冰川的)裂口,裂隙.

【例句】And crevasses can form in this upper layer of glacier. (TPO7, L, S2, C1) 在冰川的上层会形成裂缝。

【搭配】transverse crevasse 冰川横裂缝

crinkle[1] ['krɪŋkl]

【释义】v. 1. 沙沙作响 2. 变皱 n. 1. 皱纹 2. 沙沙声

【例句】I mean maybe a little snack will help the person who's eating it, but the trouble is that it makes it hard for everyone else to concentrate 'coz they have to listen to someone munching on chips or biting into an apple or crinkling paper wrappers. (TPO14, S, Q3) 我的意思是,也许吃点儿零食会帮助吃零食的人(集中注意力),但问题是别人却没法集中注意力了,因为他们不得不听见有人在咔咔地嚼薯条,或咬苹果,或沙沙的拆包装袋的声音。

cripple[1] ['krɪpl]

【释义】v. 严重削弱,使跛(disable, injure) n. 跛子

【例句】It's hard to understand why they would not be affected, whereas dinosaurs were left too crippled to cope, especially if, as some

scientists believe, dinosaurs were warm-blooded. (TPO8, R, S2, T1) 很难理解为什么它们会不受影响，而恐龙已经受到很多重创而难以应对了，尤其是如果恐龙是温血动物，就像一些科学家所认为的那样。

cruise[1] [kruːz] 

【释义】*n./v.*（航船）巡游，巡航

【例句】An objective of this particular cruise was to investigate the floor of the Mediterranean and to resolve questions about its geologic history. (TPO7, R, S1, T1) 此次特殊航行的目标之一是对地中海的海底进行调查研究，从而解决关于其地质史方面的问题

【派生】cruiser *n.* 巡游舰，游艇

【搭配】cruise missile 巡航导弹

crumble[1] ['krʌmbl] 

【释义】*v.* 1. 崩溃，坍塌（collapse）2. 弄碎（disintegrate）

【例句】But belief in this ice-free corridor began to crumble when paleoecologist Glen MacDonald demonstrated that some of the most important radiocarbon dates used to support the existence of an ice-free corridor were incorrect. (TPO9, R, S1, T1) 但当古生物学家 Glen MacDonald 证明一些用来支持不冻走廊存在的重要放射性碳的时间不正确时，对于不冻走廊的信念就被粉碎了。

cuisine[1] [kwɪ(ː)'ziːn] 

【释义】*n.* 烹饪，烹调法

【例句】It encouraged the development of new types of cuisine in southern Europe. (TPO10, L, S1, L2) 它促进了南欧新型菜肴的发展。

cult[1] [kʌlt] 

【释义】*n.* 1. 狂热崇拜 2. 宗教膜拜仪式 3. 异教

【例句】Statues were created not for their decorative effect but to play a primary role in the cults of the gods, the king, and the dead. (TPO11, R, S1, T1) 这些雕像不是做装饰用的，而是在对神、国王和死者的膜拜中起重要作用。

【同义】worship, craze

【派生】cultus *n.* 祭仪；崇拜
cultist *n.* 热衷搞迷信崇拜的人；邪教分子

cumulative[1] ['kjuːmjʊlətɪv] 

【释义】*a.* 累积的，渐增的（adding, increasing）

【例句】These changes—in plant numbers and the mix of species—are cumulative. (TPO3, R, S1, T2) 植物数量和种类混合的变化是慢慢积累的。

【派生】cumulatively *ad.* 累积地，渐增地

【搭配】cumulative process 逐步积累的渐进过程

curator[1] [kjʊə'reɪtə]

【释义】*n.*（博物馆、展览馆等的）馆长，管理者

【例句】Let's say a museum curator comes to you with a problem. (TPO5, L, S2, L1) 比方说，博物馆馆长有一个问题想问你。

curved[1] [kəːvd] 

【释义】*a.* 弧形的，曲线的，呈弯曲状的

【例句】That invention was the arch, a curved structure originally made of separate stone or brick segments. (TPO3, R, S1, T1) 这种发明便是拱，这是一种最初由独立的石头或砖块构成的弧形建筑结构。

【逆构】curve *n.* 曲线，弧线

cushy[1] ['kuʃi]

【释义】*a.*（工作）轻松的

【例句】Well, en, if you observed a 4 year-old child, for example, my daughter is 4 years old; you might read up on cushy stage of cognitive development we covered those in class. (TPO13, L, S1, C1) 举个例子，如果你观察一个 4 岁大的孩子，比如，我女儿 4 岁，你或许需要研读一下我们在课堂上讲到的认知发展较容易的阶段。

【反义】cushily *ad.* 轻松地

cute[1] [kjuːt] 

【释义】*a.* 可爱的，聪明伶俐的（smart, pretty）

【例句】And lately her favorite toy is a cute little baby doll with a big round face and lots of curly hair named Rosa. (TPO10, S, Q4) 最近，她喜欢上了一个名叫罗莎的圆脸、卷发、可爱的小玩具娃娃。

返记菜单

cruise[1]	crumble[1]	cuisine[1]	cult[1]	cumulative[1]
curator[1]	curved[1]	cushy[1]	cute[1]	

cyclical[1] ['sɪklɪk(e)l] 

【释义】*a.* 轮转的，循环的

【例句】What's important for you to understand is that these three movements, well, they are cyclical and they work together to form, ah, to produce complex but regular variations in Earth's climate and lead to the growth or decline of glaciers. (TPO17, L, S1, L2) 你重点要明白的是这些运动：它们是周期性的，并且共同形成了复杂但规律的地球气候变化，而且导致了冰川的增加或削减。

deadly[1] ['dedlɪ] 

【释义】*a./ad.* 1. 致命的（地）2. 极端的（地），非常的（地）

【例句】The virus was less deadly to the offspring of surviving rabbits, however, and it caused less and less harm over the years. (TPO17, R, S2, T2) 然而，这种病毒对于生存下来的兔群的后代就没有那么致命了，而且这种伤害会逐渐减少。

【派生】deadiness *n.* 致命

【逆构】dead *a.* 死去的，已故的

【搭配】a deadly weapon 致命武器

deceased[1] [dɪ'si:st] 

【释义】*a.* 已故的（dead）

【例句】Thus it made sense to show the statue looking ahead at what was happening in front of it, so that the living performer of the ritual could interact with the divine or deceased recipient. (TPO11, R, S1, T1) 如此一来，让雕像直视前方正在发生的事就很合理了，这样可以便于礼仪的执行者与神灵或死者进行交流。

【逆构】decease *v.* 死，死亡

defer[1] [dɪ'fɜ:] 

【释义】*v.* 1. 尊重，顺从 2. 推迟，延期

【例句】And let's say, both John and Mary defer to her leadership. (TPO6, L, S2, L1) 约翰和玛丽都服从她的领导。

deflect[1] [dɪ'flekt] 

【释义】*v.*（使）偏斜，（使）偏离，（使）转向（avert, bend, distract）

【例句】The possibility that mass extinctions may recur periodically has given rise to such hypotheses as that of a companion star with a long-period orbit deflecting other bodies from their normal orbits, making some of them fall to Earth as meteors and causing widespread devastation upon impact. (TPO15, R, S2, T2) 大规模物种灭绝可能会周期性发生的可能性引发了这样的假想：一个在长周期轨道上运行的伴星从其正常的轨道偏向其他天体，从而造成某些天体以流星的形式坠落到地球上，而这种撞击就造成了大范围的破坏。

【派生】deflection *n.* 偏向；偏差

deflective *a.* 偏斜的，偏倚的

【逆构】deflect from 从…偏斜

degrade[1] [dɪ'greɪd]

【释义】*v.* 1. 受侵蚀，老化，退化 2. 使降级，贬低

【例句】The main reason was that steel cables degrade very, very quickly in contact with salt water. (TPO2, L, S1, L2) 主要原因是钢丝绳长时间与盐水接触会导致其老化得非常快。

【反义】upgrade

【派生】degradation *n.* 降级；退化

degradable *a.* 可降解的

【搭配】degrade oneself by doing sth. 做某事降低自己的人格

deity[1] ['di:ɪtɪ] 

【释义】*n.* 神，神性（divinity, god）

【例句】Apart from statues representing deities, kings, and named members of the elite that can be called formal, there is another group of three-dimensional representations that depicts generic figures, frequently servants, from the nonelite population. (TPO11, R, S1, T1) 除了代表神明、国王和上层精英人士的这种正式的雕像以外，还有另外一种立体的表现手法，用以描绘一般民众，通常是来自非上层人群中的仆人。

delete[1] [dɪˈliːt]

【释义】*v.* 删除(erase, cancel)

【例句】Second, even if the original entry in the online encyclopedia is correct, the communal nature of these online encyclopedias gives unscrupulous users and vandals or hackers the opportunity to fabricate, delete, and corrupt information in the encyclopedia. (TPO6, W, Q1) 其次,即使在线百科全书在一开始的时候是正确的,但其公共性也会给那些无道德的用户、破坏者以及黑客们提供一些伪造、删除或更改百科全书中的信息的机会。

【派生】deletion *n.* 删除,删除部分

delight[1] [dɪˈlaɪt]

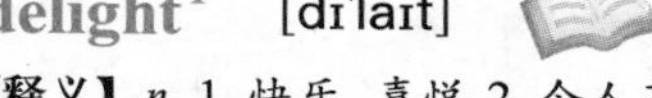

【释义】*n.* 1. 快乐,喜悦 2. 令人高兴的事 *v.* (使)高兴,(使)欣喜

【例句】It is the work of architects to create buildings that are not simply constructions but also offer inspiration and delight. (TPO3, R, S1, T1) 建筑师们的工作就是要让创造出来的建筑物并不单纯地是建筑物,还要为人们带来灵感和愉悦。

【反义】grief, sorrow

【派生】delighted *a.* 喜欢的,高兴的
delightful *a.* 令人愉快的,可喜的

delineate[1] [dɪˈlɪnɪeɪt]

【释义】*v.* 描绘,叙述,画出

【例句】The traditon of religious sculpture extends over most historical periods but is less clearly delineated than that of stonewares or porcelains. (TPO10, R, S1, T1) 瓷质神像的制作方式在历史上的大部分时段都不断的改进,但它们对人物的描绘并不像石制瓷器以及瓷器描绘的那么清晰。

【派生】delineator *n.* 描绘器

deluge[1] [ˈdeljuːdʒ]

【释义】*n.* 洪水,暴雨期 *v.* 淹没,使…泛滥

【例句】Then, about 5. 5 million years ago came the deluge. (TPO7, R, S1, T1) 随后,大约550万年前,发生了洪水。

【搭配】be deluged with… 涌来

demise[1] [dɪˈmaɪz]

【释义】*n.* 终止,结束,死亡(death, termination)

【例句】Paleontologists have argued for a long time that the demise of the dinosaurs was caused by climatic alterations. (TPO8, R, S2, T1) 在很长一段时期,古生物学家都争辩说,恐龙的灭绝是由气候变化引起的。

democratization[1] [diˌmɔkrətaiˈzeiʃ ən]

【释义】*n.* 民主化

【例句】The nineteenth century passed relatively peacefully for these countries, with progressive democratization taking place in all of them. (TPO18, R, S1, T1) 伴随着先进的民主化的发生,这些国家都相对平静地度过了19世纪。

【派生】democratic *a.* 民主的

【逆构】democratize *v.* 使民主化

demographic[1] [deməˈgræfɪk]

【释义】*a.* 人口统计的,与人口统计有关的

【例句】Still, the process is uncertain, and peaceful migration—or simply rapid demographic-growth—may have also caused the Bantu explosion. (TPO7, R, S2, T2) 然而,这一过程是不确定的,而和平迁徙——或者单纯的人口增长——也有可能促成了班图人数量的激增。

【派生】demography *n.* 人口统计学

demonstration[1] [ˌdeməns'treɪʃ ən]

【释义】*n.* 1. 表明;示范 2. 游行示威

【例句】Demonstrations of infants' and toddlers' long-term memory have involved their repeating motor activities that they had seen or done earlier, such as reaching in the dark for objects, putting a bottle in a doll's mouth, or pulling apart two pieces of a toy. (TPO6, R, S2, T2) 婴儿长期记忆形成的表现涉及到重复他们之前看到的或者自身经历的活动,比如:在黑暗的环境里取东西,把瓶子塞到洋娃娃的嘴里,或者将玩具撕成两半等。

返记菜单

delete[1] delight[1] delineate[1] deluge[1] demise[1]
democratization[1] demographic[1] demonstration[1]

【派生】demonstrator *n.* 游行者；示范者
demonstrative *a.* 感情外露的
【逆构】demonstrate *v.* 示范，演示

denominator[1] [dɪ'nɒmɪneɪtə] 

【释义】*n.* 分母；平均水平
【例句】There are variations on this model of course, but the common denominators are always an idea of creating a shopping space that will get people to shop in the city without needing their cars. (TPO13, L, S1, L1) 虽然设计模式多种多样，但是共同的特征是创建一个让人们不需要开车就能购物的商业步行街的理念。

deprecate[1] ['deprɪkeɪt] 

【释义】*v.* 声明不赞成，抨击，反对
【例句】Many older theories implicitly deprecated the navigational abilities and overall cultural creativity of the Pacific islanders. (TPO5, R, S2, T1) 许多古老的理论含蓄地否定了太平洋岛民的航海能力和综合文化创造力。

derrick[1] ['derɪk] 

【释义】*n.* 1. 油井塔 2. 动臂起重机
【例句】Permanent towers, called derricks, used to be built to handle the long sections of drilling pipe. (TPO4, R, S2, T2) 常设塔，也称油井塔，过去是用来处理长钻杆的。
【搭配】oil derrick 井架；油井架；钻油塔

desiccation[1] [ˌdesɪ'keɪʃən] 

【释义】*n.* 干燥
【例句】Their migration may have been set in motion by an increase in population caused by a movement of peoples fleeing the desiccation, or drying up, of the Sahara. (TPO7, R, S2, T2) 其迁徙可能是由人口激增引起的，而这种人口增长是由于人们逃离撒哈拉地区干旱气候的活动导致的。

designate[1] ['dezɪgneɪt] 

【释义】*v.* 把…定名为，指定，指派，任命(assign, appoint, nominate)
【例句】Mendeleyev designated this element "eka-aluminum" and predicted its properties. (TPO16, R, S2, T1) 门捷列夫将这种元素命名为"铝类元素"，并预测了其属性。
【派生】designation *n.* 指定，选派，任命

desolate[1] ['desəlɪt] 

【释义】*a.* 1. 荒凉的，荒芜的(barren, bleak) 2. 阴郁的，孤独的 *v.* 1. 使痛苦，使忧伤 2. 使(某地)荒凉
【例句】Today it's pretty desolate, barren and extremely hot. (TPO9, L, S2, L1) 如今这里已经极度荒芜、贫瘠且非常热。
【派生】desolation *n.* 荒芜，荒废；忧郁
【搭配】a desolate life 凄凉的一生

detour[1] ['diːtʊə (r)] 

【释义】*n./v.* 绕路，绕道而行
【例句】Today, we are taking a little detour from the grand styles of public architecture we've been studying to look at residential architectures in the United States. (TPO11, L, S1, L2) 今天，我们会稍微偏离我们一直在学习的风格宏伟的公共建筑，来了解一下美国的居民建筑。
【搭配】make a detour 迂回

detract[1] [dɪ'trækt] 

【释义】*v.* 贬损，诋毁
【例句】One mistake is not going to detract from your achievement. 一个错误不会抹杀你的成就。
【派生】detraction *n.* 诽谤
detractor *n.* 贬低者
【搭配】detract from 贬损，诋毁

Word List 42

detritus[1] [dɪˈtraɪtəs] 

【释义】*n.* 岩屑，碎石

【例句】These unassignable animals include a large swimming predator called Anomalocaris and a soft-bodied animal called Wiwaxia, which ate detritus or algae. (TPO5, R, S2, T2) 这些无法划分的动物包括一种叫“奇虾”的大型的游动肉食动物和一种叫做“威瓦亚虫”的以岩屑和藻类为食的软体动物。

【搭配】detritus feeder 食腐屑生物

diagonal[1] [daɪˈægənl]

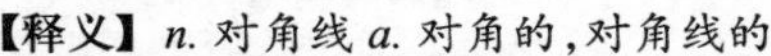

【释义】*n.* 对角线 *a.* 对角的，对角线的

【例句】You can still see the diagonal marks of the ladders in the plaster on the inside wall. (TPO 1, L, S2, L1) 你仍然能够在屋内墙上的石灰上看到那些梯子斜斜的痕迹。

【派生】diagonalizable *a.* 对角化的
diagonalize *v.* 使对角化

diesel[1] [ˈdiːzəl]

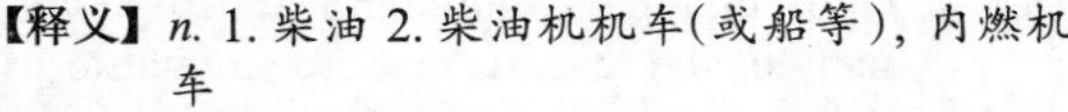

【释义】*n.* 1. 柴油 2. 柴油机机车(或船等)，内燃机车

【例句】One of the main problems with the internal-combustion engine is that it relies on petroleum, either in the form of gasoline or diesel fuel. (TPO9, W, Q1) 内燃机最大的一个问题是它依靠原油，无论是汽油还是柴油。

【派生】dieselize *v.* 柴油机化

dim[1] [dɪm]

【释义】*v.* 1.（使）变暗淡，（使）变模糊 2.（使）减弱 *a.* 1. 暗淡的，昏暗的 2. 隐约的，模糊不清的

【例句】So, on that note, let's dim the lights, so we can see these slides and actually look at the techniques they used. (TPO3, L, S2, L1) 因此，基于以上的背景知识，让我们把灯光调暗，来看看这些幻灯片以及幻灯片中壁画用到的技术。

【反义】bright, light

【派生】dimmish *a.* 暗淡的，朦胧的
dimly *ad.* 暗淡地，朦胧地

【搭配】take a dim view of 不赞成

diploma[1] [dɪˈpləʊmə] 

【释义】*n.* 毕业文凭，毕业证书，资格证书

【例句】I understand you need this in order to process my diploma. (TPO8, L, S1, C1) 我明白，你需要这个来处理我的毕业证书。

diplomacy[1] [dɪˈpləʊməsɪ] 

【释义】*n.* 外交，外交手腕；处世之道

【例句】By the Middle Ages, spices were regarded as so important and expensive that they were used in diplomacy, as gifts by heads of state and ambassadors. (TPO18, L, S2, L1) 到中世纪时，香料被视为非常重要且昂贵的东西，因而被各国元首和大使们用作外交中的礼物。

【派生】diplomat *n.* 外交家，外交官
diplomatic *a.* 外交的，老练的

【搭配】a masterstroke of diplomacy 外交上绝妙的表现

discomfort[1] [dɪsˈkʌmfət] 

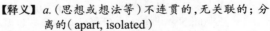

【释义】*n.* 不舒适，不愉快，苦恼(distress, uneasiness)

【例句】These contradictions can cause a kind of mental discomfort known as cognitive dissonance. (TPO3, S, Q4) 这些矛盾可能会引起一种被称为“认知失调”的心理不适感。

【反义】comfort

disconnected[1] [ˌdɪskəˈnektɪd] 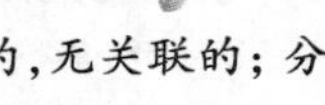

【释义】*a.*（思想或想法等）不连贯的，无关联的；分离的(apart, isolated)

【例句】The psychological effects of all these extraordinary sounds can be profound, especially when they seem so disconnected from human doing drumming or chanting. (TPO14, L, S2, L2) 这种奇特的声音产生的心理效应非常深刻，尤其是当其似乎与人类的击鼓和吟唱行为无关时。

【逆构】disconnect *v.* 使分离，断开，切断

返记菜单

detritus[1] diagonal[1] diesel[1] dim[1] diploma[1]
diplomacy[1] discomfort[1] disconnected[1]

discredit[1] [dɪs'kredɪt]

【释义】v. 1. 怀疑(disbelieve) 2. 损坏…的名誉(disgrace) n. 丧失名誉
【例句】So they were discredited. (TPO8, L, S2, L2) 所以,没人相信他们。
【搭配】bring discredit on/to 给(某人或某物)带来耻辱

discrete[1] [dɪs'kriːt]

【释义】a. 分离的,不相关联的,不连续的(separate, individual)
【例句】Another thing that distinguishes a real language is a property we call "discreteness". (TPO9, L, S2, L2) 另一个与真正语言区分的特性是我们所称的"不关联性"。
【派生】discretely ad. 分离地,离散地

disdain[1] [dɪs'deɪn]

【释义】n. 鄙视,轻视,蔑视(despise, scorn)
【例句】"Had the Greeks held novelty in such disdain as we," asked Horace in his Epistles, "what work of ancient date would now exist?" (TPO7, R, S2, T1) 贺拉斯在他的使徒信中提到:"如果希腊人当初跟我们一样守旧,不创新,那么古代也就没什么作品可以留存至今了。"
【反义】admire, respect
【派生】disdainful a. 鄙视的,轻蔑的
【搭配】a look/tone/expression of disdain 鄙夷的神态/语气/表情

disgust[1] [dɪs'gʌst]

【释义】v. 使(某人)反感,厌恶
【例句】Modern attitudes to Roman civilization range from the infinitely impressed to the thoroughly disgusted. (TPO7, R, S2, T1) 现代人对罗马文明的态度从无限的感动到彻底的厌恶,各执己见。
【派生】disgusting a. 令人作呕的,令人厌恶的

disintegrate[1] [dɪs'ɪntɪgreɪt]

【释义】v.(使)瓦解,(使)碎裂(crumble, separate)
【例句】An asteroid of this size would be expected to leave an immense crater, even if the asteroid itself was disintegrated by the impact. (TPO15, R, S2, T2) 这么大的一个小行星,即使自身受到冲击碎裂,也应该会留下一个巨大的陨石坑的。
【逆构】integrate v. 使完整

dismantle[1] [dɪs'mæntl]

【释义】v. 1. 拆开,拆卸(disassemble) 2. 废除,取消(demolish)
【例句】Now portable drilling machines are set up and are then dismantled and removed. (TPO4, R, S2, T2) 现在的便携式钻井器械可以安装,然后再拆卸移走。
【反义】assemble
【搭配】dismantlement n. 拆卸,拆除的行动

disorganized[1] [dɪs'ɔːgənaɪzd]

【释义】a. 紊乱的,无组织的;杂乱无章的
【例句】They are rather disorganized. (TPO12, L, S2, C1) 它们组织相当混乱。
【逆构】organized a. 有秩序的
disorganize v. 扰乱,使混乱

dispense[1] [dɪs'pens]

【释义】v. 分配,分发,施与(allot, distribute)
【例句】Their members command and dispense many of the rewards that are so vital to us and that make our lives seem worthwhile. (TPO13, R, S1, T1) 他们的成员掌管并分配许多对我们至关重要并且使我们的生活看起来有意义的奖励。
【派生】dispenser n. 自动售货机
dispensary n.(尤指医院的)配药处,药房
【搭配】dispense with 免除,省却

dissuade[1] [dɪ'sweɪd]

【释义】v. 劝阻,阻止(dehort, discourage)
【例句】The administrator dissuade the student from starting a job right away. (TPO18, L, S1, C1) 这位管理者劝阻学生不要立刻开始工作。
【反义】persuade

distress[1] [dɪs'tres]

【释义】 *n.* 1. 悲痛，忧伤(discomfort, affliction) 2. 贫困，窘迫 *v.* 使痛苦，使忧伤

【例句】 The noise itself was distressing. (TPO10, S, Q6) 这种声音本身就让人很悲伤。

【派生】 distressed *a.* 极为心烦的，十分痛苦的
distressing *a.* 使人不安的，让人忧虑的

【搭配】 in distress 遇难；在困境中
distress signal 求救信号

district[1] ['dɪstrɪkt]

【释义】 *n.* 地区，行政区(area, region)

【例句】 The district courts decide in if the university entitle to any of our professors' profits? (TPO14, L, S2, C1) 地方法院决定大学是否有权给予教授红利。

【搭配】 business district 商务区
urban district 市区

distrust[1] [dɪs'trʌst]

【释义】 *v./n.* 不信任，怀疑

【例句】 Widely reported, if somewhat distrusted, accounts by figures like the famous traveler from Venice. Marco Polo, of the willingness of people in China to trade with Europeans and of the immensity of the wealth to be gained by such contact made the idea irresistible. (TPO17, R, S1, T1) 如果大量的报告还有那么一点不可信的话，那么威尼斯著名的旅行家马可波罗的描述则会使这种想法变得无法抗拒，马可波罗描述了中国人希望和欧洲人通商的意愿，并且通过这样的交易，获得了取之不尽的财富。

【反义】 trust

【派生】 distrustful *a.* 不信任的，怀疑的

【搭配】 look at sb. with distrust 怀疑地打量着某人

divine[1] [dɪ'vaɪn]

【释义】 *a.* 1. 神的，神圣的(holy) 2. 极好的 *v.* 发现，猜出

【例句】 Thus it made sense to show the statue looking ahead at what was happening in front of it, so that the living performer of the ritual could interact with the divine or deceased recipient. (TPO11, R, S1, T1) 如此一来，让雕像直视前方正在发生的事就很合理了，这样可以便于礼仪的执行者与神灵或死者进行交流。

【派生】 divinely *ad.* 像神一样地

【搭配】 divine law 神法
divine service 祭礼，礼拜

devote[1] [dɪ'vəut]

【释义】 *v.* 为…付出(时间、精力等)；献身于(dedicate, contribute)

【例句】 It gave the troubadours time to devote themselves to writing poetry. (TPO13, L, S2, L1) 它使行吟诗人有时间投入到诗作中。

【派生】 devotion *n.* 热爱，忠诚

【搭配】 devote oneself/sth. to sb./sth. 为某人/某事物付出(时间、精力等)

dizziness[1] ['dɪzɪnɪs]

【释义】 *n.* 头昏眼花，眩晕

【例句】 In fact, the sounds can cause headaches, feelings of dizziness, increase heartache, that sort of thing, you see. (TPO14, L, S2, L2) 实际上，这种声音能引起人头痛、产生眩晕感、心跳加速，诸如此类的反应。

【逆构】 dizzy *a.* 眩晕的

downright[1] ['daʊnraɪt]

【释义】 *ad./a.* 彻底地(的)，完全地(的)(entire, complete, thorough)

【例句】 First, contributors to a communal online encyclopedia often lack academic credentials, thereby making their contributions partially informed at best and downright inaccurate in many cases. (TPO6, W, Q1) 在线百科全书的编撰者经常缺乏学术可信度，因此使他们的成果只有一部分比较好，而大部分都是完全不准确的。

【搭配】 a downright insult 十足的侮辱

downturn[1] ['dauntə:n]

【释义】 *n.* 低迷时期

【例句】 Four-day employees are likely to be the first to lose their jobs during an economic downturn. (TPO1, W, Q1) 那些一周只工作四天的人很可能在经济低迷的时期最先失去工作。

dozen[1] ['dʌzn] 

【释义】n. 一打,十二个(twelve)
【例句】It suddenly became public—an experience that the viewer shared with dozens, scores, and even hundreds of others. (TPO2, R, S2, T2) 电影一夜之间走向大众——观众能够和几十人、甚至上百人共同观看一部电影。
【搭配】dozens of 几十个

drench[1] [drentʃ] 

【释义】v. 使湿透(wet, flood)
【例句】Then, as blazing sunshine alternated with drenching rains, the harsh, barren surfaces of the black rocks slowly began to soften. (TPO9, R, S2, T2) 然后,经过了炙热阳光和湿润雨水的交替作用之后,荒芜的黑色岩石表面慢慢开始变软。
【反义】dry
【搭配】a drench of rain 大雨倾盆

dual[1] ['djʊ(:)əl] 

【释义】a. 双(重)的,两重的
【例句】In 1929 the United States motion picture industry released more than 300 sound film-a rough figure, since a number were silent films with music tracks, or films prepared in dual versions, to take account of the many cinemas not yet wired for sound. (TPO12, R, S2, T1) 1929 年,美国电影业推出了 300 多部有声电影——这是一个粗略的数值,因为有一些电影只是带有音乐的无声电影,或者是有两个版本的电影,那是考虑到很多影院还没有安装音响设备。
【派生】duality n. 二元性
【搭配】dual carriage 双行道

dwindle[1] ['dwɪndl] 

【释义】v. 逐渐变少或变小(decline, decrease)
【例句】It's not a remnant of some huge population that is dwindled in last few hundred years for some reason. (TPO6, L, S1, L2) 在过去几百年里,这种树的数量没有因为某些原因减少哪怕一小部分。
【反义】increase
【搭配】dwindle in size 体积缩小

eagerness[1] ['i:gənɪs]

【释义】n. 渴望;热忱(keenness, zeal)
【例句】He is impressed with her eagerness to continue. (TPO5, L, S2, C1) 他对她想要继续下去的热忱印象深刻。
【逆构】eager a. 渴望的,热心的

edible[1] ['edɪbl]

【释义】a. 可食用的(eatable)
【例句】Also they live in open field where there is lots of edible vegetation. (TPO1, L, S2, L2) 同样,它们生活在开阔的田野里,那里有很多可以食用的植物。
【派生】edibleness n. 食用价值

edifice[1] ['edɪfɪs] 

【释义】n. 宏伟的建筑物(mansion)
【例句】It had over 2,004 apartment complexes, a great market, a large number of industrial workshops, an administrative center, a number of massive religious edifices, and a regular grid pattern of streets and buildings. (TPO8, R, S1, T1) 它已经拥有超过 2004 座的公寓楼、一个巨大的市场、大量的工业厂房、一个行政中心、许多大型的宗教建筑和常规的网格形街道和建筑物。

efficacious[1] [ˌefɪ'keɪʃəs] 

【释义】a. 有效的,灵验的(effective, efficient)
【例句】When this occurs, the first step has been taken toward theater as an antonomous activity, and thereafter entertainment and aesthetic values may gradually replace the former mystical and socially efficacious concerns. (TPO1, R, S2, T1) 这时候,戏剧作为一种自发的活动迈出了自己的第一步,接着,戏剧的娱乐和审美价值开始渐渐取代先前的带有神话色彩的、在社会上灵验的关注。
【派生】efficaciously ad. 有效地,灵验地

electrify[1] [ɪ'lektrɪfaɪ]

【释义】 v. 1. 使电气化,使通电 2. 使激动,使震惊
【例句】 They are electrifying the battery. 他们正在给电池通电。
【派生】 electrifying a. 令人振奋的,惊人的

electrode[1] [ɪ'lektrəʊd] 

【释义】 n. 电极
【例句】 If you put electrodes on the throat and measure muscle potential—muscle activity—you discover that when people are thinking, that there is muscular activity in the throat region. (TPO2, L, S1, L1) 如果在喉部放入电极来测量肌肉电势——也就是肌肉活动——你会发现当人们思考问题时,在喉部会有肌肉运动。

elevate[1] ['elɪveɪt] 

【释义】 v. 提拔,抬高,使上升(lift, promote, raise)
【例句】 Soon they will elevate you to a high rank in their society. 很快他们就会提拔你到社会中较高的阶层。
【反义】 lower, degrade
【派生】 elevation n. 提高,晋级
elevator n. 电梯,升降机

elongated[1] ['iːlɒŋgeɪtɪd] 

【释义】 a. 瘦长的,细长的
【例句】 It had an elongated skeletal structure. (TPO10, L, S1, L1) 它有一个很长的骨骼结构。

emblem[1] ['embləm] 

【释义】 n. 标志,象征,徽章(symbol)
【例句】 The pine tree, peach, and crane are emblems of long life. (TPO10, R, S1, T1) 松树、桃树以及鹤都是长寿的象征。
【搭配】 national emblem 国徽

embody[1] [ɪm'bɒdɪ] 

【释义】 v. 使具体化,体现
【例句】 This "atmospheric engine," invented by Thomas Savery and vastly improved by his partner, Thomas Newcomen, embodied revolutionary principles. (TPO6, R, S1, T1) 这一由托马斯·赛福瑞发明并由他的合作伙伴托马斯·纽卡曼进行改良的"大气发动机"体现了革命性的工作原理。
【派生】 embodiment n. 体现,化身

empathize[1] ['empəθaɪz] 

【释义】 v. 移情,有同感
【例句】 Literature encourages us to exercise our imaginations, empathize with others, and expand our understanding of language. (TPO11, W, Q1) 文学鼓励我们运用自己的想象力,与他人产生共鸣,并拓展对语言的理解力。
【派生】 empathy n. 同情,同感

empress[1] ['emprɪs] 

【释义】 n. 女皇,皇后(queen)
【例句】 The dragon represented the emperor, and the phoenix, the empress. (TPO10, R, S1, T1) 龙代表了帝王,凤凰代表了皇后。

encroach[1] [ɪn'krəʊtʃ] 

【释义】 v. 逐步侵占,蚕食(infringe, intrude, invade)
【例句】 A worsening of the plight of deer was to be expected as settlers encroached on the land, logging, burning, and clearing, eventually replacing a wilderness landscape with roads, cities, towns, and factories. (TPO4, R, S1, T1) 随着移民侵占土地、伐木烧林和清理等活动的进行,最终空旷的原野会被公路、城镇和工厂所取代,可以预见鹿群的处境会越来越恶劣。
【派生】 encroacher n. 侵入者
encroachment n. 侵犯

entertainer[1] [entə'teɪnə (r)] 

【释义】 n. 表演者,供人娱乐者(performer)
【例句】 They did not require live entertainer. (TPO2, R, S2, T2) 它们不需要现场表演者。
【派生】 entertainment n. 娱乐,消遣
【逆构】 entertain v. 使快乐;款待

返记菜单

electrify[1]	electrode[1]	elevate[1]	elongated[1]	emblem[1]
embody[1]	empathize[1]	empress[1]	encroach[1]	entertainer[1]

entrepreneurial[1] [ˌɔntrəprəˈnjuriəl] 

【释义】*a.* 企业家的,创业者的

【例句】On the open market, the loyalty of one's fellows, and entrepreneurial skill make all the difference. (TPO16, R, S1, T1) 在自由市场中,伙伴的忠诚和创业技能有着重要作用。

【逆构】entrepreneur *n.* 企业家;主办者

【搭配】entrepreneurial management 创业管理

eradicate[1] [ɪˈrædɪkeɪt] 

【释义】*v.* 根除,根绝,消灭(eliminate, exterminate)

【例句】This disruption of food chain and climate would have eradicated the dinosaurs and other organisms in less than fifty years. (TPO8, R, S2, T1) 这种食物链和气候的破坏使得恐龙和其他生物在不到50年中就灭绝了。

【派生】eradication *n.* 根除,杜绝

esteem[1] [ɪsˈtiːm] 

【释义】*v./n.* 尊重,尊敬

【例句】They esteem symbols of Roman power, such as the massive Colosseum. (TPO7, R, S2, T1) 他们尊重罗马权利的象征,比如宏大的罗马圆形剧场。

【反义】despise

【派生】self-esteem *n.* 自尊

【搭配】esteem for 尊重

ethnology[1] [ˌeθˈnɒlədʒɪ] 

【释义】*n.* 人种学,民族学

【例句】The professor talking about speciation is to tell the man about a new research area in ethnology. (TPO7, L, S1, C1) 教授谈论物种形成是想告诉此人民族学的新研究领域。

【派生】ethnologist *n.* 人种学者,民族学者

【搭配】National Museum of Ethnology 国立民族学博物馆

exclude[1] [ɪksˈkluːd]

【释义】*v.* 排除,不包括在内,排斥(leave out of, keep out of)

【例句】The traditional encyclopedia provides a considered view of what topics to include or exclude and contains a sense of proportion that online "democratic" communal encyclopedias do not. (TPO6, W, Q1) 传统的百科全书对于哪些话题该包括、哪些不该包括都有很周全的考虑,这种合理的规划是充满民主性的在线百科全书所不能具备的。

【反义】include

【派生】exclusive *a.* 排他的,专有的

exclusion *n.* 排除,除外

excluding *prep.* 不包括,除去

【搭配】exclude and reject all 排斥一切

execute[1] [ˈeksɪkjuːt] 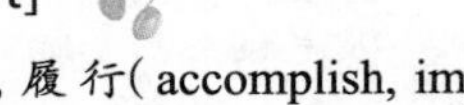

【释义】*v.* 1. 完成,执行,履行(accomplish, implement) 2. 处决

【例句】The color changes are executed by two different kinds of cells in the octopus' skin, mainly by color cells on the skin's surface called chromatophores. (TPO17, L, S2, L2) 颜色变化是由章鱼皮肤上两种不同的细胞完成的,主要由皮肤表面上叫做色素细胞的颜色细胞完成。

【派生】executed *a.* 已执行的

execution *n.* 实施,执行;处决

exemplary[1] [ɪgˈzemplərɪ] 

【释义】*a.* 模范的,典型的(typic, model)

【例句】I say this because your work on the lab project was exemplary. (TPO15, L, S2, C1) 我这样说是因为你在实验室项目上的工作堪称楷模。

【逆构】example *n.* 例子

exert[1] [ɪgˈzɜːt] 

【释义】*v.* 1. 运用,施加 2. 尽力,努力

【例句】That's because magnetic fields reduce the pressure exerted on the gases inside of them, making the spots cooler than the rest of the Sun's surface. (TPO18, L, S1, L1) 那是因为磁场降低了施加在其内部的气压,使得斑点比太阳表面其他地方的温度低。

【派生】exertion *n.* 努力,尽力

【搭配】exert oneself 努力;尽力

exert an influence on 对…产生影响

expire[1] [ɪks'paɪə]

【释义】 v. 期满,到期 2. 呼气(exhale)

【例句】 So the shell somehow has to be broken down before this…um…germination ability expires. (TPO6, L, S1, L2) 所以在种子还有发芽能力之前,种子的壳必须得有机会破开。

【派生】 expiry n. 期满,到期

explosive[1] [ɪks'pləusɪv]

【释义】 n. 爆炸物,炸药 a. 1. 爆炸的 2. (易)爆发的 3. 剧增的 4. (脾气)暴躁的

【例句】 In particular, we talked about cotton fibers, which we said were very useful, not only in the textile industry, but also in the chemical industry, and in the production of many products, such as plastics, paper, explosives, and so on. (TPO2, L, S1, L2) 我们特别探讨了棉花纤维,它用途很广,不仅可用于纺织业、化学工业,还可用来制造很多物品,如塑料、纸张、炸药等等。

【派生】 explosively ad. 爆发地,引起爆炸地

【逆构】 explode v. 爆炸

explosion n. 爆炸;激增

extraterrestrial[1] [ˌekstrətə'restrɪəl]

【释义】 a. 地球(或其大气圈)外的,行星际的 n. 外星人

【例句】 If an extraterrestrial being or two appear before us and say, what is your society like, what is this Earth thing all about, you could do worse than take that creature to an opera. (TPO12, L, S2, L1) 要是有一两个外星生物出现在你面前并且问:你们的社会是什么样的,这个地球上的事物都是关于什么的,你最好带领这个生物去看场歌剧。

eye-opening[1] ['aiˌəupəniŋ]

【释义】 a. 使人吃惊的,很有启发的(surprising, inspiring)

【例句】 That's really eye-opening news. (TPO1, L, S1, L2) 那真是让人瞠目的消息。

fabricate[1] ['fæbrɪkeɪt]

【释义】 v. 编造,捏造,虚构

【例句】 Second, even if the original entry in the online encyclopedia is correct, the communal nature of these online encyclopedias gives unscrupulous users and vandals or hackers the opportunity to fabricate, delete, and corrupt information in the encyclopedia. (TPO6, W, Q1) 其次,即使在线百科全书的原始录入是正确的,但其公共性也会给那些无道德的用户、破坏者以及黑客们提供一些伪造、删除或更改百科全书中的信息的机会。

【派生】 fabrication n. 制作,构成;伪造物

【搭配】 fabricate a rumour 捏造谣言

faith[1] [feɪθ]

【释义】 n. 1. 信仰,信条(belief) 2. 信任(trust)

【例句】 Nothing could make me waver in my faith. 任何事情都不能动摇我的信仰。

【派生】 faithful a. 守信的,忠实的,可靠的

fanciful[1] ['fænsɪful]

【释义】 a. 爱空想的,充满幻想的(imaginative)

【例句】 In the absence of solid linguistic, archaeological, and biological data, many fanciful and mutually exclusive theories were devised. (TPO5, R, S2, T1) 由于没有确凿的语言学、考古学和生物学数据,人们想出了很多充满幻想、互相矛盾的理论。

【派生】 fancifully ad. 空想地,奇异地

fancifulness n. 奇异

fantastic[1] [fæn'tæstɪk]

【释义】 a. 1. 极好的(excellent, extraordinary) 2. (计划、建议等)不实际的

【例句】 Well, these students, they'll be making fantastic meals and it's gonna be cheaper than going out to one of these reataurants. (TPO5, S, R2) 嗯,这些学生,他们将会烹饪出极好的菜肴,而且这比起去饭店吃要便宜得多。

【派生】 fantastical a. 空想的,奇异的

【逆构】 fantacy n. 幻想,白日梦

返记菜单

expire[1] explosive[1] extraterrestrial[1] eye-opening[1] fabricate[1]
faith[1] fanciful[1] fantastic[1]

fanwise[1] ['fænwaiz] 

【释义】*ad.* 如扇地，成扇形地

【例句】The water usually spreads out fanwise. (TPO1, R, S2, T2) 水通常会呈扇形扩散开去。

farsighted[1] ['fɑː'saitid] 

【释义】*a.* 有远见的，能看到远处的(forward-looking)

【例句】Yet both chemists were sufficiently farsighted to leave gaps. (TPO16, R, S2, T1) 不过，两位化学家都很有远见，在元素周期表上留有空隙。

【派生】farsightedly *ad.* 有远见地

【逆构】farsight *n.* 远见

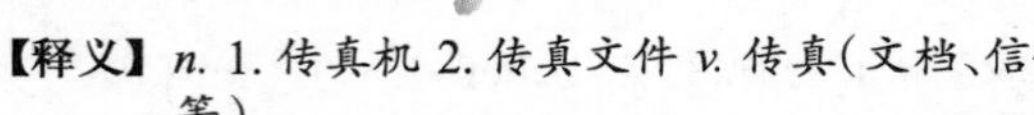

fax[1] [fæks] 

【释义】*n.* 1. 传真机 2. 传真文件 *v.* 传真(文档、信件等)

【例句】Sorry, but you will need to fill out those forms again and then I will fax them over the payroll office. (TPO12, L, S2, C1) 对不起，你得重新填写那些表格，然后我会从财务部门把它们传真过来。

festive[1] ['festɪv]

【释义】*a.*(宗教)节日的，适合于节日的

【例句】At the ceremonies, they ate festive meals and then discarded the pots in which the meals had been prepared or served. (TPO5, W, Q1) 在仪式期间，他们吃掉节日大餐，然后把用来准备或盛放食物的锅锅罐罐丢掉。

【派生】festival *n.* 节日，庆祝，纪念活动

fibrous[1] ['faibrəs] 

【释义】*a.* 纤维的，纤维性的

【例句】Leatherbacks do not have blubber, but they do have a reptilian equivalent: thick, oil-saturated skin, with a layer of fibrous, fatty tissue just beneath it. (TPO15, R, S2, T1) 棱皮龟没有那样的脂肪，但是它们和爬行类动物有着相等同的结构：厚厚的满含油脂的皮肤，皮下有一层纤维性的脂肪组织。

【逆构】fiber *n.* 纤维；光纤

fierce[1] [fɪəs] 

【释义】*a.* 强烈的，凶猛的(wild, brutal, cruel)

【例句】Fierce interspecies competition has been proposed as a possible cause of mass extinctions. (TPO15, R, S2, T2) 物种间激烈的竞争是导致大规模灭绝的一个可能的原因。

【反义】gentle, meek

【派生】fiercely *ad.* 猛烈地

flank[1] [flæŋk] 

【释义】*n.* 胁，侧腹，侧边 *v.* 位于…之侧面

【例句】Spores light enough to float on the breezes were carried thousands of miles from more ancient lands and deposited at random across the bare mountain flanks. (TPO9, R, S2, T2) 孢子很轻，可以随着微风，从更古老的陆地飘过几千英里，然后被随意地撒播在荒芜的山腰上。

【搭配】be flanked by 两侧有…

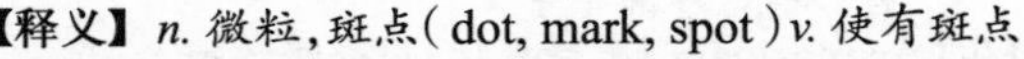

fleck[1] [flek]

【释义】*n.* 微粒，斑点(dot, mark, spot) *v.* 使有斑点

【例句】All you do is train the microscope on tiny flecks of paint and analyze them. (TPO5, L, S2, L1) 你需要做的就是把显微镜瞄准那些微小的颜料粒，然后做分析。

【搭配】fleck sth. with sth. 使…上满是斑点

fledgling[1] ['fledʒlɪŋ] 

【释义】*n.* 刚学飞的幼鸟；无经验的人(newcomer, starter)

【例句】So if there are people or dogs on the beach, the eggs and fledglings in the nest are really vulnerable. (TPO8, L, S1, L1) 所以，如果沙滩上有人或狗，那么这些巢中的蛋和刚会飞的小鸟就极容易受伤害。

Word List 43

flicker[1] ['flɪkə]

【释义】*v.*（通常指灯光）闪烁，摇曳（glimmer）

【例句】Coal gas rivaled smoky oil lamps and flickering candles, and early in the new century, well-to-do Londoners grew accustomed to gaslit houses and even streets. (TPO6, R, S1, T1) 煤气在与冒烟的油灯及忽闪的蜡烛的比较中占尽优势，而且在新世纪伊始，经济富裕的伦敦人也开始习惯将煤气用于家用照明及街道照明。

【派生】flickering *a.* 闪烁的，摇曳的

【搭配】a weak flicker of hope 一线希望的闪现

fling[1] [flɪŋ]

【释义】*v.* 1. 猛动（身体或身体部位）2.（尤指生气地）扔，掷，抛 3. 粗暴地（向某人）说

【例句】During courtship and aggressive displays, the turkey enlarges its colored neck collar by inflating sacs in the neck region and then flings about a pendulous part of the colored signaling apparatus as it utters calls designed to attract or repel. (TPO17, R, S2, T1) 在求爱期和发起挑衅时，火鸡会使自己颈囊充气，从而张开艳丽的颈圈，当其发出吸引异性或驱逐敌人的叫声时，便晃动这个色彩绚烂的信号器官的下垂部分。

【派生】flinger *n.* 投掷的人

【搭配】fling up a plan 放弃一项计划

floe[1] [fləʊ]

【释义】*n.* 海面上所结的浮冰

【例句】That is why a gull can stand on an ice floe without freezing. (TPO15, R, S2, T1) 这就是为什么海鸥可以站在浮冰上而不被冻结。

flowery[1] ['flaʊərɪ]

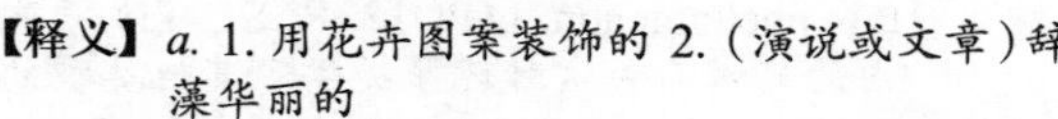

【释义】*a.* 1. 用花卉图案装饰的 2.（演说或文章）辞藻华丽的

【例句】It let him make these really intricate flowery designs for stained glass, which are used in lamp shades. (TPO16, L, S2, L2) 这让他为彩色玻璃设计了这些着实复杂的花朵图案，用来做灯罩。

footprint[1] ['fʊtprɪnt]

【释义】*n.* 脚印，足迹（footmark）

【例句】There are no footprints, no tyre tracks and no heavy machinery like a bulldozer…uh, nothing was ever brought in to move these heavy rocks. (TPO4, L, S2, L1) 没有脚印、车辙，也没有推土机之类的重型机器的痕迹…，没有任何东西被带入到这里用来移动这些岩石的迹象。

forbid[1] [fə'bɪd]

【释义】*v.* 1. 禁止，不许（prevent, prohibit）2. 阻止，妨碍

【例句】Some oil lies under regions where drilling is forbidden, such as national parks or other public lands. (TPO4, R, S2, T2) 一些原油所在的区域是禁止开采的，比如国家公园或其它公有土地。

【反义】allow, permit

【派生】forbidding *a.* 可怕的，令人难亲近的
forbidden *a.* 被禁止的

【搭配】forbid sb. from doing sth./forbid sb. to do sth. 禁止某人做某事

forbidding[1] [fə'bɪdɪŋ]

【释义】*a.* 可怕的，令人生畏的（frightening, harsh）

【例句】A few of these spores found a toehold on the dark, forbidding rocks and grew and began to work their transformation upon the land. (TPO9, R, S2, T2) 一些孢子在漆黑险恶的岩石中找到了立足点，生长起来，并开始向整个陆地蔓延。

foresight[1] ['fɔːsaɪt]

【释义】*n.* 远见，深谋远虑（forethought, precaution）

【例句】That showed good judgment, real foresight. (TPO16, L, S2, L2) 那显示出了很好的判断，真的是有远见。

【逆构】foresee *v.* 预见，预知

返记菜单

flicker[1]	fling[1]	floe[1]	flowery[1]	footprint[1]
forbid[1]	forbidding[1]	foresight[1]		

forgetful[1] [fə'getful]

【释义】*a.* 1. 健忘的，记性差的 2. 不经心的，疏忽的（careless, mindless）
【例句】Since I'm so busy now at the end of the semester, I'm getting pretty forgetful these days. (TPO2, L, S1, C1) 因为在学期末特别忙，最近我变得非常健忘。
【反义】remindful
【派生】forgetfully *ad.* 健忘地
forgetfulness *n.* 健忘
【逆构】forget *v.* 忘记

forked[1] ['fɔːkt]

【释义】*a.* 成叉的，叉状的
【例句】The result is a forked lightning that strikes the ground in two places. (TPO18, R, S2, T2) 结果就是叉状的闪电击中了地面的两处地方。
【逆构】fork *v.* 叉起

formalize[1] ['fɔːməlaɪz]

【释义】*v.* 使正式化
【例句】The group repeats, refines, and formalizes those actions into fixed ceremonies, or rituals. (TPO1, R, S2, T1) 这个群体将那些动作进行重复、改良和正式化后形成了固定的庆祝或是宗教仪式。
【派生】formalization *n.* 正式化
formalized *a.* 正式化的，形式化的
【逆构】formal *a.* 正式的

formerly[1] ['fɔːməlɪ]

【释义】*ad.* 以前，从前（previously, aforetime）
【例句】This is the time period in which most scientists formerly believed the area to be inhospitable for humans. (TPO9, R, S1, T1) 在这一时期，大部分科学家此前都认为该地区不适合人类居住。
【逆构】former *a.* 过去的，在前的

fragrance[1] ['freɪgrəns]

【释义】*n.* 芳香，香味（aroma）
【例句】Uh, two was exotic taste and fragrance. (TPO18, L, S2, L1) 呃，第二是它有一种奇异的香味。
【派生】fragrant *a.* 香的，芬芳的

frigid[1] ['frɪdʒɪd]

【释义】*a.* 1. 寒冷的（chilly, cold）2. 冷淡的，不友好的（unfriendly）3.（指女性）性冷淡的
【例句】The summers were not too warm, nor the winters too frigid. (TPO8, R, S2, T1) 那时候，夏天不太热，冬天也不太冷。
【派生】frigidly *ad.* 冷淡地

fungal[1] ['fʌŋgəl]

【释义】*a.* 真菌的，由真菌引起的
【例句】As an example, plants make chemicals toxic to fungal and bacterial parasites, along with ones toxic to predatory animals (sometimes they are the same chemicals). (TPO17, R, S2, T2) 比如说，植物可以产生某些对真菌和细菌类寄生物有害的化学毒剂以及一些对食肉动物有害的化学毒剂（有时候是同一种化学物）。
【派生】fungus *n.* 真菌
【搭配】fungal infection 真菌感染

furious[1] ['fjʊərɪəs]

【释义】*a.* 1. 狂怒的，暴怒的（angry）2. 激烈的，猛烈的（violent）
【例句】Then, if he tries to talk with her, maybe her father get furious, for no apparent reason. (TPO7, L, S1, L1) 那么，如果他试图跟她说话，她父亲可能会莫名其妙的愤怒。
【反义】gentle
【派生】furiously *ad.* 狂怒地；猛烈地
【搭配】fast and furious（指游戏、聚会、表演等）生动活泼的

furnish[1] ['fɜːnɪʃ]

【释义】*v.* 1. 提供（provide, supply）2. 布置，装备（equip）
【例句】Cave art furnishes other types of evidence of this phenomenon. (TPO12, R, S1, T1) 洞穴内的艺术品为这种现象提供了其他类型的证据。
【派生】furnishment *n.* 装置，装备

furniture *n.* 家具
furnishing *n.*（家庭中包括家具及其他的）设备
【搭配】furnish with 供给，提供

fuss[1] [fʌs]

【释义】*n./v.* 大惊小怪，小题大做（bother, fret, worry）
【例句】They wanted to see what's causing all the fuss. (TPO4, L, S1, C1) 他们想看看是什么让人们争论不休。
【搭配】fuss about 大惊小怪；忙乱
make a fuss of/over 对…体贴备至，过分宠爱
kick up a fuss about（因…）大吵大闹

gem[1] [dʒem]

【释义】*n.* 宝石，美玉
【例句】They traded grain for raw materials, such as timber and stones, as well as for metals and gems. (TPO16, R, S1, T1) 他们用谷物交换原材料，比如木料和石头，以及金属和宝石。

generalizable[1] ['dʒenərəlaizəbl]

【释义】*a.* 可概括的，可归纳的
【例句】So they become less identifiable, more generalizable to any audience. (TPO5, L, S2, L2) 所以它们对任何观众来说，（在根源上）变得更加不易辨认，但（在接受上）却更加大众化了。
【逆构】general *a.* 一般的，普通的

genotype[1] ['dʒenəutaip]

【释义】*n.* 基因型，遗传型
【例句】Apparently, genotypes (the genetic make-up of an organism) in the rabbit population were selected that were better able to resist the parasite. (TPO17, R, S2, T2) 显然，该兔群的遗传性状（生物体的基因结构）经过了自然选择之后，已经具备了更好地抵抗粘液瘤病毒的能力。
【派生】genotypic *a.* 遗传型的
【搭配】genotype and phenotype 基因型与表现型

geophysical[1] [ˌdʒiːəu'fizikəl]

【释义】*a.* 地球物理学的
【例句】For instance, apparently normal daily periods of biological activity were maintained for about a week by the fungus Neurospora when it was intentionally isolated from all geophysical timing cues while orbiting in a space shuttle. (TPO13, R, S2, T1) 例如，当被有意地从地理时间线索中隔离时，脉孢菌的正常生物活动显然会在环绕宇宙飞船里维持大概一周左右。

gesture[1] ['dʒestʃə]

【释义】*n.* 手势，姿态 *v.* 用手势表达
【例句】When we speak with other people face-to-face, the nonverbal signals we give—our facial expressions, hand gestures, body movements, and tone of voice—often communicate as much as, or more than, the words we utter. (TPO4, S, Q4) 当我们和人面对面交流时，我们所使用的非语言信号——面部表情、手势、肢体动作和声调——所传达的信息通常跟我们说的话一样多，甚至更多。
【派生】gestural *a.* 手势的；示意动作的
【搭配】make a gesture 做手势

gigot[1] ['dʒigət]

【释义】*n.* 羊脚形袖子
【例句】The wave forms were very even, but an oak which has fewer but bigger leaves with stronger reflections, produces a gigots wave form, or what we called: a rough echo. (TPO7, L, S1, L2) 这些声波的形状是平的，但是橡树这样的叶子少而大的树会产生强反射，产生出锯齿状声波，或者叫做粗糙回声。

gill[1] [dʒɪl] 

【释义】*n.* 腮
【例句】They breathe through lungs, not through gills and give birth to live young. (TPO2, R, S2, T1) 它们通过肺呼吸，而不是通过腮呼吸，为胎生动物。
【搭配】to the gills［口语］完全地，彻底地

giraffe[1] [dʒɪ'rɑːf]

【释义】*n.* 长颈鹿

【例句】Anyway, it's this fossilized pollen along with the aquifers（蓄水层）and the rock paintings, these three things are all evidence that the Sahara was once much greener than it is today, that there were hippos（河马）and probably elephants and giraffes and so on. (TPO6, L, S2, L2) 无论如何，化石花粉、蓄水层和岩石壁画这三样都是表明撒哈拉沙漠曾经比现在更加葱郁的证据，而且还有河马，可能还有大象和长颈鹿等动物。

glare[1] [gleə]

【释义】*n.* 1. 强光 2. 怒视 *v.* 1. 发出眩光 2. 怒目而视

【例句】Actually, it'd be hidden in the glare of the Sun. (TPO17, L, S2, L1) 实际上，它是被太阳的强光给隐藏了。

【派生】glaring *a.* 耀眼的，刺目的

【搭配】glare at 怒视

glimpse[1] [glɪmps]

【释义】*n.* 一瞥，一闪（glance）*v.* 瞥见

【例句】It takes geniuses, people like, say, Shakespeare, who're unique because when they have a glimpse at this truth, this universal truth, they pay attention to it and express it and don't just dismiss it like most people do. (TPO4, L, S1, L2) 这需要天赋，像莎士比亚这样的人是独一无二的，因为他们只需瞥一眼这普遍的真理，就会对其予以关注并将其表达出来，而不像大多数人那样把它忽略掉。

【反义】gaze, stare

【搭配】catch/get a glimpse of 瞥见
glimpse at 看到，瞥见

glory[1] ['glɔːrɪ]

【释义】*n.* 1. 光荣，荣誉（honor）2. 壮丽，辉煌

【例句】There is not much glory, but we are looking for someone with some knowledge of anthropology who can enter the articles. (TPO7, L, S1, C1) 没什么吸引人的，但是，我们确实在寻找一个能懂这些文章的人，这个人要懂人类学知识。

【反义】dishonor, disgrace, shame

【派生】glorify *v.* 赞美，颂扬

【搭配】in one's glory 得意；在（某人的）鼎盛时期
morning glory 牵牛花；昙花一现的人或物

gourmet[1] ['gʊəmeɪ]

【释义】*n.* 美食家

【例句】The university has announced that it will charge a small additional fee for these dinners in order to pay for the special gourmet food ingredients that will be required. (TPO5, S, Q1) 学校已经宣布这些晚餐会收取一点儿额外的费用用以支付这些特别的美味所需要的原材料。

【搭配】gourmet festival 美食节
gourmet powder 味精

grace[1] [greɪs]

【释义】*n.* 优雅，优美，风度（elegance, charm）*v.* 使优美

【例句】Admiration for the performer's skill, virtuosity, and grace are seen as motivation for elaborating the activities into fully realized theatrical performances. (TPO1, R, S2, T1) 人们对于表演者的技巧、精湛的技术和优雅的崇拜被看作是一种激励，促使表演者将这些活动完全成为戏剧表演。

【派生】graceless *a.* 无礼貌的，粗野的，难看的
graceful *a.* 优美的
disgrace *v.* 玷污

gravitas[1] ['grævɪtæs]

【释义】*n.* 庄严，庄重

【例句】In turn, a deep attachment to the land, and to the stability which rural life engenders, fostered the Roman virtues: gravitas, a sense of responsibility, pietas, a sense of devotion to family and country, and justitia, a sense of the natural order. (TPO7, R, S2, T1) 反之，对土地和平稳的乡村生活的深深依恋孕育了罗马人的美德：庄重，一种责任感；敬重，对祖国和家庭奉献的使命感；正义，对自然秩序的遵循。

grid[1] [grɪd]

【释义】*n.* 1. 网状物，电网 2.（地图上的）坐标方格 3.（汽车赛中的）赛车出发点

【例句】It had over 2,004 apartment complexes, a great market, a large number of industrial workshops, an administrative center, a number of massive religious edifices, and a regular grid pattern of streets and buildings. (TPO8, R, S1, T1) 它已经拥有超过2004座的公寓楼、一个巨大的市场、大量的工业厂房、一个行政中心、许多大型的宗教建筑和常规的网格形街道和建筑物。

grind[1] [graɪnd] 

【释义】*v.* 磨,碾碎(crush) *n.* 苦事,无聊的工作

【例句】Unlike formal statues that are limited to static poses of standing, sitting, and kneeling, these figures depict a wide range of actions, such as grinding grain, baking bread, producing pots, and making music, and they are shown in appropriate poses, bending and squatting as they carry out their tasks. (TPO11, R, S1, T1) 这些雕像不像正规雕像那样只有静止的站立、坐和跪的姿态,而是表现了各种不同的动作,比如磨谷物、烤面包、造壶罐,还有奏乐,而且进行这些活动时的姿态都很恰当,或弯腰,或蹲坐着。

【派生】grinder *n.* 研磨机
grindstone *n.* 磨刀石

【搭配】daily grind 日常工作
an axe to grind 另有所图;有不同意见
grind up 磨碎

gripe[1] [graɪp] 

【释义】*n./v.* 抱怨,牢骚

【例句】People on the job often develop close relationships with coworkers as they come to share gripes, jokes, gossip, and satisfactions. (TPO13, R, S1, T1) 工作中的人们经常会通过在一起发发牢骚、讲讲笑话、聊聊八卦和乐事儿来和同事发展亲密关系。

hail[1] [heɪl]

【释义】*v.* 呼喊 *n.* 雹,冰雹

【例句】Tulips actually hail from an area that Chinese call the Celestial Mountains in Central Asia. (TPO6, L, S1, L1) 郁金香实际上来自于亚洲中部一个中国人叫作天堂山的地区。

【搭配】hail from 来自
hail sb./sth. as 把…称作

hands-on[1] ['hændz'ɔn] 

【释义】*a.* 亲自动手的,躬亲的

【例句】But when Rome collapsed in the fifth century and the Middle Ages began, direct trade stopped, and so did that kind of hands-on knowledge of travel and geography. (TPO18, L, S2, L1) 但是当五世纪罗马崩塌、中世纪开始时,直接贸易中断了,有关旅行和地理的实用知识也中断了。

harbor[1] ['hɑːbə] 

【释义】*n.* 1. 海港,港口(port) 2. 避难所 *v.* 1. (船)入港停泊 2. 庇护,藏匿 3. 心怀,持有

【例句】The people of the Netherlands, with a long tradition of fisheries and mercantile shipping, had difficulty in developing good harbors suitable for steamships. (TPO18, R, S1, T1) 有着悠久渔业和商船业传统的荷兰人难以开发出适合轮船的好港口。

【搭配】pearl harbor 珍珠港
safe harbor 安全港,避风港
harbor bureau 港务局

hard-to-reach[1] 

【释义】*a.* 难于接近的,难通过的

【例句】The paintings were found in hard-to-reach places away from the inhabited parts of the cave. (TPO4, R, S2, T1) 这些画作是在远离人们居住的洞穴的难以到达的地方被发现的。

harp[1] [hɑːp]

【释义】*n.* 竖琴 *v.* 1. 弹奏竖琴 2. 喋喋不休

【例句】Previously, it was quite rare for a woman to perform on anything, but maybe a harp or maybe she sang. (TPO16, L, S1, L2) 在此之前,女人用乐器表演很罕见,但她们可能会吹竖笛或唱歌。

【搭配】harp on/about sth. 喋喋不休地说…

返记菜单

grind[1] gripe[1] hail[1] hands-on[1] harbor[1]
hard-to-reach[1] harp[1]

heal[1] [hiːl]

【释义】*v.*（使）愈合，治愈（cure）

【例句】The skeleton of a 40- or 50-year-old Nabatean warrior buried 2,000 years ago in the Negev Desert, Isreal, had multiple healed fractures to the skull, the left arm, and the ribs. (TPO12, R, S1, T1) 在以色列内盖夫的戈壁中埋葬了2000多年的一个40-50岁之间的Naba tean勇士的骨架，在他的头部，左臂和肋骨上有多处已愈合的骨折。

【派生】healing *a.* 有治疗功用的
healer *n.* 医治者；治疗物

【搭配】heal up 愈合
heal sb. of sth. 治疗某人的某病

hectic[1] [ˈhɛktɪk]

【释义】*a.* 忙碌的，忙乱的（busy）

【例句】Students' lives are hectic. (TPO8, S, Q3) 学生的生活很忙碌。

helicopter[1] [ˈhelɪkɒptə]

【释义】*n.* 直升飞机

【例句】In severely damaged forests, much of the lumber can be recovered only by using helicopters and other vehicles that are expensive to use and maintain. (TPO14, W, Q1) 在遭受严重破坏的森林里，多数木材只有用使用费和维护费都相当昂贵的直升机和其他交通工具才能得以恢复。

【派生】helicopterist *n.* 直升机驾驶员

hemlock[1] [ˈhemlɒk]

【释义】*n.* 1. 铁杉 2. 毒芹，毒芹汁

【例句】Even with snow on the ground, the high bushy understory is exposed; also snow and wind bring down leafy branches of cedar, hemlock, red alder, and other arboreal fodder. (TPO4, R, S1, T1) 即便白雪覆盖了大地，高而浓密的林下叶层依然不会被掩盖；风雪也吹落了雪松、铁杉、赤阳木和其他树木的茂密枝叶。

heredity[1] [hɪˈredɪtɪ]

【释义】*n.* 遗传；遗传特征（genetics, inheritance）

【例句】It is expressed in the form of a rigid hierarchy based largely on heredity. (TPO14, R, S2, T2) 它是以主要基于遗传的严格的等级制度形式来表现的。

【派生】hereditary *a.* 世袭的，遗传的

heroic[1] [hɪˈrəʊɪk]

【释义】*a.* 英雄的，英勇的（brave）

【例句】Now they were called songs of deeds because strangely enough, they were written to describe the heroic deeds or actions of warriors, the knights during conflicts. (TPO13, L, S2, L1) 现在，之所以称其为英雄颂歌，很大程度上是因为它们往往描写勇士的英雄事迹和行为，比如战争中的骑士。

【搭配】heroic deeds 英雄事迹

hexagonal[1] [hekˈsægənəl]

【释义】*a.* 六角形的，六边的

【例句】Snowfalls as hexagonal crystals, but once on the ground, snow is soon transformed into a compacted mass of smaller, round grains. (TPO15, R, S1, T1) 雪花以六角晶体的形式飘落，但一旦落在地上，雪花便迅速转换成大量密集的小而圆的颗粒。

hike[1] [haɪk]

【释义】*n./v.* 徒步旅行，远足

【例句】If someone on a hike knocks a couple of rocks over, they could be unwittingly destroying a microclimate that an animal or organism relies on. (TPO14, L, S1, L2) 如果有人在远足时敲击几块走过的岩石，他们就可能在无意间破坏了一种动物或有机体赖以生存的微气候。

hooked[1] [hʊkt]

【释义】*a.* 1. 钩状的 2. 对…成瘾的（addicted）

【例句】When I saw my name, I mean my byline in print, I was hooked. (TPO14, L, S2, C1) 当我看见我的名字时，我是说看见我的署名印

在上面时,我着迷了。
【逆构】hook *n.* 钩子

hospitalize[1] ['hɒspɪtəlaɪz] 

【释义】*v.* 就医,使住院
【例句】Most people remember only a few events—usually ones that were meaningful and distinctive, such as being hospitalized or a siblings birth. (TPO6, R, S2, T2) 大部分人只记得很少的事情——通常是那些有意义的和特殊的事情,比如住院或者弟弟妹妹的出生。
【派生】hospitalization *n.* 医院收容,住院治疗

hostile[1] ['hɒstaɪl] 

【释义】*a.* 怀有敌意的,不友善的,反对的(unfriendly, antagonistic)
【例句】As oil becomes increasingly difficult to find, the search for it is extended into more-hostile environments. (TPO4, R, S2, T2) 随着原油越来越难找,对原油的探索也扩展那到了更危险的环境中。
【反义】amicable, friendly
【派生】hostility *n.* 敌对,敌意

hug[1] [hʌg] 

【释义】*v.* 1. 紧靠着,挨着 2. 热烈地拥抱(embrace, hold) *n.* 拥抱,搂抱
【例句】Even if they hugged the African coastline, they had little chance of surviving a crossing of the Indian Ocean shortly after 1400. (TPO17, R, S1, T1) 1400年后不久,即使是紧贴着非洲的海岸线行驶,这种船也很难穿越印度洋。
【派生】huggable *a.* 逗人喜爱的,令人想拥抱的
【搭配】to give someone a hug 紧紧拥抱某人

humanity[1] [hjʊ(ː)'mænɪtɪ] 

【释义】*n.* 1. 人类(总称) 2. 人性 3. 博爱,仁慈
【例句】Humanity has been trying to use the sun's light as a reliable source of energy for centuries. (TPO12, L, S2, L2) 几个世纪以来,人类总是试图使用阳光作为一种可靠的能量来源。

humid[1] ['hjuːmɪd] 

【释义】*a.* 潮湿的,多湿气的(wet, moisty)
【例句】Properly speaking, tropical rainforests grow in high-rainfall equatorial areas that remain wet or humid all year round. (TPO14, R, S2, T1) 准确地说,热带雨林生长在降雨量较高的赤道地带,那里终年都是湿润的。
【反义】dry
【派生】humidify *v.* 使潮湿,使湿润
【搭配】humid climate 湿润气候

hurricane[1] ['hʌrɪkən] 

【释义】*n.* 飓风,暴风(storm)
【例句】The ancient Maya were presumably more experienced and did better, but nevertheless they too must have faced risks of crop failures from droughts and hurricanes. (TPO14, R, S2, T1) 古玛雅人可能经验更丰富,做得也更好,但他们也一定会面临因干旱和飓风所带来的农作物减产的风险。
【搭配】hurricane lamp 防风灯;飓风灯

hydroponic[1] [ˌhaɪdrəʊ'pɒnɪk] 

【释义】*a.* 水栽法的
【例句】Much of the research on nutrient deficiencies is based on growing plants hydroponically. (TPO5, R, S1, T1) 很多有关营养缺乏的研究都是通过水栽种植植物进行的。
【派生】hydroponical *a.* 水栽种植法的
hydroponically *ad.* 水栽种植法地

hysterical[1] [hɪs'terɪkəl] 

【释义】*a.* 情绪异常激动的,歇斯底里般的
【例句】But, there's a type of rapid expansion, what might be called the hysterical or irrational boom that pretty much always leads to a bust. (TPO6, L, S1, L1) 但是也有一种快速的经济扩张,可能会被称作疯狂的或不理智的扩张,并且极易导致萧条的结局。
【派生】hysterically *ad.* 歇斯底里地
【搭配】a hysterical statement 情绪激动的声明

返记菜单

hospitalize[1] hostile[1] hug[1] humanity[1] humid[1]
hurricane[1] hydroponic[1] hysterical[1]

iceberg[1] ['aɪsbəg]

【释义】*n.* 冰山

【例句】For a glacier to grow or maintain its mass, there must be sufficient snowfall to match or exceed the annual loss through melting, evaporation, and calving, which occurs when the glacier loses solid chunks as icebergs to the sea or large lakes. (TPO15, R, S1, T1) 为了保持或增加一个冰川的体积，就必须要有足够多的降雪量，这些降雪量需要能够抵销或者超过每年因融雪、蒸发或者因冰川以冰山的形式飘向海洋或湖泊而形成的裂冰损失的量。

ideologically[1] [ˌaɪdɪə'lɒdʒɪkli]

【释义】*ad.* 思想上；意识形态上

【例句】This mode of craft production favored the growth of self-governing and ideologically egalitarian craft guilds everywhere in the Middle Eastern city. (TPO16, R, S1, T1) 这种工艺生产模式有利于中东城市中自治的、意识上平等的工艺品行会的发展。

ill-equipped[1] [ˌɪlɪ'kwɪpt]

【释义】*a.* 装备不良的

【例句】Consumer protection groups and parents believe that children are largely ill-equipped to recognize such techniques and that often exaggeration is used at the expense of product information. (TPO14, R, S1, T1) 消费者保护团体和父母认为，大部门孩子都无法识别这些伎俩，而且这种夸张通常都是以产品信息为代价来使用的。

imagery[1] ['ɪmɪdʒərɪ]

【释义】*n.* 1. 影像，意象 2. 比喻，象征

【例句】In the very broadest sense, we said it's written to evoke, to make you, the audience, have some kind of the emotional experience through the use of imagery, en, some kinds of predictable rhythm. (TPO13, L, S2, L1) 在最宽泛的意义上，它是用来唤起，让你们听众通过使用意象、通过某种可预知的节律而产生某种情感上的经历。

immersion[1] [ɪ'mɜːʃən]

【释义】*n.* 沉浸，浸入

【例句】Remarkably resistant to the vicissitudes of ocean travel, they can survive prolonged immersion in saltwater when they come to rest on warm beaches and the conditions are favorable, the seed coats soften. (TPO9, R, S2, T2) 它们对洋流变动有着极强的抵抗力，因此可以在长时间的海水浸泡中存活下来。当它们停歇在温暖的海滩上且条件适宜时，种子的外皮就会变软。

【逆构】immerse *v.* 浸，浸没

【搭配】immersion in study 埋头研究

immune[1] [ɪ'mjuːn]

【释义】*a.* 免疫的，有免疫力的；不受影响的

【例句】In vertebrates, the immune system provides a multiple defense against internal parasites. (TPO17, R, S2, T2) 而对于脊椎动物来说，其身体的免疫系统可以对体内的寄生物进行多层防御。

【派生】immunity *n.* 免疫，免疫性

【搭配】immune system 免疫系统

impending[1] [ɪm'pendɪŋ]

【释义】*a.* 即将发生的，迫在眉睫的（imminent, impendent）

【例句】This accords with anecdotal evidence that people often yawn in situations where they are neither tired nor bored, but are preparing for impending mental and physical activity. (TPO18, R, S2, T1) 有轶事证据表明通常人们打呵欠的时候既不是因为疲倦，也不是因为无聊，而是在为即将进行的精神和身体活动做准备。这与该说法是一致的。

【逆构】impend *v.* 悬挂，逼近

【搭配】impending death 濒死，垂死

Word List 44

imperative[1] [ɪm'perətɪv] 

【释义】*n.* 命令；需要，必要的事（command, order） *a.* 必要的；强制的（necessary, essential）

【例句】Certainly, in trying to explain the Roman phenomenon, one would have to place great emphasis on this almost animal instinct for the territorial imperative. (TPO7, R, S2, T1) 毫无疑问，当人们想说明罗马现象时，就必须关注其接近于动物本能式的领土原则。

impermeable[1] [ɪm'pɜːmjəbl] 

【释义】*a.* 不可渗透的，透不过的

【例句】Beneath this active layer is the second layer called "permafrost", which is frozen all year around, and is impermeable to water. (TPO9, L, S1, L2) 在这个活跃层的下面是被称作"永久冻土"的第二层，此层终年冻结，且不透水。

impersonation[1] [im,pəːsə'neiʃən] 

【释义】*n.* 扮演，模仿，装扮

【例句】Thus, the recalling of an event is elaborated through the narrator's pantomime and impersonation. (TPO1, R, S2, T1) 这样，对于某一件事情的回忆会通过讲述者的哑剧表演或是模仿而得以详细化。

【逆构】impersonate *v.* 模仿，扮演

implausible[1] [im'plɔːzəbl] 

【释义】*a.* 难以置信的，似乎不合情理的（questionable, unbelievable）

【例句】Animals had migrated from the inland to the coasts, an indication that a midcontinental ice-free corridor was actually implausible. (TPO9, R, S1, T1) 动物从内陆迁移到沿海，表明半大陆无冰走廊的存在是不合情理的。

【派生】implausibility *n.* 难以置信

【搭配】an implausible explanation 令人难以相信的解释

imprisonment[1] [ɪm'prɪzənmənt] 

【释义】*n.* 监禁，下狱

【例句】And the opera was no longer about teaching religion as it was about satire and about expressing the ideas of society and your government without committing yourself to writing and risking imprisonment or persecution. (TPO12, L, S2, L1) 而且歌剧不再与教授宗教教义有关，而是与讽刺有关，与表达对社会对政府的看法有关，这样一来就可以使你免于写作和冒被囚禁或是被迫害的风险了。

【同义】internment

【逆构】imprison *v.* 监禁，关押

impurity[1] [ɪm'pjʊərɪtɪ] 

【释义】*n.* 1. 杂质 2. 不纯，肮脏

【例句】The purpose of heating an element in a spectroscopic flame testis to remove impurities from the element. (TPO3, L, S2, L2, Q15) 在光谱火焰测试中，加热一种元素的目的是去除元素中的杂质。

【反义】purity

【搭配】impurity in ideology 思想不纯

inadequacy[1] [ɪn'ædɪkwəsɪ] 

【释义】*n.* 1. 不充分，不足，缺陷 2. 不胜任，缺乏信心

【例句】These critics were making a common assumption that the technological inadequacies of earlier efforts (poor synchronization, weak sound amplification, fragile sound recordings) would invariably occur again. (TPO12, R, S2, T1) 这些评论家门做了一个共同的假设，即，先前的努力中存在的技术上的不足（同步性差、扩音微弱、录音差）将一定会再次出现。

【逆构】inadequate *a.* 不足的，不适当的

incense[1] [ɪn'sens] 

【释义】*n.* 香 *v.* 使发怒，激怒（enrage, anger）

【例句】They were used as medicines to ward off diseases, and mixed into perfumes, incenses. (TPO18, L, S2, L1) 它们被用作医药来抵抗疾病，也会被加入香水或香中。

返记菜单

imperative[1] impermeable[1] impersonation[1] implausible[1] imprisonment[1]
impurity[1] inadequacy[1] incense[1]

【派生】incensation *n.* 熏香，焚香

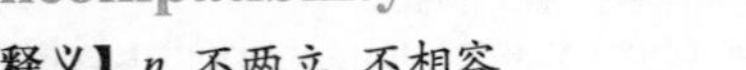

incompatibility[1] [ˈɪnkəmˌpætəˈbɪlɪtɪ]

【释义】*n.* 不两立，不相容

【例句】A third likely explanation for infantile amnesia involves incompatibilities between the ways in which infants encode information and the ways in which older children and adults retrieve it. (TPO6, R, S2, T2) 对于婴幼儿期记忆缺失的第三种可能的解释是婴幼儿记忆信息的方式与年龄大些的儿童及成人不一致。

【逆构】incompatible *a.* 合不来的，不能和谐相处的

【搭配】incompatibility of temperament 性格不合

incongruous[1] [ɪnˈkɒŋgrʊəs]

【释义】*a.* 不协调的，不一致的（incompatible, discordant）

【例句】Such yawning is often referred to as "incongruous" because it seems out of place, at least on the tiredness view: soldiers yawning before combat, musicians yawning before performing, and athletes yawning before competing. (TPO18, R, S2, T1) 这种打呵欠的行为通常被称为是"不合适"的，因为这看起来很不得体，至少从疲倦论的观点来看是这样的：士兵在战斗前打呵欠，音乐家在表演前打呵欠，运动员在竞赛前打呵欠。

inconsistent[1] [ˌɪnkənˈsɪstənt]

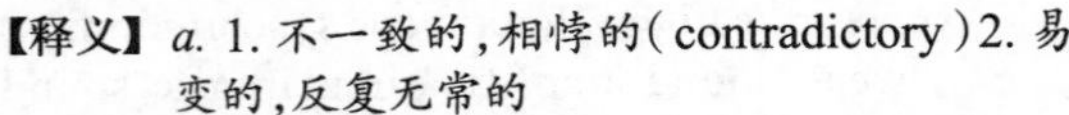

【释义】*a.* 1. 不一致的，相悖的（contradictory）2. 易变的，反复无常的

【例句】First, there is something inconsistent about the way the woman in the portrait is dressed. (TPO3, W, Q1) 首先，画像中女人的穿着方式本身就有着矛盾之处。

【反义】consistent

【派生】inconsistently *ad.* 不一致地

【搭配】be inconsistent with the facts 与事实不符

indistinct[1] [ˌɪndɪsˈtɪŋkt]

【释义】*a.* 不清楚的，模糊的（obscure, blurred, illegible）

【例句】A color or pattern that is relatively indistinct in one kind of light may be quite conspicuous in another. (TPO17, R, S2, T1) 在某一种光照下相对较难辨认的颜色或式样在另外一种光照下也许会变得相当显眼。

【反义】definite, distinct

【搭配】an indistinct image 模糊的影像

indistinguishable[1] [ˌɪndɪsˈtɪŋgwɪʃəbl]

【释义】*a.* 不能区别的，无法辨别的

【例句】Stone meteoroids, if they lie around exposed to the weather for a few years, well, they're made of rock, so they end up looking almost indistinguishable from common terrestrial rocks—once that originated on earth. (TPO13, L, S2, L2) 如果把石质流星体暴露于恶劣天气下，经过几年的时间，嗯，它们是由岩石组成的，因此最后看起来与那些源自地球的普通的地球岩石也几乎没什么区别了。

【搭配】indistinguishable speech 难以理解的谈话

inedible[1] [ɪnˈedɪbl]

【释义】*a.* 不适于食用的，不能吃的（uneatable, unedible）

【例句】So it's no wonder that people once considered potatoes and tomatoes to be inedible too, even poisonous. (TPO10, L, S1, L2) 难怪人们曾经认为马铃薯和西红柿不能吃，甚至是有毒的。

【反义】edible

infestation[1] [ɪnfesˈteɪʃən]

【释义】*n.* 感染；侵扰

【例句】So by removing rotting wood, salvage logging helps minimize the dangers of insect infestation, thus contributing to the health of the forest. (TPO14, W, Q1) 所以通过移除腐烂的树木，抢救性砍伐可以把森林遭受虫害的危险降到最低，因而有利于森林的健康生长。

【逆构】infest *v.* 侵扰，猖獗

infrared[1] [ˈɪnfrəˈred]

【释义】*a.*〈物〉红外线的

【例句】Well, we put an infrared microscope—a spectroscope—on tiny bits of paint. (TPO5, L, S2, L1) 我们把一些颜料的微粒放在一台

红外显微镜——一台分光镜下。

【搭配】infrared ray 红外线

infrasound[1] ['infrəsaund]

【释义】*n.* 次声(风暴产生的低频音波)

【例句】So, that is how elephant uses infrasound. (TPO7, L, S1, L2) 那么,那就是大象是如何使用次声的。

【搭配】infrasound monitoring 次生监控

infusion[1] [ɪn'fjuːʒən]

【释义】*n.* 1. 注入,灌输(pouring) 2. 草药泡剂

【例句】The rapid expansion in international trade also benefitted from an infusion of capital, stemming largely from gold and silver brought by Spanish vessels from the Americas. (TPO10, R, S2, T2) 由西班牙商船从美国带来的大量金银成为了促进国际贸易快速发展的资本注入。

【搭配】capital infusion 资本输入,扩充资本

ingenious[1] [ɪn'dʒiːnjəs]

【释义】*a.* 有独创性的(inventive, creative)

【例句】Unlike in the Americas, where metallurgy was a very late and limited development, Africans had iron from a relatively early date, developing ingenious furnaces to produce the high heat needed for production and to control the amount of air that reached the carbon and iron ore necessary for making iron. (TPO7, R, S2, T2) 美洲的冶金业起步晚,发展也极为缓慢,而与此不同的是,非洲在相对很早的时候就出现了铁,并发明了精妙的熔炉,来提供冶铁所需要的热量,并对冶铁过程中作用于碳和铁矿的空气量进行控制。

【派生】ingenuity *n.* 独创性,巧妙

【搭配】an ingenious device 精巧的装置

inherit[1] [ɪn'herɪt]

【释义】*v.* 继承,遗传而得(receive)

【例句】Her musical talents were inherited from her parents. (TPO16, L, S1, L2) 她的音乐才华从父母遗传而来。

【派生】inheritance *n.* 遗传,遗产

inheritor *n.* 继承人,后继者

inject[1] [ɪn'dʒekt]

【释义】*v.*(给…)注射(液体)(infuse)

【例句】Somewhat more promising have been recent experiments for releasing capillary water (water in the soil) above the water table by injecting compressed air into the ground. (TPO3, R, S1, T1) 最近一些更有希望获得成功的实验试图通过向土壤中注入压缩空气来释放地下水位线以上的毛管水(土壤中的水)。

【派生】injection *n.* 注射; 投入

innate[1] ['ɪneɪt]

【释义】*a.* 天生的,与生俱来的; 固有的(inborn, congenital)

【例句】Birds' innate bearings keep them oriented in a direction that is within 15 degrees of the Suns direction. (TPO11, R, S2, T1) 鸟类天生的方向感使它们能保持在朝着太阳方位15度以内的方向飞行。

【搭配】innate immunity 先天免疫; 自然免疫

innate ability 天赋才能

inorganic[1] [ˌɪnɔː'gænɪk]

【释义】*a.* 无机的,非自然生长的

【例句】We've been talking till now about the two basic needs of a biological community—an energy source to produce organic materials and the waste recycling or breakdown of materials back into inorganic molecules. (TPO15, L, S2, L2) 到现今为止,我们一直在讨论一个生物群体的两个基本需求——提供有机物的能量来源和对有机物的废物循环或将有机物分解成无机分子的系统。

【逆构】organic *a.* 有机的

insecure[1] [ˌɪnsɪ'kjʊə]

【释义】*a.* 不安全的,不稳定的,不牢靠的(unstable, unsafe)

【例句】Peripheral peoples therefore had a great advantage in their dealings with the center, making government authority insecure and anxious. (TPO16, R, S1, T1) 因此,周边地区

返记菜单

infrasound[1] infusion[1] ingenious[1] inherit[1] inject[1]
innate[1] inorganic[1] insecure[1]

的人们在和中心地区的人们交易时很有优势，这让政府机构感到焦虑不安。

insert[1] [ɪn'sɜːt]

【释义】 *v.* 插入，放入（inject, input）*n.* 插入物；插页广告

【例句】 You would insert it into the machine and you read it into the copies. (TPO7, L, S2, C1) 你要把它插入并把数据读到复印机里。

【派生】 insertion *n.* 插入；插入物

【搭配】 insert a key into a lock 把钥匙插进锁中

insure[1] [ɪn'ʃʊə]

【释义】 *v.* 1. 给…保险，为…投保 2. 保证，确保（assure, guarantee, ensure）

【例句】 Second, conservation has been insured by limiting times for and types of hunting. (TPO4, R, S1, T1) 其次，确立了对狩猎限时、限种类的保护措施。

【派生】 insurer *n.* 保险公司，保险人
insurance *n.* 保险，保险费
insured *a.* 被保险的

intake[1] ['ɪnteɪk]

【释义】 *n.* 1.（食物、饮料等的）摄取量，吸入量 2.（一定时期内）纳入的人数 3.（液体等的）进入口

【例句】 It had a negative effect on the nutritional intake of people living near the Mediterranean Sea. (TPO10, L, S1, L2) 它对住在地中海附近的人的营养摄入有消极的影响。

【搭配】 water intake 进水口

intellect[1] ['ɪntɪlekt]

【释义】 *n.* 1. 思维能力，智力 2. 知识分子

【例句】 In order for art to communicate, to appeal to the emotions or the intellect, it has to combine various visual elements to express meaning or emotion. (TPO4, S, Q6) 为了使艺术能够传达信息、感染情绪或思维，必须要将各种不同的视觉元素结合起来表达其意义或情感。

【派生】 intellectual *a.* 智力的

interbedded[1] [ˌintə'bedid]

【释义】 *a.* 互层的（层间的，镶嵌的，混合的）

【例句】 Interbedded with the salt were thin layers of what appeared to be windblown silt. (TPO7, R, S1, T1) 与这些结晶盐相互嵌在一起的薄层像是被风吹起的泥沙层。

【搭配】 interbedded clay 粘土夹层

interchangeable[1] [ɪntə'tʃeɪndʒəb(ə)l]

【释义】 *a.* 可互换的

【例句】 They are similar enough to be interchangeable. (TPO12, S, Q6) 它们非常相似，可以互换。

【逆构】 changeable *a.* 可替换的

interdependent[1] [ˌɪntə(ː)dɪ'pendənt]

【释义】 *a.* 相互依赖的

【例句】 The species in the system err…and even the landscape itself, they are interdependent. (TPO13, L, S1, L2) 生态系统中的物种之间、甚至和陆地本身，都是相互依赖的。

【派生】 interdependence *n.* 相互依赖

interdisciplinary[1] [ˌɪntə(ː)'dɪsɪplɪnərɪ]

【释义】 *a.* 各学科间的，跨学科的

【例句】 It seems that Mr. Grable has mastered the interdisciplinary approach to teaching—the way we've been talking about in class. (TPO1, L, S2, C1) 看样子Grable先生已经掌握了教学中的一些跨学科的方法——就是我们在课上一直讨论的那种方法。

interrelationship[1] [ˌintəri'leiʃənʃip]

【释义】 *n.* 相互关系

【例句】 The main thing to keep in mind here is the interrelationships. (TPO13, L, S1, L2) 需要记住的主要事情就是相互关系。

【搭配】 interrelationship study 相互关系研究

intestine[1] [ɪn'testɪn]

【释义】 *n.* 肠

【例句】 An example of a parasite is a tapeworm that

lives inside the intestines of a larger animal and absorbs nutrients from its host. (TPO17, R, S2, T2) 一种典型的寄生物是绦虫，它生存在较大型动物的肠道中，并吸收寄主体内的营养。

【派生】 intestinal *a.* 肠的

【搭配】 small intestine 小肠

intimate[1] ['ɪntɪmɪt] 

【释义】 *a.* 1. 亲密的（close, familiar）2. 知识渊博的（deep, profound）

【例句】 A primary group involves two or more people who enjoy a direct, intimate, cohesive relationship with one another. (TPO13, R, S1, T1) 主要群体是由两个或两个以上的人组成的，他们彼此之间有着直接、亲密、有凝聚性的关系。

【搭配】 an intimate friendship 亲密的友情

intricate[1] ['ɪntrɪkɪt] 

【释义】 *a.* 复杂的，错综的，缠结的（complex, complicated, entangled）

【例句】 It let him make these really intricate flowery designs for stained glass, which are used in lamp shades. (TPO16, L, S2, L2) 这让他为彩色玻璃设计了这些着实复杂的花朵图案，用来做灯罩。

【反义】 simple

inundate[1] ['ɪnəndeɪt] 

【释义】 *v.* 浸水，淹没（flood, overflow）

【例句】 So they had a 354-day agricultural calendar that was designed to help them determine when the Nile would inundate the land. (TPO17, L, S2, L1) 所以他们设计了一套354天的农用历法来帮助他们确定尼罗河何时会淹没土地。

【派生】 inundated *a.* 洪泛的
inundation *n.* 泛滥

invalidate[1] [ɪn'vælɪdeɪt] 

【释义】 *v.* 1. 使无效，使作废 2. 证明…错误，使站不住脚

【例句】 That expectation causes the researcher to act in ways that influence the behavior of the experiment participants, hereby invalidating the results of the experiment. (TPO15, S, Q4) 那一预期使得研究者的做法影响到了实验参与者的行为，从而导致实验结果无效。

involuntary[1] [ɪn'vɒləntərɪ] 

【释义】 *a.* 无意识的，不知不觉的（automatic, unintentional）

【例句】 Now the other type of attention is passive attention when it's involuntary. (TPO6, L, S, Q6) 当处于无意识时，另一种形式的注意力叫做被动注意。

【反义】 voluntary, conscious

【派生】 involuntarily *ad.* 非自愿地，非出于本意地

【搭配】 an involuntary injury 无意的伤害

iodine[1] ['aɪədiːn] 

【释义】 *n.* 碘，碘酒

【例句】 For example, tellurium comes before iodine in the periodic table, even though its atomic mass is slightly greater. (TPO16, R, S2, T1) 例如，在元素周期表中，碲排在碘前面，尽管其原子质量略大。

【搭配】 iodine solution 碘溶液

irresistible[1] [ˌɪrɪ'zɪstəbl] 

【释义】 *a.* 1. 无法抗拒的，无法抵抗的（overwhelming）2. 诱人的（temping, charming）

【例句】 Widely reported, if somewhat distrusted, accounts by figures like the famous traveler from Venice. Marco Polo, of the willingness of people in China to trade with Europeans and of the immensity of the wealth to be gained by such contact made the idea irresistible. (TPO17, R, S1, T1) 如果大量的报告还有那么一点不可信的话，那么威尼斯著名的旅行家马可波罗的描述则会使这种想法变得无法抗拒，马可波罗描述了中国人希望和欧洲人通商的意愿，并且通过这样的交易，获得了取之不尽的财富。

【派生】 irresistiblity *n.* 不能抵抗

irreversible[1] [ˌɪrɪ'vɜːsɪbəl] 

【释义】 *a.* 不可逆转的，不可挽回的（unchangeable）

【例句】 The collision between Earth and a large

返记菜单

intimate[1] intricate[1] inundate[1] invalidate[1] involuntary[1]
iodine[1] irresistible[1] irreversible[1]

asteroid resulted in massive damage and generated enough heat to cause irreversible changes in Earth's atmosphere. (TPO15, R, S2, T2) 地球和一颗大行星之间的撞击导致了巨大的破坏并且产生了大量的热，从而对地球的大气产生了无法逆转的影响。

【反义】reversible

jade[1] [dʒeɪd]

【释义】*n.* 玉，翡翠；浅绿(色)

【例句】Ancient demands for obsidian (a black volcanic rock useful for making mirrors and tools) led to trade with Armenia to the north, while jade for cutting tools was brought from Turkistan, and the precious stone lapis lazuli was imported from Afghanistan. (TPO16, R, S1, T1) 古代对黑曜石的需求(一种黑色的火山岩，用来做镜子和工具)促成了与北方的亚美尼亚的贸易往来，而用于切削工具的玉是从突厥斯坦引进的，珍贵的宝石青金石是从阿富汗进口的。

【派生】jaded *a.* (因经历过多而)厌倦的

jawbone[1] [dʒɔːˈbəʊn]

【释义】*n.* 颚骨，下颌骨

【例句】The skull is cetacean-like but its jawbones lack the enlarged space that is filled with fat or oil and used for receiving underwater sound in modern whales. (TPO2, R, S2, T1) 这个头盖骨和鲸类动物的很像，但它的下颌骨和现代鲸类略有不同，现代鲸类动物的下颌骨中含有额外的空间储存脂肪或油脂，并用来接收水下的声音。

jeopardize[1] [ˈdʒepədaɪz]

【释义】*v.* 危及，使处于危险境地(endanger, hazard)

【例句】He thought that disagreeing with them might jeopardize his chances of getting a promotion by not looking like a team player. (TPO1, S, Q4) 他认为，不同意他们的意见可能会因为看起来不像是个团队合作者而毁了他的晋升机会。

【派生】jeopardy *n.* 处于危险中

jot[1] [dʒɒt]

【释义】*v.* 草草记下，匆匆记下

【例句】I carry a little pad with me all the time and jot down questions or ideas that I don't want to forget. (TPO2, L, S1, C1) 我一直都会随身带一个小记事本，记下不想忘记的问题或想法。

【搭配】jot down 草草记下
not a jot 一点也不

jut[1] [dʒʌt]

【释义】*v.* 突出，伸出，凸出

【例句】Moreover, just look at the sculpture: several 60-foot long steel plates, jutting out of the earth at odd angles! (TPO1, S, Q3) 而且，就看看雕塑本身吧：有好几块60英尺的钢板，以奇怪的角度突兀出地面！

kindergarten[1] [ˈkɪndəˌɡɑːtn]

【释义】*n.* 幼儿园

【例句】About the closest any research has come to supporting the tiredness theory is to confirm that adults yawn more often on weekdays than at weekends, and that school children yawn more frequently in their first year at primary school than they do in kindergarten. (TPO18, R, S2, T1) 支持疲倦论的最有说服力的研究是证实了成年人在工作日比周末打呵欠多，孩子们在小学一年级比在幼儿园时打呵欠多。

kinship[1] [ˈkɪnʃɪp]

【释义】*n.* 亲属关系，血缘关系

【例句】They lived in the same neighborhoods, and often had assumed (or real) kinship relationships. (TPO16, R, S1, T1) 他们住在同一个街区，通常有假设(或真正)的亲属关系。

【搭配】Uterine kinship 母系社会
maternal kinship 外亲

Word List 45

knack[1] [næk]

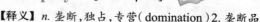

【释义】*n.* 技能，本领(talent, skill, aptitude)

【例句】From his first shows, Loutherbourg showed a knack for imagination and stage design, all in the interest of creating illusions that allowed the audience to suspend disbelief completely. (TPO 9, L, S1, L1) 通过他的第一场表演，鲁斯伯格显示出了他的想象力和舞台设计的卓越才华，意在使创造出来的幻觉足以使人们相信那些本不可信的东西。

【搭配】have a knack of doing sth. 有…的本领

lace[1] [leɪs]

【释义】*n.* 1. 鞋带，系带 2. 花边 *v.* 用带子束紧

【例句】In one study, college students were asked to each put on a pair of shoes—shoes with laces they would have to tie. (TPO2, S, Q4) 在一次实验中，所有的大学生被要求做穿鞋的动作——而且需要系鞋带。

【派生】lacy *a.* (有)花边的

shoelace *n.* 鞋带

【搭配】lace up 用带子束紧

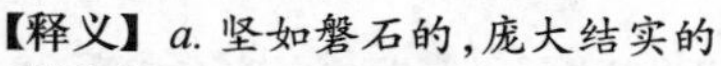

monolithic[1] [ˌmɒnəˈlɪθɪk]

【释义】*a.* 坚如磐石的，庞大结实的

【例句】Like the stones of a Roman wall which were held together both by the regularity of the design and by that peculiarly powerful Roman cement, so the various parts of the Roman realm were bonded into a massive, monolithic entity by physical, organizational, and psychological controls. (TPO7, R, S2, T1) 如同罗马墙是通过规律的设计和独特有效的罗马水泥构筑而成一样，罗马王国的各个部分也是通过对物质、组织和心理层面的支配而联结成一个规模宏大、坚如磐石的统一体的。

【搭配】a monolithic worldwide movement 世界范围内的统一运动

monopoly[1] [məˈnɒpəlɪ]

【释义】*n.* 垄断，独占，专营(domination) 2. 垄断品

【例句】By 1800 more than a thousand steam engines were in use in the British Isles, and Britain retained a virtual monopoly on steam engine production until the 1830s. (TPO6, R, S1, T1) 到19世纪时，在不列颠群岛，使用中的蒸汽机有1000多台，而一直到19世纪30年代以前，英国在蒸汽机的生产方面一直都处于实质性的垄断地位。

【派生】monopolize *v.* 独占，垄断

【搭配】monopoly capital 垄断资本

mortgage[1] [ˈmɔːgɪdʒ]

【释义】*v.* 抵押 *n.* 抵押借款

【例句】And people were borrowing, mortgaging their homes in many cases to obtain those bits of paper because they were sure they'd find an easy way to make money. (TPO6, L, S1, L1) 并且人们在很多情况下通过借款、抵押房屋的方式去获得那些小支票，因为他们确信这些支票是他们很快赚钱的一个手段。

【搭配】redeem a mortgage 赎回抵押品

be mortgaged to the hilt 把全部家当抵押出去

laissez-faire[1] [ˌleseɪˈfeə]

【释义】*n.* 自由放任政策 *a.* 自由放任的

【例句】Production flourished in this laissez-faire environment. (TPO16, R, S1, T1) 在宽松自由的环境中生产量激增。

landslide[1] [ˈlændslaɪd]

【释义】*n.* 1. 山崩，滑坡(landslip, mudslide) 2. (选举)压倒性胜利

【例句】Pipelines carrying oil can be broken by faults or landslides, causing serious oil spills. (TPO4, R, S2, T2) 输油管道可能会因断层或滑坡受损，从而引发严重的漏油事件。

larynx[1] [ˈlærɪŋks]

【释义】*n.* 喉，喉头

【例句】Watson thought laryngeal habits…you know,

返记菜单

knack[1] lace[1] monolithic[1] monopoly[1] mortgage[1]
laissez-faire[1] landslide[1] larynx[1]

from larynx, in other words, related to the voice box. (TPO2, L, S1, L1) 换句话说, Waston 认为喉部习惯与喉有关。

lateen[1] [læ'tiːn]

【释义】*a.*(有)大三角帆的

【例句】In the largest caravels, two main masts held large square sails that provided the bulk of the thrust driving the ship forward, while a smaller forward mast held a triangular-shaped sail, called a lateen sail, which could be moved into a variety of positions to maneuver the ship. (TPO17, R, S1, T1) 在最大型的轻快帆船上,有两根主桅杆撑起大块的船帆,以便提供推动帆船前进的足够推力,同时有一个小型的前桅杆来撑起一块三角形船帆,这个船帆叫做三角帆,它是用来在移动中控制帆船行驶的方向的。

launch[1] [lɔːntʃ]

【释义】*v.* 1. 发起,发动(尤指有组织的活动) 2. 发射 *n.* 1. 发射;(船)下水;(新产品)投产 2. 汽艇,游艇

【例句】Furthermore, he noticed that as they fluttered around in the cage, they often launched themselves in the direction of their normal migratory route. (TPO11, R, S2, T1) 此外,他注意到,每当它们在笼子里扇动翅膀时,它们总是让自己朝向其平常迁徙的路线。

【派生】launcher *n.* 发射装置,发射器

【搭配】launch on 开始,着手
launch into 进入,投入;突然开始
launch out 出航;开始新的事情(尤指有风险的事)

leap[1] [liːp]

【释义】*v./n.* 跳跃(jump, hop)

【例句】Fish leaping from waves indicated success in the civil service examinations. (TPO10, R, S1, T1) 鱼跳出水面意味着在科举上会高中状元。

【搭配】leap year 闰年

leftover[1] ['left,əuvə]

【释义】*n.* 1. 剩饭 2. 残留物 *a.* 剩余的,未用完的

【例句】The pots in the pile could be regular trash too, leftover from the meals of the construction workers. (TPO5, W, Q1) 土堆里的罐子可能也就是些普通的垃圾,是建筑工人用餐之后留下的。

legend[1] ['ledʒənd]

【释义】*n.* 1. 传说,传奇故事 2. 传奇人物

【例句】Add to that, spices themselves had always been considered special or magical not just for eating and this was already true in the ancient world where legends about spices were abundant. (TPO18, L, S2, L1) 香料本身已被认为是独特而神奇的,而不仅仅是只能食用,这在关于香料的传说盛行的古代社会已是一个事实。

【派生】legendary *a.* 传奇的

legion[1] ['liːdʒən]

【释义】*n.* 古罗马军团

【例句】The key to the Greek world lay in its high-powered ships; the key to Roman power lay in its marching legions. (TPO7, R, S2, T1) 希腊的成功在于其强大的海军;罗马的成功在于其强大的陆军。

【搭配】Caesar's legions 凯撒军团

legislation[1] [ˌledʒɪs'leɪʃən]

【释义】*n.* 1. 法律,法规(laws, statutes) 2. 立法(lawmaking)

【例句】The author's primary purpose is to explain how technology and legislation help reduce oil spills. (TPO4, R, S2, T2) 作者的主要目的是解释技术和立法是如何减少漏油的。

【派生】legislature *n.* 立法机关

【逆构】legislate *v.* 制定法律,立法

【搭配】labour legislation 劳工法,劳动法规

legume[1] ['legjuːm]

【释义】*n.* 豆类,豆荚

【例句】Many members of the mustard family, spurge family, legume family and grass family are top hyperaccumulators. (TPO5, R, S1, T1) 很多十字花科、牧草科、豆科和禾本科植物都是顶级的重金属超富集植物。

lessen[1] ['lesn]

【释义】v.(使)减少,(使)减轻

【例句】As the air space around them is lessened by compaction and melting, the grains become denser. (TPO15, R, S1, T1) 由于压缩和融化,这些颗粒周围的空间变少,颗粒随之变得更加稠密。

【反义】increase, raise

【派生】lessened a. 减少的

liberate[1] ['lɪbəreɪt]

【释义】v. 解放,使摆脱束缚,使自由(free, release)

【例句】It liberated industry from dependence on running water. (TPO6, R, S1, T1) 它解放了依赖流水的工业。

【反义】restrict

【派生】liberation n. 解放
liberator n. 解放者

【搭配】liberate sb. from sth. 把某人从某事中解放出来

liberty[1] ['lɪbətɪ]

【释义】n. 自由,自由权,特权

【例句】Well, I think we'd all rather focus on cases that deal with personal liberties, questions about freedom of speech, things like that. (TPO4, L, S2, C1) 我觉得大家都更愿关注诸如个人自由的案例、演讲自由权的问题,一些诸如此类的问题。

【派生】liberation n. 解放,释放
liberal a. 自由主义的

【搭配】at liberty 自由,随意
take the liberty 冒昧,擅自
set someone at liberty 解放(或释放)某人

likelihood[1] ['laɪklɪhʊd]

【释义】n. 可能性(possibility)

【例句】A number of conditions enhance the likelihood that primary groups will arise. (TPO13, R, S1, T1) 众多条件提高了主要群体增加的可能性。

【搭配】in all likelihood 极有可能地

limelight[1] ['laɪm,laɪt]

【释义】n. 众人注意的中心

【例句】A male bird of paradise may put himself in the limelight by displaying his spectacular plumage in the best stage setting to attract a female. (TPO17, R, S2, T1) 雄性极乐鸟会让自己置身于聚光灯下,在最佳的舞台背景下展现自己缤纷绚烂的羽翼,以吸引雌鸟的注意。

【搭配】be fond of the limelight 爱出风头

line-up[1] ['laɪnʌp]

【释义】n. 全体参与人员〔尤指演员〕

【例句】Tonight's line-up includes Suzanne Vega. 今晚的演出阵容中有苏珊妮·维加。

liver[1] ['lɪvə]

【释义】n. 1. 肝脏 2. (供食用的)肝

【例句】That first of all starts drawing water away from the center of its body, so the middle part of the frog, its internal organs, its heart, lungs, liver, these start getting drier and drier while the water that's being pulled away is forming a puddle around the organs just underneath the skin. (TPO18, L, S2, L2) 首先把水从身体中抽出,这样当抽出的水在皮肤下面的器官周围形成一个小水坑时,林蛙的中心内脏部位,包括心脏、肺、肝脏,就会变得越来越干。

【搭配】liver cancer 肝癌

locale[1] [ləʊ'kɑːl]

【释义】n. 事件发生的现场,地点

【例句】A slightly younger fossil formation containing animal remains is the Tommotian formation, named after a locale in Russia. (TPO5, R, S2, T2) 另一个稍微年轻的含有动物遗骸的化石构造是托莫特构造,它是以俄罗斯境内的一处地点命名的。

locomotion[1] [ləʊkə'məʊʃ(ə)n]

【释义】n. 行动(力),运动(力)(motion, movement)

【例句】The whale retained a tail and lacked a fluke,

返记菜单

lessen[1]	liberate[1]	liberty[1]	likelihood[1]	limelight[1]
line-up[1]	liver[1]	locale[1]	locomotion[1]	

the major means of locomotion in modern cetaceans. (TPO2, R, S2, T1) 这只鲸仍有尾巴，但是缺少现代水生鲸类动物用于行动的主要身体部位——尾片。

【派生】locomotive *a.* 移动的，机车的 *n.* 火车头

loggerhead[1] ['lɔgəhed]

【释义】*n.* 红海龟

【例句】Large loggerhead and green turtles can maintain their body temperature at a degree or two above that of the surrounding water. (TPO15, R, S2, T1) 大型的红海龟和绿海龟可以将自己的体温保持在高于周围水温的一两度以上。

loner[1] ['ləʊnə (r)]

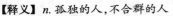

【释义】*n.* 孤独的人，不合群的人

【例句】Well, they are really territorial, and loners, and just so aggressive even with other Eastern marmots. (TPO1, L, S2, L2) 它们都相当具有领地意识，而且独来独往，所以即使是对其它的东部旱獭也极具攻击性。

【派生】lonely *a.* 孤独的，寂寞的

longitude[1] ['lɒndʒɪtju:d]

【释义】*n.* 经度，经线

【例句】It operated by measuring the height of the Sun and the fixed stars: by calculating the angles created by these points, it determined the degree of latitude at which one stood (The problem of determining longitude, though, was not solved until the eighteenth century.) (TPO17, R, S1, T1) 它通过测量太阳和固定星星的高度来运作，并且通过计算这些点所呈现的夹角来确定一个人所处的纬度（而测量经度的难题直到 18 世纪才得以解决）。

【反义】latitude

loosen[1] ['lu:sn]

【释义】*v.* 解开，松开，放松

【例句】You need to take some exercises to loosen up your muscles. 你需要活动一下以放松肌肉。

【反义】tighten

【逆构】loose *a.* 宽松的，松散的

【搭配】loosen the soil 疏松土壤

lopsided[1] ['lɒp'saɪdɪd]

【释义】*a.* 1. 不对称的，倾向一方的 2. 不平衡的（imbalanced）

【例句】Maybe a particular sunspot was sort of square, then later it would become more lopsided, then later something else. (TPO18, L, S1, L1) 也许有个别独特的太阳黑子有点像正方形的，然后变得更加不对称，再变成别的什么样子。

【派生】lopsidedness *n.* 不匀称；不平衡

lubricant[1] ['lu:brɪkənt]

【释义】*n.* 润滑剂

【例句】This layer of water reduces friction is...is like a lubricant. (TPO7, L, S2, L2) 这层水层就像润滑剂一样，减少了摩擦。

lucent[1] ['lju:snt]

【释义】*a.* 发光的，透明的，清澈的

【例句】And that's followed by the final dramatic element—the denouement or the resolution, when all the lucent have to be tied up in the logical way. (TPO7, L, S1, L1) 这之后就是最终的戏剧元素——结局或解释，此时所有清楚明白的情节都要以一种符合逻辑的方式串联起来。

lug[1] [lʌg]

【释义】*v.* 用力拖（drag, haul）*n.* 手柄，把柄

【例句】And lugging a big piece of wood 40 or 50 yards is hard work, takes a lot of energy. (TPO16, L, S2, L1) 拖着一块木头行进 40 或 50 码是一项艰难的工作，需要耗费大量能量。

luxurious[1] [lʌg'zjʊərɪəs]

【释义】*a.* 奢侈的，豪华的（sumptuous, lavish）

【例句】She is wearing a white linen cap of a kind that only servants would wear—yet the coat she is wearing has a luxurious fur collar that no servant could afford. (TPO3, W, Q1) 她戴着一顶白色亚麻布的帽子，这种帽子只有

仆人才会戴,但她穿的上衣却有着华丽的毛领,而这是任何一个仆人都买不起的。

【反义】 economical, modest

【逆构】 luxury *n.* 豪华,奢侈

【搭配】 luxurious tastes 奢侈的爱好

makeover[1] ['mekovɚ] 

【释义】 *n.* 外表的大变化,彻底改变

【例句】 So one day, a coworker and I suggested we should give our computers a design makeover, make them look more up to date. (TPO1, S, Q4) 所以有一天,我和同事建议,我们应该给我们的电脑做一个设计上的大转变,使它们看上去更加新潮。

makeshift[1] ['meɪkʃɪft] 

【释义】 *a.* 临时代用的,权宜之计的(expedient, make-do)*n.* 临时代用品,权宜之计(substitute, shift)

【例句】 These early projection devices were used in vaudeville theaters, legitimate theaters, local town halls, makeshift storefront theaters, fairgrounds, and amusement parks to show films to a mass audience. (TPO2, R, S2, T2) 这些早期的投影机可以在众多场合为广大观众播放电影,如:杂技剧团、正式影院、当地礼堂、临时店面影院、露天游乐场和游乐园等。

manageable[1] ['mænɪdʒəbl] 

【释义】 *a.* 易处理的,易管理的(accessible, achievable)

【例句】 Dialect accommodation is a more manageable sort of topic. (TPO6, L, S2, C1) 方言互融是一个较容易处理的课题。

【派生】 manageability *n.* 易管理,易处理

mandatory[1] ['mændətərɪ] 

【释义】 *a.* 法定的,义务的(compulsory, required)

【例句】 A mandatory policy requiring companies to offer their employees the option of working a four-day workweek for four-fifths (80 percent) of their normal pay would benefit the economy as a whole as well as the individual companies and the employees who decided to take the option. (TPO1, W, Q1) 一项法律强制要求公司给其员工一周工作四天并领取正常工资的五分之四的选择权,这将在总体上有利于经济发展以及那些想要行使这项权力的公司和个人。

maneuver[1] [mə'nuːvə] 

【释义】 *v.* 1. 操纵 2. 策划 *n.* 策略,谋略,花招(tactic, strategy)

【例句】 In the largest caravels, two main masts held large square sails that provided the bulk of the thrust driving the ship forward, while a smaller forward mast held a triangular-shaped sail, called a lateen sail, which could be moved into a variety of positions to maneuver the ship. (TPO17, R, S1, T1) 在最大型的轻快帆船上,有两根主桅杆撑起大块的船帆,以便提供推动帆船前进的足够推力,同时有一个小型的前桅杆来撑起一块三角形船帆,这个船帆叫做三角帆,它是用来在移动中控制帆船行驶的方向的。

manifestation[1] [ˌmænɪfes'teɪʃən] 

【释义】 *n.* 1. 显示,表明,表示 2. (幽灵的)显现,显灵

【例句】 What Watson did was to observe muscular habits because he viewed them as a manifestation of thinking. (TPO2, L, S1, L1) Waston的做法是观察肌肉的运动习惯,因为他将肌肉运动视为反映大脑思想的表现形式。

【同义】 demonstration, reflection

【逆构】 manifest *v.* 表现,显示

marathon[1] ['mærəθən] 

【释义】 *n.* 1. 马拉松 2. 耐力比赛

【例句】 I don't go because I'm training for a marathon or anything. (TPO5, S, Q2) 我不是为了马拉松训练或是其它原因才去体育馆的。

【派生】 marathoner *n.* 马拉松运动员

marble[1] ['mɑːbl] 

【释义】 *n.* 大理石

【例句】 Then they shipped these plaster casts to workshops all over the empire, where they were replicated in marble or bronze. (TPO18,

L, S1, L2) 然后他们将这些石膏像通过水路运送到全国各地的车间作坊，在那里它们被复制成青铜或大理石的塑像。

【派生】 marbled *a.* 有大理石花纹的

【搭配】 white marble 汉白玉，白色大理石

march[1] [mɑːtʃ] 

【释义】 *v./n.* 行进，前进（parade, advance）

【例句】 The key to the Greek world lay in its high-powered ships; the key to Roman power lay in its marching legions. (TPO7, R, S2, T1) 希腊的成功在于其强大的海军；罗马的成功在于其强大的陆军。

marshal[1] ['mɑːʃəl] 

【释义】 *n.* 1. 元帅 2. 消防局长 3. 典仪官，司仪 *v.* 整理，组织，控制

【例句】 Only iron smelting and mining required marshaling a significant amount of capital. (TPO10, R, S2, T2) 只有冶铁和采矿需要投入大量的资金。

【搭配】 field marshal 陆军元帅

massif[1] ['mæsiːf] 

【释义】 *n.* 1. 山峦 2. 断层地块

【例句】 These are generally fed by groundwater springs, and many issue from limestone massifs. (TPO12, R, S2, T2) 这些通常都是源自地下泉水，还有很多是从石灰岩断层中流出的。

【派生】 massify *v.* 使成整体，使一体化

maximize[1] ['mæksmaɪz] 

【释义】 *v.*（使）达到最大值；充分利用

【例句】 Exhibitors, however, wanted to maximize their profits. (TPO2, R, S2, T2) 但是，影院老板想使他们的收益最大化。

【反义】 minimize

【派生】 maximization *n.* 最大化

【逆构】 maximum *n.* 最大值 *a.* 最大的

【搭配】 maximize profit/revenue 收益 / 收入最大化

mediate[1] ['miːdieɪt] 

【释义】 *v.* 1. 调停，调解（arbitrate, intervene）2. 使…受影响

【例句】 Sociologists view primary groups as bridges between individuals and the larger society because they transmit, mediate, and interpret a society's cultural patterns and provide the sense of oneness so critical for social solidarity. (TPO13, R, S1, T1) 社会学家认为主要群体是个体和社会之间的桥梁，因为这些群体会传递、调整、诠释社会的文化形态并提供对促进社会团结极为关键的整体感。

【派生】 mediator *n.* 调停者

melodrama[1] ['melədrɑːmə] 

【释义】 *n.* 情节剧，音乐戏剧

【例句】 It is the melodious drama of ancient Greek theater, the term "melodious drama" being shortened eventually to "melodrama" because operas frequently are melodramatic, not to say unrealistic. (TPO12, L, S2, L1) 它是古希腊剧场里悦耳的戏剧，"melodious drama（悠扬的戏剧）"这一术语最终被缩改成"melodrama（音乐戏剧）"，是因为戏剧不切实际不说，还经常情节夸张。

【逆构】 drama *n.* 戏剧

memorize[1] ['meməraɪz] 

【释义】 *v.* 记住，背熟（remember, keep in mind）

【例句】 They were positioned as if they were heading in the direction of the points on the sea horizon where certain stars would appear and young would-be navigators set by the stones at night and turned in different directions to memorize the constellations they saw, so they could recognize them and navigate by them later on when they went out to sea. (TPO14, L, S2, L1) 它们被放置成好像要朝向海平面的样子，那里会有固定的星座出现，而想要成为航海家的年轻人夜晚时会留些石头在那里并变换不同的方向，以此来记录他们所看见的星座，这样他们日后出海时就可以认出这些星座并凭借它们进行导航。

【派生】 memorization *n.* 记住，背诵
memorable *a.* 值得纪念的，难忘的
memorial *a.* 纪念的，记忆的 *n.* 纪念物，纪念馆

【逆构】 memory *n.* 记忆力,记忆

microhabitat[1] [ˌmaikrəuˈhæbətæt] 

【释义】 *n.* 小环境

【例句】 Some plants can even survive in favorable microhabitats above the snow line. (TPO1, R, S1, T1) 一些植物甚至可以在雪线以上的舒适的小环境里存活。

millet[1] [ˈmɪlɪt] 

【释义】 *n.* 粟,小米

【例句】 Agriculture seems to have reached these people from the Near East, since the first domesticated crops were millets and sorghums whose origins are not African but West Asian. (TPO7, R, S2, T2) 非洲农业很可能来源于近东地区,因为非洲最初种植的农作物是小米和高粱,它们都是源于西亚,而不是非洲。

minstrel[1] [ˈmɪnstrəl] 

【释义】 *n.*(中世纪)游吟诗人,音乐家

【例句】 Previously, large audiences had viewed spectacles at the theater, where vaudeville, popular dramas, musical and minstrel shows, classical plays, lectures, and slide-and-lantern shows had been presented to several hundred spectators at a time. (TPO2, R, S2, T2) 先前,大批观众在剧院观看表演,在那里,数百名观众可以同时观看轻歌舞剧、流行戏剧、音乐剧或歌唱表演、古典音乐、演讲和幻灯片放映。

minuscule[1] [mɪˈnʌskjuːl] 

【释义】 *a.* 1. 微小的(small, tiny, minute) 2.(字母)小写的 *n.* 小写字母

【例句】 At the same time, the image that the spectator looked at expanded from the minuscule peepshow dimensions of 1 or 2 inches (in height) to the life-size proportions of 6 or 9 feet. (TPO2, R, S2, T2) 与此同时,观众所看到的图像大小也从狭小的1至2英寸扩展到与实物契合的6至9英尺。

misbehave[1] [ˈmɪsbɪˈheɪv] 

【释义】 *v.* 行为不端,举止不当

【例句】 So at the beginning, they might, I don't know, interrupt the teacher, walk around the classroom when they are supposed to be sitting down, you know just misbehaving in general. (TPO7, S, Q4) 因此,在开始的时候,他们可能会打断老师,应该坐着的时候却在教室里走来走去,你知道的,笼统地说就是举止不端。

【派生】 misbehaviour *n.* 不良行为

【搭配】 misbehave oneself 行为不端

mishear[1] [ˈmisˈhiə] 

【释义】 *v.* 误听,听错

【例句】 People who misheard sentences were most likely to make poor decisions. (TPO14, L, S1, L1) 将句子听错的人最容易做出糟糕的决定。

【逆构】 hear *v.* 听,听到

misinterpret[1] [ˈmɪsɪnˈtɜːprɪt] 

【释义】 *v.* 误解,曲解(misunderstand)

【例句】 She thinks the researchers misinterpreted the high-pitched barks as warming signals. (TPO9, L, S2, L2) 她认为研究员错误地将高声吠叫理解成了警报信号。

【派生】 misinterpretation *n.* 误解,曲解

misprint[1] [misˈprint] 

【释义】 *n.* 印刷错误

【例句】 To point out a misprint in the textbook. (TPO7, L, S2, L1) 为了指出课本里的印刷错误。

misreport[1] [ˈmisriˈpɔːt] 

【释义】 *v.* 误报,谎报

【例句】 The movement pattern of the rocks was misreported by researchers. (TPO4, L, S2, L1) 岩石的运动模式被研究人员误报了。

返记菜单

microhabitat[1]	millet[1]	minstrel[1]	minuscule[1]	misbehave[1]
mishear[1]	misinterpret[1]	misprint[1]	misreport[1]	

misrepresent[1] ['mɪsˌreprɪ'zent]

【释义】*v.* 故意对…作错误的描述，歪曲（distort, disguise）

【例句】You think that the viewer would reach the logical conclusion that the slogan…er… misrepresents the product. (TPO3, S, Q6) 你会认为顾客会觉得广告语并没有真实地反映产品。

【派生】misrepresentation *n.* 不实的陈述

【搭配】misrepresent the author's meaning 歪曲作者的原意

mite[1] [maɪt]

【释义】*n.* 小虫

【例句】For example, a well-known Burgess Shale animal called Sidneyia is a representative of a previously unknown group of arthropods (a category of animals that includes insects, spiders, mites, and crabs). (TPO5, R, S2, T2) 例如，一种叫做西德尼虫的著名伯吉斯页岩动物就是之前一类并不知名的节肢动物的代表(这类动物包括昆虫、蜘蛛、小虫及蟹类等。)

moderate[1] ['mɒdərɪt]

【释义】*a.* 温和的；适度的，有节制的（temperate, gentle, mild）*v.* 使稳定，使缓和（temper, appease）

【例句】All exhibited moderate growth rates in the course of the century (Denmark the highest and Sweden the lowest) , but all more than doubled in population by 1900. (TPO18, R, S1, T1) 在该世纪中，所有（国家）都保持了中等的增长率（丹麦最高，瑞典最低），但到1900年时人口全都达到两倍以上。

【反义】immoderate

【派生】moderation *n.* 适度，合理

【搭配】moderate price 公平的价格
moderate climate 温和的气候

moist[1] [mɔɪst]

【释义】*a.* 潮湿的，多雨的（damp, humid）

【例句】It ranges from sea level in the polar regions to 4,500 meters in the dry subtropics and 3,500-4,500 meters in the moist tropics. (TPO1, R, S1, T1) 它从极地地区的海平面延伸到4500米高的干燥的亚热带地区以及3500至4500米的潮湿的热带地区。

【反义】dry

【派生】moisture *n.* 潮湿，湿气；湿度
moisten *v.* 弄湿，使湿润

mold[1] [məʊld]

【释义】*n.* 1. 模型，模子（frame）2. 真菌 *v.* 制模，塑造（shape, model）

【例句】What they did was they made plaster casts from molds of the sculptures. (TPO18, L, S1, L2) 他们所做的就是根据雕像的模具制成石膏像。

【派生】molder *n.* 铸工
moldy *a.* 发霉的

monastery[1] ['mɒnəstrɪ]

【释义】*n.* 修道院，寺院

【例句】Ah, remember, before printing books were made mainly in monasteries. (TPO15, L, S2, L1) 啊，记住，在印刷术之前，书籍主要是在寺院制成的。

monetary[1] ['mʌnɪtərɪ]

【释义】*a.* 货币的，财政的（financial, fiscal）

【例句】The development of new international trade routes could undermine the monetary base and erode state power. (TPO16, R, S1, T1) 新国际贸易路线的开发可能会削弱货币基础，并侵蚀国家政权。

【搭配】monetary policy 货币政策
monetary system 货币制度
international monetary fund 国际货币基金组织

Word List 46

peg[1] [peg] 

【释义】*v.* 1. 钉,固定 2. 限定 *n.* 1. 钉,桩 2. 琴栓,弦轴

【例句】By contrast, wooden statues were carved from several pieces of wood that were pegged together to form the finished work, and metal statues were either made by wrapping sheet metal around a wooden core or cast by the lost wax process. (TPO11, R, S1, T1) 相比之下,木雕是由钉在一起的几块木头雕刻而成的,而金属雕塑要么是金属片包裹着一块木质核心,要么是用脱蜡铸造法铸成的。

【搭配】on the peg 在拘捕中,在监禁中
off the peg 现成的
peg down 用木钉钉住;约束
peg away at 坚持不懈地做
take sb. down a peg 煞某人的威风

pendulous[1] ['pendjʊləs] 

【释义】*a.* 吊着的,下垂的;摆动的

【例句】During courtship and aggressive displays, the turkey enlarges its colored neck collar by inflating sacs in the neck region and then flings about a pendulous part of the colored signaling apparatus as it utters calls designed to attract or repel. (TPO17, R, S2, T1) 在求爱期和发起挑衅时,火鸡会使自己颈囊充气,从而张开艳丽的颈圈,当其发出吸引异性或驱逐敌人的叫声时,便晃动这个色彩绚烂的信号器官的下垂部分。

mountainous[1] ['maʊntɪnəs]

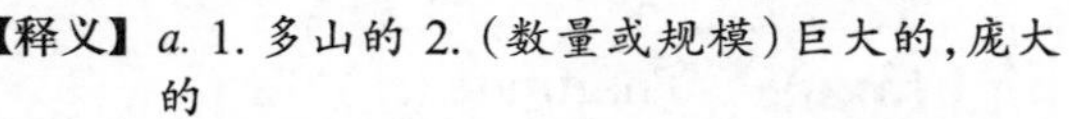

【释义】*a.* 1. 多山的 2. (数量或规模)巨大的,庞大的

【例句】Tulips actually hail from an area that Chinese call the Celestial Mountains in Central Asia. A very remote mountainous region. (TPO6, L, S1, L1) 郁金香实际上来自于亚洲中部一个中国人叫作天堂山的地区,一个很遥远的山区。

【逆构】mountain *n.* 山,山丘;山脉

【搭配】a mountainous country 一个多山的国家

multimedia[1] [ˌmʌlti'miːdiə] 

【释义】*n.* 多媒体

【例句】In this, he synthesized all his tricks from Drury Lane: mechanical motions, sound, light, other special effects to create, if you will, an early multimedia production. (TPO9, L, S1, L1) 在"Eidophusikon"中,他运用了在朱瑞巷剧院里的所有技巧:机械运动、声音、灯光以及其他特效,如果你愿意承认,那便是早期的多媒体产品。

【搭配】a multimedia presentation 多媒体的演出

municipal[1] [mjʊ(ː)'nɪsɪpəl] 

【释义】*a.* 市政的,市的(civic, metropolitan)

【例句】We are looking at the impact of recent cases on property rights, municipal land use cases, owning disputes. (TPO4, L, S2, C1) 我们在评估最近财产权和市政土地使用权宜归属争端案例的影响。

【派生】municipality *n.* 市政当局,自治市

mutate[1] [mjuː'teɪt] 

【释义】*v.* (使)变异,(使)突变

【例句】An organism often cannot survive with a mutated gene. (TPO5, L, S1, L1) 存在变异基因的机体是不能存活的。

【派生】matation *n.* 突变

naked[1] ['neɪkɪd] 

【释义】*a.* 赤裸裸的,无遮蔽的,裸露的(bare, nude)

【例句】Thus the seed's chances of survival are greatly enhanced over those of the naked spore. (TPO9, R, S2, T2) 因此,种子的成活率相对于那些裸露的孢子大大提高了。

【反义】covered, clothed

【搭配】a naked hillside 光秃秃的山坡

narrate[1] [næ'reɪt] 

【释义】*v.* 讲故事;叙述,描述(tell, recount)

【例句】The opportunity to hear chronologically narrated stories may help three-year-old children produce long-lasting memories. (TPO6, R, S2, T2) 按时间顺序讲述故事给一个三岁的孩子听可以帮助孩子形成持久记忆。

【派生】narratation *n.* 讲故事；(电影、戏剧等的)旁白，解说
narrative *n.* 叙述，记叙
narrator *n.* 讲解人，叙述者

navigable[1] ['nævɪgəbəl]

【释义】*a.* (水域)可航行[通航]的

【例句】Europe's maritime tradition had developed in the context of easily navigable seas—the Mediterranean, the Baltic, and, to a lesser extent, the North Sea between England and the Continent—not of vast oceans. (TPO17, R, S1, T1) 欧洲的航海传统是在比较容易航行的海域中建立和发展起来的——地中海、波罗的海，以及在较小的程度上，处于英格兰和欧洲大陆之间的北海，而这些海都不是什么广阔的大洋。

【派生】navigation *n.* 航行，航海(术)

【逆构】navigate *v.* 航行，航海

【搭配】a navigable channel 可以通航的河道

necessity[1] [nɪ'sesɪtɪ]

【释义】*n.* 1. 必要(性)；(迫切)需要(need, demand) 2. 必需品

【例句】All else being equal, this means they must exploit larger areas of land than do agriculturalists to secure the same amount of food, clothing, and other necessities. (TPO14, R, S2, T2) 在其他条件相同的情况下，这意味着他们必须要比务农者开拓出更广阔的土地才能确保等量的食物、衣物和其他必需品。

【逆构】necessitate *v.* 使需要，成为必要

【搭配】of necessity 必然地，不可避免地
out of necessity 出于需要，必定
by necessity 不得已；必然地

nectar[1] ['nektə]

【释义】*n.* 1. 花蜜 2. 甘美的饮料，甘露

【例句】It drinks a lot of nectar from flowers and feeds on some insects, but it's energy-efficient too. (TPO3, L, S1, L1) 它从花中吸取很多花蜜，并且以一些昆虫为食，而这也很节省能量。

【派生】nectareous *a.* 神酒似的，甘美的

negligible[1] ['neglɪdʒəbl]

【释义】*a.* 可忽略的，无足轻重的(insignificant)

【例句】This unprecedented development of a finite groundwater resource with an almost negligible natural recharge rate—that is, virtually no natural water source to replenish the water supply— has caused water tables in the region to fall drastically. (TPO3, R, S1, T1) 考虑到几乎没有补充率(实质上没有自然水资源进行补充)，这种有限的地下水资源的前所未有的发展已经造成了该地区地下水位的急剧下降。

【派生】negligent *a.* 疏忽的，粗心大意的

neutral[1] ['nju:trəl]

【释义】*a.* 中立的；中性的(impartial) *n.* 中立者

【例句】In this picture, the boy is just holding the cake, basically no emotion on his face, everything very neutral. (TPO12, S, Q5) 在这幅图片里，这个男孩子就是拿着蛋糕，脸上基本没有表情，一切都很中性。

【派生】neutralize *v.* 抵销；使中立；中和

neutralize[1] ['nju:trəlaɪz]

【释义】*v.* 1. 使中立 2. 使无效，抵消 3. 中和

【例句】The coming together of the oppositely charged particles neutralizes the electrical tension and releases a tremendous amount of energy, which we see as lightning. (TPO18, R, S2, T2) 相反的带电粒子的结合中和了电压并释放出强大的能量，这就是我们所见到的闪电。

【派生】neutral *a.* 中立的

nightmare[1] ['naɪtmeə (r)]

【释义】*n.* 恶梦，梦魇般的经历

【例句】It's been a total nightmare since constructions started next door on the science hall. (TPO16, L, S1, C1) 从隔壁科学大厅开始建设以来，简直就是一场噩梦。

nobility[1] [nəʊ'bɪlɪtɪ]

【释义】*n.* 1. 贵族阶层(aristocracy) 2. 崇高,高贵

【例句】That is—they were written for the knights and the lords—the nobility that they served. (TPO13, L, S2, L1) 即,它们是写给骑士和上层社会的——他们所效劳的贵族。

【逆构】noble *a.* 高贵的,贵族的 *n.* 贵族

nominate[1] ['nɒmɪneɪt]

【释义】*v.* 提名;任命(appoint, designate)

【例句】I mean, there were so many other people nominated. (TPO16, L, S2, C1) 我的意思是,有很多其他的人获得了提名。

【派生】nomination *n.* 提名,任命
nominator *n.* 提名者,任命者
nominee *n.* 被提名的人,被任命者

nonetheless[1] [ˌnʌnðə'les]

【释义】*ad.* 虽然如此,但是

【例句】There are nonetheless some intriguing differences. (TPO10, R, S2, T1) 但仍存在一些引人发问的差异。

non-literary[1]

【释义】*a.* 非文学性的

【例句】Do these non-literary activities lower cultural standards? (TPO11, W, Q1) 这些非文学性质的活动降低文化标准了吗?

nonspecialist[1]

【例句】Traditional encyclopedias are written by trained experts who adhere to standards of academic rigor that nonspecialists cannot really achieve. (TPO6, W, Q1) 传统百科全书是由一些受过专业培训的专家严格按照学术标准所写的,这些标准是非专家所不能达到的。

normative[1] ['nɔːmətɪv]

【释义】*a.* 标准的,规范的(standard)

【例句】A maritime code known as the *Consulate of the Sea* which originated in the western Mediterranean region in the fourteenth century, won acceptance by a majority of sea goers as the normative code for maritime conduct; it defined such matters as the authority of a ship's officers, protocols of command, pay structures, the rights of sailors, and the rules of engagement when ships met one another on the sea-lanes. (TPO17, R, S1, T1) 14世纪时起源于西地中海地区的一部叫作《康索拉度海法》的海运法典赢得了大多数航海人的认可,并把它作为海上行为的规范指南。法典规定了船长的职权范围、指令的礼节、工资结构、水手们的权利以及船与船在海上相遇时的交战方式。

【派生】normatively *ad.* 标准地,规范地

【搭配】normative grammar 规范语法

notation[1] [nəʊ'teɪʃən]

【释义】*n.* 记号;标记法

【例句】He believes that as far back as 30,000 B. C., hunters may have used a system of notation, engraved on bone and stone, to mark phases of the Moon. (TPO4, R, S2, T1) 他认为,早在公元前30000年,猎人们可能就使用了一种符号标记系统,把月相标记在骨头和石头上面了。

【逆构】notate *v.* 以符号表示

notepad[1] ['nəut'pæd]

【释义】*n.* 记事本

【例句】Keep a small notepad and record what you see. 带一个小记事本,记录下你的见闻。

notify[1] ['nəʊtɪfaɪ]

【释义】*v.* 通知,告知,报告(announce)

【例句】The woman came to the office to notify the university of her change of address. (TPO3, L, S1, C1, Q1) 女子来办公室是为了通知学校她换地址的事。

【派生】notification *n.* 通知,通知单

【搭配】notify in advance 预先通知
notify sb. of 通知某人…

nurture[1] ['nɜːtʃə]

【释义】*v.* 养育;培育,培养(foster, feed, nourish) *n.*

返记菜单

nobility[1]	nominate[1]	nonetheless[1]	non-literary[1]	nonspecialist[1]
normative[1]	notation[1]	notepad[1]	notify[1]	nurture[1]

教养，培育

【例句】So in that much shorter period of time, all the Olympic marmots, male and female, eat, play, work and nurture the young together. (TPO1, L, S2, L2) 所以在那个非常短的时间里，所有的奥林匹亚旱獭，无论公母，都在一起觅食、游戏、工作和养育幼崽。

nutmeg[1] ['nʌtmeg]

【释义】*n.* 肉豆蔻，肉豆蔻种子中的核仁

【例句】And in the Middle Ages, Europeans were familiar with lots of different spices, the most import being pepper, cloves, ginger, cinnamon, maize and nutmeg. (TPO18, L, S2, L1) 在中世纪时期，欧洲人熟知许多种香料，其中引进最多的是胡椒、丁香、生姜、桂皮、玉米和肉豆蔻。

oar[1] [ɔː]

【释义】*n.* 桨，橹

【例句】The principal seagoing ship used throughout the Middle Ages was the galley, a long, low ship fitted with sails but driven primarily by oars. (TPO17, R, S1, T1) 中世纪最为主要的海船是单层甲板帆船，其低矮狭长的船体装配着船帆，但主要还是靠船桨来操控。

【派生】oarless *a.* 无桨的

【搭配】put/stick one's oar in 插嘴，插话

obliterate[1] [ə'blɪtəreɪt]

【释义】*v.* 除去，涂掉，擦掉(delete, erase, efface)

【例句】By the early thirteenth century, Western Europeans had also developed and put into use the magnetic compass, which helped when clouds obliterated both the Sun and the stars. (TPO17, R, S1, T1) 在13世纪初，西欧人也开始使用指南针，以此来帮助他们在云层遮盖太阳和星星的情况下辨别方向。

【派生】obliteration *n.* 删除

obstruct[1] [əb'strʌkt]

【释义】*v.* 1. 阻塞(道路等)(block) 2.(故意)妨碍，阻挠，阻碍(hamper, hinder, impede)

【例句】In forests, visual signals can be seen only at short distances, where they are not obstructed by trees. (TPO17, R, S2, T1) 在森林中，视觉信号只能在不被树木阻碍的情况下进行短距离传播。

【派生】obstruction *n.* 阻塞；妨碍

【搭配】obstruct sb. in/from doing sth. 阻挠某人做某事

off-limits[1] [ɒf'lɪmɪts]

【释义】*a.* 禁止进入的

【例句】So I am sure you can see how heavy an area that off-limits to automobile traffic would be ideal for a heavily populated city where, well, the streets will otherwise be bustling with noise, unpleasant traffic congestion. (TPO13, L, S1, L1) 所以我相信你会看到，在拥挤的城市中，限制机动车辆通行，没有了不断的噪声和交通阻塞，是多么理想啊。

onrushing[1] ['ɒnˌrʌʃɪŋ]

【释义】*a.* 汹涌的；猛冲的；顾前不顾后奔跑的

【例句】The onrushing water arising from these flash floods likely also formed the odd teardrop-shaped "islands" (resembling the miniature versions seen in the wet sand of our beaches at low tide) that have been found on the plains close to the ends of the outflow channels. (TPO8, R, S2, T2) 这突如其来的洪水产生的急流可能也形成了这种奇特的泪滴形状的"岛屿"(类似于我们在落潮的沙滩湿地上看到的微型版本)，这些"岛屿"已经在靠近泄水渠末端的平原上被发现了。

open-ended[1] [ˌoʊpən'endəd]

【释义】*a.* 可修整的；末端开口的；自由回答的

【例句】Human language is productive and open-ended communication system, whereas no other communication system has this property. (TPO9, L, S2, L2) 人类的语言是一种多产且开放的交流系统，而这是任何其它交流系统所不具备的特性。

【搭配】open-ended fund 开放式基金

opponent[1] [ə'pəʊnənt]

【释义】*n.* 对手，敌手；(争论的)对方(antagonist, adversary) *a.* 敌对的，反对的(hostile, adverse)

【例句】Why and how these people spread out into central and southern Africa remains a mystery, but archaeologists believe that their iron weapons allowed them to conquer their hunting-gathering opponents, who still used stone implements. (TPO7, R, S2, T2) 这些人们为何以及是如何迁徙至非洲中南部的，至今仍是未解的谜题。不过考古学家们认为，他们的铁制武器使其能够战胜那些仍然使用石质工具、以狩猎为生的对手。
【搭配】a political opponent 政敌

optional[1] [ˈɒpʃənəl] 

【释义】*n.* 任选的，非强制的或随意的（elective）
【例句】See, the classes they are eliminating are all optional. (TPO7, S, Q3) 看吧，他们取消的这些课都是任选课。
【反义】compulsory
【逆构】option *n.* 选择（权），可供选择的人或物

orient[1] [ˈɔːrɪent] 

【释义】*v.* 1. 确定方向 2. 使适应
【例句】At seven sites he found that 57 percent of the flakes were right-oriented, and 43 percent left, a pattern almost identical to that produced today. (TPO12, R, S1, T1) 在7处遗址中，他发现有57%的碎片是右侧朝向，43%的是左侧朝向，就和我们今天（生产那种工具）所产出的结果一样。
【派生】oriental *a.* 亚洲的，东方的
orientation *n.* 定向；介绍性指导

originality[1] [ˌərɪdʒɪˈnælɪtɪ] 

【释义】*n.* 独创性，创意，新奇（creativity, novelty）
【例句】Egyptian art lacks the originality of European art. (TPO11, R, S1, T1, Q2) 埃及艺术缺乏欧洲艺术的独创性。
【逆构】original *a.* 独创的

ostracize[1] [ˈɒstrəsaɪz] 

【释义】*v.* 排斥；放逐
【例句】Should the use of rewards fail, members can frequently win by rejecting or threatening to ostracize those who deviate from the primary group's norms. (TPO13, R, S1, T1) 如果没有有效利用奖励，成员就可以时常通过拒绝或威胁来排斥那些偏离主要群体行为规范的人，以此来达到目的。
【派生】ostracism *n.* 流放，放逐，排斥

ounce[1] [aʊns] 

【释义】*n.* 盎司
【例句】For every ounce of body mass, there is proportionately less surface through which heat can escape. (TPO15, R, S2, T1) 对于体重的每一盎司来说，该动物表面积越小热量流失地越少。

outlook[1] [ˈaʊtlʊk] 

【释义】*n.* 1. 观点，见解（viewpoint）2. 景色（view）3. 前景，展望（prospect）
【例句】Young children are trusting of commercial advertisements in the media, and advertisers have sometimes been accused of taking advantage of this trusting outlook. (TPO14, R, S1, T1) 年轻的小孩容易相信媒体上的商业广告，而有些商家有时则被指控利用了这种信任。
【搭配】world outlook 世界观
outlook on life 人生观
on the outlook for 注视着；留心；物色中，寻找中

outnumber[1] [aʊtˈnʌmbə] 

【释义】*v.* 数量上超过（overnumber, exceed）
【例句】The balance of deer species in the Puget Sound region has changed over time, with the Columbian white-tailed deer now outnumbering other types of deer. (TPO4, R, S1, T1) 皮吉特海湾地区鹿群种类的平衡已经随着时间而改变了，目前是哥伦比亚白尾鹿的数量多于其他种类的鹿群。

out-of-date[1] 

【释义】*a.* 1. 过时的，老式的 2. 废弃的
【例句】But I think the problem is the route's out of date. (TPO2, S, Q3) 但我认为问题在于原来的公交路线已经过时了。
【反义】up-to-date

返记菜单

optional[1] orient[1] originality[1] ostracize[1] ounce[1]
outlook[1] outnumber[1] out-of-date[1]

outrigger[1] ['aʊtrɪɡə] 

【释义】*n.* 舷外支架；悬臂梁

【例句】Just as important, the culture also possessed the basic foundation for an effective maritime adaptation, including outrigger canoes and a variety of fishing techniques that could be effective for overseas voyaging. (TPO5, R, S2, T1) 同样重要的是，该文化还有着能够有效适应海洋生活的基础，包括桅杆船以及各种有效适应出海航行的捕鱼技术。

outright[1] ['aʊt'raɪt]

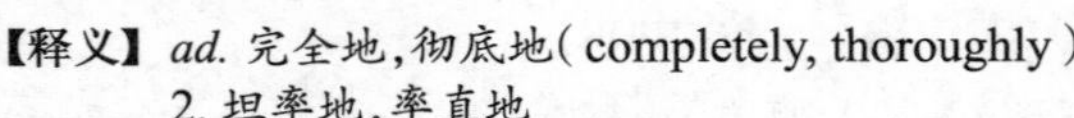

【释义】*ad.* 完全地，彻底地（completely, thoroughly）2. 坦率地，率直地

【例句】Birds that eat the poisoned insects or drink contaminated water can die as a result, and even if pesticides do not kill birds outright, they can prevent them from reproducing successfully. (TPO17, W, Q1) 鸟类吃了被毒死的昆虫或者喝了受污染的水会导致其死亡，即便不会导致鸟类的立刻死亡，也会影响其成功繁殖。

【逆构】buy a house outright 以一次性付款方式买房

overabundance[1] ['əʊvərə,bʌndəns] 

【释义】*n.* 过多，过于丰富

【例句】An overabundance of certain minerals can be toxic. (TPO5, R, S1, T1) 过量的某些化学物质可能是有毒的。

【逆构】overabundant *a.* 过多的，过于丰富的

overcultivation[1] ['əuvə,kʌlti'veiʃən] 

【释义】*n.* 过度耕种（overcropping）

【例句】Four specific activities have been identified as major contributions to the desertification process: overcultivation, overgrazing, firewood gathering, and overirrigation. (TPO2, R, Sl, T1) 四种特定活动被确定为促进沙漠化进程的罪魁祸首：过度耕种、过度放牧、伐木做柴以及过度灌溉。

【逆构】overcultivate *v.* 过度耕种

overgraze[1] ['əʊvə'ɡreɪz] 

【释义】*v.* 过度放牧

【例句】Four specific activities have been identified as major contributions to the desertification process: overcultivation, overgrazing, firewood gathering, and overirrigation. (TPO2, R, Sl, T1) 四种特定活动被确定为促进沙漠化进程的罪魁祸首：过度耕种、过度放牧、伐木做柴以及过度灌溉。

overhear[1] [,əʊvə'hɪə] 

【释义】*v.* 偷听到（某人说话等）；无意中听到

【例句】Now, ah, I just have overheard some graduates students talking. (TPO7, L, S1, C1) 现在，啊，我刚刚无意中听到了一些研究生的谈话。

【搭配】overhear sb. saying sth. 偷听到某人说某事

overland[1] ['əʊvəlænd] 

【释义】*a./ad.* 经由陆路的，陆上的

【例句】In the fourteenth century, a number of political developments cut Europe's overland trade routes to southern and eastern Asia, with which Europe had had important and highly profitable commercial ties since the twelfth century. (TPO17, R, S1, T1) 14世纪，一系列政治的发展切断了欧洲大陆与南亚以及东亚的贸易路线，通过这些贸易路线欧洲在12世纪时就已经与东亚和南亚建立起了高度互利的商业纽带。

overlap[1] ['əʊvə'læp] 

【释义】v. 部分重叠，与…交叉

【例句】Two old trees overlapped their upper branches. 那两棵古树的上端分枝相互交搭复生。

overlay[1] [,əʊvə'leɪ]

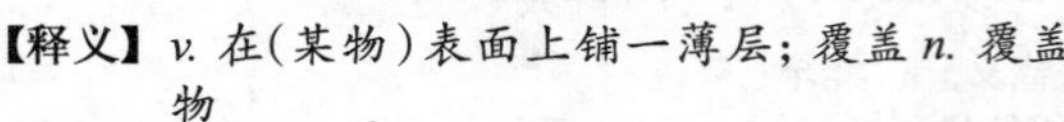

【释义】*v.* 在（某物）表面上铺一薄层；覆盖 *n.* 覆盖物

【例句】What happens is that the ice of the base of the glacier is under gradual depression—the depression coming from the weights of the

overlaying ice. (TPO7, L, S2, L2) 发生的情况是冰川底部的冰面不断受到上部覆盖冰面的重量带来的压力。

overnight[1] ['əuvə'naɪt]

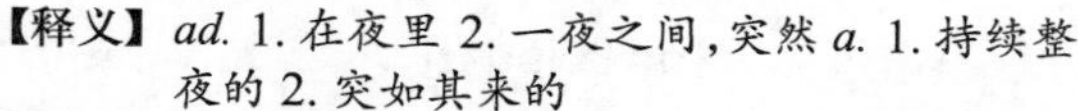

【释义】*ad.* 1. 在夜里 2. 一夜之间,突然 *a.* 1. 持续整夜的 2. 突如其来的

【例句】Look, people from town hardly ever come to games because our teams always lose and they are not suddenly going to improve overnight. (TPO13, S, Q3) 看看吧,镇上的人几乎不会来看比赛,因为我们队老是输,而且也不会一夜之间取得突破。

【搭配】an overnight trip 一整夜的旅行

overrun[1] [ˌəuvə'rʌn]

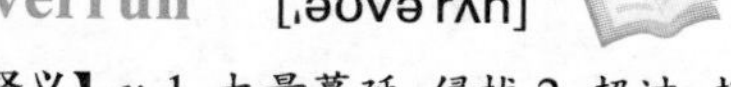

【释义】*v.* 1. 大量蔓延,侵扰 2. 超过,超出

【例句】For example, Australia during the 1940s was overrun by hundreds of millions of European rabbits. (TPO17, R, S2, T2) 例如,在二十世纪四十年代时,澳大利亚被数亿只欧洲兔所侵扰。

【搭配】be overrun with mice 老鼠猖獗

overstate[1] ['əuvə'steɪt]

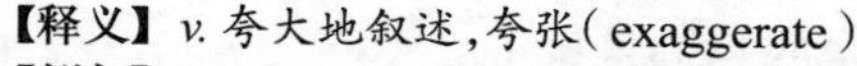

【释义】*v.* 夸大地叙述,夸张(exaggerate)

【例句】It overstates the connection between sociology and marketing. (TPO18, L, S2, C1) 它夸大了社会学与市场营销的联系。

【反义】understate

【派生】overstatement *n.* 大话,言过其实

overt[1] ['əuvɜːt]

【释义】*a.* 公开的,不隐蔽的(open)

【例句】As the individual matures, that overt talking to oneself becomes covert talking to oneself. (TPO2, L, S1, L1) 当个体逐渐成熟起来后,这种公开的自我对话就转变为秘密的自我交谈。

【反义】covert

【派生】overtly *ad.* 公开地

overview[1] ['əuvəvjuː]

【释义】*n.* 概述,概要(outline)

【例句】The lecture is mainly about an overview of vision correction over time. (TPO8, L, S2, L1) 这个讲座主要是对时间推移过程中视力矫正的概述。

paddle[1] ['pædl]

【释义】*n.* 1. 短桨 2. 趟水,涉水 3. 球拍 4. 搅拌器 *v.* 1. 用桨划船 2. 趟水,赤脚涉水

【例句】Some of the most priced tulips were white with purple stricks, or red with yellow stricks on the paddles, even a dark purple tulip that was very much priced. (TPO6, L, S1, L1) 一些很贵重的郁金香是有着紫条的白色花,或是有着黄条的红色花,甚至暗紫色的郁金香也是很值钱的。

【派生】paddler *n.* 涉水者

【搭配】paddle one's own canoe 靠自己的力量,自力更生

palace[1] ['pælɪs]

【释义】*n.* 宫,宫殿;豪华住宅(castle, mansion)

【例句】So you get more details about the characters, about where the action takes place, what people's houses were like, ur, whether they're small cabins or grand palaces. (TPO5, L, S2, L2) 所以你可以得到更多的信息:关于人物,关于事情发生的地点,关于人们的房子是什么样的,是小木屋还是大宫殿。

pantomime[1] ['pæntəmaɪm]

【释义】*n.* 哑剧(dumb show, mime)

【例句】Thus, the recalling of an event is elaborated through the narrator's pantomime and impersonation. (TPO1, R, S2, T1) 这样,对于某一件事情的回忆会通过讲述者的哑剧表演或是模仿而得以详细化。

parallel[1] ['pærəlel]

【释义】*a.* 平行的 2. 类似的,相对应的 3.〈电子学、计算机〉并联的 *n.* 类似,相似;类似的事物 *v.* 1. 与…平行 2. 与…媲美,比得上

【例句】The railway lines run parallel to the road. 铁路线和那条道路平行。

【派生】paralleled *a.* 并行的,平行的

返记菜单

overnight[1]	overrun[1]	overstate[1]	overt[1]	overview[1]
paddle[1]	palace[1]	pantomime[1]	parallel[1]	

unparalleled *a.* 无比的，空前的
【搭配】 parallel with 与…平行

parish[1] ['pærɪʃ]

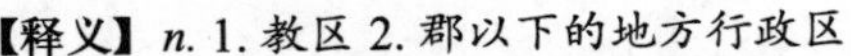

【释义】 *n.* 1. 教区 2. 郡以下的地方行政区
【例句】 When he grew older, William Smith taught himself surveying from books he bought with his small savings, and at the age of eighteen he was apprenticed to a surveyor of the local parish. (TPO6, R, S2, T1) 长大后，威廉·史密斯开始用微薄的积蓄买书自学测量，18岁的时候，他成为了当地教区测量员的学徒。
【搭配】 institute sb. into a parish 任命某人为教区牧师

partition[1] [pɑː'tɪʃən]

【释义】 *v.* 区分，隔开，分割（separate, divide）*n.* 1. 划分（division, separation）2. 隔离物
【例句】 What that meant was that the sky could be partitioned, divided up, much more symmetrically than it could farther away from the equator. (TPO14, L, S2, L1) 这就意味着天空在赤道这里比在其他远离赤道的地方被分割、划分得对称得多。
【派生】 partitioned *a.* 分配的，隔离的
【搭配】 partition off 分隔成，隔开
hard disk partition 硬盘分区

paste[1] [peɪst]

【释义】 *v.* 粘贴，裱糊 *n.* 1. 酱 2. 浆糊，糊状物 3. 人造宝石
【例句】 In this piece he illustrates a story about the adventures and pasted them into his own painted illustration of trees, flowers and grass. (TPO11, S, Q4) 在这幅画中，他描绘了冒险的故事，并把它们贴到他自己画的树木、花草上去。

pasture[1] ['pɑːstʃə]

【释义】 *n.* 牧草地，牧场（grassland, meadow）*v.* 放牧
【例句】 And, like the pastoralists, Middle Eastern merchants unhappy with their environment could simply pack up and leave for greener pastures. (TPO16, R, S1, T1) 并且，如果中东地区的商人对周围的环境不满意，他们也可以像牧人一样收拾行装、去往更好的牧场。
【派生】 pastureland *n.* 牧场
【搭配】 put out to pasture 放牧

pathology[1] [pə'θɒlədʒɪ]

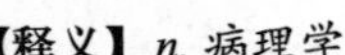

【释义】 *n.* 病理学
【例句】 People who do not live alone, for example, tend to make healthier life choices and develop fewer pathologies than people who live by themselves. (TPO13, R, S1, T1) 例如，不单独生活的人们往往比单独生活的人们更能做出更加健康的生活选择而且很少偏离常态。
【派生】 pathologist *n.* 病理学家

peep[1] [piːp]

【释义】 *n.* 1. 吱吱叫 2. 窥视，偷看 *v.* 窥视，偷看（peek）
【例句】 These loud cheeps and peeps might give the location of the nest away to a listening hawk or raccoon, resulting in the death of the defenseless nestlings. (TPO11, R, S2, T2) 这些吱吱的叫声会把其巢穴的位置暴露给正在全神聆听的老鹰或者浣熊，从而导致了毫无防备的雏鸟的死亡。
【搭配】 peep at 偷看，偷窥

Word List 47

redistribute[1] [ˌriːdis'tribjuːt]

【释义】 *v.* 重新分配，再区分

【例句】 You know planetary researchers love studying deep craters until they learn about the impacts that created them, how they redistributed pieces of a planet's crust and in this case, we especially want to know if any of the mantle, the layer beneath the crust, was exposed by the impact. (TPO5, L, S1, L2) 你知道的，行星研究者们热衷于研究深火山口，直到了解形成火山的冲击力以及这些冲击力是如何对一颗行星的地壳进行重新分配的，在这样的情况下，我们尤其想知道是否有地幔(地壳下面的一层)在这种冲击之下暴露了出来。

【派生】 redistribution *n.* 重新分配

perch[1] [pɜːtʃ]

【释义】 *n.* 1. 栖木 2. 高处 *v.* 1. 栖息 2. 就位，位于

【例句】 For example, there's a bird, the "wood thrush", anyway, when the "wood thrush" is in an attack-escape conflict, that is, it's caught between the two urges to escape from or to attack an enemy, if it's sitting on a horizontal branch, it'll wipe its beak on its perch. (TPO4, L, S1, L1) 比如，有一种鸟，"鸫科鸣鸟"，当它在处在攻击还是逃跑的矛盾中时，也就是说，它陷入了逃跑还是攻击敌人的两种想法中，如果它位于水平的树枝上，它会用鸟喙啄其所栖息的树枝。

perimeter[1] [pə'rɪmɪtə]

【释义】 *n.* 1. 边缘，周边地带(border) 2. 周长(circumference)

【例句】 There are slight variations in these two perimeters. (TPO6, L, S2, L2) 在这两个星球的距离中间存在一些轻微变动。

permeate[1] ['pɜːmieɪt]

【释义】 *v.* 弥漫，遍布(pervade)；渗入，渗透(penetrate)

【例句】 Part of the limestone rock layer is permeated by water from below. (TPO16, L, S1, L1,) 石灰岩下面的水渗入到石灰岩的部分岩层里。

【派生】 permeability *n.* 渗透性
permeable *a.* 有渗透性的，能透过的

【搭配】 permeat through 渗透入，弥漫

persecution[1] [ˌpɜːsɪ'kjuːʃən]

【释义】 *n.* 迫害

【例句】 And the opera was no longer about teaching religion as it was about satire and about expressing the ideas of society and your government without committing yourself to writing and risking imprisonment or persecution. (TPO12, L, S2, L1) 而且歌剧不再与教授宗教教义有关，而是与讽刺有关，与表达对社会对政府的看法有关，这样一来就可以使你免于写作和冒被囚禁或是被迫害的风险了。

【逆构】 persecute *v.* 迫害

perspire[1] [pəs'paɪə]

【释义】 *v.* 出汗，流汗，分泌(sweat)

【例句】 Like when you walk outside on a hot day, you perspire, and your body cools itself down, a classic example of how mammal regulates its own body temperature. (TPO14, L, S1, L2) 就像当你在酷热的天里在外面行走时，你会出汗，然后你的身体就会凉快下来，这是松鼠调节其体温的经典例子。

【派生】 perspiration *n.* 汗水；出汗

petiole[1] ['petiəul]

【释义】 *n.* 叶柄

【例句】 Anthocyanin discoloration occurs on stems, petioles, and low leaf surfaces. (TPO5, R, S1, T1) 花青素变色会出现在枝干、叶柄和低处的叶子的表面。

返记菜单

redistribute[1] perch[1] perimeter[1] permeate[1] persecution[1]
perspire[1] petiole[1]

petrify[1] ['petrɪˌfaɪ]

【释义】v. 1.（使）石化 2. 使发呆

【例句】Private collectors have been selling and buying fossils, the petrified remains of ancient organisms, ever since the eighteenth century. (TPO13, W, Q1) 私人收藏家从18世纪起就一直在买卖化石这种石化了的古生物遗迹。

【派生】petrifaction n. 石化

phoenix[1] ['fiːnɪks]

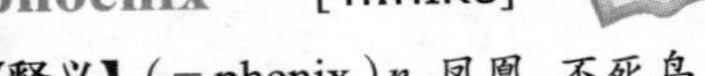

【释义】(= phenix) n. 凤凰，不死鸟

【例句】The dragon represented the emperor, and the phoenix, the empress. (TPO10, R, S1, T1) 龙代表了帝王，凤凰代表了皇后。

piecework[1] ['piːswək]

【释义】n. 计件工作（taskwork）

【例句】Production was generally in the hands of skilled individual artisans doing piecework under the tutelage of a master. (TPO16, R, S1, T1) 生产通常都是由熟练的工匠在大师的指导下进行的。

【搭配】piecework wage 计件工资
piecework system 计件制

piercing[1] ['pɪəsɪŋ]

【释义】a. 1.（指声音等）尖锐的，刺耳的 2.（感情）深切的，刻骨的 3. 锋利的，锐利的

【例句】The piercing cries of the rhinoceros hornbill characterize the Southeast Asian rain forest, as do the unmistakable calls of the gibbons. (TPO17, R, S2, T1) 马来犀鸟的尖锐叫声是东南亚雨林的代表性特色，长臂猿那确凿无误的叫声也一样。

【派生】piercingly ad. 刺透地；感动地

【逆构】pierce v. 深深感动；刺入

pinkish[1] ['piŋkiʃ]

【释义】a. 略带桃色的

【例句】The sky is kind of in a natural pinkish yellow. (TPO1, L, S1, L1) 天空有一种自然的略带粉红的黄颜色。

pitfall[1] ['pɪtfɔːl]

【释义】n. 陷阱（snare, trap）

【例句】But, here I need to warn you about a possible pitfall. (TPO6, L, S2, L1) 但是我在这里想提醒一下大家可能会遇到的陷阱。

plaque[1] [plɑːk]

【释义】n. 匾，饰板

【例句】Many of your cultural establishments in the United States will have a plaque somewhere acknowledging the support—the money they received from whatever corporation. (TPO4, L, S2, L2) 在美国，许多文化机构都会挂有一个牌匾，用以标明它们所得到的支持——从某些公司获得的资助。

【搭配】senile plaque 老年斑

plaza[1] ['plɑːzə]

【释义】n. 1. 广场（square）2. 集市

【例句】And musical drama moved from the church to the plaza right outside the church. (TPO12, L, S2, L1) 音乐戏剧从教堂里搬到了教堂外面的广场上。

pliable[1] ['plaɪəbl]

【释义】a. 1. 易弯的，柔韧的（flexible, limber）2. 易受影响的，顺从的

【例句】Well, birch bark is pliable and very easy to bend. (TPO7, L, S2, C1) 啊，桦树皮柔韧性很强，极易弯曲。

【派生】pliability n. 柔韧性

plight[1] [plaɪt]

【释义】n. 困境，苦境（misfortune, predicament）

【例句】A worsening of the plight of deer was to be expected as settlers encroached on the land, logging, burning, and clearing, eventually replacing a wilderness landscape with roads, cities, towns, and factories. (TPO4, R, S1, T1) 随着移民侵占土地、伐木烧林和清理等活动的进行，最终空旷的原野会被公路、城镇和工厂所取代，可以预见鹿群的处境会越来越恶劣。

【搭配】 in a dreadful plight 深陷困境

plural[1] ['plʊərəl]

【释义】 *a.* 复数的 *n.* 复数
【例句】 It's the plural of the word opus from Latin. (TPO12, L, S2, L1) 它是拉丁语中"opus"一词的复数。
【反义】 singular
【派生】 pluralise *v.* 使…成复数
pluralism *n.* 多元主义; 多元论

plywood[1] ['plaɪwʊd]

【释义】 *n.* 夹板,合板
【例句】 One way of dealing with the aftermath of these disasters is called salvage logging, which is the practice of removing dead trees from affected areas and using the wood for lumber, plywood, and other wood products. (TPO14, W, Q1) 对待这些灾难造成的后果的方法之一是抢救性砍伐,就是将受灾地区死掉的树木移除,将其制成木材、胶合板以及其他木制产品。
【搭配】 faced plywood 贴面胶合板

pointer[1] ['pɔɪntə]

【释义】 *n.* 1. 忠告,点子 2. 线索 3. 指针,指示棒
【例句】 So, you want some pointers where to go for information on the subject? (TPO6, L, S2, C1) 所以你想得到一些去哪里了解该课题相关信息的指点?
【搭配】 the mouse pointer 屏幕光标

populous[1] ['pɒpjʊləs] 

【释义】 *a.* 人口稠密的,人口多的
【例句】 The central state, though often very rich and very populous, was intrinsically fragile. (TPO16, R, S1, T1) 中心的州虽然很富裕,人口也很多,但是实际上很脆弱。
【搭配】 populous nation 人口大国

port[1] [pɔːt] 

【释义】 *n.* 1. 港口,口岸 2. (船或飞机的)左舷
【例句】 This, along with other policy shifts toward free trade, resulted in a significant increase in traffic through the Sound and in the port of Copenhagen. (TPO18, R, S1, T1) 该措施与其他倾向自由贸易的政策一起,使得松德海峡以及哥本哈根港的交通运输量显著上升。
【搭配】 port city 港口城市
port area 码头区,港口区

portage[1] ['pɔːtɪdʒ]

【释义】 *v.* (两条河之间的)陆运
【例句】 They could travel throughout the area only occasionally having to portage, to carry the canoe over a land short distance to another nearby stream. (TPO7, L, S2, L1) 他们在大部分区域内都可以航行,只是偶尔需要陆运,经过一段陆上运输把木舟运到另一条附近的溪流中。

postpone[1] [pəʊst'pəʊn] 

【释义】 *v.* 延期,推迟(delay, defer)
【例句】 Well, since not everyone has gotten back to you, why don't you just postpone the trip, you know, until your mom's van is repaired? (TPO13, S, Q5) 啊,既然不是所有人都回电话了,那你为什么不推迟旅行,直到你妈妈的车修好呢?
【反义】 hasten, hurry
【派生】 postponable *a.* 可以延缓的

pragmatic[1] [præg'mætɪk]

【释义】 *a.* 务实的,实事求是的,注重实效的(realistic, pratical)
【例句】 And all communication systems serve a purpose, a pragmatic function of some sort. (TPO9, L, S2, L2) 所有的交流系统都是服务于一个目的,或者说一个实用功能。
【派生】 pragmatical *a.* 独断的
pragmatist *n.* 实用主义者

prattle[1] ['prætl]

【释义】 *n./v.* 喋喋不休,闲扯,唠叨
【例句】 Anyway, he decided that the best way to serve the people of the city, of his city, was actually get out there in it and experience the things that they experienced, so he rode

返记菜单

plural[1] plywood[1] pointer[1] populous[1] port[1]
portage[1] postpone[1] pragmatic[1] prattle[1]

around the city in, you know, all parts of it, and he saw all the prattles. (TPO12, L, S1, L2) 至少，他决定出服务这个城市，他的城市，的人们的最好的方法就是走近它，经历那里的人们经历的东西，因此，他漫步城市的所有地方，了解那里人们所有的闲聊。

preconceive[1] ['pri:kən'si:v]

【释义】*v.* 预想，预先形成

【例句】Well, we have all kinds of preconceived ideas about how artistic styles develop. (TPO17, L, S1, L1) 对于艺术风格的发展我们有很多预想。

precursor[1] [prɪ(:)'kɜ:sə]

【释义】*n.* 先驱，先兆（forerunner）

【例句】Error is often the precursor of what is correct. 错误常常是正确的先导。

【派生】precursory *a.* 先驱的；前兆的

predispose[1] [ˌpri:dis'pəuz]

【释义】*v.* 使预先倾向于；使易感染

【例句】As always, there are the power worshippers, especially among historians, who are predisposed to admire whatever is strong, who feel more attracted to the might of Rome than to the subtlety of Greece. (TPO7, R, S2, T1) 通常总会有对权威的崇拜者，尤其是在历史学家中，他们倾向于钦佩强大的事物，相对于希腊的微妙，罗马的强大威力对他们更有吸引力。

【搭配】predispose sb. to/towards sth. 事先（在某方面）影响某人

preen[1] [pri:n]

【释义】*v.* 1. 整理羽毛 2. 精心打扮 3. 沾沾自喜

【例句】You may have seen, for example, a bird that's in the middle of a mating ritual, and suddenly it stops and preens, you know, takes a few moments to straighten its feathers, and then returns to the mating ritual. (TPO4, L, S1, L1) 比如，你们会看到鸟在配对过程中会突然停下来梳理羽毛，你们知道，它们会花一阵功夫理顺羽毛后，再回到配对过程中。

preferential[1] [ˌprefə'renʃəl]

【释义】*a.* 优先的，优待的，特惠的

【例句】We are the only mammal with a preferential use of one hand. (TPO12, R, S1, T1) 我们是唯一优先使用一只手的哺乳动物。

【派生】preferentially *ad.* 优先地，优惠地

【逆构】prefer *v.* 更喜欢；宁愿

prejudice[1] ['predʒʊdɪs]

【释义】*n.* 成见，偏见，歧视（bias, partiality）*v.* 1. 使有偏见 2. 有损于

【例句】The criticisms in the reading are largely the result of prejudice against and ignorance about how far online encyclopedias have come. (TPO6, W, Q1) 这篇文章中提出的评论很大程度上是由于对在线百科全书离我们有多近抱有偏见和对此的无知造成的。

【派生】prejudiced *a.* 怀有偏见的
prejudicial *a.* 引起偏见的

preliminary[1] [prɪ'lɪmɪnərɪ]

【释义】*a.* 初步的，预备的，开端的（initial, preparatory）

【例句】Absolutely! Maybe you should do some preliminary research on that. (TPO9, L, S1, C1) 完全正确！或许你应该提前做一些相关的研究。

【搭配】preliminary to 为…作准备；先于

primate[1] ['praɪmɪt]

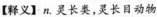

【释义】*n.* 灵长类，灵长目动物

【例句】Today, I'd like to look at some communication systems found in mammals, particularly in primates, such as orangutans, chimpanzees, gorillas...(TPO9, L, S2, L2) 今天我们将研究哺乳动物的一些交流系统，尤其是灵长目动物，例如猩猩、大猩猩、黑猩猩等…

【派生】primatial *a.* 大教主的

primordial[1] [praɪ'mɔ:djəl]

【释义】*a.* 原始的，根本的（original, fundamental）

【例句】The primordial cloud of dust and gas from which all the planets are thought to have condensed had a composition somewhat similar to that of Jupiter. (TPO16, R, S2, T2) 由尘埃和气体形成的最初的云使所有行星变紧密了，它的成份同木星上的最初的云的成份有些相似。

princess[1] [prɪn'ses] 

【释义】 *n.* 1. 公主 2. 王妃
【例句】 Oh, that's another common element, royalty—a prince or princess. (TPO5, L, S2, L2) 哦，那是另外一个元素，皇室成员——一位王子或是公主。

privacy[1] ['praɪvəsɪ] 

【释义】 *n.* 隐私，私生活
【例句】 These new units will allow students to have privacy and work in isolation and will therefore eliminate noise in the library so students can concentrate. (TPO17, S, Q3) 这些新单元将允许学生拥有私人空间，可以单独工作，从而消除图书馆里的噪音，让学生们可以集中精力学习。
【逆构】 a person's right to privacy 个人隐私权

prizefight[1] ['praiz,fait] 

【释义】 *n.* 职业拳击赛
【例句】 For the price of 25 cents (or 5 cents per machine) , customers moved from machine to machine to watch five different films (or, in the case of famous prizefight, successive rounds of a single fight). (TPO2, R, S2, T2) 观众花 25 美分(或者每台播放器的观看价格是 5 美分)，便可以从一个播放器换到下一个播放器依次观看 5 场不同的影片(例如观看著名的职业拳击赛时，观众可以连续观看同一场比赛的几轮战况)。
【派生】 prizefighter *n.* 职业拳击选手

problematic[1] [prɒblə'mætɪk]

【释义】 *a.* 成问题的，产生困难的；有疑问的(doubful, complicated)
【例句】 It is problematic because it goes too far beyond the generally available data. (TPO6, L, S2, L2) 这是有问题的，因为这远远超过了一般可接受的数据。
【派生】 problematical *a.* 问题的，有疑问的
【逆构】 problem *n.* 问题
【搭配】 a problematic future 茫然未知的前途

propel[1] [prə'pel] 

【释义】 *v.* 推进，促进(drive, impel, push)
【例句】 They propel the octopus through the water. (TPO17, L, S2, L2) 它们推动章鱼在水中行进。
【派生】 propellant *n.* 推进物 *a.* 推进的
propeller *n.* 推进器

proponent[1] [prə'pəʊnənt] 

【释义】 *n.*(某事业、理论等的)支持者，拥护者(supporter, advocate)
【例句】 The most influential proponent of the coastal migration route has been Canadian archaeologist Knut Fladmark. (TPO9, R, S1, T1) 海岸移民路线的最有影响力的支持者是加拿大考古学家 Knut Fladmark。
【反义】 opponent *n.* 对手，敌手

prosper[1] ['prɒspə]

【释义】 *v.* 成功，兴旺，繁荣(flourish, succeed, thrive)
【例句】 So, here we've got all the conditions for an irrational boom: a prospering economy, so more people had more disposable income—money to spend on luxuries, but they weren't experienced at investing their new wealth. (TPO6, L, S1, L1) 现在我们已经具备了非理性繁荣的所有条件：繁荣的经济，因此会有更多的人们有更多的可支配收入来用于奢侈品上，而非用于创造新财富的投资上。
【反义】 decline; decay
【派生】 prosperous *a.* 繁荣的，成功的
prosperity *n.* 繁荣，兴旺

prostrate[1] [prɒs'treɪt] 

【释义】 *a.* 卧倒的，匍匐的
【例句】 There is much bare ground with occasional mosses and lichens and some prostrate cushion plants. (TPO1, R, S1, T1) 那里有大片贫瘠的土地，长着苔藓、青苔和一些匍匐的垫状植物。

返记菜单

princess[1] privacy[1] prizefight[1] problematic[1] propel[1]
proponent[1] prosper[1] prostrate[1]

protocol[1] ['prəʊtəkɒl]

【释义】*n.* 1. 礼节,礼仪 2. 协议,草案

【例句】A maritime code known as the *Consulate of the Sea* which originated in the western Mediterranean region in the fourteenth century, won acceptance by a majority of sea goers as the normative code for maritime conduct; it defined such matters as the authority of a ship's officers, protocols of command, pay structures, the rights of sailors, and the rules of engagement when ships met one another on the sea-lanes. (TPO17, R, S1, T1) 14世纪时起源于西地中海地区的一部叫作《康索拉度海法》的海运法典赢得了大多数航海人的认可,并把它作为海上行为的规范指南。法典规定了船长的职权范围、指令的礼节、工资结构、水手们的权利以及船与船在海上相遇时的交战方式。

【搭配】trade protocol 贸易议定书

prototype[1] ['prəʊtətaɪp]

【释义】*n.* 原型,典型(archetype)

【例句】The Mutoscope was a less sophisticated earlier prototype of Kinetoscope. (TPO2, R, S2, T2) 早期电影放映机是活动电影放映机的早期原型,它相对而言没有那么复杂。

protrusion[1] [prə'tru:ʒən]

【释义】*n.* 1. 伸出,突出 2. 伸出物,突出物

【例句】It resembles a small green dragon with leaf-like protrusions sticking out like arms. (TPO13, S, Q6) 它与一种小型的、绿色的、有着像手臂一样的叶片状突出物的龙相似。

【搭配】protrusion of intervertebral disc 椎间盘突出症

provision[1] [prə'vɪʒən]

【释义】*n.* 1. 供应,供应品(preparation, supply) 2. 规定,条款,条件(agreement)

【例句】Increased capital was required for the provision of credit throughout Europe as well as in more distant markets overseas. (TPO10, R, S2, T2) 增加的资本被要求在整个欧洲以及更遥远的海外市场提供信用。

【搭配】make provision for 为…预先采取措施;为…作好准备

provoke[1] [prə'vəʊk]

【释义】*v.* 激起,引起,激怒(arouse, evoke)

【例句】What kinds of feelings were it meant to provoke? (TPO13, L, S2, L1) 这是想激发起一种什么样的情感呢?

【反义】appease

【派生】provoking *a.* 气人的,恼人的

prowl[1] [praʊl]

【释义】*v.* 潜行,徘徊,闲荡(hang about, wander about) *n.* 觅食

【例句】The ecology of the region also permitted armed predators to prowl the surrounding barrens. (TPO16, R, S1, T1) 该地区的生态环境也允许有武器装备的掠食者在其周围的贫瘠之地觅食。

【搭配】on the prowl 在潜行,在四处寻觅

puff[1] [pʌf]

【释义】*v.* 1. 使喷出(烟或蒸汽等) 2. 急促喘息 *n.* 1. 吸烟,抽烟 2. (风、空气、烟雾等的)一团,一阵

【例句】In some industrial regions, heavily laden wagons, with flanged wheels, were being hauled by horses along metal rails; and the stationary steam engine was puffing in the factory and mine. (TPO6, R, S1, T1) 在一些工业地区,承载重物的四轮马车都配备有带凸的缘轮,并且是通过几匹马拉动而在铁轨上行驶的;而静止的蒸汽发动机则被用于工厂和矿井之中。

【派生】puffy *a.* 膨胀的,肿胀的

【搭配】in all one's puff 一生中
puff up 使膨胀,使鼓起
puff out your cheeks/chest 鼓起双颊/挺起胸膛

purification[1] [ˌpjuərɪfɪ'keɪʃən]

【释义】*n.* 提纯,精炼(refinement)

【例句】To get pure hydrogen from water or natural gas, you have to use a purification process that requires lots of energy that's obtained by burning coal or oil. (TPO9, W, Q1) 要想从水或者天然气中获得纯净的液体氢，需要进行提纯的步骤，这个步骤需要耗费很多能量，而这些能量只能通过燃煤或者燃油而得到。

【逆构】 purify *v.* 使纯洁，净化

【搭配】 environmental self-purification 环境自净

push[1] [pʊʃ]

【释义】 *v./n.* 1. 推，按 2. 推动，促进

【例句】 So, moving on, we don't actually see any real government involvement in the arts again until the early 1960s, when President Kennedy and other politicians started to push for major funding to support and promote the arts. (TPO4, L, S2, L2) 于是，往后，我们再没有见到政府真正参与任何艺术项目，直到20世纪60年代，肯尼迪总统和其他政治家开始奋力筹集资金来支持和推动艺术发展。

quill[1] [kwɪl]

【释义】 *n.* 大翎毛，羽茎，(豪猪等的)刺

【例句】 Pressing a key of a harpsichord causes a tiny quill that's connected to the key to pluck the strings that are inside the instrument. (TPO16, L, S1, L2) 按下大键琴的一个键，就会使得连接该琴键的微小琴拨拉动大键琴内部的琴弦。

raccoon[1] [rəˈkuːn]

【释义】 *n.* 浣熊，浣熊的毛皮

【例句】 These loud cheeps and peeps might give the location of the nest away to a listening hawk or raccoon, resulting in the death of the defenseless nestlings. (TPO11, R, S2, T2) 这些吱吱的叫声会把其巢穴的位置暴露给正在全神聆听的老鹰或者浣熊，从而导致了毫无防备的雏鸟的死亡。

racket[1] [ˈrækɪt]

【释义】 *v.* 发出大响声 *n.* 1. 喧嚷，吵闹 2. 敲诈，诈骗 3. 球拍

【例句】 It was about 5000 years ago, even before the first Egyptian pyramid, that some of amazing Neolithic monuments—tombs, were racketed at the very size around ironed Great Britain and coastal islands nearby. (TPO14, L, S2, L2) 大约在5000年以前，甚至要早于埃及的第一个金字塔，一些令人惊奇的新石器时代建筑——陵墓，就已在钢铁般的大不列颠和附近的沿海岛屿大肆兴起。

【派生】 racketeer *n.* 敲诈者

【搭配】 tennis racket 网球拍

radiate[1] [ˈreɪdɪeɪt]

【释义】 *v.* 1. 放射出(光、热等)；辐射(spread, effuse) 2. (使品质或情感)显出，流露

【例句】 The iron eventually heats to the point that it radiates light. (TPO3, L, S2, L2) 将铁加热直到发光。

【派生】 radiative *a.* 辐射的

ragged[1] [ˈrægɪd]

【释义】 *a.* 1. 衣着破烂的，褴褛的(shabby, tattered) 2. 参差不齐的，凹凸不平的

【例句】 Be careful not to make him into the cliché of the "ragged mountain dweller". (TPO6, L, S2, L1) 千万不要用"一个穷苦的深山隐居者"这种陈词滥调来形容他。

【逆构】 rag *n.* 破布，碎布

reburial[1] [riˈberiəl]

【释义】 *n.* 再掩埋

【例句】 After several years of cultivation and reburial, the site would be restored at a cost much lower than the price of excavation and reburial, the standard practice for remediation of contaminated soil. (TPO5, R, S1, T1) 经过几年的耕种和再掩埋，这块地就会恢复原貌，比起挖掘和重埋这种标准的整治受污染土地的方法，这种方法的花费要少得多。

recap[1] [ˈriːkæp]

【释义】 *v.* 扼要重述，摘要说明

【例句】 So let's look at the effect the preference can have by looking at some examples, but first let's recap. (TPO8, L, S1, L1) 让我们通过一些例子看一下喜好可能产生的影响，但我们先回顾一下重点。

返记菜单

push[1] quill[1] raccoon[1] racket[1] radiate[1]
ragged[1] reburial[1] recap[1]

receptionist[1] [rɪ'sepʃənɪst]

【释义】n.（旅馆、事务所等雇用的）接待员
【例句】Listen to a conversation between a student and a receptionist at the Registrar's Office. (TPO3, L, S1, C1) 听一段在注册主任办公室里学生和接待员之间的对话。
【逆构】reception n. 接待处；欢迎会

receptiveness[1] [ri'septivnis]

【释义】n. 善于接受
【例句】Once the idea of planting diffused, Africans began to develop their own crops, such as certain varieties of rice, and they demonstrated a continued receptiveness to new imports. (TPO7, R, S2, T2) 栽培的想法一经传播，非洲就开始培养自己的农作物了，比如某些水稻品种，并且他们一直愿意接收新的进口物种。

receptor[1] [rɪ'septə]

【释义】n. 接受器，感受器，受体，受话器
【例句】There are no photo receptors in the area where the nerve connects to the eye. (TPO14, L, S1, L1) 在这块神经连接眼睛的区域没有图像接受器。

recipe[1] ['resɪpɪ]

【释义】n. 烹饪法，食谱；处方
【例句】But now what if one ingredient to this planning recipe is missing? (TPO13, L, S1, L1) 但是，如果这个计划食谱中失去了一种原料会怎样呢？
【搭配】recipe books 烹饪书
be a recipe for 是…的秘诀

reciprocate[1] [rɪ'sɪprəkeɪt]

【释义】v. 1. 往复运动 2. 回报，答谢
【例句】Then he devised a way to make the piston turn a wheel and thus convert reciprocating (back and forth) motion into rotary motion. (TPO6, R, S1, T1) 随后，他又发明了一种新的方法，使得活塞可以转动轮子，从而使原来的往复运动（来回运动）演变成为旋转运动。
【派生】reciprocal a. 相互的；互惠的
reciprocation n. 互给，互换
reciprocityn. 相互性；互惠

recital[1] [rɪ'saɪtl]

【释义】n. 独奏，吟诵
【例句】She gave her first public recital at age 9. (TPO16, L, S1, L2) 她在九岁时进行了她的第一次公开演奏。

reddish[1] ['redɪʃ]

【释义】a. 带红色的，微红的（cherry-red, ruby）
【例句】More or less, they look like regular oranges from the outside (although they sometimes get a reddish hue on their skin, as well), so you have to keep an eye out for them. 从外观上看，它们和普通的橙子差不多（虽然它们有时在表皮上也有微红的色调），所以，你需要留心寻找它们。
【搭配】reddish brown 红棕色，赭色

Word List 48

reef[1] [riːf] 

【释义】*n.* 暗礁 *v.* 缩帆

【例句】Accidents involving oil tankers occur when tankers run into shore reefs or collide with other vessels. (TPO4, R, S2, T2) 涉及到油轮的意外事件包括油轮触礁或者是与其它船只相撞。

【搭配】coral reef 珊瑚礁
great barrier reef 大堡礁

soar[1] [sɔː] 

【释义】*n.* 1. 急升，猛增(ascend) 2. 高飞，翱翔 3. 高耸，屹立

【例句】And as a result, the nutrition of the general population improved tremendously and population soared in the early 1800 and so the shift of power from southern to northern Europe continued. (TPO10, L, S1, L2) 结果，普通人群的营养有了极大的提高，到1800年早期时，人口急剧增长，所以，权力继续从南欧向北欧转移。

reevaluate[1] [ˌriːɪˈvæljueɪt]

【释义】*v.* 再评估，重新估计(reestimate)

【例句】Perhaps we could reevaluate the initial campaign and revise the allocations of our budget. 我们也许可以重新评估最初的广告计划，调整预算的分配。

refuge[1] [ˈrefjuːdʒ] 

【释义】*n.* 避难所，庇护(shelter, haven)

【例句】He theorized that with the use of watercraft, people gradually colonized unglaciated refuges and areas along the continental shelf exposed by the lower sea level. (TPO9, R, S1, T1) 他得出了这样一个理论：通过船只的使用，人们逐渐殖民没有冰冻的地方以及到沿着大陆架的、由于海平面较低而裸露出来的地区。

【派生】refugee *n.* 难民，流亡者

【搭配】a harbour of refuge 避风港

regime[1] [reɪˈʒiːm] 

【释义】*n.* 政治制度，政权，政体

【例句】What we do know is that as we include longer time intervals, the record shows increasing evidence of slow swings in climate between different regimes. (TPO10, R, S2, T1) 我们所知道的是，当我们包括的时间间隔越长，记录显示出不同国家之间气候缓慢变化的痕迹就越明显。

regrettable[1] [rɪˈgretəbl] 

【释义】*a.* 可悲的，可叹的，可惜的，遗憾的

【例句】The trend of reading less literature is all the more regrettable because it is taking place during a period when good literature is being written. (TPO11, W, Q1) 文学作品阅读量下降这一趋势是更令人遗憾的，因为这发生在有大量好的文学作品被创作出来的时代。

reinterpret[1] [ˌriːinˈtəːprit]

【释义】*v.* 重新解释

【例句】I reinterpreted my situation. (TPO3, S, Q4) 我开始重新看待我所处的情形。

【派生】reinterpretation *n.* 重新诠释

reliance[1] [rɪˈlaɪəns] 

【释义】*n.* 依靠，依赖；受信赖的人或物(dependence, trust)

【例句】Reliance on trade had several important consequences. (TPO16, R, S1, T1) 依赖贸易有几项重要的结果。

【逆构】rely *v.* 依靠，依赖
reliant *a.* 依靠的，信赖自己的

【搭配】reliance on 依靠，信赖

remuneration[1] [rɪˌmjuːnəˈreɪʃən] 

【释义】*n.* 酬金，工资；赔偿金(compensation, payment)

【例句】Members of poor peasant families spun or wove cloth and linens at home for scant remuneration in an attempt to supplement

返记菜单

reef[1] soar[1] reevaluate[1] refuge[1] regime[1]
regrettable[1] reinterpret[1] reliance[1] remuneration[1]

meager family income. (TPO10, R, S2, T2) 为了补贴本已经微薄的家庭收入，贫困潦倒的农民们通过在家纺织衣料或亚麻来换取少量的报酬。

【派生】 remunerate *v.* 酬劳

repercussion[1] [ˌriːpə (ː) ˈkʌʃən]

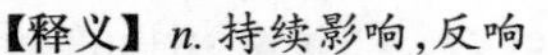

【释义】 *n.* 持续影响，反响

【例句】 And we know what important historical repercussions some of those voyages had. (TPO18, L, S2, L1) 我们知道那些航海经历所带来的重大历史影响。

【派生】 repercussive *a.* 反响的，反射的

【搭配】 chain repercussion 连锁反应

replenish[1] [rɪˈplenɪʃ]

【释义】 *v.* 补充(refill, restock)

【例句】 This unprecedented development of a finite groundwater resource with an almost negligible natural recharge rate—that is, virtually no natural water source to replenish the water supply— has caused water tables in the region to fall drastically. (TPO3, R, S1, T1) 考虑到几乎没有补充率(实质上没有自然水资源进行补充)，这种有限的地下水资源的前所未有的发展已经造成了该地区地下水位的急剧下降。

【派生】 replenisher *n.* 补充物，补偿物
replenishment *n.* 补给，补充

【搭配】 replenish the stock 补充库存

resell[1] [ˈriːˈsel]

【释义】 *v.* 再卖，转售

【例句】 The buyers of these pieces of paper would resell the notes and mark up prices. (TPO6, L, S1, L1) 这些本票的持有者将以更高的价格将它们售出去。

【派生】 reseller *n.* 分销商，代理销售商

【搭配】 resell goods 转卖货物

residue[1] [ˈrezɪdjuː]

【释义】 *n.* 残留物，余留物(leftover, remnant)

【例句】 Gypsum residue accumulated to form decorative structures. (TPO16, L, S1, L1) 石膏的残留部分堆积起来形成装饰性结构。

【派生】 residual *a.* 残余的，剩下的

resolution[1] [ˌrezəˈljuːʃən]

【释义】 *n.* 1. 决定，决议 2. 决心

【例句】 And that's followed by the final dramatic element—the denouement or the resolution, when all the lucent have to be tied up in the logical way. (TPO7, L, S1, L1) 这之后就是最终的戏剧元素——结局或解释，此时所有清楚明白的情节都要以一种符合逻辑的方式串联起来。

【逆构】 resolute *a.* 坚决的，毅然的

【搭配】 make/keep good resolutions 下定决心

resonance[1] [ˈrezənəns]

【释义】 *n.* 1. (声音)洪亮，响亮 2. 共鸣；回响；共振

【例句】 And another bit of physics I played here is something called Resonance. (TPO14, L, S2, L2) 在此我想展示的另一种物理现象叫做共振。

【逆构】 resonant *a.* (声音)洪亮的，回荡的；引起共鸣的

【搭配】 nuclear magnetic resonance 核磁共振
resonance vibration 共振；谐振

restrain[1] [rɪsˈtreɪn]

【释义】 *v.* 抑制，遏制，克制(inhibit, repress)

【例句】 He didn't let the conventional thinking of his day restrain his ideas. (TPO10, L, S1, L2) 他没有让他那个时代的传统观念制约他的想法。

【派生】 restraint *n.* 抑制，克制
unrestrained *a.* 无限制的

【搭配】 restrain oneself 自制，约束自己
restrain from 抑制；制止

retard[1] [rɪˈtɑːd]

【释义】 *v.* 妨碍，阻碍(curb, hinder, impede)

【例句】 The high costs of converting to sound and the early limitations of sound technology were among the factors that suppressed innovations or retarded advancement in these other areas. (TPO12, R, S2, T1) 转化成有声影像的高花费和早期声音技术的局限性都是制约创新或妨碍这些领域进步的

因素。

【派生】retardance *n.* 迟缓；阻止

retarded *a.* 智力发育迟缓的，弱智的

reuse[1] ['riːˈjuːz]

【释义】*n./v.* 重新使用，再利用

【例句】Some of the waste material can be reworked for reuse. 有些废料可以重新加工再次利用。

revenue[1] ['revɪnjuː]

【释义】*n.*（大宗的）收入（益）；税收

【例句】Another goal is to provide the university with an extra source of revenue. (TPO12, S, Q5) 另一个目标就是为大学提供一个额外的收入来源。

【派生】revenuer *n.* 税务官员；缉私船

revitalize[1] ['riːˈvaɪtəlaɪz]

【释义】*v.* 使复活，使重新充满活力

【例句】With financial assets considerably greater than those in the motion picture industry, and perhaps a wider vision of the relationships among entertainment and communications media, they revitalized research into recording sound for motion picture. (TPO12, R, S2, T1) 因为他们占有的资产要比电影产业多得多，又或许是因为对娱乐业和传播媒体之间的联系有着更广阔的愿景，所以他们复兴了对电影录音方面的研究。

【派生】revitalization *n.* 新生，复苏

revive[1] [rɪˈvaɪv]

【释义】*v.*（使）苏醒，（使）复原，使再流行（refresh, recover, renew）

【例句】Well, that's the amazing thing and how it revives is pretty amazing too. (TPO18, L, S2, L2) 那是非常令人震撼的一件事，同样令人惊讶的还有它是如何复活过来的。

【派生】revival *n.* 复苏，复活；重新流行

【搭配】revive an old dream 重温旧梦

rewrite[1] [riːˈraɪt]

【释义】*v.* 重写，改写

【例句】I think you could learn a lot by rewriting it. (TPO12, L, S1, C1) 我想，通过改写你能学到不少东西。

【逆构】write *v.* 写

【搭配】rewrite man 报馆改稿员

rhythmic[1] ['rɪðmɪk]

【释义】*a.* 有节奏的，有韵律的

【例句】It was secondary to the rhythmic flow of language. (TPO12, L, S2, L1) 比起有节奏的语流，它是第二位的。

【派生】rhythmical *a.* 有节奏的，有韵律的

【逆构】rhythm *n.* 节奏，韵律

rim[1] [rɪm]

【释义】*n.*（圆形物体的）边，缘（border, edge, margin）*v.* 绕…边缘

【例句】The Hellas Basin, which measures some 3,000 kilometers across and has a floor that lies nearly 9 kilometers below the basin's rim, is another candidate for an ancient Martian sea. (TPO8, R, S2, T2) 海拉斯盆地的直径有 3000 公里，并且其盆底位于盆地边缘约 9 公里以下，该盆地是古老的火星海的另一个可能的地点。

【搭配】Pacific Rim 泛太平洋，太平洋沿岸地区

roam[1] [rəʊm]

【释义】*v.* 漫步，漫游（ramble, wander）

【例句】He received rudimentary village schooling, but mostly he roamed his uncle's farm collecting the fossils that were so abundant in the rocks of the Cotswold hills. (TPO6, R, S2, T1) 他只在村里接受了最基本的教育，而大部分的时间都是在他叔叔的农场里搜寻化石，这些化石大量存在于科茨沃尔德山的岩石中。

【派生】roamer *n.* 流浪者，漂泊者

【搭配】roam about the world 漫游世界

roast[1] [rəʊst]

【释义】*v.* 烤，烘焙（bake, toast）*n.* 1. 烤肉 2. 户外烧烤野餐 *a.* 烤好的，烤制的

【例句】The first bulb to show up in the Netherlands, the merchant who received them roasted and ate them. (TPO6, L, S1, L1) 当第一株郁金

返记菜单

reuse[1] revenue[1] revitalize[1] revive[1] rewrite[1]
rhythmic[1] rim[1] roam[1] roast[1]

香出现在荷兰时，得到它的商人将其烤制后吃掉了。

【搭配】 roast turkey 烤火鸡

rotary[1] ['rəʊtərɪ]

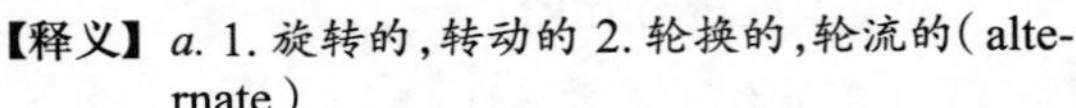

【释义】 *a.* 1. 旋转的，转动的 2. 轮换的，轮流的（alternate）

【例句】 Then he devised a way to make the piston turn a wheel and thus convert reciprocating (back and forth) motion into rotary motion. (TPO6, R, S1, T1) 随后，他又发明了一种新的方法，使得活塞可以转动轮子，从而使原来的往复运动（前后运动）演变成为旋转运动。

【逆构】 rotate *v.* 旋转，转动；轮流

rub[1] [rʌb]

【释义】 *v.* 1. 擦，摩擦，搓 2. 惹恼 *n.* 擦

【例句】 The signs of rubbing on their left side indicate that their users were right-handed. (TPO12, R, S1, T1) 它们左侧摩擦过的痕迹表明它们的使用者是惯用右手的。

【搭配】 rub sth. with sth. 用…擦…

ruffle[1] ['rʌfl]

【释义】 *v.* 1. 弄皱，弄乱 2. 激怒，扰乱 *n.* 褶饰，花边

【例句】 I mean if a bird's feathers get ruffled or an animal's fur, maybe it's not so strange for them to stop and tidy themselves up at that point. (TPO4, L, S1, L1) 我是说，假如鸟或者动物竖起毛发，也许它们停下来整理自己的毛发，这并不奇怪。

rug[1] [rʌg]

【释义】 *n.* 地毯，毯子，旅行毯（carpet）

【例句】 Say you pick green and then use a light shade of green for the walls and maybe a somewhat darker shade for the fabric on the sofa, and finally complement that with a matching green in the rug. (TPO11, S, Q6) 假设你选择绿色，然后在墙上用浅绿色，也许沙发布料选择深点的绿色，最后再用一条相配的绿色的小地毯来互补一下。

rumor[1] ['ruːmə]

【释义】 *n./v.* 谣言，谣传，传闻（gossip）

【例句】 And the other might mention a rumor about the mysterious gentleman who just moved into the town with his beautiful daughter. (TPO7, L, S1, L1) 另外一个人可能会提到关于一个神秘的绅士和他的女儿刚刚搬进城的传闻。

sacred[1] ['seɪkrɪd]

【释义】 *a.* 1. 神圣的，不可冒犯的（divine, holy）2. 宗教的，祭祀的

【例句】 It resembled sacred church music. (TPO12, L, S2, L1) 它类似于一种神圣的教堂音乐。

【派生】 sacredness *n.* 神圣；受人尊敬

【搭配】 sacred and inviolable 神圣不可侵犯

satire[1] ['sætaɪə]

【释义】 *n.* 讽刺，讥讽；讽刺作品

【例句】 And the opera was no longer about teaching religion as it was about satire and about expressing the ideas of society and your government without committing yourself to writing and risking imprisonment or persecution. (TPO12, L, S2, L1) 而且歌剧不再与教授宗教教义有关，而是与讽刺有关，与表达对社会对政府的看法有关，这样一来就可以使你免于写作和冒被囚禁或是被迫害的风险了。

【派生】 satiric *a.* 讽刺的，挖苦的
satirist *n.* 讽刺作家

sauce[1] [sɔːs]

【释义】 *n.* 调味汁，酱汁 *v.* 给…增加趣味或风味

【例句】 But what about all those Italian tomato sauces, humburger or my favorite, French fries? (TPO10, L, S1, L2) 那么，那些意大利番茄酱、汉堡包或者我最爱的薯条怎么样呢？

【搭配】 tomato sauce 番茄酱

scant[1] [skænt]

【释义】 *a.* 不足的，缺乏的（insufficient, short, defi-

返记菜单

rotary[1]	rub[1]	ruffle[1]	rug[1]	rumor[1]
sacred[1]	satire[1]	sauce[1]	scant[1]	

cient）

【例句】Members of poor peasant families spun or wove cloth and linens at home for scant remuneration in an attempt to supplement meager family income. (TPO10, R, S2, T2) 为了补贴本已经微薄的家庭收入，贫困潦倒的农民们通过在家纺织衣料或亚麻来换取少量的报酬。

【派生】scanty *a.* 不够的，勉强够的

【搭配】scant of 缺乏…的

scream[1] [skriːm] 

【释义】*v.* 尖叫，大叫大嚷 *n.* 尖叫声

【例句】I almost felt like screaming, but I didn't want to upset my daughter, so I said, "Don't worry, honey, it's nothing." (TPO4, S, Q4) 我差点都要叫出来了，但我不想吓到女儿，所以我说："别担心，宝贝，没事。"

【搭配】scream for 强烈要求；为…而尖叫
scream out 大叫，尖声喊叫

scrubland[1] ['skrʌbˌlænd] 

【释义】*n.* 灌木丛林地

【例句】This species, which lives in the rain forests and scrublands of the east coast of Australia, has a brown-to-black plumage with bare, bright-red skin on the head and neck and a neck collar of orange-yellow loosely hanging skin. (TPO17, R, S2, T1) 这一物种生活在澳大利亚东海岸的雨林和灌木丛中，有着黑棕色的羽毛，光秃秃的头部和脖子上的皮肤是鲜亮的红色，脖子上还有一圈橙黄色的松垮的皮肤。

seagull[1] ['siːgʌl] 

【释义】*n.* 海鸥

【例句】First, it's true that urban growth has been bad for some types of birds, but urban development actually provides better and larger habitats for other types, so much so, that city and suburban dwellers often complain about increased bird populations—seagulls at landfills, pigeons on the streets and so on. (TPO17, W, Q1) 第一，城市的发展的确对某些种类的鸟来说是不好的，但是城市的发展事实上为其它一些种类的鸟儿提供了更好、更大的栖息环境，以至于城市和郊区的居民常常抱怨鸟太多了——垃圾填埋场上的海鸥、街道上的鸽子等等。

sect[1] [sekt] 

【释义】*n.* 宗派

【例句】They were usually members of the same guild and religious sect. (TPO16, R, S1, T1) 他们通常是同一工会或宗教的成员。

【搭配】religious sect 宗教派别

seedling[1] ['siːdlɪŋ] 

【释义】*n.* 幼苗

【例句】Late-lying snow reduces the effective growing season to the point where seedlings cannot establish them. (TPO1, R, S1, T1) 久积不化的雪缩短了植物的有效生长时间，导致树苗无法存活。

segment[1] ['segmənt] 

【释义】*n.* 部分，片段（sector, portion, section）

【例句】That invention was the arch, a curved structure originally made of separate stone or brick segments. (TPO3, R, S1, T1) 这种发明便是拱，这是一种最初由独立的石头或砖块构成的弧形建筑结构。

【派生】segmental *a.* 部分的
segmentation *n.* 分割

【搭配】see segment of a whole 窥见一斑

self-assertion[1] [ˌselfə'səːʃən] 

【释义】*n.* 自信，自作主张，一意孤行

【例句】It is an act of self-assertion wholly impossible in most other civilizations throughout history. (TPO16, R, S1, T1) 纵观历史，在大多数的其他文明中，自作主张几乎是不可能的。

self-explanatory[1] ['selfiks'plænətəri] 

【释义】*a.* 毋需（多加）解释的；清楚的

【例句】Echolocation is pretty self-explanatory, using echoes reflected sound waves to locate things. (TPO7, L, S1, L2) 回声定位能力，不言而喻，就是通过反射声波来定位。

self-governing[1] [ˌselfˈgʌvəniŋ]

【释义】*a.* 自治的，自己管理自己的（autonomous）

【例句】This mode of craft production favored the growth of self-governing and ideologically egalitarian craft guilds everywhere in the Middle Eastern city. (TPO16, R, S1, T1) 这种工艺生产模式有利于中东城市中自治、意识上平等的工艺品行会的发展。

【搭配】self-governing power 自治权

self-sufficiency[1] [ˈselfsəˈfiʃənsi]

【释义】*n.* 自给自足

【例句】So, by and large, nomadism implies a high degree of self-sufficiency and inhibits the appearance of an extensive division of labor. (TPO14, R, S2, T2) 所以，总的来说，游牧意味着一种高度的自给自足，并抑制了大规模劳动分工的出现。

【逆构】self-sufficient *a.* 自己自足的

semicircular[1] [ˌsemiˈsəːkjulə]

【释义】*a.* 半圆的

【例句】Roman builders perfected the semicircular arch made of separate blocks of stone. (TPO3, R, S1, T1) 罗马建造者完善了由独立的石块组成的半圆拱形。

sensory[1] [ˈsensərɪ]

【释义】*a.* 感官的，感觉上的

【例句】Furthermore, one sensory ability may back up another. (TPO11, R, S2, T1) 而且，一种感官能力可能会支持另一种。

【逆构】sensor *n.* 传感器，感应装置

【搭配】sensory stimuli 感官刺激

serial[1] [ˈsɪərɪəl]

【释义】*n.* 连载小说，电视连续剧 *a.* 连续的，一系列的，一连串的

【例句】Now during TV shows that young people watch, you know shows with pop music or teen serials, they create the commercial that emphasizes how fun the phone is. (TPO5, S, Q4) 现在，在年轻人经常看的电视节目期间，你知道的，就是那些流行音乐节目或青少年连续剧期间，他们创造了商业广告来强调这款手机有多好玩。

【派生】serialize *v.*（小说等）连载，连播

【搭配】serial killer 连环杀手
serial number 连续编号

shame[1] [ʃeɪm]

【释义】*n.* 羞耻，羞愧 *v.* 使蒙羞 *v.* 感到惭愧

【例句】And one says, "Oh, what a shame master's son is still not married." (TPO7, L, S1, L1) 一人说道："主人的儿子现在还没结婚，多丢脸啊！"

【派生】ashamed *a.* 羞愧的，惭愧的

【搭配】put…to shame 使自愧不如，使相形见绌

shepherd[1] [ˈʃepəd]

【释义】*n.* 1. 牧羊人 2. 指导者 *v.* 看管，带领

【例句】The shepherds of tribal confederacies were left alone by their leaders. (TPO16, R, S1, T1) 放牧部落联盟不是由他们的头来管理。

【搭配】shepherd dog（= sheepdog）牧羊犬

shower[1] [ˈʃaʊə]

【释义】*n.* 1. 淋浴（器）2. 阵雨 3. 送礼会 *v.* 1. 抛洒；倾注 2. 淋浴 3. 下阵雨

【例句】If we had rock samples to study, we'd know whether the small craters were formed by impacts during the final stages of planetary formation, or if they resulted from later meteor showers. (TPO5, L, S1, L2) 如果我们有岩石样本可供研究，我们就能知道那些小火山是不是由行星形成后期的冲击力形成的，或者是不是由后来的流星雨造成的。

【派生】showerproof *a.* 防水的
showery *a.* 阵雨的，多阵雨的

【搭配】take a shower 洗淋浴
meteor shower 流星雨

shroud[1] [ʃraʊd]

【释义】*v.* 1. 笼罩，遮蔽，隐藏 *n.* 1. 寿衣 2. 遮蔽物，覆盖物

【例句】Their origins were shrouded in exotic travels. (TPO18, L, S2, L1) 它们的起源充满奇异的色彩。

simulate[1] ['sɪmjuleɪt] 

【释义】*v.* 1. 模拟，模仿(imitate) 2. 假装，冒充(pretend)

【例句】To simulate the shifting of light the birds would encounter along their regular migratory route (TPO11, R, S2, T1) 来模仿鸟类在定期的迁徙路途中遇到的光线的变化

【派生】simulation *n.* 仿真；假装
simulative *a.* 模拟的；假装的

sincerity[1] [sɪn'serɪtɪ] 

【释义】*n.* 真诚，诚意(earnestness, seriousness)

【例句】His absence spoke for his lack of sincerity. 他不肯来证明他缺乏诚意。

【逆构】sincere *a.* 真诚的

【搭配】in all sincerity 十分真诚地，衷心地

situate[1] ['sɪtjʊeɪt] 

【释义】*v.* 使位于，使处于…环境中(locate, posit)

【例句】Melanesia is situated to the north of Micronesia. (TPO5, R, S2, T1) 马来西亚位于密克罗尼西亚的北部。

【派生】situation *n.* 位置；形势，情况

【搭配】be situated to 位于，坐落于

skim[1] [skɪm] 

【释义】*v.* 1. 浏览，略读 2. 掠过，擦过 3. 从液体表面撇去(浮油等)

【例句】When you go into the databases and electronic sources, you have the option to display the abstracts on the computer screen, skimming those to decide whether or not you want to read the whole article. (TPO1, L, S1, C1) 当你接触到那些数据和电子原始材料时，你就可以选择在电脑屏幕上显示那些摘要，浏览那些摘要，以决定是否要阅读整篇文章。

【派生】skimmed *a.* 脱脂的

【搭配】skimming and sanning 快速阅读
skim over/through 浏览，快速阅读
skimmed milk 脱脂牛奶

slender[1] ['slendə] 

【释义】*a.* 1. 苗条的，修长的(thin) 2. 微薄的，微弱的

【例句】Stems are short and slender. (TPO5, R, S1, T1) 枝干短而细。

【派生】slenderize *v.* 使苗条；使成细长状

smash[1] [smæʃ] 

【释义】*v.* 1. 猛击，猛撞(crash) 2. 打碎，粉碎(shatter) *n.* 破碎，撞击

【例句】And of course, stupid me, I wasn't being very careful and I smashed my thumb with the hammer. (TPO4, S, Q4) 当然，我太傻了，我不小心用锤子把自己的拇指给砸到了。

【派生】smashing *a.* 粉碎性的，猛烈的

【搭配】smash up 撞毁，击毁
smash hit 非常流行的东西；轰动的演出

snowdrift[1] ['snəʊdrɪft] 

【释义】*n.* 雪堆

【例句】At this great height, rocks, warmed by the sun, melt small snowdrifts. (TPO1, R, S1, T1) 在这样的高度上，被太阳温暖了的石头把一些小雪堆融化了。

返记菜单

simulate[1] sincerity[1] situate[1] skim[1] slender[1]
smash[1] snowdrift[1]

Word List 49

solitary[1] ['sɒlɪtərɪ]

【释义】n. 1. 孤独的，独居的（isolated, alone）2. 单个的，唯一的

【例句】The hero in the Romance Poetry is independent, purely solitary in a way, not like the Chanson poet who was always surrounded by his fighting companions. (TPO13, L, S2, L1) 浪漫主义诗歌的主人公较为独立，在某种方式上是孤独的，与香颂诗人总是有战友相伴不同。

【派生】solitude n. 孤独，独处

【搭配】a solitary walk 独自一人的散步

sonar[1] ['səʊnɑː]

【释义】n. 声纳，声波定位器

【例句】Other areas under investigation include magnetism, landmarks, coastlines, sonar, and even smells. (TPO11, R, S2, T1) 其它正在研究的领域包括磁性、地标、海岸线、声纳，甚至还有气味。

soon-to-be[1]

【释义】即将成为…的

【例句】Well, as you know, the career fair is generally an opportunity for local businesses to recruit new employees, and for soon-to-be graduates to have interviews with several companies they might be interested in working for. (TPO6, L, S1, C1) 你知道，人才招聘会主要是为当地企业招聘新员工和为即将毕业的大学生与他们比较感兴趣的一些公司进行面试提供机会。

sought-after[1] ['sɔːtɑːftə]

【释义】a. 很吃香的；广受欢迎的

【例句】Spices were the most sought-after commodities. (TPO17, R, S1, T1) 香料开始变成最受欢迎的日用品。

spacious[1] ['speɪʃəs]

【释义】a. 宽广的，宽敞的（wide, vast）

【例句】It's not a very big car at all, but you get the sense that it's pretty spacious. (TPO3, S, Q6) 汽车实际上并不是很大，但给你的感觉是它真的很宽敞。

【搭配】light and spacious 敞亮

spaghetti[1] [spə'getɪ]

【释义】n. 意大利式细面条

【例句】And I spilt spaghetti sauce all over it. (TPO15, S, Q5) 我把意大利面的汁儿全洒在上面了。

speckle[1] ['spekl]

【释义】v. 点缀，弄上斑点 n. 小斑点（mottle, spot）

【例句】Its normal skin color, the one it generally presents, is either red or brown or even grey, and it's speckled with dark spots. (TPO17, L, S2, L2) 它正常的肤色，即通常所呈现的肤色，要么是红色，要么就是棕色甚至灰色，上面点缀有黑色的斑点。

【派生】speckled a. 有斑点的
speckless a. 无斑点的

spew[1] [spjuː]

【释义】v.（使）喷出，（使）涌出

【例句】The force of collision spewed large amounts of debris into the atmosphere, darkening the skies for several years before the finer particles settled. (TPO15, R, S2, T2) 碰撞的力量把大量碎片喷射到大气中，在这些小颗粒沉淀之前天空会黑上好几年。

【派生】spewer n. 呕吐者

【搭配】spew up〈英口〉呕吐

spider[1] ['spaɪdə]

【释义】n. 蜘蛛

【例句】For example, a well-known Burgess Shale animal called Sidneyia is a representative of a previously unknown group of arthropods (a category of animals that includes insects, spiders, mites, and crabs). (TPO5, R, S2,

返记菜单

T2）例如，伯吉斯页岩化石群中的一种著名动物，Sidneyia，就是一种典型的以前还不为人知的节肢动物（一种动物分类，它包括昆虫、蜘蛛、螨虫和螃蟹）。

【派生】spiderman *n.* 高空作业的人
spiderweb *a.* 蛛网形的
spidery *a.* 细长足的

spike[1] [spaɪk] 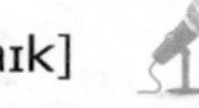

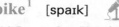

【释义】*n.* 1. 尖状物 2.（防滑）鞋钉 *v.* 1. 把尖状物钉入 2. 加烈酒于

【例句】They are like spikes, sticking out of the plant that are so numerous and dense that they prevent insects from landing on the leaves. (TPO9, S, Q6) 它们如同针状物，从植物中间伸出来，它们的数量如此之多、密度如此之大，从而阻止昆虫降落在叶子上。

【派生】spiky *a.* 有尖刺的；难对付的

【搭配】spike someone's guns 挫败某人的计划

spiky[1] ['spaɪkɪ] 

【释义】*a.* 1. 有尖刺的 2.（指人）难对付的，难取悦的，易怒的

【例句】Its leaves have little spiky hairs all over them. (TPO9, S, Q6) 它的叶子上面满是小的尖刺。

spiral[1] ['spaɪərəl] 

【释义】*v.* 盘旋上升（或下降）（rise, coil, twist）*a.* 螺旋的，盘旋的

【例句】The late Ice Age rope found in the French cave of Lascaux consists of fibers spiraling to the right, and was therefore tressed by a right hander. (TPO12, R, S1, T1) 在法国拉斯科洞中发现的冰河时代晚期的绳子中含有向右侧盘旋的纤维丝，因此这些绳子是由一个惯用右手的人拧成的。

【派生】spirality *n.* 螺旋形
spirally *ad.* 成螺旋形地

【搭配】spiral up 盘旋状上升；扶摇直上

spiritual[1] ['spɪrɪtjuəl] 

【释义】*a.* 1. 精神的，心灵的（immaterial）2. 教会的，宗教的

【例句】Pastoralist communities do not have social classes in the usual sense because they value spiritual attainment over material wealth. (TPO14, R, S2, T2) 游牧群体中没有通常意义上的社会阶级，因为他们把精神成就看得比物质财富重。

【反义】material, physical

【派生】spiritualism *n.* 唯心论；灵性
spiritualist *n.* 唯心论者；巫师
spirituality *n.* 灵性

【逆构】spirit *n.* 精神，灵魂

【搭配】spiritual pillar 精神支柱
spiritual civilization 精神文明

spurge[1] [spəːdʒ] 

【释义】*n.*（植物）大戟属

【例句】Many members of the mustard family, spurge family, legume family and grass family are top hyperaccumulators. (TPO5, R, S1, T1) 很多十字花科、牧草科、豆科和禾本科植物都是顶级的重金属超富集植物。

squash[1] [skwɒʃ] 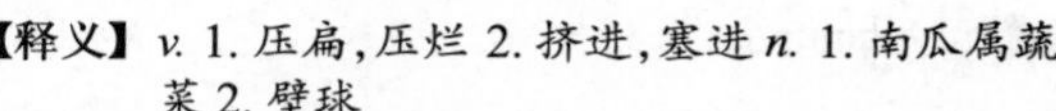

【释义】*v.* 1. 压扁，压烂 2. 挤进，塞进 *n.* 1. 南瓜属蔬菜 2. 壁球

【例句】The Americas provide Europe and Asia with food like squash, beans, turkey, peanuts. (TPO10, L, S1, L2) 美洲向欧洲和亚洲提供南瓜、豆子、火鸡、花生等食品。

【派生】squashy *a.* 软而多汁的
squashed *a.* 挤碎的，压扁的

squat[1] [skwɒt] 

【释义】*v.* 1. 蹲下，蹲坐 2. 擅自占地 *a.* 粗矮的，矮胖的 *n.* 1. 蹲 2. 擅自占用的土地

【例句】Unlike formal statues that are limited to static poses of standing, sitting, and kneeling, these figures depict a wide range of actions, such as grinding grain, baking bread, producing pots, and making music, and they are shown in appropriate poses, bending and squatting as they carry out their tasks. (TPO11, R, S1, T1) 这些雕像不像正规雕像那样只有静止的站立、坐和跪的姿态，而是表现了各种不同的动作，比如磨谷物、烤面包、造壶罐，还有奏乐，而且进行这

些活动时的姿态都很恰当，或弯腰，或蹲坐着。

【派生】squatter *n.* 蹲着的人
squatty *a.* 矮胖的

【搭配】squat down 蹲下，坐下

squid[1] [skwɪd]

【释义】*n.* 枪乌贼，鱿鱼

【例句】Take the cuddle fish, a fish that's closely related to the squid and octopus. (TPO13, S, Q6) 以拥抱鱼为例，这是一种与乌贼和章鱼非常相似的鱼。

stamp[1] [stæmp]

【释义】*n.* 1. 邮票 2. 印，图章 *v.* 1. 贴邮票于 2. 在…上盖章

【例句】A stamp on the back of the picture indicates that the blank canvas was sold by a man named William Legg. (TPO12, W, Q1) 这幅画后面的戳记表明那块空白的帆布画布是一个名叫 William Legg 的人售出的。

【派生】stamped *a.* 盖上邮戳的；铭刻的

【搭配】stamp out 扑灭，踩灭

stark[1] [stɑːk]

【释义】*a.* 1. 显而易见的，明摆着的 2. 简陋的，荒凉的 3. 全然的，十足的

【例句】Of course, the contrast is not quite so stark: in Alexander the Great the Greeks had found the greatest territorial conqueror of all time; and the Romans, once they moved outside Italy, did not fail to learn the lessons of sea power. (TPO7, R, S2, T1) 当然，二者的对比并不是十分鲜明：在亚历山大大帝时代，希腊人就已经发现了最伟大的领土征服者，而罗马人在撤出意大利之后也没有忘记过海上军事力量的重要性。

【搭配】in stark contrast 成鲜明对比

sting[1] [stɪŋ]

【释义】*v.* 刺，蛰，叮；刺痛(bite, prick) *n.* 1. (某些昆虫的)毒刺，螯针，(植物的)刺 2. 螯伤，刺伤

【例句】They sting other insects and large herbivores (animals that eat only plants) and even clip surrounding vegetation that grows near the tree. (TPO17, R, S2, T2) 它们会叮咬昆虫和大型食草动物(只以植物为食的动物)，甚至会攻击生长在树周围的其他植物。

【派生】stingingly *ad.* 有刺地，尖锐地
stingy *a.* 少量的，不足的；小气的

【搭配】sting in the tail 意外结局

stitch[1] [stɪtʃ]

【释义】*v.* 缝(sew, knit)

【例句】The bark was stretched over frames made from tree branches, stitched together and sealed with resin. (TPO7, L, S2, C1) 树皮依照用树枝做好的框架进行延展，然后缝合在一起，并用树脂密封好。

【搭配】stitch sth. up 缝合某物

storey[1] ['stɔːrɪ]

【释义】*n.* 楼层(floor)

【例句】The houses are rectangular, one storey made of sun dried bricks. (TPO 1, L, S2, L1) 这些房子是长方形的，其中一个楼层是由晒干的砖头建成的。

【派生】storeyed *a.* 有…层楼的

stratification[1] [ˌstrætɪfɪ'keɪʃən]

【释义】*n.* 层化，成层

【例句】The…uh…the stratification technique gives us the minimum age of an object which isn't necessarily its true age. (TPO17, L, S1, L1) 地层技术给我们提供了物体的最小年龄，这并不一定是它的真实年龄。

【派生】stratified *a.* 分层的

【搭配】social stratification 社会分层

sturdy[1] ['stɜːdɪ]

【释义】*a.* 1. (人)强壮的，结实的(robust, strong) 2. (物)稳固的(firm)

【例句】They would peel large sheets of bark from the tree to form light-weight yet sturdy canoes. (TPO7, L, S2, C1) 他们会将大块的树皮剥下来，做成轻而坚固的独木舟。

subconscious[1] ['sʌb'kɒnʃəs]

【释义】*a.* 下意识的；潜意识的

【例句】It is a largely subconscious process. (TPO6, L, S2, C1) 这很大程度上是一个下意识的过程。
【派生】subconsciously *ad.* 潜意识地
【搭配】a subconscious motive 下意识的动机

submarine[1] ['sʌbməriːn] 

【释义】*a.* 海底的,水下的 *n.* 潜水艇,潜艇
【例句】Offshore drilling platforms extend the search for oil to the ocean's continental shelves—those gently sloping submarine regions at the edges of the continents. (TPO4, R, S2, T2) 寻找石油的近海钻井平台已经拓展到了大陆架——那些大陆边缘逐渐向海底倾斜的区域。
【搭配】submarine pipeline 海底管道;水下管道
nuclear submarine 核潜艇
submarine cable 海底电缆

subscribe[1] [səb'skraɪb]

【释义】*v.* 1. 赞同 2. 定期交费;定期捐款 3. 订阅 4. 签名
【例句】But the other idea and this is the one that I personally subscribe to, is of the changes in the temperature pattern had been brought about by the loss of wetlands. (TPO11, L, S2, L1) 但是另外一个观点,也是我个人赞同的一个观点,就是温度场的变化是由于湿地的消失引起的。
【派生】subscriber *n.* 订阅者;会员;签名者
subscription *n.* 订阅费;会员费;捐款
【搭配】subscribe for 认购(股票)
subscribe to 同意,赞同

subsidy[1] ['sʌbsɪdɪ]

【释义】*n.* 津贴,补助金(pension, allowance)
【例句】The idea was that there be a federal subsidy…um…uh…financial assistance to artists and artistic or cultural institutions. (TPO4, L, S2, L2) 这一意见是设立联邦津贴,为艺术家及艺术文化机构提供财政支持。
【派生】subsidization *n.* 补助,津贴
【逆构】subsidize *v.* 给…补助,资助

subtropic[1] [sʌb'trɑpɪk] 

【释义】*a.* 亚热带的
【例句】It ranges from sea level in the polar regions to 4500 meters in the dry subtropics and 3,500-4,500 meters in the moist tropics. (TPO1, R, S1, T1) 它从极地地区的海平面延伸到4500米高的干燥的亚热带地区以及3500至4500米的潮湿的热带地区。

succulent[1] ['sʌkjʊlənt] 

【释义】*a.* 美味多汁的
【例句】The early explorers and settlers told of abundant deer in the early 1800s and yet almost in the same breath bemoaned the lack of this succulent game animal. (TPO4, R, S1, T1) 19世纪初期的探险家和移民们描述有大量的鹿群,而几乎与此同时又哀叹这种肉质鲜嫩的猎物的不足。
【派生】succulence *n.* 鲜美多汁
succulently *ad.* 多汁地
【搭配】succulent plant 肉质植物
succulent fruit 多汁的水果

superficial[1] [sjuːpə'fɪʃəl] 

【释义】*a.* 1. 肤浅的,浅薄的(shallow)2. 表层的,表皮的 3. 表面上的
【例句】These are usually superficial poorly written, and intellectually undemanding. (TPO11, W, Q1) 这些书通常都写得很肤浅,而且对知识要求不高。
【派生】superficiality *n.* 表面性的事物;浅薄

supermarket[1] ['sjuːpəˌmɑːkɪt] 

【释义】*n.* 超级市场,超市
【例句】Well, the head of the company, had Dortans' top executives walk around supermarkets, um, asking shoppers what they thought of Dortans' soup. (TPO12, L, S1, L2) 公司的领导让Dortan公司的高管们在超市里四处走动,询问顾客们对于Dortan公司制作的汤的看法。

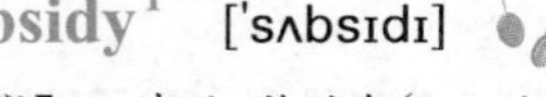

submarine[1] subscribe[1] subsidy[1] subtropic[1] succulent[1]
superficial[1] supermarket[1]

supportive[1] [sə'pɔːtɪv]

【释义】*a.* 支持的，拥护的，给予帮助的
【例句】And they're always very supportive of the university and our students. (TPO 9, L, S1, C1) 他们一直非常支持大学和我们的学生。
【逆构】support *v.* 支撑，支持

surrender[1] [sə'rendə]

【释义】*v.* 1. 投降，屈服 2. 放弃，交出 *n.* 投降，屈服，让步
【例句】There are a lot of pressures to become something you are not, and people often surrendered to that pressure. (TPO10, L, S1, C1) 有很多压力会让你变得不像自己，而很多人都经常会屈服于那种压力。
【反义】resist
【搭配】unconditional surrender 无条件投降

suspect[1]

【释义】[sə'spɛkt] *v.* 怀疑，猜想（doubt）['sʌspɛkt] *a.* 令人怀疑的，不可信的（doubtful, dubious）
【例句】With these sophisticated observational assessment and electro physiological measures, we know that the neonate of only a few days is far more perceptive than previously suspected. (TPO13, R, S2, T2) 通过这些复杂的观察评估和电子生理学的测量，我们知道，一个几天大的新生儿的感知能力远远超出我们之前的猜想。
【派生】suspectable *a.* 可疑的，有嫌疑的
【搭配】suspect sb.'s motives 怀疑某人的动机

sweep[1] [swiːp]

【释义】*v.* 1. 席卷，掠过 2. 清扫，打扫（clean）*n.* 伸展，延伸
【例句】Take a painting that, say, uses a lot of strong colors like reds and oranges and uses brush strokes that are broad—wide, sweeping brush strokes that suggest a rough texture. (TPO4, S, Q6) 以一幅画为例，比如这幅，画中运用了大量强烈的色彩，如红色和橘色，还使用了很宽的笔触——这种宽大的扫笔表现了一种粗糙的肌理。
【搭配】sweep away 清除；一扫而空
clean sweep 全胜；快速整理
sweep up 大扫除，收拾干净
sweep out 清除，扫除
sweep down 突袭

swirl[1] [swɜːl]

【释义】*v.*（使）打旋，盘旋（whirl）*n.* 旋转，打旋；漩涡
【例句】And then it runs along the ground swirling left and right you know like running around a little rocks and sticks. (TPO11, L, S1, L1) 然后它沿着地面左右盘旋着跑，你知道的，就像绕着小石子和树枝跑一样。
【派生】swirly *a.* 成漩涡形的
【搭配】swirl chamber 涡流室

syllable[1] ['sɪləbl]

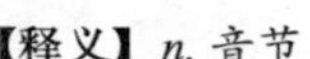

【释义】*n.* 音节
【例句】They had to count the number of syllables in different words. (TPO15, L, S1, L1) 他们得数出不同单词中音节的个数。

symmetrically[1] [sə'metrikli]

【释义】*ad.* 对称地，匀称地，均衡地（evenly）
【例句】What that meant was that the sky could be partitioned, divided up, much more symmetrically than it could farther away from the equator. (TPO14, L, S2, L1) 这就意味着天空在赤道这里比在其他远离赤道的地方被分割、划分得对称得多。
【逆构】symmetrical *a.* 对称的

synchronize[1] ['sɪŋkrənaɪz]

【释义】*v.* 同步，同时发生
【例句】The disorienting effects of this mismatch between external time cues and internal schedules may persist, like our jet lag, for several days or weeks until certain cues such as the daylight/darkness cycle reset the organism's clock to synchronize with the daily rhythm of the new environment. (TPO13, R, S2, T1) 外部时间与内在循环的这种不协调所产生的令人困惑的影响就像我们的时差综合症，可能会持续几天或者几个星期，直到诸如白昼和黑夜的循环之类的

特定信号重新设定生物体的生物钟，使其与新环境的昼夜节律同步。
【搭配】synchronize sth. with sth. 使某物同步

synthesis[1] ['sɪnθɪsɪs]

【释义】*n.* 综合物，综合体；合成，综合
【例句】Then you will write a paper that is not so much about the observations, but a synthesis of what you have observed and read. (TPO13, L, S1, C1) 然后，你要写一篇论文，观察部分不要写太多，而是要将重点放在对你所观察到的和读到的综合分析上。
【逆构】synthesize *v.* 综合，合成

tamper[1] ['tæmpə]

【释义】*v.* 1. 篡改，干预(meddle, interfere) 2. 玩弄 3. 贿赂
【例句】Once changes have been made to the original text, an unsuspecting user cannot tell the entry has been tampered with. (TPO6, W, Q1) 一旦原来的文本被改变之后，忠实的用户是看不出入口是被人篡改过的。
【搭配】tamper with a document 涂改文件

tangential[1] [tæn'dʒenʃ(ə)l]

【释义】*a.* 1.(评论、情况等)不直接相关的 2. 切线的，相切的 3.(线条、道路等)分岔的
【例句】All that tangential material just distracted from the main argument. (TPO12, L, S1, C1) 所有那些无关的材料都偏离了主论据。
【派生】tangentiality *n.* 言不及义
【逆构】tangent *n.* 离题；切线

tasty[1] ['teɪstɪ]

【释义】*a.* 1. 好吃的 2. 有品位的，有趣的
【例句】There was this Soup Shop, the soup was really tasty, but there weren't a lot of customers. (TPO11, L, S2, L2) 有一家汤店，所供应的汤味道非常好，但是光顾的客人却并不多。

tear[1] 

【释义】[teə] *v.* 1. 撕掉，扯下 2. 流泪 [tɪə] *n.* 眼泪
【例句】Turbulent waters tore into the hardened salt flats, broke them up, and ground them into the pebbles observed in the first sample taken by the Challenger. (TPO7, R, S1, T1) 汹涌的海水把已经硬化了的盐面击碎，并使之形成了鹅卵石，正如从"挑战者号"带回的第一个样本中观察到的那样。
【搭配】tear at 撕扯；严重伤害
tear away 使勉强离开
tear down 拆毁；贬低

teardrop[1] ['tɪərdrɒp] 

【释义】*n.* 泪珠，泪珠状物
【例句】The onrushing water arising from these flash floods likely also formed the odd teardrop-shaped "islands" (resembling the miniature versions seen in the wet sand of our beaches at low tide) that have been found on the plains close to the ends of the outflow channels. (TPO8, R, S2, T2) 这突如其来的洪水产生的急流可能也形成了这种奇特的泪滴形状的"岛屿"(类似于我们在落潮的沙滩湿地上看到的微型版本)，这些"岛屿"已经在靠近泄水渠末端的平原上被发现了。

tenfold[1] ['tenfəuld] 

【释义】*ad./a.* 十倍地(的)
【例句】Unfortunately, the cost of water obtained through any of these schemes would increase pumping costs at least tenfold making the cost of irrigated agricultural products from the region uncompetitive on the national and international markets. (TPO3, R, S1, T1) 不幸的是，通过其中任何一种方式获得的水资源都会将抽水的成本提高十倍以上，从而使得这一地区的农产品灌溉成本在国内和国际市场上都毫无竞争力。

terrifying[1] ['terɪfaɪɪŋ] 

【释义】*a.* 可怕的，骇人听闻的
【例句】There is also the long, rather terrifying call of the orangutan, which carries over considerable distance to advertise his presence. (TPO17, R, S2, T1) 还有猩猩发出的长而吓人的吼叫，这种叫声可以穿越很长的距离来炫耀它的存在。

返记菜单

synthesis[1] tamper[1] tangential[1] tasty[1] tear[1]
teardrop[1] tenfold[1] terrifying[1]

【逆构】terrify *v.* 使害怕，使恐惧

【搭配】terrifying waves 惊涛骇浪

thither[1] [ˈðɪðə]

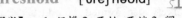

【释义】*ad.* 到那边，向那边

【例句】It's also interesting to know that microclimates thither or near each other can have very different conditions. (TPO14, L, S1, L2) 非常有趣的是，那边或者周围的微气候条件也会有很大不同。

【搭配】hither and thither 到处

threshold[1] [ˈθreʃhəʊld]

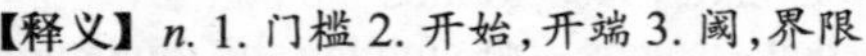

【释义】*n.* 1. 门槛 2. 开始，开端 3. 阈，界限

【例句】This phenomenon—the perception of a stimulus just below the threshold of conscious awareness—is called subliminal perception. (TPO12, S, Q5) 这种现象——对意识知觉阈限以下的刺激的感知——叫做阈下知觉。

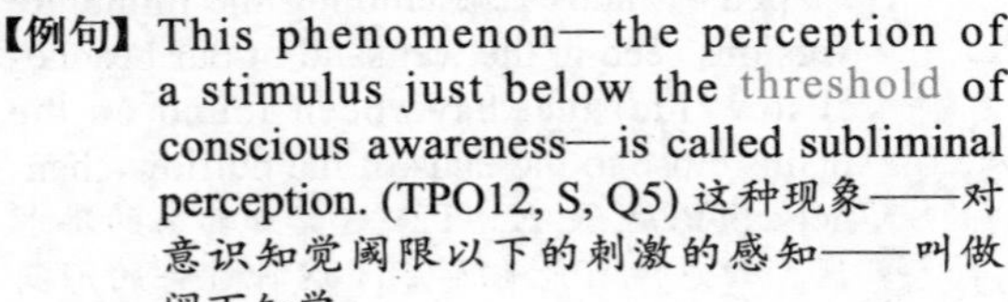

thrust[1] [θrʌst]

【释义】*n.* 推力，冲 *v.* 插入，用力刺

【例句】In the largest caravels, two main masts held large square sails that provided the bulk of the thrust driving the ship forward, while a smaller forward mast held a triangular-shaped sail, called a lateen sail, which could be moved into a variety of positions to maneuver the ship. (TPO17, R, S1, T1) 在最大型的轻快帆船上，有两根主桅杆撑起大块的船帆，以便提供推动帆船前进的足够推力，同时有一个小型的前桅杆来撑起一块三角形船帆，这个船帆叫做三角帆，它是用来在移动中控制帆船行驶的方向的。

【搭配】a rocket with a powerful thrust 具有强大推进力的火箭

tile[1] [taɪl]

【释义】*n.* 瓦片，瓷砖 *v.* 铺瓦于，贴瓷砖于

【例句】The ceramics fall into three broad types—earthenware, stoneware, and porcelain—for vessels, architectural items such as roof tiles, and modeled objects and figures. (TPO10, R, S1, T1) 陶制瓷器从广义上可以被分为3大类：陶器、石器以及瓷器，比如容器、瓦片等建筑材料以及物体和人物模型。

【派生】tiled *a.* 平铺的

tin[1] [tɪn]

【释义】*n.* 1. 锡 2. 罐 3. 罐头 *a.* 锡制的

【例句】It would fill an empty space between cadmium and tin. (TPO16, R, S2, T1) 它会填补镉和锡之间的空隙。

【搭配】tin oxide 二氧化锡
tin ore 锡矿

tolerance[1] [ˈtɒlərəns]

【释义】*n.* 宽容，容忍，忍耐（力）（endurance）

【例句】Nor have merchants and artisans ever had much tolerance for aristocratic professions of moral superiority. (TPO16, R, S1, T1) 商人和工匠不再容忍有着道德优越感的贵族同行们。

【逆构】tolerate *v.* 忍受，容忍
tolerant *a.* 容忍的，忍受的

toll[1] [təʊl]

【释义】*n.* 1. 通行费（charge, fee）2. 伤亡人数 3. 钟声 *v.* 敲钟，鸣钟

【例句】In 1857, in return for a payment of 63 million kronor from other commercial nations, Denmark abolished the Sound toll dues, the fees it had collected since 1497 for the use of the Sound. (TPO18, R, S1, T1) 1857年，作为来自其他商业国家6300万克朗的付款的交换，丹麦废除了松德海峡的通行税，这笔费用是从1497年开始征收并用于松德海峡的。

【派生】tollbooth *n.* 过路收费亭
tollfree *a.* 免通行费的
toller *n.* 鸣钟人；征收通行税的人

【搭配】death toll 死亡人数
road toll 养路费；道路收费
toll station 收费站
take a toll 产生负面影响；造成损失

torrential[1] [tɒˈrenʃəl]

【释义】*a.* 似急流的，猛烈的，汹涌的，倾泻的

【例句】According to the study, two factors were

important for lake formation in the Empty Quarter: first the rains that fell there were torrential. (TPO9, L, S2, L1) 根据这项研究，“空白之地”的湖泊的形成有两个重要因素：第一是倾盆大雨。

【逆构】torrent *n.* 湍流，急流

【搭配】torrential rain 暴雨

torrid[1] ['tɒrɪd] 

【释义】*a.* 1.（天气）灼热的，炎热的 2.（尤指性爱）热烈的

【例句】If true, though, why did cold-blooded animals such as snakes, lizards, turtles, and crocodiles survive the freezing winters and torrid summers? (TPO8, R, S2, T1) 然而，如果情况属实的话，那么为什么冷血动物，比如蛇、蜥蜴、龟、鳄鱼，却能在寒冷的冬天和炎热的夏天幸存下来？

toss[1] [tɒs]

【释义】*v./n.* 1. 投，掷，抛（cast, hurl, throw）2. 摇荡，颠簸

【例句】Over the next couple hundred years, a lot of hypotheses were tossed around. (TPO18, L, S1, L1) 在接下来的数百年里，有很多假设被提出来。

【搭配】toss and turn 辗转反侧
argue the toss 争论已决定的事，作无谓的争执
toss a coin 抛硬币决定问题
toss off 一饮而尽

trample[1] ['træmpl] 

【释义】*v.* 1. 踩，踏（tramp, tread, stamp）2. 无视；侵犯

【例句】The consequences of an excessive number of livestock grazing in an area are the reduction of the vegetation cover and the trampling and pulverization of the soil. (TPO2, R, Sl, T1) 在某一地区放牧过多家畜的后果就是：植被减少，土壤被牲畜践踏、踩碎。

【搭配】trample sb/sth underfoot 把某物 / 某人踩在脚下

transient[1] ['trænzɪənt] 

【释义】*a.* 1. 短暂的，片刻的（temporary）2. 暂住的，流动性的 *n.*〈美〉流浪者；游民

【例句】You know, one of the challenges for people who study theater is to find ways of talking about something that's really so transient, about something that, in a sense, doesn't exist. (TPO17, L, S1, C1) 你知道，对于研究戏剧的人们来说，挑战之一就是找到一些方法来谈论那些稍纵即逝的东西，那些在一定程度上根本不存在的东西。

【反义】permanent, lasting

【派生】transience *n.* 短暂，稍纵即逝

【搭配】transient phenomenon 暂时现象

traverse[1] ['trævə (:) s] 

【释义】*v.* 跨过，穿越

【例句】Rock paintings in the Sahara indicate that horses and chariots were used to traverse the desert and that by 300-200 B. C., there were trade routes across the Sahara. (TPO7, R, S2, T2) 撒哈拉地区的岩画表明，马匹和战车被用来穿越沙漠地带，并且在公元前 300 至 200 年间，该地区已出现商贸通道。

返记菜单

torrid[1] toss[1] trample[1] transient[1] traverse[1]

Word List 50

triangle[1] ['traɪæŋgl] 

【释义】*n.* 三角形,三角形物体
【例句】Polynesia is the central Pacifc area in the great triangle defined by Hawaii, EasterIsland and New Zealand. (TPO5, R, S2, T1) 波利尼西亚是太平洋地区的中心,位于夏威夷岛、复活节岛和新西兰围成的三角形区域里。
【派生】triangular *a.* 三角形的

tribal[1] ['traɪbəl] 

【释义】*a.* 部落的;种族的
【例句】The shepherds of tribal confederacies were left alone by their leaders. (TPO16, R, S1, T1) 放牧部落联盟不是由他们的头来管理。
【逆构】tribe *n.* 部落
【搭配】tribal society 部落社会

triple[1] ['trɪpl] 

【释义】*v.* (使)成为三倍 *a.* 1. 三倍的(threefold) 2. 三方的 *n.* (棒球中的)三垒打
【例句】Even if this process proves successful, however, it would almost triple water costs. (TPO3, R, S1, T1) 然而,即使这样行之有效,抽水成本也会是原来的三倍。
【派生】triply *ad.* 三重地

trustworthy[1] ['trʌstˌwɜːði] 

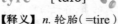

【释义】*a.* 值得信赖的,可靠的(dependable, reliable)
【例句】We tend to think they are trustworthy. (TPO3, S, Q6) 我们觉得这些名人值得信赖。
【反义】dubious
【派生】trustworthily *ad.* 可信赖地;确实地
【搭配】a trustworthy friend 靠得住的朋友

tunnel[1] ['tʌnl] 

【释义】*n.* 1. 隧道 2. (动物挖掘的)洞穴 *v.* 挖隧道
【例句】There are wide passages, narrow ones at all different depths, like underground tunnels in the limestone. (TPO16, L, S1, L1) 有宽阔的和狭窄的通道,深度不一,就像石灰岩下的地下隧道一样。

turbulent[1] ['tɜːbjʊlənt] 

【释义】*a.* 1. (指空气或水)汹涌的,狂暴的 2. 骚乱的,暴乱的
【例句】Turbulent waters tore into the hardened salt flats, broke them up, and ground them into the pebbles observed in the first sample taken by the Challenger. (TPO7, R, S1, T1) 汹涌的海水把已经硬化了的盐面击碎,并使之形成了鹅卵石,正如从"挑战者号"带回的第一个样本中观察到的那样。
【反义】calm, peaceful
【派生】turbulence *n.* 湍流;骚乱,骚动

tutelage[1] ['tjuːtɪlɪdʒ] 

【释义】*n.* 监护,指导(guidance, direction)
【例句】Production was generally in the hands of skilled individual artisans doing piecework under the tutelage of a master. (TPO16, R, S1, T1) 生产通常都是由熟练的工匠在大师的指导下进行的。
【搭配】under sb.'s tutelage 在某人的指导下

tyre[1] ['taɪə]

【释义】*n.* 轮胎(=tire)
【例句】There are no footprints, no tyre tracks and no heavy machinery like a bulldozer…uh, nothing was ever brought in to move these heavy rocks. (TPO4, L, S2, L1) 没有脚印、车辙,也没有推土机之类的重型机器的痕迹…,没有任何东西被带入到这里用来移动这些岩石的迹象。

ubiquitous[1] [juːˈbɪkwɪtəs] 

【释义】*a.* 〈正〉普遍存在的,无处不在的
【例句】Limestone may be found in the Cambrian or—300 million years later—in the Jurassic strata, but a trilobite—the ubiquitous marine arthropod that had its birth in the Cambrian—will never be found in Jurassic strata, nor a dinosaur in the Cambrian. (TPO6, R, S2, T1) 人类可能在侏罗纪时期的地层中发

现了寒武纪或者三亿年后的石灰岩，但绝不可能在侏罗纪时期的地层中发现三叶虫化石（三叶虫化石是寒武纪时期非常普遍的水生节肢动物），也不可能发现寒武纪时期的恐龙化石。

【派生】ubiquitously *ad.* 无所不在地

unacceptable[1] [ˈʌnəkˈseptəbl]

【释义】*a.* 不能接受的，不受欢迎的

【例句】The situation at the health center is unacceptable. (TPO16, S, Q3) 医疗中心的条件是不能接受的。

unassignable[1] [ˈʌnəˈsainəbl]

【释义】*a.* 不可转让的，无法分配的

【例句】These unassignable animals include a large swimming predator called Anomalocaris and a soft-bodied animal called Wiwaxia, which ate detritus or algae. (TPO5, R, S2, T2) 这些无法划分的动物包括一种叫“奇虾”的大型的游动肉食动物和一种叫做“威瓦亚虫”的以岩屑和藻类为食的软体动物。

【搭配】assignable *a.* 可分配的

unbiased[1] [ˈʌnˈbaɪəst]

【释义】*a.* 无偏见的，不偏不倚的（impartial, unprejudiced）

【例句】However, an unbiased opinion will tell you otherwise. 然而，没有偏见的意见将会告诉你另一面。

【逆构】bias *n.* 偏见，偏好 biased *a.* 有偏见的

【搭配】an unbiased opinion 不偏不倚的见解

uncanny[1] [ʌnˈkænɪ]

【释义】*a.* 不可思议的，异乎寻常的（myserious, weird）

【例句】It gives him films an uncanny feature: the familiar made unfamiliar, the normal made suspicious. (TPO3, L, S1, L2) 这赋予了他的电影一种奇异的特点：熟悉的东西让人感觉不熟悉，正常的东西让人怀疑。

【派生】uncannily *ad.* 惊异地，神秘地，危险地

uncompetitive[1] [ˌʌnkəmˈpetətɪv]

【释义】*a.* 无竞争力的，非竞争性的

【例句】Unfortunately, the cost of water obtained through any of these schemes would increase pumping costs at least tenfold, making the cost of irrigated agricultural products from the region uncompetitive on the national and international markets. (TPO3, R, S1, T1) 不幸的是，通过其中任何一种方式获得的水资源都会将抽水的成本提高十倍以上，从而使得这一地区的农产品灌溉成本在国内和国际市场上都毫无竞争力。

【逆构】compete *v.* 比赛，竞争
competitive *a.* 竞争性的，有竞争力的

uncorrupt[1] [ˈʌnkəˈrʌpt]

【释义】*a.* 廉洁的，未堕落的，不腐败的

【例句】Efforts to create a new, uncorrupt police force are moving very slowly. 创建新型、廉洁奉公的警力的工作也收效甚微。

undated[1] [ʌnˈdeɪtɪd]

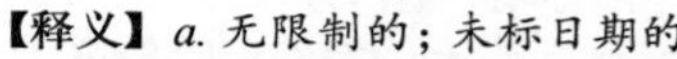

【释义】*a.* 无限制的；未标日期的

【例句】Third, although the painting is unsigned and undated, there is evidence that it was painted when Austen was a teenager. (TPO12, W, Q1) 第三，尽管画作上既没有标署名，也没有标日期，但是有证据显示，这幅画是奥斯汀还是个少女的时候所作的。

【逆构】date *v.* 标日期 *n.* 日期，时期

undemanding[1] [ʌndɪˈmɑːndɪŋ]

【释义】*a.* 容易的，要求不高的，不严格的

【例句】These are usually superficial poorly written, and intellectually undemanding. (TPO11, W, Q1) 这些通常都写得很肤浅，而且对知识要求不高。

【逆构】demanding *a.* 要求高的

undeniable[1] [ˈʌndɪˈnaɪəbl]

【释义】*a.* 无可争辩的，不可否认的，确定无疑的

【例句】Yet the essential difference is undeniable. (TPO7, R, S2, T1) 然而，本质上的区别却是毋庸置疑的。

【搭配】undeniable facts 无可否认的事实

undercut[1] ['ʌndəkʌt]

【释义】*v.* 削价(与…抢生意)

【例句】Now this happens when the market is already saturated with the product and the strategy is to undercut its competitors. (TPO8, S, Q6) 这种情况发生在当市场已经充满了这种产品的时候,应对策略是通过削价来与竞争对手竞争。

undergraduate[1] [ˌʌndə'grædjuɪt]

【释义】*n.*(未获学士学位的)大学生,大学肄业生

【例句】I even worked on a commercial fishing boat in Alaska a couple of summers while I was an undergraduate. (TPO9, L, S1, C1) 在我大学的时候,我甚至在阿拉斯加的一个商业渔船上工作了几个夏天。

understatement[1] [ʌndə'steɪtmənt]

【释义】*n.* 轻描淡写,有保留地陈述

【例句】That's an understatement. (TPO5, L, S1, C1) 那是保守的说法。

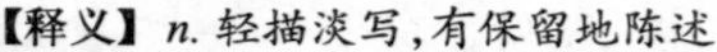

【反义】overstatement

undertaking[1] [ˌʌndə'teɪkɪŋ]

【释义】*n.* 任务,事业(task, project, career)

【例句】Unlike short-term financial cooperation between investors for a single commercial undertaking, joint-stock companies provided permanent funding of capital by drawing on the investments of merchants and other investors who purchased shares in the company. (TPO10, R, S2, T2) 与由投资家组成的以单个商业项目为目的的短期金融合作不同,合资公司会通过吸收购买公司股票的商人和投资者的投资来提供长期的融资资本。

undo[1] ['ʌn'duː]

【释义】*v.* 1. 松开,解开 2. 取消

【例句】Then if we want to undo some bad restoration attempts, we can determine what kind of process we can use to remove them to dissolve the paint and uncover the original. (TPO5, L, S2, L1) 那么,如果我们想要取消一些糟糕的修复结果,我们可以决定通过怎样的过程将其去除,将油漆溶解,从而复原本相。

【派生】undoable *a.* 做不了的;不能做的

unearth[1] [ʌn'ɜːθ]

【释义】*v.* 1. 发掘,挖出(dig up, excavate) 2. 揭露(discover)

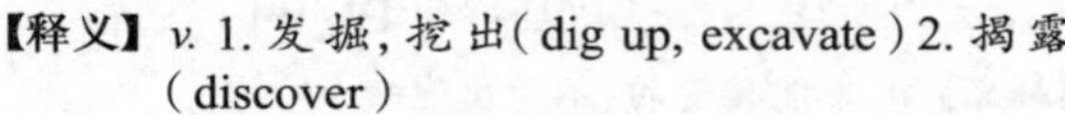

【例句】Moreover, commercial fossil collectors often destroy valuable scientific evidence associated with the fossils they unearth. (TPO13, W, Q1) 此外,商业化石收藏者常常会破坏与出土的化石相关的宝贵科学证据。

【搭配】unearth buried treasure 挖掘深埋的宝藏

unevenly[1] ['ʌniːvənlɪ]

【释义】*ad.* 不均衡地,不平坦地,不平行地(disproportionally)

【例句】Revenue from trade was unevenly distributed. (TPO16, R, S1, T1) 贸易收入分配不均。

unexplored[1] ['ʌnɪks'plɔːd]

【释义】*a.* 1. 未想到的,未考虑过的 2. 未经勘探的,尚未考察的

【例句】There appear to be many unexplored matters about the motivation to reflect—for example, the value of externally motivated reflection as opposed to that of teachers who might reflect by habit. (TPO9, R, S2, T1) 关于反思的动力存在许多未知的问题,例如,由外部驱动的反思的价值与教师通过习惯进行反思的价值是不同的。

【逆构】explore *v.* 探险;探索,探究

unfavorably[1] [ʌn'feivərəbli]

【释义】*ad.* 不利地,反对地,令人不快地

【例句】In fact, a lack of understanding concerning the purposes of Egyptian art has often led it to be compared unfavorably with the art of other cultures. (TPO11, R, S1, T1) 事实上,因为对埃及艺术的目的缺乏理解,所以经常会把埃及艺术与其他文化中的艺术进行不利的比较。

【逆构】favorable *a.* 有利的

unglaciated[1] [ʌn'gleɪsɪeɪtɪd]

【释义】*a.* 未冻结成冰的

【例句】He theorized that with the use of watercraft, people gradually colonized unglaciated refuges and areas along the continental shelf exposed by the lower sea level. (TPO9, R, S1, C1) 他得出了这样一个理论：通过船只的使用，人们逐渐殖民到没有冰冻的地方以及沿着大陆架的、由于海平面较低而裸露出来的地区。

uninformed[1] ['ʌnɪn'fɔːmd]

【释义】*a.* 信息不足的；情况不明的

【例句】Ah, not to seem uninformed. (TPO7, L, S1, C1) 啊，好像知道点儿。

【反义】informed

uninhabited[1] ['ʌnin'hæbitid]

【释义】*a.* 无人居住的，无人烟的，荒凉的(deserted, unoccupied)

【例句】Why they placed their art in dark, uninhabited places? (TPO3, L, S2, L1) 为什么他们要把艺术品置放在这些阴暗、没有人居住的地方？

【逆构】inhabited *a.* 有人居住的

uninspired[1] [ˌʌnɪn'spaɪrd]

【释义】*a.* 无想象力的，无灵感的

【例句】That sounds uninspired, and won't make any shows. (TPO10, L, S1, C1) 那听起来很乏味，而且不会做任何的表演。

unobtainable[1] ['ʌnəb'teɪnəbl]

【释义】*a.* 无法得到的，难获得的(unreachable)

【例句】From the Middle East the Chinese acquired a blue pigment—a purified form of cobalt oxide unobtainable at that time in China—that contained only a low level of manganese. (TPO10, R, S1, T1) 中国人从中东地区得到了一种蓝色的颜料，这种颜料在当时的中国还没有，是氧化钴经过提纯后的一种成分，只含有少量的锰。

unpaved[1] ['ʌn'peɪvd]

【释义】*a.*（路等）未铺砌的

【例句】The university has about three miles of unpaved dirt running trails that pass through the forest near campus. (TPO15, S, Q3) 在学校附近的森林里有长约三英里的未经铺砌的泥土跑道。

【逆构】pave *v.* 铺砌

unplug[1] [ˌʌn'plʌg]

【释义】*v.* 拔掉(电源或插座)；去掉障碍

【例句】We're also hoping that, if we provide the music, students will unplug their personal music devices—their walkmans and mp3 players or whatever—and will spend more time talking to each other. (TPO8, S, Q3) 我们还希望，如果我们提供音乐，学生们会拔下他们个人的音乐播放器——他们的随身听和MP3什么的——会多花些时间相互交谈。

【逆构】plug *n.* 插头，插座；塞子 *v.* 塞住

unpredicted[1] [ˌʌnprɪ'dɪktɪd]

【释义】*a.* 不可预料的(unexpected)

【例句】So assisted migration can have unpredicted outcomes for the new environment. (TPO17, W, Q1) 因此，帮助它们迁徙可能会给新环境带来无法预料的结果。

【反义】predicted

【派生】unpredictable *a.* 不可预测的
unpredictability *n.* 不可预测性，不可预知性

unravel[1] [ʌn'rævəl]

【释义】*v.* 1. 解开，松开(unwind, untangle) 2. 弄清楚秘密

【例句】It means not help you tie your shoe but that little plastic tip keeps the rest of the shoelace, the shoe string from unraveling into weak and useless threads. (TPO12, L, S1, L1) 它并不意味着能帮你系住你的鞋，但是那个小小的塑料末端却能使鞋带剩余的部分免于松散成不结实且无用的线。

【逆构】ravel *v.* 解开；弄清

unregulated[1] [ʌn'regjuleɪtɪd]

【释义】*a.* 未受管理的，不规范的
【例句】And finally, you have an unregulated market place, no government constrains, where price could explode. (TPO6, L, S1, L1) 最后，你将会看到一个不规范的市场，没有政府限制，价格激增。

unreturned[1] [ˌʌnrɪ'tɜnd]

【释义】*a.* 没有回报的，没有还的
【例句】They're not allowed to check anything out because of unreturned books. (TPO9, L, S2, C1) 因为他们没有还书，因此他们不被容许借任何书。

unscrupulous[1] [ʌn'skruːpjʊləs]

【释义】*a.* 肆无忌惮的，不道德的（unprincipled）
【例句】Second, even if the original entry in the online encyclopedia is correct, the communal nature of these online encyclopedias gives unscrupulous users and vandals or hackers the opportunity to fabricate, delete, and corrupt information in the encyclopedia. (TPO6, W, Q1) 其次，即使在线百科全书的原始录入是正确的，但其公共性也会给那些无道德的用户、破坏者以及黑客们提供一些伪造、删除或更改百科全书中的信息的机会。
【派生】unscrupulously *ad.* 不客气地，无道德原则地
【搭配】unscrupulous merchant 奸商

unsigned[1] [ʌn'saɪnd]

【释义】*a.* 未签约的，未签名的，无符号的
【例句】Third, although the painting is unsigned and undated, there is evidence that it was painted when Austen was a teenager. (TPO12, W, Q1) 第三，尽管画作上既没有标署名，也没有标日期，但是有证据显示，这幅画是奥斯汀还是个少女的时候所作的。
【逆构】sign *v.* 签名

unsound[1] ['ʌn'saʊnd]

【释义】*a.* 谬误的，无根据的，靠不住的（unreasonable, unsafe）
【例句】It is scientifically unsound. (TPO12, L, S2, L2) 这在科学上是行不通的。
【派生】unsounded *a.* 未经探测的，未说出的
unsoundness *n.* 不健全；不牢靠

unspecified[1] ['ʌn'spesifaid]

【释义】*a.* 未指定的，未加规定的
【例句】With fairy tales, however, the location is generally unspecified. (TPO5, L, S2, L2) 但是在童话故事里，地点往往不那么明确。
【反义】specified
【逆构】specify *v.* 明确

unsuspecting[1] ['ʌnsəs'pektɪŋ]

【释义】*a.* 不怀疑的，无疑心的
【例句】Once changes have been made to the original text, an unsuspecting user cannot tell the entry has been tampered with. (TPO6, W, Q1) 一旦原来的文本被改变之后，毫无疑心的用户并看不出入口是被人篡改过的。
【派生】unsuspectingly *ad.* 信任地

unusable[1] [ˌʌn'juːzəbl]

【释义】*a.* 无法使用的
【例句】Large areas of land would become unusable by humans. (TPO13, L, S1, L2) 人们将无法使用大片土地。
【反义】usable
【搭配】unusable byproducts 无法使用的副产品

unwind[1] [ʌn'waɪnd]

【释义】*v.* 放松，松弛；解开，展开
【例句】By the time Friday afternoon rolls around, all of you are probably exhausted, and um, all you want to do is relax and um, unwind. (TPO6, S, Q5) 周五下午到来的时候，你们大家可能都会感觉筋疲力尽，你们都需要放松。
【反义】wind, fasten

unwittingly[1] [ʌn'wɪtɪŋlɪ]

【释义】*ad.* 不知不觉地，无意地（unconsciously, unknowingly）
【例句】If someone on a hike knocks a couple

of rocks over, they could be unwittingly destroying a microclimate that an animal or organism relies on. (TPO14, L, S1, L2) 如果有人在远足时敲击几块走过的岩石，他们就可能在无意间破坏了一种动物或有机体赖以生存的微气候。

【反义】wittingly

utility[1] [juːˈtɪlɪtɪ] 

【释义】*n.* 1. 公用事业 2. 功用，效用（function, usefulness）

【例句】Right now the utility companies are interested in increasing the capacity of Cremer Junction Plant. (TPO12, L, S2, L2) 现在公共事业公司对提高Cremer枢纽工厂的生产力很感兴趣。

【派生】utilitarian *a.* 功利主义的；功利的；实用的

vacuum[1] [ˈvækjʊəm]

【释义】*n.* 真空 *v.* 用真空吸尘器清理

【例句】Early in the century, a pump had come into use in which expanding steam raised a piston in a cylinder, and atmospheric pressure brought it down again when the steam condensed inside the cylinder to form a vacuum. (TPO6, R, S1, T1) 在（19）世纪早期，泵曾被用于（发动机的）汽缸，在气缸中，膨胀的蒸汽推动活塞上升，而当汽缸内部的蒸汽被压缩形成真空环境时，气压又使得活塞下降。

validate[1] [ˈvælɪdeɪt] 

【释义】*v.* 证实，使生效，使合法化

【例句】In addition, children feel validated in their choice of a product when a celebrity endorses that product. (TPO14, R, S1, T1) 另外，儿童在选择商品时觉得名人所赞同的商品是有保障的。

vandal[1] [ˈvændl]

【释义】*n.* 破坏他人或公共财产者（demolisher, destroyer）

【例句】Second, even if the original entry in the online encyclopedia is correct, the communal nature of these online encyclopedias gives unscrupulous users and vandals or hackers the opportunity to fabricate, delete, and corrupt information in the encyclopedia. (TPO6, W, Q1) 其次，即使在线百科全书的原始录入是正确的，但其公共性也会给那些无道德的用户、破坏者以及黑客们提供一些伪造、删除或更改百科全书中的信息的机会。

vapor[1] [ˈveɪpə] 

【释义】*n.* 蒸汽，水汽（steam）

【例句】Aside from some small-scale gullies (channels) found since 2000, which are inconclusive, astronomers have no direct evidence for liquid water anywhere on the surface of Mars today, and the amount of water vapor in the Martian atmosphere is tiny. (TPO8, R, S2, T2) 除了自2000年以来发现的一些没有说服力的小规模的沟渠（渠道）之外，如今天文学家们没有直接证据能证明火星表面的任何地方有过液态水，而且在火星大气中的水蒸汽的量很小。

【派生】vaporous *a.* 蒸汽的，雾状的
vaporization *n.* 蒸发，汽化

vernacular[1] [vəˈnækjʊlə] 

【释义】*n.* 本地话，方言

【例句】The vast majority of the population used their own regional vernacular in all aspects to their lives. (TPO12, L, S2, L1) 他们中的大多数在生活中的方方面面都使用他们当地的方言。

versatile[1] [ˈvɜːsətaɪl] 

【释义】*a.* 1. 多才多艺的（talented）2. 有多种用途的

【例句】Well, she is really versatile. (TPO7, L, S1, C1) 啊，她真是多才多艺。

【派生】versatility *n.* 多才多艺；用途广泛

【搭配】a versatile mind 多面手

vestigial[1] [vesˈtɪdʒɪəl] 

【释义】*a.* 1.（器官等）退化的（degenerated）2. 残存的，残留的（remaining）

【例句】Basilosaurus was undoubtedly a fully marine whale with possible nonfunctional,

返记菜单

utility[1] vacuum[1] validate[1] vandal[1] vapor[1]
vernacular[1] versatile[1] vestigial[1]

or vestigial, hind legs. (TPO2, R, S2, T1) 龙王鲸必定是完全水生的鲸鱼，它们的后肢已经不起任何作用，或者说已经退化了。

【派生】vestigially *ad.* 残留地

【逆构】vestige *n.* 残留(物)；退化器官

vibrant[1] ['vaɪbrənt]

【释义】*a.* 1.（色彩）鲜明的 2. 活跃的，充满活力的

【例句】And there are vibrant colors. (TPO1, L, S1, L1) 还有些明亮的颜色。

【派生】vibrantly *ad.* 充满活力地

vibrate[1] [vaɪ'breɪt]

【释义】*v.*（使）振动；（使）颤动（quake, quiver, shake）

【例句】Maybe the ground vibrates, or maybe the ground itself is shifting, tilting. (TPO4, L, S2, L1) 也许是地面在震动，或者地面自己移动了，倾斜了。

【派生】vibration *n.* 振动，颤动

vicissitude[1] [vɪ'sɪsɪtjuːd]

【释义】*n.* 改变，变迁

【例句】Remarkably resistant to the vicissitudes of ocean travel, they can survive prolonged immersion in saltwater when they come to rest on warm beaches and the conditions are favorable, the seed coats soften. (TPO9, R, S2, T2) 它们对洋流变动有着极强的抵抗力，因此可以在长时间的海水浸泡中存活下来。当它们停歇在温暖的海滩上且条件适宜时，种子的外皮就会变软。

【派生】vicissitudinous *a.* 有变化的，变迁的

victimize[1] ['vɪktɪmaɪz]

【释义】*v.* 不公正地对待，使受害

【例句】Baby birds of species that experience high rates of nest predation should produce softer begging signals of higher frequency than nestlings of other species less often victimized by nest predators. (TPO11, R, S2, T2) 被捕食频率高的雏鸟种类会比其它较少受到捕食者伤害的雏鸟种类发出更柔和、更频繁的乞食信号。

【派生】victim *n.* 受害者

【搭配】fall victim to 成为…的牺牲品

videotape[1] ['vɪdiəuteɪp]

【释义】*v.* 将（节目）录到带子上 *n.* 录像（磁）带，录影带

【例句】From what I read, that production, like, it influenced every other production of the play that came after it, so I just assume that it'd been filmed or videotaped. (TPO17, L, S1, C1) 据我所知，那部作品影响了在其之后出现的每一部作品，所以我推断，它应该已经被拍成电影或制成录像带了。

virtue[1] ['vɜːtjuː]

【释义】*n.* 美德（merit, goodness）

【例句】In turn, a deep attachment to the land, and to the stability which rural life engenders, fostered the Roman virtues: gravitas, a sense of responsibility, pietas, a sense of devotion to family and country, and justitia, a sense of the natural order. (TPO7, R, S2, T1) 反之，对土地和平稳的乡村生活的深深依恋孕育了罗马人的美德：庄重，一种责任感；敬重，对祖国和家庭奉献的使命感；正义，对自然秩序的遵循。

【派生】virtuous *n.* 有品德的

virtually *ad.* 事实上，实际上

【搭配】by virtue of sth. 由于或因为某事物

virtuosity[1] [ˌvɜːtjʊ'ɒsɪtɪ]

【释义】*n.*（表演方面的）精湛技巧

【例句】Admiration for the performer's skill, virtuosity, and grace are seen as motivation for elaborating the activities into fully realized theatrical performances. (TPO1, R, S2, T1) 人们对于表演者的技巧、精湛的技术和优雅的崇拜被看作是一种激励，促使表演者将这些活动完全成为戏剧表演。

virtuoso[1] [vɜːtjʊ'əʊzəʊ]

【释义】*n.* 演艺精湛的人，大师

【例句】Clara grew up to become a well-known and respected piano virtuoso, a performer of extraordinary skill who gave concerts across Europe. (TPO16, L, S1, L2) 克拉拉成长为了一个著名的、受人尊敬的钢琴演奏家，才

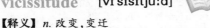

返记菜单

vibrant[1] vibrate[1] vicissitude[1] victimize[1] videotape[1]
virtue[1] virtuosity[1] virtuoso[1]

华卓越，在欧洲各地巡回演出。
【派生】 virtuosity *n.*（表演方面的）精湛技艺

walkway[1] ['wɔːkweɪ]

【释义】 *n.* 走道，人行通道（pavement）
【例句】 Well, design doesn't necessarily include things like sculptures or decorative walkways or…or even eye-catching window displays, you know, art. (TPO13, L, S1, L1) 设计不一定包括像雕塑、装饰过的走道或者或是吸引眼球的陈列窗等之类的东西，就是所说的艺术。
【搭配】 a pedestrian walkway 人行道

walrus[1] ['wɔːlrəs]

【释义】 *n.* 海象
【例句】 However, unlike the cases of sea otters and pinnipeds (seals, sea lions, and walruses, whose limbs are functional both on land and at sea) , it is not easy to envision what the first whales looked like. (TPO2, R, S2, T1) 然而，想知道世上第一只鲸长什么样并非易事，不像还原海獭及鳍足类动物（四肢水陆两用，如海豹、海狮、海象）的原貌那么简单。

ward off[1]

【释义】 *phr.* 避开，挡住
【例句】 They were used as medicines to ward off diseases, and mixed into perfumes, incense. (TPO18, L, S2, L1) 它们被用作防止疾病的药物，也会被加入香水或香中。

watershed[1] ['wɔːtəʃed]

【释义】 *n.* 转折点，分水岭，重要关头
【例句】 Despite all the highly visible technological developments in theatrical and home delivery of the moving image that have occurred over the decades since then, no single innovation has come close to being regarded as a similar kind of watershed. (TPO12, R, S2, T1) 尽管在那之后的几十年中，电影在剧场和家庭传输方面都有很显著的技术性发展，但是没有哪项单独的创新能与电影界的这一分水岭相提并论。

watertight[1] ['wɔːtətaɪt]

【释义】 *a.* 1. 不透水的（waterproof）2. 周密的，无懈可击的
【例句】 And when it dries, it's watertight. (TPO7, L, S2, L1) 当它干了以后就密不透水了。
【搭配】 a watertight alibi 无懈可击的借口

wax[1] [wæks]

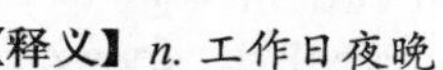

【释义】 *n.* 蜡 *v.* 1. 给…上蜡 2.（月亮）渐圆
【例句】 By contrast, wooden statues were carved from several pieces of wood that were pegged together to form the finished work, and metal statues were either made by wrapping sheet metal around a wooden core or cast by the lost wax process. (TPO11, R, S1, T1) 相比之下，木雕是由钉在一起的几块木头雕刻而成的，而金属雕塑要么是金属片包裹着一块木质核心，要么是用脱蜡铸造法铸成的。
【派生】 waxy *a.* 苍白的；光滑的
【搭配】 on the wax 正在变大，在增加
wax and wane 兴衰，盈亏

weeknight[1] ['wiːknaɪt]

【释义】 *n.* 工作日夜晚
【例句】 Well, I work weeknights, except for Friday. (TPO17, L, S2, C1) 我在工作日晚上工作，除了周五。

well-documented[1] [ˌwel 'dɑkjəˌmentɪd]

【释义】 *a.* 存档完好的，证据充分的
【例句】 And this phenomenon is so widespread and well-documented it has a name. (TPO10, L, S2, L2) 这种现象太普遍了，它被证实有一个名字。

well-to-do[1] [ˌweltə'duː]

【释义】 *a.* 富有的，宽裕的（rich, affluent, wealthy）
【例句】 Coal gas rivaled smoky oil lamps and flickering candles, and early in the new century, well-to-do Londoners grew accustomed to gaslit houses and even streets. (TPO6, R, S1, T1) 煤气在与冒烟的油灯及忽闪的蜡烛的比

较中占尽优势，而且在新世纪伊始，经济富裕的伦敦人也开始习惯将煤气用于家用照明及街道照明。

【反义】poor

whiteware[1] ['waitwɛə]

【释义】*n.* 白色陶瓷

【例句】Whitewares produced in Hebei and Henan provinces from the seventh to the tenth centuries evolved into the highly prized porcelains of the Song dynasty. (TPO10, R, S1, T1) 河北以及河南省在7到10世纪出产的白瓷逐渐演变成为了宋朝时广为称道的瓷器。

windblown[1] ['wɪndbləʊn]

【释义】*a.* 被风吹(散)的

【例句】Interbedded with the salt were thin layers of what appeared to be windblown silt. (TPO7, R, S1, T1) 与这些结晶盐相互嵌在一起的薄层像是被风吹起的泥沙层。

withdrawal[1] [wɪð'drɔːəl]

【释义】*n.* 收回；撤回，撤退(secession)

【例句】It is estimated that at current withdrawal rates, much of the aquifer will run dry within 40 years. (TPO3, R, S1, T1) 按现今的下降速度来估计，大部分地下蓄水将在40年内耗尽。

【逆构】withdraw *v.* 取消，撤回；撤退

workload[1] ['wɜːkləʊd]

【释义】*n.* 工作量，工作负荷

【例句】If many full-time employees started working fewer hours, some of their workload would have to be shifted to others. (TPO1, W, Q1) 如果很多全职雇员开始减少工作时间，那他们的工作量就会不得不转移到其他人身上了。

worship[1] ['wɜːʃɪp]

【释义】*v./n.* 爱慕，崇敬，崇拜(esteem, honor)

【例句】As always, there are the power worshippers, especially among historians, who are predisposed to admire whatever is strong, who feel more attracted to the might of Rome than to the subtlety of Greece. (TPO7, R, S2, T1) 通常总会有对权威的崇拜者，尤其是在历史学家中，他们倾向于钦佩强大的事物，相对于希腊的微妙，罗马的强大威力对他们更有吸引力。

【派生】worshipper *n.* 礼拜者

worshipful *a.* 尊敬的，敬爱的

yummy[1] ['jʌmɪ]

【释义】*a.* 美味的，好吃的，愉快的(delicious)

【例句】Those yummy fried potatoes. (TPO10, L, S1, L2) 那些美味的炸薯条啊！

zillion[1] ['zɪljən]

【释义】*n.*〈非正式〉极大的数目

【例句】Well, there is the job itself, and salary of course, and working conditions, I mean, would I have an office, or would I work in a big room with a zillion other employees, and...and maybe about opportunities for advancement. (TPO6, L, S1, C1) 那就是工作本身，当然还有工资、工作环境，我指的是，我是否会有自己的办公室，还是和其他很多同事在一个大房间里工作…另外，可能还有升迁的机会。

【搭配】zillions of mosquitoes 无数的蚊子

zoom[1] [zuːm]

【释义】*v.* 1. 疾行，飞速地(做某事) 2. 陡升，猛涨

【例句】Once a pronghorn starts running, zooming, none of its present-day predators, like the bobcat or coyote, can even hope to catch up with it. (TPO17, S, Q4) 一旦叉角羚开始快速奔跑，任何一只现在的捕食动物，例如山猫或小狼，都没有希望追上它。

【搭配】zoom in/out (镜头)拉近 / 推远

分类词汇表

1 Biology 生物学

Classifying Living Things 生物的分类

taxonomy *n.* 分类法，分类学
categorize *v.* 加以类别，分类
species *n.* 种类
genus *n.* 属
family *n.* 科
order *n.* 目
class *n.* 纲
phylum *n.* 门
kingdom *n.* 领域，界

Heredity & Evolution 遗传和进化

heredity *n.* 遗传
trait *n.* 显著的特点，特性
genetic *a.* 遗传的，起源的
gene pool 基因库
DNA（deoxyribonucleic acid）脱氧核糖核酸（遗传物质）
chromosome *n.* 染色体
dominant *a.* 显性的
recessive *a.* 隐性的；*n.* 隐性性状
distribute *v.* 散布，分布
atavism *n.* 隔代遗传，返祖现象
variety *n.* 变化；品种；变种
mutation *n.* 变化；（生物物种的）突变
hybrid *n.* 杂种，混血儿；*a.* 混合的，杂种的
offspring *n.*（单复数同形）子孙，后代
evolution *n.* 演变，进化
adaptation *n.* 适应性的改变；感官适应性调节
survival of the fittest 适者生存
natural selection *n.* 自然选择，物竞天择说
naturalist *n.* 自然主义者，博物学者

Cell 细胞

cytology *n.* 细胞学
specimen *n.* 样品，样本
building block 构件
tissue *n.* 组织
protoplasm *n.* 原生质
metaplasm *n.* 后成质
cytoplasm *n.* 细胞质
membrane *n.* 膜，隔膜
nucleus *n.* 细胞核
nucleic acid *n.* 核酸
vacuole *n.* 空泡，液泡

Biochemistry 生物化学

biochemistry *n.* 生物化学
organism *n.* 生物体，有机体
microbe *n.* 微生物，细菌
microscopic *a.* 用显微镜可见的；极小的
metabolism *n.* 新陈代谢
aerobic *a.* 依靠氧气的，与需氧菌有关的
anaerobic *a.* 没有空气而能生活的，厌氧性的
anabolism *n.* 合成代谢
catabolism *n.* 异化作用，分解代谢
photosynthesis *n.* 光合作用
respiration *n.* 呼吸，呼吸作用
secretion *n.* 分泌，分泌物（液）
osmotic pressure 渗透压
amino acid *n.* 氨基酸
enzyme *n.* 酶
yeast *n.* 酵母，发酵粉
ferment *n.* 酵素，发酵
gland *n.* 腺
mineral *n.* 矿物；无机物
protein *n.* 蛋白质；*a.* 蛋白质的

一般生物学用词

biologist *n.* 生物学家
fauna *n.* 动物群；动物志
flora *n.* 植物群；植物志
symbiotic *a.* 共生的
parasitic *a.* 寄生的
communicable *a.* 传染的，可传染的
mammary *a.* 乳房的，乳腺的
population *n.* 虫口；种群（量）
natural enemy 天敌
enmity *n.* 敌意

host *n.* 寄主，宿主
circulation *n.* 循环
nervous system 神经系统
conjugation *n.*（两个生殖细胞的）接合（作用）
culture *n./v.* 培育；培植
nest *n.* 巢，窝
niche *n.* 小生境
natural death 正常死亡
feature *n.* 特征，特色
crust *n.* 外壳，硬壳；表层，外皮
sucker *n.*（寄生植物的）吸枝，腋芽；吸盘
fin *n.* 鳍，鱼翅
beak *n.* 鸟嘴，喙
bill *n.*（水禽等细长而扁平的）嘴
agility *n.*（动作）敏捷，轻快
homeostasis *n.*（社会群体的）自我平衡，原状稳定
uniformity *n.* 同样，一致；均匀性
intake *n.* 吸入，摄取；吸收之量
larva *n.* 幼虫，幼体（*pl.* larvae）
ornithology *n.* 鸟类学，禽学
sense *n.* 感官，官能
infest *v.* 大批滋生
piscatorial *a.* 渔业的，渔民的
angle *v.* 用钩和钓钓鱼
hobble *v.* 蹒跚，跛行
lacerate *v.* 撕碎，撕裂；*a.*（叶子等）撕裂状的
annihilate *v.* 消灭，摧毁
endangered *a.* 有危险的，将要绝种的
defunct *a.* 死了的
exterminate *v.* 消灭，根除
extinction *n.* 消灭；（生物等的）灭绝
terminate *v.* 终止，结束

2 Zoology 动物学

Animal Kingdom 动物界

chordate *a.* 有脊索的，脊索动物的；*n.* 脊索动物
invertebrate *a.* 无脊椎的；*n.* 无脊椎动物
sponge *n.* 海绵，海绵状物；寄生虫
mollusk *n.* 软体动物
echinoderm *n.* 棘皮类动物
coelenterate *n.* 腔肠动物；*a.* 腔肠动物的
arthropod *n.* 节肢动物；*a.* 节肢动物的
arachnid *n.* 蜘蛛类动物；蜘蛛纲
crustacea *n.* 甲壳纲动物
bug *n.* 小虫，臭虫
vertebrate *n.* 脊椎动物；*a.* 有椎骨的，有脊椎的
fish *n.* 鱼，鱼类
amphibian *a.* 两栖类的；*n.* 两栖动物
reptile *n.* 爬虫动物；*a.* 爬行的，爬虫类的
bird *n.* 鸟，禽
mammal *n.* 哺乳动物
cyclostomata *n.* 环口目
primate *n.* 灵长类的动物
rodent *a.* 咬的，啮齿目的；*n.* 啮齿动物
livestock *n.* 家畜，牲畜
finch *n.* 雀科鸣禽（如燕雀，金翅雀等）
ruminant *a.* 反刍动物的；*n.* 反刍动物
parasite *n.* 寄生虫
herbivore *n.* 草食动物
carnivore *n.* 食肉动物
omnivore *n.* 杂食动物
biped *n.* 两足动物
quadruped *n.* 四足动物
scavenger *n.* 食腐动物
predator *n.* 食肉动物，捕食其他动物的动物
carrion *n.* 死肉，腐肉；*a.* 腐肉的，吃腐肉的
prey *n.* 被捕食的动物
game *n.* 猎物
moose *n.* 驼鹿
antelope *n.* 羚羊
sperm *n.* 鲸油
killer whale *n.* 逆戟鲸，虎鲸
serpent *n.* 蛇（尤指大蛇或毒蛇）
raptor *n.* 猛禽，肉食鸟
dinosaur *n.* 恐龙
tadpole *n.* 蝌蚪

Reproduction 繁殖

reproduction *n.* 繁殖
sexual reproduction 有性生殖
asexual reproduction 无性生殖
egg cell 卵细胞
sperm *n.* 精液，精子
fertilization *n.* 授精；受孕（受精）作用
female *n.* 女性，雌兽；*a.* 女性的，雌的
hermaphrodite *n.* 具有两性者，两性体；*a.* 雌雄同体的
breed *v.* 生育，繁殖
mate *n.* 配偶；*v.* 交配
bear *v.* 生（孩子）
hatch *n./v.* 孵，孵化
lay *v.* 产（卵），下蛋
descend *v.* 遗传

Characteristics 特征

precocial *a.* 早熟性的，生下就有很高程度独立活动能力的
altricial *a.* 孵出后需母鸟照顾一段时期的，晚成雏的
nocturnal *a.* 夜出的，夜间活动的
rampant *a.*（兽类）跳起的，用后腿直立的
ferocious *a.* 残忍的，凶猛的
aggressive *a.* 好斗的，攻击性的
cold blooded *a.* 冷血的
ambidextrous *a.* 两只手都很灵巧的
torpid *a.* 麻痹的，迟钝的；蛰伏的
dormant *a.* 睡眠状态的，蛰伏的，休眠的
hibernate *v.* 冬眠
aestivate *v.* 夏眠
live off *v.* 靠…为生
inhabit *v.* 居住于，栖息
migrate *v.* 移动，（鸟类的）迁徙
burrow *n.* 洞穴；*v.* 挖地洞
camouflage *v./n.* 伪装
capture *v./n.* 捕获，捕捉
procure *v.* 获得
swoop *n./v.* 突然下降，猛扑
fend *v.* 保护，避开
pant *n./v.* 喘气，喘息
claw *n.* 爪，脚爪
paw *n.* 手掌;（动物的）爪子，脚爪
spine *n.* 脊柱，脊椎骨；棘状突起，刺
mane *n.* 鬃毛
proboscis *n.* 鼻子，长鼻
shell *n.* 贝壳，壳
tentacle *n.*（动物）触须，触角
leathery *a.* 似皮革的，坚韧的
chambered *a.* 隔成房间的

一般动物学用词

flock *n.* 羊群，（禽、畜等的）群，大量
herd *n.* 兽群，牛群，牧群
lair *n.* 野兽的巢穴，躲藏处
den *n.* 兽穴，洞穴
habitat *n.*（动植物的）生活环境，栖息地
scrap
behavioral *a.* 动作的，行为的
transparent *a.* 透明的，透光的
hollow *n.* 洞，窟窿；*a.* 空的，凹的
pervasive *a.* 弥漫的，遍布的
bare *a.* 赤裸的，无遮蔽的
mature *a.* 成熟的；*v.* 成熟

3 Botany 植物学

Plant Parts 植物各部分

vein *n.* 叶脉；翅脉
foliage *n.* 树叶，植物
stoma *n.*（植物）气孔
bough *n.* 大树枝，主枝
stem *n.* 茎，干，柄，梗
trunk *n.* 树干
taproot *n.* 主根，直根
fibrous roots 须根

Photosynthesis 光合作用

photosynthesis *n.* 光合作用
chlorophyll *n.* 叶绿素
carbon dioxide *n.* 二氧化碳
oxygen *n.* 氧
glucose *n.* 葡萄糖
cellulose *n.* 纤维素
starch *n.* 淀粉
absorb *v.* 吸收

Reproduction 繁殖

fertilization *n.* 受精作用（现象）
pollination *n.* 授粉
alternation of generations 世代交替
hermaphrodite *n.* 两性体；*a.* 雌雄同体的
sprout *n.* 苗芽；*v.* 萌芽
burgeon *n.* 嫩芽；*v.* 萌芽
kernel *n.*（硬壳果）仁，核
germinate *v.* 发芽，发育
spore *n.* 孢子
proliferous *a.* 繁殖的
Parts of a Flower 花的各部分
bloom *n.* 花；*v.* 开花
petal *n.* 花瓣
corolla *n.* 花冠
pollen *n.* 花粉
sap *n.* 树液，汁液
nectar *n.* 花蜜
stamen *n.* 雄蕊，雄性花蕊
anther *n.* 花粉囊
carpel *n.* 心皮
ovary *n.*（植物）子房
stigma *n.*（植物）柱头
sepal *n.* 萼片

Characteristics 特征
transpiration *n.* 蒸发
respiration *n.* 呼吸，呼吸作用
parasite *n.* 寄生植物
perennial *a.* 四季不断的，(植物)多年生的
nocturnal *a.* 夜晚的，夜间活动的
brittle *a.* 易碎的
airborne *a.* 空气传播的
juicy *a.* 多汁的
feral *a.* 野生的
indigenous *a.* 土产的，本地的
rampant *a.* 蔓生的，繁茂的
lush *a.* 茂盛的，青葱的
densely *ad.* 浓密地
seasonally *a.* 季节性的
tropism *n.* 向性，向性运动
gravitropism *n.* 向重力性
hydrotropism *n.* 向水性
phototropism *n.* 趋光性，向光性
extract *n.* 精，汁，榨出物
take hold 抓住
flourish *n./v.* 茂盛，兴旺
prune *v.* 剪除，修剪
shed *v.* 脱落
wilt *v./n.* 枯萎，畏缩

一般植物学用词
vegetation *n.* 植被，(总称)植物
conifer *n.* 松类，针叶树
evergreen tree *n.* 冬青树，常青树
deciduous tree 落叶树
lumber *n.* 木材
underbrush *n.* 树林下的草丛，下层林丛
thorn *n.* 刺，棘，荆棘
sapling *n.* 树苗，小树
seedling *n.* 秧苗，树苗
turf *n.* 草根土，草皮
weed *n.* 野草，杂草
fern *n.* 蕨类植物
lichen *n.* 青苔，地衣，苔藓
fungus *n.* 菌类，蘑菇
context *n.* 菌肉层
maize *n.* 玉米
cob *n.* 玉米棒子
roost *n.* 栖木
annul ring 年轮
resin *n.* 树脂
stubble *n.* 断株，茬
bark *n.* 树皮
husk *n.* (果类或谷物的)外壳
tentacle *n.* (植物)腺毛
pigment *n.* 色素，颜料
auxin *n.* 茁长素，植物激素
graft *n.* 嫁接，(接技用的)嫩枝
devastating *a.* 破坏性的，毁灭性的
dire *a.* 可怕的
formidable *a.* 可怕的，令人生畏的
emerge *v.* 显现，暴露；形成
invade *v.* 侵袭
disperse *v.* (使)分散，(使)散开
conserve *v.* 保存，保藏
habitat *n.* (动植物的)生活环境，产地、栖息地
marshland *n.* 沼泽地
meadow *n.* 草地，牧场

4 Entomology 昆虫学

Insect 昆虫
termite *n.* 白蚁
leaf cutter ant 切叶蚁
wasp *n.* 黄蜂
bumblebee *n.* 大黄蜂
honeybee *n.* 蜜蜂
moth *n.* 蛾，蛀虫
tiger moth *n.* 虎蛾，灯蛾
cicada *n.* 蝉
treehopper *n.* 角蝉
mosquito *n.* 蚊子
fly *n.* 苍蝇，两翼昆虫
firefly *n.* 萤火虫
mayfly *n.* 蜉蝣类，飞蝼蛄
dragonfly *n.* 蜻蜓
butterfly *n.* 蝴蝶
grasshopper *n.* 蚱蜢，蝗虫
locust *n.* 蝗虫，蚱蜢
ladybug *n.* 瓢虫
thornbug *n.* 刺椿象
cockroach *n.* 蟑螂
flea *n.* 跳蚤
mite *n.* 小虫，(乳酪上的)蛆；螨类
spider *n.* 蜘蛛
worm *n.* 虫，蠕虫，蚯蚓
centipede *n.* 蜈蚣
beetle *n.* 甲虫

Structure 结构

exoskeleton *n.* 外骨骼
endoskeleton *n.* 内骨骼
shell *n.* 贝壳，壳
sensor *n.* 传感器
compound eye（昆虫的）复眼
antenna *n.* 触角，触须
mandible *n.* 下颚，下颚骨
proboscis *n.* 鼻子，长鼻
abdomen *n.* 腹，腹部
spiracle *n.*（昆虫的）气门
sac *n.* 囊，液囊
gland *n.* 腺
spinneret *n.*（蜘蛛、蚕等的）吐丝器
rear *n.* 屁股

Attack and Defense 攻击和防御

assault *n./v.* 攻击，袭击
threat *n.* 威胁，凶兆
destructor *n.* 破坏者
victim *n.* 牺牲者，牺牲品
infestation *n.*（害虫等）群袭，出没
adaptation *n.* 适应
protection *n.* 保护
camouflage *n./v.* 伪装
avoidance *n.* 避免
coloration *n.* 染色，着色
warning color 警告(颜)色
sonar *n.* 声纳，声波定位仪
scale *n.* 尺度，刻度；规模，大小
nocturnal *a.* 夜间发生的，夜间活动的
toxic *a.* 有毒的，中毒的
inedible *a.* 不适于食用的，不能吃的
scare off 吓跑，吓退
startle *v.* 震惊
swathe *v.* 绑，裹，包围
shield *v.* 遮蔽；保护，防护
anchor *n.* 锚；*v.* 抛锚，锚定
ensnare *v.* 诱捕
encapsulate *v.* 装入胶囊，压缩

Characteristics 特征

elasticity *n.* 弹力，弹性
viscosity *n.* 粘质，粘性
spiral *a.* 螺旋形的；*n.* 螺旋
resilient *a.* 弹回的，有回弹力的
flagelliform *a.* 鞭状的，细长而柔软的
insectivorous *a.* 食虫的，食虫动植物的
multiply *v.* 繁殖，增加
mate *n.* 配偶，对手；*v.* 交配
excrete *v.* 排泄，分泌
suck *v.* 吸，吮
feed on *v.* 以…为食

Life Cycle 生活周期

egg *n.* 蛋，鸡蛋，卵
larva *n.* 幼虫
caterpillar *n.* 毛虫
chrysalis *n.* 蛹，茧
pupa *n.* 蛹
pupate *v.* 化蛹
imago *n.* 成虫期，成虫

一般昆虫学用词

colony *n.* 集群，群体
hive *n.* 蜂房，蜂箱
population *n.* 虫口
metamorphosis *n.* 变形
deformed *a.* 不成形的，丑陋的
misshapen *a.* 奇形怪状的，畸形的
hollow *n.* 洞；*a.* 空的
sturdy *a.* 强健的；*n.* 家畜晕倒病
versatile *a.* 多方面的，多种的
dwindle *v.* 缩小，减少
eradicate *v.* 根除
degradation *n.* 降级，退化
insecticide *n.* 杀虫剂
parasite *n.* 寄生虫
pest *n.* 害虫，有害动物
segment *n.* 段，节
diameter *n.* 直径
vibration *n.* 振动，摇动
yield *v.* 出产，生产

5 Ecology 生态学

Ecosystem 生态系统

ecological system 生态系统
ecological efficiency 生态效应
biomass *n.*（单位面积或体积内）生物的数量
biodiversity *n.* 生物品种
biosphere *n.* 生物圈
biome *n.*（生态）生物群系
fauna *n.* 动物群，动物志
flora *n.* 植物群，植物志

organism *n.* 生物体，有机体
species *n.* 种类，（原）核素
community *n.* （生物）群落
natural enemy 天敌
habitat *n.*（动植物的）生活环境，产地、栖息地
rain forest *n.* 雨林
permafrost *n.* 永久冻结带
wetland *n.* 潮湿的土壤，沼泽地
watershed *n.* 分水岭
aquatic *a.* 水的，水生的，水栖的
terrestrial *a.* 陆地的
woodland *n.* 森林地，林地
alpine *a.* 高山的，阿尔卑斯山的
valley *n.*（山）谷，流域
endangered *a.* 有危险的，有灭绝危险的
extinct *a.* 灭绝的
wildlife *n.* 野生动植物
nekton *n.* 自游生物
omnivore *n.* 不偏食的人
carnivore *n.* 食肉动物，食虫植物
herbivore *n.* 草食动物
vegetation *n.* 植被，（总称）植物
section *n.* 部分，断片，节
span *n.* 跨度，范围
poach *v.* 偷猎
jeopardize *v.* 危害
perish *v.* 毁灭，死亡

Cycle of Material 物质循环

cycle of matetial 物质循环
energy flow 能流
food chain 食物链
food web 食物网
ecological niche 生态龛位，生态位
producer *n.* 生产者
consumer *n.* 消费者
decomposer *n.* 分解体
accumulate *v.* 积聚，堆积
decay *v.* 腐朽，腐烂

一般生态学用词

chemosynthesis *n.* 化学合成
tract *n.*（土地等）的一大片
hectare *n.* 公顷
elevation *n.* 上升，海拔
reservoir *n.* 水库，蓄水池
timber *n.* 木材，木料
deforestation *n.* 采伐森林，森林开伐
desertification *n.* 荒漠化，沙漠化
climatic *a.* 气候上的
isolated *a.* 隔离的，孤立的
evolutionary *a.* 进化的
aboriginal *a.* 土著的，原来的；*n.* 土著居民
abundant *a.* 丰富的，充裕的
emerge *v.* 显现，浮现，暴露
advance into 进入到…
intrude *v.* 闯入，侵入
recede *v.* 后退
tarnish *v.* 失去光泽，锈蚀
erode *v.* 侵蚀，腐蚀
enforce *v.* 强迫，加强

6 Geology 地质学

Rock 岩石

igneous rock 火成岩
plutonic rock *n.* 火成论
metamorphic rock 变质岩
sedimentary rock 水成岩
limestone *n.* 石灰石
granite *n.* 花岗岩
extrusive *a.* 挤出的，喷出的
molten *v.* 熔化；*a.* 熔铸的
alluvial *a.* 冲积的，淤积的
eject *v.* 逐出，撵出；喷射
crystallize *v.* 使结晶，晶化
deposit *n.* 堆积物，沉淀物；*v.* 沉淀
debris *n.* 碎片，残骸
metamorphosis *n.* 变形
stalactite *n.* 钟乳石
stalagmite *n.* 石笋
accumulation *n.* 积聚，堆积物
sediment *n.* 沉淀物，沉积
lithification *n.* 岩化

Tectonics 筑造学

tectonics *n.* 筑造学
tectonic plate（地球表面的）构造板块
continental drift theory 大陆漂移说
supercontinent *n.* 超大陆
plate *n.*（形成地壳的）板块
plate tectonics 板块构造论
earthquake *n.* 地震
earth's axis *n.* 地轴
seismic *a.* 地震的

seismic intensity 地震强度，地震烈度
seismic wave 地震波
epicenter *n.* 震中，中心
Richter scale *n.* 里氏震级
tremor *n./v.* 震动，颤动
tsunami *n.* 海啸
crust *n.* 外壳，硬壳
mantle *n.* 地幔
magma *n.*（有机物或矿物的）稀糊，岩浆
volcanic eruption 火山爆发
volcanic zone 火山带
crater *n.* 火山口
lava *n.* 熔岩，火山岩
liquefy *v.*（使）溶解，（使）液化
drift *n.* 冲洗，漂流物；*v.*（使）漂流

Stratigraphy 地层学

stratigraphy *n.* 地层学
law of superposition 地层层序律
terrane *n.* 岩层
rift *n.* 裂缝，裂口
correlation *n.* 相互关系，相关（性）
stratify *v.*（使）成层
stratum *n.* 地层
unconformity *n.* 不整合，不整合面
specimen *n.* 标本，样品，样本
chronological *a.* 按年代顺序排列的
subterranean *a.* 地下的

一般地质学用词

chasm *n.* 深坑，裂口
upheaval *n.* 隆起
bulge *n.* 凸出部分；*v.* 凸出，膨胀
aurora *n.* 北极光
transformation *n.* 变化，转化
mechanics *n.*（用作单数）机械学，力学
wear away/down/off/out 磨损
weather *v.* 风化，侵蚀
meander *n./v.* 蜿蜒而流

7 Oceanography 海洋学

Tide 潮汐

tidal energy 潮汐能
tidal wave 潮汐波，浪潮
tsunami *n.* 海啸
wave *n.* 波，波浪
gyre *n./v.* 旋回，旋转
whirlpool *n.* 漩涡，涡流
current *n.* 水流，气流
downwelling *n.*（海洋在地壳板块压力下的）下降
upwelling *n.* 上涌，上升流（指海水由较深层上升到较浅层的过程）
circulation *n.* 循环，环流
counterclockwise *a./ad.* 反时针方向的（地）
drift *n./v.* 漂流

Submarine Topography 海底地形

submarine *a.* 水下的，海底的
topography *n.* 地形，地形学
ocean floor 洋底，海底
continental shelf *n.* 大陆架
submarine valley 海底谷
strait *n.* 地峡，海峡
seamount *n.* 海山
trench *n.* 溪谷，峡谷

一般海洋学用词

Pacific Ocean 太平洋
Atlantic Ocean 大西洋
Indian Ocean 印度洋
Antarctic Ocean 南冰洋，南极海
saliferous *a.*（岩层等）含盐的
salinity *n.* 盐分，盐度
plankton *n.* 浮游生物
mooring *n.* 停泊处
peak *n.*（物体的）尖端，隆起部分；山顶
submerge *v.* 淹没
submersible *a.* 可潜入水中的；*n.* 潜水艇，潜水器

8 Astronomy 天文学

Celestial Body 天体

Mercury 水星
Venus 金星
Earth 地球
Mars 火星
Jupiter 木星
Saturn 土星
Uranus 天王星
Neptune 海王星
Pluto 冥王星
planet *n.* 行星
asteroid *n.* 小游星，小行星
comet *n.* 彗星
meteor *n.* 流星

meteorite n. 陨星，陨石
heavenly bodies 天体
celestial sphere 天球(一个想象假设的无限大球体)
ecliptic n. 黄道；a. 黄道的，日(或月)食的，
solar system 太阳系
galaxy n. 星系，银河系
nebular a. 星云的
cluster n. 串，丛
constellation n. 星群，星座
Polaris n. 北极星
variable star 变星
rotation n. 旋转
revolution n. 绕转，旋转
solar eclipse 日食
lunar eclipse 月食

Astrophysics 天体物理学

antimatter n. 反物质
interstellar matter 星际物质
stellar a. 恒星的
proton n. 质子
sunspot n. 太阳黑子
pulsar n. 脉冲星
magnetic storm 磁暴
supergiant star 超巨星
supernova n. 超新星
white dwarf star 白矮星
red giant star 红巨星
inactivity n. 静止，不活泼，休止状态
air resistance 空气阻力
friction n. 摩擦，摩擦力
repulsion n. 推斥，排斥
gravitational a. 重力的
weightlessness n. 无重状态
Van Allen Radiation Belt 范艾伦辐射带
apogee n. 远地点
perigee n. 近地点

Astronautics 太空航空学

aerospace n. 航空宇宙
astronaut n. 太空人，宇航员
astronautics n. 太空航空学
vessel n. 船，舰；飞船
carrier rocket 运载火箭
booster rocket 助推火箭
combustion chamber 燃烧室
blast off v. 点火起飞
circumlunar flight 环月飞行
blackout n. 中断
telemetry n. 遥感勘测
HST =High Speed Tester 高速试验机
balloon satellite 气球卫星
application satellite 应用卫星
broadcasting satellite 广播卫星

一般天文学用词

eccentricity n. 偏心率(度)；偏心距
axis n. 轴
orbit n. 轨道；v. 绕…轨道而行，进入轨道
track n. 轨迹；v. 追踪
observatory n. 天文台，气象台
observe v. 观察，观测
detect v. 侦查，探测
luminous a. 发光的，明亮的
stationary a. 静止的，不动的
transparency n. 透明，透明度
naked eye 肉眼
concentration n. 集中，集合
condense v. (使)浓缩
congeal v. (使)冻结，(使)凝结
astrology n. 占星术，占星学
leap year 闰年

9 Meteorology 气象学

Weather Forecast 天气预报

Weather Bureau 气象局
temperature n. 温度
wind chill (factor)风寒
below freezing 零下
Celsius n. 摄氏度
Fahrenheit n. 华氏度
precipitation n. 降雨量，降水(量)
downfall n. 暴雨，大雪
humidity n. 湿气，湿度
cold front n. 冷锋，冷面
warm front n. 暖锋
trough n. 低压槽；槽形低压
anticyclone n. 反气旋，高气压
wind velocity 风速
wind direction 风向
westerlies n. 西风带
trade wind n. 信风
typhoon n. 台风
hurricane n. 飓风，狂风

cyclone *n.* 旋风，暴风
gale *n.* 大风
blast *n.* 一阵(风)，一股(气流)
squall *n.* 暴风，暴风雪
frost *n.* 霜，霜冻
sleet *n.* 冰雨，雨夹雪，霰
blizzard *n.* 暴风雪
hail *n.* 冰雹
hailstorm *n.* 雹暴
tempest *n.* 暴风雨
heavy snow 大雪
sprinkle *n.* 小雨，间断雨
drizzle *n.* 细雨，毛毛雨
shower *n.* 阵雨
downpour *n.* 倾盆大雨
torrential rain 暴雨
cloudburst *n.* 倾盆大雨
thunderstorm *n.* 雷暴
haze *n.* 薄雾，阴霾
mist *n.* 薄雾
fog *n.* 雾
dew *n.* 露

Weather 天气

inclement weather
inclement *a.* 险恶的，严酷的
frigid *a.* 寒冷的
bleak *a.* 寒冷的，阴冷的
dreary *a.* 沉闷的
chilly *a.* 寒冷的
torrid *a.* 很热的，炽热的
scorching *a.* 灼热的
sweltering *a.* 闷热的，酷热的
stuffy *a.* 闷热的，不通气的
sultry *a.* 闷热的，酷热的
heat wave 热浪
serene *a.* 平静的，晴朗的
halcyon *a.* 太平的，平静的
overcast *a.* 阴天的，阴暗的
dense *a.* 密集的，浓厚的
arid *a.* 干旱的，干燥的
damp *n.* 湿气；*a.* 潮湿的

Climate 气候

continental climate 大陆性气候
oceanic climate 海洋性气候
desert climate 沙漠气候
subtropical climate 亚热带气候
tropical climate 热带气候
temperate climate 温带气候
monsoon climate 季风气候
highland climate 高原气候
subarctic climate 副极带气候
polar climate 极地气候

一般气候学用词

equinox *n.* 昼夜平分点，春分或秋分
spring equinox 春分
autumnal equinox 秋分
summer solstice 夏至
winter solstice 冬至
air current 气流
air mass 气团
atmosphere *n.* 大气，空气
atmospheric pressure 大气压力
barometric *a.* 气压的
lightning rod 避雷针
fallout *n.* 辐射微尘，原子尘
avalanche *n.* 雪崩
drought *n.* 干旱
deluge *n.* 洪水，大水灾
flood *n.* 洪水，水灾
inundation *n.* 洪水
geyser *n.* 天然喷泉，间歇泉
glacial epoch 冰川时期
glacier *n.* 冰河
icecap *n.* 常积不消的冰，冰盖
moisture *n.* 潮湿，湿气
droplet *n.* 小滴
soaked *a.* 湿透的
parched *a.* 炎热的
evaporate *v.* 蒸发，消失
shiver *v.* 颤抖，打冷战

10 Physics 物理学

Electric Current 电流

ammeter *n.* 电表
alternating current 交流电
direct current 直流电
electrode *n.* 电极
anode *n.* 阳极，正极
cathode *n.* 阴极
terminal *n.* 终端，接线端
charge *n.* 负荷，电荷

voltage *n.* 电压，伏特数
voltmeter *n.* 伏特计
electromagnetic wave 电磁波
magnetic field 磁场
magnetism *n.* 磁，磁力
generator *n.* 发电机，发生器
conductor *n.* 导体，导线
semiconductor *n.* 半导体
insulation *n.* 绝缘

Dynamics 动力学

dynamics *n.* 动力学
mechanics *n.* 机械学，力学
force *n.* 力，力量
universal gravitation 万有引力
free fall 自由降落
theory of relativity 相对论
strain *n.* 拉力，张力
torsion *n.* 扭(力)矩，转(力)矩
hydrodynamics *n.* 流体力学，水动力学
fluid *n.* 液体，流质；*a.* 液体的，流体的
buoyancy *n.* 浮力
vacuum *n.* 真空
sound wave 声波，音波
wavelength *n.* 波长
resonance *n.* 共鸣，回声；谐振，共振
vibration *n.* 振动，颤动
amplitude of vibration 振幅
pendulum *n.* 摆，钟摆
symmetrize *v.* 使对称，使均衡
proton *n.* 质子
neutron *n.* 中子
particle *n.* 粒子；质点
electron *n.* 电子
meson *n.* 介子
quantum *n.* 量子，量子论
quark *n.* 夸克
fission *n.* 裂开，裂变
fusion *n.* (核)聚变，核合成
critical mass 临界物质

Law of Motion 运动定律

inertia *n.* 惯性，惯量
mass *n.* 质量
friction *n.* 摩擦，摩擦力
velocity *n.* 速度，速率
accelerated velocity 加速度
centrifugal force 地心引力
centripetal force 向心力
elasticity *n.* 弹力，弹性
kinetic energy 动能
potential energy 势能
radiant energy 辐射能
mechanical energy 机械能

Optics 光学

visible rays 可视光线
ultraviolet rays 紫外线
infrared rays 红外线
disperse *v.* 使(光线)分散，使弥散
deviation *n.* 背离
radiation *n.* 放射，辐射；辐射线
reflection *n.* 反映，反射；映像
refraction *n.* 折光，折射
anaclastic *a.* 屈折的，由折射引起的
concave lens 凹透镜
convex lens 凸透镜
diameter *n.* 直径
radius *n.* 半径，半径范围

一般物理学用词

specific gravity 比重
volume *n.* 体积；量
density *n.* 密度
pressure *n.* 压，压力
capillarity *n.* 毛细管作用，毛细管现象
surface tension 表面张力
cohesive *a.* 凝聚性的，内聚性的
virtual *a.* 虚的
impulsive *a.* 瞬动的，冲击的
spatial *a.* 空间的，立体的，三维的
static *a.* 静态的，静力的
application *n.* 施加力，荷载
annihilation *n.* 湮灭
malleability *n.* 有延展性，柔韧性
flexibility *n.* 弹性，挠性
fluctuation *n.* 波动，起伏
lever *n.* 杆，杠杆
foundation *n.* 基础；基本原理

11 Chemistry 化学

Periodic Table(元素)周期表

periodic table(元素)周期表
element *n.* 元素

oxygen *n.* 氧
hydrogen *n.* 氢
nitrogen *n.* 氮
carbon *n.* 碳
silicon *n.* 硅
chlorine *n.* 氯
helium *n.* 氦
zinc *n.* 锌
tin *n.* 锡
manganese *n.* 锰
lead *n.* 铅
uranium *n.* 铀
cadmium *n.* 镉
aluminum *n.* 铝
isotope *n.* 同位素
sulfuric acid 硫磺酸
hydrochloric acid 盐酸
phosphate *n.* 磷酸盐

Chemical Reaction 化学反应

chemical action 化学反应
chemical symbol 化学符号
chemical equation 化学反应方程式
replacement 移位，置换
ingredient *n.* 成分；拼份，拼料
content *n.* 含量，容积(量)
solution *n.* 溶液
solvent *a.* 溶解的，有溶解力的；*n.* 溶媒，溶剂
solute *n.* 溶解物，溶质
insoluble *a.* 不能溶解的
stable *a.* 稳定的
molecular *a.* 分子的，由分子组成的
saturation *n.* 饱和(状态)，饱和度
concentration *n.* 浓缩，浓度
osmosis *n.* 渗透(作用)，渗透性
diffusion *n.* 扩散；渗滤
dilution *n.* 稀释；稀释法
combustion *n.* 燃烧
composition *n.* 合成物，混合物
decomposition *n.* 分解
enzyme *n.* 酶
catalyst *n.* 催化剂
reactant *n.* 反应物
acceptor *n.* 接收器
acid *n.* 酸
alkalinity *n.* 碱度
compound *n.* 混合物，化合物
inorganic compounds 无机化合物
oxide *n.* 氧化物
oxidize *v.* (使)氧化
neutralize *v.* 中和
corrode *v.* 腐蚀，侵蚀
reagent *n.* 反应物，试剂
oxidizing agent 氧化剂
reducing agent 还原剂
additive *n.* 添加剂
coolant *n.* 冷冻剂，冷却液
brine *n.* 盐水

Matter 物质

gas *n.* 气体
liquid *n.* 液体
solid *n.* 固体
freezing point 冰点，凝固点
melting point 熔点
boiling point 沸点
steam *n.* 蒸汽，水汽
evaporation *n.* 蒸发(作用)
vaporization *n.* 汽化器，蒸馏器
liquefaction *n.* 液化
solidification *n.* 凝固
sublimation *n.* 升华，升华物
colloid *n.* 胶质，胶体
filter *n.* 过滤器，滤纸
deposit *n.* 沉淀物；*v.* 沉淀
condense *v.* 浓缩

一般化学用词

alchemy *n.* 炼金术
alloy *n.* 合金
plate *n.* 镀金或镀银器皿；*v.* 镀(金，银等)，电镀
inject *v.* 注射，注入
purify *v.* 使纯净，净化
crude *a.* 天然的，未加工的；*n.* 原(生)材料，天然物质
viscous *a.* 粘性的，粘滞的
exothermic *a.* 发热的，放出热量的
incandescent *a.* 遇热发光的，白炽的
explosive *a.* 爆炸(性)的；*n.* 爆炸物，炸药
toxic *a.* 有毒的
venomous *a.* 有毒的，分泌毒液的
moldy *a.* 发霉的，腐臭的
lukewarm *a.* (指液体)微温的
thermometer *n.* 温度计

outcome *n.* 结果
crystal *a.* 结晶状的；*n.* 结晶，晶体
property *n.* 性质，特性
texture *n.* 结构，组织
amylum *n.* 淀粉
protein *n.* 蛋白质
carbohydrate *n.* 碳水化合物
mineral *n.* 矿物

12 Mathematics 数学

Algebra 代数学

algebra *n.* 代数学
equation *n.* 方程式，等式
par *n.* 同等，同位，同价
variable *n.* 变数，变量
square *n.* 平方
cube *n.* 立方
arithmetic *n.* 算术，算法
addition *n.* 加，加法
subtraction *n.* 减，减法
multiplication *n.* 乘法
division *n.* 除法
plus *prep.* 加，加上；*n.* 加号，正号
minus *prep.* 减去；*n.* 减号，负号
times *prep.* 乘，乘以
calculation *n.* 计算
reckon *v.* 计算，总计

Number Theory 数论

real number 实数
imaginary number 虚数
odd number 奇数
even number 偶数
fraction *n.* 分数
decimal *a.* 十进的，小数的
decimal system 十进制
dozen *n.* 一打，12 个

Geometry 几何学

geometry *n.* 几何学
triangle *n.* 三角形
quadrangle *n.* 四角形，四边形
trapezoid *n.* 梯形，不等边四边形
parallelogram *n.* 平行四边形
rhombus *n.* 菱形，斜方形（diamond）
rectangle *n.* 长方形，矩形
square *n.* 正方形
pentagon *n.* 五角形，五边形
hexagon *n.* 六角形，六边形
heptagon *n.* 七角形，七边形
octagon *n.* 八边形，八角形
parallel *a.* 平行的，相同的；*n.* 平行线
circle *n.* 圆周
circumference *n.* 圆周
arc *n.* 弧，弓形
periphery *n.* 圆柱（体）表面，外围
diameter *n.* 直径
radius *n.* 半径
sector *n.* 扇形
sphere *n.* 球，球体
cylinder *n.* 圆柱体
cone *n.* 锥形物，圆锥体
prism *n.* 棱柱
pyramid *n.* 角锥，棱椎
central angle 圆心角
degree *n.* 度数，度
grade *n.* 等级，级别
level *n.* 水平线，水平面；*a.* 水平的
vertical *a.* 垂直的；*n.* 垂直线，垂直面
perpendicular *a.* 垂直的，正交的；*n.* 垂线
convergent *a.* 会集于一点的，会聚性的
diagonal（line）对角线
parabola *n.* 抛物线
ellipse *n.* 椭圆，椭圆形
width *n.* 宽，宽度

一般数学用词

algorithm *n.* 运算法则
calculus *n.* 微积分学
function *n.* 函数
set *n.* 集合
matrix *n.* 矩阵
probability *n.* 概率
statistics *n.* 统计学，统计表

13 Engineering 工程学

Electrical Engineering 电气工程

galvanic cell 原电池，自发电池
grounding *n.* 接地
superconductor *n.* 超导（电）体
semiconductor *n.* 半导体
conductor *n.* 导体，导线
conduit *n.* 导线管，（电缆）管道
integrated circuit（IC）集成电路

leakage *n.* 漏，渗漏
tuning *n.* 调谐
transistor *n.* 晶体管
scramble *v.* 扰频，改变频率
radio *n.* 无线电广播
reception *n.* 接收（力）
transmission *n.* 播送，传输
teleprinter *n.* 电传打字机
insulation *n.* 绝缘
tensile *a.* 张力的，拉力的
propulsion *n.* 推进，推进力

Chemical Engineering 化学工程

polymer chemistry 高聚物化学
polymer *n.* 聚合体
resin *n.* 树脂
thermosetting resin 热固树胶
rubber *n.* 橡胶
vulcanization *n.*（橡胶的）硫化（过程）
cure *n.* 硫化，固化
accelerator *n.* 加速器
elastic *a.* 弹性的
pneumatic *a.* 空气的，气体的
compression *n.* 浓缩，压缩
mold *n.* 结晶器，坩埚
solder *n.* 焊料；*v.* 焊接
laminate *v.* 碾压

一般工程学用词

factory automation（FA）工厂自动化
abrasion *n.* 磨损
corrosion *n.* 侵蚀，腐蚀状态
obsolete *a.* 废弃的；过时的
obsolete equipment 陈旧设备
pilot 排障器；操纵器
prototype *n.* 原型
pathfinder *n.* 探险者，开创者
breakthrough *n.* 突破

14 Computer 计算机

Hardware 硬件

CPU（central processing unit）中央处理器
microprocessor *n.* 微处理器
peripheral device 外围设备
memory unit 存储单元，存储装置
access time *n.* 存取时间
optical memory 光存储器
memory chip 存储器片
mouse *n.* 鼠标
terminal *n.* 终端，接线端
laptop computer 膝上型计算机

Software 软件

freeware *n.* 免费软件
configuration *n.* 构造，配置
operating system 操作系统
retrieval system 检索系统
assembler *n.* 汇编程序
code *n.* 代码，编码
binary code 二进制码
runtime *n.* 运行时间

一般计算机用词

algorithm *n.* 运算法则
volatile *a.* 易失的（电源切断后信息消失）
compatible *a.* 一致的，兼容的
realtime 实时
interactive *a.* 交互式的
portable *a.* 手提（式）的，便携式的
equivalent *a.* 相等的，等价的
office automation 办公自动化
throughput *n.* 吞吐量
capacity *n.* 容量，负载量
store up 贮存
microchip *n.* 微芯片
wetware *n.* 湿件

15 Energy 能源

Energy 能源

alternative energy 代用能源
clean energy 清洁能源
renewable energy 可再生能源
solar energy 太阳能
energy efficient *a.* 节约能源的
energy conservation 能源节约
energy consumption 能量消耗
energy resources 能源资源
natural resources 天然资源
electricity *n.* 电，电力
generator *n.* 发电机
nuclear power 核能
power supply 电源，电力供应
power plant（station）发电厂，发电站
tidal power plant 潮水发电厂

hydroelectric power station 水电站
thermal power station 热电站，火力发电站
thermal *a.* 热的，热量的
renewable *a.* 可更新的，可再生的
sustainable *a.* 足可支撑的，可持续的
enrich *v.* 使丰富，富集化

Fuel 燃料

synthetic fuel 合成燃料
fossil fuel 矿物燃料，化石燃料
gas station 加油站
gaseous *a.* 气体的，气态的
LPG（Liquefid Petroleum Gas）液化石油气体
LNG（Liquefied Natural Gas）液化天然气
gasoline *n.* 汽油
diesel *n.* 柴油机，内燃机
petroleum *n.* 石油
kerosene *n.* 煤油
crude oil 原油
oil drilling 石油钻探
oil field 油田
oil refinery 炼油厂
oil producing country 石油生产国
oil tanker *n.* 油船，油轮
pipeline *n.* 管道，管线
reserve *n.* 储备(物)，储藏量
reserve power 备用功率，备用动力
reservoir *n.* 水库，蓄水池

一般能源用词

harness *v.* 利用(河流、瀑布等)产生动力(尤指电力)
power *n.* 动力；*v.* 供以动力
drive *n.* 推进力，动力；*v.* 推动、发动(机器等)
exploit *v.* 开发，开采；使用
extract *v.* 提取，榨出
mine *n.* 矿，矿山，矿井；*v.* 开矿，开采
submerge *v.* 浸没，淹没
compress *v.* 压缩，浓缩
deplete *v.* 耗尽，使衰竭
immense *a.* 广大的，巨大的
formidable *a.* 强大的，强有力的
inherent *a.* 固有的，内在的
substantial *a.* 坚固的，实质的
site specific 特定地点
unspoiled *a.* 未损坏的
vulnerable *a.* 脆弱的，易受损害的
daylight saving time 夏令时
blackout *n.* 灯火管制
chamber *n.* 燃烧室
combustion *n.* 燃烧
internal combustion engine 内燃机
swell *v.* 使膨胀，使增长
maintenance *n.* 维护，维修，保养
quest *n./v.* 探索，寻找
byproduct *n.* 副产品
drawback *n.* 困难，障碍

16 U.S. History 美国历史

Government 政府

Federal government 联邦政府
American Revolution 美国独立战争
the Declaration of Independence 独立宣言
Independence Day 美国独立日
federalism *n.* 联邦政治，联邦制度
feudalism *n.* 封建制度
monarchy *n.* 君主政体，君主政治
imperialism *n.* 帝国主义，帝制
colonization *n.* 殖民地化，殖民
Capitol *n.* 国会大厦，州议会大厦
Representative *n.* 众议院议员
framer *n.* 组成者，筹划者

Law 法律

the Bill of Rights《人权法案》
provision *n.* 规定，条款
convention *n.* 条约，协议，契约
privilege *n.* 特权，特别待遇；基本公民权力
women's suffrage 妇女投票权
Supreme Court 最高法院
circuit court 巡回法庭
patent *n.* 专利，专利权
Prohibition 禁酒令
Bootlegging *n.* 非法制造、运送、销售(酒类等)
unconstitutional *a.* 违反宪法的
ratify *v.* 批准，认可
consolidate *v.* 统一，合并
promulgate *v.* 发布，公布

The Civil War 美国内战

American Civil War 美国内战(南北战争)
Emancipation Proclamation《解放黑人奴隶宣言》
the Union 联邦
the Confederacy 南部邦联
thrall *n.* 奴隶，束缚

slavery *n.* 奴隶身份，奴隶制度
persecute *v.* 迫害
suppression *n.* 镇压
segregation *n.* 种族隔离
racial discrimination 种族歧视
integration *n.* 取消种族隔离
armed conflicts 武装冲突
class warfare 阶级斗争
carnage *n.*（尤指在战场上的）残杀，大屠杀
massacre *n.* 残杀，大屠杀
casualty *n.* 伤亡，伤亡人员
captive *n.* 俘虏
armistice *n.* 停战，休战
cavalry *n.* 骑兵
artillery *n.* 炮，炮兵
rifle *n.* 来复枪，步枪
musket *n.* 步枪
sweeping *a.* 扫荡的
tactic *n.* 策略，战略
disarmament *n.* 裁军，裁减军备
dismemberment *n.* 分割，瓜分（国土等）

Society 社会

Pilgrim Fathers 清教徒前辈移民
Puritan *n.* 清教徒
Quaker *n.* 基督教教友派成员，贵格会教徒
early settlers 早期定居者
covered wagon 有篷大马车；篷车
wagon train 马车队
migrate *v.* 移动，移往
blaze a trail 开辟道路，作先导
famine *n.* 饥荒
hardship *n.* 困苦，艰难
ranch *n.* 大农场
pasture *n.* 草原，牧场
plantation *n.* 种植园，大农场
public domain（美国政府的）公有土地
agrarian *a.* 有关土地的，耕地的
arid *a.* 干旱的，贫瘠的（土地等）
Sutter's Mill 苏特矿场
bonanza *n.* 富矿带
locomotive *n.* 机车，火车头
Roaring Twenties 兴旺的20年代
crusade *n.* 十字军东侵，宗教战争
Great Depression 大萧条
regrate *v.* 囤积（粮食，商品等），倒卖
flowering *a.* 开花的；*n.* 成熟
（the）Dust Bowl 风沙浸蚀区
greenback *n.* 美钞
hierarchy *n.* 等级制度
peer *n.* 贵族（指公、侯、伯、子、男中的任一爵位）
baron *n.* 男爵（英国世袭的最低级的贵族爵位）
commoner *n.* 平民，无爵位的人
redemptioner *n.* 出卖劳力来抵偿船资之移民
itinerant preacher 巡回牧师，巡回传教士
upheaval *n.* 动乱，剧变
uprising *n.* 起义

关于美国的一般情况用词

Indian reservation 印第安人保留地
minority *n.* 少数，少数民族
philanthropist *n.* 慈善家
benefactor *n.* 捐助者，赠送者
Pulitzer Prize 普利策奖
steel magnate 钢铁大亨
deity *n.* 神，神性
muckraker *n.* 搜集并揭发丑事的人
anomaly *n.* 不规则，异常的人或物
doctrine *n.* 教条，学说
trial and error *n.* 反复试验

17 Anthropology 人类学

Cultural Anthropology 文化人类学
philology *n.* 语言学，文献学
mythology *n.* 神话
legend *n.* 传说
epic *n.* 史诗
folk story 民间故事
speculation *n.* 思索；做投机买卖
animism *n.* 万物有灵论
primitive religion 原始宗教
religious cult 宗教崇拜
sanctuary *n.* 圣所，圣殿；避难所
worship *n./v.* 崇拜，礼拜
aboriginal *a.* 土著的，原来的；*n.* 土著居民
indigenous *a.* 本土的
funerary *a.* 葬礼的，埋葬的
nomadic *a.* 游牧的
acquired *a.* 已获得的，已成习惯的；习得的
antiquity *n.* 古代
forebear *n.* 祖先，祖宗
descendant *n.* 子孙，后裔
descend *v.* 下来，遗传
custom *n.* 习惯，风俗

dwelling *n.* 住处
implement *n.* 工具，器具
weaver *n.* 织布者，织工
loom *n.* 织布机，织机
erect *v.* 使竖立，树立
flourish *n./v.* 繁荣，茂盛
restoration *n.* 恢复，重建
pillar *n.* 柱子
watercourse *n.* 水道，河道
Social Anthropology 社会人类学
community *n.* 社区，团体
clan *n.* 部落，氏族
lineage *n.* 血统，世系
tribe *n.* 部落，部族
chieftain *n.* 酋长，首领
regime *n.* 政权，政权制度
legitimism *n.* 正统主义
monogamous *a.* 一夫一妻的
matrilineal *a.* 母系的
matriarchy *n.* 女家长制，女族长制
patriarchy *n.* 家长统治，父权制
monarchy *n.* 君主政体，君主政治
hereditary *a.* 世袭的，遗传的
hierarchy *n.* 等级制度
class *n.* 阶级，社会等级
status *n.* 身份，地位
aristocrat *n.* 贵族
patrician *n.* 贵族；*a.* 贵族的
plebeian *n.* 平民，庶民；*a.* 平民的
turmoil *n.* 骚动，混乱
depredation *n.* 掠夺；毁坏
retaliation *n.* 报复，报仇
ups and downs 盛衰，沉浮（rise and fall）

一般人类学用词

biological anthropology 生物人类学
pluralism *n.* 多数状态；多重性
enigma *n.* 谜
juxtaposition *n.* 并置，并列
labyrinth *n.* 迷宫，难解的事物
phenomenon *n.* 现象
adjustment *n.* 调整，调节
adaptive *a.* 适应的
radical *a.* 基本的，激进的；*n.* 激进分子
inchoate *a.* 初步的，早期的
ominous *a.* 恶兆的，不吉利的
medieval *a.* 中世纪的

elapse *v.*（时间）过去，消逝
persist *v.* 坚持，持续
testify *v.* 证明，证实

18 Archaeology 考古学

Excavation 出土文物

excavate *v.* 挖掘，挖出
digging *n.* 挖掘
site *n.* 地点，遗址
relics *n.* 遗物，遗迹
artifact *n.* 人造物品
mound *n.* 土墩，护堤
dolmen *n.* 巨石墓，史前墓石牌坊
mummy *n.* 木乃伊
skeletal *a.* 骨骼的，骸骨的
authentic *a.* 可信的
sampling *n.* 取样；样品
specimen *n.* 样品，样本
fragment *n.* 碎片，断片
shard *n.*（玻璃或陶瓷器皿的）碎片
pottery *n.* 陶器
haft *n.* 柄，把手
scraper *n.* 刮器，刮刀

Paleontology 古生物学

paleontology *n.* 古生物学
fossil *n.* 化石
progenitor *n.* 祖先，始祖
progeny *n.* 后裔
Homo Erectus 直立人
hominoid *n.* 人科之动物，类人猿
ape *n.* 猿
trilobite *n.* 三叶虫
ammonite *n.* 菊石
mammoth *n.* 猛犸，长毛象
tusk *n.* 长牙，獠牙
stratum *n.* 地层，岩层
stratigraphy *n.* 地层学
anachronism *n.* 时代错误
date *n.* 年代，时期
decipher *v.* 译解（密码等）
archive *n.* 档案文件
hieroglyph *n.* 象形文字，图画文字
cuneiform *n.* 楔形文字；*a.* 楔形的，楔形文字的
geometric pattern 几何图样

Age 时代

prehistoric *a.* 史前的
primeval *a.* 原始的
pristine *a.* 原始的，早期的
Ice Age 冰河时代
glacial epoch *n.* 冰川时期
Pleistocene Epoch 更新世
Stone Age *n.* 石器时代
Paleolithic *a.* 旧石器时代的
Mesolithic *a.* 中石器时代的
Neolithic *a.* 新石器时代的
Bronze Age 青铜器时代
Iron Age 铁器时代
chronology *n.* 年代学，年表

一般考古学用词

origin *n.* 起源，由来
sculpture *n.* 雕刻，雕塑
scythian *n.* 斯基台人
unprecedented *a.* 空前的
extant *a.* 现存的，尚存的
prevalent *a.* 普遍的，盛行的
die out 灭绝
engrave *v.* 雕刻，铭刻
depict *v.* 描述，描写
polish *n./v.* 磨光，擦亮
deform *v.*（使）变形
attest *v.* 证明，证实

19 Politics 政治

Election 选举

by election 递补选举
campaign *n.* 活动，竞选运动
canvass *v.* 游说，拉选票
address *n./v.* 演讲，演说
debate *n./v.* 争论，辩论
candidate *n.* 候选人
aide *n.* 助手，副官
delegate *n.* 代表；*v.* 委派…为代表
demagogue *n.* 煽动政治家
referendum *n.* 公民投票
ballot box 投票箱
suffrage *n.* 投票，选举权
vote *n./v.* 投票，选票
abstention *n.* 弃权
poll *n.* 选举之投票
plurality *n.*（选举中获得的）相对多数，相对多数票
unanimous *a.* 意见一致的，无异议的

Government 政府

authorities *n.* 当局，官方
sovereignty *n.* 主权，主权国家
autonomy *n.* 自治
inaugurate *v.* 举行就职典礼
inaugural *a.* 就职的，开始的；*n.* 就职演说
summit conference（talk）峰会
protocol *n.* 草案，协议
ratify *v.* 批准，认可
publicize *v.* 宣扬，宣传
autarchy *n.* 独裁，专制
appointment *n.* 任命，选派；职位，职务
cabinet *n.* 内阁
bicameral *a.* 两院制的
the House 议院
senator *n.* 议员
Congress *n.*（美国）国会
Parliament *n.*（英国）议会
independent *n.* 中立派，无党派议员
opposition party 反对党
secession *n.* 脱离，分裂主义
hard liner *n.* 不妥协者
official *n.* 官员，公务员；*a.* 官方的，正式的
consul *n.* 领事
deputy *n.* 议员，下院议员
rehabilitation *n.* 复职，复位
subvert *v.* 颠覆，策反

一般政治学用词

bureaucracy *n.* 官僚，官僚作风，官僚机构
democracy *n.* 民主政治，民主主义
communism *n.* 共产主义
totalitarianism *n.* 极权主义
hegemony *n.* 霸权
abolition *n.* 废除，废除奴隶制度
petition *n.* 请愿，请愿书
frontier *n.* 国境，边境
airspace *n.* 空域，领空
subject peoples
minority *n.* 少数，少数民族
racialism *n.* 种族主义，种族歧视
oppression *n.* 压迫，镇压
ouster *n.* 驱逐，剥夺
riot *n.* 暴乱，骚动
turmoil *n.* 骚动，混乱
political impasse 政治僵局

impasse *n.* 僵局
stalemate *n.* 僵持，僵局
status quo 现状
stopgap *n.* 临时替代的人或物，权宜之计
intransigent *a.* 不妥协的，难和解的
anonymous *a.* 匿名的

20 Economics 经济学

Economy 经济

GNP（Gross National Product）国民生产总值
trade cycle 贸易循环，商业周期
financial crisis 金融危机
panic *n.* 惊慌，恐慌
moratorium *n.* 延期偿付
recession *n.*（经济）衰退，不景气
stagnation *n.* 停滞
depression *n.* 萧条，不景气
inflation *n.* 通货膨胀
stagflation *n.* 通货滞胀，不景气状况下之物价上涨
deflation *n.* 通货紧缩
depreciation *n.* 贬值
devaluation *n.* 贬值
revaluation *n.* 升值
price fluctuation 物价波动
slump *n./v.* 衰退，（物价）暴跌
skyrocket *v.* 使…迅速上升，飞涨
rapid growth 迅速增长
boom *n./v.* 繁荣
expansionary policy 经济扩张政策
buoyant *a.*（价格等）有上涨倾向的;（国家收入等）趋向增长的
Finances 金融
fiscal year 财政年度
fiscal *a.* 财政的，国库的
national treasury 国库
budget *n./v.* 预算
bottom line *n.* 底线
fund *n.* 资金，基金
subsidy *n.* 补助金，津贴
annuity *n.* 年金
tariff *n.* 关税
preferential *a.* 优先的，特惠的
declare *v.* 申报（纳税品等）
revenue *n.* 收入，税收
defraud the revenue
Value Added Tax 增值税
levy *n./v.* 征收，征税
assess *v.* 确定（税款等）的数额；征收（税款等）
monetary circulation 货币流通
monetary system 货币体系
fiat money 不兑现纸币
paper note 纸币
counterfeit *n.* 假币；*a.* 假冒的，假装的；*v.* 仿造，伪造
principal *n.* 资本，本金
interest *n.* 利息
passbook *n.* 存款簿，银行存折
installment *n.* 分期付款
stock *n.* 股票
bond *n.* 公债，债券
stocks and bonds 股票和债券
blue chip 执行股票，蓝筹股
bill *n.* 纸币，钞票
bill of debt 债票
bill of dishonor 拒付汇票
clearing house 票据交换所
endorse *v.* 在（票据）背面签名，签署
pecuniary *a.* 金钱的，金钱上的
due *n.* 应得物;[复]应付款；*a.* 应得的；应付的，到期的
business 商业
small and medium sized enterprises 中小企业
incorporation *n.* 合并，组成公司；公司
consolidation *n.* 巩固，合并
mergers & acquisitions 收购兼并，并购
audit *n./ v.* 审计，稽核
output *n.* 产量
increment *n.* 增加；盈余，利润
gains *n.* 利润，获利
surplus *n.* 剩余，盈余；*a.* 过剩的
the black ink balance 贷方余额
deficit *n.* 赤字
futility *n.* 无益，无用
shutdown *n.* 关门，停工
bankruptcy *n.* 破产
bust *n.* 萧条，破产
liquidate *v.* 清算
proprietary name *n.* 注册商标，专利商品名
tycoon *n.* 企业界大亨
recruit *n.* 新兵，新人；*v.* 招募，招聘
transaction 交易
transaction *n.* 办理，交易
monopoly *n.* 垄断
oligopoly *n.* 寡头垄断

monopoly and oligopoly 垄断与寡头垄断
proprietary *a.* 专利的，有专利权的；*n.* 所有者，所有权
retail *n./v.* 零售；*a.* 零售的
wholesale *n./v.* 批发；*a.* 批发的
rush *n.* 匆促，抢购热潮
glut *n./v.* 充斥，供过于求
bargain *n.* 交易，成交商品；便宜货；*v.* 议价
commodity *n.* 日用品
line *n.* 运输公司
inventory *n.* 详细目录，存货清册；*v.* 盘存，盘点
stocktaking *n.* 存货盘点
current price 现价，时价
appraise *v.* 评价，估价
barter *n./v.* 物品交换，实物交易
swap *v./n.* 交换，作交易
advance *n./v.* 预付(款)
voucher *n.* 凭证，凭单；〈美〉优惠购货券
waive *v.* 搁置，延期进行
cession *n.* 让与(他人)债权
gratuitous conveyance 免费转让
gratuitous *a.* 免费的(free)
stipulate *v.*(在协议、条约或契约上)规定
covenant *n./v.*(缔结)盟约，契约
subcontract *n.* 转包合同
mortgage *n./v.* 抵押
security *n.* 安全
reimbursement *n.* 偿还，补偿；报销

一般经济学用词

check and balance 制约平衡，制衡原则
the trade imbalance 贸易不平衡
equilibrium *n.* 平衡，均衡
outlay *n.* 费用
profligacy *n.* 极度的浪费，恣意的挥霍
extravagance *n.* 奢侈，铺张
avocation *n.*(个人)副业，业余爱好
auction *n./v.* 拍卖
bidding *n.* 投标，出价
competitive bidding 竞标，竞争出价
tender *v.*(~for)投标
appropriation *n.* 拨款
smuggle *n./v.* 走私
speculate *v.* 做投机买卖
detriment *n.* 损害，有害物
fiasco *n.* 惨败，大失败

21 Sociology 社会学

Family Relationship 家庭关系

kinship *n.* 血族关系
lineage *n.* 血统，世系
consort *v.* 配偶(特指在位君主的夫或妻)
spouse *n.* 配偶(指夫或妻)
offspring *n.*(单复数同形)子孙，后代
sibling *n.* 兄弟姐妹，同胞
half brothers 同母异父(或同父异母)兄弟
illegitimate *a.* 私生的
pedigree *n.* 血统，家谱
bastard *n.* 私生子
adoption *n.* 收养
testament *n.* 遗嘱
engagement *n.* 婚约
fiancé *n.*〈法〉未婚夫
fiancée *n.*〈法〉未婚妻
go between *n.* 媒介者，中间人(middleman)
separation *n.* 分开，夫妻法定分居
alimony *n.*(离婚或分居后在诉讼期间男方给女方的)赡养费，生活费
divorce *n./v.* 离婚
break up 破坏，解体
infancy *n.* 婴儿期，幼年时代
juvenile *a.* 青少年的；*n.* 青少年
adolescence *n.* 青春期
climacteric *n.* 更年期
senile *a.* 老年的，高龄的
senescent *a.* 老了的，衰老了的
precocious *a.* 早熟的，发育过早的

Social Issue 社会问题

social integration 社会融合，社会整体化
walkout *n.* 罢工
disorder *n.* 混乱，无秩序状态
uproar *n.* 喧嚣，骚动
delinquency *n.* 行为不良，错失
juvenile delinquency 青少年犯罪
alienation *n.* 疏远，异化
minority *n.* 少数
bystander *n.* 旁观者
cultural bias 文化偏见
population density 人口密度
overpopulation *n.* 人口过剩
underpopulated *a.* 人口稀少的
exodus *n.* 大批的离去

congestion n.（交通的）拥挤;(人口）稠密
pollution n. 污染
skyscraper n. 摩天大楼
metropolitan a. 大城市的，大都会的
satellite n. 人造卫星
outer city 市郊

Social Welfare 社会福利

social security n. 社会保障
institution n. 公共机构，协会
infrastructure n. 基础建设
public facilities 市政设施
public utilities（works）公用事业
prosperity n. 繁荣
charity n. 慈善，慈善团体
life annuity n. 终身年金
average life expectancy 平均寿命预期值
longevity n. 长命，寿命
community n. 社区，团体

一般社会学用词

throng n. 人群；v. 群集
peer group 同年龄组，同年龄群体
gregarious a. 社交的
altruism n. 利他主义
egoism n. 自我主义，利己主义
contrariety n. 矛盾，相反物
consensus n. 多数人的意见，舆论
culminate v. 达到顶点
heyday n. 全盛期，年富力强时期
denomination n. 命名
alias n. 别名，化名
pseudonym n. 假名，笔名
paradigm n. 范例，典范
demography n. 人口统计学
census n. 人口普查

22 Geography 地理学

Topography 地形学

topography n. 地形学
rugged a. 高低不平的，崎岖的
highland n. 高地，丘陵地带
plateau n. 高地，高原
canyon n. 峡谷，溪谷
waterfall n. 瀑布
gorge n. 山峡，峡谷
ridge n. 山脊，山脉
pass n. 关口
cliff n. 悬崖，绝壁
bluff n. 断崖，绝壁
basin n. 盆地
plain n. 平原，草原
flood plain 河漫滩，洪泛区
delta n. 三角州
coast n. 海岸
sand dune n. 沙丘
cape n. 海角，岬
peninsula n. 半岛
archipelago n. 群岛
inland river 内河
watershed n. 分水岭
meander n. 曲流；v. 蜿蜒而流
tributary a. 支流的；n. 支流
estuary n. 河口，江口
lagoon n. 泻湖，礁湖，盐水湖
eutrophic lake 富营养湖，滋养湖
freshwater lake 淡水湖
swamp n. 沼泽，湿
hot spring 温泉
geyser n. 间歇泉

Location 位置

geographical a. 地理学的，地理的
GPS（Global Position System）全球定位系统
compass n. 罗盘，指南针
latitude n. 纬度
longitude n. 经度，经线
altitude n.（尤指海拔）高度
rotational axis 旋转轴
the North Pole 北极
true north n. 真北(非地磁北）
magnetic north n. 磁北
Northern Hemisphere 北半球

一般地质学用词

erosion n. 腐蚀，侵蚀
corrosion n. 侵蚀，腐蚀状态
weather v. 侵蚀，使风化
landmass n. 大陆
cavern n. 巨洞，洞窟
colliery n. 煤矿
canal n. 运河

23 Transportation 交通运输

Traffic 交通

public transportation 公共交通
round n. 环形路；v. 绕弯，绕行
traffic congestion 交通拥堵
traffic jam 交通阻塞
traffic light 红绿灯
isolation n. 封锁交通
pedestrian n. 步行者；a. 徒步的
traverse v. 横越，横向乱走
jaywalk v. 擅自穿越马路
derail v. 出轨
license plates 牌照
turn signal n.（车辆的）转向灯
spare tire n. 备用轮胎
puncture n. 穿孔，车胎穿孔
maintenance n. 维护，保养

Road 公路

thoroughfare n. 通路，大道
highway n. 高速公路，大路
freeway n. 高速公路
expressway n. 高速公路
toll road 收费公路
bypass n. 旁路
overpass n. 天桥，立交桥
underpass n. 地下道，高架桥下通道
sidewalk n. 人行道
crosswalk n. 人行横道
lane n.（乡间）小路；航线
alley n. 小路，小径
back road 支路，乡间的道路
shortcut n. 捷径
detour n. 便道，绕路；v. 绕路而行
devious a. 偏僻的，曲折的

一般交通用词

carriage n. 四轮马车，（铁路）客车厢
wagon n. 四轮马车，货车
raft n. 筏，救生艇，橡皮船
liner n. 班机
charter v. 租，包（船、车等）
embark v. 上船，上飞机
embargo n./ v. 禁止出入港口，禁运
manifest n. 载货单，旅客名单
freight n. 货运；运费
manned a. 有人驾驶的，有人操纵的
convoy v. 护航，护送

24 Environment 环境

Water Pollution 水污染

BOD（Biochemical Oxygen Demand）生化需氧量
COD（Chemical Oxygen Ded mand ）化学需氧量
oil spill 漏油
seep v. 渗出，渗漏
discharge v./n. 排出（气体、液体等），流出
abound in 富于
heavy metal 重金属
lead poisoning 铅中毒
fresh water 淡水
groundwater n. 地下水
wastewater n. 废水
sewage n. 下水道，污水
bleacher n. 漂白剂
detergent n. 清洁剂，去垢剂
water soluble 可溶于水的
noxious a. 有害的
untreated a. 未处理的，未加工的
aquatic a. 水的，水生的，水栖的

Air Pollution 空气污染

greenhouse effect 温室效用
global warming 全球气候变暖
ozone hole 臭氧层空洞
emission n. 排出物，排放
exhaust v./n. 排气，排气装置
release v./n. 释放，放出
diffuse v. 漫射，扩散；a. 散开的，弥漫的
photochemical smog 光化烟雾
acid rain 酸雨
aerial a. 生活在空气中的，空气的

Soil Pollution 土壤污染

fertilizer n. 肥料（尤指化学肥料）
herbicide n. 除草剂
pesticide n. 杀虫剂
pest n. 害虫
landfill n. 垃圾掩埋
garbage n. 垃圾，废物
plastic bag 塑料袋
disposable a. 一次性的，用后即可丢弃的
waste disposal 废物处理
toxic waste 有毒废物

industrial waste 工业废弃物
radioactive waste 放射性废物
discard *v.* 丢弃，抛弃；*n.* 废品(物)，废料
absorb *v.* 吸收
ruin *n.* 废墟，遗迹

Pollution 污染
contaminate *v.* 污染
public hazards 公害
pollutant *n.* 污染物质
PCB 多氯联苯
biphenyl *n.* 联苯
biochemical *a.* 生物化学的
carcinogenic *a.* 致癌物(质)的
catastrophic *a.* 悲惨的，灾难的
lethal *a.* 致命的
detrimental *a.* 有害的
sick house syndrome 致病建筑综合症

Environmental Protection 环境保护
environmentally friendly *a.* 环保的，环保型的
environmental watchdog 环境监察机构
environmentalist *n.* 环境保护论者，环境论者
advocate *n.* 提倡者，拥护者；*v.* 提倡，拥护
conservationist *n.*(天然资源的)保护管理论者
conserve *v.* 保存，保藏
shield *n.* 护罩，盾；*v.* 保护，防护
purify *v.* 使纯净，净化
rescue *v./n.* 援救，救助
rebuild *v.* 重建，改造
repair *n./v.* 修理，修补，补救
replant *v.* 再植，移植
reprocess *v.* 再加工
recycle *v./n.* 再循环，重复利用
recycled paper 再生环保纸
salvage *v./n.* 废品回收
reclamation *n.* 改造，(废料等的)收回
reserve *n./v.* 储备，保存；保护区
bulwark *n.* 防波堤
reproductive *a.* 再生的
sustainable *a.* 可持续的
shortsighted *a.* 近视的，眼光短浅的
superficial *a.* 表面的
countermeasure *n.* 对策

一般环境用词
environment *n.* 环境
underpinning *n.* 基础，基础材料
consequence *n.* 结果，后果
depletion *n.* 损耗
peril *n.* 危险
plight *n.* 情况，困境
outbreak *n.* 爆发
vulnerable *a.* 易受攻击的，脆弱的
inadvertent *a.* 疏忽的，因疏忽所致的
endangered *a.* 有危险的
shallow *a.* 浅的，浅薄的
profound *a.* 深刻的，意义深远的
tranquil *a.* 安静的
rooted *a.* 根深蒂固的
flourishing *a.* 繁茂的，繁荣的
fertile *a.* 肥沃的，富饶的

25 Education 教育

Campus Life 校园生活
academic adviser 学业导师
associate professor 副教授
faculty *n.* 全体教员；(大学的)系，学院
dean *n.*(大学)院长，系主任
chancellor *n.* 大学校长
freshman *n.* 新生，大学一年级学生
sophomore *n.* 大学二年级学生
junior *n.* 大学三年级学生
senior *n.* 大学四年级学生
dean's list(大学中定期公布的)优秀学生名单
repeater *n.*(不及格)重考者，重修(某课程)者
undergraduate *n.* 在校大学生
varsity *n.* 大学；大学运动代表队
alumnus *n.* (*pl.* alumni)男毕业生，男校友
alumna *n.* (*pl.* alumnae)女毕业生，女校友
scholarship *n.* 奖学金
grant *n.* 补助金，助学金
government aid 政府救济
student loan 助学贷款
sign up for 签约从事
extracurricular activities 课外活动
quote *v.* 引用，引证
submit *v.* 提交，递交
assignment *n.* 任务，作业
plagiarism *n.* 剽窃
bibliography *n.* 书目，参考书目
reference book 参考书
reserved book 保留图书
handout *n.* 分发的印刷品，散页

roll *n.* 名单
signboard *n.* 布告板
Academic Affairs Management 学校事务管理
curriculum *n.* 课程
syllabus *n.* 课程提纲
semester *n.* 学期
term paper *n.* 学期报告
credit *n.* 学分
absolute evaluation 绝对评价
relative evaluation 相对评价
scale *n.* 刻度，范围；阶梯
preliminary *a.* 预备的，初步的；*n.* 预考，预赛
grade *n.* 等级，级别；*v.* 评分，评级
GPA（Grade Point Average）平均成绩点数
academic performance 学业成绩
academic probation 试读，见习
withdraw *v.*（从学校）领回
flunk *n./v.* 失败，考试不及格
drop out *n.* 中途退学的人
skip *v.* 跳，跳读
transfer *n.* 转移，转学
application form 申请书，申请表
enrollment *n.* 登记，注册
matriculate *v.* 被录取入学；*n.* 被录取者
commencement *n.* 毕业典礼，学位授予典礼
dissertation *n.*（学位）论文
monograph *n.* 专论
diploma *n.* 文凭，毕业证书
bachelor's degree 学士学位
master's degree 硕士学位
doctor's degree 博士学位
certificate *n.* 证书，证明书
transcript（academic）*n.* 成绩单
report（card）*n.* 成绩单
recommendation *n.* 推荐(信)

Subject 科目

major subject 主要科目
liberal arts 文科
required/mandatory subject 必修课
optional subject 选修课
pedagogy *n.* 教育学
ethics *n.* 伦理学
pharmacy *n.* 药剂学
medicine *n.* 药，医学
earth science 地球学
geography *n.* 地理学
social studies（social science）社会科学
economics *n.* 经济学
politics *n.* 政治，政治学
history *n.* 历史，历史学
world history 世界历史
language arts 语言艺术学科
fine arts 美术
physical education 体育

Educational Institution 教育机构

community *n.* 团体，社团，界
college *n.*（综合大学中的）学院，(独立的）学院
university *n.*（综合）大学
graduate school 研究生院
administration office 行政办公室
auditorium *n.* 会堂，礼堂
gymnasium *n.* 健身房，体育馆
dormitory *n.* 宿舍
sorority *n.* 女学生联谊会
fraternity *n.* 兄弟互助会，兄弟会

一般教育用词

primary education 小学教育，初等教育
secondary education 中等教育(指初、高中)
lecture based education 以授课为基础的教育
audiovisual education 视听教育
distance education 远程教育
lifelong education 终身教育
alternative education 选择性教育

26 Law 法律

Crime 犯罪

criminal *n.* 罪犯，犯罪者 *a.* 犯罪的，犯法的
principal *n.* 主犯
suspect *n.* 嫌疑犯
accessory *n.* 从犯，同谋者；*a.* 同谋的
outlaw *n.* 歹徒，逃犯
ex convict *n.* 从前曾被判刑的人
delinquency *n.* 行为不良，错失
misdemeanor *n.* 轻罪
felony *n.* 重罪
arson *n.* 纵火，纵火罪
homicide *n.* 杀人
robbery *n.* 抢掠，抢劫
rape *n.* 强奸
sexual harassment 性骚扰
larceny *n.* 盗窃罪

fraud *n.* 欺骗，欺诈罪
blackmail *n./v.* 敲诈，勒索
perjury *n.* 伪誓，伪证
embezzle *v.* 盗用，挪用
manipulate *v.* 篡改(账目等)
bug *v.* 装置窃听器，窃听
commit *v.* 犯(法)，干(坏事)
violate *v.* 违犯，侵犯
conspiracy *n.* 共谋，阴谋
illegal *a.* 违法的
iniquity *n.* 不公正
injustice *n.* 不公平
contingency *n.* 意外事故，偶然错误
lucre *n.* 钱财，利益

Lawsuit 诉讼

lawsuit *n.* 诉讼
criminal suit 刑事诉讼
procedure *n.* 程序，手续
sue *v.* 控告，提出诉讼
indict *v.* 起诉，控告
accuse *v.* 控告
appeal *n.* 上诉
lose a suit (case) 败诉
withdraw (drop) a suit 撤诉
prosecution *n.* 起诉，诉讼；原告，控方
complaint *n.* 申诉，控告
petition *n.* 申请书，上诉状
warrant of attorney(给诉讼代理人或律师的)委托书
warrant of arrest (arrest warrant) 逮捕证，拘票
search warrant 搜查证
writ *n.* 文书，正式文件
plaintiff *n.* 起诉人，原告
arbitrator *n.* 仲裁人，公断者
defendant *n.* 被告
suspicion *n.* 猜疑，怀疑
summon *v.* 传唤，传唤到庭
alleged *a.* 声称的，有嫌疑的
false charge 编造的罪名
invalidity *n.* 无效力
autopsy *n.* (为查明死因而做的)尸体解剖，验尸

Trial 审判

courtroom *n.* 法庭，审判室
hearing *n.* 听证，听证会
default *n./v.* 缺席
jury *n.* 陪审团，陪审员
judge *n.* 法官，审判员
prosecutor *n.* 原告，起诉人，公诉人
lawyer *n.* 律师
defense *n.* 辩护词；辩护律师
testimony *n.* 证词(尤指在法庭所作的)
testify *v.* 证明，作证
witness *n.* 证人，证词；*v.* 作证
cross examine *v.* 诘问(对方证人)，反复询问
interrogation *n.* 审问
take the fifth *v.* 以美国宪法第五条修正案为庇护(避而不答)
mute *n.* 拒不答辩的被告
plea *n.* 辩解，抗辩
verdict *n.* (陪审团的)裁决，判决
sentence *n./v.* 判决，宣判
jeopardy *n.* 有罪受刑的可能性，刑事案件中被告的处境
conviction *n.* 定罪，宣告有罪
guilt *n.* 罪行
precedent *n.* 先例

Punishment 处罚

capital punishment 死刑
execution *n.* 执行法庭决议；处死，死刑
life imprisonment 无期徒刑
imprisonment *n.* 关押
custody *n.* 拘留，监禁
monetary penalty 罚款处分
suspended sentence *n.* 缓刑
probation *n.* 缓刑
bail *n./v.* 保释

一般法律用词

constitution *n.* 宪法
criminal law 刑法
penal *a.* 刑事的，刑法上的
judicial *a.* 司法的，法院的
judicature *n.* 司法
act *n.* 法案，法令
agreement *n.* 契约，协议
code *n.* 法典，法规，章程
bylaw *n.* 次要法规
due process 法定诉讼程序
amnesty *n.*(尤指对反政府政治犯的)特赦
implication *n.* 牵连
double jeopardy 一罪不受两次审理原则，双重危境
feasible *a.* 可行的，切实可行的

enforce v. 推行，实施(法律等)

27 Medicine 医学

Body Organs 人体器官

respiratory organ 呼吸器官
circulatory organ 循环器官
cerebrum n. 大脑
cerebellum n. 小脑
cranium n. 头盖，头盖骨
marrow n. 髓，骨髓
spinal cord n. 脊髓
nostril n. 鼻孔
esophagus n. 食道
bronchus n. 支气管
breast n. 胸部，乳房
abdomen n. 腹，腹部
aorta n. 大动脉
artery n. 动脉
pancreas n. 胰腺
intestine n. 肠
liver n. 肝脏
kidney n. 肾
ovary n.(生物)卵巢
limb n.(四)肢，手足
joint n. 关节
epidermis n. 表皮，上皮
chromosome n. 染色体
nerve n. 神经
tissue n. 组织
membrane n. 膜，隔膜

Disease 疾病

germ n. 细菌
carrier n. 带菌者
immunity n. 免疫性
HIV(Human Immunodeficiency Virus)艾滋病病毒
antibody n. 抗体
acute a. 急性的
lethal a. 致命的
progressive a. 进行性的
hereditary a. 遗传的
contagious a. 传染性的，会感染的
epidemic a. 流行的，传染的；n. 时疫，流行病
latency period 潜伏期
stroke n.(疾病)突然发作，中风
paralysis n. 瘫痪，麻痹
dementia n. 痴呆
cardiac n. 强心剂
heart attack 心脏病发作
high blood pressure 高血压(症)
influenza n. 流行性感冒
sore throat n. 喉咙痛
sore a. 疼痛的
asthma n. 哮喘
tuberculosis n. 肺结核
pneumonia n. 肺炎
leukemia n. 白血病
breast cancer n. 乳癌
diabetes n. 糖尿病，多尿症
gastric ulcer n. 胃溃疡
hepatitis n. 肝炎
arthritis n. 关节炎
neuralgia n. 神经痛
bruise n. 瘀伤，擦伤
measles n. 麻疹，风疹
smallpox n. 天花
polio n. 脑灰质炎，小儿麻痹症
cataract n. 白内障
hyperopia n. 远视
athlete's foot n. 脚癣，脚气
intoxication n. 中毒
drug addiction 吸毒成瘾，药瘾
hallucination n. 幻觉，幻想
hypnosis n. 催眠状态，催眠
mental illness 精神病
trauma n. 外伤，损伤；精神创伤
amnesia n. 健忘症
insomnia n. 失眠，失眠症
phobia n. 恐怖病，恐惧症
obsession n. 强迫症
neurosis n. 神经症，神经衰弱症
anorexia n. 食欲减退，厌食
bulimia n. 易饿病
depression n. 抑郁症
manic depression 躁郁症

Symptom 症状

onset n. 发作
fit n. 突然发作，痉挛
anemia n. 贫血，贫血症
vertigo n. 眩晕
dizzy a. 晕眩的
syncope n. 昏厥
nausea n. 反胃，恶心

dyspepsia *n.* 消化不良
constipation *n.* 便秘
diarrhea *n.* 痢疾，腹泻
excrement *n.* 排泄物，大便
sperm *n.* 精液，精子
saliva *n.* 口水，唾液
sputum *n.* 唾液，痰
sneeze *n.* 喷嚏；*v.* 打喷嚏
choke *v.* 窒息，哽住
side effect（药物等的）副作用
aftereffect *n.* 副作用

Treatment 治疗

remedy *n.* 药物；治疗法
heal *v.* 治愈，医治
recuperate *v.* 复原
panacea *n.* 万能药
inoculate *v.* 预防注射，接种疫苗
vaccination *n.* 接种疫苗，种痘
alleviate *v.* 使（痛苦等）减轻
palliate *v.* 减轻，缓和（疾病、痛苦等）
soothe *v.* 使（痛苦，疼痛）缓和或减轻
pain reliever 镇痛药
tranquilizer *n.* 镇定剂
disinfect *v.* 消毒
antiseptic *a.* 杀菌的，消过毒的；*n.* 杀菌剂
toxic *a.* 有毒的，中毒的
antidote *n.* 解毒剂
administer *v.* 给药，用药
ointment *n.* 药膏
antibiotic *n.* 抗生素
antioxidant *n.* 抗氧化剂
prescription *n.* 处方，药方
dose *n.* 剂量，（一）剂，（一）服
pharmaceutical *n.* 药物；*a.* 制药（学）上的

Hospital 医院

surgeon *n.* 外科医生
physician *n.* 医师，内科医师
nursing staff 护理人员
ward *n.* 病房
stethoscope *n.* 听诊器
diagnose *v.* 诊断
medical certificate *n.* 健康证明；诊断书
endoscopy *n.* 内窥镜检查法
early detection of cancer 癌症的早期发现
recurrence *n.* 复发
surgical instruments 外科器械
bleeding *n.* 出血，流血
coagulation *n.* 凝结，血凝固
transfusion *n.* 输血，输液
transplantation *n.* 移植（术）
anesthesia *n.* 麻醉
coma *n.* 昏迷
vegetable *n.* 植物人
cerebral death 脑死亡
euthanasia *n.* 安乐死

一般医学和健康用词

internal medicine 内科医学
surgery *n.* 外科，外科学；手术室
plastic surgery 整形手术，整形外科
orthopedics *n.* 矫形术
dermatology *n.* 皮肤医学，皮肤病学
ophthalmology *n.* 眼科学
otolaryngology *n.* 耳鼻喉学
obstetrics and *n.* 妇产科
gynecology *n.* 妇科医学
pediatrics *n.* 小儿科
psychiatry *n.* 精神病学，精神病治疗法
anatomy *n.* 解剖学
hygiene *n.* 卫生，卫生学
sanitary *a.*（有关）卫生的
corporal *a.* 肉体的，身体的
feeble *a.* 虚弱的，无力的
meager *a.* 瘦的（人体部分）
malnutrition *n.* 营养不良
obesity *n.* 肥胖
regimen *n.* 食物疗法；养生法
diet therapy 饮食疗法
vegetarian *n.* 素食者
strain *n.* 过度的疲劳，紧张；（身体的）扭伤，拉伤
barren *a.* 不生育的，不孕的
pregnancy *n.* 怀孕
miscarriage *n.* 流产
delivery *n.* 分娩
sterilization operation 节育手术
contraceptive（pill）*n.* 避孕药
complexion *n.* 面色，气色
afflict *v.* 使痛苦，折磨
exacerbate *v.* 恶化
incapacitate *v.* 使无能力，使不能

28 Philosophy 哲学

Logic 逻辑学

universal *a.* 全称的；*n.* 全称命题
concept *n.* 概念
gist *n.* 要义
term *n.* 项
middle *n.* 中项
proposition *n.* 命题
premise *n.* 前提
antecedent *a.* 前提的，前件的；*n.* 前提，前件
hypothesis *n.* 假设，前提
contingent *a.* 或有的，不是逻辑上必然的
implication *n.* 蕴涵
connotation *n.* 内涵，含义
denotation *n.* 外延，指称
association *n.* 联想，联合
analogy *n.* 类比
conjecture *n./v.* 假设
reasoning *n.* 推理，推论
demonstrate *v.* 证明
statement *n.* 陈述，综述
counterargument *n.* 驳论，抗辩
incompatible *a.* 不能同时成立的(两个以上的命题)
inconsistency *n.* 矛盾，不相容性
contradiction *n.* 矛盾，矛盾命题
undistributed *a.* 不周延的
conclusion *n.*(三段论的)性质判断
fallacy *n.* 谬误，谬论
dichotomy *n.* 二分法
syllogism *n.* 三段论法
induction *n.* 归纳(法)
deduction *n.* 演绎(法)
dialectic（s）*n.* 逻辑论证，辩证法

Psychology 心理学

hang up *n.*(尤指精神或感情上摆脱不掉的)烦恼，焦虑
drive *n.* 内驱力
stimulus *n.* 刺激
resistance *n.* 抵抗，阻抗
attribute *n.* 属性，性质
pattern *n.* 模式
intention *n.* 意图，意念
identity *n.* 同一性，一致
feedback *n.* 反馈
abnegation *n.* 放弃
egocentrism *n.* 自我中心主义
egoism *n.* 自我主义
altruism *n.* 利他主义
extrovert *n.* 性格外向者
introvert *n.* 性格内向的人
affirmative *a.* 肯定的
caution *n.* 小心，谨慎，警告

Philosophies 哲学

stoicism *n.* 斯多葛哲学
sophism *n.* 诡辩
sophist *n.* 诡辩家，诡辩者
skepticism *n.* 怀疑论
skeptic *n.* 怀疑论者
empiricism *n.* 经验主义，经验论
epistemology *n.* 认识论
hedonics *n.* 享乐(主义)论
ontology *n.* 存在论
theism *n.* 有神论
pantheism *n.* 泛神论
parallelism *n.* 心身平行论
determinism *n.* 决定论
idealism *n.* 唯心主义，唯心论
materialism *n.* 唯物主义，唯物论
utilitarianism *n.* 功利主义
humanism *n.* 人本主义理论
humanitarianism *n.* 人道主义
pessimism *n.* 悲观，悲观主义
positivism *n.* 实证论，实证主义
structuralism *n.* 构造主义

一般哲学用词

ideology *n.* 意识形态
substance *n.* 性质
awareness *n.* 觉知
paradigm *n.* 范式
principle *n.* 原则
disciple *n.* 信徒，弟子
erudite *a.* 博学的
oncoming *a.* 即将来临的，接近的；*a.* 基础的，基本的
fundamental *n.* 基本原则，基本原理
adamant *a.* 固执的
specific *a.* 特殊的
perceive *v.* 感知，察觉
simplify *v.* 单一化，简单化

29 Religion 宗教

Theology 神学

theology *n.* 神学
salvation *n.* 灵魂得救，超度
redemption *n.* 救赎，赎罪
mission *n.* 传道，传道权
missionary *n.* 传教士
pilgrim *n.* 圣地朝拜者，朝圣者
eschatology *n.* 末世学，来世论
Adventism *n.* 耶稣复临论
Advent *n.* 基督降临，降临节
atheism *n.* 无神论
monotheism *n.* 一神论，一神教
polytheism *n.* 多神教，多神论
satanism *n.* 恶魔崇拜，恶魔主义
diabolism *n.* 魔法，妖术
Christianity 基督教
Christianity *n.* 基督教
Catholicism *n.* 天主教
Protestantism *n.* 新教
Baptist Church *n.* 浸礼会教堂
Quakers *n.* 教友派信徒，贵格教徒
denomination *n.* 教派
orthodox *a.* 正统的，东正教的
heterodox *a.* 异端的，异教的
pagan *n.* 异教徒
infidel *n.* 无信仰者，异教徒
convert *v.* 使…改变信仰
Providence *vt.* 天意，上帝的保佑；神，上帝
Province *n.* 大教区
parish *n.* 教区
chapel *n.* 小礼拜堂
worship *v.* 礼拜，拜神
Mass *n.* 弥撒
benediction *n.* 礼拜末尾的祝祷，(餐前餐后的)谢恩祷
hymn *n.* 赞美诗，圣歌
sermon *n.* 布道，说教
intone *v.* 唱或吟咏(圣歌)
New (Old) Testament 新(旧)约全书
apocalypse *n.* 启示录
devil *n.* 魔鬼
omnipotence *n.*(全能的)上帝
lord *n.* 上帝
crucify *v.* 把…钉在十字架上
apostle *n.* 使徒(指耶稣十二使徒)
doom *n.* 末日审判
doomsday *n.* 最后审判日
resurrection *n.* 人类的复活
Easter *n.* 复活节
clergyman *n.* 牧师，教士
archbishop *n.* 大主教
cardinal *n.* 枢机主教，红衣主教
minister *n.* 牧师，(某些教派的)教长
persecution *n.* 迫害时期
martyrdom *n.* 殉难，殉道
martyr *n.* 殉道者，殉教者
Other Religions 其它宗教
Islam *n.* 伊斯兰教
Muslim *n.* 穆斯林，伊斯兰教徒
mosque *n.* 清真寺
Hinduism *n.* 印度教
Hindi *n.* 北印度语，印地语
Hindu temple 印度庙宇
sutra *n.* 佛经
Judaism *n.* 犹太教
rabbi *n.* 拉比(犹太人的学者)，犹太传教士
synagogue *n.* 犹太人集会，犹太教会堂
Buddhism *n.* 佛教
Buddhist *n.* 佛教徒
meditation *n.* (尤指宗教的)默想
nirvana *n.*(佛教)涅，极乐世界
karma *n.* 因果报应，羯磨
Samsara (transmigration) *n.* 轮回
reincarnation *n.* 再投胎，再生
Confucianism *n.* 孔教，儒教

一般宗教用词

religious dispute 宗教冲突
religious cult 宗教崇拜
primitive religion 原始宗教
ritual *n.* (宗教)仪式
foresight *n.* 预见
deification *n.* 神格化，奉若神明
spell *n.* 符咒
circumcision *n.* 割礼
immolation *n.* 祭物
fabulous *a.* 神话般的，奇异的
pious *a.* 虔诚的
sacred *a.* 神的，神圣的
sanctity *n.* 圣洁
spirit *n.* 灵魂，幽灵
incorporeal *a.* 灵魂的

secular *a.* 尘世的，世俗的
profane *a.* 亵渎的
blasphemy *n.* 亵渎(的言行)
malediction *n.* 诅咒

30 Literature 文学

Genres of Literature 文学体裁

genre *n.* 类型，流派
epic *n.* 史诗
lyric *n.* 抒情诗
ode *n.* 颂诗，颂歌
elegy *n.* 挽歌
sonnet *n.* 十四行诗
anthology *n.* 诗选，文选
verse *n.* 韵文，诗
prose *n.* 散文
biography *n.* 传记
autobiography *n.* 自传
chronicle *n.* 编年史
fiction *n.* 小说
narrative *n.* 记叙文，记叙体
folklore *n.* 民间传说
fairy tale 童话
anecdote *n.* 轶事，奇闻
fable *n.* 寓言
allegory *n.* 寓言
satire *n.* 讽刺文学
epigram *n.* 警句，讽刺短诗
innuendo *n.* 暗讽，影射
parody *n.* 歪改，(模仿他人文体所做的)游戏诗文
setting *n.* 背景
protagonist *n.* 主角
denouement *n.* 结局

Rhetoric 修辞学

rhetoric *n.* 修辞学
metaphor *n.* 隐喻，暗喻
allusion *n.* 隐喻，暗示
irony *n.* 反话，讽刺
paradox *n.* 自相矛盾的话
ellipsis *n.* 省略，省略符号
alliteration *n.* 头韵
rhyme *n.* 韵，押韵
style *n.* 文体
stylist *n.* 文体学家
terse *a.* 简洁的，精练的
flowery *a.* 绚丽的，华丽的
archaic *a.* 古老的，古体的
colloquial *a.* 口语的，通俗的
civilized *a.* 文雅的
dialect *n.* 方言，土语
cliché *n.* 陈词滥调
stereotype *n.* 陈腔滥调，老套
archetype *n.* 原型
wit *n.* 妙语，趣语

Writing 写作

version *n.* 译本，版本
installment *n.* 连载；连续剧
orthography *n.* 正确拼字，正字法
gloss *v./n.* 作注释，评注
annotation (footnote, comment) *n.* 注解，评注
commentator *n.* 注释者，评论员
bibliography *n.* 书目，参考书目
synopsis *n.* 提纲，情节摘要
compendium *n.* 纲要，概略
epitome *n.* 摘要
draft *n.* 草稿，草案
abridge *v.* 删节，精简
punctuate *v.* 加标点于
paraphrase *v.* 解释
proofread *v.* 校正，校对
revise *v.* 修订，修改

Copyright 版权

copyright *n.* 版权，著作权
pirate *n.* 盗印者，盗版者
piracy *n.* 侵犯版权，非法翻印
royalty *n.* 版税，特许权使用费
posthumous *a.* 死后的，作者死后出版的
anonymous *a.* 匿名的
pseudonym *n.* 笔名
authenticity *n.* 确实性，真实性
authorship *n.* 原创作者
censorship *n.* 审查制度
crib *v.* 抄袭
plagiarize *v.* 剽窃
excerpt *v.* 摘录，引用

一般文学用词

catharsis *n.* 净化；宣泄
metaphysical *a.* 形而上学的，超自然的
cynicism *n.* 犬儒主义，愤世嫉俗
deconstruction *n.* 解构

libel *n.* 以文字损害名誉，诽谤
eulogy *n.* 赞词，颂词
literacy *n.* 有文化，有读写能力
phonetics *n.* 语音学
scoop *n.* 内幕消息，独家新闻
subscribe *v.* 订阅
recite *v.* 背诵，朗读

31 Music 音乐

Composition 乐曲

composition *n.* 乐曲
compose *v.* 作曲
arrange *v.* 改编，编曲配器
masterpiece *n.* 杰作
movement *n.* 乐章
note *n.* 音符
musical notation 音符
clef *n.* 音部记号
scale *n.* 音阶，音列
major（scale）*n.* 大音阶
minor（scale）*n.* 小音阶
chromatic（scale）*n.* 半音阶
tune *n.* 曲调，调子
beat *n.* 拍子
upbeat *n.* 弱拍
refrain *n.* 叠句，副歌
word *n.* 词

Playing 演奏

execution *n.* 演奏，（演奏）技巧
improvisation *n.* 即席演奏
variation *n.* 变奏，变调
accompaniment *n.* 伴奏
undertone *n.* 低音
andantino *n.* 小行板
chord *n.* 弦，和音
cacophony *n.* 不协和音，杂音
harmonious *a.* 和谐的，协调的
bow *n.* 乐弓
pluck *v.* 弹，拨
strike *v.* 击打，弹奏
fingering *n.* 用指弹奏，指法
instrument *n.* 乐器
percussion（instrument）打击乐器
string *n.*（弓，乐器的）弦
string quartet 弦乐四重奏曲
fiddle *n.* 小提琴
recorder *n.* 八孔长笛
harpsichord *n.* 大键琴
conductor *n.*（乐队）指挥
philharmonic *n.* 交响乐团

Western Music 西方音乐

polyphony *n.* 复调音乐，对位法
orchestra music 管弦乐
symphonic *a.* 交响乐的，和声的
concerto *n.* 协奏曲
chamber music 室内乐
opera *n.* 歌剧
march *n.* 进行曲
national anthem *n.* 国歌
overture *n.* 序曲，前奏曲

一般音乐用词

musical literature 音乐文献
conservatory *n.* 音乐学校
contemporary *a.* 当（现）代的
radical *a.* 根音的
solemn *a.* 庄严的，隆重的
threnody *n.* 悲歌，哀歌
tone *n.* 音调
tone deaf *a.* 音盲的
marine band 海军乐队
inventiveness *n.* 原创，独创性
enthusiasm *n.* 热情，狂热

32 Art History 艺术史

Artistic Movements 艺术运动

School *n.* 画派

manner *n.* 风格，手法
Gothic *n.* 哥特式
Rococo *n.* 罗可可艺术
Impressionism *n.* 印象派
Pointillism *n.*（印象派画家的）点画法
Post Impressionism *n.* 后期印象派
Symbolism *n.* 象征派
Art Nouveau 新艺术派
Avant Garde *n.* 先锋派
Abstractionism *n.* 抽象派
Fauvism *n.* 野兽派
Cubism *n.* 立体派
Dadaism *n.* 达达派
Surrealism *n.* 超现实主义
Expressionism *n.* 表现主义

Futurism *n.* 未来派
Art Deco *n.* 装饰艺术
Postmodernism 后现代主义
Pop Art *n.* 流行艺术
Performance Art 表演艺术
Environmental Art 环境艺术
Op Art 光效应绘画艺术，欧普艺术

Painting 绘画

watercolor painting 水彩画
oil painting 油画
mural painting 壁画
figure painting 人物画
still life painting 静物画
landscape painting 风景画
portrait *n.* 肖像，人像
hue *n.* 色调(tint)，颜色(color)
pigment *n.* 色素，颜料
chromatic *a.* 彩色的
monochrome *n.* 单色
motley *a.* 五颜六色的，杂色的
azure *n.* 天蓝色
chiaroscuro *n.* (绘画中的)明暗对照法
transparent colors 透明色
limpid *a.* 清澈的，透明的
translucent *a.* 半透明的
opaque *a.* 不透明的
obscure *a.* 暗的，朦胧的
luminous *a.* 明亮的
lucent *a.* 光亮的，透明的
luster *n.* 光彩，光泽
brushstroke *n.* 一笔，一画，绘画的技巧
fresco *n.* 壁画
tempera *n.* 蛋彩画

Sculpture 雕塑

sculpture *n.* 雕刻，雕塑
sculptor *n.* 雕刻家，雕塑家
mason *n.* 泥瓦匠，石匠
three dimensional artwork 三维艺术品
statue *n.* 雕像
carve *v.* 雕刻
wood carving 木雕刻品，木刻
woodprint *n.* 木版画
marble *n.* 大理石雕刻品
lithograph *n.* 石版画，平版画
copperplate print 铜板画
etching *n.* 蚀刻版画，蚀刻术
engraving *n.* 雕刻术，雕版
emboss *v.* 饰以浮饰，使浮雕出来
plaster cast 石膏模型
bust *n.* 半身像，胸像
symmetry *n.* 对称，匀称

Architecture 建筑

architecture *n.* 建筑，建筑学
architect *n.* 建筑师
layout *n.* 规划，设计
floor plan 建筑的平面图
profile *n.* 剖面，侧面
vertical *n.* 垂直线，垂直面
ornate *a.* 装饰的，华丽的
stately *a.* 庄严的，宏伟的
structural *a.* 结构的，建筑的
ratio *n.* 比，比率
decoration *n.* 装饰，装饰品
exterior *a.* 外用的
style *n.* 风格
order *n.* 次序，顺序
feature *n.* 特色，特征
support *n.* 支撑，支柱
column *n.* 圆柱
base *n.* 底部，基座
shaft *n.* 轴，杆状物
capital *n.* 柱头，柱顶
scroll *n.* 卷轴，涡管
grave *n.* 墓穴，坟墓
Doric *n./a.* 多立克式(的)
Ionic *n./ a.* 爱奥尼亚式(的)
Corinthian *n./a.* 科林斯式(的)

一般艺术用词

fine arts 美术
formative arts 造型艺术
appreciation *n.* 欣赏，鉴赏
connoisseur *n.* 鉴赏家，鉴定家
vandal *n.* 汪达尔人，摧残文化艺术者
reproduction *n.* 复制(品)，仿制(品)
gallery *n.* 美术陈列室，画廊
aesthetic *a.* 美学的，审美的
vantage point *n.* 有利位置，优越地位
composition *n.* 结构，构图
deformation *n.* 在绘画中由于明暗、色调不准而歪曲了原来的形象

rendering *n.*（艺术品的）复制图;（建筑物等）透视图，示意图
lurid *a.* 过分渲染的，（画的颜色等）刺目的
decadence *n.* 颓废
lambent *a.* 闪烁的
blur *v.* 涂污，弄得模糊不清
symbolize *v.* 象征
illustrate *v.* 图解，加插图于
caricature *n.* 讽刺画，漫画
retouch *v.* 修饰，润色

33 Film 电影

Film Industry 电影行业

filmmaker *n.* 电影摄制者，制片人
film/movie director *n.* 电影导演
blockbuster *n.* 消耗巨资拍摄的影片，大片
box office 票房，票房收入
preview *v.* 预演，试映
running/show time 放映时间
rating *n.* 等级，级别
restricted *a.* 受限制的，R级的
exclusive *a.* 独家享有的，专有的
distribute *v.* 发行
release *v.* 发行
first run theater 首映式
ticket agency 售票代理处
usher *n.*（电影院，戏院等公共场所的）招待员，引座员
horror *n.* 恐怖片
independent film 独立短片
documentary film 纪录片，文献片
monochrome film 黑白影片
continuity *n.*（电影、广播、电视节目的）连续
dramatist *n.* 剧本作者
adaptation *n.* 改编，改写本
casting *n.* 挑选演员，扮演
cinematic *a.* 电影的，影片的

Technique 技艺

technique *n.* 方法，技艺
computer graphics 电脑图形图像
stop action *a.* 瞬时摄影的，连续摄影的
special effects 特技，特效
visual effects 视觉效果
optical illusion *n.* 幻觉，错觉
close up *n.* 特写镜头
double exposure shot 两次曝光拍摄
shot *v.* 拍摄
montage *n.* 蒙太奇，文学音乐或美术的组合体
dissolve *v.* 使(电影，电视画面)渐隐
fade *v.*（电影或广播中画面和声音的）渐变
echo *n.* 回声，回音
prop *n.* 道具
scenery *n.* 风景；舞台布景
score *n.* 配乐
subtitle *n.* 字幕
sound track 声轨，音轨

一般电影用词

motion picture 电影
nouvelle vague（法）新浪潮
criticism *n.* 评论，评论性文章
commentary *n.* 按语，评论
critical *a.* 批评性的，评论性的
sentimental *a.* 感伤性的，情感的
macabre *a.* 恐怖的，令人毛骨悚然的
outdated *a.* 过时的，不流行的
malfunction *n.* 故障，失灵
jam *n.* 堵塞
latest *a.* 最近的，最新的
alteration *n.* 变更，改造
innovation *n.* 改革，创新